Life and Death Planning for Retirement Benefits

The Essential Handbook for Estate Planners

Fifth Edition, Revised
2003

Natalie B. Choate

Ataxplan Publications, Boston, Massachusetts

For future updates of this book, visit our website:

www.ataxplan.com

Life and Death Planning for Retirement Benefits

The Essential Handbook for Estate Planners
Fifth edition, revised

By Natalie B. Choate

Published by: Ataxplan Publications
Post Office Box 1093-K
Boston, Massachusetts 02103-1093

Publisher's Cataloging-in-Publication Data
Choate, Natalie B.
        Life and Death Planning for Retirement Benefits: The Essential Handbook for Estate Planners—5th ed. / Natalie B. Choate
        p.   cm.
Includes bibliographical references and index.

ISBN 0-9649440-5-6

        1. Estate planning - United States. 2. Tax planning - United States. 3. Retirement income - Taxation - United States. 4. Inheritance and transfer tax - United States. I. Choate, Natalie B. II. Title

KF 6585 .C43 2003

To my mother

Jhan English Choate

who has had to put up with a lot

Warning and Disclaimer

The rules applicable to qualified retirement plan benefits and IRAs are among the most complex in the tax code. I have read few works on this subject that were, in my view, completely accurate; in fact most that I have seen, including, unfortunately, earlier incarnations of this work, contain errors. Furthermore, even accurate information can become outdated quickly as IRS or Congressional policy shifts. Despite my best efforts, it is likely that this book, too, contains errors. Citations are provided so that estate planning practitioners can check any statements made in this book and reach their own conclusions regarding what the law is.

This book is intended to provide general information regarding the tax and other laws applicable to retirement benefits, and to provide suggestions regarding appropriate estate planning actions for different situations. It is not intended as a substitute for the practitioner's own research, or for the advice of a qualified estate planning specialist. The author and publisher shall have neither liability nor responsibility to any person or entity with respect to any loss or damage caused, or alleged to be caused, directly or indirectly by the information contained in this book.

If you do not wish to be bound by the above, you may return this book to the publisher for a full refund.

Summary of Contents

Table of Contents: Detailed

Abbreviations Used in this Book
(And where to find definitions)

Code	Internal Revenue Code of 1986.
COLA	Cost-Of-Living Adjustment.
CRT	Charitable Remainder Trust; ¶ 7.5.04.
DNI	Distributable Net Income; ¶ 6.1.03.
EGTRRA	Economic Growth and Tax Relief Reconciliation Act of 2001 (P.L. 107-16)
ERISA	Employee Retirement Income Security Act of 1974 (P.L. 93-406).
GST tax	Generation Skipping Transfer tax; see "Estate Plan" Glossary, page 531.
IRA	Individual Retirement Account; see "Plan Types" Glossary, page 533..
IRD	Income in Respect of a Decedent; ¶ 2.2.
IRS	Internal Revenue Service.
IRT	Individual Retirement Trust; see IRA.
LSD	Lump Sum Distribution; ¶ 2.3.
MRD	Minimum Required Distribution; ¶ 1.2.02.
PLR	IRS private letter ruling.
Prop. Reg.	Proposed Treasury Regulation.
QDRO	Qualified Domestic Relations Order; § 414(p).
QJSA	Qualified Joint and Survivor Annuity; ¶ 3.4.02.
QPSA	Qualified Pre-retirement Survivor Annuity; ¶ 3.4.02.
QRP	Qualified Retirement Plan; "Plan Types" Glossary.
RBD	Required Beginning Date; ¶ 1.3.00.
REA	Retirement Equity Act of 1984 (P. L. 98-397); ¶ 3.4.
Reg.	Treasury Regulation.
TAMRA '88	The Technical and Miscellaneous Revenue Act of 1988 (P. L. 100-647).
TAPRA '97	Taxpayer Relief Act of 1997 (P. L. 105-34).
TEFRA '82	The Tax Equity and Fiscal Responsibility Act of 1982 (P. L. 97-248).
TRA '84	The Tax Reform Act of 1984 (P. L. 98-369).
TRA '86	The Tax Reform Act of 1986 (P. L. 99-514).
UCA '92	Unemployment Compensation Amendments of 1992 (P. L. 102-318).

Introduction

The purpose of this book is to explain, for the benefit of my fellow estate planning lawyers, and all other tax and financial services professionals involved in helping individuals plan for distribution of their retirement benefits, as many of the applicable rules as I can fit into almost 600 pages. I hope the book will serve as both a handy reference source for the expert and a basic guide for the novice.

Limitations of this Book

Many important aspects of planning for retirement distributions are *not* covered in this book, such as annuity payouts, investment alternatives and financial planning considerations generally. This book also does not cover: § 457 plans; qualified domestic relations orders (QDROs); stock options and other non-qualified forms of deferred compensation; ESOPs; creditors' rights; prohibited transactions; state tax issues; and community property. Other sources for some of these topics are mentioned in the Bibliography.

This book is designed to explain estate planning and tax planning issues for the benefit of estate and financial planners who are counseling individuals (and their beneficiaries) who have assets in retirement plans. It does not cover plan distribution issues which are of concern to plan administrators, but which do not have a significant impact on planning decisions for the individual participant, such as distribution notice requirements.

This book deals with the *federal* tax law applicable to retirement benefits, but in a few instances state law has a bearing on the subject. When state law has a significant impact, planners will need to determine the law applicable to their clients.

Terminology Used in this Book

The Glossary at the end of the book contains definitions of estate planning (p. 531) and descriptions of the various types of retirement plans discussed in this book (p. 533). If confronted with an unfamiliar term in the text be sure to check the Glossary; also see ¶ 1.2.02. In this book:

Section numbers refer to the Internal Revenue Code of 1986, as amended through January 2003, unless otherwise specified. Reg. stands for "Treasury Regulation" unless otherwise specified. Prop. Reg. means "Proposed Treasury Regulation."

Retirement plan means a corporate or self-employed ("Keogh") pension, profit sharing and stock bonus plan that is "qualified" under § 401(a), an individual retirement account (IRA) created under § 408, a Roth IRA established under § 408A, or a tax-sheltered annuity (or mutual fund) arrangement established under § 403(b). The narrower term qualified plan or qualified retirement plan (QRP) includes only 401(a) plans. For more description of these plan types see the Glossary at page 533.

The "Participant" is the person whose benefits we are dealing with: the employee who has benefits in a pension or profit sharing plan, or for whom a tax-sheltered annuity was purchased; or the account-holder in the case of an IRA. For ease of understanding, throughout this book, except in some specific examples and case studies, "Participant" is male and the feminine pronoun refers to Participant's spouse. Of course any statement would apply equally to a female Participant and her male spouse. There are certain matters (lump sum distributions, ¶ 2.3; plan-owned life insurance, ¶ 8.3) that apply only to qualified plans; in discussing these matters, sometimes "employee" is used instead of Participant. When discussing an issue from the point of view of advising an individual client I sometimes refer to the Participant as "the client," and in Chapter 4 (and maybe elsewhere) the Participant is sometimes called the "Decedent."

How to Use Cross References

The book is divided into numbered Chapters. Chapters are divided into *sections* (which are numbered "x.y"), and sections are divided into *subsections* (which are numbered "x.y.zz"). "X" is the number of the Chapter, "y" is the number of the section, and "zz" is the number of the subsection. Cross references to other parts of the book, indicated by the "¶" symbol, are liberally provided. A cross reference to "¶ 1.7.04" refers to Chapter 1, section 7, subsection .04.

Case studies in Chapter 11 illustrate some of the planning principles and real life issues created by the labyrinth of rules discussed in the earlier Chapters. Throughout the book, the text contains cross references to related case studies in Chapter 11.

Appendix B provides beneficiary designation forms for some common situations, along with some related trust provisions and other miscellaneous forms suggested in the text. Whenever a drafting suggestion or planning idea in the text is illustrated by a form in Appendix B, that form is cross-referenced. If there is no form reference, you can assume no form is provided.

Other Hints for Using this Book

There are many "gray areas" in the tax treatment of retirement benefits—questions the regulations do not answer; points of law subject to different interpretations; or regulatory positions that seem contrary to law or for some other reason likely to be changed in the future. When a practitioner encounters one of these in practice, the response may differ depending on whether he is doing advance planning for a client, or is dealing with a *fait accompli*. For this reason, from time to time in this book, in suggesting ways to deal with an issue, I distinguish between "planning mode" and "cleanup mode."

"Planning mode" deals with advance planning, and suggests a "safe harbor" course of action—the steps that should produce a predictable result and offer peace of mind. "Cleanup mode" deals with the *fait accompli* situation, when it is too late for advance planning, because Participant has already died. In cleanup mode, a more aggressive position may be appropriate on the issue, since there is often nothing to lose.

At the end of each Chapter, there is a summary of the planning principles developed in that Chapter. Bear in mind that most of these are general guidelines and do not apply to every case. The more detailed discussion in the Chapter provides the basis for these principles, and points out limitations and exceptions.

Acknowledgments

Reviewers and contributors

I am most grateful to those who took the time to read sections of the book and send me their thoughtful comments, almost all of which were incorporated into the book. For this and the prior 4th edition, these "peer reviewers" were Alan S. Acker, Esq., of Columbus, Ohio; Stephan R. Leimberg, Esq., of Bryn Mawr, PA; Barry S. Picker, CPA, of Brooklyn, NY; Ed Slott, CPA, of Rockville Centre, NY; Steven E. Trytten, Esq., Calleton & Trytten, LLP, Pasadena, CA; and Mark W. Worthington, Esq., of Worcester, MA. I know that their material reward for this effort (free copies of the book) is trivial in view of the time and effort they expended to help me improve the accuracy and readability of the work.

I also thank, most especially, my personal in-house Harvard Law Review editor, Ian M. Starr, Esq., who pitched in to proofread, cite check and edit several chapters, and who is also my booking agent, tour-arranger and husband, and who makes it all worth it.

I am grateful too to the many other professionals who on countless occasions have willingly shared their expertise in person, by phone, letter and email, including Jonathan Blattmachr, Frank S. Berall, Don DiCarlo, Dave Foster, Seymour Goldberg, Chris Hoyt, Mike Jones, Bob Keebler, Stephen J. Krass, and Lou Mezzullo.

The work of many who helped with earlier editions is still evident in this one:

From the 1999 edition: "Above and beyond the help one could reasonably hope to receive from volunteer peer reviewers, Guerdon T. Ely, MBA, CFP, a financial planner and investment advisor in Chico, California, and Michael Jones, CPA, of Monterey, California, re-ran number-intensive case studies and examples throughout the book, and thereby killed a number of bugs; and Ellen K. Harrison, Esq., of Washington, DC, made major contributions to Chapter 4.

" I am very grateful to the lawyers and others who took the time to review parts of the 1999 or 1996 edition and give me their comments, most of which led directly to improvements in the work (though I retain responsibility for all deficiencies in the finished product): Virginia Coleman, Esq., Boston; Paul Frimmer, Esq., Los Angeles; Randall J. Gingiss, Esq., Chicago; Zoe M. Hicks, Esq., Atlanta;   Jerold I. Horn, Esq., Peoria; Larry Katzenstein, Esq., St.

Louis; James H. Landon, Esq., Atlanta; my Bingham McCutchen LLP colleague George Mair, Esq.; Al Martin, Esq., Overland Park, KS; Ronald T. Martin, Esq.; David W. Polstra, CFP, Norcross, GA; Michael G. Riley, Esq., Cleveland; Kathleen R. Sherby, St. Louis; Lee Slavutin, M.D., C.P.C., New York; and Mark W. Worthington, Esq., Worcester."

In over thirty years of consciously or unknowingly gathering material for this book, I have talked with, listened to, or read the work of hundreds of estate planners, actuaries, accountants, lawyers, financial planners, retirees, trust officers, mutual fund personnel, plan administrators, IRS and DOL staffers, plan participants and writers who have studied the subject matter. Since almost everyone who spends time thinking about these issues or working with the actual problems of real life employers and employees has some interesting and new insight into the subject, I have learned from almost every encounter. In earlier editions I have listed the names of those whose questions and insights had led to something new or better in the book. It is no longer possible to do that, partly because there are now too many, and partly because so often I learn something from a seminar attendee whose name I never get. To all who have shared thoughts, questions, comments and suggestions for improvement, thank you!

I used to wonder why authors thanked their typists. Now having had first hand experience with the fantastic dedication and skill of the principal "word processor" of this book, Maureen Cash, I know. I relied heavily on her problem-solving ability and perfectionism, as well as the skills, professionalism and hard work of the others who worked on the production of the manuscript: in chronological order, Jeri Arbo, Sheila Irvine, Pat Longo and Joan Breen.

The Minimum Distribution Rules

The minimum distribution rules dictate when benefits must be paid out of retirement plans. Understanding these rules is key to successful tax planning for retirement benefits.

1.1 MRD Basic Training

1.1.01 *Speed summary of the minimum distribution rules*

This speed summary of the minimum distribution rules may be all you need to know; if it isn't, read ¶ 1.1.02 to figure out where to find more detailed information.

The minimum distribution rules dictate when Participants and beneficiaries must take money out of their retirement plans whether they want to or not.

During Participant's life, the Participant must start taking annual "minimum required distributions" (MRDs) at a certain point. Generally that point is age 70½, but if you need to know exactly when it is, see ¶ 1.3, because the "Required Beginning Date" is different for different types of retirement plans. Once commenced, the required distributions continue for the Participant's entire lifetime. Each year's required distribution is computed by dividing the prior year end account balance by a factor from the Uniform Lifetime Table (Appendix A). The table is designed to assure (by keeping required distributions small enough) that the retirement plan will last for the Participant's entire lifetime. If the Participant's spouse is sole beneficiary of the account and is more than 10 years younger than Participant, required distributions can be even smaller, so the account can last even longer. ¶ 1.4 explains how to compute required lifetime distributions, and the special rule for a more-than-10-years-younger spouse. Chapter 10 (¶ 10.1.01, ¶ 10.1.02) has some planning tips for lifetime distributions.

After Participant's death, the beneficiaries of the plan must start taking distributions (regardless of how young or old Participant was when he died). The general rule is easy: annual distributions are required over the life expectancy of the beneficiary.

There are quite a few twists and exceptions to the easy general rule. For example, the beneficiary's life expectancy is computed using a different table (Single Life Table; Appendix A) than was used during Participant's lifetime, and also a different basic method (fixed term rather than annual recalculation; see ¶ 1.2.06). One BIG problem is that retirement plans are not required to offer this favorable payout form—many plans offer only a lump sum (see ¶ 1.5.09).

The other BIG problem is that only certain beneficiaries, called "designated beneficiaries" (basically, individuals and qualifying trusts) qualify for this life expectancy payout. Many Participants die without having named the right kind of beneficiary; for example, the Participant's "estate" cannot be a "designated beneficiary" (see ¶ 1.7.04). If there is no qualifying ("designated") beneficiary at Participant's death, things get more complicated. The benefits must be paid out over a default period.

The default period is different depending on when Participant died. It is either (1) what would have been the Participant's remaining single life expectancy period had he lived (if Participant died on or after his "Required Beginning Date") (see ¶ 1.5.05) or (2) within five years after Participant's death (if Participant died before his "Required Beginning Date") (see ¶ 1.5.04). The good news is that these default rules also operate as a "floor" payout period that can be used even if there is a "designated beneficiary."

More good news is: if the beneficiary is the surviving spouse of the Participant, there may be even more favorable options available; see ¶ 1.6. There is even some leeway to "fix" defective beneficiary designations after the Participant has died. See ¶ 1.8.

Now, if that summary didn't tell you everything you need to know, ¶ 1.1.02 tells you where to find more detail:

1.1.02 *Where to find things in this Chapter*

This Chapter covers, throughout, both *planning* and *compliance* issues regarding the minimum distribution rules.

The rest of this ¶ 1.1 explains the importance of the minimum distribution rules, for planning as well as compliance reasons (¶ 1.1.04), and describes the Code provisions and regulations that will be referred to throughout Chapter 1 (¶ 1.1.05).

¶ 1.2.01 illustrates the financial effects of the "life expectancy payout method." *You cannot do proper estate planning for retirement benefits without understanding these financial effects.*

The rest of ¶ 1.2 provides the nuts and bolts of MRDs, starting with the terminology such as "designated beneficiary," "distribution year," MRD and RBD (¶ 1.2.02), and the basic rules that apply across the board (such as when each year's distribution must be taken, and why taking more in one year does not mean you can take less in a later year; ¶ 1.2.03). You need to read those sections even if you are not responsible for calculating MRDs, just to get the lay of the land. If you are in "compliance mode," and you need to actually calculate an MRD, you need to read all of ¶ 1.2, to find out which "life expectancy table" to use (¶ 1.2.04), what a person's "age" means for MRD purposes (¶ 1.2.05), the difference between fixed-term and recalculation life expectancy payouts (¶ 1.2.06) and what account balance the calculations apply to (¶ 1.2.07, ¶ 1.2.08).

¶ 1.3 is all about the "Required Beginning Date" for lifetime required distributions: when it is (differs depending on the type of plan; ¶ 1.3.00-¶ 1.3.04), and such knotty problems as what "retirement" means (no-one knows; ¶ 1.3.06), what a "5% owner is" (you may be surprised; ¶ 1.3.05), and the special rules for rollover contributions (¶ 1.3.08). You need to read ¶ 1.3 if you are advising a living Participant when he/she must start taking required distributions. If you are advising survivors of a deceased Participant who died somewhere around age 70½, you must read about the "limbo period" (¶ 1.3.07) to figure out which post-death distribution rules apply.

¶ 1.5 gives exhaustive precise detail regarding post-death required distributions for every possible combination of beneficiaries: non-spouse individual, spouse, non-individual, and multiple beneficiaries, whether death is before or after the Required Beginning Date (¶ 1.5.02, ¶ 1.5.03), and shows how to compute the MRD in each case. While most of ¶ 1.5 is purely for compliance purposes, every planner needs to be aware of the 5-year rule (¶ 1.5.04), Participant's-remaining-life-expectancy rule (¶ 1.5.05), what happens if the beneficiary dies after the Participant (¶ 1.5.07), and how the "law of the plan" can override everything else (¶ 1.5.09).

¶ 1.6 explains the special distribution rules that apply if the beneficiary is the Participant's spouse, including the "trap" that can occur if both spouses die young (¶ 1.6.05). Read this if advising a surviving spouse, or advising a living Participant who is considering leaving benefits to his/her spouse.

Planning success hinges on having the right beneficiary. ¶ 1.7 explains the importance of having a "designated beneficiary" (¶ 1.7.01), the difference between a plain-old "beneficiary" and a *designated* beneficiary" (¶ 1.7.02, ¶ 1.7.03), what happens if the "estate" is the beneficiary (¶ 1.7.04), the all-important planning tool known as the separate accounts rule (¶ 1.7.06), and why sometimes it all just doesn't matter (¶ 1.7.07). All of ¶ 1.7 is key information for success in planning and compliance.

¶ 1.8 explains the "Designation Date" concept and rules: what changes can (and cannot) be made to "improve" the Participant's beneficiary designation after he has already died. Read this section if you are doing any post-mortem planning, or if you are doing an estate plan (for a living Participant) that may depend on post-death actions for its success.

¶ 1.9 covers all the other MRD rules that didn't fit in anywhere else such as how to take MRDs if there are multiple plans (¶ 1.9.01); where the money in the account goes if the originally-named beneficiary survives the Participant but then dies while there's still money in the account (¶ 1.9.02); and what kinds of distributions "count" towards the MRD requirement (¶ 1.9.03, ¶ 1.9.04).

¶ 1.10 deals with enforcement. This is the section you don't want to have to read. It explains who enforces the rules and the penalties for violating the rules. Since advising someone who has missed taking some of his MRDs usually requires going back into past years, this part provides more detail about the effective dates of the various rounds of MRD regulations.

Finally, ¶ 1.11 summarizes the planning principles that derive from the minimum distribution rules.

1.1.03 *What this Chapter does not cover*

The minimum distribution system discussed in this Chapter applies to "individual account plans," including money purchase pension plans, profit sharing plans, 401(k) plans, 403(b) plans and IRAs. If benefits are paid in the form of an *annuity*, different rules apply. See Temp. Reg. § 1.401(a)(9)-6T. This book does not cover annuity payouts. See ¶ 5.1.03 for explanation of which rules in this

Chapter do, and which do not, apply to Roth IRAs.

This Chapter discusses certain distribution options that are available to *individual beneficiaries* and *qualifying trusts* (see ¶ 1.7.03); the definition of what constitutes a qualifying trust is in a different Chapter (¶ 6.2.04).

This Chapter discusses only the rules applicable to 2002 and later years under the IRS's 2001-2002 proposed and final minimum distribution regulations (¶ 1.1.05). For explanation of the old rules (under the 1987 proposed regulations) consult Chapter 1 of the 1999 edition of this book (see Bibliography). Those old rules could be used through the 2002 distribution year, but after 2002 they will be of interest only in rare situations, such as catch-up distributions for individuals who failed to take required distributions for past years (¶ 1.10.02), or for individuals who revoke "TEFRA 242(b) designations" (¶ 8.5.02).

Finally, while this Chapter explains the minimum distribution rules applicable to most qualified retirement plans and IRAs, there are grandfather rules and exceptions which exempt some individuals and plans from some or all of the requirements. See ¶ 8.5.

1.1.04 Why the minimum distribution rules are important

Congress wants tax-favored retirement plans to be *retirement* plans—not estate-building, wealth transfer vehicles. To that end, Congress enacted § 401(a)(9), which compels certain annual "minimum required distributions" (MRDs) from plans beginning generally at age 70½ or, if earlier, death. Failure to distribute the required minimum results in a 50% penalty tax on amounts that should have been distributed but were not. § 4974; ¶ 1.10.02. § 401(a)(9) and its related regulations are called the "minimum distribution rules."

Despite the apparent goal of these rules (assuring that tax-favored retirement plans are used primarily to provide retirement income), § 401(a)(9) permits tax deferral to continue long past the death of the participant whose work created the benefit—*if* the participant leaves his retirement benefits to the right kind of beneficiary. If various requirements (described in this Chapter) are met, Congress allows the retirement benefits to be paid out gradually, after the worker's death, over the life expectancy of the worker's beneficiary. The financial benefit of the long-term tax deferral permitted by the minimum distribution rules (see ¶ 1.2.01) puts a premium on naming a beneficiary who will qualify for (and make best use of) this "life expectancy payout method."

The IRS's simplification of the minimum distribution rules in 2001-2002 (¶ 1.1.05) has lulled some practitioners into thinking that favorable tax treatment is now assured for everyone, without the need for careful planning. As the length and complexity of this Chapter attest, this impression is false. Tax and estate planning professionals still need to study these rules, for both planning and compliance reasons.

<u>Planning</u> has become easier, but maximizing the value of the client's retirement benefits still depends on naming the right beneficiary. Changes in the Internal Revenue Code in 2001 permit larger contributions to retirement plans, and the 2001-2002 minimum distribution rule changes allow participants to leave money in their retirement plans longer; together, these changes mean that clients will be able to pass larger sums on to their chosen beneficiaries in the form of tax-favored retirement plans. The regulations also give older participants more flexibility than pre-2001 rules allowed to change beneficiaries to achieve a favorable estate planning result. Thus, there will be *more money* riding on the "right" choice of beneficiary and *less excuse* for not making the best choice.

<u>Compliance</u> has probably become more important. It seems likely (see ¶ 1.10.02) that the IRS, post-2002, will be less forgiving of errors in computing minimum distributions and more stringent in enforcing the 50% penalty tax. Paying this penalty would be a painful experience for any client (and for any advisor held responsible for the mistake).

1.1.05 *The minimum distribution regulations*

Congress established the minimum distribution system of § 401(a)(9) in substantially its present form in the Tax Reform Act of 1986. In 1987, the IRS issued proposed regulations § 1.401(a)(9)-1 and -2, and § 54.4974-2, interpreting and implementing the minimum distribution rules. One section of these 1987 proposed regulations was amended in December 1997. The 1987 proposed regulations, as amended in 1997, are referred to in this Chapter as "the 1987 proposed regulations."

In January 2001, the IRS issued revised proposed regulations, replacing the 1987 version, and issued a corrected version March 12,

2001 (2001-11 I.R.B. 865). With some further changes, these 2001 proposed regulations were re-issued as (mostly) final regulations in April 2002. The 2002 regulations are Reg. § 1.401(a)(9)-0 through § 1.401(a)(9)-5; Reg. § 1.401(a)(9)-7 through § 1.401(a)(9)-9; § 1.403(b)-3; § 1.408-8; and § 54.4974-2; and Proposed and Temporary Reg. § 1.401(a)(9)-6. The regulations begin with preliminary matter entitled "Supplementary Information." This preliminary material is referred to in this book as the "Preamble."

Regulations § 1.401(a)(9)-0 through § 1.401(a)(9)-9 are addressed to qualified plans, but the same rules apply (with certain variations) also to IRAs and 403(b) plans, consistent with the Congressional mandate that rules "similar to" the rules of § 401(a)(9) shall apply to IRAs (§ 408(a)(6)) and 403(b) plans (§ 403(b)(10)). Reg. § 1.408-8, A-1(a) (IRAs) and § 1.403(b)-3, A-1(a) (403(b) plans).

1.1.06 *Effective dates of the proposed and final regulations*

Although the final regulations completely restate, and replace, both versions of the proposed regulations, all three sets (1987 proposed, 2001 proposed and 2002 final) applied in varying degrees in 2002. "For determining required minimum distributions for calendar year 2002, taxpayers may rely on" either the "final regulations, the 2001 proposed regulations, or the 1987 proposed regulations." Preamble, "Effective Date."

The final regulations apply to all plans, participants and beneficiaries for calendar years beginning on or after January 1, 2003. Reg. § 1.401(a)(9)-1, A-2. There is no "grandfather rule" that would allow any person to keep using the 1987 proposed regulations to calculate his or her required distributions. However, a few individuals were already "grandfathered" from even the 1987 proposed regulations by virtue of a "TEFRA 242(b) election" made prior to 1984; these individuals can continue their grandfathered status under the final regulations. See ¶ 8.5.02.

The final regulations confirm that post-death MRDs are determined under the final regulations *regardless of when the Participant died.* When determining MRDs from the account of a Participant who died prior to the existence of these regulations, "the designated beneficiary must be redetermined....and the applicable distribution period must be reconstructed" in accordance with the new rules. Reg. § 1.401(a)(9)-1, A-2(b). The switch from basing the

Applicable Distribution Period (ADP) for post-death distributions on the beneficiaries *as of the required beginning date* (RBD) (under the old rules) to basing it on the beneficiaries *as of the date of death* will help many beneficiaries.

Example: On his RBD in 1995, Dan named his wife Trish as primary beneficiary of his IRA and named his children as contingent beneficiaries. He never changed his beneficiary designation. Trish died in 1999 and Dan died in 2001. The children inherited the IRA. Under the old rules, the children would have to withdraw the benefits over the remaining joint life expectancy (if any) of Dan and Trish. Under the final regulations, the designated beneficiary and ADP are redetermined as of the date of Dan's death, as if the new rules had been in effect then. This redetermination changes the designated beneficiary from wife Trish (under the old rules) to the four children (under the new rules), and changes the ADP to the oldest child's life expectancy. The children can even use each child's individual life expectancy, if they established "separate accounts" by December 31, 2002; see PLR 2002-48030 for example. The applicable date for determining who are the "designated beneficiaries" of this account for purposes of post-death required distributions has shifted from *Dan's RBD* (back in 1995, when the beneficiary was Trish) to *the date of Dan's death* (by which time the children, not Trish, are the beneficiaries).

Glitch in final regulations

If a decedent died in 2000, the beneficiaries had until 12/31/01 (under the 2001 proposed regulations) to "finalize" the beneficiary designation; see ¶ 1.8. If the beneficiary is re-determined under the final regulations' rules, as required by Reg. § 1.401(a)(9)-1, A-2(b), however, the beneficiaries would have had only until 9/30/01 to clean up the decedent's mistakes. What if they had paid out all non-individual beneficiaries by 12/31 but not by 9/30? Presumably the IRS did not intend that the final regulations would un-do valid beneficiary designations carried out in good faith under proposed regulations issued only 15 months previously.

1.2 Overview of the
Life Expectancy Payout Method

1.2.01 *How life expectancy method works; economics of MRDs*

The minimum distribution rules dictate when a retirement plan participant ("Participant"), or a beneficiary, must begin taking money out of the plan, and, once required distributions begin, how much must be taken out of the plan each year. Under most methods of computing required distributions, the annual "minimum required distribution" (MRD) is calculated by dividing an annually-revalued account balance by a life expectancy factor. (The exception is the "5-year rule"; see ¶ 1.5.04.)

The basic idea is that, during retirement, Participant must take annual withdrawals from his retirement plans (except Roth IRAs; ¶ 5.1.03). These mandated withdrawals are designed to reduce the retirement plan balance to a negligible amount over the joint and survivor life expectancy of Participant and a hypothetical beneficiary. The way the formula works (¶ 1.4.01), if Participant takes only the MRD each year, the account will have a positive balance for his entire lifetime (unless it is wiped out by investment losses).

In fact, depending on the rate of investment return, there may well be more in the account when Participant dies than there was when required distributions began. For example, if Participant takes only the MRD starting at age 70½, and the account has a steady 6% annual investment return, the account will have more dollars in it at his death than it did when he started taking required distributions if he dies prior to age 89. If investment returns are higher than 6%, the account value will stay above its age-70½ value to an even later age.

Once Participant dies, the rules become more restrictive. *If* the account is payable to the right type of beneficiary (individuals or qualifying trusts; see ¶ 1.7), *and* the life expectancy payout method is available under the plan in question (see ¶ 1.5.09), the rules require the beneficiary to take annual withdrawals designed to reduce the retirement plan account balance to zero over the life expectancy of the beneficiary. More favorable payout options are available if the beneficiary is Participant's spouse; see ¶ 1.6.

Again depending on the rate of investment return, if the beneficiary is young, and takes no more than the required minimum each year, the value of the inherited plan can double or triple, under the life expectancy payout method, by the time the *beneficiary* reaches retirement age.

Example: Two brothers died. Both were younger than age 70½. Each brother left his entire estate, including a $500,000 IRA, to his daughter. Both daughters, Lena and Tina, turned age 38 in the year following the year of the brothers' deaths. Each of the daughters, after taking a round-the-world cruise, buying a new house, and paying the estate taxes on her father's estate, was left with just one asset, the $500,000 IRA. Each daughter resolved to: withdraw from the inherited IRA only the minimum amount required by law; invest the after-tax proceeds of the withdrawals; and regard the inherited IRA plus the accumulated after-tax distributions as her retirement fund.

Each daughter kept her resolve, investing both in-plan and out-of-plan assets in 8% bonds, and paying income taxes at the rate of 36% on all plan withdrawals and bond interest, but there was one difference: Tina's father had named Tina as his "designated beneficiary," so Tina was entitled to withdraw her father's IRA in installments over her 45.6-year life expectancy. Lena's father had named no beneficiary; he never got around to filling out a designation of beneficiary form. Under the terms of the account agreement governing his IRA, since he had not named any beneficiary, his "beneficiary" was his estate. In minimum distribution rule jargon, he had "no designated beneficiary." Lena, the sole beneficiary of the estate, had to withdraw all money from her father's IRA within five years after his death.

After 30 years, Lena has a $1,517,000 investment portfolio, not in any IRA. Tina has $1,432,000 outside the IRA, plus $1,696,000 still *inside* the IRA she inherited from her father. Tina has 15.6 years left in her "life expectancy" over which to withdraw the remaining IRA balance. So, after 30 years, the daughter who used the life expectancy payout method has almost twice as much money as the daughter who withdrew benefits under the 5-year rule. Projections prepared using Brentmark Pension & Roth Analyzer® (Tina) and NumberCruncher® (Lena) software; see Appendix C.

The most valuable feature of retirement plans is the ability to invest without current taxation of the investment profits. In most cases, investing through a retirement plan defers income tax not only on the investment profits but also on Participant's compensation income that was originally contributed to the plan. This income tax is deferred until the date the money is distributed out of the plan to Participant or beneficiary. ¶ 2.1.01. The longer this deferral continues, the better, because, generally, the deferral of income tax increases the ultimate value of the benefits. See ¶ 10.1.01 for discussion of when deferral may be less attractive than other alternatives.

So long as assets stay in the retirement plan, Participant is investing not just "Participant's own" money, but also "Uncle Sam's share" of Participant's compensation and investment profits, i.e., the money that Participant otherwise would have had to pay to the IRS (and will eventually have to pay to the IRS) in income taxes. Keeping the money in the retirement plan enables Participant to reap a profit from investing "the IRS's money" along with his own. Once funds are distributed from the plan, they are included in the gross income of Participant or beneficiary (see ¶ 2.1.03 for exceptions), and Participant or beneficiary pays the IRS its share. Thereafter Participant (or beneficiary) will no longer enjoy any investment profits from the government's share of the plan.

Congress allows this tax-deferred investing to continue past the death of the worker whose "retirement plan" this is supposed to be—and even past the death of the worker's surviving spouse—but only if the account is left to a "designated beneficiary" (¶ 1.7). Congress allows the tax-deferred investing to continue over the life expectancy of a "designated beneficiary" regardless of how young that beneficiary may be.

The maximum theoretical duration of a retirement plan account is almost two full life-spans. Consider a 16-year old who contributes $3,000 from his summer job earnings to an IRA in 2003, lives to be 102 and then dies leaving the account to his newborn great grandchild, who has a life expectancy of 82.4 years. If Participant and beneficiary take only minimum required distributions, the last dollar of the 2003 summer job earnings may not be taxed until 2171. If you add in the possibility of a rollover by Participant's surviving spouse (¶ 3.2) the final distribution could occur even later than that.

Calculating minimum distributions by dividing an annually-revalued account balance by the beneficiary's life expectancy tends to produce gradually increasing installments over the years, so long as the plan has a positive investment return. As long as the beneficiary's remaining life expectancy is greater than [100 ÷ the plan's annual growth rate], the plan balance will be growing faster than the beneficiary is withdrawing it. For example, if the plan is growing at 8% per year, and the beneficiary's life expectancy is 20 years, the first year's required distribution (1/20, or 5%), is less than the plan's earnings for the year (1/12.5, or 8%).

Eventually the beneficiary's life expectancy is reduced to the point that he is withdrawing more than the year's investment return. If the plan is growing at 8% per year, this crossover point would be reached 12.5 years before the end of the payout period. Even after this crossover point, the annual required minimum distributions tend to keep getting larger; though the plan balance is now shrinking, the fraction applied to it grows larger.

Note: the discussion above assumes a fixed, unwavering, investment return, which is impossible to achieve in real life. See Appendix C for discussion of software products available to help make this type of financial projection.

1.2.02 *Minimum distribution terminology*

The most important term in the minimum distribution dictionary is "**designated beneficiary**." The favorable "life-expectancy-of-the-beneficiary" payout method is available only if Participant's death benefits pass to a "designated beneficiary." A designated beneficiary is one or more individuals or qualifying trusts; see ¶ 1.7 for details. Since not every beneficiary is a *designated* beneficiary, the planner must understand what a designated beneficiary is, how to go about getting one, and why and when it matters. ¶ 1.7 explains all of those points.

Other minimum distribution terms are less mysterious, and less crucial to proper planning (though important for understanding and complying with the rules).

A year for which a minimum distribution is required is called a "distribution calendar year" in the regulations (in this book, "**distribution year**" for short). Reg. § 1.401(a)(9)-5, A-1(b).

The life expectancy period over which distributions must be made is called the "applicable distribution period" in the regulations ("**Applicable Distribution Period**" in this book). Reg. § 1.401(a)(9)-5, A-1(a). The life expectancy factor used to determine required distributions is sometimes called the "**applicable divisor**."

In this book, "**MRD**" stands for **minimum required distribution**. What is called in this book an MRD is called in the IRS regulations a "required minimum distribution" or "RMD." This book uses "MRD" rather than "RMD" only to head off confusion with the abbreviation "RBD" (required beginning date).

"RBD" stands for required beginning date; the concept of the **"required beginning date"** is explained at ¶ 1.3.

For abbreviations not explained here see the list of "Abbreviations Used in This Book," page xx. For definitions of types of retirement plans, see the Glossary at page 533.

1.2.03 *Basic rules of MRDs and life expectancy payout method*

MRDs (except in the case of the "5-year rule"; ¶ 1.5.04) are computed by dividing an annually-revalued account balance by a declining life expectancy factor. Reg. § 1.401(a)(9)-5, A-1(a). The first step in calculating MRDs, therefore, is to figure out the correct account balance and life expectancy factor to use. You also need to figure out when the distributions must start, the deadline for taking each year's distribution, and who is the right person to take the distribution. This Chapter provides all those details. In the meantime, here are some overall guidelines explaining how the life expectancy payout method works:

1.   Annual distributions required: Once required distributions begin, Participant (or beneficiary) generally must take a distribution every calendar year. Reg. § 1.401(a)(9)-5, A-1. The 5-year rule (¶ 1.5.04) is the only "minimum distribution rule" that does not require annual distributions.

2.   No maximum distribution: The formula (account balance divided by life expectancy factor) tells you the *minimum required* distribution. The rules impose no maximum distribution; Participant (or beneficiary) is always free, as far as the IRS is concerned, to take more than the minimum.

3.   Each year stands on it own: Taking more than the required amount in one year does not give you a "credit" you can use to reduce distributions in a later year. Reg. § 1.401(a)(9)-5, A-2. (Taking larger distributions in one year indirectly reduces later required distributions by reducing the account balance.)

4.   The "Law of the Plan": Just because a Participant or beneficiary qualifies for the life expectancy payout method under the law does not mean he will actually get to use it; the plan must allow it too. See ¶ 1.5.09.

5.   Deadline is December 31 (except...): The final date for taking each year's required distribution is December 31 of the year in question. Reg. § 1.401(a)(9)-5, A-1(c). The only exception is that, in the case of certain lifetime required distributions, the distribution for the first "distribution year" can be postponed until April 1 of the following year. ¶ 1.3.00, ¶ 1.3.07. For unusual situations in which an MRD can be delayed beyond these deadlines, see ¶ 1.10.02.

6.   Distributions before RBD irrelevant: Distributions taken prior to the RBD have no effect on how required distributions are calculated when Participant reaches the RBD. There is neither an advantage nor a disadvantage (in terms of what the MRD formula will be) to taking distributions prior to the RBD. Reg. § 1.401(a)(9)-2, A-4, A-6. If Participant irrevocably elects a particular form of distribution (such as an annuity payout) prior to the RBD, the payments under the form of benefit he has elected must conform to the minimum distribution requirements once he reaches the RBD. For whether there is some *other* advantage to taking distributions prior to the RBD, see ¶ 10.1.01-¶ 10.1.02.

7.   Divisors are not percentages: The divisors in the applicable life expectancy table are divided into the account balance to produce the MRD; the divisor ("Applicable Distribution Period") is not a percentage amount. For example, in the year a person turns age 70, his "divisor" under the Uniform Lifetime Table is 27.4. That means his MRD is 1/27.4 times the account balance (about 3.65%)—not 27.4% times the account balance.

8.   Maximum distribution is 100%: "...the required minimum distribution amount will never exceed the entire account balance on the date of the distribution." Reg. § 1.401(a)(9)-5, A-1(a). This rule helps out when investment losses have caused the account to decline in value so much that the total value is

less than the required distribution for the year.

1.2.04 *How to determine a person's life expectancy*

Calculating MRDs requires you to look up a life expectancy ("Applicable Distribution Period") in an IRS-supplied table. The tables currently in use are:

1.   The "Uniform Lifetime Table" at Reg. § 1.401(a)(9)-9, A-2, will normally be used for determining lifetime required distributions to the Participant for 2003 and later years (¶ 1.4.01; see Appendix A). For the 2002 distribution year, a Participant could use either the Uniform Lifetime Table *or* the prior version of it (2001 Uniform Table) that was issued in the 2001 proposed regulations; or the method that applied to such Participant under the 1987 proposed regulations. For earlier years, see ¶ 1.10.04.

2.   The "Joint and Last Survivor Table" (Reg. § 1.401(a)(9)-9, A-3) is used, in 2003 and later years, for determining lifetime required distributions of a Participant whose sole beneficiary is his more-than-10-years-younger spouse (¶ 1.4.02). This table can be found in IRS Publication 590. For the 2002 distribution year, such a Participant may use either that table or the Joint Life and Last Survivor Expectancy Table from Reg. § 1.72-9, which is reproduced in Appendix E of IRS Publication 590 (where it is called "Table II").

3.   The "Single Life Table" (Reg. § 1.401(a)(9)-9, A-1) is used, in 2003 and later years, for determining post-death required distributions to an individual designated beneficiary or qualifying trust (¶ 1.5.06). It is also used for determining the remaining life expectancy of a Participant or spouse when that calculation is required; see ¶ 1.5.05 and ¶ 1.6.06. The Single Life Table is in Appendix A of this book.

All these tables are "unisex" (life expectancy for men and women is the same). The IRS uses still another set of actuarial tables for estate and gift tax valuations; see § 7520.

1.2.05 *What is a person's "age" for MRD purposes*

A person's "age" for purposes of the life expectancy tables (¶ 1.2.04) means the age he will attain on his birthday in the "distribution year." Stated another way, it is the age he will be at the end of the distribution year. Reg. § 1.401(a)(9)-5, A-4(a), (b); A-5(c).

Example: Clark turns age 70½ in 2002. 2002 is the first "distribution year" for his IRA, even though he does not actually have to take this first year's distribution until April 1, 2003. ¶ 1.3.00. To compute the 2002 required distribution, he looks up the "Applicable Distribution Period" for his age in the Uniform Lifetime Table. The age he will use is the age he will attain on his 2002 birthday, which will be 70 if he was born before July 1, or 71 if he was born after June 30.

Example: Bonnie died in 2001, before her RBD, leaving her IRA to Diane as designated beneficiary (¶ 1.7). Diane plans to use the life expectancy payout method to take distributions from the IRA. To determine the Applicable Distribution Period, she finds her life expectancy in the Single Life Table as of the first distribution year, which is 2002 (the year after the year in which Bonnie died; ¶ 1.5.06). The age she looks up in that table is her age as of her birthday in 2002 (i.e., her age as of the end of 2002).

Example: Josephine, surviving spouse of Napoleon, was sole beneficiary of Napoleon's 401(k) plan. She is taking annual MRDs as Napoleon's beneficiary; she did not roll over the benefits to her own retirement plan (¶ 3.2). Each year, the plan sends a required distribution to Josephine based on her life expectancy in that year. The life expectancy (Applicable Distribution Period) the plan uses each year (from the Single Life Table) is that for Josephine's attained age on her birthday *in the year of the distribution* (i.e., her age as of the end of each distribution year). ¶ 1.6.06.

1.2.06 *Recalculation of life expectancy vs. fixed term method*

There are two methods of computing life expectancy for minimum distribution purposes. The Participant or beneficiary taking the distribution has no choice in this matter—the regulations dictate which method must be used in which situation.

Under the "fixed term method," you determine the applicable life expectancy in the first distribution year; then in each subsequent year, you just deduct one year from that initial number. Some people call this the "reduce-by-one" method. The fixed term method is used to determine required distributions to non-spouse beneficiaries, including a qualifying trust of which the spouse is not the sole beneficiary. ¶ 1.5.06, ¶ 1.5.08.

Example: Bonnie died in 2001 and left her IRA to Diane, who is younger than Bonnie, as designated beneficiary. Diane plans to use the life expectancy payout method to take distributions from the IRA. The Applicable Distribution Period is Diane's single life expectancy (¶ 1.2.04) as of the first distribution year, which is 2002 (the year after Bonnie's death). Diane turns 46 on her birthday in 2002, so her life expectancy from the Single Life Table is 37.9. For calculating her required distributions for 2003 (and later years), Diane just deducts one from the prior year's life expectancy (so her 2003 "divisor" is 36.9, 2004 is 35.9, and so on). She never goes "back to the table" again after the first distribution year.

When the fixed term method applies, the distribution period runs out eventually. In the case of Bonnie and Diane, the final required distribution will occur in the 38th year after Bonnie's death and it will wipe out the remaining balance of the account. Thus, even though Diane may well live more than 37.9 years after Bonnie's demise, her inherited IRA will run out of money no later than 2039. If Diane dies before her life expectancy runs out, her death does not change the calculation of MRDs: required distributions to whoever succeeds to the account at that point will still be based on what's left of Diane's original life expectancy. ¶ 1.5.07.

Under the "recalculation" method, the life expectancy is "redetermined" every year. Instead of just deducting one from last year's life expectancy, you go back to the applicable table and look up the new life expectancy (or "Applicable Distribution Period" or "divisor") based on the new age. Recalculation is used for determining *all* lifetime required distributions to Participant (¶ 1.4.01, ¶ 1.4.02), and for determining post-death required distributions to a surviving spouse who is sole beneficiary (¶ 1.6.06). Under the recalculation method, life expectancy never runs out as long as the distributee is alive.

Example: Josephine, the surviving spouse of Napoleon and sole beneficiary of Napoleon's 401(k) plan, is taking required distributions based on her life expectancy. She turned 46 in the year after Napoleon's death, so her "divisor" (Applicable Distribution Period) for the first distribution year was 37.9, just like Diane's first year divisor in the preceding example. For the second distribution year, however, Josephine's divisor is not 36.9 (37.9 minus one—as it would be if she were using the fixed term method); instead Josephine's second year divisor is 37.0 (the single life expectancy of a person age 47). The fixed term method doesn't apply when the surviving spouse is the sole beneficiary. Josephine, as a surviving spouse-sole beneficiary, determines her divisor each year by going back to the life expectancy table and determining her new life expectancy based on her new age (recalculation method).

1.2.07 *What account balance the "divisor" applies to*

Each year, the MRD is determined by dividing the prior year-end account value by the applicable life expectancy factor (divisor). Exactly which "account value" is used depends on the type of retirement plan involved; and once the account value is ascertained, it may require certain adjustments (¶ 1.2.08) before it is ready to be used in the MRD formula.

In the case of a *qualified plan*, the account value used is "the account balance as of the last valuation date in the calendar year immediately preceding" the distribution year. Reg. § 1.401(a)(9)-5, A-3(a). A plan might have only one valuation date per plan year (such as "the last day of the plan year"), or it might have more than one. If the plan's last valuation date in the prior calendar year was December 31, you just use the account value as of that date and move on to ¶ 1.2.08.

If the plan's last valuation date in the prior calendar year was earlier than December 31, the last-valuation-date account balance must be:

1.   Increased by any forfeitures that were allocated to the account, and any contributions that were actually added to the account, on any date that is after the valuation date but is still within the "valuation calendar year." Contributions that were *allocated to* the account for the valuation calendar year, but not actually *added to* the account until after the end of the calendar year, do

not have to be included in the account balance; this feature is a change from the 2001 proposed regulations, under which the account balance had to include contributions allocated to the account for the year even if they were not made until after the close of the year; and

2.   Decreased by any distributions from the account made after the valuation date but before the end of the valuation calendar year. Reg. § 1.401(a)(9)-5, A-3(b), (c)(1).

Example: Tana is taking MRDs from a profit sharing plan. The plan operates on a November 30 fiscal year, and has only one annual valuation date, namely, November 30. To calculate Tana's MRD for calendar 2003, you would start with her November 30, 2002, account balance. This account balance is then increased by any forfeitures that are allocated to the account (and contributions made to the account) on any date that is after the valuation date but is still within the "valuation calendar year"; in this example, that would mean the account balance is increased, for purposes of performing the MRD calculation, by contributions made, and forfeitures (but not investment profits) allocated, to Tana's account as of any date in December, 2002. Contributions *allocated* to her account during December, but not actually *contributed* until 2003, can be ignored. Second, assume Tana took a distribution of $10,000 in December, 2002. This $10,000 distribution is deducted from her November 30, 2002, account balance for purposes of calculating her 2003 required distribution.

If the plan in question is an *IRA*, the account balance is "the value of the IRA upon close of business" on December 31 of the calendar year immediately preceding the distribution year. Reg. § 1.408-8, A-6. No adjustment is required for contributions or distributions occurring between the plan's "last valuation date" and the end of the calendar year, because the last valuation date of an IRA *is* the end of the calendar year.

1.2.08 *Required (and forbidden) adjustments to the account balance*

Once you have the correct "prior year-end account balance" (ascertained as provided in ¶ 1.2.07) two further adjustments may be required.

First, under the 2001 proposed regulations, *but not under the final regulations*, in computing the required distribution for a living Participant's second distribution year, the prior year-end account balance is reduced by the amount of any MRD for the first distribution year that had not yet been taken as of the close of the first distribution year—provided Participant actually takes that first-year MRD no later than the RBD. Compare proposed and final Reg. § 1.401(a)(9)-5, A-3(c). *This adjustment cannot be used in 2003 or later years.*

Example: Ramsey turned age 70½ in 2001. The MRD for her IRA for that year was $5,000. As permitted by law (¶ 1.3.07), she did not take that distribution until January 2002. The December 31, 2001, value of the IRA was $140,000, but that value includes the not-yet-distributed 2001 MRD of $5,000. To calculate her 2002 MRD *under the 2001 proposed regulations*, the account value she will use is $140,000 minus $5,000, or $135,000. To calculate her 2002 MRD *under the final regulations*, the account value is $140,000 with no deduction allowed for the undistributed 2001 MRD.

Second, you must *increase* the prior year-end balance by any amount that was added to the account in the distribution year ("Year 2") but which represented a rollover from another plan or IRA, if the amount in question was distributed from such other plan or IRA in the *prior* calendar year ("Year 1"). For purposes of MRDs from the *receiving* plan, such a rollover amount is deemed to have been received in the prior calendar year (i.e., Year 1) and not the year it was actually received (Year 2). Reg. § 1.401(a)(9)-7, A-2 (last sentence). If this rule did not exist, people could cheat by moving money around from account to account at the end of the year, so as to avoid having the funds count as part of the year-end account balance of *either* plan.

Example: Whit has two IRAs, IRA # 1 and IRA # 2, each of which holds $100,000. On December 1, Year 1, he closes IRA # 1, and withdraws the $100,000. On January 2, Year 2, he deposits the $100,000 into IRA # 2, to complete the tax-free rollover (see ¶ 2.5). In Year 2, there is no MRD from IRA # 1 because it no longer exists. The balance of IRA # 2 on December 31, Year 1, was only $100,000. If it weren't for Reg. § 1.401(a)(9)-7, A-2, Whit's MRD from IRA # 2 would be based on only $100,000. Because of this regulation, however, he has to use the adjusted account balance, $200,000. The $100,000 that was added to IRA # 2 after the beginning of the year by means of a rollover distribution from another plan "counts" because the distribution came out of the other plan in the prior year.

Reg. § 1.401(a)(9)-7 contains other lengthy rules regarding the effect of rollovers and plan-to-plan transfers on the calculation of required distributions, but (with the exception noted in the preceding paragraph) a rollover *into* a plan or IRA has no effect on MRDs *from* that plan or IRA until the year after the rollover is received. Reg. § 1.401(a)(9)-7, A-2. The rollover contribution has the effect of increasing the plan balance of the receiving plan, which affects the calculation of the MRD for the year *following* the rollover.

1.3 The Required Beginning Date (RBD)

1.3.00 RBD: definition and significance; definition of 70½

The date on which Participant must begin taking distributions from his retirement plan is called his "required beginning date" (RBD). § 401(a)(9)(A). Though the first "distribution year" is the year the Participant reaches age 70½ (or, in some cases, retires; see ¶ 1.3.02), the "RBD" is not until April 1 of the *following* year; see ¶ 1.3.07 for more on this distinction. The RBD is not the same for every type of retirement plan.

The RBD matters mainly for *compliance* purposes. The Participant must start taking out the required distributions by that date to avoid penalty. Also, the calculation of required distributions after Participant's death is somewhat different depending on whether death occurred before, or on or after, the RBD; compare ¶ 1.5.02 with ¶ 1.5.03. The RBD has no special significance in *planning* beyond the fact that its arrival means that Participant must start drawing down his benefits.

In the Code, "required beginning date" refers only to the required commencement date of lifetime distributions to Participant. The date by which post-death distributions to the *beneficiary* must begin does not have an official name; compare § 401(a)(9)(A) and (C) with § 401(a)(9)(B). In this Chapter, "required commencement date" is used for the date by which a beneficiary must start taking distributions.

The starting point for determining the RBD is the attainment of age 70½, i.e., "the date six calendar months after the 70th anniversary of the employee's birth." Reg. § 1.401(a)(9)-2, A-3. If the participant's date of birth is December 31, 1933, it is not clear whether he attains age 70½ on June 30, 2003, or July 1, 2003, but it doesn't matter because either way he attains age 70½ in calendar 2003 and his age on his 2003 birthday is 70. In response to many questions on this point, the author does not know why Congress selected age 70½ as the trigger for required distributions.

1.3.01 *RBD for IRAs and Roth IRAs*

Roth IRAs have NO RBD. A living Participant is *never* compelled to take distributions from his Roth IRA. ¶ 5.1.03. Minimum distribution requirements do not apply to a Roth IRA until after Participant's death; see ¶ 1.5.02.

For "traditional" (i.e., non-Roth) IRAs, the RBD is generally April 1 of the calendar year following the year in which Participant reaches age 70½. § 401(a)(9)(C)(i)(I), (ii)(II). See ¶ 1.3.08 for an exception for certain rollover contributions. With a traditional IRA, there is no possibility of postponing required distributions until after a post-age 70½ retirement as there is for qualified plans and 403(b) plans (¶ 1.3.02) as long as the money remains in the IRA.

However, if an over-age-70½ IRA owner is still working, and the company he is working for has a qualified plan that will accept IRA rollovers, the employee can roll the IRA into his employer's plan. If the employee is not a 5% owner, the former IRA money now becomes eligible for the postponed RBD discussed in the next subsection. It is no longer an IRA; it is now part of the qualified retirement plan, and as such the RBD can be postponed until the employee retires from the employment of the employer that maintains the plan.

1.3.02 *Certain plans: RBD can be postponed until retirement*

The RBD for a non-5% owner (¶ 1.3.05) in a qualified plan, or for any employee in a 403(b) plan, is generally "April 1 of the calendar year following the *later of* the calendar year in which the employee attains age 70½, or the calendar year in which the employee retires from employment with the employer maintaining the plan." § 401(a)(9)(C); Reg. § 1.401(a)(9)-2, A-2(a). Emphasis added.

The ability to postpone the RBD until a late (i.e., post-age 70½) retirement is of no interest to workers who retire before age 70½; or to the business owner who owns more than 5% of his company and thus is not eligible. The typical Participants making use of the postponed RBD are executives and service professionals who work for large firms, own either no interest or just a small interest—5% or less—in the sponsoring employer, and want to work past age 70½.

Note: the above definition of RBD applies for 1997 and later years. Under the definition that was in effect between 1986 and 1997, postponing the RBD until after a post-age 70½ retirement was not an option unless a "grandfather rule" applied; see ¶ 8.5.03.

1.3.03 *RBD for qualified plans*

A qualified retirement plan (QRP) is not required to recognize the postponed RBD authorized by § 401(a)(9)(C)(i) (¶ 1.3.02). A QRP may choose to require *all* employees (even those who are not 5% owners) to commence distributions by April 1 of the calendar year following the year they reach age 70½. Reg. § 1.401(a)(9)-2, A-2(e).

If the plan does require all employees to commence distributions by April 1 of the calendar year following the year they reach age 70½, then things get a little complicated. The employee has one RBD for certain purposes, yet some of his "required" distributions from the plan are not considered "required" distributions for other purposes. Specifically, for purposes of *determining required distributions from that plan*, and *determining whether the employee died before or after his RBD for that plan*, the employee's RBD is the RBD set by the plan, *not* the RBD described in the statute—regardless of whether he owned 5% or less of the sponsoring employer and regardless of whether he had retired. Reg. § 1.401(a)(9)-2, A-6(b).

However, any distributions the employee receives during the period that is after the employee has passed *the plan's* RBD but not the *statutory* RBD are eligible for tax-free rollover. Such distributions are not considered "minimum required distributions" for purposes of the definition of eligible rollover distribution until after the employee's *statutory* RBD. IRS Notice 97-75, 1997-51 I.R.B. 18, A-10(c).

Example: Russ is 72 years old and works for Law Firm, Inc. The Law Firm, Inc. retirement plan requires all employees to commence distributions by April 1 of the calendar year following the year they reach age 70½, so Russ has passed the plan's RBD and must take required distributions. Because Russ has never retired and is not a 5-percent owner, however, his "statutory" RBD has not yet occurred, so he can roll these distributions over to an IRA. Then he dies. His death has occurred "after the RBD" for purposes of determining required distributions after his death from the Law Firm, Inc. plan

Note: If Participant was born before June 30, 1917, or has a valid pre-1984 "TEFRA 242(b) designation" in effect, there may be a later RBD than described here; see ¶ 8.5.

1.3.04 RBD for 403(b) plans

The regulations state that the RBD for all 403(b) plans is April 1 of the calendar year following the later of the year Participant reaches age 70½ and the year Participant retires. There is no possibility of a different rule for "5% owners" because all 403(b) plans are maintained by tax-exempt charitable organizations that have no "owners." Reg. § 1.403(b)-3, A-1(c)(1).

A "grandfather rule" applies to certain pre-1987 balances in 403(b) plans if separately identified. See ¶ 8.5.03 and Reg. § 1.403(b)-3, A-2, A-3.

1.3.05 Definition of "5% owner"

The ability to postpone the RBD under a QRP until after a post-age 70½ retirement is not available for "an employee who is a 5-percent owner (as defined in section 416) with respect to the plan year ending in the calendar year in which the employee attains age 70½." § 401(a)(9)(C)(ii)(I); Reg. § 1.401(a)(9)-2, A-2(c). "Once an employee is a 5-percent owner described in the preceding sentence, distributions must continue to such employee even if such employee ceases to own more than 5 percent of the employer in a subsequent year." IRS Notice 97-75, 1997-51 I.R.B. 18.

§ 416(i)(1)(B)(i) defines 5-percent owner as someone who owns "*more than* 5 percent of the outstanding stock of the corporation or stock possessing more than 5 percent of the total combined voting power of all stock of the corporation, or (II) if the employer is not a corporation, any person who owns more than 5 percent of the capital or profits interest in the employer" (emphasis added). Note that someone who owns exactly 5% is not a 5% owner—you have to own more than 5% to be a 5% owner.

In determining ownership percentages under § 416, a modified version of the "constructive ownership" rules of § 318 applies. Under these complicated rules, Participant could be deemed, for purposes of the 5% test, to own stock held by various family members, trusts, estates, partnerships or corporations; and stock options must be taken into account. When advising an employee regarding his eligibility for the postponed RBD, the advisor needs to identify not only ownership interests held by the employee himself but also those held by these related individuals and entities. Explanation of the constructive ownership rules is beyond the scope of this book.

1.3.06 What does "retirement" mean?

How many hours must Participant work, in what time frame, in order to be considered not "retired?" The author has found no definition of "retirement" in any IRS publication. Although they purport to define RBD, neither the regulations nor IRS Notice 97-75, 1997-51 I.R.B. 18 (which provides guidance to employers on the tax law changes made by the Small Business Jobs Protection Act of 1996) says anything on this point. Thus it is not clear whether "retirement" means a complete termination of employment (separation from service), or whether some less drastic reduction of employment would be considered "retirement" for this purpose.

Example: Robin, a non-5% owner, age 74, works at Geo Dezik Co. She is a participant in the Geo Dezik Profit Sharing Plan. In 2002, she reduces her hours from full time (40 hours a week) to part time (8 hours a week). The Profit Sharing Plan provides that an employee is not entitled to withdraw benefits from the plan until he "retires," but the plan defines retirement as reduction in hours worked to less than 20 hours per week if over age 65. Robin does not want to start taking distributions from the Profit Sharing Plan until she is legally required to. Is she required to start taking distributions on April 1, 2003, because she has met the plan's definition of "retirement"? Or can she wait until she has ceased all employment with this company?

For purposes of triggering required distributions, "retirement" means retirement "from employment with the employer maintaining the plan." Reg. § 1.401(a)(9)-2, A-2(a).

Example: Archibald, age 73, works at Acme Widget Co. Archibald is not a 5% owner of Acme Widget. He is a participant in the Acme Profit Sharing Plan. This plan holds funds contributed to Archibald's account by Acme Widget as well as funds rolled over into this plan from the retirement plan of Archibald's prior employer, Western Widget Corp., and funds rolled over from an IRA to which Archibald had contributed $2,000 a year for several years. Even though the funds in Archibald's accounts in the Acme Profit Sharing Plan partly represent funds from a former IRA (which, if they were still held in an IRA, would not be eligible for the postponed RBD), and from the plan of a former employer (from whose employment Archibald has "retired"), Acme Widget is "the employer maintaining the plan" which now holds these funds, and accordingly Archibald is not required to take any distributions from any part of this plan until April 1 following the year in which he retires from Acme Widget.

How this concept applies to some 403(b) plans is not clear. Although some 403(b) plans truly are "plans" maintained by a particular employer, other 403(b) "plans" are merely annuity contracts (or mutual fund custodial accounts) purchased for the employee by the employer, where the employer does not "maintain" the "plan" after the initial funding.

Example: Rolf, age 75, is a professor who is still working at Y.O.U. He has several 403(b) accounts established for him at Pari Mutual Fund Company by Y.O.U. He also has several 403(b) accounts established for him at the same mutual fund company by his former employer, Eiluv U. Since he no longer works at Eiluv U., it appears he must take distributions from the Eiluv U. 403(b) accounts unless he can roll them over into a "plan" that is "maintained" by his current employer, Y.O.U.

Another unsolved mystery: can a person retire more than once? The statute reads as though there is only one "retirement" per employee. The IRS has issued no guidance on this question.

Example: Carmen retires from the Royal Cigar Company at age 72 and starts receiving MRDs from the RCC plan. She is in the Palm View

Senior Condo Development and hates it. She is bored and the Company needs her back because business is booming. So at age 73 she goes back to work for RCC. Can her required distributions be suspended until she retires *again*?

1.3.07 *"RBD" versus "first distribution year": the limbo period*

When the RBD is April 1 of the calendar year following the year Participant reaches age 70½ (or retires, if that is the applicable event), the distribution required on that date is actually the required distribution for the *preceding* year—the year in which Participant reached age 70½ (or retired, whichever is applicable). Participant's "first distribution year" is the year he reaches age 70½ (or retires, whichever is applicable). Reg. § 1.401(a)(9)-5, A-1(b). Any distributions he takes on or after January 1 of the "first distribution year" count towards the distribution that is required to be taken by the RBD.

The fact that the first distribution year is actually the year *before* the RBD is significant for several rules; see "Rollovers" (¶ 2.5), Roth IRA conversions (¶ 5.4.07) and how to calculate the required distribution for the second distribution year (¶ 1.2.08).

Normally the deadline for taking a distribution that is required "for" a particular distribution year is December 31 *of that year*. However, in the case of lifetime required distributions, when the requirement of taking distributions is triggered by attaining age 70½ or retirement, the deadline for the first distribution year is postponed to April 1 of the *following* year. Reg. § 1.401(a)(9)-5, A-1(c). This postponement of the required distribution for the first year does not apply to death benefits (¶ 1.5), or to the first required distribution triggered by a rollover contribution (¶ 1.3.08).

If Participant takes advantage of the postponement, and delays his first required distribution until April 1 of the following year, he will have two required distributions from that plan in the second distribution year:

Example: Bernie turns age 70½ in 2002. 2002 is the "first distribution year" for his IRA. He can take the 2002 required distribution at any time in calendar 2002, or in 2003 (on or before April 1, 2003). There will be another required distribution for the year 2003, for which the deadline is December 31, 2003. He decides to postpone the 2002 distribution until March 2003. This postponement will mean his required distributions are "bunched up" in 2003 (because he will receive and pay tax on two years' distributions in that one year). It will also mean that his 2003 MRD will be larger than it would be if he took the 2002 distribution in 2002, because the "prior year-end" account balance used to compute the 2003 MRD will not be reduced by the amount of the 2002 MRD unless the 2002 MRD is actually taken out during 2002; see ¶ 1.2.08. Bernie doesn't care about these negative aspects of deferring the first year's MRD, however, because he expects his *other* income to be much lower in 2003, so deferring the first year's MRD will still lower his overall income taxes.

The difference between the "first distribution year" and the "RBD" also creates a confusing situation if Participant happens to die during the "limbo period"(from January 1 of the first distribution year to March 31 of the following year):

Example: Otto, who retired in 1998, reaches age 70½ in June 2001. The minimum distribution rules have already started to affect him, beginning back in January of the year he reached age 70½; for example, he cannot roll over a distribution from his company's retirement plan in the year 2001 until after he has taken out that plan's MRD for 2001. ¶ 2.5.06. January 2002 rolls around. Now another MRD (the one for 2002) is triggered, and still Otto has taken nothing out of the plan, but there is no rush because he has until April 1, 2002. He dies on March 31, 2002. He has died *before* his RBD. The requirement of taking MRDs for 2001 and 2002 is simply erased, because he never reached the RBD. Furthermore, even if he HAD taken part or all of his 2001 and 2002 MRDs before his death, his death would still be "before" his RBD for purposes of computing post-death required distributions. Reg. § 1.401(a)(9)-2, A-4, A-6.

1.3.08 *First required distribution date for rollover contributions*

If a rollover contribution (¶ 2.5) is made into a brand new IRA (an account which contained nothing at the time it received the rollover), there is no distribution required for the year in which the rollover contribution comes into the new account, because the prior year-end account balance was zero (see ¶ 1.2.08 and ¶ 3.2.05 for possible exceptions). The rollover will be part of the plan balance that determines the required distribution for the *following* year. The RBD for the new account is the later of (1) April 1 of the year after the year Participant reaches age 70½ or (2) December 31 of the year after the year of the rollover. PLRs 2001-23070; 1999-31049;1999-30052.

Example: Matt works for Lowden Tree. He is not a 5% owner. He turns 70½ in 2001. He has not retired yet. He is a participant in the Lowden Tree Profit Sharing Plan and also has an IRA (IRA # 1) which has been in existence for many years. The Lowden Tree Plan does not require all employees to commence distributions by April 1 of the calendar year following the year in which they reach 70½, so Matt does not yet have any required distributions from that plan (see ¶ 1.3.03). In July 2001, he takes an in-service distribution from the Lowden Tree Plan. He rolls half the distribution into his pre-existing IRA (IRA # 1) (for which his RBD is April 1, 2002, by which date he must take the 2001 required distribution). He rolls the other half into a *new* IRA (created just to receive this contribution) (IRA # 2). Although normally the RBD for an IRA is April 1 of the calendar year following the year Participant reaches age 70½, the RBD for this newly-created rollover IRA (IRA # 2) is December 31, 2002, i.e., the end of the calendar year following the rollover contribution, because the account balance was zero as of the December 31 preceding the rollover (i.e., December 31, 2000, when IRA # 2 did not exist).

In terms of *the amount Participant is required to take out as an MRD*, it doesn't matter whether the rollover is made to a new or a pre-existing IRA. In either case the rollover contribution will form part of the year-end account balance for the year in which the rollover occurred, and the dollars will have the same effect on the next year's required distribution. However, it does make a difference for *determination of the RBD*. If the amount is rolled to a pre-existing account, the RBD for that account may have already passed (or could occur earlier than December 31 of the following year, as in the case of Matt's IRA # 1). If the amount is rolled to a new account, the RBD for that account does not occur until December 31 of the following year.

The RBD makes little or no difference in terms of planning considerations, but can be significant for compliance purposes. Compare ¶ 1.5.04 and ¶ 1.5.05. In the above example, if Matt dies after April 1, 2002, but before December 31, 2002, he has died *after* his RBD for his pre-existing IRA # 1 but *before* his RBD for IRA # 2.

1.4 Computing Required Lifetime Distributions

Once Participant reaches his RBD, § 401(a)(9) forces him to start taking money out of his retirement plans (except for Roth IRAs; the lifetime distribution requirements do not apply to Roth IRAs. ¶ 5.1.03). This ¶ 1.4 explains how to compute those distributions under the final regulations; for other options for pre-2003 years see ¶ 1.10.04. Although the computation of *post-death* required distributions can be radically different depending who is the beneficiary of the plan (see ¶ 1.5), *lifetime* required distributions are computed the same way for most people.

1.4.01 *"Uniform Lifetime Table" to determine lifetime MRDs*

Once Participant reaches his RBD, how much does he have to take out of his retirement plan each year?

As usual, minimum distributions are determined by dividing Participant's prior year-end account balance (revalued annually) by a life expectancy factor ("Applicable Distribution Period" or "divisor"). The regulations allow two choices of "divisor": one that applies only to a Participant whose sole beneficiary is his spouse who is more than 10 years younger than he is (¶ 1.4.02); and the other, called the "Uniform Lifetime Table" (¶ 1.2.04; Appendix A, Table 1), to be used by everyone else. Reg. § 1.401(a)(9)-5, A-4(a).

The divisors in the Uniform Lifetime Table represent the joint life expectancy of a Participant age 70 (or older) and a hypothetical beneficiary who is ten years younger than Participant. Thus, the initial divisor under this table (for a Participant age 70) is 27.4 years (the joint life expectancy of someone age 70 and someone age 60).

To calculate lifetime MRDs under the Table, first determine Participant's age on his birthday in the distribution year (¶ 1.2.05). Then divide the prior year-end account balance (¶ 1.2.07, ¶ 1.2.08) by the divisor in the Uniform Lifetime Table that corresponds to that age.

Example: Kenny, a widower, turns age 73 on his birthday in the year 2002. Under the Uniform Lifetime Table, the applicable divisor for age 73 is 24.7. On December 31, 2001, the value of his IRA was $750,000. Divide $750,000 by 24.7; the result ($30,364) is Kenny's MRD for 2002.

The joint life expectancy factors in the Uniform Lifetime Table are redetermined annually (¶ 1.2.06). In other words, the table does not start with a 27.4-year life expectancy (divisor) and then reduce it by one each year. If the table used such a "fixed term method," then all money would have to be distributed out of the plan by the time Participant reached age 97 (70 + 27). Instead, the table's factors are recomputed annually, so the divisor decreases by less than one each year. At age 75, the divisor is 22.9 (not 22.4), at age 89 it is 12.0 (not 8.4). The divisor never goes below 1.9 (age 115 and older). This means that, if Participant takes only the MRD, the account balance will never go down to zero, regardless of how long Participant lives.

The Code requires that benefits be distributed either in full on the RBD, or, "beginning not later than the required beginning date...over the life of such employee or over the lives of such employee and a designated beneficiary (or over a period not extending beyond the life expectancy of such employee or the life expectancy of such employee and a designated beneficiary)." § 401(a)(9)(A)(ii). The regulations carry out this provision by using the joint life expectancy of the participant and a "hypothetical beneficiary" (rather than the real beneficiary). Reg., Preamble, "Uniform Lifetime Table."

1.4.02 *Lifetime MRDs if sole beneficiary is much-younger spouse*

"If the sole designated beneficiary of an employee is the employee's surviving spouse, for required minimum distributions during the employee's lifetime, the Applicable Distribution Period is *the longer of* the distribution period determined in accordance with [the Uniform Lifetime Table; ¶ 1.4.01] or the joint life expectancy of the employee and spouse using the employee's and spouse's attained ages as of the employee's and the spouse's birthdays in the distribution calendar year." Reg. § 1.401(a)(9)-5, A-4(b) (emphasis added). Note that this formulation mandates annual recalculation (¶ 1.2.06) of Participant's and Spouse's life expectancies.

The joint life expectancy table (¶ 1.2.04) will produce larger "divisors" and smaller required distributions than the Uniform Lifetime Table if the spouse-beneficiary was born in a year more than ten years later than the year of Participant's birth.

Example: Tallula was born February 25, 1925. Her spouse Irving was born August 25, 1945. In 2002, Tallula turns 77 and Irving turns 57. If

Tallula names Irving as sole beneficiary of her IRA for the 2002 distribution year, Tallula's MRD for 2002 will be calculated using the joint life expectancy of one person age 77 and one person age 57 (from the Joint and Last Survivor Table). The resulting Applicable Distribution Period (28.6; about 3.5%) produces a smaller required distribution than the Uniform Lifetime Table divisor (21.2; about 4.72%) for a person Tallula's age, because the Uniform Lifetime Table is based on the joint life expectancy of one person age 77 and one person age 67—a shorter life expectancy.

Example: Johnny's date of birth was February 25, 1925. His spouse Evelyn's date of birth was August 25, 1935. Even though in real life Evelyn is more than 10 years younger than Johnny (she is 10 years and six months younger to be exact), she is *not* more than 10 years younger for minimum distribution purposes. For MRD purposes, she is exactly 10 years younger (i.e., she turns 67 in the year he turns 77). Use of the true joint life expectancy of Johnny and Evelyn will not produce smaller MRDs than the Uniform Lifetime Table.

1.4.03 *Spouse-as-sole-beneficiary determined yearly*

The spouse is "sole designated beneficiary" for purposes of determining Participant's required distributions "if the spouse is the sole beneficiary of the employee's entire interest at all times during the distribution calendar year." Reg. § 1.401(a)(9)-5, A-4(b)(1). For purposes of determining whether the spouse is the Participant's sole beneficiary for the entire calendar year:

1. Marital status is determined on January 1; therefore death (of either spouse) or divorce during the year does not cause spouse to lose her status as "spouse" until the *following* calendar year.

2. Spouse is deemed to be "sole beneficiary" for the entire year if she is sole beneficiary on January 1 of the year *and* Participant does not change his beneficiary designation prior to the end of the calendar year (or prior to spouse's death, if earlier). Note that Participant's changing his designated beneficiary after the spouses' divorce but prior to the end of the calendar year *would* cause spouse to lose her status as sole beneficiary. Reg. § 1.401(a)(9)-5, A-4(b)(2).

1.5 MRDs After Participant's Death

1.5.01 Overview of post-death required distributions

When Participant dies, distributions must commence (or continue) after his death. The determination of required distributions after Participant's death depends on several factors; if decedent died before 2003, see also ¶ 1.1.06.

1.   <u>Did Participant die before or after his RBD</u>? This factor is not significant for planning purposes, but the calculation of required distributions is somewhat different depending on whether death occurred before (¶ 1.5.02) or on-or-after (¶ 1.5.03) the RBD. Since the RBD can be different for different plans (¶ 1.3), it is possible that Participant's death occurred before the RBD for some of his retirement plans and after the RBD for other plans. In case of any difficulty in deciding whether Participant died before or after the RBD, re-read ¶ 1.3.00-¶ 1.3.07. Death "on" the required beginning date is treated as death "after" the RBD. Reg. § 1.401(a)(9)-2, A-6(a). The post-RBD rules apply when the Participant dies on or after the RBD, regardless of whether Participant actually took any distributions before he died. Reg. § 1.401(a)(9)-2, A-6(a).

2.   <u>Are there are multiple beneficiaries</u>? If yes, then you need to determine whether the "separate accounts" rule (¶ 1.7.06) applies. If the retirement benefit is payable to multiple beneficiaries, but their interests constitute "separate accounts payable to different beneficiaries," then the rules in ¶ 1.5.02 or ¶ 1.5.03 may be applied separately to each such "separate account." See full explanation at ¶ 1.7.06. The distribution options described in ¶ 1.5.02 and ¶ 1.5.03 either apply to Participant's *entire benefit under the plan,* or (if the separate accounts rule is to be used) apply to *each separate account.*

3.   <u>Do the benefits pass to a "designated beneficiary," and if so who is that designated beneficiary</u>? See ¶ 1.7 for explanation of how to determine who is Participant's "beneficiary" and whether there is a "*designated* beneficiary"; this Code-defined

term does not simply mean any beneficiary who is designated by Participant! Understanding the meaning of designated beneficiary is crucial to both planning and compliance with the minimum distribution rules. Also, the identity of Participant's beneficiary is not fixed, for purposes of these rules, until September 30 of the year following the year of Participant's death (the "Designation Date"; ¶ 1.8). The rules in ¶ 1.5.02 or ¶ 1.5.03 apply *once the identity of the beneficiary is finalized on the Designation Date.*

4.   <u>Does the plan put limits on distribution options?</u> See ¶ 1.5.09.

In most cases these rules are nowhere near as complicated as the following description makes them appear; it's just that there are enough little variations and possible exceptions to make it impossible to state the rules simply.

The Code has two sets of post-death required distribution rules, one for participants who die before the RBD and one for participants who die on-or-after the RBD.

If Participant dies before the RBD, benefits must be distributed within five years after Participant's death (the 5-year rule; ¶ 1.5.04) (§ 401(a)(9)(B)(ii)), unless the benefits are left to a "designated beneficiary" (¶ 1.7), in which case the benefits can be distributed over the life expectancy of the designated beneficiary. § 401(a)(9)(B)(iii), (iv). ¶ 1.5.02. The regulations follow this scheme.

If Participant dies after the RBD, the Code says that "the remaining portion of such interest will be distributed at least as rapidly as under the method of distributions being used" to calculate Participant's MRDs during his life. § 401(a)(9)(B)(i). This is called the "at least as rapidly rule." The regulations pay lip service to the "at least as rapidly rule" (Reg. § 1.401(a)(9)-2, A-5), but make no attempt to comply with it. When a Participant dies after the RBD the size of his lifetime MRDs has no bearing whatever on the determination of required distributions after his death (¶ 1.5.03). So, despite § 401(a)(9)(B)(i), the "at least as rapidly rule" has been administratively repealed by the IRS.

1.5.02 *Required distributions if Participant dies before RBD*

This ¶ 1.5.02 explains what distributions are required after Participant's death (a) for all of Participant's Roth IRAs (regardless of how old Participant was when he died; see ¶ 5.1.03); and (b) for all of Participant's other retirement plans as to which Participant died *before* his RBD (¶ 1.3).

There is no required distribution for the year of Participant's death. See ¶ 1.3.07. Required distributions begin, at the earliest, in the year after the year of Participant's death. The exact required commencement date, like the calculation of the distribution itself, depends on the identity of the beneficiary (see ¶ 1.7.02).

A. Spouse is sole beneficiary. If there is only one beneficiary, and that beneficiary is Participant's surviving spouse, the distribution options and required commencement date are described in ¶ 1.6.

B. One, individual, non-spouse beneficiary. If there is only one beneficiary, and that beneficiary is an individual (¶ 1.7.03) who is not Participant's surviving spouse, then that individual is Participant's "designated beneficiary." The designated beneficiary may take required distributions in annual instalments (beginning no later than the end of the year after the year in which Participant died) over a period not longer than the designated beneficiary's life expectancy, if that option is permitted by the plan (¶ 1.5.09). For how to compute that life expectancy, see ¶ 1.5.06. Alternatively, the designated beneficiary may take distributions using the 5-year rule (¶ 1.5.04), if that option is permitted by the plan. Reg. § 1.401(a)(9)-3, A-1. See ¶ 1.5.10 for the ability to switch from one method to the other.

C. If a qualifying trust (¶ 6.2.04) is the sole beneficiary, then the individual beneficiary(ies) of the trust are Participant's "designated beneficiary(ies)." If the sole beneficiary of the trust is Participant's spouse, see ¶ 6.3.12 for applicable rules; otherwise, the trust may take required distributions in annual instalments (beginning no later than the end of the year after the year in which Participant died) over a period not longer than the life expectancy of the oldest beneficiary of the trust (or of the sole beneficiary of the trust, if the trust has only one beneficiary), if that option is permitted by the plan (¶ 1.5.09). For how to compute that life expectancy, see ¶ 1.5.06 (if the trust has only one beneficiary) or ¶ 1.5.08 (if the trust has more than one beneficiary). Alternatively, the trust may take distributions using the 5-year rule (¶ 1.5.04), if that option is permitted by the plan. Reg. § 1.401(a)(9)-4, A-5(a). See ¶ 1.5.10 for the ability to switch from one method to the other.

D.   One beneficiary, not an individual or qualifying trust. If there is only one beneficiary, and that beneficiary is neither an individual (¶ 1.7.03) nor a qualifying trust (¶ 6.2.04), then Participant is treated as having "no designated beneficiary." The benefits must be distributed under the 5-year rule (¶ 1.5.04). Reg. § 1.401(a)(9)-3, A-4. Distributions do not have to commence in the year after death, as long as all benefits are distributed by the end of the year that contains the fifth anniversary of the Participant's date of death, as explained at ¶ 1.5.04. See also ¶ 1.5.09.

E.   Multiple beneficiaries (all individuals or qualifying trusts). If there are two or more beneficiaries, and they are all either individuals (¶ 1.7.03) or qualifying trusts (¶ 6.2.04), then all of the individual beneficiaries (and all beneficiaries of the qualifying trusts) are Participant's "designated beneficiaries." If the only beneficiaries are the spouse individually and one or more qualifying trusts of which the spouse is the sole beneficiary, see ¶ 6.3.12 for applicable rules; otherwise, the beneficiaries (including any trusts that are beneficiaries) may take distributions in annual instalments over a period not longer than the life expectancy of the oldest beneficiary, if that option is permitted by the plan (¶ 1.5.09). Reg. § 1.401(a)(9)-5, A-7(a). This rule applies even if one of the individual beneficiaries (or one of the beneficiaries of any qualifying trust) is Participant's surviving spouse, because she is not the sole designated beneficiary; however, she may still have the option to roll over the portion payable to her (¶ 3.2.09). For how to compute the oldest designated beneficiary's life expectancy, see ¶ 1.5.08. Distributions must begin no later than the end of the year after the year in which Participant died. Reg. § 1.401(a)(9)-3, A-3(a). Alternatively, the beneficiaries may take distributions using the 5-year rule (¶ 1.5.04), if that option is permitted by the plan. Reg. § 1.401(a)(9)-3, A-1. See ¶ 1.5.10 for the ability to switch from one method to the other.

F.   Multiple beneficiaries (*not* all individuals or qualifying trusts). If there are two or more beneficiaries, but any beneficiary is neither an individual (¶ 1.7.03) nor a qualifying trust (¶ 6.2.04), then Participant is treated as having "no designated beneficiary." Reg. § 1.401(a)(9)-4, A-3. The benefits must be distributed under the 5-year rule (¶ 1.5.04). Reg. § 1.401(a)(9)-3, A-4. This rule applies even if one of the beneficiaries is Participant's surviving spouse; however, she may still have the option to roll over the portion payable to her (¶ 3.2.09). Distributions do not have to commence at any particular time, as long as all benefits are distributed by the end of the year that contains the fifth anniversary of the Participant's date of death, as explained at ¶ 1.5.04. See also ¶ 1.5.09.

1.5.03 *Required distributions if Participant dies after RBD*

Here are the requirements for post-death distributions if Participant dies on or after his RBD. These rules apply to all types of retirement plans covered by this book (except Roth IRAs, as to which Participant's death is always "before" the RBD; see ¶ 1.5.02, ¶ 5.1.03).

MRD for the year of Participant's death:

When Participant dies on or after his RBD, the required distribution for the year of Participant's death is still based on whatever method Participant was using prior to death—the Uniform Lifetime Table or the joint life expectancy of Participant and Spouse, whichever is applicable (¶ 1.4). If Participant had not yet taken the full required distribution for the year of death, the balance must be taken by the end of that year by the *beneficiary* of the account, *not* by Participant's estate (unless the estate is the beneficiary of the account). Reg. § 1.401(a)(9)-5, A-4(a)(1). The beneficiary owns the account once Participant dies, and the estate has no right to take any distribution from it (unless of course the estate is the beneficiary). See, e.g., PLR 1999-30052.

MRD for later years:

Beginning with the year after the year of Participant's death, required distributions depend on who is the beneficiary (¶ 1.7.02); in all cases, a distribution must be taken in the year following the year of Participant's death, and every year thereafter, until the account has been entirely distributed. The 5-year rule (¶ 1.5.04) is NEVER available if Participant died on or after his RBD!

A.   Spouse is sole beneficiary. If Participant's surviving spouse is the sole beneficiary, the distribution options are described at ¶ 1.6.

B.   One, individual, non-spouse beneficiary. If there is one beneficiary, and that beneficiary is an individual (¶ 1.7.03) but is *not* Participant's surviving spouse, then the beneficiary must take required distributions in annual instalments (beginning no later than the end of the year after the year in which Participant died) over a period not longer than the longer of (1) the beneficiary's remaining life expectancy (¶ 1.5.06) or (2) the Participant's remaining life expectancy (¶ 1.5.05). Reg. § 1.401(a)(9)-5, A-5(a)(1).

C.   If a qualifying trust (¶ 6.2.04) is the sole beneficiary, then the individual beneficiaries of the trust are Participant's "designated beneficiaryies." If the sole beneficiary of the trust is Participant's spouse, see ¶ 6.3.13 for applicable rules; otherwise, the trust must take required distributions in annual instalments over a period not longer than the longer of (1) the life expectancy of the oldest beneficiary of the trust (or of the sole beneficiary of the trust, if the trust has only one beneficiary) (¶ 1.5.06), or (2) the Participant's life expectancy (¶ 1.5.05). Reg. § 1.401(a)(9)-4, A-5(a), -5(A-5(a)(1).

D.   One beneficiary, not an individual or qualifying trust. If there is only one beneficiary, and that beneficiary is neither an individual nor a qualifying trust (¶ 6.2.04), then Participant is treated as having "no designated beneficiary." ¶ 1.7.03. The Applicable Distribution Period is Participant's remaining life expectancy. Reg. § 1.401(a)(9)-5, A-5(a)(2). See ¶ 1.5.05 for how to compute this.

E.   <u>Multiple beneficiaries (all individuals or qualifying trusts)</u>. If there are two or more beneficiaries, and they are all either individuals (¶ 1.7.03) or qualifying trusts (¶ 6.2.04), then all of the individual beneficiaries and all beneficiary(ies) of the qualifying trust(s) are Participant's "designated beneficiaries." If the only beneficiaries are the spouse individually and one or more qualifying trusts of which the spouse is the sole beneficiary, see ¶ 6.3.12; otherwise, the beneficiaries (including any trusts that are beneficiaries) may take required distributions in annual instalments over a period not longer than the longer of (1) the life expectancy of the oldest designated beneficiary (¶ 1.5.08) or the Participant's remaining life expectancy (¶ 1.5.05). This rule applies even if Participant's surviving spouse is one of the beneficiaries, or is the oldest beneficiary, because she is not the sole designated beneficiary; however, she may still have the option to roll over the portion payable to her (see ¶ 3.2.09). Reg. § 1.401(a)(9)-5, A-5(a)(1), A-7(a).

F.   <u>Multiple beneficiaries (*not* all individuals or qualifying trusts)</u>. If there are two or more beneficiaries, but any of the beneficiaries is neither an individual (¶ 1.7.03) nor a qualifying trust (¶ 6.2.04), then Participant is treated as having "no designated beneficiary." ¶ 1.7.03. Reg. § 1.401(a)(9)-4, A-3. The Applicable Distribution Period is Participant's remaining life expectancy. Reg. § 1.401(a)(9)-5, A-5(a)(2). See ¶ 1.5.05 for how to compute this. This rule applies even if one of the beneficiaries is Participant's surviving spouse; however, she may still have the option to roll over the portion payable to her (¶ 3.2).

1.5.04 *Death before RBD with no DB: the 5-year rule; how to determine whether 5-year rule or life expectancy applies*

The 5-year rule is the only distribution method available if Participant dies before his RBD with no designated beneficiary (unless the lack of designated beneficiary can be cured before the Designation Date; see ¶ 1.8). It *may* be available as an option in other cases of death before the RBD; see the last two paragraphs of this ¶ 1.5.04.

The 5-year rule ceases to have any application once Participant reaches his RBD. The 5-year rule is never available as an option in case of death on or after the RBD. (Since Roth IRAs have no RBD, however, the 5-year rule may apply to a Roth IRA even after Participant has passed his RBD on all his other retirement plans.)

The 5-year rule operates differently from the rest of the MRD rules. Under the 5-year rule, there is no annual required distribution. The only requirement is that the entire plan balance must be distributed by December 31 of the year that contains the fifth anniversary of Participant's date of death. Reg. § 1.401(a)(9)-3, A-2; § 54.4974-2, A-3(c). Thus, a beneficiary taking distributions under this rule could spread them over all the years in the period (which could be up to six *taxable* years), or could wait until the end of the period and take out all the money on that date. However, as with other legally allowed distribution options, the terms of the particular retirement plan might require distribution in one lump sum, with no option even to spread the distributions over five years; see ¶ 1.5.09.

There are two basic options under the tax law if Participant dies before his RBD leaving benefits to a designated beneficiary: benefits must be paid out either under the 5-year rule or over the life expectancy of the designated beneficiary; ¶ 1.5.02. How do you know which one applies?

1.　　If there is no designated beneficiary it's easy—only the 5-year rule is available.

2.　　The retirement plan may provide that one or the other method *must* be used in some or all situations. Reg. § 1.401(a)(9)-3, A-4(b). For example, a plan could provide that the 5-year rule applies even if the participant had a designated beneficiary.

3.　　A retirement plan may (but is not required to) allow its participants and/or their beneficiaries to elect which method will apply. This election must be made by the following deadline:

　　(a)　　If Participant's surviving spouse is the sole beneficiary, then no later than the *earlier* of the end of the year in which the first distribution would be required to be made to her under the life expectancy payout method (see ¶ 1.6.04) or the end of the year containing the fifth anniversary of the employee's death.

(b)   In all other cases, by the end of the year after the year of the employee's death. Reg. § 1.401(a)(9)-3, A-4(c).

If the plan permits participants and/or beneficiaries to choose between the 5-year rule and the life expectancy payout (# 3 above), then the following additional rules apply:

I   The election generally becomes irrevocable by the deadline for making the election; see ¶ 1.5.10 (transition rule for 2002-2003) for exception.

II   The plan can provide a default rule that will apply if Participant and beneficiary fail to elect a method. If the plan does not contain a default rule, the default rule is the life expectancy of the designated beneficiary. Reg. § 1.401(a)(9)-3, A-4(c). (This is a change from the 1987 proposed regulations, under which the default rule in this situation was the 5-year rule.)

1.5.05 *Death after RBD with no DB: Participant's life expectancy*

The Applicable Distribution Period is the remaining years of Participant's single life expectancy if Participant dies after his RBD either (i) with no designated beneficiary (¶ 1.7.03) or (ii) leaving the benefits to a designated beneficiary whose remaining life expectancy (¶ 1.5.06) is shorter than Participant's remaining life expectancy. The Participant's life expectancy is NEVER available as a distribution period in cases of death before the RBD (and NEVER applies to Roth IRAs, as to which death is always "before the RBD").

To calculate Participant's remaining life expectancy, use the IRS's single life expectancy table (¶ 1.2.04) and find the expectancy factor based on the age Participant had attained (or would have attained had he lived long enough) on his birthday in the year of his death. The life expectancy for the year of Participant's death, *reduced by one year*, is used as the "divisor" for the first distribution year (i.e., the year *after* Participant's death). The divisor is reduced by one each year thereafter (fixed-term method; ¶ 1.2.06). Reg. § 1.401(a)(9)-5, A-5(a)(2), (c)(3).

The largest divisor that could apply under this rule is 15.3. If

Participant turned 70 in the year he reached age 70½, then died in the following year (but after his RBD), his age on his year-of-death birthday would be 71, for which the single life expectancy is 16.3 years, meaning the "divisor" for the first distribution year (year after Participant's death) would be 15.3. If Participant dies later than the year he turns 104, the beneficiary will have to take out the entire balance in the year after Participant's death (because after age 103 the single life expectancy declines to less than 2, meaning the divisor for the year after Participant's death in the age-104-year would be less than one).

1.5.06 *How to compute distributions: one non-spouse beneficiary*

This section explains how to calculate distributions when the Applicable Distribution Period is the life expectancy of one non-spouse designated beneficiary. If there is one, individual, designated beneficiary, who is not Participant's spouse, the Applicable Distribution Period is the designated beneficiary's (single) life expectancy (¶ 1.2.04), determined based on his age on his birthday in the year after the year in which Participant died (¶ 1.2.05), and reduced by one each year thereafter ("fixed-term method"; ¶ 1.2.06). This method applies regardless of whether Participant died before, on or after his RBD, with one exception: if the Participant died on or after his RBD, and the Participant's remaining life expectancy is longer than the beneficiary's life expectancy, use the Participant's life expectancy (determined under ¶ 1.5.05) instead of the beneficiary's life expectancy. See ¶ 1.5.02, B, and ¶ 1.5.03, B.

These post-death required distributions begin the year after the year of death; in other words, the beneficiary's first "distribution year" (¶ 1.2.02) is the year after Participant's death.

Example: Jack dies in 2002. Dennis, who is not Jack's spouse, and who is younger than Jack, is sole beneficiary of Jack's IRA as of the date of death and does not disclaim the benefits. Dennis turns 65 on his birthday in 2003. The single life expectancy of a person age 65 is 21.0. By the end of 2003, Dennis must withdraw from the IRA at least 1/21th of the 12/31/02 account balance. If Jack died on or after April 1 of the year following the year in which he reached age 70½, and Jack had not withdrawn the MRD for 2002 by the time of his death, Dennis *also* must withdraw the balance of the 2002 MRD (computed using the Uniform Lifetime Table and Jack's age as of Jack's birthday in 2002) prior to the end of 2002 (¶ 1.5.03).

1.5.07 *Effect of subsequent death of designated beneficiary*

Once the Applicable Distribution Period has been established based on the life expectancy of Participant's non-spouse designated beneficiary, the subsequent death of the designated beneficiary prior to the end of the Applicable Distribution Period has no effect on required distributions. Distributions can continue to be made over the remaining life expectancy of the now-deceased designated beneficiary. Reg. § 1.401(a)(9)-5, A-7(c)(2).

Example: In the preceding example, assume Dennis dies in 2013, 10 years into his 21-year Applicable Distribution Period. At Dennis's death, ownership of the remaining balance of Jack's IRA passes to Regis, a successor beneficiary named by Dennis (see ¶ 1.9.02). Required distributions to Regis continue to be calculated based on Dennis's life expectancy; he uses what's left of the 21-year Applicable Distribution Period established at Jack's death.

As far as the *period of time for required distributions* after the original beneficiary's death, the regulations are clear: the payout period is established irrevocably once the original beneficiary is established as "the" designated beneficiary, unless his/her interest in the benefits is entirely distributed to him/her (or disclaimed by him/her) prior to the Designation Date (¶ 1.8). Any subsequent beneficiary who is merely a "successor" to the original beneficiary's interest is ignored in determining the Applicable Distribution Period. Reg. § 1.401(a)(9)-4(a)(4)(c), -5(a)(7)(c). As to who that successor beneficiary is, see ¶ 1.9.02.

For different rules that apply on the designated beneficiary's death if the designated beneficiary was the spouse of the Participant, see ¶ 1.6.05 and ¶ 1.6.06.

1.5.08 *How to compute distributions: multiple beneficiaries*

Before applying the following rule, be sure to read the caveats at ¶ 1.5.01, 2, regarding whether there really are "multiple beneficiaries" (as opposed to "separate accounts payable to different beneficiaries," ¶ 1.7.06). The following multiple beneficiary rule usually applies when determining required distributions to qualifying trusts (¶ 6.2.04), because most trusts have more than one beneficiary.

If there are multiple designated beneficiaries as of the Designation Date, and all are individuals, the Applicable Distribution Period is the life expectancy of the oldest designated beneficiary ("designated beneficiary with the shortest life expectancy"), determined based on his age on his birthday in the year after the year in which Participant died, and reduced by one each year thereafter. Reg. § 1.401(a)(9)-5, A-7(a)(1). This method applies:

A.   Regardless of whether Participant died before, on or after his RBD, with one exception: if the Participant died on or after his RBD, and the Participant's remaining life expectancy is longer than the oldest beneficiary's life expectancy, use the Participant's life expectancy (determined under ¶ 1.5.05) instead of the oldest beneficiary's life expectancy; and

B.   Regardless of whether the surviving spouse is one of the beneficiaries or is the oldest designated beneficiary.

The oldest beneficiary's life expectancy is calculated as described in ¶ 1.5.06.

Example: Natalie leaves her IRA to her sister and brother-in-law, Cindy and John. Cindy and John prefer to leave the IRA intact as a single account. This is more convenient for them for investment purposes and also for "dispositive" purposes since they both want the survivor of them to own the account solely if one of them dies (each will name the other as successor beneficiary for his or her interest in the account; see ¶ 1.9.02). They are close in age, so treating the IRA as two separate accounts payable to each of them individually would not reduce the required distributions. They want the convenience of having to compute only one required distribution annually, and of not having to track "separate accounts" within the IRA. They decide to compute distributions by treating the inherited IRA as a single account that is payable to multiple beneficiaries. Their required distributions will be based on the life expectancy of whichever one of them is the older.

Example: Percy dies in 2002 at age 66. As of the date of death and as of the Designation Date (September 30, 2003), the beneficiary of Percy's IRA is a trust for the benefit of Percy's wife Olivia for life, with remainder to Percy's children at Olivia's death. The trust complies with the "trust rules" (¶ 6.2), and Olivia (who turns 65 on her 2003 birthday) is the oldest beneficiary of the trust as of the Designation Date. The single life expectancy of a person age 65 is 21.0. By the end of 2003, the trust must withdraw from the IRA at least 1/21th of the 12/31/2002 account value.

1.5.09 *Plan is not required to offer life expectancy payout*

A retirement plan is not required to offer all the payout options that the law allows. Reg. § 1.401(a)(9)-3, A-4(b). While most IRAs permit the life expectancy payout, the situation is just the opposite with qualified plans. Most qualified retirement plans offer death benefits only in the form of lump sum distributions (or in some cases annuities), and do not offer the "life expectancy payout method." A plan is not even required, when the 5-year rule (¶ 1.5.04) applies, to allow the beneficiary to spread out distributions over the five years. See Fallon case study, Chapter 11, and ¶ 10.4.01, second paragraph, for use of a charitable remainder trust or an annuity contract to solve the problem of a plan that does not permit the life expectancy payout.

1.5.10 *Switching between 5-year rule and life expectancy method*

If a Participant died before his RBD, leaving his benefits to one or more designated beneficiaries, those beneficiaries may have elected to take benefits using the 5-year rule and then later change their minds; or may be using the 5-year rule because thought they didn't qualify for the life expectancy method; or may have wanted to use the life expectancy method but were defaulted into the 5-year rule by the plan. If two conditions are met, beneficiaries in this situation can switch to the life expectancy payout method. The two conditions are:

1.   "...[A]ny amounts that would have been required to be distributed under the life expectancy rule...for all distribution calendar years before 2004" must be distributed by the earlier of December 31, 2003, or the end of the 5-year rule period. This effectively limits the benefits of this transition rule to (i)

beneficiaries of decedents who died in 1997 where the beneficiaries take all the catch-up distributions by 12/31/02 and (ii) beneficiaries of decedents who died in 1998-2001 where the beneficiaries take all the catch-up distributions by December 31, 2003.

2.   The plan must provide for this switch. Reg. § 1.401(a)(9)-1, A-2(b)(2).

The catch-up distributions taken under this provision are penalty-free. The penalty applies only to *required* distributions that are not timely taken. § 54.4974-2, A-1; see ¶ 1.10.02. The catch-up payments under this special "switching" provision were not required distributions, because the beneficiary was "receiving distributions" under the 5-year rule, not the life expectancy method. Reg. § 1.401(a)(9)-1, A-2(b)(2) refers to the catch-up payments as the payments that "*would have been required*" under the life expectancy method, not that "*were required*" (emphasis added).

Ironically, this special transition rule does not help a beneficiary who properly elected to use (or who was defaulted into) the life expectancy method but then failed to take one or more payments in years 1-4. Reg. § 1.401(a)(9)-1, A-2(b)(2) applies only to "A designated beneficiary that is receiving payments under the 5-year rule of section 401(a)(9)(B)(ii), either by affirmative election or default provisions." A designated beneficiary who elects or is defaulted into the life expectancy method and then misses one or more payments must pay the penalty for the missed payments (or seek a waiver of it); see ¶ 1.10.02.

Except for this special temporary transition rule in Reg. § 1.401(a)(9)-1, A-2(b)(2), there is *no way* for a designated beneficiary who has either elected or been defaulted into the 5-year rule to switch from the 5-year rule to the life expectancy method after the deadline for making that election, which is (for a non-spouse designated beneficiary) December 31 of the year after the year of Participant's death; see ¶ 1.5.04, 3.

Can beneficiaries switch in the other direction, from the life expectancy method to the 5-year rule? Basically no, with the following exceptions:

A.   If permitted by the plan, any beneficiary can change his or her election prior to the deadline for making the election (¶ 1.5.04).

B.   If a beneficiary is using the life expectancy method, then, unless the plan prohibits withdrawing more than the MRD (which would be rare), the beneficiary can take out the entire remaining balance of his or her share of the benefits any time, including by the end of the 5-year period if all that is desired is a faster distribution. This has no effect on the penalties unless "C" applies:

C.   If there is *only one* designated beneficiary, and he/she withdraws all of the benefits by the end of the 5-year period, the penalty for any missed distributions in earlier years is automatically waived (see ¶ 1.10.02), so to that limited extent a beneficiary can make a penalty-free switch between the methods even after the initial deadline.

1.6 Special Rules for the Surviving Spouse

This section describes the special distribution rules that apply when Participant's sole beneficiary is his spouse.

1.6.01 Overview of the special spousal rules

The Code provides special rules that apply when Participant's spouse ("Spouse") is named as Participant's beneficiary. One of the many positive features of the 2001-2002 changes in the minimum distribution regulations is greater clarity regarding application of these special spousal rules, including an explanation of when a "trust for the benefit of the spouse" may take advantage of certain tax provisions available to "the spouse" (¶ 6.3.12).

Note: the regulations often refer to the spouse as Participant's "surviving spouse" even while they are both alive. See, e.g., Reg. § 1.401(a)(9)-5, A-4(b). Of course, while Participant is alive his spouse is not yet (and may never become) the "surviving" spouse. In this book, as in the regulations, "spouse" and "surviving spouse" are used interchangeably.

There are four special provisions that may apply when Participant's surviving spouse is named as beneficiary:

1.   The calculation of lifetime required distributions using the Joint and Last Survivor Table rather than the Uniform Lifetime

Table, if Participant's sole beneficiary is his more-than-10-years-younger spouse. This rule is discussed at ¶ 1.4.02.

2.   Use of the special recalc/fixed-term combo method for calculating Spouse's life expectancy after Participant's death if Spouse is the sole beneficiary; see ¶ 1.6.06.

3.   The postponed commencement date for required distributions (and related rules) when Participant dies before his RBD leaving benefits to Spouse as sole beneficiary; see ¶ 1.6.04 and ¶ 1.6.05.

4.   Spouse's right to roll over to another retirement plan, tax-free, benefits inherited from a deceased spouse (or treat an IRA inherited from a deceased spouse as her own IRA). For this right, unlike numbers 1-3, Spouse does not have to be "sole" beneficiary. This is not a "minimum distribution" rule; the spouse's rollover and election rights are covered at ¶ 3.2.

1.6.02 *Definition of "sole beneficiary"*

For purposes of the special minimum distribution rules applicable to a spouse-beneficiary, Spouse must be the "sole" beneficiary. Spouse is the sole beneficiary if she, alone, will inherit all of the benefits if she survives Participant; in other words if she is the sole *primary* beneficiary. The fact that other beneficiaries are named as *contingent* beneficiaries (who will take if Spouse does not survive Participant, or does not survive him for some specified period of time) does not impair her status as "sole" beneficiary.

Example: The beneficiary designation form for Bud's IRA provides: "I name my spouse, Louise Clark, as my sole primary beneficiary, to receive 100% of all benefits payable under this Plan on account of my death if she survives me by 30 days. If she does not survive me by 30 days, or if she is not married to me at my death, the benefits shall instead be paid to my sister Gladys Williams." The spouse, Louise, is Bud's sole beneficiary so long as both spouses are alive and married to each other. She is Bud's sole beneficiary at his death if she is married to him at his death, survives him by 30 days and does not disclaim the benefits. The fact that Gladys is named as a contingent beneficiary does not impair Louise's status as sole beneficiary.

Extremely important note: If the retirement benefit in question is divided into "separate accounts" payable to different beneficiaries, then the test of whether Spouse is the "sole beneficiary" is applied only to the separate account of which Spouse is the beneficiary. Reg. § 1.401(a)(9)-8, A-2. See PLR 2001-21073 and further discussion at ¶ 1.7.06.

1.6.03 When Spouse's status as sole beneficiary is determined

The applicable time for determining whether Spouse is the sole beneficiary differs depending on which tax provision is being considered.

For purposes of computing *required distributions during Participant's life*, see ¶ 1.4.02.

For purposes of the *post-death minimum distribution rules* (¶ 1.6.04 through ¶ 1.6.06), it is not essential that Spouse be the sole beneficiary at the time of the decedent's death, only that she is "a" beneficiary on the date of death (¶ 1.7.02) and that she is sole beneficiary on September 30 of the year after the year in which Participant died (the "Designation Date"; ¶ 1.8) of the entire account (or of a "separate account" within the Participant's account, if the separate account is established no later than December 31 of the year after the year of Participant's death; Reg. § 1.401(a)(9)-8, A-2(a)(2), ¶ 1.7.06). Thus, in some cases, if Spouse is just one of several beneficiaries on the date of death, and therefore is not the "sole" beneficiary, it will be possible to "remove" the other beneficiaries (by means of disclaimer or distribution or establishing separate accounts) so that Spouse can become the sole beneficiary by the Designation Date. ¶ 1.8.01.

Spouse's right to roll over non-required distributions she receives from the retirement plan of her deceased spouse are not part of the "minimum distribution rules." See ¶ 3.2. Therefore this right does not depend on Spouse's being the sole beneficiary.

In the case of Spouse's right to elect to treat the deceased spouse's IRA as the spouse's own IRA, she can make this election at any time after the Participant's death provided that she is the *sole* beneficiary at the Designation Date. See Reg. § 1.408-8, A-5(a).

1.6.04 *Required commencement date for distributions to Spouse*

If Participant dies on or after his RBD (¶ 1.3), the required commencement date for distributions to Spouse is the same as the required commencement date for distributions to any other designated beneficiary: December 31 of the year after the year of Participant's death.

If Participant dies *prior* to his RBD, and Spouse is the *sole* designated beneficiary, however, the annual distributions to Spouse over her life expectancy do not have to begin until the end of the *later* of: the year following the year in which Participant died, or the year in which Participant would have reached age 70½. § 401(a)(9)(B)(iv)(I); Reg. § 1.401(a)(9)-3, A-3(b). In contrast, non-spouse beneficiaries must always commence MRDs by the end of the year after Participant's death (unless the 5-year rule applies; ¶ 1.5.04). § 401(a)(9)(B)(iii); Reg. § 1.401(a)(9)-3, A-3(a).

This rule applies whenever Participant dies before his RBD; however, it does not provide a special late commencement date for Spouse unless Participant dies before the year he would have reached age 69½. If he dies in the age-69½ year or later, spouse's required commencement date is the same as the required commencement date of any other beneficiary, i.e., the end of the year after the year of Participant's death.

1.6.05 *Spouse treated as "Participant" if both die young*

If Participant died before his RBD, and Spouse survives him, and Spouse is the sole designated beneficiary, § 401(a)(9)(B)(iv)(II) provides an additional rule for what happens on Spouse's later death. If Spouse dies before the date distributions to her are required to commence, then required distributions after Spouse's death will not be based on Spouse's remaining life expectancy (even though her life expectancy was the "Applicable Distribution Period" that would have applied for required distributions to her had she lived). Rather, a new distribution period starts: benefits must be distributed either by the end of the year that contains the fifth anniversary of *Spouse's* death or (if the benefits are payable to a designated beneficiary *of Spouse*) in annual instalments over the life expectancy of Spouse's designated beneficiary, commencing no later than December 31 of the year following the year in which *Spouse* died. Reg. § 1.401(a)(9)-3, A-5, A-6.

The "designated beneficiary" to whom the benefits are paid on the death of Spouse could be an individual named as beneficiary either by Spouse or by the plan; see Reg. § 1.401(a)(9)-4, A-4(b). Spouse's beneficiary will be determined as of the date of Spouse's death, but "finalized" on September 30 of the year after the year of Spouse's death (see ¶ 1.8). Unfortunately, if Spouse dies before she gets around to designating a successor beneficiary for her interest (see Reg. § 1.401(a)(9)-4, A-2), the benefits (under most plans' and IRAs' default provisions) will pass to Spouse's estate—meaning that, upon Spouse's death during the time this rule applies, the benefits will not pass to a "designated beneficiary" and the 5-year rule will apply (¶ 1.7.04).

Example: Alphonse died at age 65, leaving his IRA to his wife Heloise. Heloise died after Alphonse, but before the end of the year in which Alphonse would have reached age 70½, and before she had either rolled the funds over to her own IRA (¶ 3.2.01), or elected to treat the IRA as her own (¶ 3.2.05), or named a "successor beneficiary" for her interest in Alphonse's benefits (¶ 1.9.02). Under the terms of the IRA agreement, if a beneficiary has inherited the account, but then dies while there are still funds in the account without naming a successor beneficiary, the account becomes payable to the beneficiary's estate. Under the special rule of § 401(a)(9)(B)(iv)(II), the minimum distribution rules apply as if Heloise were the "Participant" who died before the required beginning date. Thus, the "new beneficiary" of the account is Heloise's estate and the 5-year rule applies because Heloise did not have a "designated beneficiary."

1.6.06 How to determine Spouse's life expectancy

Reminder: the rules discussed in this ¶ 1.6.06 do not apply: to benefits Spouse has rolled over to her own retirement plan (¶ 3.2.01); to an inherited IRA which Spouse has elected to treat as her own (¶ 3.2.05); or if Participant died before his RBD and Spouse dies before she was required to commence distributions (see ¶ 1.6.05).

In contrast to the "fixed-term method" of determining life expectancy that applies when there is a non-spouse designated beneficiary (see ¶ 1.5.06), if Spouse is Participant's *sole* beneficiary on the Designation Date, the Applicable Distribution Period is determined by a combination of recalculation and fixed-term methods (¶ 1.2.06).

During Spouse's lifetime, Spouse must take distributions over her life expectancy, *recalculated annually*, beginning in whatever year she is required to begin distributions (¶ 1.6.04). Her life expectancy is determined using the single life expectancy table (¶ 1.2.04) based on her age on her birthday in each year for which a distribution is required. ¶ 1.2.05. Reg. § 1.401(a)(9)-5, A-5(c)(2) (first sentence) and A-6. See "Josephine" example at ¶ 1.2.06.

Note: if Participant died on or after his RBD, and Spouse is the sole designated beneficiary, then the ADP is Spouse's remaining life expectancy or Participant's remaining life expectancy (¶ 1.5.05), whichever is longer. Reg. § 1.401(a)(9)-5, A-5(a)(1). If Participant's remaining life expectancy is longer initially, it is nevertheless possible that in a later year Spouse's remaining life expectancy would become longer, because Spouse's life expectancy is recalculated annually and Participant's remaining life expectancy is determined under the fixed term method. See ¶ 1.2.06. Thus, a Spouse who was a little older than Participant, and who starts out taking distributions over Participant's remaining life expectancy, could find herself switching from Participant's remaining life expectancy to her own remaining life expectancy down the road.

If Spouse dies on or after the date on which she was required to commence taking distributions, the required distribution for the year of her death must be paid out to the successor beneficiary to the extent Spouse had not already taken it by the time of her death. Any remaining benefits must be paid out (beginning the year after the year of Spouse's death) over the remaining *fixed term* life expectancy of Spouse. This is computed as of the age she attained (or would have attained if she lived long enough) on her birthday in the year of her death and reduced by one year for each year thereafter. Reg. § 1.401(a)(9)-5, A-5(c)(2). It is not clear whether this rule applies even if Spouse was taking distributions over Participant's remaining life expectancy (see preceding paragraph) rather than her own.

This convoluted rule gives Spouse and her heirs the advantage of recalculation during Spouse's lifetime (distributions stretch out over her lifetime) and the advantage of a fixed-term payout after her death. However, it is not as favorable, in most cases, as the spousal rollover (¶ 3.2). With the spousal rollover, distributions during Spouse's life are computed using the Uniform Lifetime Table (¶ 1.2.04), which, because its factors are based on joint life expectancies, produces smaller required distributions than Spouse's single life expectancy. Also, after

Spouse's death distributions from a rollover account are based on the life expectancy of Spouse's designated beneficiary, which (depending on the age of the designated beneficiary and of Spouse) could be a much longer distribution period than the remaining years of Spouse's single life expectancy.

Example: Harry dies in 2003 at age 75 leaving his 401(k) plan entirely to his wife Grace, age 73. Harry had taken his MRD for 2003 prior to his death. Grace does not roll over the 401(k) plan to her own IRA; she leaves it in Harry's name. As long as it stays in Harry's name, Grace's required distributions each year (beginning with the year 2004) are computed based on Grace's life expectancy as of her birthday in such year (recalculation method). Her age on her 2006 birthday will be 76. The single life expectancy of someone age 76 is 12.7, so her 2006 required distribution from the 401(k) plan for the year is the 2005 year-end account value divided by 12.7.

Now Grace dies in 2007. Even though she died before reaching her year-2007 birthday, we look at the age she *would have attained* in 2007 (not her age at her death) to calculate required distributions for the year of her death and later. She would have attained age 77 on her birthday in the year 2007 had she lived. The MRD for the year of her death is based on the single life expectancy of someone age 77 (12.1 years). Her life expectancy is then fixed at 12.1 years because of her death. MRDs to her successor beneficiaries thereafter will be based on this 12.1-year life expectancy, using the fixed-term method.

Grace had not taken the year-2007 MRD before she died. Her successor beneficiaries must now take the 2007 distribution, which is the 2006 year-end account value divided by 12.1. In 2008 they will take the 2008 MRD, which is the 2007 year-end account value divided by 11.1 (12.1 minus one). In 2009, the divisor will be 10.1.

If Grace had rolled the account over to her own IRA, she could have named her own designated beneficiaries, and they would have been able to use their own life expectancies for required distributions, instead of being limited to using the rest of Grace's life expectancy.

If, on the Designation Date, Spouse is not the sole beneficiary, but all beneficiaries are individuals and Spouse is the *oldest* beneficiary, her life expectancy is computed in the same fixed-term manner as that of any other beneficiary (see ¶ 1.5.06); the recalc/fixed term combination method described above does not apply.

1.7 Designated Beneficiary: What, Who and Why

1.7.01 *Significance of having a "designated beneficiary"*

The value of the "life expectancy payout method" has been explained. ¶ 1.2.01. While any Participant can use this method for calculating his lifetime required distributions (¶ 1.4.01), availability of this valuable tool is sharply limited once Participant dies. § 401(a)(9) allows Participant's death benefits to be distributed over the life expectancy of a "*designated* beneficiary," which is a defined term. If there is no "designated beneficiary," the payout options will generally be less favorable, as explained in ¶ 1.5. Therefore, estate planners must understand the meaning of this term and in most cases will want to take steps to assure that clients have a "designated beneficiary" to maximize the value of their retirement plans for the benefit of their family members or other chosen beneficiaries. (However, see ¶ 1.7.07 for cases in which it doesn't matter whether there is a "designated beneficiary.")

This ¶ 1.7 explains what a "beneficiary" is (¶ 1.7.02); the difference between a "beneficiary" and a "designated beneficiary" (¶ 1.7.03); the problems when an "estate" is a beneficiary (¶ 1.7.04 and ¶ 1.7.05); and the vital "separate accounts" rule (¶ 1.7.06). See ¶ 1.8 for discussion of how to modify the selection of beneficiary after Participant's death.

1.7.02 *Who is Participant's "beneficiary"*

Like life insurance proceeds, retirement benefits generally pass, as non-probate property, by contract, to the beneficiary named on the Participant's beneficiary designation form. Most retirement plans and IRAs have a printed form they expect Participant to use to name a beneficiary for his death benefits; some plans and IRA providers will accept attachments to the printed form, or a separate instrument in place of the printed form, designating a beneficiary.

Beneficiary designations offer a vast field for exploration, involving such issues as: contradictory, ambiguous and otherwise ineffective beneficiary designations; how an IRA custodial account may be considered a probate asset in some jurisdictions; and which state's law governs the interpretation of a beneficiary designation form. For a checklist of issues to consider in drafting a beneficiary designation form, see "Introduction" to Appendix B, page 477. This ¶ 1.7.02 discusses naming a beneficiary *only* from the perspective of the minimum distribution rules.

For purposes of the minimum distribution rules, the "beneficiary" means the person or persons who inherit the plan on Participant's death. In most cases, that means only the "primary beneficiary(ies)." In the standard type of beneficiary designation, a contingent beneficiary would take a share of the benefits only if the primary beneficiary (or all of the primary beneficiaries) failed to survive Participant. When Participant dies, if the primary beneficiary *does* survive Participant, the contingent beneficiary ceases to have any relevance to the determination of who is Participant's beneficiary for minimum distribution purposes (unless there is a disclaimer during the period between the date of death and the Designation Date; see ¶ 1.8.03). (See ¶ 1.9.02 for who gets the benefits if the beneficiary survives Participant but then dies before taking the benefits out of the plan.)

Example: Jan leaves her IRA to Jon as primary beneficiary, with Kate as contingent beneficiary. Jan dies and Jon survives her. Unless Jon disclaims all or part of the benefits (¶ 8.2.01) before the Designation Date, Jon is Jan's sole beneficiary.

However, if the primary beneficiary does not survive Participant, the contingent beneficiary becomes "the" beneficiary:

Example: Regina designates her children A, B and C as beneficiaries of her IRA, with the proviso that, if any child predeceases her, such child's issue take the share such child would have taken if living. B predeceases Regina, leaving two children and no other issue, so at Regina's death her "beneficiaries" are A, C and the two children of B.

If the contingent beneficiary's rights are contingent on something other than the primary beneficiary's failure to survive Participant (or the primary beneficiary's disclaimer), however, the question becomes more complicated. Normally this could not happen except in the context of a trust, because normally an IRA provider or plan administrator would not accept a beneficiary designation that had additional post-death conditions in it, unless the conditions were contained in a trust. When such a "special contingency" beneficiary can be disregarded is discussed under the trust rules (¶ 6.3.04).

1.7.03 *The definition of "designated beneficiary"*

In order for benefits to be distributable over "the life expectancy of the designated beneficiary," there must be a "designated beneficiary." Not every "beneficiary" is a *designated* beneficiary." The Code defines designated beneficiary as "any individual designated as a beneficiary by the employee." § 401(a)(9)(E).

The regulations substantially expand this definition:

"A designated beneficiary is an individual who is designated as a beneficiary under the plan. An individual may be designated as a beneficiary under the plan either by the terms of the plan or, if the plan so provides, by an affirmative election by the employee...specifying the beneficiary. A beneficiary designated as such under the plan is an individual who is entitled to a portion of an employee's benefit, contingent on the employee's death or another specified event....A designated beneficiary need not be specified by name in the plan or by the employee to the plan in order to be a designated beneficiary so long as the individual who is to be the beneficiary is identifiable under the plan. The members of a class of beneficiaries capable of expansion or contraction will be treated as being identifiable if it is possible, to identify the class member with the shortest life expectancy. The fact that an employee's interest under the plan passes to a certain individual under a will or otherwise under applicable state law does not make that individual a designated beneficiary unless the individual is designated as a beneficiary under the plan." Reg. § 1.401(a)(9)-4, A-1.

"Q-2. Must an employee...make an affirmative election specifying a beneficiary for a person to be a designated beneficiary under section 40l(a)(9)(E)?"

"A-2. No, a designated beneficiary is an individual who is designated as a beneficiary under the plan whether or not the designation under the plan was made by the employee..." Reg. § 1.401(a)(9)-4, A-2.

So, there are several key elements to achieving "designated beneficiary" status:

1.   Only "individuals" can be designated beneficiaries. An "estate"

does not qualify; ¶ 1.7.04. A trust is not an individual, but, if some tricky rules are complied with, you can look through the trust and treat the individual trust beneficiaries as if Participant had named them directly as his beneficiaries; see ¶ 6.2. A partnership, corporation or LLC is not an "individual" for this purpose, even if under some tax rules it is not treated as an entity separate from its individual owners.

2.   If there are multiple beneficiaries, all must be individuals and it must be possible to identify the oldest member of the group. ¶ 6.2.07. You also must determine whether the separate accounts rule applies. ¶ 1.7.06.

3.   Finally, the beneficiary must be designated either "by the terms of the plan" or (if the plan allows this; almost all plans do) by the employee. See ¶ 1.7.05.

If Participant fills out his beneficiary form and names "my spouse," or "my children," or "my friends Larry, Moe and Curly," as his death beneficiaries, and the named individual(s) survive Participant, there is no problem. We have individual beneficiaries who have been "affirmatively elected" by Participant, so there is a "designated beneficiary" whose life expectancy can be used to measure required distributions after Participant's death.

If Participant does not fill out a beneficiary designation form; or if all the beneficiaries he named fail to survive him, there is *still* no problem—*if* the plan fills the gap by specifying *individuals* to whom the benefits pass. Most qualified retirement plans, for example, provide that all benefits will be paid to Participant's surviving spouse if Participant fails to designate another beneficiary (or maybe even regardless of whether Participant designates some other beneficiary; see ¶ 3.4).

However, in many cases, if Participant fails to fill out the beneficiary form (or his named beneficiaries fail to survive him), the plan or IRA will provide that the benefits are paid to Participant's "estate." This will normally mean loss of the ability to use a beneficiary's life expectancy as the Applicable Distribution Period, as explained in ¶ 1.7.04.

1.7.04 *Estate cannot be a "designated beneficiary"*

If benefits are payable to Participant's "estate," Participant has "no designated beneficiary," even if all beneficiaries of the estate are individuals. Reg. § 1.401(a)(9)-4, A-3; PLR 2001-26041.

This author has argued that the IRS's position that the life expectancy method is not available if an "estate" is a beneficiary is incorrect. The Code provides that any portion of the employee's benefit payable "to (*or for the benefit of*)" a designated beneficiary may be distributed over that beneficiary's life expectancy. § 401(a)(9)(B)(iii) (emphasis added). Benefits paid to an estate are paid "for the benefit of" the estate's beneficiaries, and if the beneficiaries of the estate are all individuals (or qualifying trusts; ¶ 6.2), they should be recognized as "designated beneficiaries" and allowed to use the life expectancy method.

However, it is unquestionably the IRS's position that if any part of Participant's benefits is payable to Participant's "estate," participant has no designated beneficiary. Accordingly, this book follows that rule. For more on the contrary view, see Choate, N., "The 'Estate' As Beneficiary Of Retirement Benefits," *Trusts & Estates*, Vol. 138, No. 10 (Sept. 1999), p. 41.

See ¶ 1.8.06 for discussion of why this problem cannot be solved post-mortem by distributing the benefits out of the estate. See ¶ 3.2.09 for whether a spousal rollover may still be available. See ¶ 8.2.07 regarding disclaimers in this situation. For ways a retirement plan could be drafted to avoid this problem, see ¶ 1.7.05.

What if the Participant, in his beneficiary designation form, does not name "the estate" directly as his beneficiary, but names beneficiaries who are determined indirectly by reference to the participant's will or estate administration; for example, if the beneficiary designation form names "the beneficiaries of my estate" or "the residuary beneficiaries under my will" as beneficiaries of his IRA or retirement plan? The regulations do not require that beneficiaries be "specified by name...in order to be a designated beneficiary so long as the individual who is to be the beneficiary is identifiable under the plan." Reg. § 1.401(a)(9)-4, A-1. If the beneficiary designation sufficiently identifies the people who are to inherit the benefits, even if this is done by reference to another document such as the will, this should be sufficient to establish them as "designated beneficiaries." However, this approach could cause problems (not just in terms of meeting the definition of "designated beneficiary" but also in terms of figuring out who is entitled to the money) if the will is not closely coordinated with the beneficiary designation.

1.7.05 *Drafting retirement plan to avoid "estate" as beneficiary*

As explained at ¶ 1.7.04, the IRS has drawn a line in the sand on the question of whether the individual beneficiaries of an estate can be considered "designated beneficiaries." Some IRA providers have responded to this problem (and attempted to provide better results for their careless customers who don't fill out beneficiary designations) by designating individual beneficiaries (rather than simply "Participant's estate") who will take any benefits Participant has not effectively disposed of in his beneficiary designation form. Here are several approaches IRA providers may consider, with the pros and cons of each:

1.   One approach is to try to guess who the Participant would have selected as his beneficiary had he gotten around to it. Such an IRA might provide that benefits not effectively disposed of by Participant's beneficiary designation form will pass to Participant's surviving spouse, if any, otherwise to Participant's issue, if any. This approach will work well in some cases, but will create problems in other cases, for example when the spouse is estranged, or when Participant's will disinherited some of his issue. It was to avoid such problems that most IRA agreements pay defaulted benefits to Participant's estate.

2.   Another approach is to provide that benefits not effectively disposed of by Participant's beneficiary designation form will pass to the individuals who would have been Participant's heirs at law had Participant died intestate and had this account been an asset of Participant's probate estate. This approach successfully transforms the heirs-at-law into "designated beneficiaries," because now they are identifiable individuals designated under the plan. The drawback of this approach is that it requires the IRA provider to figure out the law of Participant's state of domicile, and, like approach # 1, it risks running contrary to Participant's wishes as demonstrated in Participant's duly allowed will.

3.   Another approach is to attempt to duplicate the estate disposition *in the retirement plan* while bypassing the estate itself, so that the beneficiary of the Participant's account will be the person or persons who would have inherited the benefits had the benefits been paid to the estate. For example, the plan could provide that (if Participant fails to name a beneficiary) the benefits will be not be paid to Participant's estate but instead will be paid to the person or persons who would have received the benefits had the account been (i) paid to the Participant's estate and (ii) not available for payment of Participant's debts, funeral expenses, expenses of administration or taxes. While there may be some promise to this approach, it would require great care to draft.

If Participant failed to name a beneficiary, can the executor or administrator of his estate name one for him? The IRS says no. See PLR 2001-26036, in which daughter, as executrix of mother's estate, attempted to establish an IRA in mother's name and named herself as beneficiary. The IRS ruled that "a beneficiary must be designated either by a plan participant, an IRA holder or, in limited circumstances, the surviving spouse of said participant or IRA holder. Neither the Code nor the proposed [regulations] provide that the executrix of the estate of a surviving spouse who elected to treat IRAs of her deceased husband as her own may designate herself as the beneficiary of the surviving spouse's IRAs."

However, that letter ruling was prior to EGTRRA. Since Congress, in EGTRRA, encouraged the IRS to provide regulations permitting post-death rollovers by the Participant's executor (see ¶ 2.5.03), presumably Congress expects that the executor would be able to name a beneficiary for a benefit account created by post-death rollover.

1.7.06 *Multiple beneficiary rules and "separate accounts"*

Under the IRS's multiple beneficiary rules, if Participant has more than one beneficiary, Participant has "no designated beneficiary" unless all of the beneficiaries are individuals. Reg. § 1.401(a)(9)-4, A-3. If all of the beneficiaries are individuals, they all must use the oldest beneficiary's life expectancy to calculate required distributions. ¶ 1.5.08.

There is an exception to these rules. If Participant's benefit under a plan "is divided into separate accounts, and the beneficiaries with respect to one separate account differ from the beneficiaries with respect to the other separate accounts of the employee under the plan, for years subsequent to the calendar year containing the date on which the separate accounts were established, or date of death if later, such separate account under the plan is not aggregated with the other separate accounts under the plan in order to determine whether the distributions from such separate account under the plan satisfy section 401(a)(9). Instead, the rules in section 401(a)(9) separately apply to such separate account..." Reg. § 1.401(a)(9)-8, A-2(a).

This is one of the most useful provisions in planning for retirement benefits. It means that when an IRA is left to several beneficiaries each one can use his or her own life expectancy to measure required distributions, if "separate accounts" are properly established. In order to have separate accounts the following requirements must be met:

1.   First, the beneficiaries' interests must be fractional or percentage interests in the benefit as of the date of death. This requirement comes from the definition of separate accounts: "Separate accounts in an employee's account are separate portions of an employee's benefit reflecting the separate interests of the employee's beneficiaries under the plan *as of the date of the employee's death* for which separate accounting is maintained. The separate accounting must allocate all post-death investment gains and losses, contributions and forfeitures, for the period prior to the establishment of the separate accounts on a pro rata basis in a reasonable and consistent manner among the separate accounts." Reg. § 1.401(a)(9)-8, A-3(a). A pecuniary bequest (see Glossary) will not meet this definition of "separate account" unless (under local law or under the terms of the beneficiary designation) it will share in post-death gains and losses pro rata with the other beneficiaries' shares. If the beneficiary designation contains any pecuniary gifts that would flunk this definition, the beneficiaries of the pecuniary gifts can be eliminated by distributing their gifts to them prior to the Designation Date (see ¶ 1.8.05). If only fractional or percentage interest beneficiaries remain as "beneficiaries" on the Designation Date, then this first requirement is met.

2.   Second, for purposes of determining the Applicable Distribution Period(s) for the benefits, the separate accounts must be established "no later than the last day of the year following the calendar year of the employee's death." Reg. § 1.401(a)(9)-8, A-2. Thus, having eliminated any non-sharing pecuniary gift-beneficiaries by September 30, the "residuary" beneficiaries have until December 31 of the year after death to establish separate accounts so that each of them can use his or her own life expectancy to measure required distributions from his or her separate account (and the surviving spouse can use the delayed commencement date for her separate account; ¶ 1.6.04)—or any one or more of them can elect to use the 5-year rule (or Participant's remaining life expectancy, if Participant died after his RBD) instead of the Participant's life expectancy payout method if that is an option under the plan.

3.   Third, even after December 31 of the year after death, multiple beneficiaries who have the appropriate fractional or percentage interests can establish separate accounts for their respective interests. Separate accounts for different beneficiaries can be established "at any time." Reg., Preamble, "Separate Accounts"; § 1.401(a)(9)-8, A-2(a)(2). For years following this "establishment," each beneficiary's MRD will be determined solely based on his or her separate account balance—though all will still have to use the Applicable Distribution Period established for the combined accounts on September 30 of the year after the year of Participant's death if the accounts were "established" after the December 31 deadline.

The following example illustrates how these rules work:

Example: Guerdon's IRA beneficiary designation reads as follows: "Upon my death, pay $10,000 each to Natalie Choate, Bob Keebler and Mike Jones. The remaining balance shall be paid in equal shares to: my favorite charity, the New England Home for Little Actuaries; Ed Slott; Seymour Goldberg; and Barry Picker." Guerdon dies in 2002, before his RBD. Under applicable state law and the terms of the account agreement, the $10,000 pecuniary gifts do not share in gains and losses occurring after Guerdon's demise. Before September 30, 2003, $10,000 is distributed from the account to each of Choate, Keebler and Jones, thus eliminating the pecuniary gifts from the determination of who is a "designated beneficiary" of the account. Before December 31, 2003, and before any non-pro rata distributions are made to the remaining ("residuary") beneficiaries, the remaining balance of the IRA is divided into two separate accounts, one equal to 25% of the remaining value (which belongs to the New England Home for Little Actuaries) and the other equal to 75% (which belongs to Slott, Goldberg and Picker). The division is exactly 25%/75% on the date of division (establishment of separate accounts), thus fulfilling the requirement that post-death gains and losses are allocated pro rata. The beneficiaries might agree to take different assets as part of their respective separate accounts—that's ok as long as the overall amount each takes is the correct percentage of the total account.

For 2003 and later years, the MRD from the separate account belonging to Slott, Goldberg and Picker will be determined based on the total balance of their combined account, and the life expectancy of the oldest member of that group of three beneficiaries, but without regard to the balance in, or identity of the beneficiary (New England Home) of, the *other* separate account.

In 2005, Slott, Goldberg and Picker have a bitter disagreement concerning the definition of required beginning date for a 457 plan, and decide to go their own ways. They divide up their combined account into three separate accounts in 2005. For 2006 and later years, Slott's MRD will be based solely on the balance in his separate account, Goldberg's MRD will be based solely on the balance in his separate account, and Picker's MRD will be based solely on the balance in his separate account—but all three will continue to use the life expectancy of the oldest member of their group of three to determine their respective MRDs.

Regardless of when the separate accounts are established, gains and losses between the date of death and date of "establishment" of the separate accounts must be allocated pro rata to all the accounts and distributions must be charged to the account of the beneficiary who receives the distribution. Reg. § 1.401(a)(9)-8, A-3.

Example: Chloe dies in 2002, leaving her IRA to her husband and daughter equally. Chloe's daughter withdraws $15,000 from the account. Between the time Chloe died and the time the husband and daughter divide up the IRA into separate accounts, some assets have declined in value and some have increased. The beneficiaries cannot retroactively decide that (for example) the assets that increased in value belonged to the daughter's separate account and the assets that declined belonged to the father's account. Furthermore, they must treat the $15,000 distribution to the daughter as a reduction in the daughter's interest in the IRA.

It is not clear in all cases what constitutes "establishment" of separate accounts. Clearly a physical division of (e.g.) an inherited IRA into separate inherited IRAs payable to the individual beneficiaries would work, if the requirements regarding allocation of pre-establishment gains, losses and distributions are met; presumably a written agreement among the beneficiaries and the plan administrator or IRA provider spelling out all the necessary elements would also suffice.

It is not clear whether separate accounts could somehow exist automatically without any post-death action. For example, suppose an IRA is left to three children equally. The IRA provider sends them all equal distributions periodically, the total of which equals or exceeds the MRD requirement by any measure. All gains and losses are allocated to the three beneficiaries equally by default, since they are all equal co-owners of the account. It is not clear whether the beneficiaries' respective "portions" of the account could? must? cannot? be considered "separate accounts" that were "established" as of the date of death if no further steps are taken. Accordingly, if separate account treatment is desired, it is recommended to take some step, over and above simply leaving the benefits in fractional or percentage shares, indicating that the parties have "established" separate accounts. For ways to do this after Participant's death, see ¶ 10.4.02.

If such "portions" *are* considered separate accounts, then virtually all pro-rata beneficiary designations would be separate accounts "established" as of the date of death. The regulations do not seem to contemplate such a result, since they refer to "establishing" separate accounts for the beneficiaries' proportionate shares after the Participant's death.

In planning mode, one way to attempt to assure separate account treatment is for Participant to specify that separate account treatment will be used. If Participant knows that separate account treatment would be beneficial; see Section 3.05, Forms 2.1, 2.2, Appendix B. Another approach is to have all the separate account language set up in the beneficiary designation form or account agreement, but leave it up to the beneficiaries themselves to elect whether they want separate application of § 401(a)(9) to their respective portions.

An IRA provider could facilitate either of these approaches by having the appropriate language in the IRA account agreement, so Participant (or beneficiaries as the case may be) simply have to check boxes rather than draft lengthy beneficiary designation forms or post-mortem agreements. Because creating separate accounts within a single IRA normally will involve some custom drafting, and complexities beyond the standard type of IRA account agreement used by most IRA providers, the separate account approach will probably be permitted only by those IRA providers that cater to larger investment accounts.

Another way to accomplish the objective is for Participant to divide his IRA into actual separate IRAs payable to the respective beneficiaries. For example, a Participant leaving his IRA partly to charity and partly to an individual beneficiary could create two totally separate IRAs, one payable to each of the respective beneficiaries. Some clients and planners find this approach easier to understand than the separate-accounts-within-a-single-IRA approach. Also, this approach may be the only one available if the IRA provider in question does not allow separate-accounts-within-a-single-IRA. Actual separate IRAs have the non-tax advantage of not requiring the beneficiaries to interact with each other after Participant's death.

The disadvantages of having multiple IRAs while Participant is still alive include the additional paperwork (multiple periodic statements from the IRA provider instead of just one statement), the difficulty of keeping the IRAs in the same relative proportion to each other when each contains different investments, and possibly increased investment management fees applicable to multiple smaller accounts compared with one larger account.

Three more notes:

If fractional or percentage share are *not* "automatically" considered separate accounts, then it is unclear whether the distribution requirement is imposed on the collective account (so that the requirement is satisfied as long as the right amount is distributed to any one or more of the account beneficiaries); or whether, alternatively, each beneficiary still has the personal obligation to take his/her pro rata share of the total MRD. The latter is indicated by the statute, but the regulations may have administratively decreed the former.

Since separate account treatment cannot be used for a gift that will not share in gains and losses post-death, it may be desirable to rework a pecuniary gift into a fractional gift as of the date of death, which should solve the problem.

Finally, separate account treatment is not available for computing lifetime MRDs. Reg. § 1.401(a)(9)-8, A-2(a)(2).

1.7.07 *When having a designated beneficiary doesn't matter*

While having a "designated beneficiary" is vital to obtaining the advantages of a payout of death benefits over the life expectancy of a beneficiary, there are situations in which this goal is unimportant. For example, when Participant's chosen beneficiary is a charity (see Chapter 7): charities are exempt from income tax and therefore have no need to try to defer income taxes after Participant's death.

Also, "designated beneficiary" status is irrelevant if the benefits will come out of the retirement plan immediately after Participant's death regardless of whether the benefits pass to a designated beneficiary. This could be the case if either: the plan doesn't offer any form of benefit other than a lump sum (¶ 1.5.09); or a lump sum distribution is the most attractive distribution form for other tax reasons (see ¶ 2.3, ¶ 2.4 for tax advantages for certain lump sum distributions); or the beneficiaries plan to cash out the plan and spend it as soon as possible after Participant's death whether they qualify for life expectancy payout or not.

If Participant is past his RBD, and his chosen beneficiary is close to him in age (or older) there is little or no advantage to using the life expectancy of the beneficiary as an Applicable Distribution Period (compare ¶ 1.5.05 and ¶ 1.5.06). In all of these situations, there is no need to jump through hoops to try to qualify for a life expectancy payout method that will not be available, or will not be advantageous, or for some other reason will not be used.

1.8 The "Designation Date"

The 2001 version of the proposed minimum distribution regulations allowed beneficiaries of a deceased employee or IRA owner until December 31 of the year after the year of the Participant's death to "finalize" the decedent's choice of beneficiary for purposes of determining required distributions, through disclaimers or distributions or possibly other means. The approach of that edition of the regulations was wide open—the designated beneficiary simply was not determined until 12/31 of the year after the year of death.

The final regulations have moved up the "Designation Date" from December 31 to September 30 of the year after the year of death, and also taken a narrower approach to what can happen between the date of death and this shortened deadline. The new approach is that the designated beneficiaries are determined as of the date of death; between the date of death and the Designation Date, you can eliminate a date-of-death beneficiary from the mix (by disclaimer or distribution), but you cannot "add" a beneficiary who was not a beneficiary on the date of death.

This ¶ 1.8 looks at the effects of various post mortem events on the identity of the participant's "designated beneficiary" for minimum distribution purposes.

1.8.01 *Beneficiaries can be "removed" up to 9/30 of year after death*

"[T]he employee's designated beneficiary will be determined based on the beneficiaries designated as of the date of death who remain beneficiaries as of September 30 of the calendar year following the calendar year of the employee's death." Reg. § 1.401(a)(9)-4, A-4(a).

Thus, post-death planning cannot somehow designate a new crop of beneficiaries. Rather, "...any person who was a beneficiary as of the date of the employee's death, but is not a beneficiary as of that September 30 (e.g., because the person receives the entire benefit to which the person is entitled before that September 30) *is not taken into account* in determining the employee's designated beneficiary for purposes of determining the distribution period for required minimum distributions after the employee's death." Reg. § 1.401(a)(9)-4, A-4(a) (emphasis added).

In other words, *if* there are "good" beneficiaries (e.g., individual beneficiaries with long life expectancies) who are *already named* by the deceased Participant (e.g., as contingent beneficiaries, or among a group of multiple beneficiaries), it is possible (by disclaimer or distribution) to eliminate other (e.g., older or non-individual) beneficiaries, so that by September 30 of the year after the year of death only the "good" beneficiaries are left.

1.8.02 *The three post-death deadlines*

Although the "Designation Date" is September 30, the deadline for supplying trust documentation to the plan administrator (¶ 6.2.09) is a little later—October 31 of the year after the year of death; and "separate accounts" for different beneficiaries do not have to be established until December 31. ¶ 1.7.06. This seems to leave the plan administrator with a problem—how does he cut a check (or checks) for distribution to multiple beneficiaries by December 31 of the year after the year of Participant's death, when he may not know until that very day whether they will establish separate accounts?

1.8.03 *Changing the designated beneficiary by disclaimer*

Qualified disclaimers (¶ 8.1.01) made before the Designation Date are given effect in determining who is the designated beneficiary. "...if a person disclaims entitlement to the employee's benefit, pursuant to a disclaimer that satisfies section 2518 by that September 30 thereby allowing other beneficiaries to receive the benefit in lieu of that person, the disclaiming person is not taken into account in determining the employee's designated beneficiary." Reg. § 1.401(a)(9)-4, A-4(a). Thus, an older beneficiary (such as a surviving spouse or child) can disclaim the benefits and allow them to pass to a younger contingent beneficiary (such as a child or grandchild) and the younger beneficiary will then be "the" designated beneficiary whose life expectancy becomes the Applicable Distribution Period. See ¶ 8.1-¶ 8.2. As a reminder, the deadline for making a "qualified disclaimer" is generally nine months after Participant's death. ¶ 8.1.11. The fact that the Designation Date is not until September 30 of the year after the year of death does *not* extend the deadline for making a qualified disclaimer.

1.8.04 *Establishing separate accounts after death*

A retirement plan account that is left to multiple beneficiaries can be divided into separate accounts for them after Participant's death. See full explanation at ¶ 1.7.06.

This can be helpful for: assuring that the existence of non-individual beneficiaries does not prevent individual beneficiaries from using the life expectancy payout method; assuring that each designated individual beneficiary can use his or her own life expectancy (rather than the life expectancy of the oldest beneficiary) to measure required distributions; and applying the special spousal rules (¶ 1.6).

1.8.05 *Eliminating beneficiaries by distributing their benefits*

Another way to cure the multiple beneficiary problem is to distribute, to any non-individual (or older) beneficiaries, the shares payable to them. If the amounts payable to the non-individual (or older) beneficiaries are entirely distributed to them by the Designation Date, then only the remaining (younger, individual) beneficiaries who still have an interest in the benefit will "count" for purposes of determining who is the designated beneficiary. Reg. § 1.401(a)(9)-4, A-4(a). This can be helpful if the separate account rule (¶ 1.7.06) is not available. See sidebar at ¶ 1.1.06 for possible glitch in the regulations applicable to deaths in the year 2000.

Example: Frank's beneficiary designation for his $1 million IRA reads "$10,000 shall be paid to Charity X and the balance shall be paid to my son." If the charity's share is distributed to it in full by the Designation Date, the son is left as the sole beneficiary. The multiple beneficiary rule (¶ 1.7.06) does not apply. Since the son is an individual, he is a "designated beneficiary," and required distributions will be determined based on the son's life expectancy.

1.8.06 *Distributing the account itself out of an estate*

The IRS states emphatically, twice, that an estate cannot be a "designated beneficiary." Reg. § 1.401(a)(9)-4, A-3(a), § 1.401(a)(9)-8, A-11. See ¶ 1.7.04. This problem can NOT be cured by distributing the retirement plan itself (intact) out of the estate to the individual beneficiaries of the estate before the Designation Date.

The executor can distribute the IRA to the estate beneficiaries; see ¶ 6.1.06 and PLR 2002-34019; that's not a problem. The problem is that such distribution will not have the effect of allowing the estate beneficiaries to use their own life expectancies for computing MRDs.

Example: Jane dies without having named a beneficiary for her IRA. Under the terms of the IRA agreement, the IRA is payable to her estate as default beneficiary, so she does not have a "designated beneficiary" at the time of death. The only beneficiaries of her estate are her children

Gray and Seymour. Before the Designation Date, the executor of her estate, before taking any distributions from the IRA, transfers the IRA account to Gray and Seymour. This transfer does not trigger any income tax, because it is an assignment of the right-to-receive-IRD to the persons entitled to receive the IRD under the decedent's will (¶ 2.2.04). On the Designation Date, the children are the sole owners of the account. However they do not qualify as "designated beneficiaries" because they are not "designated as a beneficiary under the plan."

1.8.07 *Powers of appointment*

What if Participant's beneficiary designation form gives Participant's executor (or spouse, or some other person), a power to appoint the benefits to any person the power-holder chooses (other than the power-holder himself)? If the power-holder exercises the power irrevocably prior to the Designation Date by appointing the benefits to an individual, would the beneficiary so selected be a "designated beneficiary?"

Probably not. The regulations allow only *eliminating* (by means of disclaimer or distribution) beneficiaries chosen by Participant, and do not allow *adding* new beneficiaries. Reg. § 1.401(a)(9)-4, A-4(a). Allowing someone to choose beneficiaries at random from a huge amorphous class probably violates the requirement that the beneficiary must be identifiable under the plan *as of the date of death* (not just as of the Designation Date). Reg. § 1.401(a)(9)-4, A-1. See also ¶ 6.3.06. The language in former proposed Reg. § 1.401(a)(9)-5, A-7(d)(1), providing that an employee is deemed to have no designated beneficiary if the plan permits any person to "have the discretion to change the beneficiaries of the employee...after the end of the calendar year following the calendar year in which the employee died" has been eliminated in the final regulations, along with its implication that granting someone the power to change the employee's beneficiaries *prior to* the Designation Date was not a problem.

Reg. § 1.401(a)(9)-4, A-1, provides that "An individual may be designated as a beneficiary under the plan either by the terms of the plan or, if the plan so provides, by an affirmative election by the employee *(or the employee's surviving spouse)* specifying the beneficiary." Reg. § 1.401(a)(9)-4, Q-2, asks "Must an employee *(or the employee's spouse)* make an affirmative election specifying a beneficiary for a person to be a designated beneficiary?" (Emphasis added.) Some practitioners have wondered whether these parenthetical references to Spouse's designating a beneficiary are intended to allow Spouse (but not other beneficiaries or fiduciaries) to exercise a broad power of appointment during the post-death clean-up period. That seems unlikely because these references to a designation by the employee's spouse were carried over verbatim from the 1987 proposed regulations (1987 Prop. Reg. § 1.401(a)(9)-1, D-1 and D-2), which did not allow any post-death cleanup period. Apparently the phrase is merely referring to the § 401(a)(9)(B)(iv)(II) situation (¶ 1.6.05; designated beneficiary is determined as of Spouse's death, if Participant died before his RBD leaving benefits to Spouse as sole beneficiary and she then died before the required commencement of distributions to her).

1.8.08 *Effect of beneficiary's death prior to Designation Date*

A person who is a beneficiary as of the date of death, but then dies prior to the Designation Date, does not lose his status as a "designated beneficiary." Reg. § 1.401(a)(9)-4, A-4(c). He will still be considered a designated beneficiary (unless his benefits are entirely distributed or disclaimed prior to the Designation Date); his successor beneficiaries do not step into his shoes as "designated beneficiaries." For how to determine who those successor beneficiaries are, see ¶ 1.9.02.

Example: Waylon dies on February 15, 2002, prior to his RBD, leaving his two IRAs, IRA # 1 and IRA # 2, to Willy as primary beneficiary. Willy survives Waylon, but then dies on December 1, 2002, without having withdrawn from or disclaimed either account. Prior to his death, Willy named his granddaughter (age 5) as his successor beneficiary on IRA # 1. However, Willy never got around to naming a successor beneficiary for IRA # 2, so IRA # 2 passed to Willy's estate upon his death. The Designation Date for these accounts is September 30 of the year after Waylon's death, i.e., September 30, 2003, at which time IRA # 2 is owned by Willy's estate and IRA # 1 is owned by Willy's granddaughter. Even though he is not living on the Designation Date, Willy is still the designated beneficiary of both IRAs, and distributions must be made from both accounts over Willy's life expectancy (determined as of the age he would have attained in 2003 if he had lived that long) commencing no later than December 31, 2003. The granddaughter cannot switch over to using her life expectancy for IRA # 1, even though she now owns IRA # 1 as successor beneficiary; and the estate is not compelled to use the 5-year rule for IRA # 2, even though an estate could not have been a "designated beneficiary" had it been named directly as beneficiary by Waylon.

1.9 Other Important MRD Rules

1.9.01 *Taking distributions from multiple plans*

If the client participates in more than one qualified retirement plan, the MRD must be calculated separately for each such plan, and each such plan must distribute the MRD calculated for that plan. Reg. § 1.401(a)(9)-8, A-1. Thus if the client participates in two pension plans and a 401(k) plan, he will receive three separate MRDs, one from each of these plans.

A different rule applies for IRAs. The MRD must be calculated separately for each IRA, but (subject to the exception noted below) Participant is not required to take each IRA's calculated amount from that IRA. He can total up the MRDs required from all of his IRAs and then take the total amount all from one of the IRAs, or from any combination of them. Reg. § 1.408-8, A-9.

This rule applies also to 403(b) accounts. The MRD must be calculated separately for each 403(b) account, but (subject to the exception noted below) Participant is not required to take each 403(b) account's calculated amount from that 403(b) account. He can total up the MRDs required from all of his 403(b) arrangements, and then take the total amount all from one of them, or from any combination of them. Reg. § 1.403(b)-3, A-4.

The Exception: Notice 88-38, 1988-1 C.B. 524, stated that an individual could aggregate inherited IRAs with non-inherited IRAs for MRD purposes. The 2001 proposed regulations proposed to modify, and the final regulations did modify, Notice 88-38 by providing that an individual's IRAs held as *owner* may not be aggregated with IRAs held as *beneficiary of another person*; an individual's 403(b) plans held as *employee* may not be aggregated with such individual's 403(b) plans held as *beneficiary of another person*; and an individual's IRAs (or 403(b) plans) held as beneficiary of one decedent may not be aggregated with IRAs (or 403(b) plans) held as beneficiary of another decedent. Reg. § 1.408-8, A-9, § 1.403(b)-3, A-4. The regulations are effective for 2003 and later years (¶ 1.1.06).

Note that IRAs can be combined only with other IRAs, not with 403(b)s. 403(b)s can be combined only with other 403(b)s, not with IRAs.

Note also that the rules allow the *taxpayer who must take distributions* to combine multiple IRAs he must take distributions from (see Notice 88-38, Example 4); it does not allow IRAs inherited by different beneficiaries *from a single participant* to be "pooled" so that required distributions paid to one beneficiary can fulfill the distribution requirement applicable to another beneficiary.

Example: Jeffrey dies, leaving two IRAs. One is payable to a QTIP marital trust (¶ 3.3.04), the other to a credit shelter trust. The "trust rules" (¶ 6.2) are complied with, so the beneficiaries of the respective trusts are treated as Jeffrey's designated beneficiaries, and the life expectancy of the oldest beneficiary of each trust is used to measure the post-death MRDs to that trust. Assume the credit shelter trust permits accumulation of income. To maximize income tax deferral and minimize estate taxes, the family would like to compute one single MRD for both trusts and take it entirely from the IRA payable to the marital trust. This way, the credit shelter trust would get the maximum available income tax deferral and what income taxes had to be paid would be paid by the marital trust, where at least they could reduce Spouse's future taxable estate. Neither Notice 88-38 nor the regulations appears to allow this maneuver.

1.9.02 *Who gets the account when the original beneficiary dies*

If the participant dies leaving his benefits to a beneficiary ("original beneficiary"), and the original beneficiary survives the participant, but then dies before withdrawing all of the benefits, what happens to the money in the account? ¶ 1.5.07, ¶ 1.6.05, and ¶ 1.8.08 explain the Applicable Distribution Period that applies in that situation.

This ¶ 1.9.02 explains *who is entitled to the benefits* at that point, which is a more complicated subject. The answer depends on the terms of the plan or IRA agreement. The IRS doesn't really care (for MRD purposes) who the account passes to at that point, since that has no effect on the Applicable Distribution Period.

1. <u>Beneficiary names his/her own successor beneficiary</u>. Enlightened plans and IRA providers allow the original beneficiary to name his or her own successor beneficiary. If the original beneficiary has successfully named a successor beneficiary, the successor beneficiary steps into the shoes of the original beneficiary as owner of the account.

2. <u>Beneficiary's estate</u>. Some plans and IRAs require the benefits to be paid to the original beneficiary's estate in this case; this is also likely to be where the benefits go if the beneficiary dies before naming his/her own successor beneficiary. In either case, the estate of the original beneficiary steps into the shoes of the original beneficiary as owner of the account.

3. <u>Contingent beneficiary named by original owner</u>. Many practitioners assume that, if the original beneficiary dies after the Participant, the account passes to the contingent beneficiary named by the Participant. This would typically NOT be true. Usually, the Participant's beneficiary designation form provides that the contingent beneficiary will receive the benefits only if the original beneficiary *predeceases* the Participant (or disclaims the benefits). Once the original beneficiary survives the Participant, the original beneficiary (unless he/she disclaims the benefits; see Chapter 8) becomes the absolute owner of the account and the contingent beneficiary's interest is completely eliminated. Of course, the plan documents (including the Participant's beneficiary designation) could provide otherwise, but typically they don't.

4. <u>Other provision by the Participant</u>. Some Participants would like to include provisions dictating what happens to the benefits remaining in the account if the original beneficiary dies after the Participant but before withdrawing all the benefits. There is nothing illegal about doing this, but it does raise property law and estate tax issues beyond the scope of this discussion. For that reason, some IRA providers will not accept such restrictions, unless contained in a formal trust agreement.

Unfortunately, the final regulations left out the helpful statement, which appeared in the proposed regulations, that blessed allowing a beneficiary to "designate a subsequent beneficiary for distributions of any portion of the employee's benefit after the beneficiary dies." See 2001 Prop. Reg. § 1.401(a)(9)-5, A-7(d)(1). This omission is not intended to imply that now beneficiaries cannot name their own beneficiaries; it's just an unfortunate side effect of the deletion of the mysterious never-explained old rule that no person could have the power, after the employee's death, to change the employee's beneficiary. The helpful language in the proposed regulation was appended to this now-deleted rule, and so it disappeared when the rule it was appended to disappeared.

1.9.03 *Tax-free distributions count towards the MRD*

Reg. § 1.401(a)(9)-5, A-9, and Reg. § 1.408-8, A-11, provide lists of which types of distributions do, and which do not, count towards the MRD requirement. These provisions confirm that non-taxable distributions fulfill the distribution requirement. See, e.g., PLR 9840041 in which an employee took a distribution of his entire balance from an employer plan, rolled over the taxable portion of the distribution and did not roll over the non-taxable amounts. The IRS ruled that the non-taxable distribution, which exceeded the MRD, satisfied the MRD requirement.

Certain types of retirement plans accept, or used to accept, non-deductible employee contributions. Such plans typically maintain two "accounts" on the books for each employee, the "employer contribution account" and the "employee contribution account." The employee would typically have no "basis" in the employer contribution account, but would have some basis in the employee contribution account. Distributions from the employee contribution account would therefore be partly tax-free (as a distribution of basis). ¶ 2.1.04.

Even though the two accounts are maintained as "separate accounts" on the employer's books, they must be treated as one account for MRD purposes during the employee's life. ¶ 1.7.06. Thus, an employee who has made non-deductible contributions to a qualified retirement plan can, if he wishes, use distributions from the employee contribution account to fulfill the MRD requirement with regard to both the employer and employee contribution accounts.

Unfortunately, an IRA owner cannot use the same approach (take out non-deductible amounts first), because (a) all IRA distributions generally are deemed to come proportionately from taxable and after-tax amounts, and (b) all IRAs are treated as one single account for this purpose; for detailed explanation of this rule, see ¶ 5.4.10-¶ 5.4.12.

1.9.04 *Distributions in kind*

Participant or beneficiary can take required distributions in kind as well as in cash. Plans are permitted to distribute property as well as cash. See instructions for IRS form 1099-R (2000), Box 1, where the payer is instructed "If you distribute employer securities or other property, include in box 1 the FMV of the securities or other property on the date of distribution." There is nothing in the Code, regulations, or form 1099-R instructions that indicates distributions in kind could not be used to satisfy the minimum distribution requirement.

1.10 Enforcement of the MRD Rules

1.10.01 *Who enforces the minimum distribution rules*

Compliance with the minimum distribution rules is one of the more than 30 requirements a "qualified retirement plan" must meet to stay "qualified." § 401(a). Accordingly, in the case of qualified plans, the plan administrator is the enforcer of the minimum distribution rules. Since disqualification of the plan would be a disaster for all concerned (the plan would lose its income tax exemption for example), the plan administrator is extremely concerned to make sure required distributions are distributed—even though the 50% penalty tax for failing to make a required distribution is imposed on the "payee" (non-payee?) rather than on the plan. § 4974' ¶ 1.10.02.

An IRA does not have to be "qualified" in the same way as qualified plans have to be qualified; the IRS does not issue individual determination letters for IRAs. Rev. Proc. 87-50, 1987-2 C.B. 647, Sec. 4.03. Furthermore, the IRA provider typically does not have sufficient information to enforce the minimum distribution rules; for example, the IRA provider has no way of knowing whether Participant satisfied the MRD requirement for that IRA by taking a larger distribution from another IRA held by a different provider (¶ 1.9.01). The penalty for failure to take the MRD falls on the payee, not on the IRA provider.

The IRS is drawing IRA providers in to a greater role in enforcing the minimum distribution rules. Reg. § 1.408-8, A-10. IRA providers will be required to report to the IRS annually, beginning in 2004, not only the year-end account value of each IRA (as they already do), but also the fact that an MRD is required from the account for the year in question; and the IRA provider will also be required, beginning in 2003, to inform the IRA account holder that a distribution is required, as well as either calculating or offering to calculate the amount of the MRD for the account holder. Reg., Preamble, "IRA Reporting of Required Minimum Distributions."

1.10.02 *50% penalty for failure to take MRD*

§ 4974 imposes a penalty for failure to take a required distribution. The penalty is 50% of the amount that was supposed to be, but was not, distributed. Based on anecdotal evidence, the IRS was lenient in waiving this penalty during the years of the proposed regulations, 1987-2001. Enforcement may become more vigorous now that final minimum distribution regulations are issued.

Minimum distributions can be delayed beyond the normal deadline (¶ 1.2.03) in only two situations: a review period for QDROs and (in the case of insured plans) delay caused by receivership of the insurance company. Reg. § 1.401(a)(9)-8, A-7, A-8.

There are two provisions for waiver of the penalty: In the case of a Participant who dies before his RBD, *if there is only one individual beneficiary*, the penalty is *automatically* waived if Participant's entire benefit is distributed by the end of the fifth calendar year following the calendar year in which Participant died. Reg. § 54.4974-2, A-7(b). It is not clear why the IRS limits this reasonable provision to the situation in which there is only one individual beneficiary. See also ¶ 1.5.10 for rule temporarily allowing penalty-free switches from the 5-year rule method to the life expectancy method.

The 50% penalty tax can be waived by the IRS on a case-by-case basis (§ 4974(d)) "if the payee described in section 4974(a) establishes to the   satisfaction of the Commissioner" that "(1) The shortfall...in the amount distributed in any taxable year was due to reasonable error; and (2) Reasonable steps are being taken to remedy the shortfall." Reg. § 54.4974-2, A-8(a).

Although the regulation doesn't say so, the IRS wants you to pay the penalty first and then request a refund. See IRS Publication 590 (2000), p. 35, "Excess Accumulations (Insufficient Distributions)," and instructions for Form 5329 (2000), Part VII. The form to file to report the penalty is 5329. It is supposed to be attached to Form 1040 for the year the distribution was missed. Instructions for Form 5329 (2000), "When and Where to File." According to Publication 590 and the instructions to Form 5329, you can file amended 1040's for each year in which the MRD was not taken just to add the Form 5329 for each year, or file Form 5329 as a stand-alone form.

Reminder: The point of filing amended returns is *not* to add the missed distributions back in to your income for those years. The minimum distribution rules do not create "constructive distributions" of the MRD amounts; you actually have to take the distribution in order to have income to report. The income is properly reported in the later year, when the (late) distribution is actually taken. Thus, the amended 1040 you file for a year you missed a MRD will show the same income as the return you originally filed for that year, but will show a new higher tax (because of the 50% penalty).

For how to compute the penalty, see Reg. § 54.4974-1.

Because computing the penalty may involve computing MRDs for years before the final regulations became the exclusive method of computing MRDs, the following sections are included to record the history of the effective dates of the various changes in the regulations.

1.10.03 *Final regulations' effective date: by type of plan*

Traditional and Roth IRAs: IRA owners did not have to wait until the IRA provider amended its documents to take advantage of the new rules, since "For determining required minimum distributions for calendar year 2002, taxpayers may rely on" either the "final regulations, the 2001 proposed regulations, or the 1987 proposed regulations." Preamble, "Effective Date." So, the IRA owner could determine his required distribution for 2002 under whichever of the three sets of regulations provides the smallest required distribution. The IRA owner did not have to file any election with the IRA provider or the IRS; as long as he took the amount required by whichever set of rules produced the smallest MRD, he would not be liable for a penalty.

Qualified Plans: A Participant receiving required distributions from a qualified plan was permitted to use the 2001 proposed regulations for computing his MRD for 2001—regardless of whether the plan had been amended, apparently. In IRS Announcement 2001-23, 2001-10 I.R.B. 791 (amending IRS Publication 575, "Pension and

Annuity Income"), the IRS told retirees, "Use the new rules for figuring the required distribution for 2001 that must be made by the end of 2001." There was no mention in the Announcement of any exception to this direction. This meant that if Participant received a larger distribution from the plan in 2001 than the new rules would require (because the plan was still using the old rules), Participant could roll over the excess to an IRA within 60 days, because the excess was not a minimum required distribution (MRDs cannot be rolled over; ¶ 2.5.06). (Note: a non-spouse beneficiary who received a larger-than-required distribution *cannot* use a rollover to avoid tax on the excess distribution, because non-spouse beneficiaries cannot roll over distributions from an inherited plan. ¶ 2.5.05.)

The various IRS pronouncements, read together, lead to the conclusion that the plan administrator of a qualified retirement plan can write a check that *is* an MRD when it leaves his office, but that same check is *not* an MRD when it arrives in the recipient's mailbox.

403(b) plans: The effective date provisions for 403(b) plans are the same as for traditional IRAs. Reg. § 1.403(b)-3, A-1(b).

1.10.04 *What rules apply to pre-2003 distributions?*

The final regulations must be used for calculating required distributions for 2003 and later years, as noted at ¶ 1.1.06. However, the statute requiring minimum distributions (§ 401(a)(9)) has been in effect since 1987. Therefore, for the years 1987 through 2002, taxpayers have been taking (or not taking) MRDs without the benefit of final regulations. Looking back, how do we determine what distributions were required in those years for purposes of computing a penalty?

For distribution years prior to 2002, previous IRS announcements indicated that:

1.   Taxpayers may not "rely on" the 2001 proposed regulations in computing distributions required for years prior to 2001; they "may rely" only on the 1987 proposed regulations for pre-2001 years. IRS Announcement 2001-23, 2001-10 I.R.B. 791.

2.   In determining minimum distributions for the year 2001, "taxpayers may rely on" either the 2001 or the 1987 proposed regulations. 2001 Proposed Regulations, Preamble, "Proposed

Effective Date." This Preamble may be found in the 2002 CCH Standard Federal Tax Reporter, U.S. Tax Cases Advance Sheets volume, at ¶ 49,393.

See ¶ 10.4.06 for how the changes in the regulations affect beneficiaries taking distributions from plans inherited from decedents who died before the new regulations were issued. For a complete explanation of the old rules (under the 1987 proposed regulations) consult Chapter 1 of the 1999 edition of this book (see Bibliography).

MRDs computed *in compliance with* the proposed regulations that were "in effect" at the time are in a safe harbor. Specifically, distributions for years 1987 through 2002 that are computed in compliance with the 1987 proposed regulations are protected; and distributions for 2001 or 2002 that are computed in accordance with the 2001 proposed regulations are protected. Compliance with the proposed regulations for years prior to 2003 protects the taxpayer against later changes in the law. The IRS promised that if "future guidance is more restrictive than the guidance in these regulations, the future guidance will be issued without retroactive effect." 2001 proposed regulations, Preamble, "Proposed Effective Date."

Though most beneficiaries are better off using the final regulations to calculate their distributions, some will be worse off. Those beneficiaries may ask, "Does the final regulations' requirement that the designated beneficiary and Applicable Distribution Period must be redetermined under the final rules, even for beneficiaries of decedents who died prior to 2003, violate the IRS's promise not to issue final regulations with retroactive effect harmful to those who relied on the proposed regulations?" Such a claim would be a long shot. The IRS is not imposing any penalty for *pre-2003 distributions* calculated under the proposed regulations, so there is no "retroactive" penalty; the final regulations apply only to *future* required distributions.

In fact, the final regulations make no attempt to dictate how to calculate distributions that were required for pre-2002 years. The final regulations do *not* say that, for years prior to 2003, MRDs must be calculated under the then-issued proposed regulations—or under the final regulations. The final regulations say nothing at all about required distributions for years prior to 2002.

What if the taxpayer's actions prior to 2003 were clearly *not* in compliance with the proposed regulations, but constituted a reasonable interpretation of the statute? Proposed regulations have a rather lowly legal status. They "are not entitled to judicial deference," *Natomas North America, Inc. v. Comm'r*, 90 T.C. 710, at 718, n. 11, (1988), and "are given no greater weight than a position advanced by the Commissioner on brief." *Van Wyk v. Comm'r*, 113 T.C. 441 (1999). Therefore failure to comply with proposed regulations *per se* can't be held against you. Furthermore, if the taxpayer's actions taken in conformity with proposed regulations are later prohibited by final regulations, but at the time taken constituted "a reasonable interpretation of the statute and proposed regulations," the taxpayer cannot be penalized. See, *e.g.*, discussion in PLR 9506001. If a particular interpretation of the law was explicitly adopted by the IRS in one or more letter rulings, it is presumably safe to conclude that interpretation is "reasonable." See, *e.g.*, PLR 9311037.

If pre-2003 distributions were not computed in compliance with any of the proposed regulations, the taxpayer is not entitled to the IRS's promised protection for those complying with the proposed regulations, *if* the final regulations had been later issued with retroactive effect. However, the final regulations were *not* adopted with retroactive effect. Compliance with the final regulations is required only for 2003 and later years. Therefore, it appears that distributions calculated based on "a reasonable interpretation of the statute" for the years 1986 through 2002 should be protected even if not in compliance with the proposed *or* final regulations.

For more discussion of the taxpayer's right (or lack thereof) to rely on IRS pronouncements of all types, see 2001 CCH *Standard Federal Tax Reporter* ¶ 43,282.0211.

1.11 Summary of Planning Principles

1.   The income tax deferral on plan contributions and investment income is the most valuable feature of qualified retirement plans and IRAs. Preserving the option of continued tax deferral is an important goal of estate planning for retirement benefits. The minimum distribution rules set the outer limits on deferral and establish the requirements for reaching those limits. Planning for retirement benefits therefore requires familiarity with these rules.

2.   Naming a beneficiary for retirement benefits does more than determine who will receive the benefits after Participant's death; it also determines the maximum period of income tax deferral that will

be available for those benefits.

3.   Naming Participant's "estate" as beneficiary generally reduces the opportunities for continued income tax deferral compared with naming an individual beneficiary. Naming a trust as beneficiary has the same effect as naming an estate, unless the "trust rules" (¶ 6.2) are complied with.

4.   Naming a young beneficiary will generally permit the longest possible income tax deferral.

5.   If Participant is naming more than one beneficiary, consider structuring the benefits as "separate accounts payable to different beneficiaries" (¶ 1.7.06) to enable each individual beneficiary (and qualifying trust) to use his or her own life expectancy (or the life expectancy of the trust beneficiary) to measure required distributions after Participant's death.

2

Income Tax Issues

*The impact of federal income taxes on
estate planning for retirement benefits*

This Chapter examines the federal income tax treatment of retirement benefits:

¶ 2.1 gives an overview of the subject: which Code sections govern the income tax treatment of retirement benefits (¶ 2.1.01), *when* benefits are taxed (¶ 2.1.02), summary of which distributions are taxed at lower rates or not at all (¶ 2.1.03), how to compute and recover participant's "basis" in the benefits (¶ 2.1.04), and income tax withholding (¶ 2.1.05-¶ 2.1.08).

¶ 2.2 discusses the additional income tax rules that apply to distributions after the Participant's death, when the retirement benefits become "income in respect of a decedent" (IRD), including the sometimes-overlooked income tax deduction for estate taxes paid on IRD (¶ 2.2.07-¶ 2.2.11) and the critical issue of post-death "assignments" of retirement plan benefits (¶ 2.2.05-¶ 2.2.06).

¶ 2.3 reviews the special favorable income tax treatments available for certain "lump sum distributions" to participants born before 1936, including "10-year averaging" and "capital gain."

¶ 2.4 discusses another special favorable income tax treatment, the deferral (and lower tax rate) allowed for certain distributions that include "net unrealized appreciation" (NUA) of employer securities.

¶ 2.5 explains the rules for tax-free rollovers.

¶ 2.6 summarizes planning principles arising from the income tax treatment of retirement plan distribution.

2.1 Income Tax Treatment: In General

This Section explains the federal income tax treatment of non-annuity distributions from QRPs, IRAs and 403(b) plans. This book does not cover state or local income taxes or annuity payouts.

2.1.01 *Plan distributions includible in gross income*

Income taxation of distributions from qualified retirement plans ("QRPs") is governed by § 402(a), which provides that, except as otherwise provided in § 402, "any amount actually distributed to any distributee by any employees' trust described in section 401(a) which is exempt from tax under section 501(a) shall be taxable to the distributee, in the taxable year of the distributee in which distributed, under section 72 (relating to annuities)." § 408(d)(1) provides similarly for distributions from IRAs, as § 403(b)(1) does for 403(b) plans. See ¶ 5.2 regarding distributions from Roth IRAs.

(If the distribution occurs after Participant's death, it is also subject to the rules of § 691, governing "income in respect of a decedent" (IRD); ¶ 2.2 discusses these additional rules. See also Chapter 7 for the income tax treatment of benefits paid to charity.)

§ 72 is one of the most complicated sections of the Code. It has lengthy rules dealing with: taxation of distributions (and deemed distributions) from annuity contracts, employer plans, life insurance contracts and modified endowment contracts; how the owner's "investment in the contract" (basis) is apportioned among distributions; and various penalties. Since this ¶ 2.1 covers only non-annuity distributions from QRPs, IRAs and 403(b) plans, there is no need to tackle most of the intricacies of § 72. Suffice it to say that all distributions from a QRP, IRA or 403(b) plan are includible in the distributee's gross income as ordinary income unless an exception applies. ¶ 2.1.02 lists the distributions and other events that trigger income tax; the exceptions to the general rule are listed in ¶ 2.1.03.

The only two parts of § 72 covered in depth in this book are the penalty for certain distributions before age 59½ (§ 72(t), covered in Chapter 9), and how to compute the a Participant's "investment in the contract" (basis) that may be distributed tax-free (see ¶ 2.1.04).

2.1.02 *Actual distributions and deemed distributions*

Generally, a Participant or beneficiary is taxable on QRP, IRA or 403(b) benefits only if, as and when such benefits are "actually distributed." § 402(a), § 408(d)(1), § 403(b)(1). The doctrine of "constructive receipt" (holding that income becomes taxable when it is "made available," not just when it is paid) does not apply to these benefits. Compare § 402(b), dealing with tax treatment of distributions from "nonexempt" (non-qualified) employee benefit plans, providing that the employee is taxed on amounts "actually distributed *or made available.*"

However, there are certain events that can cause a Participant or beneficiary to be currently taxable on retirement benefits without an actual distribution. For example:

1.   After Participant's death, certain "assignments" of Participant's retirement plan benefits can trigger immediate realization of the underlying income as explained at ¶ 2.2.05.

2.   If a QRP ceases to be "qualified" under § 401(a), income taxation would cease to be governed by § 402(a); the results of this event are beyond the scope of this book.

3.   Under § 72(p), certain loans made by a QRP to the Participant may be treated as distributions at the time made or if the loan is defaulted. See ¶ 2.1.04, B, for the effect of a defaulted plan loan on the Participant's basis; otherwise this book does not cover plan loans.

4.   § 408(e)(2) provides that "[I]f, during any taxable year of the individual for whose benefit any [IRA] is established, that individual or his beneficiary engages in any transaction prohibited by section 4975 with respect to such account, such account ceases to be an individual retirement account as of the first day of such taxable year." The individual is taxed "as if there were a distribution on the first day of the taxable year...of an amount equal to the fair market value on such day of all of the assets in the account on such day." Reg. § 1.408-4(d)(1). This book does not cover prohibited transactions.

5.   "If, during any taxable year of the individual for whose benefit an individual retirement account is established, that individual uses the account or any portion thereof as security for a loan, the portion so used is treated as distributed to that individual." § 408(e)(4), Reg. § 1.408-4(d)(2).

6.   The acquisition by any IRA (or by a self-directed account in a QRP) of a "collectible" (as defined in § 408(m)(2)) is treated as

a distribution of the cost of the "collectible." § 408(m)(1).

7.   Lifetime assignment of a Roth IRA to "another individual" causes a deemed distribution of the account to Participant; see ¶ 5.5.07. Presumably the IRS would apply the same rule to traditional IRAs.

2.1.03 *Catalogue of no-tax and low-tax distributions*

As noted (¶ 2.1.01), retirement plan distributions are generally taxable to the recipient as ordinary income. Here is a list of all the exceptions to that general rule, with a cross reference telling where to find more information about each:

1.   Qualified distributions from a Roth IRA are tax-free. ¶ 5.2.01.

2.   Distributions "rolled over" to another retirement plan are tax-free if various requirements are met. Tax-free rollovers are discussed at ¶ 2.5 and ¶ 3.2.

3.   Distributions of life insurance *proceeds* from a QRP are partly tax-free; see ¶ 8.3.03. Distribution of a life insurance *policy* on an employee's life to that employee may be partly tax-free as a return of basis; see ¶ 8.3.04.

4.   See ¶ 2.1.04 regarding tax-free return of Participant's non-deductible contributions (and other elements of Participant's "basis" or "investment in the contract").

5.   Certain distributions of "employer stock" from a QRP are eligible for deferred taxation at capital gains rates rather than immediate taxation at ordinary income rates. See ¶ 2.4.

6.   Certain lump sum distributions from QRPs to individuals born before 1936 are eligible for reduced tax; see ¶ 2.3.06-¶ 2.3.12.

7.   While a distribution made to a Participant's beneficiary after Participant's death is taxable just as it would have been if made to Participant during life, the beneficiary is entitled to an income tax deduction for federal estate taxes paid on the

benefits; see ¶ 2.2.07-¶ 2.2.11.

8.   If Participant's beneficiary is income tax-exempt, the
        beneficiary will not have to pay income tax on the distribution.
        See generally Chapter 7 and in particular ¶ 7.5.01.

2.1.04 *Participant's basis (investment in the contract)*

A distribution is non-taxable to the extent it represents the
recovery of Participant's "investment in the contract," or what might be
more familiarly called his "basis." § 72(b)(2). To apply this rule in any
situation requires two separate determinations. First, what *is* the
Participant's investment in the contract? Second, how much of any
particular distribution or deemed distribution is treated as a distribution
of that basis? This section ¶ 2.1.04 looks at the first question: what
dollars get added into "basis." The answers to the second question vary
depending on the type of plan, and are covered elsewhere in this book:

*   ¶ 5.4.10-¶ 5.4.12 explains how much of a distribution from a
        traditional IRA is treated as recovery of basis.

*   ¶ 5.2.03 explains how much of a non-qualified distribution
        from a Roth IRA is tax-free as recovery of basis.

*   ¶ 8.3 explains the basis rules for plan-owned life insurance.

For most Participants, the only "investment in the contract" they
have is their after-tax contributions to the plan, if any. In a traditional
IRA, this would be the $2,000 per year (maximum for years prior to
2002; limit higher for later years) contribution the Participant
contributed, if Participant did not take a tax deduction for such
contribution.

Some qualified retirement plans (QRPs) permit employees to
make after-tax contributions. In a defined contribution plan, usually the
employer maintains a separate accounting for the employ*ee*
contribution account (i.e., the employee's after-tax contributions and
the earnings thereon) and the employ*er* contribution account (i.e., the
employer's contributions and the earnings thereon). The rules of § 72
may be applied separately to these separate accounts. § 72(d)(2). This
is favorable to the employee, because typically he has a higher basis in

the employee-contribution account, so a lump sum distribution of that account might be largely tax-free if it is treated separately from the rest of his plan benefits. The employee may then choose to roll over the taxable part of that distribution tax-free to an IRA. See, e.g., PLR 9840041. As a result of EGTRRA 2001, the employee may even choose to roll over the non-taxable as well as the taxable portions of his account to another retirement plan; see ¶ 5.4.12.

Aside from non-deductible contributions, here is the treatment of other amounts that may or may not increase the employee's basis:

A.   Cost of current life insurance protection. See ¶ 8.3.02.

B.   Loans that became deemed distributions. QRPs (but not IRAs) are permitted to make loans to participants from their accounts in the plan provided various requirements are met. One of the requirements is that the loan must be repaid within a certain period of time. If the loan does not meet these requirements, or is not paid back within that time frame, the loan is treated as a "deemed distribution" and included in the employee's income. ¶ 2.1.02. If, after the loan was treated as a deemed distribution, the employee does in fact repay the loan, then such repayments are treated as employee after-tax contributions for purposes of computing the employee's investment in the contract. Reg. § 1.72(0)-1, A-21; see IRS Instructions for Form 1099-R, 2000, under heading "Loans treated as distributions."

C.   Unrelated taxable business income (UBTI). Though IRAs are generally income tax-exempt, they are subject to the tax on UBTI. § 408(e)(2). If an IRA has to pay this tax, there is no authority for treating the income thus taxed as part of the Participant's basis in the account, meaning it will be taxed *again* when it is distributed.

2.1.05 *Withholding of federal income taxes*

Retirement plan distributions are subject to withholding of federal income taxes. This fact creates problems and planning opportunities. This book does not cover state or local withholding requirements.

In general, withholding is voluntary, in the sense that it can be waived by the recipient, for all types of retirement plan distributions *except* "eligible rollover distributions" from QRPs that are not in fact rolled over; and participants can often have additional amounts voluntarily withheld (see ¶ 2.1.07).

This ¶ 2.1.05 explains the Code's general scheme for withholding from retirement plan distributions, including the different rules for different types of distributions. Exceptions and special rules are discussed at ¶ 2.1.06. ¶ 2.1.07 describes the legal authority for withholding of income tax from retirement plan distributions, including the quasi- authority for mutual voluntary withholding from IRA distributions. Finally, ¶ 2.1.08 explains how withheld income taxes are applied to the recipient's tax liability for the year.

¿ɐ¿ɐ¿ɐ

Here are the Code's opening bids on withholding from retirement distributions, including which ones the recipient can opt out of. (If the recipient wants to have a *greater* amount withheld from a plan or IRA distribution, see ¶ 2.1.07.)

The withholding requirements distinguish between "periodic payments" (§ 3405(e)(2)), "nonperiodic distributions" (§ 3405(e)(2)), and "eligible rollover distributions" (§ 3405(c)(3)).

Periodic payments from all types of retirement plans, including IRAs, are subject to withholding of taxes at the same rate as wages. § 3405(a)(1). The recipient can elect out of having anything withheld from a periodic payment, so the withholding is voluntary as far as the recipient is concerned. § 3405(a)(2). The Code defines "periodic payment" as a distribution that is "an annuity or similar periodic payment." § 3405(e)(2). The IRS says "periodic payments are pension or annuity payments made for more than 1 year that are not eligible rollover distributions," and include "substantially equal payments made at least once a year over the life of the employee and/or beneficiaries or for 10 years or more." IRS Publication 15A, "Employer's Supplemental Tax Guide" (§ 9, Pensions and Annuities). An "annuity" for this purpose is "a series of payments payable over a period greater than one year and taxable under section 72...whether or not the payments are variable in amount." Reg. § 35.3405-1T, A-9.

Nonperiodic distributions from all types of retirement plans, including IRAs, are subject to withholding at a flat rate of 10%, unless they are "eligible rollover distributions" (see next paragraph). § 3405(b)(1). "Distributions from an IRA that are payable on demand are treated as non-periodic payments." Instructions for IRS Form W-4P ("Withholding Certificate for Pension or Annuity Payments," 2002 version). The recipient can elect out of having anything withheld from a nonperiodic distribution, so again the withholding is voluntary. § 3405(b)(2).

Eligible rollover distributions from qualified retirement plans (QRP) are subject to withholding at a 20% rate, and the recipient cannot elect out. The only way to avoid the 20% withholding is to have the distribution paid directly to an eligible retirement plan ("direct rollover"). § 3405(c). An "eligible rollover distribution" is a defined term meaning basically any distribution from a qualified plan (§ 402(c)(1)(A)) or (after 2001) 403(b) plan that is eligible to be rolled over. § 3405(c)(3); § 402(f)(2)(A). For list of distributions eligible or not eligible to be rolled over, see ¶ 2.5.02. Thus, an IRA distribution cannot be an "eligible rollover distribution" for withholding tax purposes even if it is eligible to be rolled over.

The distinction between periodic payments and nonperiodic distributions is a little vague, but is not terribly important. Both types are subject to withholding by all types of plans, and with both types the recipient can elect out of having anything withheld. The only difference is the rate of withholding that applies if the recipient does not opt out of withholding.

The significant distinction is between "eligible rollover distributions" and the other types of payments, because withholding from an eligible rollover distribution is mandatory unless the distribution is sent by direct rollover to another retirement plan.

The mandatory withholding on eligible rollover distributions does not pose a problem if someone simply wants to get the money out of the QRP without paying any income tax until the following April 15. All such person has to do is have his distribution transferred directly (a "direct rollover") into an IRA, so the qualified plan doesn't have to withhold anything; and then take the money out of the IRA (electing out of withholding on the IRA distribution).

The person for whom "mandatory withholding" is *truly*

mandatory is the person who wants to take a lump sum distribution and qualify for special averaging treatment (¶ 2.3.06). This person cannot roll over any part of the distribution, and so will be forced to pay 20% income tax on it through withholding. He can get a refund when he files his tax return for the year of the distribution, if his total tax payments (including this withholding) exceed his actual tax liability.

2.1.06 *Withholding: exceptions and special rules*

A retirement plan does not have to withhold taxes from a distribution to the extent it is "reasonable to believe" that the distribution is not includible in the payee's income. For some reason this exception is not applicable to a traditional IRA. § 3405(e)(1)(B)(ii); Temp. Reg. § 35.3405-1T, A-2.

If the entire distribution consists of securities of the employer corporation (as defined in § 402(e)(4)(E)) (and up to $200 cash "in lieu of financial shares," whatever that means), there is no withholding. If the distribution consists of securities of the employer corporation plus cash and other property, the maximum amount that may be withheld is the value of the cash and other property. § 3405(e)(8). In connection with determining the amount required to be withheld from that sort of mixed distribution, "it is reasonable to believe that all net unrealized appreciation [NUA] from employer securities is not includible in gross income." Reg. § 35.3405-1T, A-30; see ¶ 2.4 regarding NUA.

There is no withholding on dividends paid to participants on employer securities held in the plan. § 3405(e)(1)(B)(ii); § 404(k)(2).

2.1.07 *Withholding: legal basis; voluntary withholding*

Chapter 24, Subchapter A, of the Internal Revenue Code, (§ 3401-§ 3406) establishes the withholding of income tax at the source of payment for certain types of income. Though primarily dealing with "Withholding from Wages" (the title of Subchapter A) it also deals with income tax withholding for pensions, annuities and retirement plan distributions. The following three subparagraphs lay out the statutory and regulatory foundation for withholding; the succeeding text discusses how all this applies to retirement plans and IRAs.

A.   <u>Withholding that is imposed on payer and payee by Congress, (or imposed unless waived by payee)</u>: § 3405, "Special Rules for Pensions, Annuities and Certain Other Deferred Income," sets forth rules for withholding from "designated distributions." A designated distribution is "any distribution or payment from or under (i) an employer deferred compensation plan [this includes pension and profit sharing plans; Temp. Reg. § 35.3405-1T(a-3)], (ii) an individual retirement plan (as defined in section 7701(a)(37)) [this includes IRAs under § 408] or (iii) a commercial annuity." There is an exception for certain distributions that are not includible in gross income; see ¶ 2.1.06. For purposes of the withholding rules, "designated distributions" are further divided into "periodic payments," "nonperiodic distributions," and "eligible rollover distributions"; see ¶ 2.1.05.

B.   <u>Withholding that the payee may impose on the payer</u>: § 3402(o) requires payers of certain types of income to withhold income tax if so requested by the payee. Thus, if the payee of this type of income requests the payer to withhold income taxes, the payer cannot refuse (assuming the request meets the applicable procedural requirements); but if the payee does not request withholding, the payer cannot withhold from this type of income. The types of income subject to such payee-requested withholding include "any amount paid to a person as a pension or annuity" (§ 3402(o)(1)(B), (2)(B))—*unless* the payment is subject to § 3405 (Temp. Reg. § 35.3405-1T, A-6).

C.   <u>Mutually voluntary withholding</u>. Finally, for categories of payments authorized by the IRS, there can be income tax withholding if mutually agreed by the payer and payee. § 3402(p)(3)(B). The IRS has used this provision to authorize greater-than-20% withholding on "eligible rollover distributions" (¶ 2.1.05) if mutually agreed upon by the "distributee" and "the plan administrator or payor." Reg. § 31.3405(c)-1, A-3. For mutually voluntary withholding on other types of "designated distributions," see next paragraph.

The (A) and (B) regimes are mutually exclusive. Thus, distributions from employer plans and IRAs (all of which generally fit

within the definition of "designated distribution" under § 3405(e)(1))
are subject to the "A" rules, and not subject to employee-initiated,
mandatory-on-the-payor, "B" withholding under § 3402(o). If the plan
administrator does not want to withhold any income taxes beyond the
amount required by § 3405, the participant or beneficiary cannot force
him to do so. Temp. Reg. § 35.3405-1T, A-6.

However, if the plan administrator or IRA provider is agreeable,
the parties can *apparently* do mutually voluntary withholding under
§ 3402(p) for such payments. I say "apparently" because, technically,
the Code allows mutually voluntary withholding only for types of
payments authorized by *regulations*. § 3402(p)(3)(B). The only
regulation dealing with mutually voluntary withholding on periodic
payments and nonperiodic distributions is Temp. Reg. § 35.3405-1T,
A-7, which was adopted in 1982 (amended in 2001). A temporary
regulation expires three years after its issuance, so this regulation has
expired. § 7805(e)(2). Furthermore, this temporary regulation only
authorized continuation of voluntary withholding agreements entered
into prior to 1982 (when the current regime for withholding from
retirement plan distributions came into effect); it says nothing about
new mutual voluntary withholding agreements.

Nevertheless, IRS Publication 575 ("Pension and Annuity
Income," under "General Information, Withholding Tax and Estimated
Tax") states, regarding nonperiodic distributions, that the recipient can
"ask the payer to withhold an additional amount using From W-4P."
The ability to request extra withholding is presumably also implied for
periodic payments because ("Unless you choose no withholding") such
payments "will be treated like wages for withholding purposes," and
mutually voluntary withholding for wages is authorized by Reg.
§ 31.3402(p)-1. Form W-4P clearly permits the recipient to request
withholding of additional amounts for all three types of payments
covered by § 3405.

2.1.08 *How withheld income taxes are applied*

In this section, the "taxpayer" is the individual plan participant
(or beneficiary) who receives a retirement plan distribution from which
federal income tax was withheld.

Withheld income taxes are applied as a credit against the
taxpayer's income tax liability for the year of the distribution.
§ 31(a)(1). Although § 31 is titled "Tax Withheld on Wages," it applies

to any amount "withheld as tax under chapter 24," which includes withholding from retirement plan distributions (since § 3402 and § 3405 are part of chapter 24).

§ 6654 (part of Subtitle F of the Code) imposes a penalty for underpayment of estimated income taxes, and also establishes the interrelation of withheld income tax to the taxpayer's obligation to make estimated tax payments. For purposes of determining the penalty, the § 31 credit for withheld income taxes "shall be deemed a payment of estimated tax, and an equal part of such amount shall be deemed paid on each due date for such taxable year, unless the taxpayer establishes the dates on which all amounts were actually withheld, in which case the amounts so withheld shall be deemed payments of estimated tax on the dates on which such amounts were actually withheld." § 6654(g)(1). This rule can help a taxpayer who has underpaid his estimated taxes "catch up" (and possibly avoid the penalty for underpayment of estimated taxes) through a late-in-the-year distribution for which he elects 100% income tax withholding.

Example: Lincoln, age 65, requests a nonperiodic distribution of $100,000 from his IRA in December, Year 1, and also (by filing Form W-4P) asks the IRA provider to withhold $100,000 of this distribution for federal income tax. The IRA provider is willing to do this (though the IRA provider could refuse to withhold more than 10%, many IRA providers apparently will withhold whatever is requested). Even though the tax is withheld in December, Year 1, it is treated as if it were four $25,000 payments of estimated tax by Lincoln on April 15, June 15, and September 15, Year 1, and January 15, Year 2, for purposes of determining whether Lincoln owes a penalty for underpayment of estimated taxes.

2.2 Income in Respect of a Decedent (IRD)

This part describes the special rules for taxation of "income in respect of a decedent" (IRD) under § 691. IRD is not defined in the Code, but may be generally defined as income earned by an individual that is not realized until after his death.

Death benefits under qualified plans, 403(b) plans, and IRAs are IRD, and thus will be subject to income tax when distributed to the beneficiary (except to the extent such distribution is excludible from gross income; see ¶ 2.1.03). Thus, retirement benefits are generally subject to *both* estate taxes and income taxes. This creates numerous planning considerations, such as the desirability of deferring the income taxes as long as possible (see Chapter 1) and leaving these benefits to beneficiaries who are in a low income tax bracket (see ¶ 2.2.03) or tax-exempt (see Chapter 7).

2.2.01 *No stepped-up basis for IRD*

An individual who inherits property from someone who dies before 2010 does not simply take over the decedent's income tax basis in the property; rather, the inheritor's future gain or loss will be computed by reference to the value of that property as of the decedent's date of death (or as of the "alternate valuation date," if that date was used to compute the decedent's federal estate tax). § 1014(c). This tax rule is usually referred to as "stepped-up basis," on the assumption that the property appreciated between the time the decedent acquired it and the date of death, although of course it might have declined in value (in which case there is really a "stepped-down basis").

However, "property which constitutes a right to receive an item of income in respect of a decedent" is an exception: IRD does not get a new basis at death. Instead of a stepped-up basis, an individual who inherits IRD takes over the decedent's basis ("carryover basis").

After 2009, § 1014(c) is repealed and "carryover basis" will apply generally to all assets. Therefore, generally, an individual who inherits an asset from someone who dies after 2009 will take the decedent's basis. This will lessen the relative disadvantage of IRD but will not eliminate it, because:

A.   Even after 2009, there will be a limited stepped-up basis: the decedent's executor will have the power to allocate $1 million of "basis step-up" among the decedent's appreciated assets. Even more "step-up" can be allocated among assets left to the surviving spouse. Retirement plans and other IRD will not be eligible for the allocation of basis step-up.

B.   Retirement plan distributions will be taxable as ordinary income, while the built-in gain in other inherited assets may be eligible for capital gain treatment.

C.   Section 901 of EGTRRA reinstates § 1014(c) (as in effect prior to EGTRRA) for deaths after 2010.

2.2.02 *When IRD is taxed*

§ 691 governs the income tax treatment of IRD. Under § 691(a)(1), IRD is includible (when received) in the gross income of the person or entity who acquired, from the decedent, the right to receive such income. This could be the estate (if the right to receive the income passes to the estate as a result of decedent's death); or a person who is entitled to receive the income directly as decedent's beneficiary under a retirement plan or similar arrangement; or a beneficiary who is entitled to receive the IRD asset by virtue of a bequest under the decedent's will.

§ 691(a)(2), in addition, imposes a tax on the transfer of the right-to-receive IRD by the person or entity who received the right-to-receive the IRD from the decedent. However, there is an exception: the tax is *not* imposed on a transfer of the right-to-receive IRD to the person who is *entitled* to the IRD by reason of the decedent's death or as a result of a bequest from the decedent.

So, § 691 makes a distinction between "IRD" and "the right-to-receive IRD." Generally, IRD is taxed to the recipient upon receipt; but if the right-to-receive the IRD is transferred, the transfer will trigger an income tax unless the exception applies. A distribution from a retirement plan or IRA after the owner's death is IRD; the retirement plan or IRA *itself* is a "right-to-receive IRD."

2.2.03 *Drawback of making IRD payable to a trust*

IRD paid to a trust is generally subject to trust income tax rates. A trust generally pays higher tax than an individual taxpayer on the same amount of income. See ¶ 6.1.02. Thus, making retirement benefits payable to a marital, credit shelter or other trust may result in the benefits' being taxed more heavily than if the benefits were paid to individual family members.

Note that IRD distributed from a retirement plan to a trust is generally "principal" for trust accounting purposes. However, for *income tax purposes*, it is "income." See ¶ 6.1.07.

2.2.04 *Tax treatment of IRD paid to an estate*

IRD items will be taxed to the estate if paid to the estate. However, if the estate, before actually receiving the income, distributes the *right to receive* the income, then:

(a)   the distributee will be taxable on the income, if he/she acquired it by specific bequest or as residuary legatee of the estate; Reg. § 1.691(a)-2(b), Examples (1) and (2); § 1.691(a)-4(b). A "specific bequest" is a bequest of a specific item of property.

(b)   If the distribution is treated as a "sale," however, the estate is taxable on the greater of the value of the right transferred, or the consideration—if any—received for the transfer. Reg. § 1.691(a)-4(a). See ¶ 2.2.05.

If the will leaves retirement benefits to a particular beneficiary, but the benefits are paid to the estate before the estate gets a chance to assign the "right-to-receive" the benefits to that beneficiary, distributing the benefits to the beneficiary upon receipt should carry out the taxable income to the beneficiary. See ¶ 6.1.03. Although normally all items of income are pro-rated proportionately among beneficiaries who receive distributions, a different allocation specified in the governing instrument is respected. Reg. § 1.661(b)-1; § 1.663. See ¶ 7.4.05.

The following examples illustrate these rules.

Example 1: Larry names Liz as beneficiary of his IRA. Liz is taxable on IRA distributions she receives after Larry's death.

Example 2: Mike names his estate as beneficiary of his IRA. His will bequeaths "all IRA benefits" to Liz. After Mike's death, the estate assigns the IRA to Liz. Liz pays the tax on the IRA distributions.

If the right-to-receive IRD is distributed as a specific "bequest" from a *trust*, rather than an *estate*, the same principles should apply: the beneficiary who is entitled to the item, and not the trust, bears the income tax. Reg. § 1.691(a)-(4)(b); § 1.663.(c)-2(b)(3).

If the right-to-receive is distributed to the trust beneficiaries under a discretionary power to distribute principal, do the beneficiaries pay the income tax? Presumably the answer is yes, although the regulations provide only that if a trust *terminates* and distributes the right-to-receive to the beneficiaries, the beneficiaries pay the tax. Reg. § 1.691(a)-4(b)(3). Professor Jeffrey Pennell points out that possibly a discretionary distribution of principal would be considered a "partial termination" of the trust and thus fit within the regulation cited.

2.2.05 *Assignment of the right-to-receive IRD*

The major planning pitfall of IRD has to do with "assignments" of the right-to-receive such income, which trigger immediate tax under § 691(a)(2). The problem of assignment of the right-to-receive IRD does not exist when IRD assets are divided up to fulfill fractional bequests; see, *e.g.*, PLR 9537005, Ruling 7. The pitfall comes when the right-to-receive IRD is used to satisfy a pecuniary bequest.

It is axiomatic among estate planners that a distribution of the right-to-receive IRD in fulfillment of a pecuniary bequest triggers immediate realization of income by the estate or other funding entity.[1]

---

[1]See, *e.g.*, Acker, A.S., *Income in Respect of a Decedent*, 862 Tax Mgmt. (BNA), at A-11; Blattmachr, J.G., "Income in Respect of a Decedent," 12 Probate Notes 47 (1986), 50; Choate, N.B., *Life and Death Planning for Retirement Benefits*, 1st ed., (Foundation for Continuing Education, 1993); CCH 1997 *Standard Federal Tax Reporter*, ¶25,306.0112; Ferguson, M.C., *et al.*, *Federal Income Taxation of Estates, Trust and Beneficiaries* (2d ed. 1997) at 3:27; Gamble, E.J., "Planning for Distributions from Retirement Plans," *N.Y.U. Proceedings of the Forty-Fifth Institute on Federal Taxation*, Vol. 1, Ch. 27, § 27.04[5] last paragraph (1987, p. 27-15); Lane, N.H., and Zaritzky, H.M., *Federal Income Taxation of Estates and Trusts*, 2d Ed., (Warren Gorham & Lamont, 1988-1997) ¶ 15.08, pp.15-54,55; Martin, A., Esq., "Recent Developments/Estate Planning/Post Mortem Planning for QRPs and IRAs," in course materials for ALI-ABA seminar *Professional Organizations, Qualified Plans, etc.*, 2/98, at p. 103; Mezzullo, L.A., *Estate and Gift Tax Issues for Employee Benefit Plans*, 378 Tax Mgmt. (BNA) A-31; Mulligan, M.D., "Planning for Income in Respect of a Decedent Can Minimize Effects of Double Taxation," 57 J. Tax'n 22, pp. 106-112 (1982); Thompson, W.B., "How to Structure a Trust as Beneficiary of a Qualified Plan or IRA Death Benefits," *Estate Planning*, Jan./Feb. 1988 at p. 10.

In view of the universality of this belief, it is surprising to learn that this result is not specified in any Code section, Treasury regulation or Revenue Ruling, nor has any reported case ever so held.

However, this widely held belief does not spring out of thin air. It derives partly from the regulations under § 691(a)(2). The IRS, in its regulations, does not come right out and say that transferring the right-to-receive IRD in fulfilment of a pecuniary bequest is treated as a non-exempt transfer of the right-to-receive, but implies it. Reg. § 1.691(a)-4(b)(2) says that, if the right-to-receive IRD is transferred to "a *specific* or *residuary* legatee" (emphasis added), only the legatee includes the IRD in income. The negative implication is that fulfilling a *pecuniary* bequest with the right-to-receive IRD does *not* carry out the income tax burden to the legatee. In other words, the regulation implies that satisfying a pecuniary bequest with the right-to-receive IRD should be treated as a "sale," just as (under Reg. § 1.661(a)-2(f)(1)) satisfying a pecuniary bequest with appreciated property is treated as a "sale."

Furthermore, the IRS has indicated in several private letter rulings that it considers the "sale" principle of §1.661(a)-2(f)(1) applicable to funding a pecuniary bequest with the right-to-receive IRD. PLRs 9123036 (using an installment obligation to fund a pecuniary credit shelter gift would trigger realization of gain); 9315016 and 9507008 (satisfying pecuniary legacies with Series E or H bonds triggers realization by the funding entity of the untaxed interest accruals on the bonds, which were IRD).

IRD, however, is taxed under § 691, not §§ 661-663. It is taxed only when § 691 says it is taxed. § 691's standards for carrying out the income tax burden to the beneficiaries are not the same as the "DNI" rules of §§ 661-663. Thus, it is quite logical, under the Code, that a pecuniary bequest funded with *IRD* could carry the income tax burden to the beneficiary when funding the same bequest with *appreciated property* would not.

Example: Ron dies, leaving his $1 million IRA payable to his trust as beneficiary. The trust contains a pecuniary formula marital bequest, under which the marital trust is entitled to $400,000. The trust holds no other assets except the IRA. Ron's trustee transfers $400,000 of the IRA to the marital trust and keeps the rest for the residuary credit shelter trust. In this example, surely the IRA is transferred to the marital trust "by bequest from the decedent." The funding trust is not "selling" or "exchanging" the IRA—it is fulfilling the pecuniary marital bequest, and a transfer in fulfillment of a bequest is not taxable under § 691(a)(2). The trust has no choice regarding which asset to use to fund the marital trust—the IRA is the only asset available.

Most commentators assume that transferring IRD in fulfillment of a pecuniary bequest is exactly the same as fulfilling such a bequest with appreciated property in kind, but the rationale for taxing the transfer of appreciated property in fulfillment of a pecuniary bequest does not exist in the case of Ron's IRA. When a pecuniary bequest is fulfilled by a transfer of appreciated property in kind, the transaction is treated as a "sale" of that property because the residuary estate has, by this transaction, realized the benefit of the appreciation that has occurred between the date of death and the date of funding the bequest. The residuary estate has an asset which has grown in value, and uses this to satisfy a fixed dollar liability, thereby in effect "cashing in" that appreciation to satisfy its obligation. The recipient of the pecuniary bequest did *not* benefit from the appreciation, because he would have received the same dollar value either way, whether in cash or in property.

IRD, however, is different. The right-to-receive IRD is not "appreciated property." In fact a retirement plan such as an IRA, which is a common form of "right-to-receive IRD," could easily have *depreciated* in value between the date of death and the date of funding particular bequests. The residuary estate has not necessarily realized any "profit" by funding the pecuniary bequest with IRD, or, if it has realized a gain, it is only to the extent there has been appreciation after the date of death, not to the extent of the entire value of the asset.

Although the precise question discussed here has never been decided, the principle that § 691 overrides the §§ 661-662 scheme is established in other contexts. On the question of whether an estate can take a distributions deduction (¶ 6.1.03) for distributing the right-to-receive IRD, the Tax Court (in holding that the estate can not take such a deduction despite the specific language of § 661(a), which appears to allow deduction) has stated that, "We hold as a general principle that section 691 overrides sections 661 and 662" (*Edmund D. Rollert Residuary Trust*, 85-1 USTC ¶ 9139 (C.A. 6); 752 F2d 112) and "...the transfer by an estate of section 691 property is treated as a neutral event, and is not subject to the distribution rules of section 661 and 662" (*Estate of Jack Dean*, 46 TCM 184 (1983)). As one source put it, "the general distribution rules of subchapter J...do not apply to distributions of rights to [IRD]...[the DNI] scheme is antagonistic to the rules of section 691...Section 691...prevails over the rules relating generally to distributions, and a transfer to a beneficiary of property representing [IRD] is treated as a neutral event." James J. Freeland, *et al.,* "Estate and Trust Distribution of Property in Kind After the Tax Reform Act of 1984," 38 Tax L. Rev. 449, 463 (1985).

2.2.06 *Letter rulings allow fulfilling pecuniary bequests with IRD*

Letter rulings indicate that the IRS *may* have recognized that transferring retirement benefits in fulfillment of a pecuniary marital bequest is not a § 691(a)(2) transfer. In PLR 9524020 an estate was allowed to transfer an IRA directly to a surviving spouse in fulfillment of a pecuniary spousal share under state statute.

PLR 9608036 involved the transfer of an IRA by a pourover trust in fulfillment of a pecuniary formula marital gift. The ruling treated the IRA, for purposes of the spousal rollover rules, as acquired by the spouse "from the decedent," not "from the trust." If the IRA were deemed acquired "from the trust" (a "third party") rather than "from the decedent," it would not have been eligible for rollover under § 408, according to the ruling. This logic is similar to that of § 691(a)(2), under which a transfer of the right-to-receive IRD to one who is entitled to it by bequest *from the decedent* is not a taxable event, while a transfer to any other person *is* taxable.

In PLR 9623056 the decedent's IRA was payable to a trust which was also the residuary beneficiary of his will. The trust created a marital trust by means of a pecuniary marital formula, and a residuary credit shelter trust. The IRA was not payable to either of these specific subtrusts. The IRS permitted a tax-free rollover by the spouse of the portion of the IRA allocated to the marital trust.

In PLR 9808043 an IRA was payable to Participant's estate. The will left a "pecuniary formula marital bequest outright to" the spouse, and left "the remainder" to a "credit shelter trust." Because the surviving spouse, as executrix, was entitled to and did use the IRA to fund the pecuniary marital bequest, and the bequest was outright, the IRS ruled that the surviving spouse was entitled to roll over the IRA proceeds distributed to her via the pecuniary bequest.

In none of these four rulings did the IRS say that the transfer of the IRA generated current income to the funding entity. Although the IRS did not mention IRD or § 691(a)(2) in any of these rulings, in view of the emphasis on the fact that pecuniary bequests were involved it is hard to believe the IRS is overlooking the § 691(a)(2) issue time after time.

A possible explanation, which would make these rulings consistent with the otherwise apparently inconsistent letter rulings (holding that Reg. § 661(a)-2(f)(1) applies to funding a pecuniary bequest with the right-to-receive IRD), *may* be found in the statutory conflict between §§ 402 and 408, on the one hand, and § 691(a)(2) on the other. The Code provides that the income represented by qualified plans and IRAs is included in gross income only when it is "actually distributed" (§ 402(a)) or "paid or distributed" (§ 408(d)(1)). These provisions override other normal income tax rules such as the doctrine of constructive receipt (¶ 2.1.02). Perhaps they also override § 691(a)(2).

For more on this issue, see Choate, N., "Mysteries of IRD," *Tax Management Memorandum*, Vol. 38, No. 20, p. 235 (Tax Management Inc., Washington, D.C., 9/29/97). See also discussion at Acker, *supra*, at § VII(A)(1)(g),(h), p. A-27; and PLR 1999-25033 in which the IRS ruled that a non-pro rata division of community property, in which a surviving spouse took the decedent's IRA as part of the surviving spouse's share of the community property, did not constitute a § 691(a)(2) "assignment."

Planning mode: To avoid the whole issue of whether funding a pecuniary bequest with IRD is a taxable transfer, planners are advised to avoid having retirement benefits pass through a pecuniary funding formula. If benefits must pass to a trust, make them payable to a trust that is not going to have to be divided up. If the benefits are going to a trust which will be divided among various shares (*e.g.*, a marital and a family share), either specify clearly (in both the designation of beneficiary form and in the trust instrument) which trust share these retirement benefits go to (so that the benefits pass to the chosen share directly, rather than through the funding formula), or use a fractional formula (fulfillment of which does not trigger immediate realization of IRD) rather than a pecuniary formula (which may).

Cleanup mode: Although it is advisable to steer clear of funding a pecuniary bequest with qualified plan or IRA benefits, inevitably some participants will leave their benefits payable to a trust which contains a pecuniary funding formula. In these circumstances, first look into the possibility of using disclaimers to get the benefits payable to the "right" beneficiary (see Chapter 8). If that course is not available, and the retirement benefit must pass through the pecuniary funding formula, see if the benefits can be passed through the pecuniary formula to the spouse for a spousal rollover (see letter rulings cited above), and the other arguments cited above for why funding the pecuniary gift with this asset does not trigger tax.

2.2.07 *Income tax deduction for estate tax paid on IRD*

The federal estate tax paid on IRD is deductible for federal income tax purposes. § 691(c). To determine the amount of the deduction, first determine the estate tax due on the entire estate. Next, determine the net value of all items of IRD that were includible in the estate. For definition of net value see § 691(c)(2)(B). The estate tax attributable to the IRD is the difference between the actual federal estate tax due on the estate, and the federal estate tax that would have been due had all the IRD had been excluded from the estate.

Example: Harvey dies in 1999, leaving his $2 million taxable estate (including a $1 million pension plan) to his daughter Emma. The federal estate tax on a $2 million taxable estate, after deducting the unified credit and the maximum credit for state death taxes, is $469,900. If the $1 million IRA were excluded from the taxable estate, the taxable estate would be only $1 million, and the federal estate tax would be $101,300. Thus the amount of federal estate tax attributable to the IRA is $469,900 minus $101,300, or $368,600. Emma will be entitled to an income tax deduction of $368,600 which she can claim when she receives the $1 million pension distribution.

Note also the following:

1.   The deductible portion of the estate tax is computed at the marginal rate, not the average rate; this is favorable to the taxpayer. In the Harvey and Emma example above, even though the IRA constituted only 50% of the taxable estate, it accounted for 75% of the estate tax, so the IRD deduction equals 75% of the total estate tax.

2.   Under EGTRRA, federal estate taxes are scheduled to be

reduced (through increasing exemptions and declining top rates) for deaths in years 2002 through 2009; the federal estate tax is repealed for deaths in 2010; and the estate tax is reinstated (under EGTRRA's sunset provision, § 901) for deaths in 2011 and later. EGTRRA did not repeal or amend § 691, so if federal estate taxes are paid (because Participant died in a year in which the estate tax was in effect), they can be deducted when the beneficiary receives a distribution from the plan, even if the distribution occurs when the estate tax no longer exists.

3.   State estate taxes are *not* deductible. Under EGTRRA, the credit allowed against the federal estate tax for *state* death taxes paid by the estate, is phased out (for estates of decedents dying in 2002-2004) and then repealed (for deaths in 2005 or later). § 2011. The immediate effect of this change, for beneficiaries of decedents in "sponge tax" states, is to make a higher proportion of the total estate tax bill deductible for income tax purposes under § 691. "Sponge tax" states are those which impose no death tax other than the amount allowed as a credit against federal estate taxes under § 2011. In these states, the state death tax will automatically disappear as the credit disappears. These states may react by imposing new forms of death taxes, in which case the benefit beneficiaries receive from their increased § 691(c) deduction will presumably be taken away by other means.

4.   The computation of the § 691(c) deduction becomes more complex if a marital or charitable deduction is involved; this topic is beyond the scope of this book. See Westfall and Mair, *Estate Planning Law and Taxation* (3d ed., Warren, Gorham & Lamont, Boston, 1998), ¶ 14.02.

2.2.08 *Planning for client with short life expectancy*

There are times when an estate planner is called upon to advise a client who, due to accident or illness, has a severely shortened life expectancy. One suggestion to consider is cashing out retirement plan benefits that will have to be cashed out anyway shortly after the client's demise (either because of minimum distribution requirements, or to pay estate taxes, or just because the beneficiaries will want the money).

When an IRA or other tax-deferred retirement plan will have to be cashed out shortly after Participant's death, *and* the estate will be subject to estate taxes, there are several reasons why it is better to cash out the account immediately *before* death rather than immediately after:

First, if the plan is cashed out before death, the income taxes on the benefits are thereby removed from the estate for estate tax purposes—in effect, both the federal *and* state income taxes on the benefits become 100% deductible for estate tax purposes. If the plan is cashed out *after* death, the recipient of the benefits gets a federal income tax deduction under § 691(c) for the *federal* estate taxes paid on the benefits (¶ 2.2.07)—but *not* for the *state* estate taxes.

Second, the § 691(c) deduction is an itemized deduction, and as such may not be fully deductible; see ¶ 2.2.11. Finally, the recipient may not be able to take the § 691(c) deduction in determining his *state* income tax.

For all these reasons, paying the income taxes "first" and the estate taxes "second" may produce a lower tax burden overall than doing it the other way round. Another way to get the same advantages is to convert to a Roth IRA if the client is eligible; see ¶ 5.5.06.

On the other hand, if the death benefits are going to be paid to charity (so they will not be subject to income taxes—see Chapter 7), or will be paid to a designated beneficiary over a long life expectancy (so the income taxes can be deferred for a long time—see Chapter 1) this arbitrage advantage disappears. Similarly, if the beneficiary is in a lower income tax bracket than Participant, that may reduce the arbitrage advantage. Finally, if the estate will not be subject to estate tax, there is no known tax advantage to cashing out the plans before death.

2.2.09 *Who gets the § 691(c) deduction*

The § 691(c) deduction goes to the person who receives the IRD, not the person who paid the estate tax. If there are several beneficiaries who receive the IRD, the deduction is apportioned among them in proportion to the amounts of IRD each received.

Example: Jack dies with an estate of $3 million. He leaves his $1 million IRA (which is entirely IRD) to his daughters Jill and Holly. He leaves his $2 million probate estate (which is not IRD) to his son Alex. Alex pays the federal estate tax of $897,500. The § 691(c) deduction goes equally to Jill and Holly because they received the IRD, even though Alex is the one who paid the estate tax.

2.2.10 § 691(c) deduction for installment and annuity payouts

Calculating the § 691(c) deduction is easy when the beneficiary receives a distribution of the entire benefit all at once. What if the retirement benefit is not distributed as a lump sum but rather in installments over the life expectancy of the beneficiary? Clearly the deduction will also be spread out; but how much of the deduction is allocated to each payment? How much of each distribution represents "IRD" that was included in the gross estate, and how much represents income earned by the retirement plan after the date of death?

When IRD is in the form of a joint and survivor *annuity*, the Code requires that the deduction be amortized over the surviving annuitant's life expectancy and apportioned equally to the annuity payments received by the survivor. § 691(d). However, no official source discusses the allocation of the deduction to non-annuity payouts, such as instalment payments. For a catalogue of several possible alternative methods, see Hoyt, C.R., "Inherited IRAs: When Deferring Distributions Doesn't Make Sense," *Trusts & Estates*, June 1998, p. 52. For possible future developments in this area, keep an eye on QDOT regulations and rulings, where deciding which retirement plan distributions constitute IRD and which constitute post-death earnings is critical to application of the deferred estate tax; see Chapter 4.

Meanwhile, the method used by many practitioners could be called the "IRD comes out first" method. All distributions from the retirement plan are assumed to be coming out of the IRD (rather than out of the post-death earnings of the plan) until the § 691(c) deduction has been entirely used up. However, as noted, there is no authority for use of this or any other approach.

Example: In the Jack and Jill example above, the total § 691(c) deduction was $427,600, which is 42.76% of the total $1 million IRA. Suppose the IRA has grown to be worth $1.2 million by the time Jill and Holly, the beneficiaries, take their first withdrawal of $30,000 each. They assume the distributions come entirely from the $1 million original principal of the IRA (from the IRD, in other words) and none of it from the $200,000 post-death earnings, so each daughter takes a deduction equal to 42.76% of her $30,000 distribution, or $12,801. Each daughter keeps doing this until she has received a total of

$500,000 of distributions from the IRA, at which point she has used up all of her $218,800 share of the § 691(c) deduction.

2.2.11 § 691(c) deduction on the income tax return

The § 691(c) deduction is reported as an "other miscellaneous deduction" on the beneficiary's income tax return. As such, it is not subject to the 2% "floor" applicable to "miscellaneous itemized deductions." § 67(b)(7); see line instructions to IRS Form 1040, Schedule A. However, it is an "itemized deduction," and as such it is subject to the reduction of itemized deductions by up to 3% of AGI in excess of $132,950 (as of 2001), if paid to an *individual*. § 68.

The impact of the 3% reduction rule will vary from beneficiary to beneficiary depending on the size of the distribution and the amount of the beneficiary's other income and deductions. In the case of a high-income taxpayer, with few itemized deductions, the benefit of the § 691(c) deduction could be substantially reduced by the § 68 adjustment.

Example: In 2001, Joyce receives a $500,000 distribution from her deceased mother's IRA. She is single. Assume the § 691(c) deduction allocable to this distribution is $200,000, and that Joyce has other AGI of $2 million in excess of the $132,950 § 68 threshold, and no other itemized deductions. If she did not receive the $500,000 IRA distribution, her taxable income would be $2,132,950.

With the distribution, her income is:

Gross:		$2,632,950
Less: itemized deduction	200,000	
Reduced by (3% x $2,500,000)	-75,000	
	125,000	-125,000
Taxable income		$2,507,950

In the above example, the § 691(c) deduction is chopped from $200,000 to $125,000. The fact that the 3% reduction rule does not apply to trusts tends to offset somewhat the higher income tax bracket generally applicable to trusts (¶ 2.2.03).

Under EGTRRA, the reduction applicable under present law to

itemized deductions of high income taxpayers is *itself* reduced in the years 2006-2009, so in those years high-income taxpayers will be entitled to deduct a higher proportion of their itemized deductions. EGTRRA then repeals § 68 effective in 2010 (but EGTRRA's sunset provision reinstates it in 2011 at 2001 levels). A high-income beneficiary who inherits a retirement plan that was subject to a large estate tax may want to consider deferring receipt of the income from the plan until 2010, if that's possible under the plan terms and the minimum distribution rules; deferring receipt until the repeal of § 68 is effective may increase the amount of the § 691(c) deduction such person can take.

2.3 Lump Sum Distributions

See ¶ 2.1.05 regarding income tax withholding on lump sum distributions.

2.3.01 *Introduction to lump sum distributions*

Through the years, the Code has provided a special gentle treatment for "lump sum distributions" (LSD) from qualified plans. A person who wishes to obtain this special treatment is confronted with some of the most convoluted requirements known to post-ERISA man.

Congress has changed the rules on LSD treatment so often that the IRS has been unable to keep pace with regulations. There are only assorted proposed and temporary regulations issued from 1975 through 1979 (under old Code § 402(c)), which became obsolete before they could be finalized. The instructions for IRS Forms 4972 and 1099-R are often the best indication of the IRS's interpretation of the LSD rules.

From 1992 through 1999, the definition of LSD was found in § 402(d); after 1999, it went back to its pre-1992 home, § 402(e).

For years prior to 2000, an LSD from a qualified plan, as defined in § 402(d), could be eligible for various special tax treatments, including "five year forward averaging" ("5YFA") (§ 402(d)(1)); "10-year averaging" (¶ 2.3.06-¶ 2.3.08); "20% capital gain tax" for benefits attributable to pre-1974 participation (¶ 2.3.09); and the postponement of tax on the "net unrealized appreciation" of employer securities distributed as part of the LSD (¶ 2.4). As a result of changes made by the Small Business Jobs Protection Act of 1996, *one* of these special deals, 5YFA, ceased to be available for distributions after 1999. The requirements applicable to 5YFA are not covered in this edition of this book; for details see pages 101-106 of the 1999 edition of this book.

To achieve the favorable tax treatment, the taxpayer must clear various requirement "hurdles," many of which are surrounded by hidden issue "land mines." The requirements that must be met in order for a distribution to qualify as an LSD, under both pre-2000 and post-1999 law, are summarized in ¶ 2.3.02 through ¶ 2.3.05. If a distribution clears the three hurdles described in ¶ 2.3.02 through ¶ 2.3.05 it is an LSD. That doesn't mean much, however, unless it meets further tests necessary to qualify for particular favorable tax treatments:

1.   If the LSD meets numerous *additional* tests, it can qualify for special averaging treatment; see ¶ 2.3.06 through ¶ 2.3.12.

2.   If the LSD includes employer stock, see ¶ 2.4.

This ¶ 2.3 does not exhaust the intricacies of § 402(d). The following aspects of LSDs are not treated here: LSDs under QDROs; interplay with the § 691(c) deduction; an LSD paid to multiple recipients; and distribution of annuity contracts as part of an LSD.

2.3.02 *First hurdle: type of plan*

Only distributions from § 401(a) "qualified plans" (pension, profit sharing or stock bonus) can qualify as LSDs. Both corporate plans and self-employed ("Keogh") plans can give rise to LSDs, but a distribution from an IRA, SEP-IRA or 403(b) plan can never qualify for LSD treatment. § 402(e)(4)(D)(i).

2.3.03 *Second hurdle: "reason" for distribution*

The distribution must be made either:

(i)   On account of the employee's death; or
(ii)   After the employee attains age 59½; or
(iii)   On account of the employee's "separation from service."

§ 402(e)(4)(D)(i)(I-III).

Reason (iii) is not available to the self-employed person; a distribution to a self-employed person is eligible for LSD treatment only under reasons (i) or (ii), or if he is "disabled," which for this purpose means "unable to engage in any substantial gainful activity by reason of any medically determined physical or mental impairment which can be expected to result in death or to be of long continued and indefinite duration." § 402(e)(4)(D)(i)(IV).

These LSD "triggering events" are of significance primarily for determining whether there has been a distribution of 100% of the balance to the credit of the employee (¶ 2.3.04).

(a)   Landmine: separation from service

A treatise could be written on the subject of what constitutes "separation from service." If the employee in question was fired, moved to another state and is now working for a competing company while engaged in bitter litigation with his former company, he has probably "separated from service." On the other hand, if the employer from which he "separated" sold all its assets to a new company, which rehired the employee the next day to do the same job at the same desk, you may need a ruling to determine whether there has been a "separation from service." See, *e.g.*, PLR 1999-27048. Defining "separation from service" is beyond the scope of this book.

The frustrating technicalities of the term "separation from service" caused Congress to change to a different term—"severance from employment"—in defining when an elective deferral account may properly be distributed from a 401(k) plan; see § 401(k)(2)(B)(k)(I), effective for distributions after 2001. Unfortunately, Congress did not similarly amend § 402(e), so "separation from service" is still the term applicable in the definition of lump sum distribution. All the cases and rulings generated in recent years on the meaning of separation of service came from 401(k) plans; post-2001 401(k) rulings etc. will no longer be of use in the analysis of lump sum distribution issues, since the two Code sections now use different terms.

(b)   Landmine: "on account of"

Occasionally taxpayers have had problems asserting that a particular LSD was made "on account of" an LSD triggering event. For example, if an employee receives a distribution upon separation from service, but at the same time the plan is terminating and *everyone* is receiving a full distribution whether or not he separated from service, the IRS may say the distribution is "on account of" the plan termination (which is not an "LSD triggering event") and *not* "on account of" the separation from service. But see PLR 2003-02048, in which a distribution received 10 years after taxpayer's separation from service was ruled to be "on account of" the separation from service.

2.3.04 *Third hurdle: distribution all in one taxable year*

The distribution, to qualify, must be a "distribution within one taxable year of the recipient of the balance to the credit of [the] employee... from the plan." § 402(e)(4)(D)(i). This hurdle is surrounded by land mines. The general guiding principle is that the employee's entire balance in all "aggregated plans," determined as of the most recent triggering event (¶ 2.3.03) must be distributed to him within one calendar year. For exceptions to this rule, see ¶ 2.3.05.

Clearly, if an employee takes out, say, one-third of his plan balance in 1997 and leaves two-thirds in the plan, the distribution of the one-third portion in 1997 does not qualify for LSD treatment because it is not a distribution of the entire balance. Now suppose the employee takes out the remaining two-thirds of his balance in 1998. He has taken out 100% of his (remaining) plan balance in 1998. Is the 1998 distribution an LSD?

It *would* be a distribution of 100% of the balance to his credit in one calendar year *if* the "balance to his credit" simply meant the entire balance as of the date of distribution—but that is not what it means. Rather, the rule means that, in order to qualify for LSD treatment, there can be distributions in only one taxable year following the most recent triggering event (¶ 2.3.03). See Prop. Reg. §1.402(e)-2(d)(1)(ii); Rev. Rul. 69-495, 1969-2 C.B. 100. The "balance to the credit" of the employee is determined as of the first distribution following the most recent triggering event. This is the balance that must be distributed "in one taxable year." IRS Notice 89-25, 1989-1 C.B. 662, A-6.

Example: After Elaine retired from Acme Widget in 1997 at age 64, she withdrew $60,000 from her $800,000 Acme Widget Profit Sharing Plan account in order to fulfill her lifelong dream of traveling around the world in a submarine. Returning to the U.S. in 1998, paler but wiser, she takes a distribution of the rest of her profit sharing account. This final distribution would not qualify for LSD treatment because the entire balance that existed on the date of the most recent triggering event (separation from service) was not distributed all in one calendar year.

In contrast to this, suppose that Elaine, upon returning from her cruise, died on her way to the Acme benefits office. Now there is a new triggering event, the death of the employee. Her beneficiary can elect LSD treatment for her remaining plan balance even though Elaine, had she lived, could not have done so. Another alternative: suppose Elaine had withdrawn the $60,000 for her cruise *before* she retired. Then her later separation from service would have been a new triggering event, and the final distribution would qualify for LSD treatment.

The IRS instructions for Form 4972 (2000) make no reference to this requirement. Prior distributions from the same plan are referred to only in connection with the rule that if any prior distribution from the same plan was rolled over, subsequent distributions cannot receive special averaging treatment (¶ 2.3.07). These instructions give the impression that the IRS regards the triggering events as obsolete. However, unless the IRS has had an unpublicized change of heart, Notice 89-25 is still in effect. The Code's definition of LSD still includes the requirement that the distribution be of the "balance to the credit" of the employee which becomes payable "after the employee attains age 59½," or "on account of" Participant's death, separation from service (non-owner employees) or disability (owner-employees).

Here are other land mines surrounding this hurdle:

(a)   Landmine: Post year-end vesting and other adjustments

If you THINK you have withdrawn 100% of your plan balance, but then after the end of the year you receive a little extra due to a previous bookkeeping error, you have probably lost your LSD eligibility. However, if the post-year-end increase comes about because the employee is rehired, and prior forfeited amounts are reinstated, see ¶ 2.3.05.

Here is an example of how this requirement can unexpectedly pose a problem:

Example: Lewis terminated his Keogh plan and took a lump sum distribution of the entire balance in 1997. He diligently closed every account the plan had and distributed all the assets to himself before the end of the calendar year. Then in January 1998 he received a notice from a federal court: because of certain securities transactions that had occurred in his Keogh plan account in 1993, he (in his capacity as trustee of the plan) was a plaintiff in a class action suit against the Aging Bull Brokerage Firm. Enclosed with the notice is a check for $1.98, representing his share of the winnings in the now-settled class action suit. The check is payable to (and presumably constitutes an undistributed asset of) the Keogh plan. The balance of his plan, in other words, was NOT distributed all in one year.

To avoid this problem, when distributing all assets of an account (or when terminating the plan altogether), have the plan trustee sign a blanket assignment of all remaining assets, claims, etc., known and unknown, to the recipient (Participant or the beneficiary, as the case may be). Thus, the recipient, not the plan trustee, becomes the owner of the stray interest, dividends, and class action claims that seem inevitably to turn up after the plan is liquidated, and the newly-discovered dollars do not upset the LSD status of the terminating distribution.

(b)   Landmine: aggregation of plans

In determining whether the entire balance to the credit of an employee has been distributed, certain plans must be aggregated. Specifically all profit sharing plans of the same employer are considered to be one plan for this purpose; all pension plans of the employer are treated as one plan; and all stock bonus plans are treated as one. § 402(e)(4)(D)(ii).

Unfortunately it is not always easy to determine what type a particular retirement plan is. The employee is entitled to a summary plan description for each plan; that should tell what type it is. If not, you could request the answer from the company benefits office; or request a copy of the most recent IRS annual report (Form 5500 series) filed by the employer. Form 5500 requires the employer to check a box indicating whether the plan is a profit sharing, pension or stock bonus plan, and the employer is required to provide a copy of this form to the employee on request.

Finding out what type of plan a particular retirement plan is does not necessarily end the problems with this requirement. For one thing plans may have to be aggregated, even if they are *not* both of the same type, if they have interrelated benefit formulas. Also, it may be impossible to obtain distribution of 100% of all similar plans. For example, the employer may have two pension plans (a defined benefit and a money purchase), which must be aggregated for purposes of this requirement, but the employer may permit lump sum distributions from only one of them.

If the employer maintains more than one plan, and it is proposed to take an LSD from only one of them, it may require a legal opinion of an ERISA lawyer, or the employer's counsel, to be sure that this requirement is met for the proposed distribution.

(c)   Landmine: employers under common control

When aggregating "plans of a similar type" of the "employer," who is the "employer"? Must we aggregate separate *employers*, too, if they are under common control?

When two employers are under common control (*e.g.*, a proprietorship and a corporation owned by the same person), § 414 says the two entities will be treated as one "employer" for purposes of certain Code sections relating to retirement plans. § 414(b), (c). § 402 is not among the listed sections. This would seem to imply that employers are *not* aggregated for purposes of § 402. However, the author is not aware of any authority one way or the other on this question.

If your client is taking an LSD from an employer's plan, while he still has a balance in a plan of "similar type" maintained by a different employer that is under common control, this question must be further investigated.

(d)   One taxable year of the "recipient"

Here's a stumper: Richard wants to take an LSD of his $300,000 profit sharing plan in 1999. He withdraws $200,000 in May; but due to delays in selling some stock inside the plan, the rest of the distribution is delayed a bit. Richard dies in June and the remaining $100,000 is paid in July to Richard's estate, after the end of Richard's taxable year (which ended unexpectedly at his death). Clearly the estate's $100,000 payment qualifies as an LSD (because Richard's death was a new "triggering event"); but is there any way that the entire $300,000 can be aggregated and treated as an LSD?

2.3.05 *Exceptions to the all-in-one-year rule*

"Accumulated deductible employee contributions" can be ignored in determining whether the employee has received a distribution of his entire plan balance. § 402(e)(4)(D)(i). This type of contribution, which was permitted under § 72(o) only for the years 1982 to 1986, is rarely encountered.

Another exception: "Dividends to ESOP participants pursuant to section 404(k)(2)(B) of the Code are not treated as part of the balance to the credit of an employee for purposes of the lump sum distribution rules...Thus, such distribution does not prevent a subsequent distribution of the balance to the credit of an employee from being a lump sum distribution." PLR 9024083.

If the employee has terminated his service and withdrawn 100% of his plan balance, but then after the end of the year the employee is rehired, and prior forfeited amounts are reinstated, technically the prior LSD is not "disqualified"; however, § 402(d)(6) (before 2000) provided a recapture provision under which the benefits received from the now defunct 5YFA treatment had to be paid back to the IRS in the year the increased vesting occurred. If the post-year-end increased vesting did not occur because of a rehire, but rather due to a plan termination (which sometimes causes 100% vesting of everyone retroactively), the status of the prior special averaging treatment is unknown.

2.3.06 *Special averaging method: Participants born before 1936*

If an LSD (as defined in ¶ 2.3.02-¶ 2.3.05) meets certain additional requirements, the LSD can receive certain tax breaks: it can be excluded altogether from the recipient's adjusted gross income and taxed separately, using "10-year averaging" (¶ 2.3.08), with or without some "20% capital gain" (¶ 2.3.09) thrown in. These two special tax deals are referred to collectively as the "special averaging method." An LSD for which a proper election is made to use these methods is excluded from the recipient's adjusted gross income (AGI). § 402(d)(3); § 62(a)(8). The fact that an LSD for which special averaging is elected is excluded from AGI can be beneficial, but it can also create additional problems.

On the good side, it means the distribution will not be included in AGI for purposes of: the income limit for obtaining a Roth IRA (¶ 5.4.04); the threshold for deducting medical expenses (7.5% of AGI)

(§ 213(a)); the threshold for reduction of itemized deductions by 3% of "excess" AGI (§ 68) ($132,950 in 2001; this deduction-reduction is phased down in 2006-2009 and repealed after 2009 by EGTRRA); the threshold for reducing personal exemptions (§151(d)(3)) ($199,450 for a married couple in 2001; this reduction is also phased down in 2006-2009 and repealed after 2009 by EGTRRA); or determining how much of the recipient's Social Security benefits for that year will be subject to income tax under § 86. On the negative side, the exclusion of the LSD from AGI may reduce the client's ability to make large charitable gifts (which are limited to a certain percentage of AGI) (§ 170(b)).

Mike Jones, CPA *extraordinaire*, who has "dominion over palm and pine" (he practices in California and Minnesota), rattled off the following observations about the special averaging treatment of LSDs, when he reviewed this chapter prior to publication:

1.   Special averaging treatment for an LSD is the only occasion in the Code when a trust or estate gets to use the *individual* income tax rate schedule rather than trust rates.

2.   The exclusion from income means a client can receive (say) a $100,000 LSD, elect special averaging, pay roughly $15,000 of income tax, donate the $100,000 to charity, and take a deduction of $100,000 from his *ordinary* income (which saves roughly $40,000 of income tax).

3.   On the negative side, if the LSD is subject to state income tax, it may generate a large deduction for state income tax, which in turn may make the taxpayer subject to the alternative minimum tax if the LSD is excluded from AGI.

2.3.07 *Requirements for special averaging method*

The special averaging method is available only for individuals born before 1936. TRA '86 § 1122(h), as amended by TAMRA '88, § 1011A(b)(11), (13)-(15). Special averaging may be elected only once with respect to a taxpayer. It must be elected for all lump sum distributions in the same year that qualify for it. Special averaging cannot be used if any portion of the distribution is rolled over. Other requirements are listed in Form 4972, which can be used as a checklist to determine qualification.

Only individuals, estates and trusts can elect (by filing Form

4972) the special averaging method. A distribution to a partnership or corporation will not qualify. § 402(d)(4)(B).

2.3.08 *How to calculate tax using 10-year averaging*

Here is how to determine the tax under the 10-year averaging method:

(i)   Divide the LSD by 10.

(ii)   Determine the tax on 10% of the LSD using 1986 rates applicable to single taxpayers (conveniently reproduced in the instructions to IRS Form 4972).

(iii)   Multiply the amount obtained in step (ii) by 10. The result is the 10-year averaging tax applicable to the distribution.

Although maximum tax rates were higher in 1986 than they are now, the effect of the 10-year averaging calculation is to tax the distribution as if it were 10 small distributions rather than one big distribution. The result can be dramatically lower-than-usual taxes, especially on smaller LSDs. See Table 4 in Appendix A.

Exceptions:

- A "minimum distribution allowance" produces an even lower tax on distributions under $70,000. See Form 4972.
- No tax is paid currently on the value of certain annuity contracts included in the distribution, though the value is still counted as part of the LSD.
- The above method determines the tax on the "ordinary income" portion of the LSD. See ¶ 2.3.09 for possible capital gain treatment of part of the distribution.

2.3.09 *20% capital gain rate for pre-1974 participation*

If the employee was born before 1936, and was a participant in the plan prior to 1974, part of the LSD for which the "special averaging method" (¶ 2.3.07) has been elected is eligible to be treated as a "capital gain" taxed at 20%. This 20% rate applies without regard to the actual tax rate on capital gain in any particular year.

Prop. Reg. § 1.402(e)-2(d) provides that the "capital gain" portion of the distribution is determined by deducting the "ordinary income portion" (OIP) from the "total taxable amount" (TTA). The OIP is determined by multiplying the TTA by the following fraction:

Numerator: Calendar years of active participation after 1973.
Denominator: Total calendar years of active participation.

In the case of pre-1974 years, the employee gets twelve months' credit for each calendar year or partial calendar year of participation. For post-1973 years a different rule applies: He gets one *month's* credit for each calendar month or part of a month in which he is an active participant.

It is possible, with smaller distributions, for the 20% "capital gain method" to produce a higher tax than would apply under 10-year averaging. In this case, Participant can elect to have his capital gain portion treated as ordinary income; or rather, technically, to "treat pre-1974 participation as post-1973 participation." See § 402(e)(4)(L) as it existed prior to repeal by TAMRA '88 § 1011A(b)(8)(G). If this election is made, the 20% treatment is waived and the entire distribution is taxed under 10-year averaging (¶ 2.3.08).

2.3.10 *Capital gain: what is an "active participant?"*

What is an "active participant" for purposes of the fraction described at ¶ 2.3.09? The regulations under § 219(g) (which limits the income tax deduction for IRA contributions by those who are "active participants" in various types of retirement plans) gives a very specific definition. Under Reg. § 1.219-2 a person is an "active participant" in a money purchase pension plan in a particular year *only* if some of the employer contribution was required to be allocated to his account for that year; or in a profit sharing plan *only* if any forfeiture or employer contribution was added to his account in that year. If this § 1.219-2 definition were applied for purposes of determining the capital gain portion of an LSD, the OIP/TTA fraction would become fixed, once and for all, when the plan discontinued contributions on behalf of the employee, since "active participation" (in the § 219 sense) ends then.

But the IRS apparently does not apply the § 219 definition of "active participation" to § 402 for this purpose. It appears that the IRS uses, for purposes of determining the "capital gain" portion of an LSD, a definition which makes no distinction between "participation" and "active participation," thus rendering nugatory the word "active" in the Code's phrase *"active* participation." The IRS definition is in a 1975 proposed regulation, § 1.402(e)-2; and is repeated in the instructions to Form 1099-R, which is the tax form used (by the employer) to report how much of each distribution is ordinary income and how much is capital gain. From the 2000 "Instructions for Form 1099-R, Box 3," p. R-6: "Active participation begins with the first month in which the employee became a participant under the plan and ends with the earliest of –"

(i)   The month the employee receives the LSD.

(ii)   The month the employee dies.

(iii)   In the case of a common law employee, the month of separation from service.

(iv)   In the case of a self-employed person who receives the LSD on account of disability, the month in which he becomes disabled.

The effect of this definition is to gradually and inexorably reduce the capital gain portion of the distribution, even if the plan has been "frozen" since 1974, since the fraction keeps changing until events (i) - (iv) occur.

This definition appears arbitrary and capricious, first, because it ignores the word "active" in the Code, and second, because the IRS used the § 219 definition intact for *another* part of the LSD determinations under § 402 (namely the "five years of participation" requirement that formerly applied when determining eligibility for the now-repealed five-year averaging method) when to do so favored the Treasury.

2.3.11 *Tax on OIP when there is a capital gain portion*

Once you have determined how much of the total taxable amount (TTA) is the "ordinary income portion" (OIP) (to be taxed under 10-year averaging), and how much is capital gain (to be taxed at a flat 20%), how do you calculate the tax on the OIP? There are two possible methods:

(i)   Calculate the 10-year averaging tax on the TTA then multiply the result by the fraction OIP/TTA; or

(ii)   Calculate the 10-year averaging tax on the OIP only.

Method (i) was required by § 402(e)(1)(B) before it was repealed by TRA '86. However, the grandfather rule which continues 20% capital gain treatment for those born before 1936 appears to adopt method (ii): see § 1122(h)(3)(b) of TRA '86 as amended by TAMRA '88 § 1101A(b)(11), (13)-(15). IRS Form 4972 clearly uses method (ii) (see part III of form). Method (ii) produces a lower tax than method (i). Thus, the treatment of "grandfathered" individuals is more favorable than the treatment they would have received prior to the change in the law that they are being grandfathered from.

2.3.12 *Certain rollovers end LSD eligibility*

The 10-year averaging and 20% capital gain tax grandfather rules were not repealed by EGTRRA and thus will continue to be available indefinitely for LSDs of benefits of employees born before 1936; however, EGTRRA did put on one new limitation. EGTRRA substantially liberalized the rollover rules (see ¶ 2.5). Congress intends the liberalized rollover rules to increase the "portability" of pensions, not to increase the amounts eligible for ancient grandfather rules. Accordingly, EGTRRA § 641(f)(3) provides that the benefits of TRA '86 § 1122(h) "shall not apply" to a distribution from an otherwise-eligible retirement plan "if there was a rollover to such plan on behalf of such individual which is permitted solely by reason of any amendment made by this section."

2.4 Net Unrealized Appreciation of Employer Stock

This ¶ 2.4 describes the special favorable tax treatment available for "lump sum distributions" (and certain other distributions) of employer stock from a retirement plan. For charitable giving with "NUA stock" see ¶ 7.6.04. For 10% penalty on distributions of stock prior to the employee's attaining age 59½, see ¶ 9.1.03.

2.4.01 NUA: Tax deferral and long-term capital gain

The Code gives special favorable treatment to distributions of "employer securities" from a qualified plan. Any growth in value of such securities which has occurred between the time the plan originally placed the securities in the employee's account and the time of the distribution is called "net unrealized appreciation" (NUA). Under certain circumstances, NUA is not taxed at the time of the distribution; rather, only the plan's cost basis in the stock is included in the employee's gross income at the time of the distribution. Taxation of the NUA is postponed until the stock is later sold. § 402(e)(4).

When the stock is later sold, the NUA is taxed as long term capital gain, regardless of how long the recipient (or the plan) actually held the stock. See Reg. § 1.402(a)-1(b)(1)(i) (sale of such stock shall be treated as sale of a capital asset "held for more than 6 months"). This regulation was written before the holding period for long-term capital gain treatment was extended, but Notice 98-24, IRB 1998-17, 4/13/98, confirms that the actual holding period need not be calculated to qualify for the long-term capital gain tax rate.

Example: Joe, age 61, retires from Baby Bell Corp. and receives an LSD of his 401(k) plan, consisting entirely of 10,000 shares of Baby Bell stock. The plan's cost basis for that stock is $10 per share; the stock is worth $100 a share at the time of the distribution. Joe will receive a 1099-R from Baby Bell, indicating a gross distribution of $1 million and a taxable amount of $100,000. The NUA is $900,000. If Joe sells the stock immediately for $1 million, he will have long term capital gain of $900,000. If he waits two months and sells the stock for $125 a share, he has a short term capital gain of $250,000 ($25 appreciation between date of distribution and date of sale, times 10,000 shares) in addition to his long term capital gain of $900,000. If he holds the stock for the required length of time after receiving the distribution, all gain on any subsequent sale will be long term capital gain.

The tax deferral/capital gain treatment is not available for all distributions of employer securities. It applies in only two situations:

1.   If the securities are distributed as part of a "lump sum distribution" (see requirements described at ¶ 2.3.02-¶ 2.3.05) *all* the NUA is non-taxable at the time of the distribution.

2.   If the distribution is *not* an LSD, then only the NUA attributable to the *employee's* contributions receives the favorable treatment.

2.4.02 *Determining the amount of NUA*

The employer is supposed to determine how much of a distribution of employer securities constitutes NUA. The employer then reports this figure in Form 1099-R, box 6. For tax planning purposes the employee will probably want to know how much of the distribution is NUA no later than the date he receives the distribution, so it is to be hoped that the employer can provide this information then, rather than making the employee wait until January of the next year, when the 1099-R is prepared. Reg. § 1.402(a)-1(b) and Notice 89-25, 1989-1 C.B. 662, A-1, tell the employer how to calculate the NUA.

2.4.03 *Distributions after the employee's death*

The favorable tax treatment of NUA also applies when employer stock is distributed to the employee's beneficiaries. So, even if the employee dies before taking a distribution of the employer securities, the beneficiary can exclude the NUA from income—*if* the beneficiary takes a lump sum distribution of the employee's balance. (If the beneficiary takes distribution of the benefits in some form other than an LSD, then the beneficiary can exclude only the NUA attributable to stock purchased with the employee's contributions.)

The IRS has held that the NUA, like other post-death retirement plan distributions, constitutes "IRD" (¶ 2.2). Rev. Rul. 69-297, 1969-1 C.B. 131. Accordingly, when Participant's beneficiaries sell the employer stock that is distributed to them from the plan in a qualifying distribution, the NUA portion of the sale proceeds is long term capital gain. They will get a § 691(c) deduction (¶ 2.2.07) for the estate taxes paid on the NUA.

2.4.04 *Basis of stock distributed during life and held until death*

When the employee receives an LSD of employer stock and the NUA is excluded from his income, his basis in the stock going forward is the value that *was* taxed upon distribution, *i.e.*, the plan's original cost basis of the stock.

If the employee still holds the stock at his death, the IRS has ruled that such stock does *not* receive a stepped-up basis (under § 1014(c); see ¶ 2.2.01) to the extent the employee benefitted from exclusion of NUA. According to the IRS, the NUA that the employee received upon distribution of the stock to him, which was not taxed when distributed to him, retains its character as NUA even after the employee's death, and will constitute IRD to the employee's heirs when they eventually sell the stock. Only to the extent, if any, that the stock appreciated in value *after* it was distributed to the employee by the plan does it receive a stepped-up basis. Rev. Rul. 75-125, 1975-1 C.B. 254.

2.4.05 *Election to include NUA in income*

The recipient can elect *out* of the favorable tax treatment, *i.e.*, can elect to have the NUA taxed as income when the distribution is received rather than deferring tax until the stock is sold. This option could be attractive if (i) the distribution qualifies for special averaging (¶ 2.3.06) and (ii) the total distribution is small enough that the tax under the special averaging method is less than the capital gain tax that will otherwise eventually have to be paid. Of course this decision is based on some guesswork, since it involves comparing the special averaging rate with tomorrow's capital gain rate.

2.4.06 *Rollovers and NUA*

For most retiring employees, rolling over (¶ 2.5) any large lump sum distribution received from an employer plan is the best tax-saving and financial planning strategy. The opportunity for continued tax-deferred growth of retirement assets inside an IRA offers the greatest financial value for *most* retirees.

An LSD that includes appreciated employer securities often provides an exception to this rule of thumb. Since the NUA is not taxed currently anyway, rolling it over does not defer tax on the NUA. The NUA, even if not rolled over, will not be taxed until the stock is sold. Furthermore, rolling over NUA will convert this unrealized long term capital gain into ordinary income, since IRA distributions are taxed as ordinary income (¶ 2.1.01). Thus, if the employee is planning to hold onto the employer stock, the rule of thumb would be: do *not* roll over NUA. (Note that NUA could be rolled over even in pre-2002 years, unlike other "tax-free" distributions. Reg. § 1.402(c)-2, A-3(b).)

The requirements that an LSD must meet to qualify for the

favorable NUA treatment are more lenient than the requirements that must be met for an LSD to qualify for special averaging treatment. Although it is a requirement for special averaging (see ¶ 2.3.07) that no portion of the LSD be rolled over, and indeed that no other qualifying distribution received in the same year be rolled over, no such requirement applies to obtaining the exclusion from income of the NUA portion of an LSD.

Accordingly, if the employee receives a distribution that (i) meets the LSD requirements (¶ 2.3.02-¶ 2.3.05) and (ii) includes employer securities, the employee can exclude from his income the NUA inherent in the securities, while rolling over to an IRA the *rest* of the distribution, *i.e.*, the assets other than the employer securities, which otherwise would be included in gross income. PLR 9721036. If he rolls over some but not all of the employer stock, a ruling should be obtained to determine proper allocation of the NUA between the rolled and the non-rolled stock.

Another alternative, if the LSD also qualifies for special averaging treatment (¶ 2.3.06), is not to roll over any part of the distribution, and pay tax on the taxable portion using the special averaging method. See IRS instructions for Form 4972. See ¶ 9.1.03 regarding the 10% "premature distributions" penalty (§ 72(t)) if the employee is under 59½.

2.4.07 *If the employee wants to sell the stock*

If the employee wants to sell the employer stock he is receiving, then more complex calculations are necessary. He can take his distribution of employer stock, not roll it over, and sell it; he will then pay tax at long-term capital gain rates, to the extent the sale proceeds consist of NUA. ¶ 2.4.01.

Or, the employee can roll the stock over to an IRA and sell it inside the IRA and pay *no* current tax. This approach could be attractive if the taxation can be deferred, via the IRA, for a very long period of time. Even if the employee's ordinary income tax bracket at the time of ultimate future distribution will be higher than the capital gain tax he would have to pay today if he sells the stock outside the plan, the advantages of deferral may overcome the bracket differential.

For another approach that may be attractive if the employee wants to sell the stock see ¶ 7.6.04.

2.4.08 *Client with shortened life expectancy*

A client faced with imminent death may want to know what steps can be taken to increase the financial protection of his family if the anticipated event occurs. If such a client is a participant in a plan which holds appreciated employer stock, one point to consider is whether distribution should be taken before death. As with any retirement plan, distribution before death may have certain tax advantages (see ¶ 2.2.08), but distribution of a plan balance that includes appreciated employer securities, with a rollover of as much of the currently taxable portion as possible, may be attractive if it is desired to continue the tax deferral on retirement benefits after the client's death.

Example: Dagwood has six months to live. He is a participant in his company's retirement plan. One-third of his account in the plan consists of employer stock which has substantially appreciated; the other two-thirds consists of mutual funds. He has made no contributions to the plan. His beneficiaries are his children. If they inherit the plan, they are faced with a disagreeable choice: either they take an LSD of the entire benefit (in order to take advantage of the favorable treatment of the NUA portion of the distribution), thus forfeiting all possibility of continued tax deferral on the non-employer stock portion of the benefit; or, they opt for continued tax deferral by taking out all the plan benefits in instalments over their life expectancy (see Chapter 1)—and forfeit the favorable capital gain treatment of the NUA. They are faced with this choice because they do not have the option of rolling over the taxable portion (see ¶ 2.5.05).

If, on the other hand, Dagwood takes an LSD of the entire plan balance while he is still living, *he* can use the partial rollover strategy to get the best of both worlds. He rolls over the portion of the distribution that is not employer stock; and the children, when they inherit this rollover IRA, can benefit from continued tax deferral by gradually withdrawing the IRA over their life expectancy. He does *not* roll over the stock with its built-in NUA; when the children inherit this stock, they can sell it and pay only long term capital gains tax on the NUA portion of the proceeds.

2.5 Rollovers and Plan-to-Plan Transfers

2.5.01 *Definition of rollover and plan-to-plan transfer*

Under § 402, generally, retirement plan distributions are not taxed in the year received if they are "rolled over" to a different retirement plan or IRA. A "rollover" is generally a distribution from one plan or IRA to Participant, followed by Participant's redepositing the distribution in the same or another plan or IRA.

A rollover differs from a "trustee-to-trustee transfer," "custodian-to-custodian transfer" or "plan-to-plan transfer." With these types of transfers (all of which are hereinafter referred to as "plan-to-plan transfers"), the money is never distributed to Participant—it goes straight from one IRA to another (or from one qualified retirement plan (QRP) to another). Many of the technical rules that apply to rollovers (such as the one-per-year limit; ¶ 2.5.07) do not apply to these transfers. Rev. Rul. 78-406, 1978-2 C.B. 157.

What makes things vastly more confusing, however, is that the direct transfer of a participant's benefits from a QRP to an IRA is called a "direct rollover" and it *is* considered a rollover at least in some respects; likewise (since TAPRA '97) the conversion of a traditional IRA to a Roth IRA (¶ 5.4.01), even if it is done by plan-to-plan transfer, must meet some (not all) requirements of a true "rollover."

Until 1992, the requirements for a valid rollover were almost as difficult and perilous as the LSD rules, but UCA (applicable to distributions after 1992) liberalized the rules and made rollovers much easier to accomplish. EGTRRA 2001 further eased the rules.

2.5.02 *Eligible distributions and plans*

Any distribution from a qualified plan, IRA or 403(b) plan can be rolled over, with only the following exceptions:

1.   A minimum required distribution (MRD) under § 401(a)(9) (see Chapter 1) cannot be rolled over. See ¶ 2.5.06.

2.   "Any distribution which is one of a series of substantially equal periodic payments" made annually or more often (a) over the life or life expectancy of Participant, (b) over the joint life or life expectancy of Participant and a designated beneficiary, or (c) over a "specified period

of 10 years or more" may not be rolled over. § 402(c)(4)(A). Reg. § 1.402(c)-2, A-5, explains how to determine whether a distribution is part of such a series of "substantially equal installments."

3.   Certain corrective or "deemed" distributions cannot be rolled over (for example, the taxable cost of insurance in a qualified plan (¶ 8.3.01), or a plan loan that is foreclosed, or the return of an excess 401(k) contribution).

4.   Non-taxable distributions (see ¶ 2.1.03) could not, prior to enactment of EGTRRA 2001, be rolled over. See § 402(c)(2) prior to amendment by EGTRRA, applicable to years before 2002; Reg. § 1.402(c)-2, A-3. For the ability to roll over after-tax amounts post-EGTRRA, see ¶ 5.4.12.

5.   Hardship distributions cannot be rolled over. § 402(c)(4). Prior to 2002, this limitation applied only to distributions from 401(k) plans; now it applies to hardship distributions from any type of plan.

Another EGTRRA change is the broadening of the definition of "eligible retirement plan," i.e., the type of plan that can receive a rollover. Before 2002, a Participant could roll a QRP distribution over into only another QRP or an IRA. After 2001, § 402(c)(8)(B) also allows tax-free rollovers from QRPs to 457 and 403(b) plans.

2.5.03 *60-day deadline for completing a rollover*

A rollover generally must be completed no later than "the 60th day following the day on which the distributee received the property distributed." § 402(c)(3)(A). Prior to EGTRRA 2001, there were almost no exceptions to this 60-day deadline. Now, § 402(c)(3)(A), added by EGTRRA, provides that the IRS "may waive the 60-day requirement under subparagraph (A) where the failure to waive such requirement would be against equity or good conscience, including casualty, disaster, or other events beyond the reasonable control of the individual subject to such requirement."

In Rev. Proc. 2003-16, the IRS issued the following guidance for such hardship waivers:

1.   Automatic waiver for certain financial institution errors. The
      deadline is *automatically* waived in the following
      circumstances: Participant received a distribution after 2001,
      and (within the 60-day limit) transmitted the funds to a financial
      institution and did everything else required (under the financial
      institution's procedures) to deposit the funds in an eligible
      retirement plan, but "solely due to an error on the part of the
      financial institution" the funds were not deposited into the
      eligible retirement plan within 60 days of the original
      distribution—provided the funds are actually deposited in the
      eligible plan within one year of the original distribution. There
      is no need to seek IRS approval in this case.

2.   Case-by-case waivers in other cases. A participant can request
      a hardship waiver of the deadline in all other circumstances
      (including financial institution errors not covered by the
      automatic waiver) by following the usual procedures (including
      the "user fee") for obtaining a private letter ruling. Although the
      legislative history of EGTRRA indicated that Congress wanted
      the IRS to issue "objective standards" for granting these
      waivers, the Rev. Proc. says only that the IRS will consider "all
      relevant facts and circumstances," such as "death, disability,
      hospitalization, incarceration, restrictions imposed by a foreign
      country or postal error;...the use of the amount distributed (for
      example...whether the check was cashed); and...the time
      elapsed since the distribution occurred."

2.5.04 *Rollover completed by Participant's executor*

If Participant receives a distribution, and is planning to roll it
over, but then dies before having completed the rollover, can the
Participant's executor complete the rollover? Apparently yes. Although
prior to 2003, the IRS was mostly hostile towards allowing the executor
to make any kind of IRA contribution on behalf of his decedent (see
items 1-5 at the end of this subsection), Rev. Proc. 2003-16 (discussed
at ¶ 2.5.03) indicates that the IRS will consider requests for waiver of
the 60-day deadline applicable to rollovers if the failure to timely
complete the rollover is "due to death" (among other causes). If the
decedent's rollover can be completed *more than* 60 days after the
distribution date (under grant of an IRS hardship waiver), then it must

be true that the executor can complete the rollover (without an IRS waiver) *within* 60 days of the original distribution.

The fact that such rollovers now appear to be permitted, however, does not solve all the problems. For one thing, if the decedent had not yet taken a distribution at the time of his death, there is nothing in § 408(d)(3) that allows the executor to initiate the rollover by taking the distribution; thus, this provision will not solve the problem of a decedent who dies with money in a plan that offers only lump sum distributions (¶ 1.5.09). For another thing, taking money out of the decedent's probate estate (where the distribution is sitting, because decedent died before rolling it over) and rolling it into an IRA could change the substantive estate plan (if the beneficiary of the IRA is not the same as the beneficiary of the estate); neither the Code nor the Rev. Proc. can tell us who decides who will be named as beneficiary of the rolled-over distribution.

Prior to the amendment of § 408 by EGTRRA, the IRS had issued the following mostly negative pronouncements on the subject of an executor's right to make IRA contributions on behalf of his decedent; query whether Congress's amendment of § 408(d)(3) will cause the Service to rethink some of these positions:

1.   An executor may not make a $2,000 IRA contribution on a decedent's behalf. PLR 8439066.

2.   Where Participant had received a distribution, but then died before rolling it over, his executor could roll over the distribution to an IRA in the decedent's name, provided the rollover was completed within 60 days after the distribution was received by Participant. *Gunther v. U.S.*, 573 F. Supp. 126, 127 (1982) (USDC MI, 51 AFTR 2d 83-1314). See AOD 1981-038 (11/10/83), in which the IRS announced it would not follow *Gunther* to the extent *Gunther* held that an executor can exercise a decedent's right to roll over a plan distribution.

3.   In a now-expired Temporary Regulation (dealing with the 15% excise tax on excess plan accumulations and distributions under since-repealed § 4981A) the IRS specifically recognized post-death rollovers. The Temp. Reg. explained the effect on the calculation of decedent's 15% excise tax in the following situation: "ROLLOVER AFTER DEATH. If any amount is

distributed from a qualified employer plan or individual retirement plan within the 60-day period ending on the decedent's date of death and is rolled over to an IRA after such date but within 60 days of the date distributed...." Temp. Reg. § 54.4981A-1T (d-5)(c).

4.   The IRS does not allow a surviving spouse's executor to exercise Spouse's "personal" right to elect to treat the deceased Participant's IRA as Spouse's own IRA (see ¶ 3.2.05).

5.   The IRS does allow Participant's executor to elect to "recharacterize" a Roth IRA contribution as a traditional IRA contribution or vice versa (see ¶ 5.8.06).

2.5.05 *Rollovers of inherited benefits*

For rollovers by a surviving spouse named as beneficiary of Participant's benefits, see ¶ 3.2. Unfortunately, a non-spouse beneficiary is not allowed to roll over inherited benefits to his own plan; a non-spouse beneficiary is not even allowed to roll over benefits from a decedent's plan into an IRA in the name of the *decedent.* § 402(c)(9), § 408(d)(3)(C).

A surviving spouse who inherits an IRA may elect to treat the decedent's IRA as his or her own; see ¶ 3.2.05. A non-spouse beneficiary cannot elect to treat the decedent's IRA as his or her own, with one "grandfather"-type exception: any beneficiary (even a non-spouse) of an IRA owner who died *before 1984* could elect to treat the decedent's IRA as his or her own IRA. See 1987 version of Prop. Reg. § 1.408-8, A-4; for some reason this grandfather rule is not mentioned in the final regulations.

2.5.06 *No rollover of minimum required distributions*

The rule that a minimum required distribution (MRD) cannot be rolled over (§ 402(c)(4)(B), § 408(d)(3)(E)) can take Participants by surprise.

For example, the first distribution received in any year for which a distribution is required ("Distribution Year") will be considered part of the MRD for that year and thus cannot be rolled over. Reg. § 1.402(c)-2, A-7. Furthermore, Participant's first

Distribution Year is not the year in which the required beginning date (RBD) (¶ 1.3) occurs; it is the year *before* the RBD. Thus the first Distribution Year is the year Participant reaches age 70½ (or retires as the case may be; see ¶ 1.3), even though the first MRD does not have to be taken until April 1 of the *following* year. Any distribution received on or after January 1 of the first Distribution Year will be considered part of the MRD for that year, and thus cannot be rolled over.

Example: Leonard turns 70½ on January 1, Year 1. On that date, he retires from his job at XYZ Corp. and asks the plan administrator of the retirement plan to distribute Leonard's benefits to Leonard's IRA in a "direct rollover." The administrator replies that it will make a direct rollover of everything except the MRD for Year 1. Leonard replies, fine, he will take the Year 1 MRD as a taxable distribution and roll over the rest. Since he has named his 40-year-old wife Louise as his designated beneficiary the MRD should be 1/44th of the account balance, based on their 44-year joint life expectancy (¶ 1.4.02). But the administrator says, "Louise is your wife and designated beneficiary now, but you are entitled to use your and Louise's joint life expectancy to measure required distributions only if she is your sole beneficiary for the entire Distribution Year. Since we don't know for sure that she will be your sole beneficiary for all of Year 1, we will distribute to you the MRD calculated using the Uniform Lifetime Table (¶ 1.4.01)—which is 1/26.5th of the account, not 1/44th."

For similar problems facing would-be Roth IRA converters, see ¶ 5.4.07.

There is one quasi-exception to the no-rollover-of-MRD rule: it is possible for a distribution that is considered a "required distribution" at the plan level to be *not* a required distribution in the hands of the Participant. This can happen in two ways. First, if the Participant would qualify for the later required beginning date (RBD) allowed for non-5% owners by § 401(a)(9)(C) ("April 1 of the calendar year following the later of the calendar year in which the employee attains age 70½, or the calendar year in which the employee retires from employment with the employer maintaining the plan"), but the plan requires all employees to commence distributions by April 1 of the calendar year following the calendar year in which the employee attains age 70½ regardless of employment status, a distribution that is received after the plan's "RBD" but before the RBD as it is defined in

§ 401(a)(9)(C), can be rolled over by the employee. IRS Notice 97-75, 1997-51 I.R.B. 18, A-10(c). ¶ 1.3.03.

Similarly, under the transition rules for the proposed minimum distribution regulations issued in 2001(see Chapter 1), the IRS recognized that plans might continue to follow the 1987 proposed minimum distribution regulations in computing "required" distributions to retired employees, even though the 2001 proposed regulations could be used to compute required distributions in 2001. An employee who received a "required" distribution, in 2001, from a qualified plan that was still following the older version of the proposed regulations could roll over the part of such distribution (if any) that would not have been required had the plan been using the 2001 proposed regulations. See IRS Announcement 2001-23, 2001-10 I.R.B. 791 (amending IRS Publication 575, "Pension and Annuity Income"). Although the IRS did not issue a similar update to Publication 575 to reflect the final regulations in 2002, presumably the same rule applies; see Preamble to final minimum distribution regulations. ¶ 1.10.04.

2.5.07 *Limit of one IRA-to-IRA rollover distribution each 12 months*

Generally, a distribution from an IRA may be rolled over tax-free to the same or another IRA, or to any other eligible retirement plan. § 408(d)(3). However, an IRA distribution may not be rolled over to any IRA "if at any time during the 1-year period ending on the day of [the receipt of the distribution] such individual received any other amount...from an individual retirement account...which was not includible in his gross income because of the application of this paragraph." § 408(d)(3)(B).

Translation: if an IRA owner receives a distribution from any IRA he owns (Distribution #1), and rolls it over tax-free to the same or any other IRA, he cannot roll over, to any IRA, any *other* distribution (Distribution #2) that he receives from either of those IRAs on or before the first anniversary of Distribution #1. Note the following:

A.   How the rule applies to multiple IRAs: Under the statute, it appears that the tax-free rollover of a distribution from *any* IRA into the same or any other IRA prevents the tax-free rollover of any *other* IRA distribution that is received less than 12 months after the first distribution—regardless of which IRA the second distribution came from. However, the IRS applies the rule on an account-by-account basis: "If you have two traditional IRAs, IRA-1 and IRA-2, and you make a tax-free rollover of a distribution from IRA-1 into a new traditional IRA (IRA-3), you can also make a tax-free rollover of a distribution from IRA-2 into IRA-3 (or into any other traditional IRA) within 1 year of the distribution from IRA-1. These can both be tax-free rollovers *because you have not received more than one distribution from either IRA within 1 year.* However, you cannot, within the 1-year period, make a tax-free rollover of any distribution from IRA-3 into another traditional IRA." IRS Publication 590, "Traditional IRAs, Waiting Period Between Rollovers"; emphasis added. Thus, under the IRS interpretation of this rule, if you have a tax-free IRA-to-IRA rollover (first rollover), you cannot roll over any distribution FROM either of the IRAs involved in the first rollover, until 12 months have elapsed since the date of the distribution involved in the first rollover. However, you can roll over a distribution from ANOTHER IRA (an IRA that was not involved in the first rollover) within that 12-month period.

B.   Not a calendar year test: The no-rollover period is twelve months from the date of receipt of the first distribution. Thus it is always necessary to look back into the prior calendar year, as well as to the current calendar year, in determining whether there has been a prior rolled-over distribution that would prevent the rollover of a second distribution.

C.   Distribution dates count, not rollover dates: The rule prevents tax-free rollover of a *distribution* that occurs within 12 months of a prior *distribution* that was rolled over. Thus, if Distribution # 2 is received less than 12 months after Distribution # 1, waiting until 12 months have elapsed since the prior *rollover* does *not* cure the problem. Similarly, there is no prohibition against two tax-free rollovers within 12 months of each other, provided that the distributions being rolled over did not occur within 12 months of each other. **Example:** Barak received Distribution # 1 from IRA-1 on January 2, Year 1, and rolled it into IRA-2 on February 28, Year 1. He received Distribution # 2 from IRA-1 on January 3, Year 2, and rolled it into IRA-2 on February 1, Year 2. Both distributions are tax-free: even though the second rollover occurred less than 12 months after the first, the second *distribution* did not occur within one year of the first *distribution*.

D.   <u>Does not apply to plan-to-plan transfers</u>: The limit of one tax-free rollover per year has no application to a direct transfer of funds or property from one IRA custodian to another IRA custodian (IRA-to-IRA transfer; see ¶ 2.5.01). In most cases, concerns about § 408(d)(3)(B) can be easily avoided by using an IRA-to-IRA transfer rather than a rollover.

E.   <u>Affects only IRA-to-IRA rollovers</u>: § 408(d)(3)(B) limits only rollovers from an IRA into an IRA; it does not prevent a tax-free rollover of Distribution # 2 into some other kind of eligible retirement plan, nor does it prevent multiple tax-free rollovers *into* an IRA from some other type of plan. Thus it would appear easy to avoid § 408(d)(3)(B) by rolling the second IRA distribution first into a QRP and then rolling it out again to another IRA shortly thereafter; but it has always been easy to avoid § 408(d)(3)(B) anyway (see "D," above), so presumably this is not a major IRS concern.

F.   <u>Can taxpayer choose, after the fact, which rollover is tax-free?</u> No. **Example:** In July, Ian withdraws $60,000 from IRA A, intending to roll it over tax-free to IRA B. Then he remembers that in the preceding March he rolled over a $1,000 distribution from IRA A to IRA B. He would rather pay tax on the $1,000 distribution than on the $60,000 distribution. Ian can not now elect to treat the $1,000 of cash he deposited in IRA B in March as not in fact a rollover of the $1,000 distribution he received from IRA A, but rather as part of his $3,000 "regular" IRA contribution for the year. Reg. § 1.402(c)-2, A-13, says that in order for a contribution to qualify as a tax-free rollover contribution the participant must elect, "at the time the contribution is made, to treat the contribution as a rollover contribution...This election is irrevocable." Thus, when Ian made his $1,000 contribution to IRA B in March he was required to irrevocably designate it either as a rollover or a "regular" contribution. If he said it was a rollover contribution when he made it, he cannot retroactively change that election.

G.   Other exceptions to the waiting period: Certain involuntary distributions are not subject to the rule; see IRS Publication 590. A Roth conversion is not treated as a distribution or tax-free rollover for purposes of this rule; see Chapter 5.

2.5.08 *Must roll over the same property that you received*

A rollover cannot be used as a way to "swap" property out of a retirement plan. If property is distributed from a retirement plan, and tax-free rollover treatment of the distribution is sought, the same property that was received from the first plan must be contributed to the recipient plan. See IRS Publication 590. The only exception, according to IRS Publication 590, is that if the Participant sells the property after receiving it from the first plan, the sales proceeds can be rolled over rather than the property itself. But the Participant cannot simply substitute some other asset of equivalent value; if he still owns the property that was distributed to him from the first plan, that is what he must re-contribute to the same or another plan to have a tax-free rollover. For an excellent discussion of this topic and recent cases dealing with related issues, see the article "Directing a 'Self-Directed' IRA," by Burgess J.W. Raby, Esq. And William L. Raby, CPA, Tax Analysts Document # Doc 2002-24485, Tax Analysts Electronic Citation 2002 TNT 211-71 (30 Oct 2002).

2.6 Summary of Planning Principles

1.   Consider the respective income tax brackets of potential beneficiaries of retirement benefits. Other things being equal, it is more tax-effective to leave retirement benefits to lower-bracket beneficiaries, and non-IRD assets to higher bracket beneficiaries.

2.   Do not use retirement benefits to fund a pecuniary bequest under a will or trust. Do not arrange retirement benefits so that they will have to pass through a pecuniary formula in a will or trust.

3.   As between the marital and the credit shelter share, it is generally better to use IRD to fund the marital share, so no part of the "credit shelter" is "wasted" paying income taxes. Income taxes paid out of the marital share will reduce the future taxable estate of the spouse.

4.   When determining what benefits each beneficiary will receive, consider the impact of the § 691(c) deduction for federal estate taxes paid on IRD. This deduction benefits the person who receives the IRD, not the person who pays the estate tax.

5.   If the client's retirement plan holds stock of the employer which sponsors the plan, evaluate the alternatives for treatment of the "NUA" before any distributions are taken from the plan (or before selling that stock inside the plan).

6.   Determine whether a client is eligible for "lump sum distribution" income tax treatment. Do not take steps (such as a rollover) which would eliminate eligibility for beneficial LSD treatment without carefully considering the alternatives.

3

Marital Matters

Rules and estate planning concerns for the married Participant and surviving Spouse

This Chapter deals with various rules that apply (and planning options available) to married Participants.

3.1 Considerations for Married Participants

3.1.01 *Checklist of considerations for married Participant*

Here is a list of factors that need to be considered when planning for disposition of retirement benefits of a married Participant, whether he is thinking of leaving those benefits to his spouse ("Spouse"), to a trust for her benefit, or to someone else entirely.

A. Determine what rights, if any, federal law ("REA") gives Spouse in Participant's benefits. REA may prevent Participant from naming who he wants to name, or from taking benefits out of his plan, without the consent of Spouse. See ¶ 3.4.

B. State law may give Spouse rights in any of Participant's plans REA does not apply to. Community property and other state law spousal property rights are beyond the scope of this book.

C. Federal tax law gives Spouse a powerful option to defer income taxes, the "spousal rollover." See ¶ 3.2 for the advantages of and rules applicable to the spousal rollover.

D. The minimum distribution rules (Chapter 1) have a variety of special provisions (intended to be favorable, through they don't always operate favorably) that apply when Spouse is named as Participant's beneficiary. These are discussed at ¶ 1.6.

E.   Whenever benefits are left to a marital trust (or even to Spouse outright; ¶ 3.3.14) special precautions must be taken to make sure the disposition qualifies for the marital deduction, if estate taxes are a concern. See ¶ 3.3.

F.   If Spouse is not a U.S. citizen, and estate taxes are a concern, read Chapter 4.

G.   Leaving benefits to a "QTIP" trust often results in substantially higher income taxes than leaving benefits to Spouse outright. See ¶ 3.3.10.

H.   Preparing the typical "credit shelter/marital share" estate plan poses special challenges when one or both spouses have no assets other than retirement plans to use to fund the "credit shelter" share. This problem is discussed at ¶ 10.5.

I.   For rules regarding Spouses and Roth IRAs, see ¶ 5.8.03.

J.   Review the "simultaneous death" issues at ¶ 3.1.02.

3.1.02 Simultaneous death clauses

If Participant names Spouse as his beneficiary, and they die simultaneously, it will be presumed under the Uniform Simultaneous Death Law that Spouse predeceased Participant. A presumption that Spouse *survived* Participant, if contained in Participant's will or trust, will NOT govern retirement plan benefits payable directly to Spouse. To have an effective presumption that Spouse survives in that case, the presumption must be contained in the designation of beneficiary form itself. Such a presumption may be used, if Spouse's estate is smaller than Participant's, to equalize the estates for estate tax purposes.

Note: Before attempting to create a presumption of spousal survival in a designation of beneficiary form, check the plan to make sure it does not create an irrefutable presumption that Participant survives the beneficiary in case of simultaneous deaths.

What is the effect of such a survivorship presumption under the minimum distribution rules? Participant's "designated beneficiary" (¶ 1.7) is determined at the time of Participant's death. If the designated beneficiary survives the Participant, the beneficiary's subsequent death does not erase his status as "designated beneficiary." This is true even if the beneficiary, having survived the Participant, dies before September 30 of the year after the year of the Participant's death (the "Designation Date"; ¶ 1.8.01), unless the beneficiary disclaims the benefits. Reg. § 1.401(a)(9)-4, A-4(c); ¶ 1.8.08. Therefore, if the presumption of survivorship is recognized for minimum distribution purposes, the Spouse should be treated as the Participant's designated beneficiary as of the date of death and as of the Designation Date.

Is the presumption of survivorship recognized for minimum distribution purposes? The IRS recognizes presumptions of spousal survival to a limited extent for purposes of the estate tax marital deduction. Reg. § 20.2056(c)-2(e). There is no comparable regulation under the minimum distribution rules.

However, a presumption that the Spouse survives, even assuming it is recognized for minimum distribution purposes, will usually produce bad results under the minimum distribution rules. The IRS's position is that the Spouse's executor cannot exercise the Spouse's right to roll over the benefits; see ¶ 3.2.07. Therefore, in *most* cases, the result of a presumption that the Spouse survives in case of simultaneous deaths will be that benefits must be distributed over the remaining single life expectancy of the Spouse (if Participant died after the end of the year in which he reached age 70½; see ¶ 1.6.06), or by the end of the fifth year after the spouses' deaths (if Participant died before the end of the year in which he reached or would have reached age 70½, and the effect of the presumption of survivorship is that the benefits pass to Spouse's estate; see ¶ 1.6.05).

3.2 Spousal Rollover of Inherited Benefits; Election to Treat Inherited IRA as Spouse's IRA

This ¶ 3.2 deals with Spouse's option to roll over, tax-free, to another retirement plan distributions made to her from the retirement plan of her deceased spouse (Participant). ¶ 2.5 explains what a rollover is and the rules governing tax-free rollovers generally; this ¶ 3.2 discusses additional rules and considerations that apply to a rollover by a surviving spouse.

When Spouse inherits an IRA she has the option to elect to treat it as her own. The effect of such an election is the same as that of a tax-free rollover. Throughout this ¶ 3.2, "spousal rollover" means "spousal rollover (or, in the case of an inherited IRA, Spouse's election to treat the inherited IRA as her own)." For particular rules dealing with the IRA election, see ¶ 3.2.05.

3.2.01 *Advantages of spousal rollover*

The surviving spouse's ability to "roll over" inherited benefits to her own retirement plan gives her a powerful option to defer income taxes not available to other beneficiaries. By rolling over benefits to her own retirement plan, or by electing to treat an inherited IRA as "her own" IRA (¶ 3.2.05), Spouse becomes the "Participant" with regard to those benefits under the minimum distribution rules and thus gains the following income tax deferral advantages compared with a beneficiary who must take the benefits solely "as beneficiary" (and even compared with taking the benefits herself as a "spouse-beneficiary," using the special options available only to a spouse-beneficiary; see ¶ 1.6):

1.   Other beneficiaries must commence distributions by the end of the year after Participant's death (¶ 1.5.02, ¶ 1.5.03). A Spouse who is under age 70½ can postpone distributions from the rollover IRA until she reaches her own RBD (¶ 1.3).

2.   The maximum deferral period for anyone (even Spouse) who takes inherited benefits as *beneficiary* is the beneficiary's *single* life expectancy. Spouse can take MRDs from a *rollover* IRA using the favorable "Uniform Lifetime Table" (¶ 1.4.01), which is based on the *joint* life expectancy of Spouse (as Participant) and a hypothetical 10-years-younger beneficiary, and thus provides small required distributions than would use of Spouse's single life expectancy.

3.   Spouse can name her own designated beneficiary for the rollover IRA. After her death, MRDs will be based on the life expectancy of her designated beneficiary. In contrast, when a beneficiary (even Spouse) takes the inherited benefits merely "as beneficiary," distributions after such beneficiary's death will generally continue to be based solely on such beneficiary's life expectancy (see ¶ 1.6.06); there is no ability for payments after a beneficiary's death to be extended over the life expectancy of *another* beneficiary (except in the rare case in

which both spouses die young; ¶ 1.6.05).

This does not mean that naming Spouse as beneficiary is necessarily the way to achieve the longest income tax deferral on benefits. Nevertheless, the spousal rollover is still an extremely valuable deferral tool for three reasons: First, most participants want to name their spouses as beneficiaries, despite the longer income tax deferral that might be available if children or grandchildren were named, so the rollover becomes a way to revive the option of longer deferral if Spouse survives Participant. Second, once Participant has died, the spousal rollover shines as a way to correct problems that exist with Participant's beneficiary designation (see ¶ 3.2.09). Third, if the only form of distribution permitted by Participant's retirement plan is a lump sum distribution (see ¶ 1.5.09), the spousal rollover is the only way to preserve the possibility of a life expectancy payout (because Spouse, as beneficiary of the lump sum distribution, can roll the distribution to a retirement plan that permits the life expectancy payout while other beneficiaries could not).

The spousal rollover is so valuable that it is frequently the object of *post mortem* planning efforts. See ¶ 8.2.03 for the use of disclaimers to redirect to Spouse retirement benefits that were left payable to the "wrong" beneficiary, so the spousal rollover can be used.

3.2.02 *Rollover if Spouse is under age 59½*

A drawback of the spousal rollover is its effect on the 10% penalty applicable to pre-age 59½ distributions (Chapter 9). If Spouse is named as beneficiary, she is entitled to withdraw benefits from the deceased Participant's plan without a penalty even if she is younger than age 59½ because the penalty does not apply to death benefits (¶ 9.4.01). If she rolls over the benefits to her own retirement plan, however, they lose their character as penalty-exempt-death benefits. She will not be able to withdraw them until she herself reaches age 59½, unless she either pays the 10% penalty or qualifies for one of the exceptions (¶ 9.2, ¶ 9.4) from that tax.

So what should a Spouse who inherits benefits while under age 59½ do? One approach is to leave the benefits in the decedent's plan until Spouse reaches age 59½. The advantage of this approach is that Spouse can draw money out of the decedent's plan, as beneficiary, penalty-free, whenever she needs it, and (once she reaches age 59½) roll over whatever is left to her own retirement plan. The *drawback* of this approach is what happens if Spouse dies before she does the rollover, which generally would result in less income tax deferral than if Spouse had rolled over the benefits prior to her death. If Spouse died after she was required to commence taking distributions (see ¶ 1.6.04), the benefits remaining in the decedent's plan at her death will have to be distributed over Spouse's remaining single life expectancy (¶ 1.6.06). If Participant and Spouse both died prior to the end of the year Participant would have reached age 70½, the 5-year rule and its exceptions will apply as if Spouse were the "participant." See ¶ 1.6.05.

Rather than leaving the benefits in the decedent's plan until she is over 59½, Spouse could roll the benefits to her own retirement plan. This option is best if she won't need any money from the account prior to age 59½. Even if she will need money after the rollover, however, she can withdraw from her rollover IRA penalty-free if she qualifies for an exception; for example, she could structure her withdrawals as a "series of substantially equal periodic payments" (¶ 9.2).

Finally, she could roll over some of the benefits and leave some of them (equivalent to what she thinks she might need before age 59½) in the decedent's plan.

An old letter ruling (PLR 9608042) suggested that, by withdrawing *any* benefits penalty-free before she herself attained age 59½, Spouse would be making an irrevocable election not to treat Participant's IRA as her own IRA. The IRS has abandoned this idea. See, e.g., Reg. § 1.408-8, A-5(a), which provides that "The surviving spouse of an individual may elect...to treat the spouse's entire interest as a beneficiary in an individual's IRA (*or the remaining part of such interest if distribution thereof has commenced to the spouse*) as the spouse's own IRA." Emphasis added. By specifying that the spousal election can be made even after Spouse has taken one or more distributions as beneficiary, the IRS confirms that taking a distribution as beneficiary does not constitute an election not to treat the remaining benefits as Spouse's own. See also PLR 2001-10033 (spouse not forced to elect between taking as beneficiary and taking as owner).

3.2.03 *Spousal rollover of QRP distribution*

§ 402(c)(9) allows Participant in a qualified retirement plan (QRP) to "roll over" certain plan distributions to another QRP, or to an individual retirement account (IRA), provided various requirements are met. ¶ 2.5. If death benefits are paid to Participant's surviving spouse, the rollover rules "apply to such distribution in the same manner as if Spouse were" the Participant.

The distribution does not have to be a distribution of the entire account balance. Partial distributions are eligible for rollover, unless they are MRDs or part of a series of substantially equal payments (see ¶ 2.5.02). The tests for determining whether a distribution is an "eligible rollover distribution," and other rollover rules, are the same for the surviving spouse as they would have been for the deceased Participant, except that there are slightly different rules regarding what type of plan Spouse may roll the distribution into (see ¶ 3.2.10).

3.2.04 *Deadline for completing spousal rollover*

There is no deadline, as such, for making a spousal rollover. Of course, once any benefits are actually distributed to Spouse, they must be rolled over within 60 days (see ¶ 2.5.03). But there is no specific time limit based on Participant's death after which it becomes "too late" for Spouse to roll over distributions. The Code provides simply that a distribution of benefits to Spouse can be rolled over by Spouse if the deceased Participant could have rolled it over had it been paid to him. § 402(c)(9).

However, there are other rules which, as a practical matter, do create "deadlines" for completing the spousal rollover, or otherwise function as limitations on Spouse's ability to roll over:

1.   If Spouse dies before completing the rollover, see ¶ 3.2.02 (for discussion of MRD drawbacks) and ¶ 3.2.07 (regarding whether Spouse's executor can complete a rollover).

2.   If Participant was already older than age 69½ when his death occurred, MRDs must start or continue until the rollover occurs; thus delay may waste deferral opportunities or even eliminate the possibility of a rollover. See ¶ 1.6.04, ¶ 2.5.06.

3.2.05 *Rollover (or spousal election) for inherited IRA*

§ 408(d), in a backhanded way, permits a surviving spouse to treat an inherited IRA as if it were Spouse's *own* IRA, and to roll over distributions from decedent's IRA to her own IRA.

The Code provides that distributions from an "inherited IRA" may not be treated as tax-free rollovers; but then goes on to say that an "inherited IRA" means an IRA acquired by reason of the death of another individual, if the person who inherited the account is not the surviving spouse of the decedent. § 408(d)(3)(C). Thus an IRA inherited by Spouse is not subject to the restrictions applicable to an "inherited IRA" (¶ 2.5.05) and by negative implication Spouse may roll over distributions to her from the deceased Participant's IRA as if it were Spouse's own IRA.

Reg. § 1.408-8, A-5(a), provides that "The surviving spouse of an individual may elect...to treat the spouse's entire interest as a beneficiary in an individual's IRA (or the remaining part of such interest if distribution thereof has commenced to the spouse) as the spouse's own IRA." The effect of such an election is that subsequent required distributions are "determined under section 401(a)(9)(A) with the spouse as IRA owner and not section 401(a)(9)(B) with the surviving spouse as the deceased IRA owner's beneficiary."

The spousal election "is permitted to be made at any time after the individual's date of death. In order to make this election, the spouse must be the sole beneficiary of the IRA and have an unlimited right to withdraw amounts from the IRA." Note that the requirement that Spouse be "sole" beneficiary to make this election is satisfied (as to a "separate account" within the retirement plan benefit) if Spouse is sole beneficiary of such separate account, even if she is not sole beneficiary of Participant's entire interest in the retirement plan. See ¶ 1.7.06.

Reg. § 1.408-8, A-5(b) explains how Spouse makes this election. Ideally, with proper advice and planning, Spouse makes the election in an affirmative manner by "redesignating the account as the account in the name of the surviving spouse as IRA owner rather than as beneficiary." However, the election can get made automatically by Spouse's taking actions deemed inconsistent with "beneficiary" status. This can happen in either of two ways. One is Spouse makes a contribution to the account (other than a rollover contribution of other benefits inherited from the same deceased spouse); since contributions to an inherited IRA (other than rollover contributions of other benefits inherited from the same deceased spouse) are not allowed, Spouse is deemed to have elected to treat the account as her own if she contributes to it. Reg. § 1.408-8, A-5(b)(2).

The other way is if Spouse fails to take an MRD that would be required to be made to her as beneficiary. Reg. § 1.408-8, A-5(b)(1).

See, e.g., PLR 2001-21073.

The spousal election is generally retroactive to the beginning of the year it is made. Thus, distributions for the year in which the election is made are determined based on the spouse as "owner" rather than as "beneficiary." The exception to this rule is that the MRD *for the year of the deceased spouse's death* is still based on the distribution rules applicable to the decedent. Reg. § 1.408-8, A-5(a). Presumably, the required distribution for the year in which the election occurs would be based on the account balance as of the preceding December 31 even though the spouse was not the "owner" as of the preceding December 31. Either that or the surviving spouse is entitled to skip a year of MRDs, which presumably is not allowed to happen.

3.2.06 *Rollover (but no election) for 403(b) plans*

The Code does not permit spousal rollovers or elections for 403(b) plans. § 403(b) has no provision comparable to § 408(d)(3)(C) permitting Spouse to treat an inherited 403(b) plan as her own. The regulations confirm that a surviving spouse as beneficiary of a 403(b) plan cannot elect to treat an inherited 403(b) account as her own; that option applies only to inherited IRAs. Reg. § 1.403(b)-3, A-1(c)(2).

§ 403(b)(8) permits rollovers by a 403(b) plan *Participant,* but has no provision for rollovers by Participant's *Spouse.* § 403(b)(8)(B) provides that "rules similar to" § 402(c)(2)-(c)(7) (dealing with rollovers of qualified plan distributions) shall apply to distributions from 403(b) plans, but § 403(b) does not "import" § 402(c)(9), the provision that allows *spousal* rollovers.

Thus there is no statutory authority for spousal rollover of a 403(b) plan distribution. Nevertheless, the IRS thinks Congress *meant* to allow such rollovers, so Reg. § 1.403(b)-2, A-1, provides that various rollover rules in § 402, including § 402(c)(9), apply to distributions from 403(b) plans. See, e.g., PLRs 2001-01018, 9713018.

3.2.07 *Rollover or election by Spouse's executor*

The IRS has not allowed the executor of Spouse's estate to exercise Spouse's "personal" right to treat the deceased Participant's IRA as Spouse's own IRA. PLRs 2001-26036, 9237038. As one lawyer put it, "She can't roll over in her grave" (Colin S. Marshall, 1997).

If Spouse has taken a distribution from the decedent's plan, but died with 60 days without completing the rollover to another plan, her executor may be able to complete the rollover; see discussion at ¶ 2.5.03. As with any post-death rollovers that may be permitted a very thorny question is who will be the beneficiary of the rollover IRA

However, nothing in EGTRRA requires the IRS to review its policy of not permitting the surviving spouse's executor to *initiate* a rollover. Therefore, after 2001 as well as before 2002, if it is desirable for Spouse to roll over amounts left to her by Participant, such rollovers should be completed as soon as possible after Participant's death.

3.2.08 *Required beginning date for rolled over benefits*

Once Spouse has completed a rollover, the minimum distribution rules apply to the rolled over amount as if she were the Participant (which she now is, with respect to the rolled over amounts). See ¶ 1.3.08 for the required beginning date for rolled over amounts.

3.2.09 *Rollover when Spouse inherits through an estate or trust*

The IRS, in letter rulings, has permitted a spousal rollover where Spouse was not named as beneficiary, but the benefits were payable to Participant's estate and Spouse was the sole beneficiary of the estate. See, *e.g.*, PLRs 2003-04038, 2001-29036, 8911006, and 9402023 (Spouse was sole beneficiary and personal representative).

In other rulings, Spouse was not the sole beneficiary, but was the residuary beneficiary and also was the executrix. As executrix, she distributed the right to receive Participant's retirement benefits (which were payable to the estate) to herself in partial fulfillment of the residuary bequest. The IRS allowed her to roll the benefits over. PLRs 2001-06047, 2001-01038, 9351041, 9545010.

In another ruling, Spouse claimed a statutory share of the estate. Under applicable state law, a surviving spouse who elected the statutory share could also specify which assets would be used to fund that share. Spouse exercised this right by directing the trustee of the decedent's QRP (which was payable to the estate) to transfer assets of the plan directly into an IRA in Spouse's own name. This was ruled to be a valid "direct rollover." PLR 9524020.

There have been letter rulings permitting a spousal rollover where benefits were payable to a trust under which Spouse had an unlimited right to withdraw the principal. Spouse exercised the power to withdraw the funds from the IRA into the trust, then out to herself and into her own IRA. PLRs 2003-04037, 2001-30056, 1999-25033, 9302022, 9426049, and 9427035.

PLR 9426049 may be the most extreme of these favorable rulings. Participant's benefits were payable to a trust that was to be divided into two subtrusts at his death. Spouse and a bank were co-trustees, but Spouse had the right to remove the bank, and become sole trustee, one year after Participant's death. After the one-year period, the trustees allocated the benefits to one of the subtrusts, and caused them to be distributed to Spouse under a discretionary power to pay her principal "in her best interest." This was held to be a valid rollover because of Spouse's power to remove the co-trustee and distribute principal to herself, even though for the first year after Participant's death she had no such power (and even though she never did exercise this power).

Based on these rulings, it is clear that Spouse is entitled to roll over not only benefits that are paid to her directly as beneficiary, but also benefits that are paid to her as an estate or trust beneficiary *provided* that she is *entitled* to the benefits. She is entitled to the benefits if either:

1.   She is the sole beneficiary of the estate or trust;

2.   She is not the sole beneficiary of the estate or trust, but under the terms of the governing instrument the benefits must be paid to her—for example because the will or trust requires that the retirement benefits be allocated to spouse, or because there are no assets available to fund her share other than the retirement plan. If under the terms of the will or trust only part of the assets would necessarily have to be allocated to her share, only that part qualifies for the rollover.

3.   If the benefits are allocated to Spouse's share as a result of the exercise of someone's discretion (rather than because the will or trust requires it) the rollover is still allowed if Spouse is the one who has the discretion (as beneficiary or as fiduciary).

These rulings can obviously be useful in cleanup mode. The approach could also be useful for planning purposes. A client who wants to divide benefits between Spouse and a credit shelter trust by a formula could leave the benefits to a trust, have the trustee apply the formula to determine how much Spouse is entitled to, and then have the trustee direct the plan administrator to pay the marital portion of the benefits directly to Spouse. Spouse would be able to roll over the amount allocated to her share if, for example, the trustee had no discretion in applying the formula and was required to fulfill Spouse's formula share to the maximum extent possible with retirement benefits. See Form 3.2, Appendix B.

If payment of the benefits to Spouse depends on the discretion of some third party, such as a trustee who is not Spouse herself, the rollover will not be allowed. The rulings have denied rollovers for an IRA payable, for example, to a QTIP trust (¶ 3.3.04) where Spouse's power to withdraw principal was not immediate and unlimited. PLRs 9322005 (Spouse could receive principal only in discretion of a third party trustee), 9321032, and 9445029.

3.2.10 *Types of plan Spouse can roll benefits into*

Spouse can roll benefits to a pre-existing IRA, or to a new IRA established to receive this rollover.

Spouse can roll over a post-2001 distribution into any type of plan a living Participant is permitted to roll into; see ¶ 2.5.02. § 402(c)(9).

The IRS has permitted Spouse to roll over benefits from Participant's plan or IRA into another IRA *still in the name of the decedent*. PLRs 9418034, 9842058. This approach may be better than a rollover to an IRA in Spouse's own name when Spouse wants to move the benefits to a different IRA provider, but wants the benefits to retain their status as "death benefits" exempt from the penalty on premature distributions (¶ 3.2.02).

3.3 Qualifying for the Marital Deduction

This ¶ 3.3 describes the requirements and effects of qualifying for the federal estate tax marital deduction for retirement benefits left to the surviving spouse (sometimes called "Spouse") of the retirement plan Participant (sometimes called the "decedent," the "client," or the "first spouse to die"), or to a trust for Spouse, if Spouse is a United States citizen. If Spouse is not a U.S. citizen, you must read Chapter 4 in addition to this ¶ 3.3.

In reading this Section, keep in mind the difference between "trust accounting income," "taxable income" and "minimum required distributions" (¶ 6.1.07); and remember that there are different tests for whether a trust qualifies for the marital deduction (¶ 3.3.03 to ¶ 3.3.09), "passes" the minimum distribution trust rules (¶ 6.2), or is entitled to special options normally available only to the spouse under the minimum distribution (¶ 6.3.12) or rollover (¶ 3.2.09) rules.

The next two subsections are designed to provide a quick introduction to the marital deduction, not a complete exposition of its many intricacies. For complete discussion of estate planning techniques involving the marital deduction, and its requirements, see sources in the Bibliography. ¶ 3.3.03 through ¶ 3.3.14 then discuss how to make sure retirement benefits left to Spouse (or a marital trust) qualify for the deduction, and other marital deduction issues.

3.3.01 *What the marital deduction is and why planners care about it*

Federal estate tax law allows a decedent's estate a deduction, in computing the taxable estate, for the value of property left to the decedent's surviving spouse if various requirements are met. § 2056(a). As long as the federal estate tax is in effect (see § 2210(a), and § 901 of EGTRRA, repealing the estate tax for estates of decedents who die in 2010), qualifying for this "marital deduction" will be an important way to reduce estate taxes for a married client.

Example: It is 2002. Sonny has a $10 million profit sharing plan. Sonny has no other assets and no debts. If he dies in 2002 his estate will be subject to estate taxes because it is over the estate tax exemption amount ($1 million for deaths in 2002), unless some deduction or other technique for estate tax reduction can be applied. Sonny wants to leave his profit sharing plan benefits to his wife, Sally. Both are U.S. citizens. If he leaves the benefits to Sally in a way that qualifies for the marital deduction there will be no estate tax on Sonny's estate because the marital deduction ($10 million) reduced the taxable estate to $0.

Using the marital deduction to eliminate the estate tax on the estate of the first of the two spouses to die is a very popular estate planning technique. Even if not seeking to *eliminate* estate taxes on the first death, the first spouse to die normally wants whatever property he leaves to the surviving spouse to qualify for the estate tax marital deduction, to keep taxes as low as possible on the first death. Therefore estate planners must know how to make bequests qualify for the marital deduction.

Of course, the estate tax may not be actually eliminated (or even reduced) by leaving assets to Spouse and taking the marital deduction. Once Spouse receives the property from decedent's estate it is now part of *her* estate. Thus the property will be subject to estate tax on Spouse's subsequent death—unless Spouse makes the property vanish through spending, gifts and/or unsuccessful investing, or unless the estate tax itself vanishes through repeal or through increased exemptions. Barring such changes, however, the idea of the marital deduction is that the property is removed from the estate of the first spouse to die and added to the surviving spouse's estate, so the tax is merely deferred not eliminated. See, e.g., § 2044.

3.3.02 *The marital deduction requirements: quick tour*

§ 2056, which creates the marital deduction, provides a general rule (the deduction is allowed for the value of property "which passes or has passed from the decedent to his surviving spouse"; § 2056(a)), followed by an exception to the general rule (no deduction is allowed if the property that passes to the surviving spouse is a "life estate or other terminable interest"; § 2056(b)(1)), followed by several exceptions to the exception (certain terminable interests do qualify for the marital deduction after all). The key to qualifying for the marital deduction, therefore, is to make sure that any property left to the surviving spouse either (1) is not a "terminable interest," or (2) if it is a terminable interest, it qualifies for one of the exceptions to the "terminable interest rule."

Here is the terminable interest rule: "Where, on the lapse of time, on the occurrence of an event or contingency, or on the failure of an event or contingency to occur, an interest passing to the surviving spouse will terminate or fail, no deduction shall be allowed under this section with respect to such interest--(A) if an interest in such property passes or has passed (for less than an adequate and full consideration in money or money's worth) from the decedent to any person other than such surviving spouse (or the estate of such spouse); and (B) if by reason of such passing such person (or his heirs or assigns) may possess or enjoy any part of such property after such termination or failure of the interest so passing to the surviving spouse...." § 2056(b)(1).

The classic "terminable interest" is a life estate:

Example: Howie leaves BigAcre to his wife Sandra for life, with remainder to Howie's children. Sandra's interest will "terminate or fail" upon her death; she has no power to control what happens to the property after her death, or to say who receives it after she is finished with it. An interest in BigAcre (i.e., the remainder interest) has passed from Howie to someone other than Sandra or her estate (i.e., Howie's children). Howie's children will "enjoy" BigAcre after Sandra's interest ends. Sandra's life estate in BigAcre is a "terminable interest."

One reason Congress is so concerned to make sure that Spouse doesn't get a terminable interest is that Congress wants to be sure the estate tax is merely *deferred* by the marital deduction, not eliminated. In the Howie and Sandra example, on Sandra's death there is nothing left to tax in Sandra's estate because all she owned was a life estate. On the death of a life tenant there is nothing to be taxed in the life tenant's estate. The life tenant has nothing she can transfer to others at her death, so the property is not includible in the gross estate of a life tenant—unless some special statutory provision applies to make it taxable. There are two such special statutory provisions under which property is included in the estate of a life tenant. One (§ 2036) applies to a person who originally owned the entire property, gave it away and *retained* a life estate; the other (§ 2044) is for "QTIP" property; see ¶ 3.3.04.

To test a bequest for qualification for the marital deduction, therefore, you need determine (1) whether any interest in the property is passing from the decedent to someone other than Spouse or her estate (i.e., a third party), (2) whether Spouse's interest in the same property will "terminate or fail" at some point and (3) whether the third party will have the property after termination of Spouse's interest. If the answer to these three questions is "yes," then the property is a terminable interest, and you need to determine (4) whether the property qualifies for any exception to the terminable interest rule.

The rest of this ¶ 3.3 looks at the most common forms of disposition of retirement benefits to Spouse and how these fit into the terminable interest rule and its exceptions. ¶ 3.3.03 through ¶ 3.3.12 look at leaving retirement benefits to a marital deduction trust ("marital trust"). ¶ 3.3.13 discusses the marital deduction rules for "survivor annuities." Finally, ¶ 3.3.14 discusses the marital deduction rules for benefits left outright to Spouse as named beneficiary under the plan.

This discussion is merely an overview of the various methods of qualifying for the marital deduction; the practitioner needs to read the applicable statutory provisions and regulations for full details on the requirements before drafting an estate plan. In expert hands, the interaction of the marital deduction and minimum distribution rules could inspire creative solutions to planning problems; see, e.g., discussion at ¶ 3.3.11. Less experienced practitioners may wish to stay within the safe harbors of tried and true solutions; see, e.g., ¶ 3.3.07.

This book does not cover other forms of marital deduction disposition, such as the charitable remainder trust of which Spouse is the sole non-charitable beneficiary (§ 2056(b)(8)), insurance or annuity contracts with power of appointment (§ 2056(b)(6)), or the "estate trust" (trust of which Spouse is sole life beneficiary, and the remainder beneficiary is Spouse's estate).

3.3.03 *"General power" marital trust*

Under § 2056(b)(5), property qualifies for the marital deduction if Spouse (1) is "entitled for life to all income from" the property, payable at least annually (see ¶ 3.3.06), and (2) has the power, exercisable by Spouse alone and in all events, to appoint the property to herself (or to her estate), and (3) there is no power in any other person to appoint any of the property to someone other than Spouse. This type of interest left to a surviving spouse is not a terminable interest because § 2056(b)(5) says that if these conditions are met no part of the property is considered to pass to someone other than Spouse. A trust that meets the requirements of § 2056(b)(5) is called a "general power marital trust" in this Chapter.

If Participant names a "general power marital trust" as beneficiary of his retirement benefits, does he need to take any *other* steps to make sure the retirement benefits qualify for the marital deduction? Yes. See ¶ 3.3.05. For income tax effects of naming a general power marital trust as beneficiary, see ¶ 3.3.11.

3.3.04 *"QTIP" marital trust*

As explained in ¶ 3.3.03, § 2056(b)(5) defines a "general power marital trust" so that such a trust is not a terminable interest. Under

§ 2056(b)(7), Congress goes further and allows the marital deduction for a type of bequest to Spouse that definitely *is* a terminable interest, namely, "qualified terminable interest property," or "QTIP."

Property qualifies for the estate tax marital deduction as QTIP if (1) Spouse is entitled for life to all of the income from the property (¶ 3.3.06), payable at least annually, and (2) no person has the power to appoint any of the property to someone other than Spouse during her lifetime, and (3) the decedent's executor irrevocably elects, on the decedent's estate tax return, to treat the property as QTIP. § 2056(b)(7). A trust that meets the requirements of § 2056(b)(7) is called a "qualified terminable interest property" marital trust, QTIP marital trust or simply "QTIP trust."

Since a QTIP trust really *is* a terminable interest, Congress needed to take one more step to insure that the estate tax would be merely deferred rather than eliminated when it allowed the marital deduction for QTIP trusts. Accordingly, § 2044 provides that the surviving spouse's estate includes any property for which the marital deduction was elected at the first spouse's death under § 2056(b)(7).

3.3.05 *Extra step required for benefits payable to marital trust*

Every estate planning lawyer should know how to draft a trust that complies with the marital deduction requirements described at ¶ 3.3.03 and ¶ 3.3.04. Many practitioners assume that, once the standard marital trust is drafted, and the trust is named as beneficiary of Participant's retirement benefits, qualification of those benefits for the estate tax marital deduction is assured (assuming Spouse survives Participant and doesn't disclaim her interest in the marital trust).

The IRS has a different view. The IRS's position is that, when a retirement plan benefit is payable to a marital trust, both the retirement plan benefit *and* the trust must meet the marital deduction requirements. In the IRS's view, the retirement plan itself is an item of "terminable interest property" separate from the marital trust. Rev. Rul. 2000-2, 2000-31 I.R.B. 305 (1/4/2000).

Does this mean that all the marital deduction language must be recited in the beneficiary designation form as well as in the trust instrument? No. Although that would be one way to comply with the IRS's directive, Rev. Rul. 2000-2 says that the various "governing instrument" requirements are satisfied with respect to a retirement benefit payable to a marital trust if (1) the marital trust document contains the required language (e.g., giving the spouse the right to all income annually) and (2) the retirement plan document does not contain any provisions which would prevent the trustee of the marital trust from complying with the trust's provisions.

Note, however, that Rev. Rul. 2000-2 requires the executor, on the estate tax return, to elect QTIP treatment for *both* the retirement benefit *and* the marital trust when retirement benefits are payable to a marital trust, confirming the approach seen in PLR 9442032 as well as Rev. Rul. 89-89, 1989-2 C.B. 231.

3.3.06 *Meaning of "entitled for life to all of the income"*

One of the requirements for either type of marital trust (¶ 3.3.03-¶ 3.3.04) is that Spouse must be "entitled for life to all of the income" of the trust. There are several ways to comply with this requirement. This ¶ 3.3.06 discusses the general problems of meeting this requirement in connection with retirement benefits payable to a marital trust. Particular methods of compliance are discussed in ¶ 3.3.07 through ¶ 3.3.09.

Regardless of which method is used to comply with the entitled-to-all-income requirement, there are two perennial issues that make marital trust administration (and drafting) more difficult when the trust is funded with retirement benefits. One is, what is the "income" Spouse is entitled to when the asset in question is a retirement plan benefit? See ¶ 6.1.07 for discussion of that question.

The second problem is the minimum distribution rules (Chapter 1). Regardless of whether the trustee is required to withdraw "income" from the retirement plan (see ¶ 3.3.07-¶ 3.3.09), the trustee must withdraw the minimum required distribution (MRD) annually. Thus, if the trust instrument requires the trustee to withdraw the "income" annually, what it is really requiring is that the trustee withdraw from the retirement plan each year the income or the MRD, whichever is the larger amount. The trustee must calculate both amounts each year in any case. The MRD may be more or less than the income. Spouse is entitled to the "income," but the marital deduction rules do not require that she receive the entire MRD (if that is larger than the income). Even though it is not a marital deduction requirement that the QTIP trustee distribute to Spouse the greater of the MRD or the income, it is sometimes appropriate to draft the trust that way; see ¶ 3.3.12.

This brings us to the crux of why it matters how a marital trust named as beneficiary of retirement benefits complies with the "entitled to all income" requirement. If the "income" of the retirement plan benefits is greater than the MRD, it would be desirable not to have to distribute the excess amount out of the retirement plan if such distribution would cause current taxation of that amount, and taxation *could* have been deferred until later under the minimum distribution rules (Chapter 1). Therefore, if the current distribution of "all income" would result in significant acceleration of income taxation, the planner will look for a way to avoid such current distribution.

The planning process on this issue is quite complex, and it is not possible to review every consideration here. A review of the following subsections will reveal that use of any method of compliance other than "distribute all income" (¶ 3.3.07) involves greater complication of the drafting and planning process. These complications are usually worth undertaking only if the result will be significantly improved income tax deferral. Therefore the planner must consider exactly what the difference will be between the amount of the income and the amount of the MRD; see further discussion at ¶ 3.3.09.

Another factor to consider when deciding how to comply with the entitled-to-all-income requirement is how cooperative Spouse is likely to be. If Spouse is likely to exercise every demand right given to her (see ¶ 3.3.08 and ¶ 3.3.09), then nothing will be achieved by substituting demand rights for mandatory income distributions.

The next three subsections review three approaches to complying with the requirement that spouse be entitled for life to all income of a marital trust. The same rules apply to both QTIP and general power marital trusts for purposes of determining whether the spouse is entitled to all income. Reg. § 20.2056(b)-7(d)(2).

3.3.07 *Distribute all income to Spouse annually*

The easiest way to comply with the all-income requirement is to require the trustee to withdraw from the retirement plan each year, and distribute to Spouse, the "income" of the retirement plan. Reg. § 20.2056(b)-5(f)(8). This method was "blessed" by the IRS in Rev. Rul. 89-89, 1989-2 C.B. 231, and is believed to be the most commonly used by estate planners. See, *e.g.*, PLRs 9321035, 9321059, 9418026, and 9348025. For an example of a form using this method, see Form 7.4, Appendix B. Unless the "income" substantially exceeds the MRD (see ¶ 3.3.09) this method does not have significant tax drawbacks (beyond the usual drawbacks of leaving retirement benefits to a marital trust in the first place; see ¶ 3.3.10).

Even if use of this method does require distribution to Spouse of an amount significantly greater than the MRD, that would not mean loss of deferral if Spouse is entitled to, and does, roll over the excess to her own retirement plan. The IRS has repeatedly ruled that a surviving spouse may roll over retirement plan distributions that are made to her through a trust if she was absolutely entitled to receive that amount. ¶ 3.2.09. This rule would appear to allow spousal rollover of income distributions from a marital trust that is named as beneficiary of a retirement plan (to the extent the distribution exceeds the MRD; MRDs cannot be rolled over; ¶ 2.5.06), provided the trust requires the trustee to distribute those amounts to Spouse. However, the application of the rollover-through-trust rules to income distributions from a marital trust has not been confirmed in any case or ruling.

Prior to 2000, the IRS's position was that the distribution from the plan of all income annually was the *only* method available for a retirement plan benefit payable to a trust to qualify for the marital deduction. Rev. Rul. 89-89. In Rev. Rul. 2000-2 the IRS reversed this position and acknowledged that a marital trust funded with retirement benefits can use other methods permitted in the regulations for meeting the "entitled for life to all income" requirement. Rev. Rul. 2000-2 announced that it "obsoleted" Rev. Rul.89-89, which has led to some confusion among practitioners. The method "blessed" in Rev. Rul. 89-89 for complying with the entitled-to-all-income requirement (namely, requiring annual distribution of all plan income to Spouse) still works; Rev. Rul. 2000-2 obsoleted Rev. Rul. 89-89 only to the extent Rev. Rul. 89-89 said this was the *only* method that worked.

3.3.08 *Treat the retirement plan as "unproductive property"*

It wouldn't make sense for Congress to say Spouse must be "entitled to all income" of the trust, then allow the trust to invest in property that doesn't produce any income. The classic example of "unproductive property" (in the trust accounting sense) is a tree farm. As the trees grow, the property may be increasing in value but there are no sales proceeds, dividends, interest payments or other cash profits coming to the trust until the trees are cut down and sold. Until then, the asset generates no "income" to be distributed to Spouse.

Accordingly, to avoid leaving Spouse with a meaningless right, the law has to prevent the trustee from thwarting Spouse's income rights by investing the trust in non-income producing property against her wishes. A marital trust does not have to forbid the trustee to invest in non-income producing property, but if the trust is *permitted* to invest in unproductive property it must protect Spouse in one of two ways:

A.   One way is for the instrument to give Spouse the right to require the trustee to make any such property productive (she could require the trustee to cut down some trees for cash sale every year) or to convert it to productive property within a reasonable time (she could require the trustee to sell the tree farm and reinvest the proceeds in something that produces current income). Reg. § 20.2056(b)-5(f)(4).

B.   If the trust corpus consists substantially of non-income producing property and Spouse does *not* have the power to compel the trustee to make it income-producing, the trust will *still* qualify for the marital deduction if Spouse can "require that the trustee provide the required beneficial enjoyment, such as by payments to Spouse out of other assets of the trust." Reg. § 20.2056(b)-5(f)(5).

If a retirement plan from which annual MRDs are small or non-existent (see ¶ 3.3.11) could be regarded as "unproductive property," current distribution of income could be avoided and income tax deferral enhanced, perhaps with fewer complications than are involved with giving Spouse an income demand right (¶ 3.3.09). Whether or how this could be done is beyond the scope of this discussion, but anyone trying it would need to deal with the following points.

First, unlike the other two methods of complying with the entitled-to-all-income requirement (¶ 3.3.07, ¶ 3.3.09), there is no Revenue Ruling or other pronouncement from the IRS explaining how this method applies to retirement plans.

Second, since the IRS regards the retirement plan as a separate item of "terminable interest property" (see discussion of Rev. Rul. 2000-2 at ¶ 3.3.05), it is not clear that distributions to Spouse from *other* (non-retirement plan) assets held by the marital trust could be used to replace the missing income payments with regard to the "unproductive" retirement plan as permitted by Reg. § 20.2056(b)-5(f)(5). This issue can be avoided by giving Spouse the right to demand that the property be made income-producing (Reg. § 20.2056(b)-5(f)(4)) rather than giving the trustee the right to substitute other distributions for the missing income payments.

Third, in view of the lack of authority regarding the definition of trust accounting income with respect to retirement benefits (see ¶ 6.1.07) it is not clear that a retirement plan is "unproductive" just because it isn't *distributing* anything. If the trust instrument requires the trustee to distribute "all income" to Spouse, the trustee may not be complying with the trust document if the trustee doesn't distribute anything from the retirement plan, even if the trust allows the trustee to hold unproductive property with Spouse's consent, unless applicable state law or the governing instrument makes clear that a retirement plan has no "income" apart from what is distributed from the plan.

3.3.09 *Give Spouse the right to demand the income*

A surviving Spouse is entitled to all income of a trust if Spouse has "the right exercisable annually (or more frequently) to require distribution to herself of the trust income, and otherwise [*i.e.*, if she does not require such distribution in any year] the trust income [for such year] is to be accumulated...." Reg. § 20.2056(b)-5(f)(8).

In Rev. Rul. 2000-2, citing Reg. § 20.2056(b)-5(f)(8), the IRS ruled that an IRA payable to a marital trust qualified for the marital deduction where the trust gave the surviving spouse "the power, exercisable annually, to compel the trustee to withdraw from the IRA an amount equal to the income earned on the assets held by the IRA during the year and to distribute that amount through the trust to" the surviving spouse, and "[n]othing in the IRA instrument" prohibited the trustee from making such withdrawals.

Use of this method of complying with the entitled-to-all-income requirement involves substantial additional complications not discussed in Rev. Rul. 2000-2. Is Spouse's right to withdraw the income from the retirement plan to be lapsing or non-lapsing? If lapsing, will her failure to withdraw the income constitute a completed gift to the remainder beneficiaries of the trust? Whether her right is lapsing or not, her failure to withdraw current income could: change the income tax treatment of the trust (by causing it to become partially a "grantor trust" as to Spouse; see § 678(a)(2)); result in inclusion of the different portions of the trust in her estate under different Code sections (§ 2036 versus § 2044), which in turn could make different estate tax apportionment rules applicable to the different parts of the trust at her death (compare § 2207B(a)(1) and § 2207A(a)(1)); and (if a "reverse QTIP" election has been made for the trust; see § 2652(a)(3)) result in the trust's having two transferors for generation skipping transfer tax purposes. These questions are not relevant to marital deduction qualification, nor applicable only to retirement benefits, and are beyond the scope of this book, but need to be considered by a practitioner who uses this method of complying with the entitled-to-all-income requirement.

Before undertaking such additional complications, the practitioner should consider whether the effort will result in significant savings. For example, in a classic QTIP trust (income to Spouse, remainder to issue), the maximum period of income tax deferral for retirement benefits left to that trust is the life expectancy of the oldest trust beneficiary (¶ 1.5.08), who is (in most cases) Spouse. If Spouse is 51 or older at the time of Participant's death, the MRD based on her life expectancy will be more than 3% of the benefits: The "divisor" at age 51 under the "Single Life Table" (see Appendix A) is 33.3, which translates to an MRD of 3% of the value of the plan. Each year the divisor declines and the corresponding percentage increases (see ¶ 1.2.01). Unless the "income" rate of the retirement benefit is more than 3%, the MRD for a Spouse over age 51 will be more than the income—meaning the trustee will have to withdraw more than the "income" *regardless* of the fact that the trust allows income to be accumulated. Thus, there is no advantage to allowing the trustee to accumulate income inside the retirement plan because the minimum distribution rules will prevent him from doing so.

3.3.10 *Income tax drawbacks of leaving benefits to QTIP trust*

Even aside from the problems with the "all income" requirement, leaving retirement benefits to a QTIP trust is no tax bargain. Compared with leaving benefits outright to Spouse, the classic QTIP trust (income to Spouse, remainder to other beneficiaries) costs substantial extra income taxes, *even if* the trust qualifies for the marital deduction and *even if* the trust complies with the minimum distribution "trust rules" (¶ 6.2).

For example, if the retirement plan benefits were payable to Spouse personally and Spouse rolled them over to Spouse's own IRA, Spouse could defer distributions altogether until she reached age 70½. When the benefits are paid to a QTIP trust, in contrast, the minimum distribution rules require annual distributions to the trust beginning the year after Participant's death. ¶ 1.5.08.

Also, with a rollover IRA, when Spouse reaches her required beginning date (¶ 1.3), Spouse must start taking MRDs from the rollover IRA. These would be computed using the factors in the "Uniform Lifetime Table" (¶ 1.4.01; see Appendix A), which represent the joint life expectancy of the IRA owner (Spouse in this case) and a hypothetical beneficiary who is 10 years younger. When the benefits are paid to a marital trust, in contrast, minimum distributions will be based (*at best*) on the single life expectancy of Spouse (if she is the oldest trust beneficiary, and the other requirements for "looking through" a trust for MRD purposes are met; ¶ 6.2.04). The use of the single life expectancy payout will produce a much more rapid depletion of the account than would use of the joint life expectancy factors in the Uniform Lifetime Table.

With a rollover IRA, there can be a long period of deferral (over the life expectancy of Spouse's oldest designated beneficiary; ¶ 1.5.08) for any benefits remaining in the IRA at Spouse's death. When the benefits are paid to a marital trust, in contrast, MRDs will continue to be calculated based solely on Spouse's single life expectancy, even after Spouse's death. The opportunity to spread distributions over the long life expectancy of members of a younger generation is forever lost.

To the extent the retirement plan distributions are treated as "principal" for trust accounting purposes (¶ 6.1.07), they can be retained in the trust during Spouse's lifetime without jeopardizing the marital deduction. For income tax purposes, however, these distributions are "income" regardless of their status for trust accounting purposes. Trust income tax rates reach the top federal bracket at a much lower amount of taxable income than individual rates do; see ¶ 6.1.02.

Thus, making benefits payable to a marital trust, as opposed to Spouse individually, often results in subjecting the benefits to income taxes sooner, and at a higher rate, than would be the case if Spouse personally were named as beneficiary. See the *Koslow* case study, Chapter 11, and more discussion at ¶ 10.5.05.

3.3.11 *Income tax treatment of other types of marital trust*

Can the QTIP trust drawbacks described in ¶ 3.3.10 be avoided by naming some other kind of marital trust as beneficiary?

A "general power marital trust" (¶ 3.3.03) has all the same

drawbacks as a QTIP trust if it gives Spouse only the right to income, or if it gives Spouse the right to income plus limited rights to principal that fall short of allowing her unconditionally to withdraw the retirement plan from the trust. Examples of such limited principal rights would be the right to principal in the discretion of the trustee (who is someone other than herself), the right to principal based on an ascertainable standard relating to her health, education, maintenance and support (§ 2041(b)(1)(A)), or a "5-and-5 power" (see § 2514(e)). The fact that Spouse has a general power of appointment at death makes a difference in terms of what particular Code section the trust qualifies for the marital deduction under, but has no impact on the income tax problems discussed at ¶ 3.3.10.

If the trust gives Spouse the unconditional right to withdraw the retirement plan from the trust, and Spouse exercises that right, she can roll over the benefits to her own IRA; see ¶ 3.2.09. If she doesn't exercise the right, so the benefits stay in the trust, see ¶ 6.3.09 for tax treatment of a trust that is a "grantor trust" as to Spouse under § 678(a).

Finally, if the trust is a "conduit trust" as to Spouse (¶ 6.3.08), and Participant died many years before he would have reached age 70½, there are slightly more interesting planning possibilities. Such a trust would be entitled to exercise Spouse's right to defer the commencement of distributions until Participant would have reached age 70½. This right combined with a provision such as that used in Rev. Rul. 2000-2 (discussed at ¶ 3.3.09) permitting accumulation of income in the retirement plan (with Spouse's consent) could substantially improve the income tax deferral compared with a standard QTIP trust. *All* plan distributions could be deferred until the year Participant would have reached age 70½. Since this approach makes a difference only for Participants who die relatively young (which most people don't), and since the conduit trust format requires all plan distributions (not just "income") to be distributed immediately to Spouse (which is not what most clients who leave benefits to a QTIP trust want), it seems unlikely this will be a widely used approach.

3.3.12 *Other considerations in naming a marital trust as beneficiary*

If the benefits are payable to a trust that is to be divided, at Participant's death, between a "marital trust" and a "credit shelter" (or bypass) trust, it is recommended that either the division be by means of a "fractional" (rather than a "pecuniary") formula, or, if a pecuniary formula is used, that the benefits be made payable directly to the marital trust so they don't become subject to the pecuniary formula for reasons explained at ¶ 2.2.05.

In addition to qualifying for the marital deduction, the practitioner will in many cases also want to be sure the trust complies with the minimum distribution "trust rules," so that benefits can be distributed to the trust over the life expectancy of the oldest trust beneficiary (¶ 6.2, ¶ 1.5.08). However, if Participant is past his required beginning date (¶ 1.3), and the oldest beneficiary of the trust (who typically is Spouse) is close in age to (or older than) Participant, compliance with the "trust rules" will make no difference: the payout period will be the same either way (compare ¶ 1.5.05 with ¶ 1.5.08).

If the client is determined not to leave any assets outright to Spouse, but is unhappy about the adverse income tax effects of a QTIP trust described at ¶ 3.3.10, consider making the retirement benefits payable to the credit shelter trust, and using other assets to fund the marital trust. Although this approach is contrary to the usual rule of thumb ("don't waste your credit shelter paying income taxes"; see ¶ 10.5), this move could substantially increase the potential income tax deferral if the only beneficiaries of the credit shelter trust are substantially younger than Spouse, because MRDs will be spread out over a longer life expectancy period (assuming the trust complies with the minimum distribution trust rules; ¶ 6.2).

3.3.13 *Automatic QTIP election for "survivor annuities"*

§ 2056(b)(7)(C) provides that "[i]n the case of an annuity included in the gross estate of the decedent under section 2039...where only the surviving spouse has the right to receive payments before the death of such surviving spouse--(i) the interest of such surviving spouse shall be treated as [QTIP], and (ii) the executor shall be treated as having made" a QTIP election for such property unless the executor elects *not* to have QTIP treatment apply. Retirement plan benefits are considered annuities, includible in Participant's estate under § 2039, whether or not paid in the form of true annuities, and thus are subject to this rule. Reg. § 20.2039-1(b).

Electing out of automatic QTIP treatment for a retirement plan death benefit means that the benefit will not subsequently be included in the surviving spouse's estate under § 2044; however, it does not mean that the asset will not be included in the spouse's estate under some other Code provision such as § 2033.

The automatic QTIP treatment for "annuities" is a nice backup when benefits are left outright to Spouse (see ¶ 3.3.14). It also can be helpful when retirement benefits are paid in the form of a true annuity and payments could continue after the surviving Spouse's death:

Example: Mona receives a monthly pension of $5,000 for her life, with a minimum guaranteed term of 10 years. She has named her husband Jeff as beneficiary to receive the balance of payments due if she dies before the guaranteed term is up. She has named her child Robin as successor beneficiary to Jeff if he also does not survive until the end of the 10-year guarantee period. On her death the value of the annuity is $400,000. Because this is included in Mona's estate under § 2039, and no one but her spouse has the right to receive any payments until his death, the $400,000 is "qualified terminable interest property" under § 2056(b)(7)(C), unless her executor elects *not* to have it so treated.

What if Mona's estate is not large enough to be taxable, and Jeff's estate is large enough to be taxable), and Jeff (having survived Mona) also dies before the end of the 10-year guarantee period? Normally, if a QTIP election applied to the annuity in Mona's estate, the remaining value of the payments would be includible in Jeff's estate under § 2044, resulting in estate taxes—even though the QTIP election did not save any estate taxes at Mona's death because her estate was too small to be taxable. However, Rev. Proc. 2001-38, 2001-24 I.R.B. 1335, makes such "unnecessary" QTIP elections automatically void; thus, if the automatic QTIP election did not reduce Mona's estate tax, it is void and the value of the annuity remaining at Jeff's subsequent death is not includible in his estate under § 2044.

3.3.14 *Marital deduction for benefits left outright to Spouse*

Death benefits payable directly to Spouse outright in a lump sum should qualify for the marital deduction, provided Spouse is a U.S. citizen and Spouse is entitled to withdraw all the benefits. See, *e.g.*, PLR 8843033. Where Spouse is named as sole beneficiary, with the unrestricted right to withdraw all the benefits, no part of Participant's interest in the plan passes to someone other than Spouse or her estate, so Spouse has not received a "terminable interest" (¶ 3.3.02).

There is one possible quibble with this conclusion. Suppose Participant has provided in his beneficiary designation form (or the plan documents provide) that, if Spouse dies before having withdrawn all the benefits, any benefits remaining in the account at Spouse's death pass to a "successor beneficiary" who is someone other than Spouse's estate. See ¶ 1.9.02.

Example: Jerry leaves his IRA outright to his wife Carol. However, Jerry's beneficiary designation form (or the account agreement governing the IRA) names his son Hanson as "successor beneficiary" to take the (remaining) benefits if Carol dies after Jerry but before she has withdrawn all the benefits. Since that successor beneficiary is someone other than Carol's own estate, Jerry asks you whether his IRA will qualify for the marital deduction for his estate, or whether it has been transformed into a nondeductible "terminable interest." He points out that an interest in the IRA (*i.e.*, the amount remaining in the account at Carol's death) will pass to someone other than Carol or her estate (*i.e.*, Hanson) upon the occurrence of an event or contingency (*i.e.*, Carol's failure to withdraw the benefits during her lifetime), which is the definition of a nondeductible terminable interest under § 2056(b)(1).

The author believes that this scenario does *not* create a nondeductible interest. For one thing, it meets the description of a deductible interest in § 2056(b)(5), which provides that an interest is deemed to pass to Spouse and only Spouse (and therefore is not a nondeductible terminable interest) if Spouse is entitled to all the income for life, at annual or more frequent intervals, and has the right (exercisable by her alone and in all events) to appoint the principal to herself with no person having the power to appoint it to someone other than her. Spouse has these rights with respect to a retirement plan benefits left outright to her, assuming there is nothing in the beneficiary designation form or plan documents that limits her right to withdraw the income or principal of the account.

The fact that the interest will pass to a successor beneficiary *if Spouse chooses not to withdraw the benefits* should not be deemed to transform this into a terminable interest. The situation is analogous to property left by wife to husband and child as joint tenants. After wife's death, husband can seek partition and take his share of the inherited joint property whenever he wishes, but *if he chooses not to withdraw his share*, it will automatically pass to child by right of survivorship on husband's death. This gift qualifies for the marital deduction. Reg.

§ 20.2056(b)-5(g)(2).

Furthermore, as explained at ¶ 3.3.13, § 2056(b)(7)(C) treats a surviving spouse's interest in a survivor annuity as "QTIP" property unless the decedent's executor elects otherwise, if Spouse is the sole beneficiary during her lifetime. Therefore, even if it were determined (wrongly, in the author's view) that Jerry's IRA in the example above *was* a terminable interest, the interest would qualify for the automatic QTIP marital deduction under § 2056(b)(7)(C).

To sidestep the issue altogether, one could include additional language such as that in Section 3.07, Forms 2.1, 2.2, Appendix B, when (1) Participant is naming Spouse outright as beneficiary and (2) either the plan document or the beneficiary designation form names a successor beneficiary (other than Spouse's estate) who will be entitled to receive the benefits that Spouse does not withdraw during her lifetime. This language explicitly recites that Spouse has the right to withdraw all income and principal of the benefits, tracking the wording of § 2056(b)(5) and Reg. § 20.2056(b)-5(f)(8).

For why it may be desirable for Participant to name a successor beneficiary see ¶ 1.6.05.

3.4 REA '84 and Spousal Consent

3.4.01 *Introduction to the Retirement Equity Act of 1984*

This ¶ 3.4 describes the federal rights granted to spouses of retirement plan participants by the "Retirement Equity Act of 1984" ("REA" or "REACT"; P.L. 98-397), and discusses the estate planning implications of these rights. The applicable law is in IRC § 401(a)(11) and § 417, and the virtually identical ERISA § 205; and Treas. Regs. § 1.401(a)-20 and § 1.417(e)-1.

The purpose of this ¶ 3.4 is to provide estate planners with an overview of REA's requirements and exemptions, with emphasis on aspects that affect estate planning. This essay by no means exhausts REA's intricacies. Practitioners who have studied the spousal consent requirements are bedeviled by such problems as precisely when (relative to the distribution date) spousal consent must be obtained in order to be valid; whether a new spousal consent is required for every distribution if installments are being paid out prior to the RBD; and whether the consent requirements limit the ability of Participant and Spouse to change the form of benefits after the RBD.

This Chapter should not be relied upon for purposes of design or administration of a retirement plan. For an explanation of REA aimed at the plan designer or administrator, see *The Pension Answer Book* by Stephen J. Krass (Panel Publications). See Bibliography for details on that Book and other recommended resources.

Retirement plans fall into three categories with respect to REA's requirements: plans that are subject to the full panoply of REA requirements (all pension plans, some profit sharing plans, some 403(b) plans; ¶ 3.4.02); plans that are subject to a modified version of the REA requirements (some profit sharing plans and some 403(b) plans; ¶ 3.4.03); and plans that are totally exempt from REA's requirements (IRAs, Roth IRAs and some 403(b) plans; ¶ 3.4.04).

3.4.02 *Plans subject to full-scale REA requirements*

If a plan is fully subject to REA, then, generally (for exceptions see ¶ 3.4.05), ANY benefits distributed by that plan to a married employee MUST be distributed in the form of a "qualified joint and survivor annuity" (QJSA), unless the employee has waived that form of benefit and the employee's spouse *consents* to the waiver. If a married employee covered by such a plan dies before retirement, then the plan MUST pay his surviving spouse a "qualified pre-retirement survivor annuity" (QPSA) unless she has *waived* the right to receive the QPSA. The spousal consent (to employee's waiver of QJSA) or spousal waiver (of right to QPSA) must meet specific requirements to be effective; see ¶ 3.4.07, ¶ 3.4.08.

A QJSA is an annuity (1) for the life of Participant with a survivor annuity for the life of Spouse which is not less than 50 percent of (and is not greater than 100 percent of) the amount of the annuity which is payable during the joint lives of Participant and Spouse, and (2) which is the actuarial equivalent of a single annuity for the life of Participant.

The definition of a QPSA is even more elaborate; basically, it is supposed to be the annuity Spouse would have received under the QJSA had the employee lived to retirement, retired with a QJSA, then died. In the case of a defined contribution plan (such as a money purchase pension plan, target benefit plan or "non-exempt" profit sharing plan), the value of the QPSA is defined as an annuity equal in value to 50% of the employee's account balance. § 417(d)(2).

All *pension plans* are subject to the QJSA/QPSA requirements that are described in this ¶ 3.4.02. Defined benefit plans, money purchase pension plans and target benefit plans are in this category. The Code's description is "all defined benefit plans and all defined contribution plans that are subject to the funding standards of § 412." § 401(a)(11)(B).

Other types of qualified retirement plans (profit sharing, stock bonus, 401(k) and ESOP) may or may not be subject to the rules described in this ¶ 3.4.02, depending on whether they fit into the "exemption" (which is not really an exemption, just a modified version of the requirements) described at ¶ 3.4.03.

3.4.03 REA requirements for "exempt" profit sharing plans

Certain qualified plans are exempt from the QJSA/QPSA requirements of REA described at ¶ 3.4.02. Although this type of plan could be any type of QRP other than a "pension" plan, i.e., it could be a profit sharing or stock bonus plan or ESOP, these plans are called here "exempt profit sharing plans." However, these plans are not truly "exempt" from *REA*, because (as a condition of being exempt from the QJSA/QPSA requirements) they still have to provide a spousal benefit. A qualified retirement plan that is not a pension plan (see ¶ 3.4.02) is not subject to the QJSA/QPSA requirements described at ¶ 3.4.02 if it meets tests A, B and C described below, and, most significantly for estate planning:

"The plan provides that the participant's nonforfeitable accrued benefit is payable *in full*, upon the participant's death, to the participant's surviving spouse (unless the participant elects, with spousal consent that satisfies the requirements of section 417(a)(2), that such benefit be provided instead to a designated beneficiary)." Emphasis added.

In other words, the only way a profit sharing plan can be "exempt" from the QJSA/QPSA requirements is by (among other requirements) providing a REA-type benefit, namely, distribution of 100% of Participant's account to Spouse at Participant's death unless Spouse consents to waive this right.

Despite the fact that an "exempt" profit sharing plan has to comply with REA, an exempt profit sharing plan is still critically different from a pension plan. Under an exempt profit sharing plan, the employee can withdraw ALL his benefits from the plan whenever the plan permits him to do so (typically, upon separation from service, although some profit sharing plans permit in-service distributions) WITHOUT the consent of Spouse. He can then roll the distributed benefits over to an IRA (¶ 2.5) and continue to enjoy tax deferral without any further obligations to Spouse under federal law (¶ 3.4.04).

The trade-off is that, if the employee dies BEFORE having withdrawn the benefits from the exempt profit sharing plan, 100% of his benefits (including proceeds of any life insurance policy held in the plan) must be paid to the surviving spouse, unless Spouse has consented to waive this right. Reg. § 1.401(a)-20, A-12(b).

In addition to providing that 100% of Participant's benefits are paid to Spouse on Participant's death, a profit sharing plan must meet the following three tests in order to be exempt from QJSA/QPSA benefits for any particular Participant:

A. <u>The Participant does not elect to have his benefits under the plan paid in the form of a life annuity</u>. As a practical matter, this means that the plan cannot *offer* retirement annuities as a form of benefit if it wants to avoid the QJSA/QPSA requirements, because if the plan offers annuities some Participants will elect them, and then the plan will be in the QJSA/QPSA business. See Reg. § 1.401(a)-20, A-4. Many profit sharing plans choose not to offer any annuity form of retirement benefit.

B. <u>The plan does not contain money transferred to it from a pension plan</u>. This refers to direct transfers, for example, if an employer terminates its pension plan and transfers its funds into a profit sharing plan. Amounts rolled over into the profit sharing plan by employees are not considered transfers for this purpose, even if the amount rolled over originally came from a pension plan. Even if a profit sharing plan does contain money that was transferred from a pension plan, there is a way of keeping the pension money (subject to REA) separate from the "pure" profit sharing plan money and avoiding the QPSA/QJSA requirements as to the latter. Reg. § 1.401(a)-20, A-5.

C. <u>No interrelated benefit formula</u>. The employees' benefits under the profit sharing plan are not taken into account as part of an interrelated benefit formula of a pension plan; Reg. § 1.401(a)-20, A-5(a)(3) (next to last sentence).

3.4.04 *IRAs, Roth IRAs and 403(b) plans*

IRAs and Roth IRAs are not subject to REA; neither ERISA § 205 nor IRC § 401(a)(11) applies to IRAs or Roth IRAs.

Finally, we come to the special case of 403(b) plans. Although 403(b) plans are subject to some of the same § 401(a) requirements as qualified plans (see § 403(b)(10), (12)), § 401(a)(11) is not one of the "401(a)" provisions "imported" into § 403(b), which would make it at first appear that 403(b) plans are not subject to REA. However, even though the Internal Revenue Code REA provisions don't apply, *some* 403(b) plans are subject to ERISA—which has its own set of QJSA/QPSA requirements. Therefore, "to the extent that section 205 [of ERISA] covers section 403(b) contracts and custodial accounts they are treated as section 401(a) plans" for purposes of the QJSA/QPSA requirements. Reg. § 1.401(a)-20, A-3(d). Therefore, some 403(b) plans are subject to REA and some are not.

The 403(b) plans NOT covered by ERISA (and therefore not subject to REA) are those funded exclusively by means of elective employee deferrals (salary reduction agreements). 403(b) plans funded in whole or in part by employer contributions are subject to ERISA and therefore also to the REA requirements.

403(b) plans that are subject to ERISA and offer annuity benefits will be subject to REA's full QJSA/QPSA requirements, just like a pension plan (¶ 3.4.02). A 403(b) plan that is subject to ERISA but that does *not* offer annuity benefits (e.g., a plan funded exclusively with mutual fund custodial accounts pursuant to § 403(b)(7)) can use the alternative compliance procedure available to "exempt" profit sharing plans (¶ 3.4.03). For full details on which 403(b) plans are covered by ERISA and which are exempt, see DOL Reg. § 2510.3-2(f).

3.4.05 *Various REA exceptions and miscellaneous points*

There are a few exceptions to the REA requirements, even for covered plans. These exceptions are rarely significant in estate planning, but are listed here in case they may be significant in your particular client's situation (but be sure to read ¶ 3.4.06).

A.   No spousal consent is required for distribution of benefits to Participant when the total value of Participant's benefits is under $5,000. Reg. § 1.411(a)-11(c)(3).

B.   REA does not require that a QPSA or 100%-death-benefit-in-lieu-of-QPSA, be paid to a spouse who was married to the Participant for less than a year prior to the date of death. § 417(d); § 401(a)(11)(D).

C.   No spousal consent is required if "it is established to the satisfaction of a plan representative that the consent...may not be obtained because there is no spouse, because the spouse cannot be located, or because of such other circumstances as the Secretary may by regulations prescribe." § 417(a)(2)(B).

D.   There are special rules for using retirement plan benefits as security for a plan loan to the employee, under which Spouse must consent to the loan but then the loan can later be "foreclosed" without further spousal consent. § 417(a)(4).

E.   There are modified rules for ESOPs. § 401(a)(11)(C).

F.   There are exceptions for plans terminated (or employees retired) before REA's effective date.

G.   Spouse loses her rights upon divorce or legal separation or her "abandonment" of the Participant (except to the extent otherwise provided in a "qualified domestic relations order" issued in connection with the divorce; see § 414(p)). Reg. § 1.401(a)-20, A-27.

3.4.06 *Plan may be more generous than REA requires*

For reasons of administrative convenience or other reasons, a retirement plan may give spouses more rights than REA requires. For example, REA does not require that a QPSA, or (in the case of an "exempt" profit sharing plan) the 100%-death-benefit-in-lieu-of-QPSA, be paid to a spouse who was married to the Participant for less than a year prior to the date of death. § 417(d); § 401(a)(11)(D). However, many retirement plan designers decided it was easier to grant the same rights to *all* spouses than to try to figure out exactly how long each employee had been married, so many plans grant these rights to all surviving spouses, regardless of the length of the marriage.

Similarly, the value of the legally-required QPSA (which is

supposed to be equivalent only to the survivor pension Spouse would have received under a joint and survivor annuity) is less than the total value of the employee's accrued benefit in the plan. However, some plans simply award every non-consenting Spouse 100% of the value of the Participant's benefit, presumably because that is administratively easier than figuring out for each individual employee and spouse what would have been the relative values of their shares under a QJSA.

3.4.07 *Requirements for spousal consent or waiver*

Spouse's consent to waive any of these mandatory benefits cannot be in any old form done at any old time. § 417 contains elaborate rules for the spousal consent, including as to its form (¶ 3.4.08) and:

1.   Timing: Participant's waiver of a QPSA, and Spouse's consent to such waiver, must be given after the beginning of the plan year in which Participant reaches age 35, and prior to the employee's death. § 417(a)(6)(B). The IRS, unlike the Code itself, permits waiver of the QPSA even *before* Participant reaches age 35, provided Participant goes through the waiver/consent process *again* after reaching age 35. Reg. § 1.401(a)-20, A-33. For exempt profit sharing plans (¶ 3.4.03), the spousal consent for waiver of the 100%-death-benefit-in-lieu-of-QPSA may be provided "at any time," including before Participant reaches age 35. Reg. § 1.401(a)-20, A-33(a).

2.   Disclosure: "No consent is valid unless [Participant] has received a general description of the material features, and an explanation of the relative values of, the optional forms of benefit available under the plan in a manner which would satisfy the notice requirements of section 417(a)(3)." Reg. § 1.417(e)-1(b)(2)(i). Although the statute requires that this disclosure be provided to *Participant* rather than Spouse, Spouse's consent to Participant's waiver of the QJSA or QPSA must "acknowledge the effect" of such waiver. This probably means Spouse should see the same disclosures provided to Participant himself, in order that Spouse may understand the effect of the waiver.

3.4.08 *Form of spousal consent or waiver*

An election in proper form "designates a beneficiary (or a form of benefits) which may not be changed without spousal consent (or the consent of the spouse expressly permits designations by Participant without any requirement of further consent by the spouse), and...the spouse's consent acknowledges the effect of such election and is witnessed by a plan representative or a notary public." § 417(a)(2)(A). See Reg. § 1.401(a)-20, A-31 for more detail about the required form of spousal consent.

Note that there are two ways Spouse can consent: she can say "I am consenting to this *particular* beneficiary designation, but I do not consent in advance to any changes, so if you change the beneficiary designation hereafter you need to get a new consent from me"; or the consent can expressly permit further changes ("designations") by Participant without the requirement of further spousal consents.

The IRS has published four sample spousal consent forms (IRS Notice 97-10, 1997-2 I.R.B. 41). They are available on "Forms on Disk" (order form at end of this book).

3.4.09 *Key points for estate planners*

REA poses many challenges to estate planners, including:

1. REA creates serious, and sad, difficulties if Spouse is unable due to mental disability to consent to the desired estate plan. In that case the consent must be provided by Spouse's legal guardian. Reg. § 1.401(a)-20, A-27. The author has seen the following situation more than once: Participant has a mentally disabled spouse, whose life expectancy is shortened due to the disability. A survivor annuity would probably never provide a dime to the disabled spouse (because of his or her shortened life expectancy), but *would* reduce Participant's pension (because the plan's actuarial formula for determining the amount of benefits does not take into account the health of the individual Participant or Spouse). Through hard work and loving care Participant has avoided the expense and humiliation of legal guardianship proceedings for the disabled spouse. Thanks to REA, and because of the importance to both spouses of maximizing the value of the pension, said expense and

humiliation must be incurred when Participant reaches retirement age. Although the regulations say that Participant may be the guardian of a disabled spouse for the purpose of providing the needed consent, the court having jurisdiction either does not allow the employee to serve as guardian because the court perceives there is a conflict of interest, or requires appointment of a guardian ad litem with attendant expense.

2.   If there is any question about Spouse's willingness to consent, or to honor a consent once given, it becomes especially important to adhere strictly to the statutory requirements regarding the form of the consent. There is no guarantee that your client's plan's standard printed spousal consent form complies with REA. Consider supplying your own form, using the IRS-provided sample spousal consent forms (¶ 3.4.08).

3.   Waiver of the QJSA benefit must occur not more than 90 days prior to the annuity starting date, so it is impossible to lock in spousal consent in advance.

4.   The Supreme Court has held that REA preempts state spousal rights laws such as community property; *Boggs v. Boggs*, 117 S. Ct. 1754 (1997). The interrelation of REA and state spousal rights laws baffles the nation's estate planning gurus.

5.   Some defined benefit plans subsidize the annuity payments to Spouse (meaning that the employee's pension is not reduced to provide the survivor annuity; the married employee and the single employee receive the same pension), and do not permit Spouse to waive the survivor annuity. This type of plan typically would provide no death benefits at all other than the required spousal annuities, and would not allow an employee to cash out the value of his pension at retirement—the employee must take an annuity. § 417(a)(5).

6.   REA rights cannot be waived in a pre-nuptial agreement, because the employee's affianced is not at that point the "spouse." "An agreement entered into prior to marriage does not satisfy the applicable consent requirements, even if the agreement is executed within the applicable election period."

Reg. § 1.401(a)-20, A-28.

7.   If Spouse is being asked to waive a QPSA or QJSA, consider whether Spouse needs to be advised of the option of retaining separate counsel. Spouse might for example wish to consent to a waiver of the QJSA (and allow Participant to roll over the benefits to an IRA) only if Participant agrees to name Spouse as beneficiary of the IRA.

8.   If Spouse consents to Participant's naming a trust as beneficiary, later amendments to the trust do not require a subsequent spousal consent. Reg. § 1.401(a)-20, A-31(a).

3.5 Summary of Planning Principles

1.   The tax laws generally, though not always, favor naming Spouse, personally, as designated beneficiary of retirement benefits and using other, non-IRD, assets to fund a credit shelter trust.

2.   IRS rulings provide clear instructions for qualifying retirement benefits payable to QTIP trusts for the estate tax marital deduction. Although the method specified in these rulings is not the only way to obtain the marital deduction for benefits payable to a QTIP trust, many practitioners are choosing to use it.

3.   Making benefits payable to a QTIP trust often results in a substantial loss of potential income tax deferral compared with leaving benefits to Spouse outright.

4.   Upon Participant's death it is extremely important for Spouse to consider her options immediately, and to roll over the benefits if that is the chosen option.

Non-Citizen Spouse

If Participant's spouse is not a U.S. citizen, the usual marital deduction is not available. A modified marital deduction is available if certain requirements are met.

This Chapter explains the tax issues involved when the Participant's spouse is not a U.S. citizen (¶ 4.1, ¶ 4.2), then examines four alternatives for retirement benefits in this situation (¶ 4.3-¶ 4.6). The Chapter ends with suggested investment and distribution strategies for a "Qualified Domestic Trust" (QDOT) (¶ 4.7) and a summary of planning principles (¶ 4.8). In this Chapter, the Participant is sometimes called the "Decedent" or "client." His spouse is called "Spouse."

4.1 Modified Marital Deduction for Non-Citizen Spouse

4.1.01 *Modified marital deduction and deferred estate tax*

Property passing to a surviving spouse who is not a United States citizen will not qualify for the normal estate tax marital deduction. § 2056(d)(1). However, if property left to Spouse in a form that would qualify for the marital deduction (but for the fact that Spouse is not a citizen) is placed in a certain kind of trust, called a qualified domestic trust ("QDOT"), either by Decedent or by Spouse, it will qualify for a *modified* version of the marital deduction. § 2056(d)(2).

Under this modified form of marital deduction, the property is not simply deducted from Decedent's estate and added to Spouse's estate, as normally occurs when the marital deduction is taken (¶ 3.3.01). Rather, the tax is merely deferred until one of three possible events triggers the requirement of paying estate tax: non-hardship distributions of principal to Spouse from the QDOT (§ 2056A(b)(1)(A), (3)(B)); the trust's ceasing to meet the QDOT requirements

(§ 2056A(b)(4)); or Spouse's death (§ 2056A(b)(1)(B)). Any payment of deferred estate tax by the QDOT is treated as an additional distribution of principal to Spouse (resulting in more deferred estate tax). § 2056A(b)(11).

When a triggering event occurs, the deferred estate tax applies to the amount of the non-hardship principal distribution, or (in the case of Spouse's death or the disqualification of the QDOT) to the entire "principal" (¶ 4.7.03) of the QDOT. The amount of the tax is the amount of tax that would have been owed if the QDOT property (or amount distributed as the case may be) had been part of Decedent's estate back when Decedent died. § 2056A(b)(2). For example, if Spouse dies when the federal estate tax exemption is $3,500,000, but when Decedent died the exemption was only $1,000,000, the deferred estate tax is computed using the $1,000,000 exemption. Note that even though this is in effect a deferred estate tax, there is no requirement of paying interest on it.

The QDOT property will *also* be subject to U.S. estate tax as part of Spouse's estate upon her death, if she is a U.S. resident or citizen, under normal estate tax principles. In that case, her estate will receive a credit for the deferred estate tax paid on the property by the QDOT, and of course *her* estate will have the benefit of whatever estate tax exemption applies for the year of her death. § 2056(d)(3); § 2001(c). So, in effect, the estate tax payable on the QDOT at Spouse's death is going to be at Decedent's marginal rate, or at Spouse's marginal rate, whichever is higher.

Adding to the already-considerable complications of this setup are the scheduled repeal of the estate tax and the scheduled sunset of the repeal; see ¶ 4.1.03. But first, a way to avoid the whole mess:

4.1.02 *If Spouse becomes a citizen, or is or becomes a non-resident*

If Spouse becomes a *U.S. citizen* prior to the filing of the estate tax return for Decedent's estate, *and* if Spouse was a U.S. *resident* at all times after Decedent's death until she became a citizen, the normal marital deduction becomes available and it is not necessary to transfer property to a QDOT or worry about the deferred estate tax. § 2056(d)(4). This is often the simplest solution to the problem if Spouse intends to remain permanently in the U.S. This approach should be explored at the planning stage if possible, otherwise as soon as possible after Decedent's death, since becoming a citizen takes time.

If Spouse becomes a U.S. citizen *after* the filing of Decedent's estate tax return, all distributions to Spouse thereafter from the QDOT (or from non-assignable property subject to an agreement with the IRS; ¶ 4.6) are free of the deferred estate tax—provided Spouse was a U.S. *resident* at all times after Decedent's death until she became a citizen. The QDOT could terminate at that point and distribute its assets to Spouse free of the deferred estate tax. § 2056A(b)(12); Reg. § 20.2056A-10(a); see PLR 9848007.

If the non-citizen spouse is or becomes a non-U.S. *resident*, different considerations may apply. This situation is beyond the scope of this book.

The rest of this chapter assumes Spouse will remain a non-U.S. citizen.

4.1.03 *QDOTs, estate tax repeal and sunset*

This ¶ 4.1.03 discusses what happens, under EGTRRA's estate tax repeal and sunset provisions, to *any* property left to a QDOT; the additional complications of *retirement plan benefits* left to a QDOT are discussed in subsequent sections.

§ 2056A(b), which imposes the deferred estate tax on QDOT property, is part of Chapter 11 (Subtitle B) of the Code (Estate and Gift Taxes). Chapter 11 "shall not apply to the estates of decedents dying after December 31, 2009." § 2210(a) This provision has no effect on the deferred estate tax on QDOTs established by decedents who died *prior* to 2010 that are still in existence in 2010.

§ 2210(b) deals with that situation. § 2210(b)(1) provides that the deferred estate tax on non-hardship distributions of principal from a QDOT "shall not apply to distributions made after December 31, 2020." However, since § 901 of EGTRRA repeals § 2210 effective after 2010, this provision will never apply.

§ 2210(b)(2) provides that the deferred estate tax imposed on a QDOT *at Spouse's death* "shall not apply" after December 31, 2009. § 2210 says nothing explicitly about the deferred estate tax imposed on a QDOT *if the trust ceases to meet the requirements* of § 2056A(a); however, since tax in that case is imposed "as if the surviving spouse died on the date" the trust ceased to qualify (§ 2056A(b)(4)), effectively the cease-to-qualify tax does not apply if the disqualification occurs in 2010 (since Spouse's death in 2010 would not trigger the deferred estate tax; § 2210(b)(2)). *Accordingly, the way the law is now written (but it's bound to be changed; see next paragraph) it would appear that all QDOTs still in existence on January 1, 2010, should take some step to make the trust disqualified in the year 2010*, and thereby eliminate all future concerns about the deferred estate tax.

There are two anomalies in § 2210. First, § 2210(a) says that the estate tax chapter will not apply to decedents dying after 2009 "except as provided in" § 2210(b); however, § 2210(b) applies *only* to estates of decedents who die *before* 2010, so it does not contain any exceptions to § 2210(a). Second, § 2210(b)(1) purports to continue to tax non-hardship distributions of principal from a pre-2010 QDOT until 2020, but seems to allow a QDOT to disqualify itself in 2010 without payment of deferred estate tax, which would make subsequent distributions non-taxable, which seems nonsensical and therefore presumably will be changed.

Here, then, is a summary of possible results if Decedent dies before 2010 and leaves property to a QDOT for the benefit of his non-citizen Spouse:

1.   If Spouse dies before or after (but not during) 2210, and before the QDOT ceases to meet the requirements of § 2056A(a) (see # 2), the property remaining in the QDOT at Spouse's death is subject to the deferred estate tax.

2.   If, prior to Spouse's death, the QDOT ceases to meet the requirements of § 2056A(a), the deferred estate tax is imposed just as if Spouse had died when the disqualification occurs (see # 1). § 2056A(b)(4).

3.   If, prior to Spouse's death, prior to the disqualification of the QDOT, and prior to 2021, the QDOT distributes principal to Spouse, and the hardship exception (¶ 4.7.01) does not apply, the distribution is subject to the deferred estate tax.

4.   If Spouse dies (or the QDOT ceases to qualify) in 2010, the deferred estate tax does not apply to the QDOT. § 2210(b)(2).

4.1.04 *Overview of ways to qualify for modified marital deduction*

If the surviving spouse is not a U.S. citizen (and will not become a U.S. citizen prior to filing the estate tax return), there are four possible ways to qualify for the modified marital deduction:

One is for Decedent to have arranged his estate plan so that property for which the marital deduction is sought will pass, on his death, directly to a QDOT. See ¶ 4.3.

If Decedent's estate plan failed to do this, the modified marital deduction is still available if Spouse herself, having inherited the property outright, transfers it to a QDOT prior to the filing of the estate tax return and no later than one year after the due date of the return. Reg. § 20.2056A-1(a)(iii). See ¶ 4.4 and ¶ 4.5.

Finally, ¶ 4.6 describes two other methods available for "non-assignable property"—that is, property (such as a non-assignable annuity) that passes to Spouse outright, but that cannot legally be transferred by Spouse to a QDOT. Spouse can get QDOT treatment for non-assignable property by entering into an agreement with the IRS whereby, when she receives a distribution from the non-assignable property, she will transfer the distributed amount to a QDOT, or, alternatively, by agreeing that she will pay the deferred estate tax on the distributed amount when she receives it. The regulations permit Spouse to elect to treat an IRA as non-assignable property.

4.1.05 *Consider not qualifying for the marital deduction*

Any strategy that requires making retirement benefits qualify for the modified marital deduction involves loss of potential income tax deferral, or substantial complications and uncertainties, or all of the above (see ¶ 4.3-¶ 4.6). Decedent can avoid these difficulties by leaving his retirement benefits to his children or other non-spouse beneficiary, or to a trust that does not qualify for the marital deduction. The disadvantages of this approach are those that exist whenever retirement benefits are paid in a non-marital deduction disposition (see ¶ 10.5).

Another alternative is to make the benefits payable to Spouse individually but not claim the marital deduction. Scheduled Federal estate tax exemption increases from $675,000 to $3,500,000 over the years 2002-2009 (§ 2010(c)) will mean that more clients can leave 100% of their estates to their non-citizen surviving spouses and not incur an estate tax even *without* qualifying for the modified marital deduction; this much less complicated approach should appeal to an increasing number of clients. Even if an estate tax has to be paid on client's death, Spouse will get the benefit of the § 691(c) deduction. ¶ 2.2.07. This approach may be especially attractive if Spouse will probably return to her country of origin, so U.S. estate taxes will not apply to her estate (because she will be a non-citizen non-resident).

If Spouse is likely to remain a U.S. resident, whether leaving all retirement benefits outright to Spouse would be an attractive approach depends on the likely future estate tax Spouse faces. If federal estate taxes will apply on Spouse's death (e.g., because she is wealthy and dies when the estate tax is in effect), this approach will not be attractive, especially if estate taxes have to be paid at the first death, because the benefits, already reduced by income taxes, and by estate taxes at Decedent's death, would be subject to estate tax again at Spouse's death (though if Spouse dies within 10 years after Decedent the estate tax credit for tax on prior transfers would be available; § 2013). On the other hand, if estate taxes are not likely to apply at Spouse's death (either because her assets are under the exemption amount, or because estate taxes will have been repealed), this approach would be attractive.

4.1.06 *The requirements of a QDOT*

The distinguishing characteristics of a qualified domestic trust are set forth in § 2056A(a) and regulations. The principal requirements are:

(a) At least one trustee of the QDOT must be an individual citizen of the United States or a United States domestic corporation. § 2056A(a)(1)(A).

(b) The trust must be "maintained" under, and the administration of the trust must be governed by, the laws of a particular state or the District of Columbia. Reg. § 20.2056A-2(a).

(c) No principal distribution may be made from the trust unless the U.S. trustee has the right to withhold from the distribution the deferred estate tax discussed at ¶ 4.1.01. § 2056A(a)(1)(B).

(d) The trust must meet any additional requirements imposed by the Secretary of the Treasury by regulations to insure collection of the tax. § 2056A(a)(2). The IRS has imposed some such additional requirements, such as bonding for non-bank trustees and limits on non-U.S. real estate investments. Reg. § 20.2056A-2.

Note that there is no requirement that all of the QDOT income be distributable annually to Spouse, or even that Spouse be the sole beneficiary of the QDOT. The *QDOT* requirements are concerned *only* with the identity of the trustee, necessary elections, and security for collection of the deferred estate tax.

In summary, in order to qualify for the modified version of the marital deduction when Spouse is not a U.S. citizen, the property must be placed (by Decedent or by Spouse) in a trust which meets the above requirements; and *in addition* the property must pass from Decedent to Spouse (or to a trust for Spouse's benefit) in a way that qualifies for the marital deduction (aside from the QDOT requirements).

4.1.07 *Differences between QDOT created by Decedent, Spouse*

Regardless of whether Spouse is a U.S. citizen, the marital deduction is not allowed for property passing from Decedent to a trust for Spouse unless the trust meets certain requirements familiar to all estate planners: a "marital deduction trust" will be a nondeductible "terminable interest" unless it fits into one of the exceptions to the "terminable interest rule." ¶ 3.3.02. This Chapter assumes that any QDOT created by transfer from Decedent will be either a "general power marital trust" (¶ 3.3.03) or a "QTIP trust" (¶ 3.3.04), and so will qualify as an exception to that rule. (Two other categories of trust that qualify for the marital deduction, the rarely-used "estate trust," and the charitable remainder trust of which the spouse is the only non-charitable beneficiary, are not discussed in this Chapter.)

If property passes from Decedent to Spouse *outright*, it qualifies for the marital deduction (except for the QDOT requirements) under § 2056(a). An outright bequest is not a "terminable interest," and accordingly does not have to comply with the marital deduction *trust* rules. Therefore, when Spouse receives an outright bequest, and transfers the inherited property into a QDOT *she* creates, there is no requirement that the terms of that QDOT be similar to those of a "normal" marital deduction trust (unless the trust also contains property transferred to it directly by Decedent); only the QDOT requirements need be met. A "QTIP election" cannot be made for a QDOT established by Spouse. Reg. § 20.2056A-4(d), example 5.

A QDOT created by Spouse need not (and normally should not) be irrevocable. A QDOT created by Spouse need not (but probably should) require annual distribution of all income to Spouse. A QDOT created by Spouse could (but probably should not) allow distributions to people other than Spouse during her lifetime. For further suggestions regarding the terms of a QDOT created by Spouse, see ¶ 4.5.

Note: if the QDOT to which Spouse transfers property *also* contains any property transferred directly to it by Decedent then the *entire trust* must qualify for the marital deduction under § 2056. Reg. § 20.2056A-4(b)(1). In this chapter, a "QDOT funded by Spouse" means a QDOT *exclusively* so funded.

4.2 Income Tax vs. Deferred Estate Tax

4.2.01 *Statute suggests possibility of double tax*

Retirement benefits generally are subject both to income tax as "income in respect of a decedent" (IRD) (¶ 2.2) and estate tax. When the benefits are paid to a non-citizen Spouse or a QDOT it is not always clear how the income tax and the deferred estate tax relate to each other.

Under the statute, it appears possible that Spouse could be required to pay *both* income tax *and* deferred estate tax on the full amount of inherited retirement benefits, with neither tax deductible in determining the other. The regulations make it clear in a couple of situations (¶ 4.2.03, ¶ 4.2.04) that amounts used to pay income tax on IRD will not *also* be subject to the deferred estate tax; in other situations (¶ 4.2.05) we are left to assume that this result is allowed, without specific authority.

If the client's retirement plan is an IRA, one way to avoid all the complications described in this section is to convert the IRA to a Roth IRA during life, so that distributions post-death will generally not be subject to income tax; see Chapter 5.

4.2.02 *§ 691(c) deduction for deferred estate tax*

Generally, the beneficiary of retirement benefits can deduct the federal estate taxes paid on the benefits in determining how much income tax the beneficiary must pay on those benefits, because § 691(c)(2)(A) allows an income tax deduction for estate taxes imposed on IRD "*under section 2001 or 2101....*" ¶ 2.2.07. Although the deferred estate tax on a QDOT is imposed by § *2056A* rather than by either of the two sections mentioned in § 691(c), the regulations provide that "The estate tax (net of any applicable credits) imposed under section 2056A(b)(1) constitutes an estate tax for purposes of section 691(c)(2)(A)." Reg. § 20.2056A-6(a).

While it is nice to know that the deferred estate tax qualifies for the 691(c) deduction, it is not clear how this will actually help Spouse. Normally, estate taxes are paid when a decedent dies, then the beneficiary collects the benefits, and the beneficiary can deduct the estate taxes paid when computing his income tax on the benefits. In the case of the *deferred* estate tax, however, Spouse (or the QDOT) normally collects the income-taxable benefits *first*, before the deferred estate tax has been "imposed" (at her death), so there is no estate tax to deduct because it hasn't been imposed yet. On the other hand, since any federal income taxes Spouse pays on the benefits are probably removed from the tax base for purposes of computing the deferred estate tax that will later be due (see the next three subsections), it makes sense that she does not also get a deduction in the other direction (i.e., deducting the estate tax for purposes of computing income tax).

If the deferred estate tax on retirement benefits has to be paid during Spouse's life (*e.g.*, if the QDOT ceases to qualify as a QDOT), Spouse can take the § 691(c) deduction for the deferred estate tax with regard to subsequent distributions. Also, to the extent there are still some benefits inside the plan at Spouse's death, the next succeeding beneficiary can take a § 691(c) deduction for the deferred estate tax (and/or for the surviving spouse's estate tax). How to compute the deduction in these situations is beyond the scope of this book.

4.2.03 *Income tax paid by Spouse on plan distributions*

The Code exempts, from the deferred estate tax, distributions to Spouse from a QDOT made to reimburse Spouse for *federal* income taxes imposed on Spouse on any item of income of the QDOT "to which [Spouse] is not entitled under the terms of the trust." § 2056A(b)(15). The IRS in its regulations has interpreted this oddly worded Code provision in such a way as to alleviate the double taxation effect in some specific situations. Under the regulations, if Spouse receives a distribution from Decedent's retirement plan and then "assigns" that distribution to the QDOT, the QDOT can, without triggering deferred estate tax, reimburse Spouse for the federal income tax she pays on the distribution, including federal income taxes paid "through withholding." Reg. § 20.2056A-5(c)(3)(iv).

Example: The Acme Profit Sharing Plan distributes $100,000 to Spouse as a death benefit (and MRD) from Decedent's account in the plan. There is no withholding (see ¶ 2.1.05). Spouse assigns the $100,000 check to the QDOT pursuant to a "(c)(3)" agreement (¶ 4.6.01). At the end of the year, when the dust settles, it turns out that Spouse's income tax liability on the $100,000 distribution was $38,000. The QDOT can reimburse her for the $38,000 without having to pay deferred estate tax on the distribution. End result: QDOT holds $62,000 cash ($100,000 distribution minus $38,000 income tax reimbursement), Spouse holds $0 ($100,000 received from plan minus $100,000 paid to QDOT, $38,000 received from QDOT minus $38,000 paid to IRS).

Example: The Acme Profit Sharing Plan distributes a $100,000 lump sum distribution to Spouse as a death benefit from Decedent's account in the plan. $20,000 of the distribution is withheld for federal income taxes (¶ 2.1.05). Spouse assigns the distribution to the QDOT pursuant to a "(c)(3)" agreement (¶ 4.6.01). It's not clear how she can assign the *entire* distribution to the QDOT since she only received $80,000 of it, but that's what the regulation says is supposed to happen. Maybe she assigns to the QDOT her rights to the withheld taxes along with her rights to the net cash. At the end of the year, when the dust settles, it turns out that Spouse's income tax liability on the $100,000 distribution was $38,000. The QDOT can reimburse her for the $38,000 without having to pay deferred estate tax on the distribution; however, since the QDOT never received the withheld tax money ($20,000), it only reimburses Spouse $18,000. End result: QDOT holds $62,000 cash ($80,000 net distribution received minus $18,000 income tax reimbursement), Spouse holds $0 ($80,000 received from plan minus $80,000 paid to QDOT, $18,000 received from QDOT minus $18,000 paid to IRS).

This estate-tax-free reimbursement is available only for taxes imposed by subtitle A, *federal* income taxes. It is not permitted for state income taxes. The reimbursable tax is calculated at the marginal rate, *i.e.*, the difference between Spouse's *actual* income tax for the year and what Spouse's tax *would* have been if the distribution had not been included in her gross income.

4.2.04 *Income taxes paid by the QDOT*

Assume Decedent left his IRA to a QTIP Trust (¶ 3.3.04) that is also a QDOT. The trust is to pay "income to Spouse for life, remainder to Decedent's issue." Because Spouse is only the income beneficiary, she is not treated as the "owner" of the trust *principal* for income tax purposes. Reg. § 1.671-3(b)(1). Accordingly, income taxes on distributions of IRD from the plan to the trust, to the extent such distributions are considered "principal" (see ¶ 6.1.07), are imposed directly on the trust. All income taxes (both federal and state, apparently) paid on any IRA distribution that is retained in the QDOT as principal are exempt from the deferred estate tax as "[p]ayments to applicable governmental authorities for income tax or any other applicable tax imposed on the QDOT" (other than the deferred estate tax itself). Reg. § 20.2056-5(c)(3)(ii).

In contrast, when benefits are payable to Spouse, and then transferred by Spouse to the QDOT, only the *federal* income taxes Spouse pays can be reimbursed by the QDOT free of deferred estate tax. § 2056A(b)(15); Reg. § 20.2056A-5(c)(3)(iv). This slight discrepancy in treatment of state income taxes argues in favor of leaving the benefits to a QTIP-QDOT, rather than outright to Spouse. The downside of leaving the benefits to a life income QTIP-QDOT is that the benefits will be taxed at trust rates, whereas income taxes might be lower if paid at Spouse's personal rate.

4.2.05 *QDOT income taxable to Spouse*

As noted (¶ 4.2.04), the regulations provide that if retirement benefits are distributed to, and taxable to, a QDOT, the income taxes paid by the QDOT are not subject to the deferred estate tax. What if, under § 678(a), Spouse, not the trust, is taxable on a plan distribution received by the trust, because she has the power to withdraw the distribution from the trust (see ¶ 4.3.02)? The regulations do not explicitly give relief here. The regulations explicitly exempt from the deferred estate tax only income taxes "imposed on the QDOT," or paid by Spouse on a plan distribution received by Spouse and assigned to the QDOT.

However, the non-taxable reimbursement of Spouse for income tax is "not limited to" the specific situations mentioned. § 20.2056A-5(c)(3)(iv). Presumably, reimbursement of Spouse by the QDOT for income tax paid by Spouse on trust income she *is* entitled to receive would also be allowed free of deferred estate tax, despite the fact that the Code allows tax-free reimbursement of Spouse only for taxes on trust income she is *not* entitled to.

The result should be the same when a distribution of IRD is made from the plan to the QDOT, and the trustee distributes the principal to Spouse under a discretionary power to distribute principal, if the principal distribution carries out "distributable net income" (DNI) to Spouse under § 661-§ 662 (¶ 6.1.03). The portion of such a principal distribution which Spouse is required to pay to the IRS as income taxes should not be subject to the deferred estate tax, but there is as yet no official confirmation on this.

෫෧෫෧

Having completed the tour of the estate and income tax considerations, we next look at the alternatives available for leaving retirement benefits to a non-citizen spouse.

4.3 Approach # 1: Decedent Leaves Benefits to Marital Trust-QDOT

4.3.01 *Advantage: safety, predictability*

At the planning stage, while the client is still living, the safest course is for the client to make his retirement benefits payable to a marital trust that will also qualify as a QDOT. With this approach, the client knows that, upon his death, the benefits will automatically pass in a manner that will qualify for the modified marital deduction; the success of the estate plan will not depend on Spouse's taking action after client's death to create a QDOT and assign assets to it (¶ 4.4, ¶ 4.5) or enter into an agreement with the IRS (¶ 4.6).

4.3.02 *Drawbacks; use of grantor trust to mitigate*

If Spouse is entitled only to annual income distributions, there are all the usual disadvantages of leaving retirement benefits to a QTIP trust. See ¶ 10.5.05. A marital trust for the benefit of a *citizen* spouse could minimize the adverse effects of at least one of the drawbacks of the standard QTIP trust, namely, the high income tax rates applicable to a principal distribution from the retirement plan to the trust, by passing some or all of the distribution out to the spouse-beneficiary, if the trust permitted this. See ¶ 6.1.03. This safety valve is not helpful in the case of a marital trust-QDOT, however, because non-hardship distributions of principal from the QDOT to Spouse will attract the deferred estate tax. ¶ 4.1.01.

Possibly, giving Spouse the unlimited right to withdraw all of the principal from the trust at all times would cause the trust's income to be taxed at her (possibly lower) rate, rather than the trust's (often higher) rate, if she is a U.S. resident, thus eliminating at least one drawback; see discussion of § 678(a)(1) "grantor trusts" at ¶ 6.3.09 for more on this and other possible advantages of a § 678 grantor trust. Spouse is unlikely to exercise such withdrawal power under a QDOT because exercise would trigger the deferred estate tax.

One risk of using this approach is that the regulations do not explicitly permit the QDOT to reimburse Spouse for income tax she is required to pay on the trust's income under § 678, without paying the deferred estate tax on the reimbursement, although it appears *likely* that this is permitted; see ¶ 4.2.05. Another question is whether it is possible for the trust to be considered entirely subject to a right of withdrawal by Spouse (within the meaning of § 678(a)(1)) when the QDOT trustee has the right (as required by § 2056A(a)(1)(B)) to withhold the deferred estate tax from any distribution to her. See discussion at ¶ 4.5.01.

4.4 Approach # 2: Spouse Rolls Over Benefits to QDOT-IRT

If property passes outright to Spouse, the modified marital deduction can still be obtained if Spouse transfers the property to a QDOT. ¶ 4.1.04. This option poses special problems in the case of retirement benefits that are paid to Spouse individually.

If Spouse is named personally as the beneficiary of Decedent's retirement plan, and she leaves the benefits in Decedent's plan, the benefits will not qualify for the marital deduction because the retirement plan is not a QDOT. If she withdraws the benefits from Decedent's plan, with the idea of transferring them to a QDOT, she will have to pay income tax on the benefits (unless the benefits are not subject to income tax; see ¶ 2.1.03).

4.4.01 *The combination QDOT-IRT*

One way out of this dilemma is for Spouse to take the benefits out of Decedent's retirement plan and roll them over tax-free (¶ 3.2) to a trust that is both a QDOT *and* an IRA under § 408(a). There is no tax or legal obstacle in the way of combining an IRA and a QDOT. An IRA can be in the legal form of a trust (§ 408(a)) or a custodial account (§ 408(h)), though most IRAs are in the form of custodial accounts. The term "individual retirement trust" (IRT) is used here to distinguish the individual retirement account in the form of a trust from the more common custodial form of IRA.

The QDOT-IRT would provide that Spouse had the right to withdraw all the income (and principal) on demand, but, as an IRT, would also provide that the minimum required distribution would have to be distributed to Spouse annually. As a rollover IRT, MRDs would begin to Spouse when she reached age 70½, using the Uniform Lifetime Table; see ¶ 3.3.10 for explanation of the income tax advantages of the spousal rollover compared with the treatment of a benefits paid to a marital trust as beneficiary.

The practical difficulties of this approach include drafting the document and finding a U.S. bank willing to serve as trustee (¶ 4.4.04). Unfortunately, this difficulty may be substantial in the case of a smaller retirement benefit. Larger banks' fee schedules make them good choices, usually, only for accounts worth $1 million or more. Smaller bank trust operations accept smaller trusts and IRAs, but in the author's experience smaller banks refuse to accept an *IRA* in the form of a trust because their IRAs are administered by an outside provider who furnishes all the forms and monitors compliance. A bank that does not have true in-house IRA capability will probably not be willing to take on a unique entity like a QDOT-IRT.

4.4.02 *Deferred estate tax on principal distributions*

There is a price to be paid for the greater income tax deferral that can be obtained with a QDOT-IRT. The price is paid when "principal" for which the marital deduction was taken in Decedent's estate is distributed from the QDOT-IRT to Spouse. At that time, the deferred estate tax, as well as income taxes, will have to be paid on the principal distribution.

Of course, deferred estate tax is due whenever principal is

distributed to Spouse from *any* QDOT. But with a regular QDOT (¶ 4.3), it is possible for the trust to exist for Spouse's entire lifetime without ever distributing principal. With a QDOT-IRT, the minimum distribution rules require certain amounts to be distributed every year after spouse reaches age 70½. See Chapter 1. "Principal" will have to be distributed out to Spouse when the minimum required distributions (MRDs) from the IRA exceed the "income" of the IRA (see ¶ 3.3.06, ¶ 6.1.07).

If (after age 70½) Spouse is taking out only the MRDs under the Uniform Lifetime Table (¶ 1.4.01), *and* undistributed income inside the IRT retains its character as "income" for purposes of the deferred estate tax (see ¶ 4.7.03), *and* the required distributions could be treated as coming first out of the "accumulated income," then it is likely that distributions to Spouse would not be coming out of "principal" (i.e., the value of the account as it existed on the participant's death) until very late in Spouse's life. The MRDs would be less than the annual income so long as the Uniform Table divisor expressed as a percentage (i.e., one, divided by the remaining life expectancy) is less than the rate of income, so for many years after Spouse's RBD the IRT will actually be accumulating some of its income.

However, this conclusion depends on treating income accumulated inside the QDOT-IRT as "income" for purposes of the deferred estate tax. If the IRS decides that "principal" for this purpose includes accumulated income (see ¶ 4.7.03), the crossover point (when MRDs must necessarily include principal and therefore trigger deferred estate tax) will be reached much sooner. Accordingly, until further clarification of the IRS's position, accumulating income inside a QDOT-IRT is not recommended without obtaining a ruling on the status of undistributed income under § 2056A. In the absence of such a ruling, Spouse should (1) withdraw all "income" of the QDOT-IRT annually and (2) in any year in which the "income" exceeds the MRD, roll over the excess to her non-QDOT-IRA (see ¶ 3.3.07).

4.4.03 *No IRS ruling on QDOT-IRT qualification*

"Receipt of a favorable opinion letter on an IRA ... is not required as a condition of receiving favorable tax treatment." Rev. Proc. 87-50, 1987-2 C.B. 647, section 2.08. Although it will issue opinion letters on prototype IRAs, "The Service will not issue rulings or determination letters to individuals with respect to the status of their"

IRAs. *Id.*, § 4.03. Fortunately, the IRS has supplied a "Model Trust Account" form for an IRA, known as Form 5305. "[I]ndividuals who adopt the Model Trust ... Account...will be treated as having an arrangement that meets the requirements of section 408(a)." *Id.*, § 5.01. By adopting Form 5305, and adding to it the provisions required for a QDOT (and other provisions deemed desirable for proper trust administration), Spouse has a QDOT-IRT. The IRT should be fully revocable by Spouse to avoid gift tax issues (see ¶ 4.5.01).

4.4.04 Trustee of QDOT-IRT must be U.S. bank

As a practical matter, the trustee of a QDOT-IRT must be a U.S. bank or other financial institution, for the following reasons:

First, in order for the trust to qualify as an IRA, the trustee must be a bank or such "other person who demonstrates to the satisfaction" of the IRS that "such other person will administer" the IRA in the required manner. § 408(a)(2). The procedure for a non-bank to seek IRS approval to serve as trustee of IRAs involves a filing fee of several thousand dollars, as well as demonstrating institutional soundness and continuity to the IRS. It is generally undertaken only by a firm which has plans to serve as trustee for many customers. It is hard to see how an individual could demonstrate the required permanence. Therefore, even though an individual can serve as trustee of a QDOT, an individual will *not* be able to be trustee (or even co-trustee) of a QDOT-IRT.

Second, in order to qualify as a QDOT, there must be at least one U.S. trustee. § 2056A(a)(1)(A). This leads to the conclusion that the trustee of a QDOT-IRT must be a U.S. bank.

4.5 Approach # 3:
Spouse Assigns IRA To A QDOT

4.5.01 Assignment of inherited IRA to a QDOT

Another approach is for Spouse to assign ownership of an inherited IRA to a revocable QDOT she creates. The QDOT would become the "owner" (account holder) of the IRA. If Spouse is treated as owner of all of the income and principal of the QDOT under the grantor trust rules (§ 676) then she should be able to elect to treat the

IRA as her own IRA despite the fact that it is owned by a trust (¶ 6.3.12). Using a *revocable* trust avoids gift tax problems; Spouse's transfer of assets into a QDOT would be subject to gift tax if it put the property irrevocably beyond her control. Even if the initial transfer to the trust is structured so as not to trigger gift tax, distributions to someone other than Spouse during her life would constitute completed gifts, resulting in a gift tax payable by her. Reg. § 20.2056A-4(d), Example 5. Therefore typically a QDOT created by Spouse would be for her own sole life benefit and fully revocable by her.

The regulations also eliminate another possible problem with this approach, namely, the possible difference between assigning *the IRA* to a QDOT and transferring *the property held in the IRA* to the QDOT. Generally, property inherited outright by Spouse must be transferred to a QDOT by a certain deadline to qualify for the modified marital deduction. ¶ 4.1.04. The regulations provide that the assignment of an IRA to a QDOT (provided various technical details are complied with) "is treated as a transfer of such property to the QDOT...." § 20.2056A-4(b)(7)(i).

Does this approach work? The following discussion argues that it does work; however, in view of the lack of precedent and clear authority, it would be advisable to get a ruling before using this approach.

<u>Can the QDOT trust be entirely a "grantor trust" as to Spouse despite the QDOT trustee's power and obligation to withhold the deferred estate tax from any distribution to Spouse?</u>

It does not seem that the QDOT trustee's power and obligation to withhold deferred estate tax from any non-hardship principal distributions to Spouse should cause the trust to be considered not fully "revocable" by Spouse (and thus ineligible for grantor trust status). By assigning inherited assets to the QDOT, Spouse was relieved of the obligation to pay the estate tax on those assets; in that sense the deferred estate tax is her obligation and its payment by the QDOT trustee is a payment "to" her, which supports the argument that this is a grantor trust. See discussion in Blattmachr, J., et al. *Income Taxation of Estates and Trusts*, 14th ed. (PLI Press, New York, NY 2000), § 3.3.7 (last paragraph, p. 3-32).

Does the assignment of the IRA to a QDOT violate the IRA rules, causing the IRA to lose its status as such?

The Code does not prohibit the assignment of an IRA; see § 408. The Code provides that *certain* assignments (to wit, pledging the IRA as security for a loan) will cause the IRA to lose its status as such (§ 408(e)(4)); this Code provision creating a negative tax effect for one specific type of assignment suggests that other types of assignments do not cause the IRA to lose its status as such. However, regardless of whether a living IRA owner might be able to make some other type of assignment of his IRA, an assignment by Spouse of an *inherited* IRA would trigger immediate realization of the income under a different Code section, § 691(a)(2), because the inherited IRA is a right to receive IRD (see ¶ 2.2.05)...unless, possibly, if the assignment is to a "grantor trust."

If the assignment is to a trust all of which is treated as owned by Spouse under § 676 (because she is a U.S. resident and has the unlimited right to revoke the trust), then the transfer should not be a taxable assignment under the IRS's doctrine that Spouse and her grantor trust are one taxpayer, not two separate taxpayers. Rev. Rul. 85-13, 1985-13, 1985-1 C.B. 184.

The IRS's pronouncements on this subject have been vague. In the Preamble to the QDOT regulations, § E, the IRS said: "In general, individual retirement accounts under section 408(a) are assignable.... However, if an [IRA] is assigned to a trust with respect to which [Spouse] is *not* treated as the owner under section 671 *et seq.* ...then the entire account balance is treated as a distribution... includible in [Spouse's] gross income" in the year of the assignment. (Emphasis added.) This implies that assignment of an IRA to a QDOT of which Spouse *is* treated as the owner (i) is possible and (ii) would *not* be treated as a distribution.

In the regulations, the IRS admits that IRAs "are assignable and subject to provisions of this paragraph (b)(7) [dealing with Spouse's assignment to a QDOT of assets she inherited outright]. *However,*" Spouse may elect to treat an inherited IRA as non-assignable (see ¶ 4.6.02). Reg. § 20.2056A-4(b)(7)(iii) (emphasis added). There is no hint in this statement why assignment to a QDOT would not be acceptable, but the "however" suggests that the IRS thinks the election to treat the IRA as non-assignable is preferable to the assignment approach.

4.5.02 *Assignment of rollover IRA to a QDOT*

The regulations mention the assignment approach only in connection with an IRA owned by Decedent of which Spouse is named beneficiary and which Spouse then assigns to a QDOT she has created, with no rollover involved. The regulations do not specifically bless a rollover of Decedent's benefits by Spouse to her *own* IRA, followed by assignment of the *rollover* IRA to a QDOT. This procedure would be of interest, for example, to a Spouse who inherits a benefit under a QRP. Typically the deferral options are better if Spouse rolls the QRP benefit over to an IRA than if she leaves the benefits in the QRP and takes them as beneficiary (see ¶ 3.2.01).

However, there should not be any difference in result. The modified marital deduction is available if Spouse assigns to the QDOT *either* the asset inherited from Decedent *or* the "proceeds from the sale, exchange or conversion" of such asset. Reg. § 20.2056A-4(b)(3). If Spouse receives a distribution from Decedent's QRP, and rolls that distribution over to her own IRA, the rollover IRA presumably constitutes "proceeds" from the "conversion" of the inherited asset and thus is suitable for assignment to a QDOT to exactly the same extent an inherited IRA would be (see ¶ 4.5.01). See PLR 1999-18039 (surviving non-citizen spouse contributed inherited real estate to a wholly-owned corporation, then contributed 94.9% of the stock to the QDOT; stock ruled to be "proceeds" of the inherited property, marital deduction allowed for the 94.9% interest transferred to QDOT).

The IRS has, in connection with other provisions, allowed Spouse to use, for a rollover IRA, provisions that the regulations specifically authorize only for an inherited IRA; see ¶ 4.6.02.

4.5.03 *Advantages, drafting issues*

The "IRA assigned to a QDOT" has one advantage over the "combination QDOT-IRT" (¶ 4.4) arising out of the fact that principal distributions from the IRA at some point during Spouse's life are unavoidable under the minimum distribution rules (Chapter 1) if she lives long enough. With an "IRA assigned to a QDOT," the inevitable principal distributions come out of the IRA but stay in the QDOT, and accordingly the deferred estate tax can continue to be deferred. In contrast, principal distributions from a QDOT-IRT to Spouse individually will trigger deferred estate tax. ¶ 4.4.02.

In order to preserve the option of income tax deferral as long as possible, the QDOT presumably must comply with the minimum distribution "trust rules" (¶ 6.2) after Spouse's death.

4.6 Approach # 4: Non-Assignable Annuities; IRAs Treated as Same

4.6.01 *Two alternatives for non-assignable assets*

The Code directs the IRS, by regulations, to permit the surviving non-citizen spouse to obtain QDOT treatment for assets, such as a life annuity, which Spouse cannot legally transfer to a QDOT before the estate tax return is filed. § 2056A(e). The regulations provide a method of obtaining QDOT-type marital deduction treatment for such annuities, as well as for any "plan, annuity or other arrangement" that cannot be transferred to a QDOT (whether because of applicable federal, foreign or state law, or because of the terms of the "plan or arrangement"). Reg. § 20.2056A-4(c)(1).

All qualified retirement plan ("QRP") benefits are considered "non-assignable" because QRP benefits cannot be assigned as a matter of federal law. § 401(a)(13); Reg. § 20.2056A-4(c)(1). A QRP benefit, therefore, is automatically a non-assignable annuity for purposes of § 2056A, even if Spouse has the option to take all the money out immediately.

For these and other "non-assignable" assets, Spouse is given a choice of two methods in lieu of immediately transferring the asset to a QDOT:

A.   Spouse can agree to pay, each year, the deferred estate tax on all non-hardship corpus distributions Spouse receives from the arrangement in that year. This right is granted in Reg. § 20.2056A-4(c)(2) and accordingly such an agreement is referred to in this Chapter as a "(c)(2) agreement."

B.   Alternatively, Spouse can agree that she will transfer to a QDOT all non-hardship corpus distributions she receives from the arrangement, as she receives them. This type of agreement is described in Reg. § 20.2056A-4(c)(3) and is referred to in this Chapter as a "(c)(3) agreement."

The advantage of the (c)(3) agreement compared with a (c)(2) agreement is that, under a (c)(3) agreement, Spouse can continue to defer estate taxes until her death (or other triggering event; ¶ 4.1.01), whereas under a (c)(2) agreement deferred estate taxes must be paid whenever principal is received. So why would anyone ever use a (c)(2) agreement? Its only advantage appears to be that it does not require drafting a QDOT. Perhaps the (c)(2) agreement would appear attractive if there is no QDOT already in existence created to receive other assets and either: Spouse expects to become a U.S. citizen in the near future and eliminate the deferred estate tax that way (¶ 4.1.02); or the asset in question is of small value. In most other cases, presumably, the (c)(3) agreement would be preferable.

In PLR 1999-04023, the spouse used some of each method in connection with a joint and survivor annuity inherited from Decedent's pension plan: she paid the deferred estate tax on the corpus portion of annuity distributions she received prior to the completion of reformation proceedings designed to bring Decedent's QDOT into conformity with final regulations and agreed under (c)(3) to pay over to the QDOT any such payments she received after reformation was complete.

Upon Spouse's death, the remaining value of the non-assignable asset is subject to the deferred estate tax. Reg. § 20.2056A-5(b)(2). With respect to assets that are assigned to a QDOT, the *QDOT trustee* is responsible for paying this tax. With a non-assignable asset, *Spouse's estate* is required to report the death and pay the tax if (as can happen under a (c)(2) agreement) there is no QDOT in existence, or if (under either form of agreement) the remaining value of the asset passes at Spouse's death to beneficiaries other than the QDOT. If Spouse's estate has no assets the enforcement mechanism is not clear. Reg. § 25.2056A-4(c)(7).

4.6.02 *Election to treat IRA as non-assignable*

The (c)(2) and (c)(3) agreement scheme applies not only to a truly non-assignable benefit payable to Spouse, that she does not (or cannot) take out of the plan and roll over to an IRA; it also applies to an IRA established by Decedent and inherited by Spouse that Spouse elects to treat as a non-assignable benefit. Reg. § 20.2056A-4(c)(1).

Is the option to treat an IRA as non-assignable available for a *rollover* (as opposed to an inherited) IRA? The regulations say that

"The Commissioner will prescribe by administrative guidance the extent, if any, to which" the election may be made for plan or IRA benefits that were distributed to Spouse and rolled over by her after Decedent's death. § 20.2056A-4(c)(1). The Commissioner has issued no such guidance, so there is no statutory or regulatory authority for a Spouse's electing to treat a rollover IRA as non-assignable.

The fact that there is no authority for such treatment, however, has not stopped the IRS from allowing surviving spouses, in at least two instances, to make the election and enter into a (c)(2) agreement regarding a rollover IRA. See PLRs 9729040 (two QRPs rolled to IRA; (c)(2) agreement allowed) and 9713018 (rollover of 403(b) annuity to IRA; (c)(2) agreement allowed).

The (c)(2)- or (c)(3)-agreement approach puts substantial responsibility on Spouse. She must make sure that her withdrawals do not exceed the "income" of the account (or, to the extent withdrawals do exceed income, i.e., to the extent such withdrawals constitute non-hardship distributions of "corpus"; ¶ 4.6.03) she must carry out the terms of her agreement with the IRS. With the other approaches (¶¶ 4.3-¶ 4.5), there is a third party (the QDOT trustee) interposed between Spouse and the IRA who can monitor compliance with these points, but with an IRA Spouse has elected to treat as non-assignable she is on her own. The spouse's ability to understand and comply with these requirements should be considered when adopting this approach.

4.6.03 *How much of each distribution is "principal?"*

Under either a (c)(2) or (c)(3) agreement (¶ 4.6.01), Spouse is agreeing that she will do something whenever she receives a "corpus" (principal) distribution from the non-assignable annuity. The regulations require use of the following formula to determine how much of each distribution from an annuity is "corpus":

Corpus portion = PV/T

Under the formula, "PV" is the "total present value of the annuity," i.e., "the present value of the nonassignable annuity ... as of the date of [Decedent's] death, determined in accordance with interest rates and mortality data prescribed by section 7520." This should be same as the date of death value of Spouse's interest in the annuity as reported on Decedent's estate tax return, since the same method is used to value the annuity for estate tax purposes.

This "Present Value" is divided by the "expected annuity term" (T) to arrive at the "corpus amount" of the annual payment. The "expected annuity term" is "the number of years that would be required for the scheduled payments to exhaust a hypothetical fund equal to the present value of the scheduled payments." To determine *this* figure, you need IRS Publication 1457 (7-1999), "Book Aleph," (Actuarial Values for Remainder, etc., interests) which can be obtained from the Government Printing Office, and the § 7520 rate used to value the annuity as of the date of death. The IRS publishes the § 7520 rate monthly; it can be found at www.tigertables.com and CCH Standard Federal Tax Reporter (Index Volume), among other places. With Book Aleph and the § 7520 rate in hand, the steps are as follows: Divide PV by the amount of the annual payment under the annuity. Take the resulting quotient and match it up with an "annuity factor" from column 1 of Table B for the applicable § 7520 rate, in Book Aleph. If it falls between two factors, use the higher one (longer term). You now have "T." Reg. § 20.2056A-4(c)(4)(ii)(B).

Example 4 in Reg. § 20.2056A-4(d) illustrates the calculations. In the IRS's Example 4, a 60-year old surviving spouse is required to recover all of the corpus portion of a life annuity within 16 years after Decedent's death, even though her life expectancy is 24.2 years (according to IRS's Table V). Yet there is nothing in the regulation indicating that Spouse can *stop* paying taxes on (or sending to the QDOT) the annuity payments once the corpus has been fully recovered under the above formula. Accordingly, this approach would appear to be disadvantageous to Spouse.

4.6.04 *Determining "corpus" portion: individual account plan*

The wording of Reg. § 20.2056A-4(c)(4) suggests that the above formula is the *only* method that may be used to determine the corpus portion of plan distributions subject to a (c)(2) or a (c)(3) agreement. However, several letter rulings have confirmed that the formula applies only when benefits are in fact taken in the form of an annuity. For determining the corpus portion of distributions from an individual account plan (see Glossary) subject to a (c)(2) or (c)(3) agreement, the general (trust accounting) rules of Reg. § 20.2056A-5(c)(2) apply; see ¶ 4.7.05. See PLRs 9746049, 9729040 and 9713018.

4.7 QDOT Investment and Distribution Strategies

This section looks at various tax rules that have an effect on the administrative policies of a QDOT (including a QDOT-IRT), and the strategies suggested by these rules.

4.7.01 *Hardship exception to deferred estate tax*

An important exception to the general rule that principal distributions to Spouse from the QDOT are subject to the deferred estate tax is that distributions to Spouse on account of *hardship* are not subject to that tax. § 2056A(b)(3). "A distribution of principal is treated as made on account of hardship if the distribution is made to [Spouse] from the QDOT in response to an immediate and substantial financial need relating to [Spouse]'s health, maintenance, education, or support, or the health, maintenance, education, or support of any person that [Spouse] is legally obligated to support. A distribution is not treated as made on account of hardship if the amount distributed may be obtained from other sources that are reasonably available to [Spouse]; e.g., the sale by [Spouse] of personally owned, publicly traded stock or the cashing in of a certificate of deposit owned by [Spouse]. Assets such as closely held business interests, real estate and tangible personalty are not considered sources that are reasonably available to [Spouse]." Reg. § 20.2056A-5(c)(1).

This generous definition of hardship will make this exception a useful planning tool in many situations. The QDOT trustee should be on the lookout for possible hardship distribution opportunities. If Spouse keeps all her non-QDOT assets illiquid, more of her living expenses can be shifted to the QDOT principal. If she needs money for living expenses, she should think of the QDOT as a resource first.

4.7.02 *Investment disincentives of a QDOT: capital growth*

The deferred estate tax problem can grow worse over the duration of the QDOT through capital growth and capital gains which augment the "corpus" of the QDOT, thus increasing the amount that will eventually be subject to the deferred estate tax. The structure of the deferred estate tax encourages investing for income and discourages investing for "growth" or capital gain.

Of course, all assets held by Spouse at her death (including

QDOT income distributions she receives during life and does not spend) will be subject to estate tax if she is either a U.S. resident or a U.S. citizen at that time, so in many cases it will make no difference if the trust's investment gain is in the form of capital appreciation (subject to deferred estate tax) or income (subject to estate tax at Spouse's death if not spent by her). But if for any reason the estate tax rate on Spouse's estate will be significantly lower than the deferred estate tax rate applicable to the QDOT (*e.g.*, because Spouse ceases to be subject to U.S. estate tax), this factor becomes significant.

4.7.03 *How income can become principal*

Distributions of "income" from a QDOT are free of the deferred estate tax, whereas all (non-hardship) "principal" (or "corpus") distributions will be subject to that tax. Therefore "income" is very valuable. Unfortunately, as the following examples illustrate, it appears that the IRS wants to herd as many dollars as possible into the "principal" corral, where they can be branded with the deferred estate tax, and make it difficult for "income" dollars to escape tax-free onto the open range.

For example, whatever was in the retirement plan at Decedent's death *should* be considered the initial principal of the QDOT-IRT. However, the IRS may have refused to rule its agreement with this simple statement in PLR 9729040 (Ruling request 4, which was withdrawn; often, a taxpayer seeking a ruling will withdraw the request if the IRS indicates it will give a negative ruling). In another letter ruling, the initial principal of the QDOT was defined as *the amount rolled over to it*, with no stated exception for post-death income that had accumulated in the retirement plan. PLR 9623063. Although possibly there *was* no post-death accumulated income (and maybe that's why the ruling doesn't discuss this subject), it's also possible that this ruling means that any accumulated income rolled to a QDOT must be added to principal for deferred estate tax purposes.

Second example: Reg. § 20.2056A-5(c)(2) states that "income does not include capital gains." This rule seems unfair: If *income* is reinvested, and the reinvestment produces capital gain in the *income* account, that should be considered income for purposes of § 2056A, even if it is taxable as capital gain.

Third example: In PLR 9729040, the surviving non-citizen spouse did not intend to take distributions from a rollover IRA until she reached age 59½. The (c)(3) agreement she signed with the IRS stipulated that "any income accumulated in the IRAs prior to" Spouse's reaching that age would be considered principal. Since it is hard to imagine that she would have suggested this stipulation, one wonders if the IRS gave her the following choice: take your "income" distributions now and avoid deferred estate tax on them (but pay income taxes now, plus 10% penalty) (see Chapter 9); or defer income tax, and avoid the 10% penalty (but agree that the accumulated income becomes "principal" for purposes of the deferred estate tax). This could be called the "get tough on young widows" policy. However, we don't need to feel too sorry for this Spouse, since she can presumably avoid both the 10% penalty and the deferred estate tax by not allowing the income to "accumulate inside the IRA." Instead, she could distribute the income to herself and roll those income distributions over tax-free *again*, to an IRA to which the (c)(3) agreement did not apply. See ¶ 4.7.04, ¶ 3.3.07.

Fourth example: On Spouse's death, the deferred estate tax can no longer be deferred. The deferred estate tax is imposed on "the value of the property remaining in a qualified domestic trust on the date of the death of the surviving spouse." § 2056(A)(b). It is not clear from this phrase that *undistributed income* held in the QDOT would be excluded from the tax base. The *proposed* QDOT regulations issued in 1992, § 20.2056A-5, specified that "the amount subject to tax is the value of the trust *corpus* on the date of Spouse's death" (emphasis added). The final regulations issued in August 1995 deleted this statement, retaining the ambiguity of the statute.

These examples suggest that the IRS intends to treat accumulated income as principal to the maximum extent possible for purposes of imposing the deferred estate tax. Therefore, the QDOT should distribute all income annually to Spouse, so the IRS cannot impose deferred estate tax on it.

4.7.04 *Rollover strategy for excess income distributions*

If the income distributed to Spouse in any particular year from a QDOT-IRT, or from an inherited or rollover IRA assigned to a QDOT, or from a rollover or inherited IRA that Spouse has elected to treat as non-assignable, is greater than the amount that would be required to be distributed to her under the minimum distribution rules (see Chapter 1), Spouse could establish a separate IRA (not a QDOT-IRT, and not an IRA held by a QDOT, and not an IRA subject to a (c)(2) or (c)(3) agreement) into which she rolls either the entire income distribution or the part of it that exceeds the MRD. See ¶ 3.3.07. This strategy would permit continued income tax deferral for the rolled amount while removing it from the reach of the deferred estate tax.

4.7.05 *What is income?*

The discussion at ¶ 4.7.03 shows how certain traditional items of "income" (capital gains in the income account; accumulated income) may be treated by the IRS as "principal" (and therefore subject to the deferred estate tax). Presumably the QDOT trustee will foil that IRS policy by promptly distributing all income to Spouse. Which leads to the question of how the trustee (and the IRS) determine whether an item (or distribution) is allocated to "income" earned after Decedent's death (not subject to the deferred estate tax), or "principal" (taxable)?

The regulations' pronouncements on this subject are all contained in Reg. § 20.2056A-5(c)(2). "Income" of the QDOT will mean income as it is defined in § 643(b), except that "income does not include capital gains....[or] any other item that would be allocated to corpus under applicable local law governing the administration of trusts irrespective of any specific trust provision to the contrary." Typically such "other items" allocated to corpus under local law would include the property originally contributed to the trust.

§ 643(b) defines "income" as "the amount of income of the estate or trust for the taxable year determined under the terms of the governing instrument and applicable local law." If local law has nothing to say on the subject, "the allocation...will be governed by general principles of law (including but not limited to any uniform state acts, such as the Uniform Principal and Income Act, or any Restatements of applicable law)."

Hopefully, "irrespective of any specific trust provision" means that the governing instrument's allocation will be respected, provided its method of determining principal and income is permitted under local law and provided it does not violate any specific QDOT rule. Or does it mean that income will be determined under local law, *without regard* to the specific provisions of the trust?

Regardless of what local law or the trust says, "income does not include items constituting" IRD unless otherwise provided in future administrative guidance. Reg. § 20.2056A-5(c)(2). Thus, a trust provision defining all retirement plan distributions as "income" will not change the character of such distributions (from taxable corpus to non-taxable income) for purposes of the deferred estate tax (because such distributions generally constitute "IRD"; see ¶ 2.2). Retirement plan distributions to a QDOT could bring to a head the never-resolved issue of which distributions from a retirement plan constitute IRD (i.e., funds that were in the plan as of the date of Decedent's death) and which distributions come from the plan's earnings and growth that occurred after the date of death; see ¶ 2.2.10.

The allocation of annuity payments between corpus and income by the method prescribed in the regulations (¶ 4.6.03) will be respected.

4.8 Summary of Planning Principles

As the discussion in this Chapter indicates, there is no problem-free way to dispose of retirement benefits when Spouse is not a U.S. citizen.

4.8.01 *Benefits that can be rolled over*

1.   If Spouse inherits QRP benefits outright, and wants to get both the income tax benefits of the spousal rollover (¶ 3.2.01) *and* the estate tax benefits of the modified marital deduction: either Spouse rolls over Decedent's benefits to a combination QDOT-IRT (¶ 4.4), or Spouse rolls over the benefits to a non-QDOT IRA that Spouse then "assigns" to a grantor-trust-type QDOT she establishes (¶ 4.5). A third choice (for which a ruling should be obtained, since "administrative guidance" is yet to be issued on this choice) is to roll over the benefits to a (non-QDOT) IRA, elect to treat the rollover IRA as non-assignable, and then sign an agreement with the IRS, agreeing either that Spouse will pay the deferred estate tax on the corpus portion of each payment as received or that Spouse will assign such corpus portion to a QDOT (¶ 4.6).

2.   If the inherited benefit is already in an IRA, things are a little easier: Spouse has all the same choices as for inherited QRP benefits, but does not need a ruling to treat the inherited IRA as non-assignable.

3.   In the planning stage, while Participant is still alive, the choice is even more complicated. The marital trust-QDOT (¶ 4.3) will

appeal to the client who wants to control the ultimate disposition of the asset, or who simply wants his estate plan to be self-executing, without requiring Spouse to undertake additional steps after his death. However, making benefits payable directly to a QDOT probably eliminates the income tax benefits of a spousal rollover (but see ¶ 4.3.02). Making benefits payable outright to Spouse will appeal to the client who has no objection to giving Spouse control, desires maximum income tax deferral and is willing to adopt a plan which requires post-death action by Spouse in order to succeed.

4.   The client may be attracted to the income tax deferral possibilities of the rollover, but reluctant to leave qualifying for the marital deduction entirely up to *post mortem* action. What this client might want, ideally, would be a plan that has all the elements in place to automatically qualify for the modified marital deduction, without foreclosing the option of the spousal rollover. One way to achieve this result (for an IRA) would be for Decedent's IRA to be in the form of an IRT which will become a QDOT-IRT on his death (this is a variation of Approach # 2, not discussed in this book). Another possibility is to leave the benefits to a marital trust-QDOT (Approach # 1), but name Spouse as contingent beneficiary, so the trust can disclaim (see Chapter 8) the benefits and they will pass to Spouse who can roll them over, on the assumption that the trust would disclaim unless Spouse was disabled or for some other reason not able to carry out the rollover.

4.8.02 *Benefits that cannot be rolled over*

5.   If the benefits are non-assignable, and Spouse cannot roll them over, Spouse can agree to deposit the benefits into a QDOT as they are paid to her ("(c)(3) agreement"). Because this approach allows the longest deferral of the deferred estate tax it appears preferable to agreeing to pay the deferred estate tax on non-assignable benefits as they are received ("(c)(2) agreement"). However, agreeing to pay the deferred estate tax may be attractive for retirement benefits subject to income tax because the income tax can be deducted from the amount that will be subject to the deferred estate tax.

4.8.03 *Other comments*

6.   If using the marital trust-QDOT option (¶ 4.3), consider giving Spouse the unlimited right to withdraw principal, if that will cause distributions of IRD from the retirement plan to the trust to be taxed at Spouse's income tax rate and if Spouse's income tax rate will be lower than the trust's income tax rate. Unless there has been further guidance from the IRS, however, it might be advisable to get a ruling confirming that Spouse (assuming she is a U.S. resident) will be personally taxable on plan distributions to the trust because of her unlimited right to withdraw from the trust (despite the trustee's obligation to withhold from her withdrawals), and that principal distributions to Spouse to reimburse her for income taxes imposed *on her* by virtue of § 678 on the distributions from the plan to the trust can be made free of the deferred estate tax before taking this route. Once the client has chosen to make the benefits payable either to Spouse or to a marital trust, consider making them "disclaimable" to the other (trust or Spouse) in case that option appears more attractive when death occurs (see Chapter 8).

7.   While the client is living, he should consider converting IRAs to Roth IRAs, if he is eligible to do so, to avoid many of these problems; see Chapter 5.

8.   In administering any QDOT, the trustee should take advantage of the hardship distribution exception whenever possible (to distribute principal to Spouse free of the deferred estate tax); and should consider investing so as to minimize growth of the original "principal," while maximizing "income." All income (whether earned inside or outside a retirement plan) should be distributed to the Spouse as soon as is practicable to avoid the risk that the IRS will say it has become "principal." If this income distribution includes retirement plan distributions in excess of the MRD, it may be that the excess can be rolled over by Spouse to her own non-QDOT-IRA.

5

Roth Retirement Plans

Roth retirement plans offer an intriguing opportunity for a limited number of people who are eligible, and can afford, to adopt them

5.1 Introduction to Roth Retirement Plans

5.1.01 *Roth retirement plans: background*

Prior to the debut of the Roth IRA in 1998, all retirement plans had the same basic tax structure: contributions to the plan might or might not be tax deductible; and all distributions from the plan (except to the extent attributable to after-tax contributions) would be includible in the recipient's gross income. Thus, income taxes on all of the plan's investment returns (and on some or all contributions to the plan) would be deferred until distributed from the plan (after retirement or after death, in most cases).

§ 408A established a new kind of IRA, called a "Roth IRA," effective in 1998. Reg. § 1.408A-9, A-1. The basic idea of the Roth IRA is that contributions are never deductible, but distributions are normally tax-free. Thus, the income tax on the plan's internal investment returns is not merely deferred, it is eliminated, at the cost of payment of income taxes up front on the plan contributions.

In 2001, EGTRRA added two more "Roth" retirement plans, the "deemed Roth IRA" (effective in 2003 and later years) (¶ 5.1.04) and the "Designated Roth Account" (beginning in 2006) (¶ 5.1.05).

5.1.02 *Overview of Roth IRAs*

All rules applicable to traditional IRAs also apply to Roth IRAs, except to the extent the Code specifically provides otherwise. § 408A(a); Reg. § 1.408A-1, A-1(b). Thus, if there is any question about Roth IRAs that is not specifically answered in § 408A or the Roth

IRA regulations, the answer should be the same as for a traditional IRA.

In addition to tax-free distributions, the Roth IRA offers other attractions: no required distributions during life (¶ 5.1.03); and no maximum age for making contributions (¶ 5.3.04).

There are two ways to create a Roth IRA. One is by non-deductible contributions on behalf of an individual who has compensation income; the IRS calls these "regular contributions." Reg. § 1.408A-3, A-1; see ¶ 5.3. The other is by rolling over a distribution from a traditional IRA (or by conversion of a traditional IRA to a Roth IRA) (¶ 5.4). The rollover (or conversion) of a traditional IRA to a Roth IRA causes the full amount of the rollover (minus any applicable basis) to be currently taxed. ¶ 5.4.09.

Each of the two methods has its own rules and eligibility requirements.

5.1.03 *How the minimum distribution rules apply to Roth IRAs*

The lifetime minimum distribution rules (¶ 1.4) do not apply to Roth IRAs. § 408A(c)(5) provides that § 401(a)(9)(A) (which contains the lifetime minimum distribution rules) and the "incidental death benefit" rule (¶ 8.3.04) do not apply to Roth IRAs. Therefore, a person who reaches age 70½ does not have to start taking distributions from his Roth IRA as he does from his traditional IRA. There is no "required beginning date" (RBD) (¶ 1.3) for a Roth IRA. This is one of the two major advantages of the Roth IRA (the other being tax-free distributions; ¶ 5.2.01). A traditional IRA will eventually be diminished by required distributions to Participant if he lives long enough; the Roth IRA can keep growing larger as long as Participant lives.

Once death occurs, the minimum distribution rules do apply to Roth IRAs. The Roth IRA is not exempted from any minimum distribution rules other than § 401(a)(9)(A) and the incidental death benefit rule, both of which apply only during Participant's life, so distributions must begin coming out of the Roth IRA after Participant's death. Since there is no RBD for a Roth IRA, the post-death minimum distribution rules will be applied "as though the Roth IRA owner died before his" RBD, regardless of when he dies (i.e., regardless of whether he dies before or after reaching age 70½). Reg. § 1.408A-6, A-14(b). For how to compute required distributions from a Roth IRA after Participant's death, see ¶ 1.5.02.

Distributions from a Roth IRA cannot be used to fulfill a

minimum distribution requirement arising from any other kind of IRA. Reg. § 1.408A-6, A-15.

5.1.04 *"Deemed" Roth IRAs (2003 and later)*

Under § 408(q), added by EGTRRA 2001, an employer that maintains a qualified retirement plan may (for plan years beginning after 2002) permit employees to make voluntary contributions to "a separate account or annuity established under the plan." The separate account must meet the requirements of § 408 (traditional IRA) or § 408A (Roth IRA). The separate account (the deemed traditional IRA or deemed Roth IRA) is then treated in all respects the same as a traditional IRA or Roth IRA, as the case may be, and is generally not subject to the qualified plan requirements.

Since a "deemed" Roth IRA is treated in all respects the same as a "real" Roth IRA, all the discussion in this Chapter about Roth IRAs applies equally to deemed Roth IRAs. See Rev. Proc. 2003-13.

The purpose of deemed traditional and Roth IRAs is, as with many of EGTRRA's provisions, to facilitate and encourage saving for retirement. The idea seems to be that the employee may find it convenient to make his annual IRA contribution right at the workplace. From the employer's perspective, adding yet another set of accounts to the company's retirement plan can only further complicate the already extremely complicated job of plan administration, especially since the deemed accounts are subject to an entirely different set of tax rules than the rest of the plan. Since employees who care about saving for retirement can easily contribute to traditional and/or Roth IRAs without employer involvement, it is hard to see what incentive an employer has to allow them to make deemed IRA contributions.

5.1.05 *Designated Roth Accounts (Roth 401(k)s) (2006 and later)*

The "designated Roth account" (also called the "Roth 401(k)") is another new type of retirement plan created by EGTRRA 2001. Under § 402A, effective for years after 2005, an employer can permit its employees to make "designated Roth contributions" to their "designated Roth accounts" under a 401(k) or 403(b) plan. § 402A(b). This option does not increase the amount that may be contributed to a 401(k) or 403(b) plan through salary reduction (elective deferral). Rather, if the employer allows these designated Roth contributions, the employee may choose to have part or all of his normal elective deferrals to a 401(k) or 403(b) plan channeled into a designated Roth account (DRAC) in the plan rather than into a regular account.

The employer must maintain separate records for the Roth and non-Roth accounts. § 402A(b)(2).

Unlike normal 401(k) or 403(b) elective deferrals, the DRAC contribution is not excluded from the employee's income. Later "qualified" distributions from the Roth account are tax-free. § 402A(a)(1), (d)(1). The Five-Year Period necessary to qualify for the tax-free distribution feature begins, in the case of a DRAC, with the first year the employee made a designated Roth contribution *to that particular plan.* § 402A(d)(2)(B). With a Roth IRA, in contrast, the Five-Year Period begins with the first year of contribution to *any* Roth IRA; ¶ 5.2.02.

The only contributions that can go into the DRAC are the employee's elective deferrals, such as are permitted under a 401(k) or 403(b) plan. § 402A(e). § 402A contains no provision: for matching or other contributions by *employers* to DRACs of their employees; or for conversion of any other types of contributions or plan accumulations to DRACs.

Although the basic tax structure of the DRAC is similar to that of a Roth IRA (pay tax when money goes into the plan, and no tax when money comes out), the DRAC is a hybrid of a qualified plan and a Roth IRA. Note the following differences between DRACs and Roth IRAs:

1.   Anyone who is otherwise eligible to make elective contributions to the 401(k) or 403(b) plan can have his elective contribution designated as a Roth contribution, if the employer permits that feature in its plan, regardless of how much adjusted gross income that person has. § 402A(a)(1). In contrast, an individual may contribute to a Roth IRA only if his income is below a specified level (¶ 5.3.03, ¶ 5.4.03).

2.   Since the DRAC will be part of a qualified plan (or part of a 403(b) arrangement, as the case may be), it will apparently be subject to the requirement of lifetime minimum required distributions (see Chapter 1). Roth IRAs have no required distributions prior to the death of the participant (¶ 5.1.03).

Ed Slott, CPA, publisher of *Ed Slott's IRA Advisor*, and Barry Picker, CPA, author of *Barry Picker's Guide to Retirement Distribution Planning,* point out that, unless EGTRRA's provisions are further amended by Congress, no-one will ever receive a "qualified distribution" from a DRAC, because (a) the earliest year a DRAC can be established, under EGTRRA, is 2006, meaning that (b) the earliest year in which a qualified distribution could be received is 2011, but (c) under EGTRRA's "sunset" provision (§ 901) DRACs and the rest of EGTRRA's provisions are repealed for years after 2010.

Distributions from a DRAC may be rolled over subject to the same rules generally applicable to rollovers of distributions from the applicable type of plan, except that DRAC distributions may be rolled only to another DRAC or to a Roth IRA. § 402A(c)(3)(A). § 402A(d)(2)(B) specifies that if DRAC money is rolled into another DRAC (in a different plan), the holding period for the transferee DRAC dates back to the date of establishment of the DRAC in the prior plan for purposes of calculating the Five-Year Period (¶ 5.2.02) necessary to have qualified distributions. However, § 402A says nothing about calculation of the Five-Year Period in case of a rollover from a DRAC to a Roth IRA, so this aspect will presumably require further clarification from Congress or the IRS.

Although the DRAC option does not increase the amount that employees can contribute to their 401(k) and 403(b) plans, it does offer employees something unique, namely the opportunity to have their salary deferral contributions placed in a Roth-type retirement plan (no deduction now, tax-free distributions later) instead of a regular-type retirement plan (plan contribution excluded from income now, taxable distributions from plan later). Employees whose income is too high to allow them to contribute to a Roth IRA (¶ 5.3.03; ¶ 5.4.03) cannot have a Roth retirement plan unless their employer offers DRACs. This makes DRACs different from deemed Roth IRAs, which add no new planning options, just (maybe, at best) greater convenience. Thus, presumably, employers will have an incentive to take on the additional burden of administering DRACs, as DRACs may be an attractive option for existing and potential employees.

The rest of this Chapter describes the rules and planning considerations applicable to Roth IRAs, emphasizing contrasts with traditional IRAs. Everything in this Chapter that applies to Roth IRAs applies equally to "deemed" Roth IRAs (¶ 5.1.04); however, the extent to which each rule will apply to "designated Roth accounts" remains to be seen. To make this Chapter easier to read, I have written simply about "Roth IRAs," rather than saying, every time, "Roth IRAs or deemed Roth IRAs."

5.1.06 *Roth IRA terminology*

In this Chapter: A **"traditional IRA"** refers to an individual retirement account or individual retirement trust established under § 408. A traditional IRA may contain deductible contributions, non-deductible contributions and/or rollovers from employer plans.

The term **"conversion"** of a traditional IRA to a Roth IRA includes a "rollover" from a traditional IRA to a Roth IRA. Conversion contributions and rollover contributions to Roth IRAs mean the same thing: a transfer, rollover or conversion of funds from a traditional IRA to a Roth IRA. See ¶ 5.4.

The **"Five-Year Period"** refers to the period of time after which distributions from a Roth IRA may be income tax-free. See ¶ 5.2.02.

The **"Ordering Rules"** dictate which contribution (or earnings) a particular Roth IRA distribution is deemed to come from; see ¶ 5.2.04.

"The **regulations**" refers to the IRS's final regulations on Roth IRAs issued February 3, 1999, effective generally for taxable years beginning after December 31, 1997 (except that to the extent they replaced IRS Notice 98-50 (1998 C.B. 569) they were effective January 1, 2000). For more Roth IRA terms see ¶ 5.2.01 and ¶ 5.4.01.

5.1.07 *State law problems: creditors, taxes*

Many states' laws exempt IRAs from creditors' claims, but in many of these states the exemption refers to a specific Code section, namely § 408—which describes only traditional IRAs. Roth IRAs would presumably not be protected in such states without a legislative change. In states whose tax laws do not automatically follow federal Code changes, Roth IRAs may not receive favorable tax treatment without a legislative change. See also ¶ 5.4.09.

5.1.08 *Basis in property distributed from a Roth IRA*

The basis of property distributed from a Roth IRA is its fair market value on the date of the distribution. Reg. § 1.408A-6, A-16.

5.1.09 *Excess contributions: 6% penalty*

There is an excise tax of 6% imposed on contributions to Roth IRAs in excess of the applicable limits, just as there is for excess contributions to traditional IRAs. § 4973; Reg. § 1.408A-3, A-7. This excise tax would apply, for example, to a person who converted a traditional IRA to a Roth IRA but was not eligible to do so—for example, because he had more than $100,000 of income (see ¶ 5.4.03). This excise is imposed *annually* on the excess contribution. § 4973(a).

The "failed" conversion would be treated as a (taxable) distribution from the traditional IRA (subject to the 10% penalty under § 72(t) if the individual is under 59½; see Chapter 9), followed by an excess contribution to the Roth IRA. To avoid the penalty, the person would have to recharacterize the contribution (¶ 5.7.02).

5.2 Tax Treatment of Roth IRA Distributions

Not all Roth IRA distributions are automatically tax-free; only "qualified distributions" from a Roth IRA are income tax-free. ¶ 5.2.01. It is relatively easy to qualify for "qualified" distributions, and even non-qualified distributions from Roth IRAs (¶ 5.2.03) get favorable treatment compared with distributions from traditional IRAs (see ¶ 5.4.09-¶ 5.4.12).

5.2.01 *Definition and tax treatment of qualified distributions*

"Qualified distributions" from a Roth IRA are not included in the recipient's gross income for federal income tax purposes, regardless of whether the recipient is the Participant or a beneficiary. § 408A(d)(1). A qualified distribution is one made after the Five-Year Period (¶ 5.2.02); and which *in addition* (§ 408A(d)(2)(A)):

1.   Is made on or after the date on which Participant attains age 59½; or

2.   Is made after Participant's death; or

3.   Is "attributable to" Participant's being totally disabled (as defined in § 72(m)(7)) (see ¶ 9.3.02); or

4.   Is a "qualified special purpose distribution." A qualified special purpose distribution is a distribution of up to $10,000 for certain purchases of a "first home" (see ¶ 9.3.09). § 408A(d)(5); § 72(t)(2)(F).

In general, these conditions for a qualified distribution from a Roth IRA resemble the requirements for avoiding the premature-distributions penalty of § 72(t) (Chapter 9), but are not identical. For example, withdrawals from a Roth IRA to pay "higher education expenses" are not qualified distributions, even though such withdrawals from a traditional IRA would be exempt from the 10% penalty. § 72(t)(2)(E).

5.2.02 *Computing Five-Year Period for qualified distributions*

The Five-Year Period (called in the statute the "nonexclusion period") for *all* of a Participant's Roth IRAs (with one exception applicable to certain surviving spouses; see ¶ 5.8.03) begins on January 1 of the first year for which a contribution was made to *any* Roth IRA maintained for that Participant. § 408A(d)(2)(B); Reg. § 1.408A-6, A-2.

Example: Fred puts $2,000 into his Roth IRA for 2001. He had never previously made any type of contribution to a Roth IRA and makes no further contributions in 2001. Fred's Five-Year Period starts January 1, 2001. The first year in which he can possibly have a qualified distribution is 2006. If he makes further contributions (either regular or rollover) to the same (or any other) Roth IRA in later years, those contributions do not start a new Five-Year Period running. This result appears to hold even if Fred cashes out the entire Roth IRA before the end of the Five-Year Period (otherwise than by means of a corrective distribution; ¶ 5.7.01).

However, if Fred *recharacterizes* his 2001 contribution (¶ 5.7.02), the Roth IRA is treated as if it never existed. Such an "unconversion" would extinguish the Five-Year Period, and he would have to start over in another year.

5.2.03 *Tax treatment of non-qualified distributions*

A non-qualified distribution is one made before the Five-Year Period is up; or which is made after expiration of the Five-Year Period but not for one of the four specified reasons (¶ 5.2.01). A non-qualified distribution is not *per se* excludible from gross income. However, even if a distribution is not "qualified" it receives favorable tax treatment compared with distributions from a traditional IRA.

A Roth IRA contains two types of money. First, it contains Participant's own regular contributions and/or conversion contributions; since these amounts were *already* included in Participant's gross income, these originally-contributed funds will not be included in his income *again* when they are later distributed. Thus, the amount of Participant's original contribution(s) to the Roth IRA (plus any after-tax contributions contained in a traditional IRA that was converted to a Roth IRA) constitutes Participant's basis (or "investment in the contract") in the Roth IRA. ¶ 2.1.04. If the account has grown to be worth more than this basis, the rest of the account value (which represents the earnings and growth that have occurred since the original contribution) has not yet been taxed (and may *never* be taxed if it is distributed in the form of a qualified distribution).

All distributions from a Roth IRA are deemed to come *first* out of Participant's contributions. § 408A(d)(4)(B); ¶ 5.2.04. Thus, if Participant needs to get money out of the Roth IRA, but the account has not been established long enough to generate qualified distributions, he can still take out money income tax-free, up to the amount he originally contributed.

In contrast to this favorable treatment afforded to Roth IRAs, all distributions from a *traditional* IRA are deemed to come *proportionately* from the "basis" (non-taxable) portion and the post-contribution earnings of all of Participant's aggregated IRAs. § 408(d)(1), (2); § 72(e)(2)(B), (5)(A), (5)(D)(iii), and (8). Thus, Participant's basis in a traditional IRA is recovered only gradually, as he makes withdrawals, and some part of every distribution is taxable. See ¶ 5.4.10 and ¶ 5.4.12.

See ¶ 5.4.09 and ¶ 5.6.03 for situations in which the distribution of Participant's own contributions may nevertheless accelerate taxation or result in a penalty.

5.2.04 *The Ordering Rules*

Any distribution from a Roth IRA (*except* a corrective distribution of an excess contribution; Reg. § 1.408A-6, A-9(e); ¶ 5.7.01) is deemed to come from the following sources, in the order indicated. § 408A(d)(4)(B); Reg. § 1.408A-6, A-9. These rules are referred to in this chapter as the "Ordering Rules."

1.   Any distribution is deemed to come, first, from Participant's *contributions* to his Roth IRA(s) (to the extent that all previous distributions from his Roth IRA(s) have not yet exceeded the contributions); and

2.   If Participant has made both "regular" (¶ 5.3) and "rollover" (conversion) (¶ 5.4) contributions, the distributions are deemed to come, first, from the regular contributions (with no rule specifying in what order contributions made in different years are deemed distributed), then from rollover contributions, on a first-in, first-out, basis; and

3.   Once it is thus determined (under the preceding paragraphs) that the distribution is deemed to come from a particular rollover contribution, the dollars that were includible in gross income by virtue of that rollover (¶ 5.4.09) are deemed distributed first, and non-taxable dollars last; and

4.   Finally, once all contributions have been distributed out, the balance of the distribution comes out of post-contribution earnings. Whew!

Fortunately, for most people, the Ordering Rules matter only for purposes of determining whether a non-qualified distribution is taxable; the Ordering Rules essentially mean that the distribution is NOT taxable until all contributions have been distributed out. See example at ¶ 5.8.01.

The only other time the Ordering Rules will have to be consulted is when someone (A) converts a traditional IRA to a Roth IRA before reaching age 59½, and then takes a distribution from the Roth IRA (B) before reaching age 59½ and (C) within the five taxable years beginning with the year of the conversion. The Ordering Rules will apply in determining whether the 10% penalty applies to the distribution. See ¶ 5.6.03.

5.2.05 *Aggregation of Roth IRAs for income tax purposes*

§ 408A(d)(4)(A) provides that § "408(d)(2) shall be applied separately with respect to Roth IRAs and other individual retirement plans." This means that the taxation of distributions from *traditional* IRAs will be computed without regard to the existence of, or distributions from, *Roth* IRAs in the same year; and that all of Participant's Roth IRAs are treated as one single account for purposes of applying the Ordering Rules. § 408A(d)(4)(A).

5.3 "Regular Contributions" to a Roth IRA

One way to fund a Roth IRA is by making what the IRS calls "regular" (as opposed to "rollover"; ¶ 5.4) contributions. This ¶ 5.3 discusses the requirements for making a regular contribution to a Roth IRA, as contrasted with the rules governing regular contributions to a traditional IRA. See ¶ 5.7.04 for discussion of how to change your mind about which type of IRA you want to contribute to after you've already contributed.

5.3.01 *Definition of compensation*

Whether an individual is entitled to make a regular IRA contribution, and if so to *which type* of IRA (traditional or Roth), depends on various eligibility factors, the first of which is the necessity of having "compensation" income for the year in question.

"Compensation income" is partly defined in § 219(f)(1): it includes self-employment income (§ 401(c)(2)), and does *not* include pension, annuity or deferred compensation payments. It includes taxable alimony and separate maintenance payments (§ 71). It includes "wages, commissions, professional fees, tips, and other amounts received for personal services." Reg. § 1.408A-3, A-4. See Rev. Proc. 91-18, 1991-1 C.B. 522, for further detail on the definition.

Compensation income does not include gifts. If a parent decides to pay his toddler a salary for performing household chores, the IRS might maintain that the child has received a gift, not compensation, and that Roth IRA contributions based on this "compensation" are excess contributions subject to the 6% excise tax (§ 4973).

5.3.02 *How much may be contributed annually*

The maximum annual regular *Roth* IRA contribution derives from the maximum annual regular *traditional* IRA contribution.

The maximum amount that may be contributed to all of a person's traditional IRAs for a particular year is the lesser of the applicable dollar limit or the individual's compensation income (¶ 5.3.01) for the year. The maximum regular contribution for a particular year to all of a person's *Roth* IRAs is the exact same amount—minus the amount of regular contributions made to any traditional IRA(s) for that person for that year. § 408A(c)(2).

So, an individual who has compensation income (and who meets the other eligibility requirements; see ¶ 5.3.03, ¶ 5.3.04 for Roth IRAs, § 219 for traditional IRAs) may contribute to either a traditional IRA or a Roth IRA (whichever one or both he or she is eligible to contribute to), provided that the total contributed to both types of accounts for the year does not exceed the applicable dollar amount (or the individual's total compensation income for the year, if less).

Contributions to a "simplified employee pension" individual retirement account (SEP-IRA) (§ 408(k)) or a "simple retirement account" (SIMPLE IRA) (§ 408(p)) are *not* treated as "IRA contributions" for this purpose, so the maximum regular contribution by a person who is otherwise eligible to make a contribution to a Roth IRA in a particular year is not reduced by the amount of a contribution made for him to a SEP-IRA or SIMPLE IRA. § 408A(f).

The applicable dollar limit was $2,000 for the years 1998 through 2001. § 219(b)(1)(A), as in effect through 2001. § 219(b)(5), added by EGTRRA 2001, increases the applicable dollar limit for 2002 and later years to:

Year	Basic Applicable Dollar Limit	Add-on for Participant over 50
2002-2004	$3,000	$ 500
2005	$4,000	$ 500
2006-2007	$4,000	$1,000
2008-2010	$5,000	$1,000

The $500 or $1,000 add-on to the applicable dollar limit is

available to a Participant who has attained age 50 by the end of the taxable year. § 219(b)(5)(B). After 2008, § 219(b)(5)(C) applies a COLA to the applicable dollar limit (but not to the over-50 add-on amount) in $500 increments. § 219(b)(5)(C). The sunset provision (§ 901(a)(2)) of EGTRRA would cause the dollar limit to revert to $2,000 for all individuals after 2010.

5.3.03 *Who may contribute to a Roth IRA: income limits*

Not just anyone who has compensation income may contribute to a Roth IRA. There is an income limit. A specially calculated version of "adjusted gross income" (see ¶ 5.4.04-¶ 5.4.08) cannot exceed the following levels. In order to be able to contribute the full dollar limit (e.g., $3,000 for 2003) to a Roth IRA, AGI may not exceed $95,000 for a single taxpayer, $150,000 for a married taxpayer filing a joint return, or zero for a married taxpayer filing a separate return.

(Note: these are the income limits applicable to "regular" Roth IRA contributions. A different income limit applies to Roth "conversion" contributions; see ¶ 5.4.03.)

The maximum dollar amount that may be contributed (e.g., in 2003, $3,500 for a person who had attained age 50 by the end of the year, or $3,000 for a younger person) is reduced if AGI exceeds these levels. The dollar contribution limit goes to zero at AGI of $110,000 (single), $160,000 (married filing jointly), or $10,000 (married filing separately). § 408A(c)(3)(A), (C)(ii). For this purpose, "a married individual who has lived apart from his or her spouse for the entire taxable year and who files separately is treated as not married." Reg. § 1.408A-3, A-3(b).

An individual who is prevented from making the maximum dollar contribution to a Roth IRA because of these income limits can contribute his reduced maximum to the Roth and the balance of the applicable dollar limit to a traditional IRA (assuming he otherwise meets the requirements for contributing to a traditional IRA). Reg. § 1.408A-3, A-3(d), Example 4.

5.3.04 *Who may contribute: age, participation in workplace plan*

There is no maximum age limit for contributing to a Roth IRA, as there is for contributions to a traditional IRA; a taxpayer can contribute to a Roth IRA even after age 70½. § 408A(c)(4); compare

§ 219(d)(1); § 408(o)(2)(B)(i).

Participation in an employer plan is *irrelevant* for purposes of determining whether (and how much) an individual may contribute to a Roth IRA. A person who meets the income test and other requirements (¶ 5.3.01-¶ 5.3.03) may contribute to a Roth IRA regardless of whether he is or is not participating in a "workplace" retirement plan in the same year.

5.3.05 *Deadline for contributions, and other rules*

As with traditional IRAs, only cash may be contributed. § 408A(a), § 408(a)(1). The trustee or custodian must be a bank (or other entity that has gone through the IRS approval procedure for serving in this capacity). § 408A(a); § 408(a)(2). The deadline for making a regular Roth IRA contribution for a particular year is the same as the deadline for traditional IRA contributions, i.e., the *unextended* due date of the tax return for that year (Reg. § 1.408A-3, A-2(b)), in other words, for most people, April 15 following the year in question. See ¶ 5.7.03-¶ 5.7.04 for more on Roth IRA deadlines.

5.4 Conversion of Traditional IRA to Roth IRA

See ¶ 5.6 for interaction of Roth conversions and the 10% penalty on pre-age-59½ distributions. See ¶ 5.7.03 regarding the deadline for completing a Roth IRA conversion.

5.4.01 *Rollover (conversion) contributions to a Roth IRA*

The second way to create a Roth IRA is to transfer funds to it from a traditional IRA. The amount so transferred is included in Participant's gross income ("treated as a distribution from" the traditional IRA) (¶ 5.4.09); thereafter the account will enjoy the favorable tax treatment afforded to Roth IRAs. § 408A(d)(3)(A), (B), (C). Since there is no limit on the amount that can be "converted" from a traditional IRA to a Roth IRA, a "conversion contribution" can be a much more substantial amount than the few thousand dollars per year maximum regular Roth IRA contribution (¶ 5.3.02).

Example: Manuel is 60 years old. He rolls over [or transfers, or converts—all these terms are used interchangeably] $300,000 from his traditional IRA to a Roth IRA in 2001. The entire $300,000 is included in his gross income for 2001. When he retires at age 65, in 2006, the Roth IRA has increased to $1.2 million. All subsequent distributions from the Roth IRA (whether made to Manuel or to his beneficiaries) will be income tax-free.

There are three ways to make this type of contribution to a Roth IRA:

1. A distribution from a traditional IRA may be rolled over to a Roth IRA. § 408(d)(3)(A)(i). See ¶ 2.5.03 for deadline for completing this rollover.

2. Money in a traditional IRA may be transferred in a plan-to-plan transfer directly from the trustee (or custodian) of the traditional IRA to the trustee (or custodian) of the Roth IRA.

3. All or part of a traditional IRA can simply be "redesignated" as a Roth IRA maintained by the same trustee or custodian. Reg. § 1.408A-4, A-1(b).

All three of these transactions are considered rollovers ("a distribution from the traditional IRA and a qualified rollover contribution to the Roth IRA"). Reg. § 1.408A-4, A-1(c). Prior to the arrival of Roth IRAs, "rollovers" were always tax-free, and most people still associate that word with tax-free transfers from one retirement plan to another (see ¶ 2.5). In contrast, the rollover of funds from a traditional IRA to a Roth IRA is taxable. The term "conversion" is often used (including in § 408A) for the rollover of funds from a traditional IRA to a Roth IRA, which is a taxable event, just as a handy way to distinguish that type of rollover from a "normal" rollover, which is non-taxable.

Both partial and total conversions are allowed. An individual may choose to convert all, part or none of his traditional IRA to a Roth IRA. There is no minimum or maximum dollar or percentage amount that must be converted.

Generally, there is no limit on the number of times an individual may convert traditional IRA funds to Roth IRA status. A person who converts part of his traditional IRA to a Roth IRA is free at any later time (in the same or a later year) to convert more of the same or another

IRA to a Roth IRA. The one exception applies to someone who did a Roth IRA conversion, then later "unconverted"; see ¶ 5.7.07.

The one-rollover-per-year limitation in § 408(d)(3)(B) (¶ 2.5.07) does not apply to a conversion to a Roth IRA, so such conversion may occur even if it is within 12 months of a tax-free rollover into a traditional IRA. Reg. § 1.408A-4, A-1(a).

5.4.02 *What type of plan may be converted to a Roth IRA*

An "individual retirement plan" may be converted to a Roth IRA. § 408A(d)(3) (B), (C); Reg. § 1.408A-4, A-5. "Individual retirement plans" include individual retirement accounts (IRAs) and individual retirement trusts (IRTs) under § 408(a), (h). However, an *inherited* traditional IRA may not be converted by the beneficiary to a Roth IRA. § 408(d)(3)(C).

A "simplified employee pension"-individual retirement account (SEP-IRA) (§ 408(k)) and a "simple retirement account" (SIMPLE IRA) (§ 408(p)) cannot be "redesignated" as Roth IRAs (§ 408A(f)). However, these types of IRAs can be rolled or converted into Roth IRAs, subject to one limit: a SIMPLE IRA distribution "is not eligible to be rolled over into" a Roth IRA "during the 2-year period...which begins on the date that the individual first participated in any SIMPLE IRA Plan maintained by the individual's employer...." Reg. § 1.408A-4, A-4(b). Once a SEP or SIMPLE IRA account has been converted to a Roth IRA, the account is not eligible to receive further contributions under the SEP or SIMPLE plan. Reg. § 1.408A-4, A-4(c).

There is no way to transfer funds directly from a qualified retirement plan or 403(b) plan to a Roth IRA, or to roll over a distribution from such a plan directly into a Roth IRA. § 408A(c)(6) says "No rollover contribution may be made to a Roth IRA unless it is a qualified rollover contribution"; and § 408A(e) defines a qualified rollover contribution as "a rollover contribution to a Roth IRA *from another such account, or from an individual retirement plan....*" (emphasis added). See also Reg. § 1.408A-4, A-5. However, a Participant in a qualified plan or 403(b) plan who receives a distribution eligible to be rolled to a traditional IRA can roll the distribution to a traditional IRA and then convert *that* to a Roth IRA.

Education IRAs cannot be converted to Roth IRAs. Reg. § 1.408A-6, A-18. Education IRAs are not covered in this book.

5.4.03 *Who may convert: income limit and filing status*

No conversion is permitted if "the taxpayer's adjusted gross income exceeds $100,000" for the taxable year. § 408A(c)(3)(B).

In the case of a *married couple filing jointly*, the $100,000 limit applies to the adjusted gross income (AGI) of the *couple*, not of each *spouse*. Reg. § 1.408A-4, A-2(b). Generally, no conversion is permitted if the taxpayer is *married filing a separate return* for the year. § 408A(c)(3)(B). However, if a "married individual has lived apart from his or her spouse for the entire taxable year, then such individual can treat himself or herself as not married for purposes of [the adjusted gross income test], file a separate return and be subject to the $100,000 limit on his or her separate modified AGI." Reg. § 1.408A-4, A-2(b).

The year you look at for applying this income limit is the year in which the distribution from the traditional IRA occurs (*i.e.*, the distribution that is rolled over to a Roth IRA), *not* the year that the contribution to the Roth IRA occurs. Reg. § 1.408A-4, A-2(a). Usually, the distribution from the traditional IRA and its recontribution to the Roth IRA occur simultaneously; this rule covers the case of a distribution from the traditional IRA that occurs in one taxable year, and is rolled over in the *next* taxable year, but still within 60 days of the distribution; see ¶ 2.5.03 for hardship extensions of the 60-day limit.

5.4.04 *Definition of AGI for both types of Roth IRA contributions*

For the years 1998 through 2004, the definition of "adjusted gross income" (AGI) is the same for purposes of determining a person's eligibility for both types of Roth IRA contributions (though the maximum permitted *amount* of AGI differs depending on which type of Roth IRA contribution you're talking about; compare ¶ 5.3.03 with ¶ 5.4.03). After 2004, there will be an additional adjustment required for purposes of the *conversion* eligibility test that does not apply for purposes of *regular* contribution eligibility; see ¶ 5.4.08.

"Adjusted gross income" is a defined term in the Code (§ 62); however, for purposes of determining Roth IRA eligibility you do not simply look at the "adjusted gross income" line on the person's Form 1040. Rather, the definition of AGI for purposes of the Roth IRA income limits starts with the modified definition of AGI used under § 219(g)(3) (income limits for making a deductible contribution to a traditional IRA when the individual is also a participant in an employer plan). The § 219(g)(3) definition of AGI includes the individual's taxable Social Security benefits (§ 86), and takes into account the disallowance of "passive activity losses" (§ 469) if applicable, then requires the following further adjustments:

1.   Certain income that is normally *excluded* from AGI is added back in, namely: income resulting from redemption of U.S. savings bonds to pay higher education expenses (§ 135); qualified adoption expenses paid by the individual's employer (§ 137); and foreign earned income and housing costs (§ 911).

2.   Certain deductions normally allowed for purposes of computing AGI are not allowed for this purpose, namely the deductions for: education loan interest expenses (§ 221); tuition expenses (§ 222); and IRA contributions (§ 219).

Once you have determined AGI as defined under § 219(g)(3), one further modification is required before you know what a person's "AGI" is for purposes of determining eligibility to contribute (or convert) to a Roth IRA; see ¶ 5.4.05. For years after 2004, an additional adjustment is made; see ¶ 5.4.08.

5.4.05 *Conversion income does not count for purposes of AGI test*

For purposes of the income limits applicable to both types of Roth IRA contributions, AGI does *not* include any amount that is included in gross income because of the conversion of a traditional IRA to a Roth IRA. § 408A(c)(3)(C)(i).

So, if, in the year being tested, Participant does a conversion to a Roth IRA, resulting in the inclusion of some or all of the conversion amount in his gross income; or if the year being tested is 1999, 2000 or 2001 and gross income includes some income on account of a 1998 conversion for which Participant used the four-year spread; the gross income resulting from the conversion (¶ 5.4.09) is disregarded SOLELY FOR PURPOSE OF DETERMINING WHETHER THE TAXPAYER'S AGI IS LOW ENOUGH TO MAKE HIM ELIGIBLE TO CONTRIBUTE TO A ROTH IRA.

This aspect of Roth IRA conversions has been the downfall of many taxpayers and tax preparers, because it requires that the taxpayer's AGI be determined twice. Determining AGI is no easy task because it involves many interrelated computations, such as how much of the individual's Social Security payments are taxable, and how much "passive activity loss" is deductible. Yet all these computations must be done twice: First, for purposes of determining the individual's eligibility to contribute to a Roth IRA, all gross income resulting from traditional IRA-to-Roth IRA conversions is ignored (and all adjustments dependent on AGI are determined in accordance with this reduced income figure). This fictional AGI has *no relevance* to the taxpayer's actual tax burden—it is a pro forma number used solely to determine eligibility to contribute to a Roth IRA. Reg. § 1.408A-4, A-9.

Then, for purposes of determining the individual's *actual* tax owed, income resulting from conversions to a Roth IRA *is* included in gross income; and all computations dependent on the taxpayer's "AGI"—such as taxability of Social Security benefits, deductibility of medical expenses, etc.—are redetermined based on this true AGI figure.

5.4.06 *Income limit: effect of minimum required distribution*

What happens if Participant will be age 70½ or older by the end of the taxable year, and withdrawing his minimum required distribution (MRD) for the year would put his income over the income limit?

Example: Jeanette is age 72. It is 2001 and she would like to convert her traditional IRA to a Roth IRA. Her AGI, before taking any IRA distributions, is $50,000, so based on this she meets the income limitation, but her MRD for 2001 from the traditional IRA is $75,000. If she has to take that much out of her IRA on a taxable basis she will be over the $100,000 income cap and cannot convert to a Roth IRA. Is there any way around this dilemma?

First question: Can the realization of deemed income that comes from converting to a Roth IRA count toward fulfilling her minimum distribution requirement for 2001? After all, the point of the minimum distribution rules is to make you pay some income tax on your retirement plan, and she will have paid tax on 100% of the traditional IRA value by converting it to a Roth. Unfortunately, there is no authority for the proposition that a Roth IRA conversion could be used, in place of an actual non-rolled-over cash distribution, to fulfill the minimum distribution requirement for the traditional IRA.

Second question: Since Jeanette is required to take an *actual* distribution in 2001, can she avoid the problem by first converting the traditional IRA to a Roth IRA, and THEN taking the distribution? The withdrawal from the brand new Roth IRA is non-taxable because it is deemed to be a return of her basis—it has already been included in her income by virtue of the conversion—and therefore the post-conversion distribution does not put her over the $100,000 income cap. Unfortunately, this maneuver is not possible either, because (1) MRDs may not be rolled over and (2) the first dollars distributed in any year are deemed to be part of the MRD for such year, until the MRD has been entirely distributed. ¶ 2.5.06. Also, a distribution from a Roth IRA does not count toward fulfilling the requirement of taking a MRD from a traditional IRA. Reg. § 1.408A-6, A-15.

Thus Jeanette must withdraw the MRD for the year from the traditional IRA, and not roll it over, before she can convert any of her *remaining* traditional IRA balance to a Roth IRA. Of course, once she withdraws the MRD of $75,000 her income will be over $100,000 and she cannot convert any part of the traditional IRA to a Roth IRA. Reg. § 1.408A-4, A-6(b). This result is not affected by the means through which the taxpayer effects the conversion, *i.e.*, whether by rollover or by trustee-to-trustee transfer, or by whether an amount greater than or equal to the year's MRD remains in the traditional IRA after the conversion.

If an amount is converted in violation of this principle, the amount is treated as a distribution to Participant, and (since it is not eligible for rollover) it would be treated as a regular contribution to the Roth IRA. Reg. § 1.408A-4, A-6(c). As such it will attract a 6% excess contribution penalty (imposed annually until the excess contribution is distributed) if it is in excess of the applicable limit on a regular Roth IRA contribution for that person for that year. Reg. § 1.408A-3, A-7.

5.4.07 *Trap for the unwary: conversions in the age 70½ year*

The rule that MRDs cannot be rolled over (¶ 2.5.06), and that the first dollars distributed in any year are deemed to come from the MRD until the MRD has been fully distributed, creates a trap for individuals in the year they turn age 70½:

Example: Jay, who is single, turns 70½ in 2001. His income (before taking any required distributions) is $80,000. He wants to convert his traditional IRA to a Roth IRA. His MRD from the traditional IRA for 2001 is $45,000, but he does not have to take that distribution until April 1, 2002 (¶ 1.3.01). Accordingly, he plans to defer that first distribution until January, 2002, so it will not count as part of his income for 2001 and therefore (he thinks) he is eligible to convert to a Roth IRA in 2001 because his income is under $100,000 (¶ 5.4.03). Unfortunately the no-conversion-until-after-taking-MRD rule applies to him just the same as it did to Jeanette in the preceding example. The $45,000 is a required distribution *for the year he turns 70½*, even though he is allowed to defer it until the next year. Therefore he cannot convert to a Roth IRA in 2001 until *after* he takes the $45,000 distribution (and once he takes the $45,000 distribution in 2001 he is ineligible to convert that year, because his income—$80,000 + $45,000—exceeds $100,000).

The moral of the story is: A person who wants to convert his IRA to a Roth IRA, and whose traditional IRA is large enough that minimum distributions could push him over the $100,000 limit, must act *before* the year he reaches age 70½.

Note that this rule does *not* preclude postponing MRDs for the age-70½-year from *other* (non-IRA) kinds of retirement plans until April 1 of the following year, as a way of keeping income low enough to allow conversion of a traditional IRA to a Roth IRA:

Example: Justin, who is single and retired, turns 70½ in 2001. His income (before taking any required distributions) is $30,000. He wants to convert his traditional IRA to a Roth IRA. His MRD from the traditional IRA for 2001 is $45,000. His 2001 MRD from his 401(k) plan is $40,000. Although he must take the traditional IRA MRD of $45,000 in 2001 prior to converting the traditional IRA to a Roth IRA, that will bring his 2001 AGI up to only $75,000—still under the $100,000 eligibility ceiling. A $40,000 distribution from the 401(k) plan, if taken in 2001, would put his income over $100,000, but he does not have to take the 401(k) distribution for the age-70½-year until April 1, 2002. Accordingly, he defers the first 401(k) plan MRD until January, 2002, so it does not count as part of his income for 2001 and therefore he is eligible to convert the traditional IRA to a Roth IRA in 2001 because his income is under $100,000.

5.4.08 *Effect of required IRA distributions: after 2004*

For years after 2004, solely for purposes of applying the $100,000 limit that determines eligibility to convert a traditional IRA to a Roth IRA, AGI will NOT include any amount that is included in AGI by reason of a required minimum distribution from an IRA (including an inherited IRA). § 408A(c)(3)(C)(i)(II).

Example: In 2005, Lucy's MRD from her traditional IRA is $130,000. Her other income is $60,000. She will still be required to take, and pay tax on, the $130,000 distribution, and she cannot roll *that* distribution over to a Roth IRA (because it is a required distribution; ¶ 2.5.06); but she will be able to convert the *rest* of her IRA to a Roth IRA in that year, because her AGI (not counting the MRD of $130,000 from the traditional IRA, or the income arising from the conversion; ¶ 5.4.05) is only $60,000, and thus under the $100,000 limit. Note that only the *required* distribution from the traditional IRA is ignored. Any amount Lucy withdraws from her traditional IRA in excess of the MRD *does* count as part of her AGI for purposes of determining her eligibility to convert to a Roth IRA.

Note also that only MRDs from IRAs (and from individual retirement annuities) are disregarded under § 408A(c)(3)(C)(i)(II); required distributions received from *other* types of retirement plans will still count for purposes of determining eligibility to convert a traditional IRA to a Roth IRA. This could be a good reason to roll money from a qualified plan or 403(b) plan into a traditional IRA—to increase the likelihood of qualifying for a Roth IRA conversion after 2004.

5.4.09 *Tax treatment of converting to a Roth IRA*

The rollover from a traditional IRA to a Roth IRA is treated as a distribution from the traditional IRA. § 408A(d)(3)(A), (B), (C). Thus, the rollover amount is included in Participant's gross income, to the extent an actual distribution of the same amount from his traditional IRA would have been taxable. ¶ 5.4.10-¶ 5.4.12 explain how to compute this amount. Note that the conversion may result in an increase in the taxpayer's required estimated tax payments for the year of the conversion (as well as in his safe harbor estimated tax levels for the following year).

For rollovers in 1998 ONLY, the inclusion in gross income could be spread equally over the four taxable years 1998, 1999, 2000 and 2001. For details on this election, and on the acceleration of taxation in case of actual distributions prior to 2001, see "1998 Conversions: The Four-Year Spread," in Chapter 5 of the 1999 edition of this book.

State income tax effects should not be overlooked in planning a Roth IRA conversion. For example, if the individual will have to pay state income tax as well as federal income tax on the conversion, and he is planning to move to a state with no income tax, he may do better to defer the conversion until after the move.

5.4.10 *Conversion of non-taxable amounts: years prior to 2002*

Since conversion of a traditional IRA to a Roth IRA is treated (for income tax purposes) as a distribution of the converted amount (¶ 5.4.09), the amount converted is includible in Participant's gross income except to the extent it can be excluded from income as a return of Participant's basis (¶ 2.1.04). To the extent the amount converted represents Participant's basis in the traditional IRA it is non-taxable.

Example: Whit's only IRA is a traditional IRA worth $70,000. He has made a total of $6,000 of non-deductible contributions to his traditional IRA over the years and has never taken a distribution from the account. If he converts the entire traditional IRA to a Roth IRA in 2001, he will have to include only $64,000 in gross income on account of the conversion ($70,000 total IRA value minus $6,000 basis).

Once you have determined what the person's basis is in his traditional IRAs (see ¶ 5.4.11), how do you determine how much of that basis can be offset against income resulting from a Roth IRA conversion, if the person converts some, but not all, of his traditional IRA funds to a Roth IRA?

The extent to which a traditional IRA distribution (or conversion) is treated as a non-taxable return of basis (*i.e.*, the return of Participant's non-deductible contributions) is determined under § 408(d). Reg. § 1.408A-4, A-7(a). Under § 408(d)(2), for years prior to 2002, for purposes of determining how much of a traditional IRA distribution rolled over to a Roth IRA is non-taxable, all (traditional) IRAs are treated as one traditional IRA, and all distributions in one taxable year are treated as one distribution. This rule trips up some taxpayers:

Example: Each year for six years Gibbs has contributed the maximum amount permitted to his traditional IRA at X Mutual Fund. His contributions (cumulative total of $12,000) were not deductible. The traditional IRA that holds these contributions is now worth $30,000. He also has a traditional IRA worth $205,000 at Y Mutual Fund. The rollover IRA contains no after-tax contributions; it contains a rollover from a QRP maintained by Gibbs's former employer plus some deductible $2,000-per-year contributions Gibbs made years ago. He has no other IRAs. In 2001, he is eligible to convert to a Roth IRA and decides to convert the smaller, $30,000, IRA. He thinks that he will be taxable on only $18,000 by virtue of this conversion, because that particular account contains his $12,000 of non-deducted contributions, so he should be taxable on only $30,000-$12,000, or $18,000. Unfortunately for Gibbs, because of § 408(d)(2), his $30,000 conversion is *deemed* to come proportionately from *both* of his IRAs (valued as of year-end 2001), even though it *actually* came from only one of them. Therefore, the amount of the Roth IRA conversion that is deemed to come from his non-deducted contributions is A/B x C, where:

A = total amount of Gibbs's basis in both IRAs ($12,000);

B = total value of both of his traditional IRA accounts as of the end of 2001, with any amounts distributed out of either traditional IRA in 2001, including amounts rolled over to the Roth IRA, added back in for this purpose. Assume the 2001 year-end value of his remaining traditional IRA is $210,000, and there were no distributions from either traditional IRA in 2001 other than the conversion of the $30,000 traditional IRA to a Roth IRA, so B = $240,000 ($210,000 + $30,000); and

C = amount of 2001 distributions; in this case, the only 2001 "distribution" was the conversion of the smaller traditional IRA to a Roth IRA, so C is $30,000.

Thus, the amount of the $30,000 conversion Gibbs can exclude as representing his non-deductible contributions is $12,000/$240,000 x $30,000, or $1,500. The amount of income he must pay tax on as a result of the conversion is therefore $28,500 ($30,000 conversion minus $1,500 basis assigned to the conversion). His remaining basis in his traditional IRA is $10,500 ($12,000 total non-deducted contributions, less $1,500 used up in the Roth conversion).

Ed Slott has analogized this system to the "cream in the coffee." Once the cream has been poured into the coffee, there's no way to remove just the cream or just the coffee. Every "distribution" includes a proportionate amount of cream and coffee. However, there are two exceptions to the "cream in the coffee" rule:

A.   Conduit IRAs. Prior to 2002, if Participant had a traditional IRA that consisted purely of distributions rolled over from a QRP (or purely of distributions rolled over from a 403(b) plan), and the Participant rolled that IRA back into the same or another QRP (or 403(b) plan), that rollover did not carry with it a proportionate amount of the Participant's basis. § 408(d)(3)(A)(ii), (iii). This type of IRA is called a "conduit" IRA, because it holds only money in transit from one QRP to another, or from one 403(b) plan to another.

B.   Rollovers from IRA to QRP. After 2001, amounts rolled over from an IRA to a QRP are deemed to come first from pre-tax dollars; see ¶ 5.4.12.

5.4.11 Determining basis in the traditional IRA (pre-2002)

For years prior to 2002, the only possible "basis" a Participant could have in a traditional IRA was the cumulative amount of the Participant's non-deductible $2,000-per-year contributions. Prior to 2002, the only funds a traditional IRA could hold that would not be includible in income upon distribution would be these accumulated non-deductible "regular" contributions. There was just no other way for non-taxable money to get into a traditional IRA. For example:

1.   A Participant in a QRP could have made non-deductible contributions to that plan, and so could have a substantial basis in the QRP; however, prior to 2002, those amounts could not be rolled over to a traditional IRA. § 401(a)(31) and § 402(c)(2), as applicable to years prior to 2002, limited rollovers from a

QRP to an IRA to amounts that "would be includible in gross income" if not rolled over.

2.   Another type of non-taxable amount that can be contained in a QRP is life insurance proceeds (¶ 8.3.03). If a Participant died leaving his QRP benefits to his surviving spouse as beneficiary, and the benefits thus becoming payable to Spouse included life insurance proceeds, a distribution of all of Participant's benefits to Spouse would include the tax-free portion of the insurance proceeds. Prior to 2002, Spouse could roll over to a traditional IRA (¶ 3.2) everything *except* the tax-free insurance proceeds, because, again, § 401(a)(31) and § 402(c)(2) prevented rollover of non-taxable amounts. Income tax-free insurance proceeds could not be generated inside Participant's traditional IRA to start with because IRAs are forbidden to hold life insurance. § 408(a)(3).

The first year for which non-deductible $2,000 IRA contributions were permitted was 1987. § 408(o), added by § 1102 of TRA '86. As of the end of 2001, therefore, the most basis a person could have in a traditional IRA would be $30,000, the amount of basis a person would have if he made the maximum $2,000 IRA contribution every year for the years 1987-2001, and if in every year his contribution was non-deductible (see § 219(g)), and if he took no distributions during that time that diminished his basis.

A Participant who makes a non-deductible contribution to his IRA is required to report the contribution to the IRS on Form 8606 (attached to Form 1040). Part of the information reported on Form 8606 is the cumulative total of such contributions. To determine a client's basis in his traditional IRAs, therefore, theoretically, you need only look at his most recent Form 8606. Whether everyone who is supposed to file this form has actually done so is another question.

5.4.12 *Conversion of non-taxable amounts: years after 2001*

Three Code provisions that are effective for 2002 and later years change the rules regarding (1) rollover of non-taxable amounts to traditional IRAs (not previously allowed, now allowed); (2) rollovers from traditional IRAs to QRPs and 403(b) plans (allowed in more cases than previously); and (3) how certain rollovers are apportioned between taxable and non-taxable amounts. These changes are mainly significant because they make it easier for Participants to save for retirement, but they also incidentally create the opportunity for tax-free or lower-tax conversions of traditional IRAs to Roth IRAs.

First change: As noted (¶ 5.4.10), prior to 2002, § 401(a)(31) and § 402(c)(2) forbade the rollover of non-taxable amounts from a QRP to a traditional IRA. As amended by EGTRRA, these sections permit non-taxable as well as taxable amounts to be rolled over to a traditional IRA after 2001. Once non-taxable amounts are rolled over to a traditional IRA from a QRP, such amounts are then positioned to be converted to a Roth IRA. For an employee who has a substantial after-tax contribution account in his qualified plan, this process (rolling the amounts to a traditional IRA, then doing a Roth IRA conversion) represents a way to get the advantages of the Roth IRA (tax-free internal growth of the account, followed by tax-free distributions) with a lower price tag, since this employee already paid the "price" (income taxes) back when he made the non-deductible contribution to the QRP.

Second change: § 402(c)(8)(B) as amended by EGTRRA generally allows rollovers from any traditional IRA to a QRP or 403(b) plan for years after 2001—but only of the *taxable* money in the traditional IRA. Prior to this amendment, money could be rolled from a traditional IRA to a QRP (or 403(b) plan) only if the traditional IRA contained no contributions other than one or more distributions rolled from the same or another QRP (or 403(b) plan) (so-called "conduit IRAs"; ¶ 5.4.10). Now funds can be rolled from *any* traditional IRA to *any* QRP or 403(b) plan that is willing to accept such contributions.

Third change: As noted above (see the "Gibbs" example at ¶ 5.4.10), § 408(d)(2) provides that (except in the case of rollovers of so-called "conduit IRAs") all of an individual's traditional IRAs are aggregated for purposes of allocating his basis to distributions from any particular traditional IRA (including a distribution that is converted to a Roth IRA), and any distribution (including a distribution that is converted to a Roth IRA) is deemed to come proportionately from the non-taxable and taxable portions of Participant's aggregated IRAs (the "cream in the coffee" rule). This method of determining the taxable and non-taxable portions of a distribution will still (after 2001) apply to Roth IRA conversions and to any distribution from the traditional IRA that is not rolled over to another retirement plan.

However, after 2001, the proportionate allocation rule will *not* apply to rollovers from a traditional IRA to a QRP or 403(b) plan (see "Second change"). Instead, after 2001, a distribution rolled from a traditional IRA to a QRP or 403(b) plan is deemed to come entirely out of the *taxable* portion of the traditional IRA. The non-taxable portion cannot be rolled to a QRP or 403(b) plan at all.§ 408(d)(3)(H)(ii).

This creates the possibility of the following sequence. In 2002, a retiring employee receives a QRP distribution that includes his after-tax contributions account. The employee rolls the distribution over to a traditional IRA. The IRA now contains $Z, consisting of the basis ($X) that would be non-taxable if distributed, plus the portion ($Y) that would be taxable upon distribution.

The employee participates in another QRP, maintained by the new business he started upon retirement from his former job. He rolls over $Y to the new QRP. Under § 408(d)(3)(H) the entire amount of this rollover is deemed to come from the *taxable* portion of the traditional IRA. After this rollover, the only money left in the traditional IRA is $X, which is all "basis." If he qualifies to convert the traditional IRA to a Roth IRA (¶ 5.4.03), he can convert the remaining traditional IRA funds to a Roth IRA tax-free. The conversion does not result in any amount being added to his gross income because the traditional IRA consisted of 100% non-taxable amounts at the time of the Roth IRA conversion, so he has gotten the benefits of a Roth IRA with no current income tax cost.

5.5 Planning Considerations for Roth IRAs

"Tax-free compounding is the best thing in the world."
–Jonathan G. Blattmachr, Esq.

5.5.00 *Mathematics of the Roth retirement plan choice*

A Roth IRA is a nice asset to own. No other vehicle offers the ability to invest in the stock and (non-municipal) bond markets and generate totally tax-free investment accumulations you can spend in retirement.

The question is what price must be paid to acquire this wonderful asset. Generally, the price is payment of income taxes on the amount going *in* to the Roth retirement plan—taxes that could have been deferred (via a traditional retirement plan) until the money in question was taken *out* of the retirement plan. Is it more profitable to pay the taxes up front and get tax-free distributions later or to defer the taxes?

If you can duck that question by not paying taxes *either* when the money goes into the Roth plan *or* when it comes out, then you can get the advantages of a Roth retirement plan "free," so that has to be a good deal; see ¶ 5.4.12 and ¶ 5.5.01 for discussion of those unusual situations.

Assuming that's not an option, you are faced with doing a mathematical analysis of which alternative produces more dollars. See the Bibliography and software listed in Appendix C for resources that can help with this analysis.

One thing is sure however: if you take $A, pay income tax on it at B%, deposit the net after-tax amount in a Roth IRA, earn an investment return of C% and withdraw the accumulated funds ($D) on date E, the amount of money you will have ($D) will be *exactly the same* as if you had deposited $A in a traditional IRA, earned an investment return of C%, withdrawn the accumulated funds on date E, and paid income tax on that distribution at B%. In other words, there is nothing magic about paying taxes earlier rather than later.

For the Roth approach to be profitable, therefore, one or more of the factors in the equation must be different as between the Roth IRA option and the traditional IRA option. There are two factors in the equation that, for many of the people eligible to convert traditional IRAs to Roth IRAs, can change enough to tilt the balance in favor of Roth IRAs. One of these factors is that the money in a Roth IRA does not have to be distributed at the same time money would have to be distributed out of a traditional IRA; it can stay in much longer, because of the different minimum distribution rules that apply to Roth IRAs (¶ 5.1.03). Thus tax-free compounding can occur to a greater extent in a Roth IRA during the owner's life than is possible with a traditional IRA (from which the owner must take lifetime distributions; ¶ 1.4).

The other factor is that the taxes on a Roth IRA conversion can be paid with money that is not in any retirement plan. Thus, the Roth IRA need not be depleted by the tax money, which can come from the non-retirement plan investment portfolio.

The complex mathematical computations that go into analyzing the Roth IRA option are beyond the scope of this book. The purpose of this ¶ 5.5 is to point out considerations that may make a Roth IRA contribution more or less attractive either purely as a financial proposition or for other reasons, and planning considerations that apply when dealing with a client who already has a Roth IRA.

5.5.01 Choosing between traditional and Roth IRA contributions

An individual who has compensation income and whose AGI is under the limits described at ¶ 5.3.03 has the option to contribute to a Roth IRA. If he is under age 70½ he also has the option to contribute to a traditional IRA instead of to a Roth IRA, or to contribute part of his maximum permitted "regular" contribution amount (¶ 5.3.02) to each type of IRA. Assuming he wants to contribute to a retirement plan, which type should he contribute to if he has a choice?

The decision is easy if the individual (or his spouse) is an active participant in an employer plan, and his (or their) AGI exceeds the amounts specified in § 219(g)(3)(B) (AGI limit for determining deductibility of traditional IRA contribution, where Participant or Spouse is an active participant in an employer plan): the only choice is between a non-deductible traditional IRA and a Roth IRA. Since he can't get a tax deduction no matter which kind of IRA he contributes to, he gives up nothing by contributing to the Roth IRA.

The decision is also easy if the individual's taxable income is so low he is not subject to income tax, since, again, he gives up nothing by opting to contribute to the Roth IRA (because the tax deduction he might get by contributing to a traditional IRA would not save him any income taxes).

If neither the individual (nor his spouse) is an active participant in an employer plan; or, if he (or his spouse) is an active participant in an employer plan, but his (or their) AGI is low enough that he can get a tax deduction for a contribution to a traditional IRA; *and* his (or their) tax bracket is higher than zero; then his choice is between a *deductible* traditional IRA contribution (which could save him some current income taxes) and the *non-deductible* Roth IRA contribution. Which is a better deal (save taxes now or save taxes later) is a very complicated question. This question will be faced by a much larger number of individuals when DRACs (¶ 5.1.05) come on stream in 2006. See further discussion in the next subsection.

5.5.02 *Risks of Roth IRA conversion*

This ¶ 5.5.02 lists risks that should be considered by anyone considering a Roth IRA conversion. Most clients considering a Roth IRA conversion will evaluate the financial impact using computer projections of one brand or another (see "Software," Appendix C). Computer projections of the benefits of converting an existing IRA to a Roth IRA are based on assumptions as to future tax rates, investment returns and withdrawal amounts. Most such projections assume a constant rate of investment return; that today's tax rates will last forever; and that participants and beneficiaries will withdraw from the account no more than required by today's minimum distribution rules. Other possible scenarios should be considered, such as a stock market decline; it would be a shame to pay income tax on today's stock values, only to find out later that this was the all-time market high. This exact scenario happened to many who converted to Roth IRAs in the halcyon investment era of 1998-1999, then endured the stock market declines of 2000-2002.

Under 2001 tax law changes, the top marginal income tax rate is scheduled to decline from 39.6% (as of 2000) to 35% (by 2006). The expectation of lower brackets will doubtless dampen enthusiasm for Roth conversions; why pay 39.6% to convert when one can wait a while and pay 35%? Of course, while the individual is waiting for new lower rates to kick in, something else (further law changes, a loss of eligibility, an increase in value that increases the cost of conversion, or death) could happen in the meantime that makes conversion more expensive or impossible.

Congress could make other changes that would make a Roth conversion less appealing. For example, Congress could decide to bring the minimum distribution rules back into line with the original purpose of tax-favored *retirement* plans, and require that all benefits be distributed within some much shorter period of time after the deaths of Participant and Spouse. Congress could decide that the Roth IRA was too good a deal, and take away some of its favorable tax features on a prospective basis. Of course future changes (such as higher income tax rates or a higher stock market) could also go the other way (and make a conversion at today's values and tax rates look good).

5.5.03 *Clients who may profit from Roth conversion*

The client most likely to profit from converting to a Roth IRA is one who: has sufficient other wealth that he will never need to draw from the account during life (not drawing anything out of the account is the way to maximize the tax-free accumulations of the Roth IRA); plans to leave the account to young generation beneficiaries, to be drawn down over their life expectancy after the client's death (¶ 1.2.01) (again, the long life expectancy payout available for distributions to a young designated beneficiary maximizes the tax-free build-up of the Roth IRA); and can afford to pay the income tax on the conversion, and the estate tax on the account's date of death value, from other assets, without sacrificing other goals such as his own financial security (so that the income tax-free Roth IRA is not depleted by paying tax bills). Add steady to rising income tax rates, no negative tax law changes and positive investment returns and the conversion is a definite winner.

Many clients who can afford to pay the taxes and take the risks will not qualify for the Roth conversion because of the $100,000 AGI limit (¶ 5.4.03). Most of the people who *are* eligible to convert simply cannot afford to write a check for the up-front tax on the conversion. Therefore, it may be that the Roth IRA conversion will mainly be of interest to: wealthy people who due to some fluke have income under $100,000 in a particular year; young people who face a long life expectancy and expect their tax bracket to rise; and those who see benefits in the Roth IRA conversion besides just the ultimate numerical payout, such as improvements in their cash flow options.

The 2001-2002 minimum distribution rule changes (¶ 1.1.05) should increase the number of individuals who qualify to convert to a Roth IRA. Since MRDs from qualified plans and (until 2005) IRAs are included in gross income, anything that has the effect of reducing a Participant's MRDs should increase the number of Participants who will have gross income under $100,000. However, the longer deferral now available to traditional IRAs under the new rules (¶ 1.4.01) decreases the relative advantages of converting to a Roth IRA.

5.5.04 *Establishing Roth IRAs for low-income relatives*

Establishing a Roth IRA for teenage children, grandchildren, etc., has great appeal. Typically these young family members have summer or after-school jobs that generate compensation income on which an IRA contribution can be based, but have little enough income that they are in a low or zero tax bracket. The projections of what a humble $3,000 contribution will grow to by the time the 15-year-old child reaches age 65 can be staggering. What gives pause is that there is no way to prevent the donee from taking the money out of the account once he reaches the age of majority.

5.5.05 *Retiree with long life expectancy*

Roth IRAs have appeal for those retirees who do not need to withdraw any funds from their IRAs during life, especially those who expect to live well beyond the average life expectancy due to their genetic heritage and/or health. A traditional IRA Participant approaching age 70½ faces forced distributions that may substantially diminish the account over a long life span. ¶ 1.4.01. With a traditional IRA, the way to maximize tax deferral is to die prematurely (leaving benefits to a younger generation beneficiary) (¶ 1.2.01).

By converting the traditional IRA to a Roth IRA, this person can eliminate the forced lifetime distributions (¶ 5.1.03) and reverse the usual rule of thumb: The way to maximize tax deferral with a *Roth* IRA is to live as long as humanly possible, deferring the commencement of ANY distributions until that way-later-than-normal death (and then leave the benefits to a young beneficiary).

5.5.06 *Conversions to improve beneficiaries' tax situation*

Converting to a Roth IRA just before death can reduce *estate taxes* by removing the income taxes due on the Roth conversion from the gross estate. See ¶ 2.2.08.

A Participant may also choose to do a Roth conversion to save *income taxes* for his or her beneficiaries:

Example: Rhonda is a widow, age 65, living happily on her Social Security payments plus $25,000 a year withdrawn from a substantial traditional IRA representing a rollover of her late husband's pension plan. For the last several years, she has withdrawn sufficient extra dollars from the traditional IRA to use up the lower income tax brackets available to her. Even though she doesn't need this extra money for her living expenses, she knows that her children are all in the highest income tax bracket, and that some day those high brackets will apply to distributions the children take from the traditional IRA they inherit at her death. The Roth IRA conversion gives her another way to accomplish the same goal. She can convert some of the traditional IRA to a Roth IRA each year to use up her lower income tax brackets, and the high-bracket children will pay no income tax on distributions from the inherited Roth IRA.

Even if the pure economics indicate no substantial advantage to having Participant pay the income tax now rather than having the beneficiaries pay it later, it would be a convenience to the beneficiaries to inherit a Roth IRA (distributions from which are tax-free) rather than a traditional IRA, so they do not to have to wrestle with the valuable but complicated IRD deduction every year as they do their income tax returns (see ¶ 2.2.07).

5.5.07 *Estate planning with a Roth IRA*

See ¶ 10.5.03, "Solution G," for discussion of funding a credit shelter trust with a Roth IRA. See ¶ 10.5.05, "Solution E," for discussion of funding a QTIP trust with a Roth IRA.

A Roth IRA could substantially ease the problems of leaving retirement benefits to a non-citizen spouse (Chapter 4). Many of the problems of leaving traditional retirement benefits to a non-citizen spouse arise from the fact that such benefits are subject to income tax and the Roth IRA eliminates this problem. See ¶ 4.2.

By funding a *generation skipping trust* (see Glossary) with Roth IRA death benefits (rather than traditional IRA death benefits), Participant still gives his beneficiaries the advantage of long-term tax-free investment accumulations (if the trust passes the MRD trust rules; ¶ 6.2); *and* this approach has the additional advantage of not "wasting" any of the GST exemption paying income taxes. This use of a Roth IRA can be attractive if the oldest beneficiaries of the generation skipping trust are young (have a long life expectancy). If the oldest beneficiary of the generation skipping trust is not young, much of the potential advantage of the Roth IRA (stretching out tax-free distributions over a long life expectancy) is wasted.

According to the IRS, assigning a Roth IRA by *lifetime gift* "to another individual" causes the Roth IRA to be "deemed" distributed to the owner-donor, and accordingly it ceases to be a Roth IRA. Reg. § 1.408A-6, A-19. Needless to say, this treatment eliminates the advantages of such a gift. For a vigorous disagreement with the IRS's interpretation, see articles by Mervin Wilf cited in the Bibliography.

5.6 10% Penalty For Pre-Age 59½ Distributions

Full details on this penalty are contained in Chapter 9. This section discusses how the penalty applies to Roth IRAs, and assumes you have read Chapter 9.

5.6.01 *Penalty does not apply to conversions*

The 10% penalty under § 72(t) (applicable to certain retirement plan distributions before age 59½) does not apply to the "deemed" distribution that results from converting a traditional IRA to a Roth IRA. § 408A(d)(3)(A)(ii); Reg. § 1.408A-4, A-7(b). Thus a young person who meets the eligibility requirements (¶ 5.4.03) may convert his traditional IRA to a Roth IRA without penalty. However, this does not mean he can forget about the 10% penalty; see ¶ 5.6.02-¶ 5.6.05.

5.6.02 *Penalty applies to certain distributions from the Roth IRA*

§ 72(t) imposes a 10% penalty on any distribution from a "qualified retirement plan (as defined in section 4974(c))" made while Participant is under age 59½ (see Chapter 9). The definition of "qualified retirement plan" in § 4974(c) includes traditional IRAs. The regulations confirm that the 10% penalty would apply to non-excepted pre-age 59½ distributions from Roth IRAs, the same as to traditional IRAs, under the rule that Roth IRAs are treated the same as traditional IRAs unless § 408A provides otherwise. Reg. § 1.408A-6, A-5.

Since (regardless of the type of retirement plan) the 10% penalty applies only to the amount of a distribution that is includible in gross income (¶ 9.1.04), it would at first appear that it can only apply to *non-qualified* distributions from a Roth IRA (¶ 5.2.03), since qualified distributions (¶ 5.2.01) are not included in gross income; and basically this would be true—generally, for Roth IRAs, the penalty only applies to non-qualified distributions (see ¶ 5.6.04)—except for the two special rules dealing with the conversion of a traditional IRA to a Roth IRA by someone who takes distributions prior to age 59½ (¶ 5.6.03, ¶ 5.6.05).

5.6.03 *Conversion followed by distribution within five years*

A person who is under age 59½, although he can convert to a Roth IRA without penalty, has to come up with the money to pay the income tax on the conversion from some source *other* than the Roth IRA (or a traditional IRA), because he will owe the penalty to the extent he taps his traditional IRA or his newly-converted Roth IRA for this money.

If a Participant who is under age 59½ receives a distribution from a Roth IRA; and if "any portion" of that distribution is allocable under the Ordering Rules (¶ 5.2.04) to funds rolled over to the Roth from a traditional IRA that were includible in gross income; and "the distribution is made within the 5-taxable-year period beginning with the first day of the individual's taxable year in which the conversion contribution was made"; then the § 72(t) penalty shall apply to the distribution. § 408A(d)(3)(F); Reg. § 1.408A-6, A-5(b).

This provision was not included in the original Roth IRA legislation (TAPRA '97), but was added by the IRS Restructuring and Reform Bill of 1998, effective retroactively to January 1, 1998. This retroactive imposition of the penalty was held to be constitutional in *Kitt v. U.S.* (Fed. Cls. 2000, KTC 2000-490).

Note that this five-year period is *not the same* as the Five-Year Period for determining "qualified distributions" (¶ 5.2.02). The latter begins in the first year *any* contribution is made to any Roth IRA; the former begins, as to any conversion of a traditional IRA to a Roth IRA, with the year of that *particular* conversion. Reg. § 1.408A-6, A-5(c). Note also that this penalty applies regardless of whether the distribution is included in gross income in the year of the *distribution*.

Example: Rand, age 32, converts his $100,000 traditional IRA to a Roth IRA in 1999. He has no basis in the traditional IRA, so the entire $100,000 is includible in his gross income in 1999. He has no other Roth IRAs, and makes no other contributions to this one. In 2002, at age 35 (in other words, before the end of the five taxable years beginning with the year of the conversion, and while he is still under 59½) he takes $20,000 out of the Roth IRA to finance the purchase of a rare edition of *The Canterbury Tales*. Under the Ordering Rules, this distribution is deemed to come out of the portion of the 1999 conversion-contribution that was includible in gross income, and therefore it is subject to the 10% penalty.

"The exceptions under § 72(t) also apply to such a distribution," so there *should* be no penalty if the distribution is made after the death (or on account of the total disability) of Participant, for example. Reg. § 1.408A-6, A-5(b). But see discussion of Reg. § 1.408A-6, A-11, at ¶ 5.8.04.

5.6.04 *Taxable portion of non-qualified distributions*

If there is a distribution from a Roth IRA before Participant reaches age 59½, then, to the extent the distribution is *not* allocable under the Ordering Rules (¶ 5.2.04) to money converted within the last five years from a traditional IRA, the penalty applies only to the portion of the distribution (if any) that is included in gross income (¶ 5.2.03). Reg. § 1.408A-6, A-5(a).

5.6.05 *Conversion while receiving "series of equal payments"*

The 10% penalty does not apply to IRA distributions that are part of a "Series of Substantially Equal Periodic Payments" (¶ 9.2). If an individual who is receiving such a series of payments from a traditional IRA converts the traditional IRA to a Roth IRA, the conversion is "not treated as a distribution for purposes of determining whether a modification" of the series (¶ 9.3.01) has occurred, so the conversion itself does not trigger the loss of the exempt status of the series. Reg. § 1.408A-4, A-12.

However, the conversion does not mean that the individual can stop taking his periodic payments. "If the original series...does not continue to be distributed in substantially equal periodic payments *from the Roth IRA* after the conversion, the series of payments will have been modified and, if this modification occurs within 5 years of the first payment or prior to the individual [sic] becoming disabled or attaining age 59½, the taxpayer will be subject to the recapture tax of § 72(t)(4)(A)." Reg. § 1.408A-4, A-12 (emphasis added); ¶ 9.3.01.

This statement in Reg. § 1.408A-4 seems to assume that the individual converted the entire traditional IRA to a Roth IRA. If he converted only part of the traditional IRA to a Roth IRA, it is not clear whether the rest of his "series" payments would have to come all from the Roth IRA, or proportionately from the new Roth IRA and the (now-diminished) traditional IRA; or whether Participant could take the payments from whichever of the two accounts he chooses.

5.7 Recharacterizations; Corrective Distributions

A taxpayer who is unhappy with the IRA contribution choices he made for a particular year, or who discovers that he was not eligible to contribute to the type of IRA he contributed to (¶ 5.3.03, ¶ 5.4.03), or who contributed more than he was entitled to contribute (¶ 5.3.02), has two ways to remedy the problem without incurring any penalty.

5.7.01 *Corrective distributions*

One way to correct mistakes (or simply act on a change of heart) is for Participant to distribute the contribution back to himself. If any Roth IRA contribution (together with its net income; ¶ 5.7.06) is distributed before the extended due date (¶ 5.7.04) of the tax return for the year for which the contribution was made, then (a) the contribution is treated, at least for purposes of the 6% penalty on excess IRA contributions (§ 4973(a)), as not having been contributed and (b) the net income on the contribution is "includible in gross income for the taxable year in which the contribution is made." Reg. § 1.408A-3, A-7, § 1.408A-6, A-1(d); see also § 408(d)(4).

Example: Wayne contributed $2,000 to a new Roth IRA in 2001. By January 2002, the investments in the Roth IRA had earned $75 of interest, so the account was worth $2,075. Wayne then changed his mind and decided he would rather spend the money on a new gas grill. He closes the account, and the $2,075 is distributed out to him in January 2002. The $75 of taxable income is included in his gross income for the year of the contribution (2001). If Wayne is under 59½, see ¶ 9.1.05 regarding the premature distributions penalty.

If Wayne has another change of heart before the due date of his 2001 tax return, can he still contribute $2,000 to an IRA for 2001 before the April 15, 2002 deadline? The answer to this is not clear. The maximum non-rollover contribution an IRA may accept for 2001 is $2,000. The IRS may say Wayne has used up his $2,000 dollar maximum for 2001 by making the original contribution to the Roth IRA (even though he unwound that contribution in early 2002).

If Wayne had a net loss inside the Roth IRA (instead of $75 of gain), is the loss treated as if it had been realized outside the Roth IRA;

in other words, is there a way it can be used to offset other income? In Publication 590, on an analogous point, the IRS describes what happens when a taxpayer cashes out all of his traditional IRAs "and the total distributions are less than your unrecovered basis, if any. Your basis is the total amount of the nondeductible contributions in your traditional IRAs. You claim the loss as a miscellaneous itemized deduction, subject to the 2% limit, on Schedule A, Form 1040."

Once the grace period (extended due date of the tax return for the year the excess contribution is made; ¶ 5.7.04) has expired, if Participant did not withdraw any excess contribution and its associated income, Participant owes the 6% excess contributions penalty for that year. The penalty will continue to accrue annually until the excess contribution is either withdrawn from the account or treated as a proper contribution for a later year (to the extent Participant is eligible to make a contribution in a later year but does not do so; Reg. § 1.408A-3, A-7).

A timely corrective distribution can be useful for undoing *regular* Roth IRA contributions, but it is not much help for someone who has *converted* a traditional IRA to a Roth IRA and then wishes he hadn't (or who discovers after the fact that he wasn't eligible; ¶ 5.4.03). This person usually doesn't want to distribute the money out to himself, he just wants to restore the pre-conversion status quo. For this person, there is a second method of fixing the problem: an "unconversion," or "recharacterization."

5.7.02 *How to undo (recharacterize) a Roth IRA contribution*

The regulations provide broad relief to taxpayers who wish to "amend" their IRA contributions by switching the contribution from a Roth IRA to a traditional IRA or vice versa. This relief is for anyone who changes his mind about which type of IRA he wants his contribution to go to; it is not limited to (though it also helps) those who need to correct Roth IRA conversions for which they were ineligible (¶ 5.4.03). Reg. § 1.408A-5, A-10, Example 2.

A "regular" contribution made, for a particular taxable year, to either type of IRA may be transferred to the other type of IRA before the "extended due date" (¶ 5.7.04) of the person's tax return for such year. The contribution, to a Roth IRA, of a traditional IRA distribution made in a particular year may be transferred back to a traditional IRA before the "extended due date" (¶ 5.7.04) of the person's tax return for the year the distribution from the traditional IRA occurred. In either case, the contribution will be treated as a contribution to the *transferee* IRA for tax purposes. § 408A(d)(6), (7).

For example, if a person converts a traditional IRA to a Roth IRA in 2001, and then discovers that his income for 2001 exceeds the $100,000 limit so he is ineligible to do that conversion, he can move the money back to a traditional IRA before the extended due date of his tax return for 2001 and it will be treated as a rollover contribution to the traditional IRA. In effect, the Roth conversion is "undone," so the taxpayer does not realize income on account of the Roth conversion.

Here are the significant requirements for effecting a recharacterization:

1.   The transfer from the Roth IRA back to the traditional IRA (or vice versa) must be by trustee-to-trustee transfer (*not* by a rollover, which is a distribution to Participant followed by a recontribution to the other account). Reg. § 1.408A-5, A-1(a).

2.   Not only the original contribution but "any net income allocable to such contribution" must be retransferred. See ¶ 5.7.06.

3.   The election to recharacterize is made by providing notice and directions to the IRA trustee(s) involved. The election to recharacterize "cannot be revoked" after the transfer back to the traditional IRA has occurred. Reg. § 1.408A-5, A-6.

A recharacterized contribution will be treated for Federal income tax purposes as having been contributed to the transferee IRA (rather than the transferor IRA) "on the same date and (in the case of a regular contribution) for the same taxable year that the contribution was made to the transferor IRA." Reg. § 1.408A-5, A-3. A recharacterization is "never treated as a rollover for purposes of the one-rollover-per-year limitation of § 408(d)(3)(B), even if the contribution would have been treated as a rollover contribution by the [transferee] IRA if it had been made directly to the" transferee IRA in the first place. Reg. § 1.408A-5, A-8; ¶ 2.5.07.

5.7.03 *Deadline for Roth IRA contributions and conversions*

The various deadlines for contributions, conversions, corrective distributions and recharacterizations are extremely confusing. Some deadlines are based on the calendar year end, some on the extended due date of the return, and some on the unextended due date; and some of the deadlines qualify for an "automatic" extension, though you don't get the "automatic" extension unless you ask for it!

Starting with the easiest one: A "regular" Roth IRA contribution (¶ 5.3) for a particular year must be made no later than the *unextended* due date of Participant's tax return for the year. For example, a $3,000 contribution "for" the year 2003 may be made at any time on or before April 15, 2004. When a participant sends in a contribution between January 1 and April 15, the IRA provider must ask which year it is for, since between those dates it could be for either the year in which the contribution occurs or the prior year. *There is no way to extend this April 15 deadline applicable to regular contributions.*

Conversions are slightly more complicated. Because the conversion is technically a "rollover" (¶ 2.5), a "conversion contribution" is tied to the traditional IRA "distribution" that is being "rolled over." Therefore a Roth IRA conversion that is supposed to be "for" the year 2003 must be tied to a *distribution* that occurred in the *calendar* year 2003. *The due date of the 2003 return is irrelevant.*

A distribution that is made from a traditional IRA in the calendar year 2003, if it is to be contributed to a Roth IRA, must be so contributed within 60 days after the date of the distribution. January 1, 2003, would be the first date in calendar 2003 on which an amount could be distributed out of a traditional IRA; therefore the earliest possible date for a "2003 Roth IRA conversion" would be January 1, 2003 (same-day conversion of a January 1 distribution). The last possible date in calendar 2003 on which an amount could be distributed out of a traditional IRA would be December 31, 2003; therefore the last possible date for a "2003 conversion" would be the 60th day after December 31, 2003 (the deadline for rolling over a traditional IRA distribution made on December 31, 2003; § 408(d)(3)(A)(i)).

Note that:

A.   Roth IRA conversions are usually accomplished by transferring sums directly from a traditional IRA to a Roth IRA. If both accounts are with the same IRA provider, the traditional IRA distribution and the Roth IRA contribution would normally occur simultaneously. Thus in this typical situation there would be no need to get involved with calculating the 60-day period.

B.   There can be an extension of the 60-day rollover deadline in cases of hardship. See ¶ 2.5.03. This would in effect also allow a longer period to complete a Roth IRA conversion in cases of hardship. See Reg. § 1.408A-4, A-1(b)(1).

5.7.04 *Recharacterization deadline: meaning of "extended due date"*

Generally, the deadline for recharacterizing an IRA contribution is the due date of the tax return for the year of the contribution that is being recharacterized, *including extensions.* § 408A(d)(6), (7). So:

1.   A regular contribution to either a Roth IRA or a traditional IRA for a particular year, that was made by the *unextended* due date of the return for that year, can be recharacterized by the *extended* due date of the return for that year.

2.   A rollover (conversion) contribution to a Roth IRA may be recharacterized by the *extended* due date of the return for the taxable year in which the taxpayer received the distribution that was rolled over.

"Due date including extensions" or "extended due date" has a special meaning under IRS regulations. The taxpayer does not actually have to get an extension of his income tax return in order to go beyond April 15 for his recharacterization decision. Reg. § 301.9100-2(b) provides an automatic six-months extension (from the *unextended* due date of the return) for all "regulatory or statutory elections whose due dates are the...due date of the return including extensions *provided* the taxpayer timely filed its return for the year the election should have been made and the taxpayer takes" necessary corrective actions (such as filing an amended return if necessary). (Emphasis added.)

What's confusing is that there are two different "automatic" extensions, for different periods of time, neither of which is totally automatic. Any taxpayer can obtain a *four-months'* "automatic" extension of time to file his income tax return (i.e., to August 15 instead of April 15)—but it's not truly automatic because to get this extension the taxpayer has to file Form 4868 by April 15.

Then there's the "automatic" *six-months'* extension of time to recharacterize an IRA contribution. This extension *is* automatic in the sense that the taxpayer doesn't have to request it; but to qualify for this automatic extension he has to "timely" file his income tax return. "Timely" filing the income tax return means filing the return on or before April 15 (*or* getting an extension of time to file from the IRS and then filing the return on or before the extended due date).

Putting all these rules together, we find that if a taxpayer wants to recharacterize a Roth IRA contribution made in Year 1 he must complete the necessary actions (¶ 5.7.02) by whichever one of the following deadlines applies:

1.   If he files his income tax return for Year 1 on or before its due date, he has until October 15 of Year 2 to complete the recharacterization. The "due date" of the Year 1 income tax return is April 15, Year 2, *unless* he obtained an extension of time to file the return, in which case the due date is whatever date the return was extended to. For example, if, on or before April 15, Year 2, he filed Form 4868 with the IRS requesting the "automatic" four months' extension of time (to August 15, Year 2), the due date of his Year 1 return is August 15, Year 2. However, *regardless* of whether he got an extension of time to file his income tax return, as long as he filed the income tax return by whatever date it was due, the deadline for recharacterizing his IRA contribution is October 15, Year 2, under the automatic extension rule of Reg. § 301.9100-2(b).

2.   If he does not file his income tax return for Year 1 on or before the date it is due (whether that due date is April 15 or a later date he qualified for by requesting an extension from the IRS), he must complete the recharacterization by April 15 of Year 2.

The following examples illustrate these rules:

Example: Sandy files his income tax return on April 15, Year 2. The deadline for recharacterizing his Year 1 IRA contribution is October 15, Year 2.

Example: On or before April 15, Year 2, Pearl files Form 4868 with the IRS requesting the automatic four months' extension of time (to August 15, Year 2) to file her Year 1 income tax return. She files her Year 1 tax return on August 10, Year 2. The deadline for recharacterizing her Year 1 IRA contribution is October 15, Year 2.

Example: Chad made a regular Roth IRA contribution in Year 1. On or before April 15, Year 2, he files form 4868 with the IRS requesting the automatic four months extension of time (to August 15, Year 2) to file his Year 1 income tax return. He does not apply for any further extensions. He does not file his Year 1 income tax return until August 20, Year 2, which is after the (extended) due date. Because he did not timely file his Year 1 tax return, his deadline for recharacterizing the Roth IRA contribution is April 15, Year 2.

For the unfortunate taxpayer who discovers he was not eligible to convert to a Roth IRA, but misses all these deadlines for recharacterizing, there is still hope. There are procedures for applying to the IRS for relief in cases of good faith errors. See Reg. § 301.9100-1 *et seq.* The IRS has been generous in using these relief provisions to grant extensions for recharacterizations of erroneous Roth conversions, where the taxpayers requested relief before the IRS caught the mistake. See, e.g., PLRs 2001-16053 (taxpayer erroneously believed that due date of her return was October 15 and that capital gain did not count toward $100,000 Roth conversion income limit); 2001-16057 (recharacterization of improper Roth conversion was late due to financial institution error); 2001-16058, 2001-19059, 2001-20040, 2001-22050, 2001-28058 and 2001-30058 (taxpayers unaware they didn't qualify for Roth conversion and unaware of recharacterization deadline); 2001-26040 (taxpayers had been erroneously advised that the Roth IRA conversion income limit was $150,000, that the deadline for 1998 conversion was 4/15/99, etc.); and 2001-29040 (taxpayer ineligible to convert, and thought she had timely recharacterized all her Roth IRAs, but missed the deadline on one of them because she forgot about that account). In each of these PLRs, and countless more issued since, the IRS granted the taxpayers additional time, after the issuance of the ruling, to complete their recharacterizations.

5.7.05 Confusion between "conversions" and "recharacterizations"

While it is nice that taxpayers have been given a way to back out of Roth IRA conversions, so they need not be punished for (*e.g.*) making an incorrect prediction of their income, the addition of the recharacterization option is bound to create confusion among IRA owners and their advisors. Here are some points that will need to be constantly restated:

First, the ability to recharacterize a "Year 1" IRA contribution until the due date of the Year 1 tax return does *not* create a new extended right to do Roth IRA conversions in Year 2 (before the tax return due date) that will count as Year 1 conversions. If, in Year 1, there was no traditional IRA distribution that was properly converted to a Roth IRA (¶ 5.4.01), there is nothing to "recharacterize."

Second, not every type of contribution to a *traditional* IRA may be recharacterized—only "regular" contributions, i.e., the $2,000-per-year (or other applicable dollar limit, depending on the year; ¶ 5.3.02) type. A tax-free rollover from an employer plan (or from another traditional IRA) to a traditional IRA may not be recharacterized as a Roth IRA conversion or contribution, because "an amount contributed to an IRA in a tax-free transfer cannot be recharacterized." Reg. § 1.408A-5, A-10, Example 4.

Similarly, employer contributions to a SEP or SIMPLE plan may not be recharacterized as contributions to a Roth IRA, because the employer could not have made direct contributions to a Roth IRA in the first place. Once the contribution has been made, the employee may be able to convert the account to a Roth IRA. Reg. § 1.408A-5, A-5; ¶ 5.4.02.

5.7.06 *Determining net income attributable to contribution*

In order to effect a recharacterization (unconversion), not only the original contribution but also any net income attributable to such contribution must be retransferred. Reg. § 1.408A-5, A-2(a). This requirement may be met in one of two ways. Note that "net income" may be a negative amount—a loss, in other words.

Method 1: If the contribution in question was made to a new, separate, Roth IRA that contained no other funds, *and* there have been no other contributions to or distributions from that separate Roth IRA, *and* the entire contribution is being recharacterized, then simply transferring the entire account balance back to a traditional IRA satisfies the requirement. Reg. § 1.408A-5, A-2(b). This method being so much simpler than Method 2, there is an advantage to keeping each year's contributions to a Roth IRA in a separate Roth IRA account (not commingled with any pre-existing Roth IRA), until the period has expired for recharacterizing such contributions.

Method 2: If Method 1 is not available, then the net income attributable to the contribution must be calculated by a formula that is contained in Reg. § 1.408-4(c)(2)(ii) (Reg. § 1.408A-5, A-2(c)), or IRS Notice 2000-39, 2000-30 I.R.B. 132.

5.7.07 *Same-year reconversions outlawed (2000 and later)*

There are limits on the ability to use the recharacterization rules to flip back and forth between traditional IRA and Roth IRA status. For the limits applicable to reconversions in 1998 and 1999, see *"Limit on the number of 'reconversions' in 1998 and 1999: IRS Notice 98-50"* at page 225 of the 1999 edition of this book.

In Reg. § 1.408A-5, A-9(a), the IRS banned same-year reconversions, effective in 2000 and later years. Once a recharacterization of a Roth IRA conversion occurs, the individual may not reconvert the amount to a Roth IRA until the taxable year following the taxable year of the original conversion, or until at least 30 days have elapsed since the recharacterization, *whichever is later*. If the individual defies this rule and attempts to reconvert before the prescribed time period ends, the result is a "failed conversion."

Query: Taxpayer converts IRA # 1 to a Roth IRA on Date 1, then timely recharacterizes the conversion, so IRA # 1 is once again a traditional IRA. Then, within 30 days, he converts IRA # 2 to a Roth IRA. Is this a forbidden "same year reconversion," or is it a conversion of an entirely different "amount," so the ban does not apply?

5.8 When the Roth IRA Owner Dies

This ¶ 5.8 collects the rules that come into play upon death of the Roth IRA owner.

5.8.01 *Five-Year Period: effect of Participant's death*

The Five-Year Period (¶ 5.2.02) does not start running over again just because the Roth IRA owner dies. The Five-Year Period applicable to distributions from an inherited Roth IRA is the Five-Year Period that applied to the account during the original owner's life. Reg.

§ 1.408A-6, A-7(a). Also, the Five-Year Period requirement is not *waived* simply because the original owner dies—even though in most cases the minimum distribution rules (¶ 5.1.03) require the beneficiaries to begin withdrawing from the account by the year following the year of death. Reg. § 1.408A-6, A-14(c).

Example: Agatha, age 83, converted her traditional IRA to a Roth IRA in 2001, shortly before her death. She had made no prior Roth IRA contributions, so the Five-Year Period for her Roth IRA starts January 1, 2001. Her designated beneficiary must begin taking required distributions in 2002 (the year after her death). Because the Five-Year Period has not elapsed, the required distributions for the years 2002-2005 are not "qualified distributions." However, all distributions to the beneficiary are deemed to come first out of Agatha's original rollover contribution (¶ 5.2.04). Since Agatha paid tax on that amount already (it was included in her gross income for the year of the conversion; ¶ 5.4.09), these distributions are still income-tax free so long as the distributions do not exceed the amount of Agatha's original contribution. See ¶ 5.2.03. Beginning in 2006 all distributions from Agatha's Roth IRA will be tax-free as "qualified distributions" (¶ 5.2.01).

5.8.02 *Income in respect of a decedent problem*

If Participant dies during the Five-Year Period, and the beneficiaries withdraw from the account before the Five-Year Period expires, and the total of their withdrawals during this period exceeds the total of Participant's contributions, the excess will constitute "income in respect of a decedent" (IRD) (see Chapter 2). However, any distribution made from the Roth IRA *after* the expiration of the Five-Year Period (and after Participant's death) will be an income tax-free qualified distribution (and so will *not* be IRD) (¶ 5.2.01). Since it is impossible to know at the time of Participant's death how much the beneficiaries will withdraw from the account prior to the end of the Five-Year Period, it is impossible to know, until the end of that period (or until total distribution of the account, if earlier), exactly how much IRD there is in the estate.

Recipients of IRD are entitled to an income tax deduction for federal estate taxes paid on IRD. The amount of the deduction depends on the amount of estate taxes paid on *all* of the IRD included in the estate and on what proportion of it each beneficiary received. § 691; ¶ 2.2.07. Thus, in an estate which pays a federal estate tax, the existence of a Roth IRA for which the Five-Year Period had not expired at death may make it impossible for tax preparers to finalize beneficiaries' IRD deductions until expiration of the Five-Year Period (or earlier distribution of the entire Roth IRA).

5.8.03 *Special rules for surviving spouses*

A surviving spouse as beneficiary of a Roth IRA can roll her share of the account over into a Roth IRA of her own, or (if she is the sole designated beneficiary) elect to treat the deceased spouse's Roth IRA as her own Roth IRA. The result of such rollover or election is that the minimum distribution rules (Chapter 1) and the 10% penalty for pre-age 59½ distributions (Chapter 9) are then applied to the surviving spouse as owner rather than as beneficiary. Reg. § 1.408A-2, A-4. For more on spousal rollovers, see ¶ 3.2.

The regulations provide a special favorable rule (not in the statute) for surviving spouses: if the beneficiary of a Roth IRA is the spouse, and the "surviving spouse treats the Roth IRA as his or her own," and the surviving spouse also owns her own Roth IRA, the Five-Year Period (¶ 5.2.02) "with respect to any of the surviving spouse's Roth IRAs" (including the inherited one that the surviving spouse has elected to treat as her own) ends at the earlier of the end of either the Five-Year Period for the deceased spouse's Roth IRA or that applicable to the surviving spouse's own Roth IRAs. Reg. § 1.408A-6, A-7(b).

If the surviving spouse receives a distribution from: (i) a Roth IRA belonging to the surviving spouse into which she has rolled distributions from a Roth IRA she inherited from the deceased spouse; or (ii) a Roth IRA inherited from the deceased spouse that the surviving spouse has elected to treat as her own Roth IRA; such distribution is *not* as a distribution "made to a beneficiary on or after the owner's death." Reg. § 1.408A-6, A-3. Thus, even after expiration of the Five-Year Period, the spouse may not receive qualified distributions from the rollover (or elected) account until she herself reaches age 59½ (or is disabled). ¶ 5.2.01.

5.8.04 *How the Ordering Rules apply to a decedent's Roth IRA*

If a Roth IRA owner dies, leaving his Roth IRA(s) to more than one beneficiary, and his death occurs at a time when the Ordering Rules (¶ 5.2.04) might matter (*i.e.*, before the end of the "Five-Year Period" necessary to have a qualified distribution; ¶ 5.2.01), the various components of the decedent's Roth IRA(s) that matter for purposes of the Ordering Rules are carried over and allocated pro rata among the beneficiaries who inherit the Roth IRA(s). Reg. § 1.408A-6, A-11.

This regulation also indicates that such carryover and allocation is necessary if the decedent died within five taxable years after doing a pre-age 59½ conversion (¶ 5.6.03), as if the 10% penalty (Chapter 9) could apply to distributions from such an account to the beneficiaries. However, distributions after death are excepted from the 10% penalty (§ 72(t)(2)(A)(ii); ¶ 9.4.01); and the regulations provide that the § 72(t) exceptions are available even for distributions within the five years following a conversion (Reg. § 1.408A-6, A-5(b)), so the author does not see how the 10% penalty could apply to such distributions.

Is this carryover and allocation in case of death within the five years following a pre-age 59½ conversion important for a surviving spouse who inherits a Roth IRA and elects to treat it as her own (¶ 5.8.03)? Generally, the regulations provide that, when a surviving spouse elects to treat an inherited Roth IRA as her own, § 72(t) is applied as if the surviving spouse, *not* the decedent, were the owner of the account. Reg. § 1.408A-2, A-4. Does Reg. § 1.408A-6, A-11, suggest that, even though the surviving spouse is now treated as the owner for purposes of § 72(t), she still carries over the decedent's potential liability for the 10% penalty, if distributions occur within five years after the *decedent's* conversion? What if the surviving spouse is already over age 59½? Further clarification from the IRS is needed on this point.

5.8.05 *Other rules for tax treatment of inherited Roth IRAs*

Non-spouse beneficiaries cannot roll over an inherited Roth IRA (or convert an inherited traditional IRA to a Roth IRA), due to the prohibition (applicable to anyone other than the surviving spouse) on rolling over inherited IRAs. § 408(d)(3)(C).

Generally, if an individual (other than the surviving spouse; ¶ 5.8.03) inherits a Roth IRA, and also has a Roth IRA funded by his own contributions, the Five-Year Period runs separately ("is determined independently") for the two types. Reg. § 1.408A-6, A-7(b). A beneficiary cannot aggregate an inherited Roth IRA with his own Roth IRA for purposes of the minimum distribution rules (¶ 5.1.03). Reg. § 1.408A-6, A-15.

5.8.06 *Conversions, unconversions, by personal representative*

"The election to recharacterize a contribution...may be made on behalf of a deceased IRA owner by his or her executor, administrator, or other person responsible for filing the final Federal income tax return of the decedent under section 6012(b)(1)." Reg. § 1.408A-5, A-6(c).

Since the regulations give the Participant's personal representative—*not* the beneficiary who inherited the account—the right to "recharacterize" Roth IRA contributions (¶ 5.7.02), this raises the possibility that a beneficiary could inherit a recently established Roth IRA, only to have Participant's executor transform the account back into a traditional IRA. How the executor will persuade the Roth IRA provider to transfer the money back to a traditional IRA when the executor does not have title to the account is unclear.

5.9 Summary of Planning Principles

1.   Generally, it is easier to get money out of a Roth IRA tax-free than out of other retirement plans. Participant can withdraw his own contributions tax-free at any time (¶ 5.2.03); and (after expiration of the initial Five-Year Period; ¶ 5.2.02) *all* distributions are tax-free after Participant reaches age 59½ (or dies) (¶ 5.2.01). The only significant exception is that a person who converts to a Roth IRA while under age 59½ may have to pay a 10% penalty if he withdraws from the account within five years of the conversion (¶ 5.6.03).

2.   Funding a Roth IRA with regular contributions is an excellent tax shelter for individuals who have "compensation income" but are in a low income tax bracket (¶ 5.5.01).

3.   Converting a traditional IRA to a Roth IRA (¶ 5.4) offers those who meet the income limit (¶ 5.4.03) a chance to eliminate required lifetime distributions (¶ 5.1.03) and (if they can pay the

income tax on the conversion from other assets; ¶ 5.5.00) a way to increase the relative portion of their investments that is inside a tax-favored retirement plan.

4.   For other reasons to convert a traditional IRA to a Roth IRA, see ¶ 5.5.06 and ¶ 5.5.07.

5.   A person under age 59½ can convert a traditional IRA to a Roth IRA without being liable for the 10% penalty (¶ 5.6.01), but must either pay the income tax on the conversion from other funds or pay a 10% penalty if he withdraws the needed money from the converted account (or from an unconverted IRA) within five years after the conversion (unless some other exception applies; see Chapter 9). ¶ 5.6.03.

6.   The decision to convert a traditional IRA to a Roth IRA is not irrevocable, since "recharacterization" (unconversion) offers a penalty-free way to back out of the conversion decision up until (if the Participant timely files his income tax return for the year of the conversion) October 15 of the year after the conversion. ¶ 5.7.02.

6

Trusts as Beneficiaries of Retirement Plans

The minimum distribution "trust rules," trust accounting, and other tax and non-tax concerns when naming a trust as beneficiary of retirement benefits.

This Chapter discusses issues that arise when retirement plan benefits are payable to a trust, as the named beneficiary under a retirement plan, upon the death of the client ("Participant") who is the retirement plan participant.

6.1 Trust as Beneficiary: in General

This ¶ 6.1 lists the factors which (in addition to all other issues you need to consider in connection with any estate plan, or any disposition of retirement benefits) you need to review when it is proposed to name a *trust* as beneficiary of the client's retirement plan.

6.1.01 *Consider leaving benefits outright rather than in trust*

In preparing the estate plan, it may at first appear easier to have all the client's assets (including retirement benefits) "pour" into one trust, such as the client's "living" trust, so that a single fiduciary has control of all the assets and can then divide them up and distribute them according to a master formula and provisions contained in the trust. In view of the substantial complications and other disadvantages (explained in this Chapter and elsewhere; see, e.g., ¶ 10.5) involved in making *retirement benefits* payable to a trust, this rule of thumb does not apply to retirement benefits. With retirement benefits, the bias is in favor of leaving the benefits outright to the intended beneficiaries unless there is a compelling reason to leave them in trust.

6.1.02 Consider trust income tax issues

Distributions to a trust after the client's death from the client's non-Roth retirement plans will generally be included in the trust's gross income as "income in respect of a decedent" (¶ 2.2).

With the exception of "grantor trusts" (¶ 6.3.09), trusts generally are taxed as separate entities, subject to a separate rate schedule that applies only to trusts and estates. § 1(e). A trust goes into the highest tax bracket (38.6%) for taxable income in excess of $9,350 (2003 rates). For an individual, the top income tax bracket applies only to taxable income above $311,950. § 1(c). Thus, in all but the wealthiest families, income taxed to a trust will be taxed at a higher rate than would apply to the individual family members. See ¶ 10.5 and ¶ 3.3.10 for the planning implications of this fact in connection with leaving retirement benefits to a credit shelter trust or QTIP trust.

If the estate plan calls for the retirement benefits to be left to a trust, consider whether the high rates could be avoided or mitigated by one of the following means:

1.   A trust is entitled to an income tax deduction for distributions the trust makes from the trust's "distributable net income" (DNI) to individual trust beneficiaries, if various requirements are met. See ¶ 6.1.03.

2.   A trust is entitled to an income tax deduction for certain distributions the trust makes to charity, if various requirements are met. § 642(c). See ¶ 7.4.

3.   If the individual trust beneficiary is a U.S. citizen or resident, and has the unlimited right to take the retirement benefits out of the trust, the trust is considered a "grantor trust" as to that beneficiary, and the distributions from the retirement plan to the trust would be taxed at the beneficiary's rate rather than at the trust's rate. See ¶ 6.3.09.

4.   If Participant's estate was liable for federal estate taxes the trust is entitled to an income tax deduction for the estate taxes paid on the retirement benefits. § 691(c). See ¶ 2.2.07.

The fact that retirement plan distributions to the trust are "income in respect of a decedent" raises another concern if the trust's assets are to be divided into separate shares or trusts upon the client's death, namely, the risk that the retirement benefits will be subjected to tax *immediately* (rather than upon distribution) if the benefits are used to fund a "pecuniary" bequest. See ¶ 2.2.05 and ¶ 6.1.05, Item 6.

6.1.03 *Trust passes out taxable income as part of "DNI"*

A trust may be able to reduce the income taxes payable on retirement plan distributions it receives by passing such distributions out to the individual trust beneficiaries. A trust gets an income tax deduction for distributions made from the trust's "distributable net income" (DNI) to individual trust beneficiaries. § 651, § 661. The beneficiaries then include the distributions in their gross income. § 652, § 662. If the distributions the trust receives from the retirement plan are passed out to the individual beneficiaries of the trust as part of DNI, the income tax burden is shifted to the individual beneficiaries, who may be in a lower tax bracket than the trust.

Computation of DNI and the allocation of DNI among beneficiaries' shares are complex topics that are beyond the scope of this book. For explanation of those subjects, I recommend the sources described in "General Note on Sources" in the Bibliography, which I have relied on in preparing this section. See also ¶ 7.4.

The purpose of this ¶ 6.1.03 is to point the way to successful drafting to take advantage of the DNI deduction. The following discussion uses the term "gross income" to refer to a retirement plan distribution that is received by a trust and is includible in the trust's gross income for the year of such receipt.

The fact that a trustee receives a retirement plan distribution and later makes a distribution to an individual trust beneficiary does *not* automatically mean that the distribution to the beneficiary carries with it the gross income arising from the retirement plan distribution. The trust might still be liable for the income tax on the retirement plan distribution it received. The question is (in trust administration lingo) whether such distribution "carries out DNI." For example:

1.   The DNI deduction is available only for gross income that either is required to be distributed, or is actually distributed, to the individual beneficiary in the same taxable year it is received by the trust (or that is distributed within 65 days after the end of

such taxable year, if the trustee elects under § 663(b) to have such distribution treated as made during such taxable year). § 651(a), § 661(a).

2.   The DNI deduction is not available for distributions in fulfillment of a bequest of a specific sum of money ("straight" pecuniary bequest) unless the governing instrument requires that such distribution is to be paid in more than three instalments. § 663(a)(1), Reg. § 1.663(a)-1. However, a "formula" pecuniary bequest is not considered a bequest of a specific sum of money for this purpose, and so can "carry out DNI." Reg. § 1.663(a)-1(b)(1). A "formula pecuniary bequest" does not mean simply any pecuniary amount determined by a formula; it means a bequest of a sum of money determined by a formula where the amount of the bequest cannot be determined as of the date of death. Many marital deduction bequests are of this type; see, e.g., Form 3.4(B), Appendix B.

3.   Finally, if there are two or more beneficiaries, and they have "substantially separate and independent shares," a distribution to one beneficiary will not carry out DNI that is allocated under the "separate shares" rule to a different beneficiary. § 663(c); ¶ 7.4.05.

With this background in mind, we look at some typical trust provisions and see whether these would cause or allow the gross income attributable to retirement plan distributions received by a trust to be "carried out" to individual trust beneficiaries (and therefore taxed to such beneficiaries rather than to the trust):

A.   A trust provides "income to spouse, remainder to issue." As explained at ¶ 6.1.07, Spouse is entitled under this provision only to "trust accounting income." Unless the trust instrument provides to the contrary, retirement plan distributions to the trust will be allocated wholly or partly to trust principal or "corpus," and thus cannot be entirely distributed to Spouse under this type of trust. Except for the portion that is properly attributable to trust accounting income (e.g., under UPIA 1997, 10% of MRDs), which will be taxable to spouse as the income beneficiary, such distributions will be taxed to the trust. For comments on including, in a QDOT, a provision that defines all retirement plan distributions as "income," see ¶ 4.7.05.

B.   A trust provides "income to spouse, plus principal to spouse in the discretion of the independent trustee, remainder to issue." Under this trust the trustee could distribute to Spouse amounts the trust receives from retirement plans, even if such amounts are allocable to trust principal, to the extent such distributions are permitted under whatever standards the trustee is given for exercise of its discretion to distribute principal to Spouse. If the trust says Spouse is entitled to principal only "if needed for her health, education and support," and she doesn't need any principal for those purposes, the trustee could not pass out to her the retirement plan distributions just to reduce income taxes. However, if the distribution is authorized by the trust instrument, it will carry with it the gross income generated by the trustee's receipt of a retirement plan distribution in the same year. The retirement plan distribution received by the trust is included in DNI (see definition at § 643(a)), deductible by the trust (§ 661(a)), and includible in the beneficiary's income. § 662(a)(2), Reg. § 1.662(a)-3.

C.   If the trust instrument requires the trustee to distribute to the individual trust beneficiary all retirement plan distributions received by the trust (without regard to whether such plan distributions are considered "income" or "corpus" for trust accounting purposes), the plan distributions received by the trustee would be part of DNI and the DNI would be carried out and taxable to the beneficiary. § 643(a), § 661(a)), § 662(a)(2); Reg. § 1.662(a)-3. For further discussion of such "conduit trusts" see ¶ 6.3.08.

6.1.04 *Consider your client's particular retirement plans*

Part of what makes planning for retirement benefits difficult is the variety of arrangements that can be encompassed in the term "retirement benefits." The trustee of a trust that is named as sole beneficiary of a typical *self-directed IRA* simply owns an investment account with special tax characteristics; the trustee can freely buy and sell assets "inside" the IRA, withdraw assets from the account at any time and in any amount, and even move the account to another IRA custodian (by means of a direct custodian-to-custodian transfer). The trustee's duties include directing the investments and making decisions regarding the timing of distributions.

In contrast to this, if a trust is named as beneficiary of remaining payments under a *defined benefit plan* (for example, if the deceased participant was receiving a life annuity with a minimum term of years, and dies before the term of years is up, leaving the remaining payments to his trust), the trustee has no control of plan investments or the size or timing of distributions, and cannot move the "account" to another plan. With this type of traditional annuity-based retirement plan the trustee owns a mere contract right to receive the future payments. The trustee's only duty is to collect the payments.

In between the self-directed IRA (over which the trustee-named-as-beneficiary has complete control) and the defined benefit or annuity plan (over which the trustee-named-as-beneficiary has absolutely no control) are a variety of other types of qualified retirement plans where the trustee has some, but less than complete, control. For example, under a 401(k) plan, the trustee-named-as-beneficiary might have a limited menu of investment choices (among one "family" of mutual funds for example), and a limited menu of distribution options (such as lump sum or instalments over a term certain).

Despite the vast differences, in terms of the degree of the trustee's control, among the various types of retirement plans, Congress, the IRS, and the drafters of state laws often do not differentiate. In many cases the same rules apply both to self-directed IRAs and to more traditional annuity-based types of retirement benefits.

Many practitioners, like the drafters of legislation, would like to have a blanket trust form that will "work" for all clients' situations without further fine tuning. This approach can be hazardous when dealing with retirement benefits. The practitioner needs to consider how the trust provisions will operate with regard to the particular client's retirement plan assets, and adjust the estate plan accordingly.

Some retirement plans offer only a limited menu of payout options for death benefits. For example, many 401(k) plans offer a lump sum distribution as the only form of death benefit. See ¶ 1.5.09. Some qualified plans may refuse to honor disclaimers (¶ 8.2.08). Some plan administrators may not allow a terminating trust to pass the retirement benefit out to the trust beneficiary, but rather require the trust to cash out the plan (¶ 6.1.06).

Whenever a retirement plan constitutes a major asset of the client's estate, it is necessary to make sure that the proposed disposition of the retirement benefits will be permitted under the terms of the client's retirement plan.

6.1.05 *Checklist of factors to consider when drafting trust*

When drafting a trust that is to be named as beneficiary of a client's retirement plan benefits, consider the following points, in addition to those discussed at ¶ 6.1.01 through ¶ 6.1.04:

1. If special provisions are to be included that deal with retirement plan benefits, you need to define "retirement benefits." See Form 7.5, Appendix B.

2. If the trust is intended to qualify for the federal estate tax marital deduction, see ¶ 3.3.

3. If the dispositive terms of the trust distinguish between "income" and "principal," consider how these terms will apply to the retirement plan and to distributions from it. See ¶ 6.1.07.

4. The minimum distribution rules of § 401(a)(9) (Chapter 1) permit death benefits to be paid out over the life expectancy of individual beneficiary who inherits the benefits. Regulations allow a trust that is named as beneficiary of retirement benefits to use this "life expectancy payout method" if various requirements are met. See ¶ 6.2.

5. When Participant's spouse ("Spouse") is named as Participant's beneficiary, certain distribution options (including most importantly the spousal rollover; ¶ 3.2) become available that are not available otherwise. These special options are usually *not* available when a trust is named as beneficiary, even if Spouse is the sole life beneficiary of the trust. If use of the special tax options available to a surviving spouse-beneficiary would be beneficial as part of the client's estate plan, consider whether it is feasible, in line with the client's other estate planning objectives, to name Spouse individually (rather than the trust) as beneficiary of the retirement plan; or if that is not

feasible, consider whether the trust can be written so that it qualifies for some of the special spousal options; see ¶ 6.3.12.

6.   If the trust's assets are to be divided into shares or subtrusts upon the client's death, read ¶ 2.2.05-¶ 2.2.06 regarding why a fractional (rather than a "pecuniary") formula should be used to divide the trust assets (see Form 3.2(B), Appendix B); or, either in the trust instrument (see Form 3.3(B), Appendix B) or the beneficiary designation form (see Form 3.4(A), Appendix B) or both, require that the retirement benefits be allocated to one particular share or trust, so that the benefits do not become subject to the formula at all.

6.1.06 *Distributing a retirement plan out of a trust*

¶ 6.1.03 discussed the tax treatment of a trust's distributing, to an individual trust beneficiary, amounts that the trust had received from a retirement plan. This subsection discusses the trust's distributing *the retirement plan itself* out of the trust to the trust beneficiary. Here are some common examples of such distributions:

Example: Foster names the Foster Revocable Trust as beneficiary of his IRA. The Foster Revocable Trust provides that, upon Foster's death, the trustee is to divide all assets of the trust into two separate trusts, the Marital Trust and the Credit Shelter Trust, pursuant to a fractional formula. All retirement benefits are to be allocated to the Marital Trust. The trustee instructs the IRA provider to change the name of the owner of the IRA from "Foster Revocable Trust, as beneficiary of Foster, deceased," to "Marital Trust, as beneficiary of Foster, deceased." The trustee has distributed (transferred) the IRA from the Foster Revocable Trust to the Marital Trust.

Example: Stanley names his testamentary trust as beneficiary of his IRA. The testamentary trust provides that, after Stanley's death, the trustee is to pay income of the trust to Mrs. Stanley for life. On her death, the principal of the trust is to be paid outright to Stanley's two children, A and B. The trustee takes annual MRDs from Stanley's IRA. Because the testamentary trust complies with the "trust rules" (¶ 6.2), these MRDs are computed using the life expectancy of Mrs. Stanley (the oldest trust beneficiary), which is 18 years. Mrs. Stanley dies 12 years later. There are six years left to go in the life expectancy payout. The trustee instructs the IRA provider to change the name on the IRA from "Stanley Testamentary Trust, as beneficiary of Stanley, deceased," to "Child A and Child B, as beneficiaries of Stanley, deceased." The trustee has distributed (transferred) the IRA from the testamentary trust to the two children.

Generally, the transfer of an inherited retirement plan after Participant's death would trigger immediate realization of the income represented by the retirement plan, because it is the transfer of a right to receive "income in respect of a decedent." § 691(a)(2); see ¶ 2.2.05. However, there is an exception to the § 691(a)(2) "trigger" rule: it does *not* apply to a "transfer to a person pursuant to the right of such person to receive such amount by reason of the death of the decedent or by bequest, devise, or inheritance from the decedent." § 691(a)(2).

This exception applies to the transfer of the right to receive income in respect of a decedent by a terminating trust to the trust beneficiaries. Reg. § 1.691(a)-4(b)(3). Thus, the distribution of a retirement plan from a trust to the trust beneficiaries, as in the above examples, does *not* cause realization of income. The same would be true in the case of distribution of a retirement plan by an estate to the estate's residuary beneficiaries.

PLR 2001-31033 (Rulings 5, 6 and 7) illustrates this rule (although the ruling didn't mention § 691). This ruling allowed the distribution of "IRA Y" from a terminating trust to Participant's children, C and D. From the ruling: "The provision of Trust X which provides for its termination does not change either the identity of the individuals who will receive the IRA Y proceeds or the identity of the designated beneficiary of IRA Y.... Furthermore, the Trust X termination language which results in distributions from IRA Y being made directly to Taxpayers C and D instead of initially to Trust X and then to Taxpayers C and D was language in Trust X approved by [Participant] during his lifetime which reflects [Participant's] intent to pay his children directly instead of through Trust X."

If the retirement benefits are in a qualified plan (see Glossary), rather than an IRA, another issue that arises concerning a transfer of the benefits from a trust to the trust's beneficiaries (or from an estate to the estate beneficiaries) is whether the transfer violates § 401(a)(13)(A) ("benefits provided under the plan may not be assigned or alienated").

Reg. § 1.401(a)-13(c)(1)(i) defines the type of assignment prohibited by § 401(a)(13) as "Any direct or indirect arrangement...whereby a party acquires from a ...beneficiary a right or interest enforceable against the plan in, or to, all or any part of a plan benefit payment which is, or may become, payable to...[the beneficiary making the assignment]." Although § 401(a)(13) is clearly aimed at pledges and garnishments of benefits, a quick reading could lead to the conclusion that it applies to this type of "transfer" as well.

However, § 401(a)(13) prohibits the employee's beneficiary from assigning the benefits to a third party, someone who is a "stranger" to the plan and who is not the beneficiary chosen by the employee. In the case of a transfer of the account from an estate or trust to the beneficiaries of the estate or trust, the benefits are being assigned from a "beneficiary" (the estate or trust) which is *no longer* entitled to receive them (because the entity is terminating, or because the terms of the will or trust require that this particular asset be distributed to the beneficiary), to the beneficiary who is *now* entitled to the benefits under the terms of the plan and under the terms of the employee's beneficiary designation.

When an estate is terminating, the terms of the employee's will (or applicable intestacy laws) require that the remaining assets be transferred to the estate's beneficiaries; the distributees of the estate *are* the employee's "beneficiaries" at that point (though they are not "designated" beneficiaries; see ¶ 1.7.03). When a trust is terminating, the terms of the trust instrument require that the remaining trust assets be transferred to the trust's beneficiaries; they *are* the employee's "beneficiaries" at that point. For the plan *not* to permit the benefits to be transferred out of the estate or trust, when the terms of the will or trust require such distribution, would be a failure to comply with the terms of the employee's beneficiary designation and therefore violate the terms of the plan itself.

§ 401(a)(13) should be applied only to a situation where the benefits would be paid to someone *other than* the beneficiaries chosen by the employee; it does not prevent the plan from carrying out the employee's wishes as expressed in the terms of his will and trust.

6.1.07 Trust accounting for retirement benefits

There are three problems in applying traditional trust concepts of "principal" and "income" to retirement benefits payable to a trust.

These are: the confusion between "trust accounting income" and "taxable income" or "federal gross income"; the confusion between "trust accounting income" and "minimum required distributions" (MRDs); and the difficulty of defining "trust accounting income" with respect to retirement benefits.

First, "income" as that term is generally used in a trust instrument means "trust accounting income," not income in the federal income tax sense. An asset can be "principal" (corpus) for trust accounting purposes and yet be "income" for purposes of the federal income tax law.

Example: Jorge dies leaving his $1 million 401(k) plan to a trust for his daughter. The trustee is to pay "income" to the daughter, and to distribute "principal" to the daughter if needed for her health, education and support until she reaches age 35, at which time the trust is to terminate and the remaining principal is to be distributed outright to the daughter. The trust specifies that the date of death value of the 401(k) plan is the "principal" of this trust. The only form of death benefit allowed by the 401(k) plan is a lump sum in cash which is received by the trustee a few days after Jorge's death. Because the trust instrument defines this asset as "principal," the trustee holds the $1 million in the trust, invests it, and starts paying the income of the investments to the daughter. Then the trustee prepares the income tax return for the trust for its first year. He has to report as "income" the $1 million distribution from the 401(k) plan. This is "income" for federal income tax purposes even though it is "principal" for trust accounting purposes.

The second source of confusion is the difference between "trust accounting income" and "MRDs." The two are totally different concepts, though it is possible to have a definition of "income" that takes into account the minimum distribution concept.

Example: Belle dies leaving her $1 million IRA to a trust for her son Burt. The trustee is to pay "income" to Burt, and distribute "principal" to Burt if needed for his health, education and support until he reaches age 35, at which time the trust is to terminate and the remaining principal is to be distributed outright to Burt. The trust specifies that the date of death value of the IRA is the "principal" of this trust and that "income" with respect to the IRA means the income earned inside the

IRA (i.e., interest and dividends on the IRA's investments) as if the IRA were itself a trust (see Form 7.6, Appendix B).

Each year, the trustee withdraws from the IRA the MRD based on Burt's life expectancy (see ¶ 6.2.04) and transfers that distribution to the trust's non-retirement plan investment account. In addition, because the trustee is required to pay Burt all "income" as that is defined in the trust, if the "income" of the IRA is larger than the MRD, the trustee has to withdraw the excess and distribute that also to Burt. (If that outcome is considered undesirable, the trust could be drafted so that the trustee was required to withdraw from the IRA and distribute to Burt the *lesser of* the "income" or the MRD; such a form could not be used for a marital trust; see ¶ 3.3.06.)

Finally, there is no generally accepted definition of what "trust accounting income" means as applied to a retirement plan benefit payable to a trust. If the trust requires the trustee to pay all "income" of the trust to A for life and distribute the "principal" of the trust to B at A's death, and the trust's only asset is a retirement plan, what is the "income" that A receives? We have seen that "trust accounting income" does not mean "federal gross income" and it does not mean "MRD"; so what does it mean?

State law will govern if the trust agreement does not cover this subject. Applicable state law may provide nothing at all on the subject, or may not provide a provision suitable for your client's situation.

For example, the Uniform Principal and Income Act (1997) ("UPIA 1997"), which has been adopted in some states, provides trust accounting rules for retirement plan *distributions*, but does not say how the trustee is to account for the retirement plan itself. Also, UPIA 1997 generally allocates 10% of any required distribution from a retirement plan to income. Amounts that are paid by the plan to the trust as dividends *per se* (for example, dividends distributed on stock held in an ESOP) are also allocated to income. All other distributions (i.e., 90% of required distributions, and 100% of non-required distributions) are generally allocated to principal. UPIA 1997, § 409.

If a client whose trust would be governed by the law of a state that has adopted UPIA 1997 wants his trust beneficiary to receive the "income" of the trust, the 10% allocation rule may or may not reflect what the client means by "income." In the Belle/Burt example above, the UPIA 1997 definition would mean that Burt would receive only 10% of each year's MRD (plus income from the trust's non-retirement plan investments, including investments created by reinvestment of the "principal" portion of the required distributions).

UPIA 1997 also provides that a *larger* portion of any distribution is allocated to income to the extent such larger allocation is necessary for the trust to qualify for the federal estate tax marital deduction—but does not specify what that larger portion would be. UPIA 1997, § 409(e). Therefore, in a state that has adopted UPIA 1997, the state law definition of "income" with respect to a retirement plan payable to a marital deduction trust would be "at least 10% of any required distribution," with the upper limit not defined.

If you are drafting a trust under which substantive rights of the beneficiaries depend on the distinction between "income" and "principal," and the trust may receive retirement benefits upon the client's death, it is advisable to include a provision explaining how retirement benefits are to be accounted for. Even if the applicable state law definition suits the client's needs perfectly, the state law could change before the trust becomes effective; for example, even the Uniform Principal and Income Act has evolved through three incarnations (1931, 1962 and 1997).

6.1.08 *Retirement benefits and the "unitrust" concept*

A recent trend in trust-drafting is to eschew "income" and "principal" concepts in favor of a "unitrust" approach: the life beneficiary receives a fixed percentage of the value of the trust's assets each year, rather than receiving trust accounting income. For an excellent, readable and practical analysis of the reasons for this trend, the different methods of implementing the idea, and its pros, cons and pitfalls, see the article by Al Golden, Esq., in the Fall, 2002, issue of *ACTEC Journal*. If using the unitrust approach for a trust that is to be named as beneficiary of retirement benefits, it would be advisable to specify in the instrument whether built-in income taxes are to be taken into account in valuing the trust assets for purposes of computing the unitrust percentage. This is not an issue for charitable remainder unitrusts (¶ 7.5.04), which are not subject to income tax.

6.2 The Minimum Distribution Trust Rules

6.2.01 *Why complying with the trust rules matters*

§ 401(a)(9) generally requires that retirement benefits be entirely distributed out of the plan (and subjected to income tax) within five years after Participant's death (if he died before his required beginning date) (¶ 1.5.04), or over what would have been the remaining single life expectancy of the deceased participant (if he died on or after his required beginning date) (¶ 1.5.05). However, if the benefits are left to an individual (human) beneficiary, *or to a qualifying trust* (¶ 6.2.04), the benefits can be distributed, instead, in annual instalments over the individual beneficiary's life expectancy (or over the life expectancy of the oldest beneficiary of the trust; ¶ 1.5.08). See Chapter 1 for a full explanation of the minimum distribution rules.

In many cases, distribution over the life expectancy of a beneficiary provides substantially longer income tax deferral than does distribution over five years or over Participant's life expectancy. Since longer income tax deferral often translates into substantially more money for the family beneficiaries (¶ 1.2.01), it is important to consider whether the trust proposed to be named as beneficiary of retirement benefits "qualifies" under the IRS's minimum distribution trust rules.

Note, however, that the fact that a trust qualifies under the minimum distribution rules does not mean that the trust is a good choice as beneficiary of retirement benefits. Making benefits payable to a trust of which Spouse is the oldest (or even the sole) beneficiary results in substantially less income tax deferral than would be available (via the spousal rollover) for benefits left to Spouse outright *even if* the trust "passes" all the minimum distribution trust rules (see ¶ 3.3.10, ¶ 10.5.05). Also, complying with the "trust rules" does not solve the problem of high trust income tax rates (¶ 6.1.02).

6.2.02 *When complying with the trust rules doesn't matter*

Complying with the IRS's minimum distribution trust rules is not a requirement of making retirement benefits payable to a trust. If a trust named as beneficiary of a retirement plan flunks the rules, the trust still receives the benefits; it just does not get to use the life expectancy of the oldest trust beneficiary as the measuring period for MRDs.

There are cases in which it makes little or no difference whether the trust complies with the trust rules. For example, many qualified plans do not permit the life expectancy payout; they offer only the lump sum distribution form of death benefit. ¶ 1.5.09. If the client's retirement benefit is in this type of plan, then the life expectancy payout will not be available regardless of whether the trust passes the rules.

The identity of the trust beneficiary(ies) also may make qualification under the rules irrelevant. For example, if Participant is past his required beginning date (¶ 1.3), and the oldest beneficiary of the proposed trust is the same age as (or older than) Participant, then the payout period will be no longer if the trust passes the rules (the longer of the life expectancy of the Participant or the life expectancy of the oldest trust beneficiary; ¶ 1.5.08) than if the trust flunks the rules (the life expectancy of Participant; ¶ 1.5.05). Similarly, if the trust that is to be named as beneficiary of Participant's retirement plan is a charitable remainder trust that meets the requirements of § 664 (¶ 7.5.04) then the trust is income tax-exempt. An income tax-exempt entity does not need to take advantage of the income tax deferral potentially available under the life expectancy payout method, so passing the trust rules is irrelevant.

Finally, in some cases complying with the trust rules involves significant compromise with the client's other estate planning goals. It may be appropriate to sacrifice the income tax deferral possibilities of the life expectancy payout method in order to realize the client's other goals, especially if the retirement benefits will be a minor asset of the proposed trust.

6.2.03 *Trust does not need to recite the MRD rules*

One thing the minimum rules do NOT require is that you specify in the trust instrument that the trustee must withdraw from the retirement plan the annual MRD. § 401(a)(9) requires the trustee to withdraw the MRD whether the trust instrument tells him to or not.

Nevertheless, practitioners frequently do mention the requirement of withdrawing the MRD in the trust instrument itself, for various reasons, such as: In a conduit trust (¶ 6.3.08), the minimum distribution rules are essentially incorporated into the substantive provisions of the trust, so they should be mentioned in that case. In other types of trusts it doesn't hurt to remind the trustee that he is supposed to comply with the minimum distribution rules. Finally, including language dealing with the minimum distribution rules makes it clear that the drafter was aware of these rules and that the dispositive terms of the trust are not meant to conflict with the minimum distribution rules. For example, in a marital deduction trust (¶ 3.3.07; Form 7.4, Appendix B) it is common to specify that the trustee must withdraw from the retirement plan "the greater of" the income (that Spouse is entitled to under the marital deduction rules) and the MRD.

6.2.04 *Trust beneficiaries can be "designated beneficiaries"*

Retirement plan death benefits generally may be distributed over the life expectancy of Participant's "designated beneficiary." ¶ 1.5.06. A "designated beneficiary" means one or more individuals who are to inherit the retirement benefits upon Participant's death. ¶ 1.7. Although the general rule is that a designated beneficiary must be an *individual*, the regulations allow you to name a *trust* as beneficiary and still have a "designated beneficiary" for purposes of the minimum distribution rules. Reg. § 1.401(a)(9)-4, A-5. These rules permit you to look through a trust instrument, and treat the *trust beneficiaries* as if they had been named directly as Participant's beneficiaries, if the following four requirements are met:

1.   The trust must be valid under state law. ¶ 6.2.06.

2.   "The trust is irrevocable or will, by its terms, become irrevocable upon the death of the" participant. ¶ 6.2.07.

3.   "The beneficiaries of the trust who are beneficiaries with respect to the trust's interest in the employee's benefit" must be "identifiable...from the trust instrument." ¶ 6.2.08.

4.   Certain documentation must be provided to "the plan administrator." ¶ 6.2.09-¶ 6.2.10.

If Participant dies leaving his retirement benefits to a trust, and the above four rules are satisfied, then, for purposes of § 401(a)(9), the beneficiaries of the trust (and not the trust itself) "will be treated as having been designated as beneficiaries of the employee under the plan..." Reg. § 1.401(a)(9)-4, A-5(a).

However, complying with these four rules does not ensure that the life expectancy method will be available. Treating the trust beneficiaries as if they had been named as beneficiaries directly does not get you very far if the trust beneficiaries themselves do not qualify as "designated beneficiaries." Accordingly, the "fifth rule" is that:

5.   All beneficiaries of the trust must be individuals. ¶ 6.2.12.

Unfortunately, the application of the rules to several commonly used trust provisions is unclear at best and unfavorable at worst. For ideas on how to fix a non-complying trust see ¶ 10.2.

6.2.05 *Date for testing trust's compliance with rules*

The relevant date for applying these tests varies.

The <u>irrevocability requirement</u> must be met as of the date of death; ¶ 6.2.08. Prior to a 1997 change in the proposed regulations, the deadline for compliance with the irrevocability requirement was the required beginning date (¶ 1.3), not the date of death—even for post-death MRDs. Some trusts that were named as beneficiaries of pre-1997 decedents, and that were trapped by that rule, can get back on track for a life expectancy payout, if the trust otherwise qualifies under the new rules, by fulfilling the documentation requirement by October 31, 2003; see ¶ 6.2.09.

The <u>documentation requirement</u> must be met by the later of October 31 of the year after the year of Participant's death or October 31, 2003. See ¶ 6.2.09.

The regulations give no specific testing date for the requirement that the trust must be <u>valid under state law</u>, but the examples in the regulation refer to a trust that is valid under state law *as of the date of death*. See ¶ 6.2.06.

The requirement that the <u>beneficiaries be identifiable</u> must be met as of the date of death, except that, if the trust flunks the requirement as of the date of death, but the problem can be fixed by disclaimer or distribution prior to the Designation Date, the trust should pass; see ¶ 6.2.08 and ¶ 10.2.

The requirement that all <u>beneficiaries must be individuals</u> must be met by the Designation Date (¶ 1.8). For example, if Participant died in 2002, any non-individual trust beneficiaries must be "removed" (through disclaimer or by distribution of their benefits) by September 30, 2003. See ¶ 6.3 and ¶ 10.2.

6.2.06 *First Rule: trust must be valid under state law*

The first rule is that "The trust is a valid trust under state law, or would be but for the fact that there is no corpus." Reg. §1.401(a)(9)-4, A-5(b)(1). A testamentary trust can pass this test, despite the fact that, at the moment of Participant's death, the trust is not yet in existence; see Reg. §1.401(a)(9)-5, A-7(c)(3), Examples 1 and 2.

6.2.07 *Second Rule: trust must be irrevocable*

The second rule is: "The trust is irrevocable or will, by its terms, become irrevocable upon the death of the employee." Reg. § 1.401(a)(9)-4, A-5(b)(2). Generally, any testamentary trust or "living trust" automatically becomes irrevocable upon the testator's or donor's death, and therefore passes this test.

Unfortunately, it is not clear what the IRS is driving at with this rule. The IRS has never given an example of a trust that does not become irrevocable at Participant's death. Perhaps the regulation-writers are thinking of a situation where someone *other than* Participant has a power to "revoke" the trust after Participant's death.

For example: Participant owns an IRA that is community property. He leaves the IRA to a trust. Spouse has the power to revoke that trust with respect to Spouse's community property interest in any property in the trust, and that power would allow her to cancel the trust with respect to the IRA. It appears that the trust is not irrevocable as to the IRA proceeds up to the maximum amount that is subject to Spouse's power. Thus, the trust "flunks" the irrevocability rule to that extent.

However, this doesn't matter, if Spouse *exercises* the power (removes the IRA from the trust): since the IRA is no longer part of the trust, we don't care whether the trust passes the trust rules. It also does not matter to the extent that the IRA exceeds Spouse's interest; if her power is to revoke 50% of the trust, and the IRA represents more than 50%, the excess is not subject to the power, and so the rule is not violated as to that excess portion.

A trustee's power, after Participant's death, to amend administrative provisions of the trust should not be considered a power to revoke, provided it is clear the trustee's power does not permit him to materially modify any beneficial interests. However, this point is not covered in the regulations or any ruling.

Including in the trust the statement "This trust shall be irrevocable upon my death" is not necessary, since any testamentary trust or "living trust" automatically becomes irrevocable upon the testator's or donor's death, and therefore passes this test. On the other hand it does no harm to include this sentence, and inclusion may avoid the necessity of argument with possible future plan administrators and auditing IRS agents who may not be familiar with estate planning.

6.2.08 *Third Rule: beneficiaries must be identifiable*

"The beneficiaries of the trust who are beneficiaries with respect to the trust's interest in the employee's benefit" must be "identifiable within the meaning of A-1 of this section from the trust instrument." Reg. §1.401(a)(9)-4, A-5(b)(3). The entirety of what "A-1 of this section" provides on the meaning of the word "identifiable" is the following: "A designated beneficiary need not be specified by name in the plan or by the employee to the plan...so long as the individual who is to be the beneficiary is identifiable under the plan. The members of a class of beneficiaries capable of expansion or contraction will be treated as being identifiable if it is possible to identify the class member with the shortest life expectancy." Reg. § 1.401(a)(9)-4, A-1.

The easy part of what this rule means is that it must be possible to determine who is the oldest person who could ever possibly be a beneficiary of the trust (because that's whose life expectancy is used as the measuring period for required distributions after Participant's death). ¶ 1.5.08. Thus, if the trust beneficiaries are "all my issue living from time to time," the members of that class of potential beneficiaries are considered "identifiable," even though the class is not closed as of the applicable date, because no person with a shorter life expectancy can be added later. See rulings discussed at ¶ 6.3.06, A. The oldest member of the class can be determined with certainty (because the Participant's issue who are born after his death are by definition younger than the oldest issue of the Participant who is living at the Participant's death). Reg. § 1.401(a)(9)-4, A-1.

Actually, there *is* theoretically a problem even with the common provision "the trust shall be distributed to my issue living at the time of my spouse's death." If people who are issue by virtue of legal adoption are to be included on the same basis as "natural" issue, there is a potential for violating the rule. After Participant's death, one of his issue could adopt someone who was born earlier than the person who was the oldest beneficiary of the trust when Participant died. It is not known whether the IRS would ever raise this "issue," but to avoid the problem, language can be included in the trust providing that older individuals cannot be later added to the class of trust beneficiaries by legal adoption. See Form 7.3, Appendix B.

The rule that it must be possible to identify the oldest member of a class of beneficiaries is similar to the rule against perpetuities, in that the mere *possibility* that an older beneficiary could be added to the trust after the applicable date is enough to make the trust flunk this rule, regardless of whether any such older beneficiary ever is *actually* added.

Example: Kit leaves his IRA to a trust that pays income to his daughter Julia for life, and after her death is to pay income to her widower (if any) for his life, with remainder to Kit's grandchildren. Kit dies, survived by Julia and several grandchildren, none of whom disclaims his or her interest in the trust. Kit's trust flunks this rule, because Julia, after Kit's death, *could* marry a new husband who is older than she. Thus an older beneficiary *could* be added to this trust after the applicable date, and we cannot tell with certainty who is the oldest person who could ever be a beneficiary of the trust.

Any "power of appointment," or trustee power to "spray" (or "sprinkle") income and/or principal of a trust among a class of beneficiaries, under which older beneficiaries *could* be added to the trust at a later date violates this rule. However, if you are permitted to disregard remainder beneficiaries of the trust (¶ 6.3.04), you can *also* disregard any power of appointment that affects only the identity of beneficiaries who could be disregarded.

Apparently, if the oldest beneficiary can be identified, there is no problem with having an extremely broad or amorphous class of potential beneficiaries, such as a power to appoint to "my son or any individual who is younger than my son." See PLR 2002-35038.

The "identifiable" test is applied, first, as of the date of death. If the trust flunks the requirement as of the date of death, but the "unidentifiable" beneficiaries can be "removed," by disclaimer or distribution, prior to the Designation Date, the trust would "pass."

The problem is that if a trust flunks this test as of the date of death it often is not the type of mistake that can be fixed by a disclaimer or distribution prior to the Designation Date. In the "Kit and Julia" example above, Julia's future husband(s) can't disclaim (and we can't distribute their share of the benefits to them) because we don't know who they are yet—that's the whole problem! In some cases the problem could be fixed by disclaimer; for example, if permitted by applicable state law, a fiduciary or beneficiary could disclaim a power of appointment that permitted appointment to "unidentifiable" beneficiaries. The disclaimer dates back to the date of death, and presumably would be recognized as effective for the purpose of fixing the problem.

6.2.09 *Fourth Rule: documentation requirement (post-death)*

The trustee of the trust that is named as beneficiary must supply certain documentation to the <u>plan administrator</u>. Reg. § 1.401(a)(9)-4, A-5(b)(4). In the case of a qualified plan, "plan administrator" is the statutory title of the person(s) or entity responsible for carrying out the plan provisions and complying with the minimum distribution rules; the employer must provide the name, address and phone number of the plan administrator to all employees in the Summary Plan Description. In the case of an IRA, the IRA trustee, custodian, or issuer is the party to whom the documentation must be delivered (IRAs don't have "plan administrators"). Reg. § 1.408-8, A-1(b).

The <u>deadline</u> for supplying this documentation is October 31 of the year after the year of Participant's death (or October 31, 2003, if later). Reg. § 1.401(a)(9)-4, A-6(b). Note that this "documentation deadline" is one month later than the "Designation Date" as of which the designated beneficiary is determined (see ¶ 1.8). The idea is that, once it is settled, on the Designation Date, exactly who the "designated beneficiaries" are, the trustee then has another month to certify this final information to the plan administrator.

Here is the <u>documentation required</u> to be supplied to the plan administrator under Reg. § 1.401(a)(9)-4, A-6(b). The trustee of the trust must *either*:

1.   "Provide the plan administrator with a final list of all beneficiaries of the trust (including contingent and remaindermen beneficiaries with a description of the conditions on their entitlement) as of September 30 of the calendar year following the calendar year of the employee's death; certify that, to the best of the trustee's knowledge, this list is correct and complete and that the [other "trust rules"] are satisfied; and

agree to provide a copy of the trust instrument to the plan administrator upon demand....;" an example of a certification intended to comply with this rule is provided at Form 6.2, Appendix B; or

2.   "Provide the plan administrator with a copy of the actual trust document for the trust that is named as a beneficiary of the employee under the plan as of the employee's date of death."

Supplying a copy of the trust is an easier way to comply than providing a summary of the trust. However, some retirement plans may decide to require the alternative method of compliance, since the alternative method relieves the plan administrator of the burden of reading the trust and determining whether it complies with all the technical requirements of the trust rules.

6.2.10 *Documentation requirement for lifetime distributions*

The identity of the trust beneficiaries is irrelevant to the determination of Participant's lifetime distributions if Participant is using the Uniform Lifetime Table (¶ 1.4.01). Therefore, Participant has no need to comply with the "trust documentation requirement" (or any other trust rules) for his lifetime distributions *unless*: (a) Participant has named a trust as Participant's sole beneficiary; and (b) Participant's spouse is the "sole" beneficiary of the trust (¶ 6.3.12); and (c) Spouse is more than 10 years younger than Participant (so that required distributions are lower if computing using the joint life expectancy of husband and wife rather than the Uniform Lifetime Table; ¶ 1.4.02); and (d) Participant wants to use the actual joint life expectancy (rather than the Uniform Lifetime Table) to measure his MRDs. In such cases, see Reg. § 1.401(a)(9)-4, A-6(a), for details regarding the documentation to be supplied.

No deadline is specified for supplying documentation in the case of lifetime distributions. The conservative assumption would be that the deadline is the beginning of the distribution year in which Participant intends to use the spouses' joint life expectancy to calculate his MRDs. Note that in the case of lifetime required distributions the person who must fulfill this requirement is *Participant* (not the trustee, as is the case when Participant dies).

6.2.11 *What happens if incorrect trust documentation is supplied*

What if the information supplied to the plan administrator is incorrect? This can happen if the Participant (in the case of lifetime MRDs) or the trustee (in the case of post-death MRDs) completed the certifications incorrectly, or sent a copy of the wrong trust instrument to the plan administrator. The regulations let the *plan* off the hook in this situation: the plan will not be disqualified "merely" because of these errors, provided "the plan administrator reasonably relied on the information provided and the required minimum distributions for calendar years after the calendar year in which the discrepancy is discovered are determined based on the actual terms of the trust instrument." Reg. § 1.401(a)(9)-4, A-6(c)(1). However, the penalty tax (which is payable by the person required to *take* the MRD) will be still be based on what should have been distributed "based on the actual terms of the trust in effect." Reg. § 1.401(a)(9)-4, A-6(c)(2).

6.2.12 *Fifth Rule: all beneficiaries must be individuals*

The result of compliance with the first four rules is that the trust beneficiaries will be treated as if Participant had named them directly as beneficiaries. ¶ 6.2.04. The next step, therefore, is to make sure that these trust beneficiaries qualify as "designated beneficiaries," *i.e.*, that they are individuals. This requirement is much trickier than it appears.

The first pitfall in this rule is that an estate is not an individual and therefore an estate cannot be a designated beneficiary. ¶ 1.7.04. Therefore, if any part of the trust's interest in the benefits will pass to an estate (see ¶ 6.2.13), Participant has "no designated beneficiary" (unless the estate can be disregarded; ¶ 6.3.04).

6.2.13 *Paying estate expenses, taxes, etc. from the trust*

Some IRS letter rulings suggest that even indirectly allowing benefits to pass to Participant's estate (as through a trust provision which allows or directs the use of trust property to pay Participant's debts or probate expenses) may be treated the same as naming the estate as a beneficiary and may result in having "no designated beneficiary." See, *e.g.*, PLR 9809059, in which part of an IRA was payable to "Trust K." In ruling that Trust K was entitled to use the "life expectancy method" for the IRA benefits payable to it, the IRS noted that "Trust K does *not* provide that trust assets shall be used to pay funeral costs," probate expenses or estate taxes (emphasis added). Although the ruling does not comment on the absence of such a provision, it merely recites the fact that the trust contained no such provision, one could conclude that the IRS ruled favorably on Trust K only because it did not contain the (forbidden?) clause.

The IRS, having apparently adopted this unfortunate position, then seems to bend over backwards in rulings to find a way around its own rule. In letter rulings regarding IRAs payable to trusts, the IRS has taken to reciting that state law exempted the IRAs from claims of creditors, without specifying what the relevance of such a state law provision is. This creates the impression that the state law exemption of the benefits from claims of creditors was significant, perhaps as "proof" that the trustee could not distribute retirement benefits to the estate to pay debts, expenses and taxes (although it doesn't prove that). See, e.g., PLR 2001-31033.

Planning mode: Amend the trust so it either prohibits this use of the retirement benefits, or requires that no such payments may be made from the retirement benefits on or after September 30 of the year after the year of the Participant's death. See Form 7.2, Appendix B. If there are no assets available to pay debts, expenses and taxes other than retirement benefits, consider specifying that only certain retirement plans may be used for this purpose, so that only the retirement plans authorized to be used to pay the debts and expenses will be "tainted," and the other(s) can be exempted from this problem; or have Participant take withdrawals during life so his estate will have sufficient non-plan assets to pay these items.

Cleanup mode: If the Participant has died, but the Designation Date (¶ 1.8.01) has not yet passed, the trustee can withdraw from the retirement plan as much money as is expected to be needed from the plan to pay debts, expenses and taxes (if any will be so needed), then have all parties (trustee, executor, beneficiaries) agree that the estate will not claim any more funds from the retirement plan under this provision. If the agreement is binding under applicable state law on all future fiduciaries and beneficiaries of the estate, it should work to insulate the benefits from being considered payable to the estate after the Designation Date. If it is not feasible to eliminate the offending trust provision by this method, the IRS may approve a fact-based argument (e.g., if you show that all realistically expected claims, debts and taxes have either been paid or provided for prior to the Designation Date, or that state law exempts retirement benefits from creditors' claims) and give a ruling.

6.3 Who Are the Beneficiaries of a Trust?

6.3.01 *Post-death distributions; benefits and "proceeds" thereof*

This ¶ 6.3 deals only with ascertaining who are the beneficiaries of a trust for purposes of applying the minimum distribution rules to required distributions after the death of Participant. The trust rules apply to lifetime required distributions only in rare cases (see ¶ 6.2.10); that topic is not discussed directly here.

Also, note that a "trust's interest in a retirement plan" includes not just the retirement plan itself and the distributions from the retirement plan, but also the "proceeds" resulting from the trust's reinvestment of the retirement plan distributions. Thus, the regulations "care about" who is the beneficiary of the trust even after the retirement plan has ceased to exist (because 100% of it has been distributed to the trustee of the trust that was named as beneficiary of the retirement plan). The tests apply to that trust as long as the trust holds any distributions that were retained ("accumulated") in the trust even though they were reinvested in other forms of investment.

Example: Olga's retirement plan is payable to a trust. The trustee of the trust is instructed to withdraw all benefits from the retirement plan over a period of time not exceeding the life expectancy of Olga's husband Bengt, and to withdraw any remaining benefits from the plan upon Bengt's death. The trustee is to pay income of the trust to Bengt for his life, and after Bengt's death is to pay income to Olga's and Bengt's son Rolf for his life. On the death of Rolf, the principal of the trust is to be paid to a remainder beneficiary. Under the minimum distribution trust rules we need to determine who that remainder beneficiary is, and include that remainder beneficiary when testing to see if (for example) all the trust beneficiaries are "individuals." Even though the retirement plan won't exist at that point (because it was all distributed to the trust no later than Bengt's death), the trust assets at that point will include the reinvested "proceeds" of the retirement plan distributions. Thus, if the remainder beneficiary who takes after Rolf's death is not an individual the trust flunks the fifth rule (¶ 6.2.12).

6.3.02 Importance of definition of "trust beneficiary"

To apply the minimum distribution trust rules to a particular trust, we need to determine who are the "beneficiaries" of that trust. Unfortunately the regulations never define "trust beneficiary," leaving doubt, in many cases, regarding whether a particular trust "passes" the rules or not.

This ¶ 6.3 discusses the question of which trust beneficiaries "count" for purposes of the minimum distribution trust rules, and which may be disregarded. If a trust has a non-individual beneficiary, the trust will "flunk" the rules—unless the rules allow that beneficiary to be disregarded. If it is not possible to identify the oldest person who could ever possibly be a beneficiary of the trust, then the trust again flunks, because its beneficiaries are not "identifiable" (¶ 6.2.08)—*unless* the rules allow you to disregard the provision that creates the possibility of an "unidentifiable" beneficiary.

The first step in the process is to see whether certain beneficiaries may be disregarded because, even though they are beneficiaries of the overall trust, they *cannot possibly* receive any of the retirement benefits payable to that trust

6.3.03 Beneficiaries with respect to "trust's interest in the benefits"

In determining who are the beneficiaries of a trust, we need be concerned only with beneficiaries who are such "with respect to the trust's interest in the employee's benefit." See Reg. § 1.401(a)(9)-4, A-5(b)(3); § 1.401(a)(9)-8, A-11 (last sentence).

Example 1: Calvin's IRA is payable to a trust. At his death the trust assets are divided between a marital trust and a credit shelter trust. However, Calvin's IRA is required to be paid to the marital trust (either because the plan beneficiary designation form names the marital trust directly as beneficiary, or because the trust requires that all retirement benefits are to be allocated to the marital trust). We need look only at the *beneficiaries of the marital trust* in applying the various tests and questions. However, if neither the beneficiary designation form nor the trust instrument requires that all benefits be paid to one share or the other, then we need to look at all beneficiaries of both shares.

Example 2: Katerina's 401(k) plan benefits are payable to a trust as beneficiary. The trust provides for distributions to be made on her death to her husband Lou, various relatives and charities. However, the trust prohibits use of retirement benefits to pay the charitable bequests. Accordingly, the charities are not trust beneficiaries "with respect to the trust's interest in the employee benefit," and can be disregarded.

Note that this is not a "separate account" rule (see ¶ 1.7.06). Disregarding beneficiaries who are prohibited from sharing in the retirement benefit does not depend on the existence of "separate accounts" at the plan level or "separate shares" (¶ 7.4.04) in the usual tax or trust accounting sense. The conclusions in the above examples are based on the regulations' statement that beneficiaries of the trust *"with respect to the trust's interest in [the] employee's benefit* are treated as having been designated as beneficiaries of the employee under the plan." Reg. § 1.401(a)(9)-8, A-11 (emphasis added).

In the rest of this ¶ 6.3, "beneficiaries of the trust" means "beneficiaries of the trust with respect to the trust's interest in the employee's benefit."

Second, we must conclude that "all" trust beneficiaries ("current" beneficiaries, as well as those who have vested or contingent remainder interests) are considered "beneficiaries of the trust" for purposes of the regulations—unless they can be excluded from consideration under the rules discussed below.

6.3.04 *Beneficiaries who may be disregarded; the A-7 rule*

If the trust rules are complied with, then all "trust beneficiaries" (except those who have no interest in the benefits because they are categorically excluded from sharing in them; ¶ 6.3.03) are treated as having been named directly as beneficiaries by Participant. If the trust has more than one beneficiary, then: "In the case of payments to a trust having more than one beneficiary, see A-7 of section 1.401(a)(9)-5 for the rules for determining the designated beneficiary whose life expectancy will be used to determine the distribution period." Reg. § 1.401(a)(9)-4, A-5(c). The same "A-7" rule is also to be used for determining whether all beneficiaries are individuals. Reg. § 1.401(a)(9)-5, A-7(c).

So what is the "A-7" rule? This provision, the test for determining which potential beneficiaries of a trust can be disregarded has been stated differently in each version of the minimum distribution regulations (1987 proposed, 2001 proposed and 2002 final). The final regulations version is as follows:

"(c). Successor beneficiary—(1) A person will not be considered a beneficiary for purposes of determining who is the beneficiary with the shortest life expectancy...or whether a person who is not an individual is a beneficiary, merely because the person could become the successor to the interest of one of the employee's beneficiaries after that beneficiary's death. However, the preceding sentence does not apply to a person who has any right (including a contingent right) to an employee's benefit beyond being a mere potential successor to the interest of one of the employee's beneficiaries upon that beneficiary's death." Reg. § 1.401(a)(9)-5, A-7(c).

Unfortunately, the meaning of A-7(c) is unclear. The regulations offer no other guiding principles and contain only two examples, one of which is a "conduit trust" (¶ 6.3.08) and the other of which is ambiguous (¶ 6.3.11). *Until the standards regarding which potential trust beneficiaries may be disregarded are further clarified by IRS guidance or litigation, practitioners are left at their peril in drafting trusts as beneficiaries of retirement benefits.*
Here is your road map through the trust minefield:

I.   The only absolutely safe harbor trusts are MRD conduit trusts (¶ 6.3.08) and trusts that cannot possibly pass to non-individual beneficiaries (¶ 6.3.07). A grantor trust is probably also safe (¶ 6.3.09).

II.   The tests applicable to the most common forms of family and marital trusts and trusts for minors are not clear. See ¶ 6.3.10. Consider obtaining a ruling.

III.   Certain trusts definitely do not pass the rules. See ¶ 6.3.05.

IV.   Finally, remember that sometimes you can just ignore these rules because you don't care about using the life-expectancy-of-the-beneficiary payout. See ¶ 6.2.02.

6.3.05 *Remainder beneficiaries generally do count*

To understand the following discussion, it is essential to bear in mind the distinctions between "trust accounting income" and "MRDs" discussed at ¶ 6.1.07.

If any distributions made from the retirement plan to the trust during the lifetime of the life beneficiary of the trust can be held for later distribution to the remainder beneficiaries, then the remainder beneficiaries must be counted as "beneficiaries." "Thus, for example, if the first beneficiary has a right to all income with respect to an employee's individual account during that beneficiary's life and a second beneficiary has a right to the principal but only after the death of the first income beneficiary (any portion of the principal distributed during the life of the first income beneficiary to be held in trust until that first beneficiary's death), both beneficiaries must be taken into account in determining the beneficiary with the shortest life expectancy and whether only individuals are beneficiaries." Reg. § 1.401(a)(9)-5, A-7(c). See also Reg. § 1.401(a)(9)-5, A-7(c)(3), Example 2.

Therefore, under the typical form of trust that provides income to one beneficiary and remainder to another (such as a "QTIP" trust) both the remainder beneficiary and the income beneficiary "count." See PLR 9820021 (a trust which provided income to spouse and remainder to charities; ruled, Participant had "no designated beneficiary"); see also, *e.g.*, PLR 9322005 (marital trust to a spouse for life, remainder to children; spouse *and children* regarded as beneficiaries).

Example: Lou names a trust as beneficiary of his IRA. The trust is to pay all trust accounting income to Judy for life, and on Judy's death the principal goes to the Community Foundation. Principal (i.e., trust accounting principal) distributed from the retirement plan during Judy's life is "accumulated" (held) in the trust until Judy dies, and then it is turned over to the Foundation. Accordingly, the Foundation, as remainder beneficiary, *is* counted as a beneficiary of the trust, and therefore this trust "flunks" the rules because not all beneficiaries are individuals. Thus, Lou has "no designated beneficiary." Benefits must be distributed from the plan to the trust over Lou's remaining life expectancy (if he died after his required beginning date) or under the 5-year rule (if he died before his required beginning date). See ¶ 1.5.04 and ¶ 1.5.05.

The same rule applies even if the trust is not *required* to "accumulate" the retirement plan distributions for the charitable (or older individual) remainder beneficiary, but *could* do so. In the Lou/Judy example above, giving the trustee discretion to distribute principal to Judy would not solve the problem; the charitable remainder beneficiary would still "count" as a trust beneficiary because the trustee also has discretion *not* to distribute principal to Judy but rather to accumulate it for the charity.

Note also that:

1. If the remainder beneficiary is an individual, but is older than the life beneficiary, the remainder beneficiary is the "oldest trust beneficiary" for purposes of measuring required distributions. Even though this result is illogical (because the remainder beneficiary will die before the life beneficiary, according to the IRS's actuarial tables, and so is not predicted to receive anything under the trust) it seems to be the IRS's position. See PLR 2002-28025, discussed at ¶ 6.3.10.

2. If the remainder beneficiary is another trust, both trusts must comply with the trust rules (unless the remainder trust can be disregarded; see ¶ 6.3.04). Reg. § 1.401(a)(9)-4, A-5(d). See ¶ 6.3.06, D.

6.3.06 *Effect of powers of appointment*

It appears that if a "countable" remainder interest is subject to a power of appointment upon the death of the life beneficiary, all potential appointees are considered "beneficiaries." Thus potential appointees should be (i) identifiable (see ¶ 6.2.08) (ii) individuals who are (iii) younger than the beneficiary whose life expectancy is the one that the parties want to use to measure distributions. The following examples illustrate the possibilities:

A. Power to appoint to "issue" apparently is acceptable. A trust that says "The trustee shall pay income to my spouse for life, and upon my spouse's death the principal shall be paid to such persons *among the class consisting of our issue* as my spouse shall appoint by her will" does not create a problem under this rule because the power is limited to a small, clearly-defined group of "identifiable" younger individuals. See, *e.g.*, PLRs 1999-03050 ("Trust B") and 1999-18065 ("Trust 2") approving trusts which contained powers to appoint principal among Participant's issue.

B.   Power to appoint to charity. A trust that says "The trustee shall pay income to my spouse for life, and upon my spouse's death the principal shall be paid to such members of *the class consisting of our issue and any charity* as my spouse shall appoint by her will," would flunk this rule, because the benefits could pass under the power to a non-individual beneficiary.

C.   Power limited to younger individuals. Under any power of appointment, if the class of potential appointees is limited to *younger individuals*, the power of appointment will not create a problem under the rules that all remainder beneficiaries must be individuals and that it must be possible to identify the oldest beneficiary of the trust. See PLR 2002-35038. However, if the class is very broad or amorphous see ¶ 6.2.08.

D.   Implied power to appoint to another trust. Under many states' laws, any power to appoint property to individuals includes the power to appoint in trust for such individuals. The IRS has never commented on the effect of such a state law in any private letter rulings or in the regulations. Since the regulations require that, if benefits are distributable under one trust to another trust, *both* trusts must comply with the rules, it would appear that any power of appointment that could be exercised by appointing in trust would cause a trust to flunk the trust rules unless the power is limited to appointing only to other trusts that comply with the rules. Reg. § 1.401(a)(9)-4, A-5(d).

E.   When a power of appointment can be ignored. Finally, if exercise of the power of appointment can affect the benefits only at a point where a successor beneficiary could be ignored, the power can also be ignored. See ¶ 6.3.04. In other words, if you could disregard a contingent beneficiary because he, she or it is "merely" a successor to the interest of another beneficiary, you can disregard a power of appointment that would determine the identity of that contingent beneficiary—regardless of whether the potential appointee is a charity, an older individual or another trust.

6.3.07 *Trust that cannot possibly pass to non-individuals*

One way to deal with the mystery of which beneficiaries don't count is to draft the trust so there are no beneficiaries you *need* to disregard. If the trust property cannot under any circumstances be distributed to a non-individual beneficiary, then it passes the rule.

For example, if the trust provides "income to spouse for life, remainder to our issue living at spouse's death; provided, if at any time during spouse's life there are no issue of ours living, the trust shall terminate and be distributed to spouse," it is impossible for the trust assets to pass to anyone other than spouse or issue, all of whom are individuals. If spouse dies before issue, issue get the benefits. If issue die before spouse, spouse gets the benefits.

6.3.08 *Conduit trusts (also called "MRD conduit trusts")*

A "conduit trust" is not an official term, but is a nickname for a trust which serves as a conduit for distributions from the retirement plan to the individual beneficiary of the trust. The trustee is required to withdraw the minimum distributions from the retirement plan over the life expectancy of the individual trust beneficiary (or of the oldest member of a group of individual trust beneficiaries) and distribute the distributions out to that beneficiary (or the members of the group). The trustee does not have the power to hold and retain inside the trust *any* plan distributions made during the lifetime of the beneficiary (or of the oldest beneficiary).

With a conduit trust, the retirement benefits are deemed paid "to" the individual conduit trust-beneficiary for purposes of the minimum distribution rules, and the "all beneficiaries must be individuals" test is met. Remainder beneficiaries can be disregarded because they are "mere potential successors" to the conduit beneficiary's interest in the benefits. Reg. § 1.401(a)(9)-5, A-7(c)(3), Example 2. *This is a guaranteed safe harbor.*

The conduit trust could be useful in some situations, such as:

A.   Aunt Emily believes that leaving her IRA to her young nephews is a fine way to provide them with a nest egg, but knows that, if she names them directly as beneficiaries, they will simply cash out the account immediately upon her death. So she leaves the IRA to a conduit trust for them. The purpose of the trust is to make sure that the nephews take advantage of the "life expectancy method," whether they want to or not, and to provide professional management for the undistributed portion of the IRA. The trustee is instructed to withdraw from the IRA, each year, the MRD (based on the life expectancy of the oldest nephew) and distribute it equally to the surviving nephews.

B. Eli wants to leave his IRA to his wife Laura, but is concerned about her ability to handle a large sum of money that becomes subject to her control all at once. He is confident that she would handle wisely a stream of installment payments from the IRA. So he makes the IRA payable to a trust. The trustee will withdraw from the IRA and distribute to Laura each year the greater of the income of the IRA (see ¶ 3.3.07) or the MRD based on Laura's life expectancy.

Under the conduit trust approach, the primary trust beneficiary is in the same position as if he had been named directly, individually, as beneficiary of the benefits, but with a variation: it is as if Participant, instead of leaving it up to the beneficiary to decide when and how to take out the benefits, had specified a payout mode as well as a beneficiary. In this case, it is as if Participant had specified that distributions would be paid in instalments over the life expectancy of the designated beneficiary. If the designated beneficiary (or life beneficiary of the conduit trust) lives to his life expectancy, he will have received 100% of the benefits and the remainder beneficiary will receive nothing.

Unfortunately, this type of trust is not useful in many situations. To work as intended it depends entirely the minimum distribution payout scheme staying exactly as it is under present law. If changes in the law require or encourage faster distributions the trust beneficiary will receive the money much sooner than Participant intended.

For discussion of using conduit trusts in connection with a non-QDOT marital trust, see ¶ 10.5.05, C; in connection with a credit shelter trust, see ¶ 10.5.03, D.

Practice Note: The life expectancy payout period under a conduit trust could last longer than the Rule Against Perpetuities would permit the trust to last. Even though the maximum payout period for post-death MRDs is an individual beneficiary's single life expectancy, the beneficiary whose life expectancy is being used as a measuring period could die more than 21 years before the end of his IRS-defined life expectancy, in which case (if his was the only measuring life), the trust could (depending on exactly what the dispositive terms are at that point) be in existence more than 21 years after the termination of "lives in being" at the commencement of the trust. The trust drafter should take care that the payout period required by the trust does not exceed the "perpetuities" period under applicable state law.

CONDUIT TRUST IRONY

If the surviving spouse is the conduit beneficiary, she is considered the sole beneficiary of the trust (¶ 6.3.12) and accordingly her life expectancy will be determined using the recalculation method (¶ 1.2.06) for purposes of calculating MRDs to the trust. Ironically, this means that she is guaranteed *not* to receive all of the benefits during her lifetime (if the trustee is limited to distributing to her only the MRD amount). Because her life expectancy will always be greater than one year (see ¶ 1.6.06), there will be money left in the retirement plan at her death if the trustee takes no more than the MRD. A conduit trust for the life of the spouse, with remainder to a charity, "passes" the MRD trust rules (because the non-individual remainder beneficiary is ignored), even though some of the benefits are *guaranteed* to pass to a non-individual—which is the result the trust rules were supposed to prevent!

6.3.09 § 678(a)(1) grantor trusts

Under the so-called "grantor trust rules" of the Code, a trust beneficiary who is a U.S. citizen or resident is treated for all purposes of the federal income tax as the "owner" of trust assets if such beneficiary has the sole unrestricted right to withdraw those assets from the trust. See § 678(a)(1), § 672(f), as interpreted in regulations (see especially Reg. § 1.671-3(b)). It would appear that if an individual beneficiary is deemed the owner of all of the trust's assets under § 678(a)(1), then retirement benefits payable to such trust must be deemed paid "to" such individual beneficiary for purposes of the minimum distribution rules, and the "all beneficiaries must be individuals" test is met. Note: the discussion in this subsection assumes the beneficiary's withdrawal power does not lapse during his lifetime.

See, *e.g.*, PLR 1999-03050 ("Trust A"), in which the IRS ruled with respect to a marital trust under which the surviving spouse had the unlimited right to withdraw all principal and income: "You are the beneficiary of Trust A because the terms of Trust A provide that you may invade principal in your absolute discretion. Thus, the beneficiaries' entitlement to benefits after your death is essentially contingent upon your death within the meaning of...the proposed regulations and they are not considered." Note, however, that this ruling was under the old (1987-2000) proposed regulations and in any case did not mention § 678.

Treating the trust beneficiary as the owner of the benefits for income tax purposes would have two results: income taxes on the trust income would be imposed at the beneficiary's rate; and the remainder beneficiary would not count as a trust beneficiary for purposes of the minimum distribution rules. Thus an estate, older individuals or charities could be named as remainder beneficiaries (to succeed to whatever part of the trust was not distributed to or withdrawn by the owner-beneficiary during his life) without loss of the use of the owner-beneficiary's life expectancy as the measuring period for MRDs. Similarly, a power of appointment that affected the trust property only after the death of the owner-beneficiary could be disregarded

Under this model, the trust beneficiary would be given the unlimited right to withdraw the benefits (and any "proceeds" thereof; ¶ 6.3.01) from the trust at any time. Until the beneficiary chooses to exercise this right, the trustee exercises ownership rights and responsibilities on the beneficiary's behalf, for example, by investing the trust funds, choosing distribution options, and distributing income and/or principal to or for the benefit of the beneficiary.

This type of trust would be uncommon, since anyone wanting to give such broad rights to the beneficiary would presumably choose to leave the benefits outright to the beneficiary rather than in trust. However, there are two situations in which this model could be useful:

1. A marital deduction "qualified domestic trust" (QDOT) for the benefit of a non-citizen spouse (§ 2056A), where the only purpose of placing a trust between the surviving spouse and the retirement benefits is to qualify for the modified marital

deduction available when the surviving spouse is not a U.S. citizen. See ¶ 4.3.02.

2.   A trust to provide for a mentally handicapped beneficiary who can exercise the right of withdrawal only through a legal guardian. For this type of beneficiary, this type of trust provides the benefits of a discretionary trust without losing the benefits of the "life expectancy" method based on the life expectancy of the handicapped beneficiary. This can be particularly helpful where the primary beneficiary does not have and is not likely to have issue, and the only likely remainder beneficiaries are the primary beneficiary's older siblings, the beneficiary's own estate or charities.

Unfortunately, the IRS has never mentioned § 678(a)(1) either in rulings or in the minimum distribution regulations, so the above conclusions are based on the author's analysis without the comforting assurance of any IRS pronouncements.

6.3.10 *Remainder contingent on premature death or "wipe-out"*

What if a remainder interest is not vested, but rather is contingent on all the family beneficiaries' dying young, or dying "out of actuarial order" (what lawyers sometimes refer to as the "wipe-out clause")? It is not clear how the "A-7" rule (¶ 6.3.04) applies here, leaving practitioners in limbo regarding whether many of the most common forms of family/marital/minors' trusts pass the "trust rules."

Example: Hunter leaves his IRA to a trust which provides "income to my wife Anita for life, and on her death the principal shall pass to Peter, if he is then living, or, if he is then deceased, shall pass to Charity X." Anita and Peter both survive Hunter. Charity X is not an individual.

Many practitioners assume that in this example we are entitled to disregard Charity X, because Peter receives his interest outright at Anita's death, so Charity X is a "mere potential successor" to Peter. However, the regulations provide no discussion of this point, no guiding principles, no definitions and no examples. What if Peter is much older than Anita, so he is likely to predecease her? We know that if he is older than Anita, he would be considered the oldest individual trust beneficiary, so his life expectancy (not Anita's) would control if the trust is entitled to use the life expectancy of the oldest trust beneficiary, but that doesn't help us decide whether the charity is considered a beneficiary.

If preparing a typical trust such as this with a charitable wipe-out beneficiary, consider applying for a ruling, or restructure the trust to eliminate the charity. See ¶ 6.3.07 for one way to do this. Another way some practitioners are considering is to name heirs at law "who are younger than [name of primary trust beneficiary]" as the wipe-out beneficiary; see PLR 2002-35038 for a similar approach. The problem with this approach is it never gets to the end—what if there are no "individual heirs-at-law younger than [X]" when the trust terminates? As indicated by the reasoning in PLR 2002-35038, the IRS has not dealt with the reality there will always be some potential for a trust to pass to non-individual beneficiaries (such as the estate of a deceased individual or even the state by escheat).

The same problem exists, even more critically, with the typical trust for young beneficiaries that calls for the trust to terminate and be distributed to them outright at a certain age. If the age for distribution is such that there is an overwhelming actuarial likelihood that the beneficiary will reach that age alive (e.g., there is an over 95% chance at birth of living to age 46), a remainder beneficiary who takes only if the individual beneficiary dies before that age *should* be considered a "mere potential successor," and therefore should not count as a beneficiary.

However, the IRS, at least judging by the one letter ruling that squarely addressed the issue, apparently doesn't see it that way. See PLR 2002-28025, which involved a trust for the benefit of two minors. The trust was to terminate and be distributed outright to the minors as each reached age 30, but if they both died before reaching that age, the trust would pass to other relatives, the oldest of whom was age 67 at participant's death. The IRS ruled that the 67-year-old "counted" and therefore his life expectancy governed computation of MRDs to the trust because he was the "oldest trust beneficiary."

In view of this letter ruling, and since the *only* examples the IRS provides of trusts that "pass the rules" are a trust that cannot (apparently; the example is ambiguous—see ¶ 6.3.11) pass to a non-individual beneficiary under any circumstance (see ¶ 6.3.07) and a conduit trust (¶ 6.3.08), a practitioner who is drafting a minor's trust should consider the following alternatives:

1.   Use a conduit trust. Even though a conduit trust (¶ 6.3.08)
      partly defeats the purpose of leaving money in trust for a young
      beneficiary, some practitioners are opting for this because it is
      a safe harbor, and does not require a letter ruling, on the theory
      that the MRDs that would have to be passed out to the minor
      beneficiary (or his guardian or custodian) would be very small
      because of his young age.

2.   Forget about the life expectancy payout. Realistically assess
      whether the life expectancy payout method is available and/or
      useful in the particular situation. If the retirement plan in
      question is a 401(k), it probably doesn't offer the life
      expectancy payout method anyway (¶ 1.5.09). If the retirement
      plan is the major asset of the trust, will the trustee be able to
      afford a life expectancy payout? Or will the benefits have to be
      distributed faster than the minor child's 60+ year life
      expectancy, to provide for the child's care, support and college
      education? If the benefits are going to have to be paid out
      during the child's youth for these purposes, qualifying for the
      life expectancy payout method is probably not an important
      goal.

3.   Buy life insurance. For many young parents, buying additional
      term insurance would be a more certain and effective way to
      protect their minor children in case of the parent's premature
      death than the uncertainties of the life expectancy payout
      method.

4.   Get a ruling. It can be hoped that the IRS would be more
      reasonable in another ruling than it was in PLR 2002-28025.

6.3.11 *Regulation's Example 1 needs clarification*

The only example the IRS provides of a non-conduit trust that
passes the rules is in Example 1 of Reg. § 1.401(a)(9)-5, A-7(c)(3). In
this example, we are told that "Under the terms of Trust P, all trust
income is payable annually to B [Spouse of the deceased participant,
A], and no one has the power to appoint Trust P principal to any person
other than B. A's children, who are all younger than B, are the sole
remainder beneficiaries of Trust P. *No other person has a beneficial*

interest in Trust P." (Emphasis added.) In this example, the IRS is making the point that B and the children of A are all considered "beneficiaries" of Trust P, so the surviving spouse is not the sole beneficiary, but her life expectancy is used to measure required distributions because she is the oldest beneficiary.

This example is defective, however, because it does not explain what happens under "Trust P" if all of A's children predecease B. Either the trust document or state law must have something to say on that point, but the IRS's example is silent. Yet the only way we would be entitled to disregard the beneficiaries ("contingent beneficiaries") who take in that case is if they are considered "mere potential successors" to the interests of A's children.

Here are all the possibilities for what happens to "Trust P" in Example 1 if all A's children die before B:

1.   Perhaps Trust P provides for further younger individual beneficiaries (such as issue of A's children) to take the remainder if A's children predecease B. But that doesn't resolve the question, because every human being in the world could predecease B, and the question is where does the trust principal go if *that* happens? The IRS ignores this question in, e.g., PLR 2002-35038.

2.   Perhaps Trust P provides for a charity (or for the children's estates) to take the remainder interest if A's children predecease B. In that case the trust would flunk, because the charity (or estates) could receive the benefits if the beneficiaries die out of actuarial order—*unless* we are entitled to disregard such contingent beneficiaries as "mere potential successors" to the children's interests. If that is the case, however, are we entitled to disregard them because we can assume that the children, being younger than B, will outlive B? Or because we can "stop" once we reach any person named as outright remainder beneficiary, regardless of how unlikely that person is to outlive the life beneficiary? If the latter, then for the client who really wants to name a charity as remainder beneficiary, there would be a premium on finding a young person with a terminal illness, to name as the nominal "remainder beneficiary," knowing that the such person is unlikely to outlive the life beneficiary but nevertheless he "counts" as "the" remainder beneficiary.

3.   The only other way that Trust P can pass the IRS's test is if the trust provides that, if all the children predecease B, the trust terminates and is distributed *to B*. Under this formulation, no non-individual has any interest in the trust. If the children survive B the children (who are individuals) get the benefits, and if B survives the children then B (who is an individual) gets the benefits, and there is no beneficiary we have to try to disregard. See ¶ 6.3.07. Since the example says that no one other than B and A's children has any beneficial interest in the trust maybe that is what the IRS means; but if so that would be an unusual trust provision.

It is hoped that the IRS will issue additional guidance on these issues soon. The ambiguity of the trust regulations has become a scandal. Without authoritative guidance, practitioners, retirees, beneficiaries, plan administrators and IRA providers are left in limbo, forced to seek letter rulings at every turn. Some of the issues may end up being resolved by litigation. In any such litigation it is hard to imagine the courts would be sympathetic to the IRS's position if the IRS has left an entire industry, and millions of taxpayers, with incomprehensible rules or no rules after 16 years of study.

6.3.12 *When is 'a trust for Spouse' the same as 'Spouse'?*

Under the Code and regulations, the surviving spouse as beneficiary is entitled to various special "deals" not available to other beneficiaries. See ¶ 1.6, ¶ 3.2. This raises the question whether a trust for the sole or primary benefit of Spouse would be entitled to any of the special privileges that apply when Spouse individually is named as beneficiary. The answer to this varies. The following is a brief summary. For full details on this topic, see the article "When a 'Trust for Spouse' Is Treated the Same as 'Spouse'" by Natalie B. Choate, *Trusts & Estates*, Sept. 2001.

If Spouse is treated as owner of all of the trust property under the grantor trust rules (¶ 6.3.09), she *should* be considered the sole beneficiary of that trust; and (although the regulations do not discuss grantor trusts) the trust should be entitled to all the privileges of Spouse individually so long as she has not made a completed transfer of the trust to anyone else. However, the regulations provide that, for purposes of Spouse's right to elect to treat an inherited IRA as Spouse's own IRA (¶ 3.2.05), Spouse must be the sole beneficiary of the IRA and this requirement is not satisfied "If a trust is named as beneficiary of the IRA...even if the spouse is the sole beneficiary of the trust." Reg. § 1.408-8, A-5(a).

If Spouse is entitled to all income (i.e., trust accounting income; ¶ 6.1.07) of the trust for life, but she does NOT have the right to demand distribution to herself of the entire amount of Participant's retirement benefits payable to the trust, and she does NOT even have the right to demand distribution to herself of whatever amounts are distributed from the retirement plan to the trust during her lifetime, then the trust is a "classic QTIP trust." ¶ 3.3.04. Many "credit shelter trusts" also fall into this model. Even if distributions to such a trust will be measured by Spouse's life expectancy (because the trust complies with the trust rules and spouse is the oldest beneficiary of the trust), "some amounts distributed from...[the retirement plan] to [the QTIP trust] may be accumulated in [the QTIP trust] during [Spouse's] lifetime for the benefit of [the] remaindermen beneficiaries." Therefore the remainder beneficiaries are considered "beneficiaries" of the trust for purposes of the multiple beneficiary rule, and Spouse is not the sole beneficiary. This type of trust is not entitled to any of the privileges of Spouse.

As previewed by Rev. Rul. 2000-2, the regulations confirm that a trust may use the delayed beginning date of § 401(a)(9)(B)(iv) (later of December 31 of the year after the year Participant died or December 31 of the year Participant would have reached age 70½; ¶ 1.6.04) for required distributions (if Participant died before his RBD) only if Spouse is the *sole* beneficiary of the trust. Therefore, the delayed commencement date (and related rules) of § 401(a)(9)(B)(iv) do *not* apply to benefits payable to a QTIP trust (¶ 3.3.04), but *do* apply to benefits payable to a conduit trust for Spouse (¶ 6.3.08) or (presumably) to a trust of which Spouse is treated as sole owner under § 678 (¶ 6.3.09). Reg. § 1.401(a)(9)-5, A-7(c)(3), Ex. 2(i). A temporary transition rule allowing some beneficiaries to switch to the life expectancy payout method may help trusts that concluded the delayed commencement date was available for QTIP trusts; see Reg. § 1.401(a)(9)-1, A-2(b)(2), discussed at ¶ 1.5.10.

Required lifetime distributions to a Participant who has named a trust as beneficiary are determined under the Joint and Last Survivor Table or the Uniform Lifetime Table, whichever produces a lower MRD, in any particular distribution year, if Participant's sole beneficiary for such year is either Spouse, or a conduit trust for Spouse, or (presumably) a 100% grantor trust for Spouse, provided Participant complies with the documentation requirement (¶ 6.2.10) and other trust rules (¶ 6.2.04). A Participant who has named a QTIP Trust as beneficiary must use the Uniform Lifetime Table (¶ 1.4.01).

The special method of computing Spouse's life expectancy (¶ 1.6.06) is available to a trust only if the trust is the sole beneficiary of Participant, and Spouse is the sole beneficiary of the trust, i.e., the trust is a conduit trust (¶ 6.3.08) as to Spouse or (presumably) a 100% grantor trust (¶ 6.3.09) as to Spouse. Reg. § 1.401(a)(9)-5, A-5(c)(2). In the case of a QTIP Trust, or any other trust, the life expectancy of the oldest trust beneficiary applies and it is calculated on a fixed-term basis as described in Reg. § 1.401(a)(9)-5, A-5(c)(1).

6.3.13 *"Separate accounts" vs. "separate trusts"*

Under the "separate accounts" rule (¶ 1.7.06), the minimum distribution rules apply separately to different beneficiaries of a single retirement plan if the plan is divided into "separate accounts" payable respectively to such different beneficiaries. A common estate planning technique is to leave assets to a trust that will be divided, immediately upon Participant's death, into several trusts (such as a marital trust and credit shelter trust, or separate trusts for individual children).

It is clear from the Regulations that the separate accounts concept applies at the *plan level*, not at the *trust level*. The *plan benefit* is not considered divided into separate accounts merely because it is payable to a *trust* that has multiple beneficiaries, even if the beneficiaries' shares constitute "separate shares" for purposes of allocating the income of the trust (§ 663). Reg. § 1.401(a)(9)-4, A-5(c) ("...the separate account rules under A-2 of § 1.401(a)(9)-8 are not available to beneficiaries of a trust with respect to the trust's interest in the employee's benefit."). See also PLR 9809059.

However, Reg. § 1.401(a)(9)-4, A-5(c) should not be interpreted as prohibiting *separate trusts* from using the separate accounts rule. If benefits are left to one "funding" trust (such as Participant's living trust), and upon Participant's death the trustee is required to create separate trusts (such as a separate trust for each child), the trustee of the trust that is named as beneficiary of the retirement plan has until December 31 of the year after the year of the Participant's death to cause the *retirement benefit* to be allocated into separate accounts, one payable to each of the separated trusts. This is no different from an account that is payable to multiple children being divided into separate accounts, one payable to each of the children.

PLR 2002-34074 illustrates this. In this ruling, Participant left his benefits to a trust. As a result of a disclaimer by the Participant's spouse, the trust became payable, at Participant's death, in fractional shares to three children and a trust for spouse. The IRS ruled each beneficiary's share of the terminating trust was a "separate account" for MRD purposes, and accordingly each child was able to use his or her individual life expectancy to measure his or her required distributions.

Nevertheless, unfortunately, plan administrators and IRS agents may read Reg. § 1.401(a)(9)-4, A-5(c), as prohibiting separate account treatment in any case in which a trust is named as beneficiary, despite the clear holding to the contrary in PLR 2002-34074 (which was issued the same month as the final regulations). To avoid the problem, in planning mode, the beneficiary designation form should name directly the beneficiaries for whom it is desired to have separate account treatment, rather than naming the "funding" trust as beneficiary. See Choate, N., "Final Minimum Distribution Regulations: Selected Issues," *ACTEC Journal*, Vol. 28, No. 3 (Winter 2002), p. 191.

6.4 Summary of Planning Principles

1.   Because of the drawbacks and complications of making retirement benefits payable to a trust, name a trust as beneficiary only when there is an important reason to do so.

2.   Despite the complications, naming a trust as beneficiary can facilitate planning techniques (such as disclaimers, and division of benefits using a tax-based formula) that may be difficult to accomplish in a beneficiary designation form.

3.   Review the trust drafting checklist (¶ 6.1.01-¶ 6.1.05) when considering naming a trust as beneficiary of retirement benefits.

4.   If "separate accounts" treatment (¶ 1.7.06) is an important goal, make the benefits payable to separate trusts at the planning stage (see ¶ 6.3.13).

7

Charitable Giving

The pros, cons and pitfalls of funding charitable gifts with retirement benefits

7.1 Introduction to Charitable Giving with Retirement Benefits

7.1.01 *What this Chapter covers*

This Chapter:

- Explains the tax advantages of leaving retirement benefits to charity. ¶ 7.1.02.
- Reviews some minimum distribution pitfalls if both charitable and individual beneficiaries are to be named as beneficiaries of the retirement benefits, and the ways around them. ¶ 7.2.
- Examines the minimum distribution problems that occur when benefits are paid to a charity under a trust that also has individual beneficiaries, and the ways around those. ¶ 7.3.
- Discusses the income tax issues that arise when retirement benefits pass through a trust or estate on their way to the charitable beneficiary, and how to solve them. ¶ 7.4.
- Describes the different types of charitable entities that exist (such as charitable remainder and lead trusts, private foundations and pooled income funds) and tells which are (or are not) suitable to be named as beneficiaries of retirement benefits. ¶ 7.5.
- Reviews other issues, and planning ideas, that involve charitable giving with retirement plan benefits. ¶ 7.6.
- Summarizes the planning principles. ¶ 7.7.

This Chapter assumes the reader is generally familiar with the tax rules of charitable giving. For more information about charitable giving, see the sources cited in the Bibliography.

The planning principles discussed in this Chapter generally do not apply to Roth IRAs (Chapter 5). Since Roth IRA distributions are generally not subject to federal income tax, there is no income tax advantage to leaving such benefits to charity. The best planning strategies for Roth IRAs therefore generally do not include leaving such plans to charity. This Chapter deals only with traditional IRAs, qualified retirement plans ("QRPs") and 403(b) arrangements.

In this Chapter, "Charitable Remainder Trust" means a trust that meets the requirements of § 664; see ¶ 7.5.04.

7.1.02 *Advantages of naming a charity as beneficiary*

Because retirement plan death benefits are subject to income tax (¶ 2.1.01), there is an advantage to naming a charity as beneficiary of the benefits: charities are generally exempt from income taxes (¶ 7.5.01), and thus can collect the entire death benefit without paying income taxes. § 501(a), § 664(c). For the client who wants to leave some assets to charity at death, using the retirement benefits for that purpose is often the most tax-effective way to fund the gift.

Example: Helen wants to leave half of her $1.2 million estate to her favorite charity, the Salk Institute, and half to her nephew Achilles. Her assets are: a $600,000 IRA and $600,000 of cash. Achilles is in the 40% income tax bracket. If Helen simply leaves half of each asset to Achilles and half to the charity, Table 7.1 shows what each receives.

Table 7.1	Charity	Nephew
½ cash	300,000	300,000
½ IRA	300,000	300,000
Gross bequest	600,000	600,000
Less: income tax on ½ IRA	-_____0	-120,000
Net bequest	600,000	480,000

If, instead, she leaves the entire IRA to the charity and all the cash to nephew Achilles, the charity receives the same amount it would have under the other approach, but the nephew receives more money than he would have received with the other approach, at the expense of the IRS, as shown in Table 7.2. This tax advantage of funding at-death charitable gifts with retirement benefits enables the client to fund his charitable gifts at a lower "cost" to the family beneficiaries.

Table 7.2	Charity	Nephew
IRA	600,000	0
Cash	0	600,000
Gross bequest	600,000	600,000
Less: income tax on IRA	- 0	- 0
Net bequest	600,000	600,000

Although it is generally desirable to use retirement benefits to fund at-death charitable gifts it is not necessarily easy to integrate this planning idea into a particular client's estate plan, as the discussion in this Chapter shows. Also, not every type of charitable organization receives the same favorable income tax treatment; see ¶ 7.5.

7.2 Pitfalls Under the Minimum Distribution Rules

7.2.01 *Relevance of minimum distribution rules*

Retirement plan benefits are generally subject to income taxes at the time of distribution, whether that distribution occurs before or after the participant's death. ¶ 2.1.01. Until distribution occurs, the investment growth inside the retirement plan incurs no income taxes and accordingly money inside a retirement plan can grow much faster than investments outside a retirement plan. See ¶ 1.2.01. Thus, a popular strategy for maximizing the value of retirement plan benefits is to keep the benefits inside the plan as long as possible.

Congress does not allow the deferral of taxation to go on forever. To avoid draconian penalties, and preserve the tax-favored status of the retirement plan, plan participants and administrators must comply with § 401(a)(9), which dictates when benefits must start to be distributed from retirement plans, and, once distribution begins, how fast distributions must be made. These "minimum distribution rules" can also be used positively, to continue deferral of income taxes for decades even after the participant's death. See Chapter 1.

Under these rules as they existed prior to 2001, for a participant over age 70½, naming a non-individual beneficiary such as a charity caused the participant to have to take larger taxable distributions from the plan during his lifetime than he would have had to take if he had named an individual beneficiary. In 2001-2002, the IRS substantially changed the minimum distribution rules. See ¶ 1.1.05. One result of the change is that the lifetime drawback of naming a charity as beneficiary of retirement benefits has been eliminated. *Under the new rules, naming a charity as beneficiary does not have a negative effect on the participant's required distributions during life.*

When Participant dies, the beneficiary who inherits the benefits must begin to withdraw the benefits. If the benefits are inherited by an individual, group of individuals or qualifying trust (¶ 6.2), the payout period for the benefits is the life expectancy of that individual beneficiary (or the oldest member of the group, or oldest beneficiary of the trust). ¶ 1.5. Benefits payable to a non-individual beneficiary (such as a charity) must generally be paid out of the plan over a shorter period of time: within five years after Participant's death if he died before his RBD (¶ 1.5.04), or over Participant's remaining life expectancy if he died on or after his RBD (¶ 1.5.05).

As discussed in detail in Chapter 1, the key to long-term income tax deferral after Participant's death is the use of an *individual* beneficiary's life expectancy as the measuring period for required distributions. A charity is not an individual, and therefore is not eligible to use the "life expectancy payout method. However, it doesn't matter, because the charity is income tax-exempt (generally speaking; see ¶ 7.5.01 for discussion of which charities are and which are not income tax-exempt). The income tax-exempt charity can receive the benefits in a lump sum or instalments or any which-way and still pay no income tax on the benefits, so the charitable beneficiary does not need the income tax deferral of a life expectancy payout to minimize taxes.

Thus there is "no problem" under the minimum distribution rules if the charity is named as sole beneficiary of the benefits.

7.2.02 *Naming a charity as one of several beneficiaries*

Naming a charity as beneficiary poses a problem in terms of post-death MRDs only if the client is not leaving the *entire* benefit to charity. If the client wants to leave part of the benefit to individuals and part to charity, and wants the individual beneficiaries to be able to use their life expectancies to compute their MRDs, the client has to overcome the IRS's "multiple beneficiary rule."

Under this rule (Reg. § 1.401(a)(9)-4, A-3), ALL beneficiaries of a retirement plan death benefit must be individuals (or qualifying trusts; ¶ 6.2), if ANY of the benefits are to be paid out over the life expectancy of a beneficiary. See ¶ 1.7.06. Under this rule, a $1 million IRA payable at death "$1,000 to the United Way and the balance to my children" would have to be entirely distributed by the end of the fifth year after the death of a Participant who died before his RBD (or over Participant's remaining life expectancy, if he died on or after his RBD), because one of the beneficiaries is not an individual. These options will in most cases provide a shorter payout period (less income tax deferral) than the "life expectancy of the designated beneficiary."

Is the IRS's position correct? The regulation appears to be harsher than the Code, which says that (at least in case of death before the RBD) if *"any portion* of the employee's interest is payable to (or for the benefit of) a designated beneficiary," *such portion* may be distributed over the life expectancy of the designated beneficiary. § 401(a)(9)(B)(iii) (emphasis added). Thus, the Code appears to permit a life expectancy payout to an individual designated beneficiary of his portion, even if some *other* "portion" of the benefit is payable to a non-individual.

Fortunately, it is easy in most cases, even under the regulations, to have a life expectancy payout to an individual of part of the benefit, and distribute the rest of the benefit to a charity. The next four subsections explain four ways to achieve this. If a client is leaving benefits to both human and charitable beneficiaries and the "life expectancy of the beneficiary" payout method for the human beneficiaries is an important goal, read the next four subsections.

7.2.03 *Separate accounts for charitable, human, beneficiaries*

The multiple beneficiary rule does not apply if the respective shares of the individual and charitable beneficiaries constitute separate accounts payable to different beneficiaries as of December 31 (or possibly September 30) of the year after the year of Participant's death. Reg. § 1.401(a)(9)-8, A-2, A-3. See ¶ 1.7.06 for explanation of the separate accounts rule.

7.2.04 *If the spouse is the only non-charitable beneficiary*

The concern about multiple beneficiaries does not arise when the only beneficiaries are Spouse and one or more charities, if *Spouse in fact survives*, because Spouse does not need to take an installment payout of the benefits over her life expectancy in order to defer income taxes; she can simply roll over her share of the benefits to her own retirement plan. ¶ 3.2.

However, even when Spouse is named as the sole non-charitable primary beneficiary, consider the possibility of Spouse's disclaimer, simultaneous death or predeceasing Participant *if* the contingent beneficiary in that case would be another non-charitable beneficiary. If the contingent beneficiary of the interest left to Spouse is another non-charitable beneficiary (such as Participant's child); *and* Spouse either (a) dies simultaneously with Participant, or (b) predeceases Participant (with Participant then failing to take steps to fix the beneficiary designation before he dies) or (c) disclaims the benefits; *and* the non-charitable contingent beneficiary would like to take his share of the benefits out over his life expectancy; then the multiple beneficiary rule will prevent child from using his/her life expectancy to measure required distributions unless the child's and the charity's interests qualify as "separate accounts"; see ¶ 7.2.03.

7.2.05 *Separate account treatment for pecuniary gifts*

Generally, separate account treatment cannot be used for a pecuniary gift. For example, suppose Participant wants his IRA benefits to be paid at his death "$50,000 to My Favorite Charity, Inc., and the balance to my daughter Gretchen." Reg. § 1.401(a)(9)-8, A-3, requires, as a condition of having "separate accounts," that investment gains and losses accruing after the date of death be allocated pro rata among the beneficiaries' shares. Unless local law or the beneficiary designation form specifically so provides, pecuniary gifts do not share in post-death gains and losses. Thus "separate accounts" generally are available only for fractional gifts.

It should not be difficult, in planning mode (i.e. when drafting a beneficiary designation form for a living client) to rework a pecuniary gift into a fractional gift as of the date of death. If Participant is already deceased, the best approach is to pay out the pecuniary bequest prior to the Designation Date. ¶ 7.2.06.

7.2.06 Distribute charity's share before Designation Date

If the client has already died, and a retirement plan has been left to both charitable and individual beneficiaries, and it is not clear that the beneficiaries are entitled to "separate account" treatment (for example, because one or more beneficiaries' shares are defined as "pecuniary" amounts rather than on a fractional or percentage basis—¶ 7.2.05), the best way to deal with the multiple beneficiary problem is to pay out to any charitable beneficiary its share of the benefits prior to September 30 of the year after the year of Participant's death (the "Designation Date"). Under Reg. § 1.401(a)(9)-4, A-4(a), as long as the charities have been totally paid out prior to that date, the beneficiaries who have not yet received a distribution of their shares (i.e., the individual beneficiaries) will be deemed to be the "only" beneficiaries for minimum distribution purposes. ¶ 1.8.05.

7.3 MRDs and Charitable Gifts Under Trusts

7.3.01 Trust with charitable and human beneficiaries

Suppose a client wants to name a trust as beneficiary of his retirement plan. His children are intended to be the primary beneficiaries of the trust, but the trust also has one or more charitable beneficiaries. He wants the plan benefits that pass to this trust to be paid out in installments over the life expectancy of his oldest child. To achieve the desired result, the various "trust rules" (¶ 6.2) must be complied with. One of these rules is that all trust beneficiaries must be individuals. This rule creates two problems in common estate planning situations involving charities.

First, *any* charitable gift to be paid from the trust at Participant's death, no matter how small, would cause the trust to flunk this requirement, unless the trustee is forbidden to use the retirement benefits to fund the charitable bequest. ¶ 6.3.03. Even the typical normally innocuous statement "this trust shall pay any bequests under my will, if my estate is not adequate to pay the same," could make the trust "flunk" if the will contains charitable bequests. However, the problem of payable-at-death charitable gifts can be cured by paying out all charitable bequests prior to September 30 of the year after the year of Participant's death; ¶ 7.2.06.

The second problem is that, generally, remainder beneficiaries are considered "beneficiaries" for this purpose. Thus, if the beneficiary of the client's retirement plan is a trust, and any part of the remainder interest in the trust passes to charity (or could be appointed to charity under a power of appointment), the trust will flunk (unless the charitable remainder beneficiary can be disregarded under the IRS's nearly incomprehensible trust rules; ¶ 6.3.04). This is not a problem with a true "charitable remainder trust" that meets the requirements of § 664 (¶ 7.5.04), because such trusts are income tax-exempt. The problem is with a trust that is primarily a family trust but which happens to have charitable gifts that will be made after the family members' deaths.

Thus, when drafting a trust that is to make charitable gifts, or that may be used to fund charitable bequests under the will, it is important to determine whether any retirement benefits may be payable to that trust, and, if so, to draft appropriate language either:

A.   To forbid use of the retirement benefits to fund the charitable gifts, if you want the benefits to be paid out over the life expectancy of individual trust beneficiaries (¶ 7.3.02). This approach only works for charitable gifts to be paid upon Participant's death, not if there are charitable remainder interests, as explained at ¶ 7.3.02. Or,

B.   To match the retirement benefits to the charitable gifts, if the goal is to have the benefits pass to the charity free of income taxes (¶ 7.4.06). Under this approach you are giving up on using the life expectancy payout method for the benefits used to pay the charitable gifts.

The first step in analyzing a trust with both charitable and non-charitable beneficiaries is to determine whether the charitable gifts are to be made immediately upon the death of the Participant (¶ 7.3.02), or are remainder interests that do not vest until some later date (such as when an individual beneficiary dies) (¶ 7.3.03).

7.3.02 *If charitable gifts occur at death of Participant*

Example: Russ leaves his $3 million IRA to a trust. The trust provides that, upon Russ's death, the trustee is to pay $10,000 to Russ's favorite charity, and hold the rest of the funds in trust for the life of Russ's wife with remainder to Russ's issue. This trust has both charitable and non-charitable beneficiaries. Unless something is done to avoid the multiple beneficiary rule, the trust will not be able to use the life expectancy of the oldest trust beneficiary to measure required distributions from the IRA to the trust after Russ's death. ¶ 1.7.06.

Here is how to solve this problem, i.e., achieve Russ's goal of paying $10,000 to the charity while still allowing the trust to qualify to use the life expectancy the oldest individual trust beneficiary to measure required distributions from the plan to the trust (see ¶ 6.2.04):

Planning mode: Include language in the trust agreement to prohibit use of the retirement plan to pay the charitable gift; this will work, assuming the trust has some other assets that can be used to fulfill Participant's charitable gifts. ¶ 6.3.03. See Form 7.2, App. B.

Cleanup mode: The trustee can "eliminate" the charitable beneficiary by paying to the charity its $10,000 bequest before the Designation Date. If the charity is paid in full prior to the Designation Date, then it is no longer a "beneficiary" of the trust as of the Designation Date, and (assuming that the one $10,000 bequest to a non-charitable beneficiary was the only "defect" of the trust under the minimum distribution trust rules) the trust has only individual beneficiaries and qualifies under the "trust rules." ¶ 6.2.05. If the trust does not contain a prohibition against paying retirement benefits to charity, and the trustee has authority to pay any asset to any beneficiary, the trustee could choose whether to use the IRA proceeds or other assets to pay the $10,000 bequest. It would make no difference, under the minimum distribution rules, which assets were used, as long as the charity has no further interest in the trust after the Designation Date.

7.3.03 *If charitable gifts are to occur after the Designation Date*

A prohibition against using retirement benefits to fund charitable gifts will not solve the multiple beneficiary problem if the charitable interest is not one that can be paid out or segregated at death.

Example: Heather's trust provides that, upon Heather's death, the trust is divided into equal shares for her four children. Each child receives income for life from his or her share, plus principal in the trustee's discretion for the child's health, education and support. At death, each child can appoint the principal of such child's share among Heather's issue and any charity. If the child fails to exercise this power of appointment, such child's share is paid to such child's issue if any, or otherwise to the other children. Assets coming to this trust at Heather's death include Heather's $2 million IRA and $3 million of other assets. The existence of potential charitable remainder beneficiaries (as appointees under the children's powers of appointment) would mean that, under the multiple beneficiary rule, this trust would flunk the IRS's minimum distribution trust rules. ¶ 6.3.06. The trust would not be able to use the life expectancy of the oldest child to measure MRDs from the IRA to the trust after Heather's death.

Adding a blanket prohibition against paying retirement benefits to charity (such as Form 7.2, Appendix B) will *not* solve the problem in Heather's trust. Because the potential charitable gifts do not occur until each child dies, the trustee, in order to carry out a blanket prohibition against using retirement benefits to fund any charitable gift, would have to segregate the IRA (and all distributions from the IRA) from the other assets of the trust immediately upon Heather's death and keep them segregated for the duration of the trust. So instead of administering four trusts (one for each child) the trustee would end up administering eight trusts (one trust for each child's share of the IRA and IRA distributions, which could not be appointed to charity on the child's death, plus a separate trust for each child's share of the non-IRA assets, which *could* be appointed to charity on the child's death). That is the only way the trustee will be able to tell, when the child dies many years from now, which assets can be appointed to charity and which assets cannot be. The trust instrument would have to give the trustee authority to establish two separate trusts for each beneficiary (or, if that provision is not included, the trustee would probably have to go to court to get authority).

Suppose the trustee sets up the eight separate trust shares. Now Child A needs a discretionary distribution of principal. Does it come out of the retirement assets trust for Child A? or the non-retirement assets trust for Child A? Again, this is a question that must be covered in the trust instrument (or, if it is not, the trustee might have to go to court for authority to pay out of one share or the other).

Moral: A catchall prohibition against paying retirement benefits to non-individual beneficiaries does not solve the problem of a charitable *remainder* interest in a trust that may receive retirement benefits.

If including a catchall paragraph does not solve the problem, what other solutions are there?

Cleanup mode: See ¶ 10.2.02 for ways to fix this problem if the participant-trustor has already died.

Planning mode: If there may be charitable remainder interests in a trust that is being created primarily for individual beneficiaries, and the trust may receive retirement benefits, here are the steps to go through and the options to consider:

A.   Jettison the less important goal. Determine which is a more important goal to the client, the charitable remainders or the life expectancy payout for the retirement benefits, then give up whichever one is less important. If the charitable gifts are high priority, consider giving up the life expectancy payout over the life expectancy of the oldest trust beneficiary. In the Heather example above, if the total value of Heather's retirement plan had been $100,000 out of her total estate of $5 million, she might decide the life expectancy payout was not of significant value, and therefore not bother to take steps to try to preserve it.

B.   Create separate trusts. Consider creating separate trusts to receive the retirement benefits and the non-retirement assets. Returning to the Heather example, if Heather places high priority on *both* the life expectancy payout of her $2 million IRA over the life expectancy of her children, *and* on allowing the children to appoint their shares of the other $3 million of assets to charity, she could direct the trustee to establish two separate trusts for each child as above described, one for the child's share of the IRA proceeds and one for the child's share of the other assets. The power to appoint to charity would apply only to the trusts that held no retirement benefits. The drawback of this approach is the administrative inconvenience and cost of extra trust bookkeeping.

C.   Consider a Charitable Remainder Trust. Consider whether an income tax-exempt Charitable Remainder Trust (¶ 7.5.04) would be a better choice of beneficiary than the client's "regular" trust.

Example: Hilda, age 68, has a $3 million IRA. Her goal is to provide a life income to her sister (age 71) and remainder to a charitable foundation. Assuming the income stream from a Charitable Remainder Trust (¶ 7.5.04) would fulfill the non-charitable objective, it would make no sense to sacrifice her charitable objectives in order to get a life expectancy payout of the IRA (especially since her sister is elderly and does not have a multi-decade life expectancy). The CRT would provide far greater tax advantages: no income tax on distribution of the benefits from the IRA to the CRT, and an estate tax deduction for the value of the charitable remainder.

D.   Consider using a "conduit trust."

A "conduit trust" is a trust under which the trustee is required, each time the trust receives any distribution from the retirement plan, to immediately pass that distribution out to the life beneficiary. The trustee is not permitted to "accumulate" (hold) any retirement plan distributions in the trust. See ¶ 6.3.08. Under the regulations, the remainder beneficiary of a conduit trust does not "count" as a beneficiary; thus, having a charity as remainder beneficiary of a conduit trust does not violate the rule that "all trust beneficiaries must be individuals." Reg. § 1.401(a)(9)-5, A-7(c)(3), Example 2.

Example: Luigi wants his daughter Lavinia, age 41, to receive a stream of income from his $3 million IRA. A stream of minimum required IRA distributions over her life expectancy would be just right.

However, he does not want her to have outright control of the entire IRA after his death. Although a stream of MRD payments from the IRA would not be guaranteed to last for Lavinia's entire life (it would last only until the end of her IRS-defined life expectancy), he thinks a stream of MRD payments probably *would* last for her lifetime because she has a below-average life expectancy due to her medical condition. If she does die prematurely, he wants to be sure that any money left in the IRA goes to the charity that funds research into Lavinia's medical condition. He could leave the benefits to a conduit trust for Lavinia with remainder to the charity. There would be no estate tax charitable deduction (because this is not a Charitable Remainder Trust; ¶ 7.5.04), but the trust would be able to use Lavinia's life expectancy to measure distributions (because the charitable beneficiary can be disregarded).

7.4 Income Tax Treatment of Charitable Gifts From a Trust or Estate

7.4.01 *Advantages of naming charity as beneficiary directly*

The way to leave retirement benefits to charity that involves the fewest difficulties and pitfalls is simply to name one or more existing "public" charities (¶ 7.5.02), private foundations (¶ 7.5.03), or Charitable Remainder Trusts (¶ 7.5.04), directly, as the beneficiary of 100% of the death benefit payable under the particular retirement plan, as in the following example:

"I name as my beneficiary, to receive 100% of the death benefits payable under the above-named retirement plan on account of my death, the Inner-City Scholarship Fund."

Because the benefits are paid directly to the charity under the beneficiary designation form, income tax on the benefits is easily avoided: § 691 causes the benefits to be included directly in the income of the charitable recipient as named beneficiary (¶ 2.2.02), and the charity's tax exemption makes the distribution non-taxable (¶ 7.5.01, A). The estate tax charitable deduction is available for the full value of the charity's interest. ¶ 7.5.01, B.

(As with any charitable gift, practitioners must consider such issues as the need to properly identify the intended recipient by using its correct legal name and adding such helpful information as the address and/or taxpayer identification number of the organization. Also, the practitioner needs to consider with the client whether to make the gift conditional on the recipient's meeting, at the time of the client's death, the applicable requirements under the Internal Revenue Code for income tax exemption and/or the estate tax charitable deduction. Since these considerations are the same for gifts of retirement benefits as for other gifts, these points will not be dealt with in this Chapter.)

7.4.02 *If benefits pass to charity through estate or trust, not directly*

Sometimes it is not feasible to name the intended charitable recipient directly as beneficiary of the retirement benefits. The most common reason for this is that some additional actions must be taken, after the client's death, to carry out the charitable gift.

For example, the intended charitable recipient may be a charitable foundation that has not been created yet; or the amount going to various charities may be based on a formula that depends on facts that cannot be determined until after the client's death, such as "Charity A shall receive an amount equal to 10% of my net estate, and the balance shall be paid to Child" (formula makes it impossible to determine how much each beneficiary receives until the estate is settled); or the client may want the charitable recipients to be selected after his death, with a designation such as "The benefits shall be distributed to such one or more educational institutions located in Massachusetts as my executor shall select from among those that are exempt from federal income taxes under § 501, and gifts to which qualify for the federal estate tax charitable deduction under § 2055."

In all of these examples, the retirement plan administrator may not be willing to accept a beneficiary designation under which the plan administrator would not be able to tell, at Participant's death, who was entitled to the benefits.

If the only problem is that the actual charitable recipients are to be selected after the Participant's death, consider leaving the retirement benefits to a tax-exempt "donor-advised fund." The Participant should create the fund prior to death, name it as beneficiary, designate who will be responsible for allocating the fund's assets to charities after his death, and provide the allocators with the guidelines they are to follow. Because the donor-advised fund is itself tax-exempt, the problems discussed in the rest of this section do not arise—and the plan administrator is happy because it knows who to make the check out to.

If the problem is that the amount passing to charity is determined by a formula, the plan administrator might be willing to accept a formula beneficiary designation if the form specifies a fiduciary (such as Participant's executor, or a trustee) who can certify the proper recipients and amounts to the plan administrator.

In some situations, however, the benefits may have to be made payable to Participant's estate or trust as beneficiary of the retirement plan, with the will (or trust instrument) specifying that the benefits are to be paid to the not-yet-created (or not-yet-selected) charitable beneficiaries. The executor of the will (or trustee of the trust) is then responsible for carrying out the post-death actions (such as forming the charitable foundation, or calculating the formula distributions, or selecting the charities), and the plan administrator can then simply follow the instructions of the executor (or trustee) in distributing the benefits. Unfortunately, this course introduces a substantial additional complexity, namely, the steps that must be taken to avoid having *income tax* imposed on the benefits at the estate (or trust) level.

The rest of this ¶ 7.4 discusses whether and how an estate or non-charitable trust can avoid income taxes on retirement plan benefits that are paid to it and used to fund charitable gifts under the instrument.

The following discussion assumes that the fiduciary receives a distribution from the retirement plan and, in the same year, funds a fractional or residuary gift to a "public" charity (¶ 7.5.02) or private foundation (¶ 7.5.03). If the charitable gift is not funded in the same year the distribution is received from the retirement plan, see ¶ 7.4.10. If, instead of taking a distribution from the plan and passing the distributed property out to the charity, the fiduciary assigns the retirement plan itself to the charity, see ¶ 7.4.09. If the bequest is a pecuniary bequest (as opposed to a fractional or residuary bequest) see ¶ 2.2.05. Gifts from an estate or non-charitable trust to a Charitable Remainder Trust (¶ 7.5.04), pooled income fund (¶ 7.5.06), or charitable lead trust (¶ 7.5.07) are beyond the scope of this discussion.

In the rest of this ¶ 7.4, "trust" means a trust that is not, itself, income tax-exempt (see ¶ 7.5.01).

7.4.03 *No DNI deduction for distributions to charity*

The income tax treatment of trusts is an extremely complex topic. This Chapter seeks only to highlight issues particularly involved when retirement plan benefits are paid to charity through a non-charitable trust, not to explain all the rules of trust income taxation. For full details, see the two sources described in the Bibliography, Blattmachr, J.G., et al., *Income Taxation of Estates and Trusts*, and Zaritsky, H., et al., *Federal Income Taxation of Estates and Trusts* (cited, in this Chapter as "Blattmachr" and "Zaritsky," respectively).

To vastly oversimplify a complex topic, the general scheme of income taxation of trusts and estates is as follows: All income items (including retirement plan distributions; ¶ 2.1.01) paid to an estate or trust are includible in its gross income just as such items would be included in the gross income of an individual if paid to such individual. A trust (unless its existence as a separate entity is ignored under the "grantor trust rules" of § 671-§ 678; see ¶ 6.3.09) or estate is a separate taxpayer and pays tax on its taxable income at the rate prescribed for trusts and estates. § 641(a); § 1(e).

However, the trust gets a unique deduction on its way from "gross income" to "taxable income": the trust can deduct certain distributions of income made to the trust's beneficiaries. § 651, § 661. The beneficiaries then pay the income tax on these distributions. § 652, § 662. Needless to say, there are complex rules governing this unique deduction. The first rule is that the amount the trust can deduct is limited to the amount of its "distributable net income" or "DNI." § 651, § 661. Because of this limitation, the deduction is often called the "DNI deduction."

The second rule is that there is no DNI deduction allowed for a distribution from an estate or trust to a charity. § 651(a)(2), § 663(a)(2). A distribution to a charity from an estate or trust is deductible, if at all, only as a charitable deduction under § 642(c). (Although the Code could be interpreted to mean that a trust can take a DNI deduction for distributions to charity that do not qualify for the deduction under § 642, the IRS has not interpreted it that way, and the courts have supported the IRS; see *Blattmachr*, § 2:6.1[J].) § 642(c) allows an estate or trust "a deduction in computing its taxable income [for] any amount of the gross income, without limitation, which pursuant to the terms of the governing instrument is, during the taxable year, paid for a" permitted charitable purpose. For meaning of "pursuant to the governing instrument" in this context, see *Zaritsky*, ¶ 4.07.

The third rule is the "separate share" rule of § 663(c). When the separate share rule applies, if a fiduciary distributes money to a beneficiary, that distribution will carry out DNI only to the extent there is DNI that is properly allocable to that particular beneficiary's "separate share." The regulations interpreting the separate share rules specifically deal with the allocation of "income in respect of a decedent" (IRD) (¶ 2.2) that is "corpus" (i.e., "principal" for trust accounting purposes; see ¶ 6.1.07) separately from other types of income that may make up DNI. The regulations' principles for dealing with IRD are different from the rules for "regular" DNI.

(Note: the "separate share rule" of § 663(c) governs the allocation of DNI among multiple beneficiaries *of a trust or estate,* and is not to be confused with the "separate accounts rule" that dictates when multiple beneficiaries *of a retirement plan* are treated separately for purposes of the required distribution rules. ¶ 1.7.06. These are *completely* different and unrelated rules.)

Having in mind these various rules, we now look at what happens to a trust that (a) has both charitable and non-charitable beneficiaries and (b) is named as beneficiary of a retirement plan. In the following example, note that the bequests are in the form of fractional or percentage portions of the trust principal. The following discussion does not necessarily apply at all or in the same way to pecuniary bequests; see ¶ 2.2.05.

Example: Tom dies leaving his $1 million IRA, $1 million of real estate and $1 million of marketable securities to a trust. At Tom's death, the trust is to terminate and be distributed 50% to Charity and 50% to Tom's son Timmy, so each beneficiary is to receive a total of $1.5 million. The trust provides that Timmy has to pay all estate taxes, if there are any, out of his 50% share. Because Tom had no basis in the IRA (see ¶ 2.1.04), all distributions from the IRA after Tom's death are includible in the recipient's gross income as "income in respect of a decedent" (IRD). If the trustee takes $1 million out of the IRA (thereby generating $1 million of gross income to the trust) and distributes that $1 million to the charity in partial fulfillment of its 50% share, can the trust take an income tax deduction for the distribution to charity?

To answer this question, we first need to determine whether the separate share rules apply in this situation.

7.4.04 *Do the separate share rules allocate income to charity?*

The trust can take a charitable deduction under § 642(c) for a distribution to charity that is paid, pursuant to the governing instrument, out of the trust's gross income. If the gross income arising from the $1 million IRA distribution is not properly allocable to the charity's share the trust cannot deduct it.

The separate share rules of § 663(c) generally tell us how much "gross income" is allocated to each beneficiary's share. Even though § 663(c) applies "For the sole purpose of determining the amount of distributable net income in the application of sections 661 and 662," it appears probable that the separate share rules also apply to determine allocation of DNI among the separate shares allocable to charitable as well as non-charitable beneficiaries (even though, after all the allocating is done, there will be no DNI deduction for distributions to charity). See Reg. § 1.663(c)-5, Example 11.

7.4.05 *Allocating IRD that is corpus under the separate share rule*

Retirement benefits paid to a trust are income in respect of a decedent (IRD). See ¶ 2.2. Here is what the regulation says regarding the allocation of IRD among beneficiaries' separate shares:

"(3) Income in respect of a decedent. This paragraph (b)(3) governs the allocation of the portion of gross income includible in distributable net income that is income in respect of a decedent within the meaning of section 691(a) and is not [trust accounting income; see ¶ 6.1.07]. Such gross income is allocated *among the separate shares that could potentially be funded with these amounts*... The amount of such gross income allocated to each share is based on the relative value of each share that could potentially be funded with such amounts." Reg. § 1.663(c)-2(b)(3). (Emphasis added).

We next look at how this rule applies in three situations: if the governing instrument dictates which beneficiary's share is to receive the IRD (¶ 7.4.06); if the governing instrument is silent on which assets are allocated to which beneficiary's share and the applicable state law requires pro rata funding (¶ 7.4.07); and if the governing instrument allows the trustee to pick and choose which assets are to be used to fund which beneficiary's share (¶ 7.4.08).

7.4.06 *If governing instrument requires funding bequest with IRD*

Suppose Tom's trust (see "Example" at end of ¶ 7.4.03)

contains the following provision: "The charity's share shall be funded to the maximum extent possible with retirement benefits, including any Individual Retirement Account or distribution therefrom (Retirement Assets). My son Timmy's share shall be funded to the maximum extent possible with assets other than Retirement Assets."

The trustee withdraws $1 million from the IRA and distributes the $1 million to the charity in partial payment of its $1.5 million 50% share of the estate. On the same date, the trustee distributes Tom's real estate (also worth $1 million) to Timmy in partial fulfillment of his $1.5 million 50% share of the estate. Is the $1 million of gross income arising from the IRA distribution properly allocated to the charity's share under the separate share regulations?

Prior to the issuance of the final separate share regulations, it appeared that the IRS would not give effect to a trust provision (such as that in Tom's trust) that purports to assign *taxable income* to one beneficiary rather than another, where the provision in question has no "substantial economic effect." This principle is explained in *Zaritsky* at ¶ 2.04[4], pages 2-16 *et seq.* The provision in Tom's trust requiring the charity's share to be funded first with IRA proceeds has no "substantial economic effect" because the provision has no effect on *how much* the charity and Timmy will receive.

However, Reg. § 1.663(c)-5, Ex. 9, indicates that a governing instrument provision that specifically allocates IRD to one beneficiary's share will be effective to cause the IRD to be allocated to that beneficiary's separate share for income tax purposes, even when such allocation has no economic effect. Accordingly, because Tom's trust directs that the retirement plan benefits must be used to fund the charity's share, the IRD resulting from cashing out the IRA is allocated to the charity's separate share.

The fact that the governing instrument specifies that this income goes to the charity's share means that the charity's share is the only share that "could potentially be funded" with these proceeds. Thus, even if the trustee does not distribute anything to the charity that year, but does make a distribution to Timmy, the distribution to Timmy does not carry out any DNI attributable to the IRA distribution. See ¶ 7.4.09 for what happens if the distribution to charity does not occur in the same year the IRA distribution is received.

7.4.07 *If there is no authority to fund disproportionately*

Suppose Tom's trust requires that the beneficiaries' shares be funded pro rata with each trust asset; or Tom's trust is silent on the subject of which assets will be used to fund which beneficiary's share, and applicable state law requires that (unless the governing instrument specifically provides otherwise) each asset must be distributed to each beneficiary proportionately.

Since "under the terms of the governing instrument or applicable local law" the fiduciary is required to allocate each asset proportionately, Timmy's share and the charity's share must be funded pro rata. Since each beneficiary's share can only "potentially be funded" with equal shares of each asset, the separate share regulations dictate that the gross income resulting from the IRA distribution must be allocated equally for purposes of § 642(c) between the charity's share and Timmy's share.

7.4.08 *If fiduciary has authority to pick and choose*

Suppose that Tom's trust, after specifying that the entire trust is to be distributed equally to Charity and Timmy, contains the following provision: "The Trustee shall not be obligated to distribute each asset equally to the two beneficiaries, but rather may make distributions in cash or in kind (including non pro rata distributions and distributions of undivided interests in property) or partly in cash and partly in kind, and may distribute different assets to each beneficiary, provided that the total amount distributed to each beneficiary is equal." In 2001, the trustee receives a $1 million cash distribution from the IRA, which it immediately distributes to Charity, and on the same date distributes Tom's real estate (also worth $1 million) to Timmy. There are no other distributions in 2001.

The trustee has exercised its authority to choose which assets to use to fund each beneficiary's share. When the trustee prepares the trust's income tax return for 2001, how does the trustee account for the $1 million of IRD the trust received from the IRA?

There are two possible interpretations of the separate share rule in this situation. The first interpretation, which is apparently the most widely accepted, is that, since the trustee *could* have elected to fund either beneficiary's share of the trust with the IRD, the trustee *must* (in computing its taxable income and DNI) allocate the IRD equally to the two shares. Under this interpretation, $500,000 of income would be allocated to Timmy's share even though the IRA proceeds were paid to the charity. While this is certainly the most obvious interpretation of the words "could potentially be funded," it has a defect, namely, that it overrides a specific provision of the governing instrument: in this example, there is specific authority in the governing instrument for the trustee to choose which assets are to be used to fund which share, and the trustee exercised that power.

A second possible interpretation of the regulation would be that, if the fiduciary has, and exercises, a power to allocate the IRD to a particular share, there is no longer an open question of which shares could "potentially be" funded, because one particular share *has* been funded with the IRD, and that is therefore the only share that can "potentially be" funded with the IRD.

Under this interpretation, when the fiduciary has a power to pick and choose which shares to allocate the IRD asset to, the proportionate allocation rule of Reg. § 1.663(c)-2 would apply only if the fiduciary did not exercise the power, and the IRD were commingled with the other assets that could be used to fund each share. Under this interpretation, the regulation would not trample on the fiduciary's rights under the instrument. Though the author is fond of this interpretation, she has not found anyone else who shares it.

7.4.09 *Avoiding deemed allocation by assigning the benefits*

As the discussion at ¶ 7.4.08 indicates, the meaning of § 1.663(c)-2(b)(3) is at best unclear and at worst negative (in the sense that the regulation may require pro rata allocation of IRD to beneficiaries' shares even when the fiduciary has, and exercises, authority for non-pro rata funding). Planning should try to avoid a situation in which the trustee may not be able to get a charitable deduction for retirement plan distributions passed out to a charitable beneficiary. There are two ways to avoid the problem.

One way is for the governing instrument to specify that retirement plan benefits shall be used to fund any bequest to charity that qualifies as a "separate share" under the regulations to the maximum extent possible (see ¶ 7.4.06).

If that approach is not available (for example, because Participant has already died, so it is too late to amend the trust to include that provision), a deemed allocation to non-charitable beneficiaries' shares of gross income arising from retirement plan distributions can still be avoided if:

1.   The trust gives the trustee authority to pick and choose which asset will be used to fund the charity's share; and

2.   The trust gives the trustee authority to distribute in kind; and

3.   The trustee, instead of taking distribution of the retirement benefits, assigns the retirement plan itself to the charity (see ¶ 6.1.06).

Following the assignment, the charity can take distributions directly from the retirement plan. The distributions do not have to be included in the gross income of the trust because the benefits are never paid to the trust (¶ 2.1.01). The assignment itself does not trigger realization of income; ¶ 2.2.04. The problem of Reg. § 1.663(c)-2(b)(3) is avoided. This approach was blessed in PLR 2002-34019, in which IRAs were payable to Participant's estate. The residuary beneficiaries of the estate were charities and individuals. The executor (pursuant to power granted in the will to make disproportionate distributions in kind) distributed cash to the individual beneficiaries in satisfaction of their shares, and proposed to distribute the IRA to the charities in payment of their shares. The IRS ruled that transfer of the IRAs to the charities would not be a taxable assignment of IRD under § 691, or create taxable income to the estate or the individual beneficiaries.

7.4.10 *Deduction if distribution to charity occurs in a later year*

The preceding discussion has dealt with retirement plan distributions that are paid to a trust and distributed by the trustee to the trust beneficiaries, where the plan-to-trust distribution and the trust-to-beneficiary distribution occur *in the same taxable year of the trust*. If the plan distribution is received by the trust in one taxable year, and properly allocated to the charity's "separate share" of the trust under the rules discussed in ¶ 7.4.05, but nothing is distributed to the charity until a later year, here is what happens:

If the amount is distributed to the charity in the year (Year 2) *following* the year the income was received (Year 1), the trustee can elect to treat the payment to the charity as if it had been made in Year

1 (and so can deduct it in Year 1). § 642(c)(1).

If the distribution to the charity does not occur until even later than that, things get tougher. An *estate* can take a charitable deduction for amounts "permanently set aside for" charity as well as for amounts "paid to" charity. § 642(c)(2). Trusts, however, generally *cannot* take a deduction for amounts that are merely "set aside for" charity; a trust generally gets a deduction only for amounts *paid* to charity, unless the trust is treated as part of the estate pursuant to a § 645 election (see Reg. § 1.645-1(e)(2)(i); this election is not discussed in this book). Therefore, if the distribution to the charity does not occur in the same year the income is received by the trust, or in the immediately following year, a trust will not get a charitable deduction for that amount, *unless* there is § 645 election in effect; or the trust is eligible for a grandfather exception for certain pre-10/9/69 instruments (see § 642(c)(2)).

7.5 Types of Charitable Entities

7.5.01 Overview of tax benefits of charitable giving

So far we have been discussing "charity" as a potential recipient of retirement plan benefits as if all charities were the same. In fact there are many different types of entities that receive some special treatment in the Code because they dedicate all or part of their income or assets to charitable purposes, and each presents unique considerations as a potential beneficiary of retirement benefits.

This ¶ 7.5 examines various types of charitable entities from the point of view of their merits as potential beneficiaries of retirement benefits. This ¶ 7.5 does not cover every type of organization that may be eligible for one or another charitable deduction; it covers only the types most commonly encountered in estate planning. This section does not attempt to describe all the detailed requirements and attributes of these different types of charitable organization; for that information consult the sources in the Bibliography. Rather, the point of this ¶ 7.5 is to look at the principal distinguishing characteristics of each entity and describe the planning problems each presents with regard to bequests of retirement benefits.

In general, when considering the tax advantages of any type of charitable gift (not just gifts of retirement plan benefits), there are several different taxes to be concerned with. This ¶ 7.5.01 provides a brief overview of these various special charitable tax provisions, with a cross reference to a more detailed discussion of the particular tax provisions involved in charitable gifts *of retirement plan benefits*. Since this Chapter is concerned with naming charities as beneficiaries of retirement benefits *at death*, the individual income tax charitable deduction (§ 170, which applies only to lifetime gifts) is not relevant.

A.   Is the charitable entity exempt from income taxes (§ 501)? Since retirement plan distributions are generally includible in gross income (¶ 2.1.01), an important advantage of leaving such benefits to charity is avoidance of income tax. Public charities (¶ 7.5.02), private foundations (¶ 7.5.03) and Charitable Remainder Trusts (¶ 7.5.04) are generally income tax-exempt, and therefore will not have to pay income tax on distributions they receive from a retirement plan. Pooled income funds (¶ 7.5.06) and charitable lead trusts (¶ 7.5.07) are not income tax-exempt.

B.   Do gifts or bequests to the entity qualify for the gift (§ 2522) or estate (§ 2055) tax charitable deduction? In the case of retirement plan benefits left to charity, the concern would be with the *estate tax* rather than the *gift tax* (but see also ¶ 7.6.01). The full value of retirement benefits left to a public charity (¶ 7.5.02) or private foundation (¶ 7.5.03) would be eligible for the estate tax charitable deduction. For benefits left to a Charitable Remainder Trust (¶ 7.5.04), pooled income fund (¶ 7.5.06) or charitable lead trust (¶ 7.5.07), only part of the total value (namely, the value of the charity's remainder or lead interest) would be deductible for estate tax purposes.

7.5.02 *Least-restricted or "public" charities*

§ 501 provides an income tax exemption for a lengthy list of organizations, including clubs, burial societies, employee benefit plans and, in § 501(c)(3), what people generally mean when they refer to "charities": "Corporations, and any community chest, fund, or foundation, organized and operated exclusively for religious, charitable, scientific, testing for public safety, literary, or educational purposes, or to foster national or international amateur sports competition (but only if no part of its activities involve the provision of athletic facilities or equipment), or for the prevention of cruelty to children or animals, no part of the net earnings of which inures to the benefit of any private shareholder or individual," and which does not engage in certain proscribed political activities. The definition is similar, though not identical, for § 2055(a)(2) (estate tax deduction for bequests to charity).

These organizations are referred to in this Chapter as "public charities," meaning 501(c)(3) organizations that are not private foundations (¶ 7.5.03).

A public charity is totally exempt from income tax (except for the tax on "UBTI"; ¶ 7.6.02). § 501(a). Lifetime gifts to such charities are fully deductible for gift tax purposes. § 2522(a). Bequests to public charities qualify for the estate tax deduction, with no limit (other than that the deduction for the transferred property may not exceed the value of such property included in the gross estate). § 2055(a).

Lifetime gifts to all domestic charities qualify for the income tax charitable deduction under § 170(c), though gifts to some charities qualify for a larger deduction (as a percentage of the donor's gross income) than others; this distinction is not relevant to at-death gifts.

Making a bequest of retirement plan death benefits directly to a public charity presents the fewest problems. The planner needs to verify that the organization is an exempt organization under § 501(c)(3) and, in the case of a major gift, the planner should review each of the Code sections under which a deduction will be claimed, to make sure that the organization in question meets the requirements. This is not generally a problem in the case of gift by a U.S. citizen to typical charities.

7.5.03 *Private foundations*

In general, a private foundation is a "501(c)(3) organization" (see ¶ 7.5.02) that is primarily supported by contributions of one donor or family. However, the definition of a private foundation is notoriously convoluted (see § 509), especially since there are several different types and not all are subject to the same restrictions. Untangling the various definitions and subsets of private foundations is beyond the scope of this Chapter.

Certain private foundations, although exempt from "regular" income taxes (except on UBTI; ¶ 7.6.02), are subject to a 2% excise tax on net investment income. § 4940. PLR 9633006 ruled that a distribution from a Keogh plan to a foundation was subject to the 2%

tax to the extent it represented investment income and gains accumulated inside the retirement plan, but not to the extent it represented contributions to the plan by the decedent or his employer. Timothy W. Mulcahy, CPA, criticized this ruling in "Is a Bequest of a Retirement Account to a Private Foundation Subject to Excise Tax?," *Journal of Taxation*, August 1996, p. 108. Apparently the IRS agreed with his comments, and a later ruling, 9838028, held that the § 4940 tax "is a limited excise tax that applies only to the specific types of income listed in that section. Amounts from retirement accounts are deferred compensation income," not part of "the gross investment income" of a foundation, and therefore are *not* subject to the tax. PLR 2000-03055 came to the same conclusion.

7.5.04 *Charitable Remainder Trusts*

A "Charitable Remainder Trust" (CRT), as that term is used in this book, means a charitable remainder trust that meets the requirements of § 664.

The general idea of a CRT (for full details on these rules, see sources cited in the Bibliography) is that the trust pays out an annual income to one or more non-charitable beneficiaries (such as the donor and/or the donor's spouse or children) either for life or for a term of not more than 20 years. At the end of the life (or term) interest, the remaining trust assets are paid to charity.

A CRT must meet rigid requirements set forth in § 664. The annual payout to the non-charitable beneficiary (which is specified in the trust instrument) must be either a fixed dollar amount, in which case the trust is a "charitable remainder annuity trust" or CRAT, or a fixed percentage of the annually-determined value of the trust, in which case the trust is a "charitable remainder unitrust" or CRUT. The annual payout rate must be at least 5% (but not more than 50%) of the initial trust value. A CRUT is slightly more flexible than a CRAT because it can provide that the annual payout to the non-charitable beneficiary is the unitrust percentage or the net income of the trust if less, and can even provide that there will be "makeup" distributions to the non-charitable beneficiary if in later years the trust's income exceeds the unitrust percentage. However, neither type of CRT can permit the non-charitable beneficiary to receive anything other than the unitrust or annuity payout amount.

A CRT pays no income tax itself because it is income tax-exempt (unless it receives "UBTI"; see ¶ 7.6.02). However, it has a unique internal accounting system called the "four-tier" system. Under this system, every dollar that the CRT receives is allocated to one of four tiers based on the federal income tax character of the receipt (ordinary income, capital gain, tax-exempt income, or principal). In effect, the CRT "remembers" what types of income it has received. Then, when the CRT makes a distribution to the non-charitable beneficiary, the distribution is deemed to come out of one of these tiers, and the federal income tax character of the amount is revived. If the distribution to the non-charitable beneficiary is deemed to come out of the ordinary income tier the beneficiary will have to include that distribution in his gross income as ordinary income.

Distributions to the non-charitable beneficiary are assigned to tiers on a "worst-first" basis, so (for example) the non-charitable beneficiary cannot receive any capital gain income from the CRT until the CRT has distributed everything it held in its ordinary income tier.

Some people mistakenly believe that, if they leave a retirement plan to a CRT, the CRT could take a distribution of the entire plan tax-free, reinvest the proceeds in municipal bonds, and pay tax-exempt municipal bond interest to the non-charitable beneficiary. This maneuver does not work, because the retirement plan distribution (to the extent it is "ordinary income"; see ¶ 2.1.01) all goes into the "ordinary income" tier. Even if the trustee *did* invest the proceeds in municipal bonds no distribution out to the non-charitable beneficiary would be treated as coming from the tax-exempt municipal bond interest "tier" until the ordinary income "tier" had been used up.

So, although the CRT pays no income tax when it receives a distribution from a retirement plan, the beneficiary of the CRT will have to pay income tax on the distributions *from* the CRT, to the extent those are deemed to represent the CRT's regurgitation of the retirement plan benefit under the four-tier system.

When a decedent leaves a retirement plan to a CRT, the estate is entitled to an estate tax deduction equal to the actuarially determined value of the remainder (using IRS-prescribed actuarial tables and interest rates), which must be at least 10% of the asset's initial value.

The attraction of leaving retirement plan death benefits to a CRT is that the benefits are paid to the CRT with no income tax, meaning that the client's non-charitable beneficiaries can receive a life income generated by reinvestment of the *entire amount* of the retirement benefit. In contrast, if the non-charitable beneficiaries inherited the benefits as named beneficiaries under the plan, they would have to pay income taxes on the benefits as those were distributed to them, meaning that (once distribution of the benefits is complete) the amount left over for the beneficiaries to invest is vastly reduced. Thus they could expect a larger annual income from the CRT than they would receive by investing the after-tax value of any retirement benefits distributed to them directly.

This is not to suggest that the client's human beneficiaries will receive more money as life beneficiaries of a CRT that is named as beneficiary of the retirement plan than they would receive if they were named directly as beneficiaries of the plan. Normally the opposite is true, because an individual named directly as beneficiary of a retirement plan receives the *entire* retirement plan benefit, not just the income from the benefit. The income beneficiary of a CRT receives only the income from the reinvested plan proceeds; the proceeds themselves (the principal of the CRT) eventually go to the charity. Also, the economic advantage of deferral of distributions over the life expectancy of the beneficiary (¶ 1.2.01) reduces the negative effects of the fact that the distributions are taxable income to the beneficiary.

On the other hand, the payout from a CRT may be more attractive than naming the individual beneficiaries directly as beneficiaries of the retirement plan if long-term deferral is not available (for example, if the retirement plan in question does not offer a life expectancy payout; see ¶ 1.5.09), especially when the estate tax benefits of the charitable deduction are taken into account. For an example of how this mode of charitable giving may actually result in a "profit" to the family, see the Fallon case study in Chapter 11.

7.5.05 *The "IRD deduction" and Charitable Remainder Trusts*

Generally, when a human beneficiary of a retirement plan receives a distribution from the plan, he must include such distribution in gross income as income in respect of a decedent (IRD) (¶ 2.2), but he is entitled to an income tax deduction for the federal estate taxes that were paid on those benefits. § 691(c); ¶ 2.2.07. If retirement benefits are paid to a Charitable Remainder Trust, that deduction for practical purposes disappears—nobody gets to use it. There is no mechanism by which a CRT can pass out the IRD deduction.

The § 691(c) deduction reduces the "taxable income" of the CRUT (i.e., income assigned to the trust's "first tier") in the year the distribution is received from the retirement plan. Reg. § 1.664-1(d)(2). All distributions to the individual beneficiary would be deemed to come out of the "net taxable income" of the CRT (first tier) until it had all been used up. The income of the CRT that was sheltered by the 691(c) deduction would effectively become "principal" that could be distributed to the individual beneficiary tax-free (fourth tier). However, the tax-free principal of the CRT is not deemed to be distributed until after all net *taxable* income has been distributed. This point would never be reached in most CRTs, unless the unitrust payout rate substantially exceeds the anticipated income.

The IRS has confirmed this explanation of how § 691(c) applies to a CRT in PLR 1999-01023. Some practitioners disagree with the result in this ruling and argue that the unitrust distributions to the non-charitable beneficiary from the CRT should retain their character as IRD and therefore carry out the IRD deduction to the non-charitable beneficiary along with the taxable income, citing Reg. § 1.691(c)-1(d).

7.5.06 *Pooled income funds*

With a pooled income fund (see definition in § 642(c)(5)), the donor makes his gift to a fund maintained by the charitable organization that ultimately will receive the gift. The fund invests the gift collectively with gifts made by other donors, and pays back to the donor (or to another beneficiary named by the donor) a share of the fund's income corresponding to the relative value of the donor's gift. When the donor (and/or the beneficiary he nominated) dies, the share of the fund attributable to that donor's gift is removed from the fund and transferred to the charitable organization.

The pooled income fund has been called the "poor man's Charitable Remainder Trust," because it provides approximately the same benefits as a Charitable Remainder Trust (irrevocable gift of remainder interest to charity generates charitable gift (§ 2522(c)(2)(A)) or estate (§ 2055(e)(2)(A)) tax, and income (§ 170(f)(2)(A)) tax, deductions, while preserving a life income to the donor and/or the donor's chosen human beneficiaries), without the expense of creating and operating a stand-alone Charitable Remainder Trust.

Unlike Charitable Remainder Trusts, however, pooled income funds are not exempt from income tax. Reg. § 1.642(c)-5(a)(2); compare § 664(c). Thus, generally, a pooled income fund will file an income tax return, and include retirement plan distributions in its gross income, like any other trust would have to do (see ¶ 7.4.03). The fund can take a deduction for its *income* distributions to the non-charitable income beneficiaries (see § 661(a)), but the fund's receipt of retirement benefits is considered a receipt of *principal*, which the fund will not distribute to the non-charitable income beneficiaries. ¶ 6.1.07.

Can the pooled income fund take an offsetting charitable deduction for the amount of any retirement benefits included in its gross income? Generally, no. Like other (non-charitable) trusts, a pooled income fund is allowed an income tax deduction for amounts actually *paid* during the year (or in the following year) to charity, but (like other trusts, and unlike an estate) a pooled income fund is generally *not* allowed a deduction for amounts that are merely permanently set aside for charity. ¶ 7.4.10.

Therefore, generally retirement plan death benefits paid to a pooled income fund will be subject to income tax in the year received by the fund to the same extent they would be taxable to an individual beneficiary. Accordingly a pooled income fund is not an attractive choice as beneficiary of retirement benefits.

7.5.07 *Charitable lead trusts*

A charitable lead trust (CLT) is the mirror image of a Charitable Remainder Trust (CRT) (¶ 7.5.04). Under a CLT, the charity receives either a fixed dollar amount (charitable lead annuity trust) or a fixed percentage of the value of the trust property (with such value being redetermined annually) (charitable lead unitrust) paid annually (or more often) for a fixed term of years, or for the life of an individual. At the end of the term of years (or upon the death of the individual who is the measuring life), the remainder interest is paid to individuals, such as the donor's children or grandchildren. With a CRT, in contrast, the lead "unitrust" or annuity interest is paid to one or more individual beneficiaries for a term of years (or for life), and the remainder interest is paid to charity. § 664(d).

The term "charitable lead trust" does not appear in the Code, but this type of entity is described in § 170(f)(2)(B).

Unlike a CRT, however, the CLT is not exempt from income taxes. Thus the CLT must include the benefits in its income when they are distributed from the retirement plan to the CLT. Because of this, leaving retirement plan death benefits to a CLT appears generally to be a disadvantageous way to fund such a trust.

Generally, the planning advantage of a CLT funded at death is that, in addition to satisfying the donor's charitable intentions, it may allow funds to pass to the donor's descendants (or other non-charitable beneficiaries) free of gift or estate taxes. This phenomenon occurs if the investment performance of the trust "beats" the IRS's § 7520 rate. When the initial bequest is made to the CLT, the IRS § 7520 tables are used to value the charity's and family's respective interests in the trust. The decedent's estate then pays estate tax on the value of the interest passing to the family. If the trust's investments outperform the § 7520 rate, the amount by which the investments outperform the § 7520 rate eventually passes to the family beneficiaries. Since the IRS rates did not predict that this value would exist, the excess value is never subjected to estate tax.

If the CLT is funded with retirement benefits, however, the CLT will generally start out at a disadvantage, since some of the principal that the IRS assumed the trust would have has in fact been used up paying income taxes. This makes it that much *less* likely that the trust will "beat" the IRS's § 7520 rate, because in effect the trust starts out with a loss. The client may well end up paying estate tax on *more* than the family beneficiaries eventually receive.

7.5.08 *Foreign charities*

Generally, an income tax charitable deduction is allowed only for gifts to charities that are "created or organized in the United States or in any possession thereof, or under the law of the United States, any State, the District of Columbia, or any possession of the United States...." § 170(c)(2)(A). The estate tax charitable deduction is not similarly limited to domestic organizations; compare § 2055.

7.6 Various Ideas and Issues

7.6.01 *Charitable gifts of retirement plan benefits during life*

How wonderful it would be if a Participant could transfer his retirement plan to a CRT, reserving the CRT income for himself and his spouse for life, never paying income tax on the underlying benefits, and even getting an income tax deduction for the value of his remainder gift. This strategy doesn't work. For one thing, qualified retirement plan benefits are non-assignable (with limited exceptions, but this isn't one of them). § 401(a)(13). For another, the income tax deduction for a charitable gift of ordinary income property is limited to the donor's basis, which, in the case of an IRA, is generally either zero or a relatively small amount. § 170(e)(1)(A); ¶ 2.1.04.

If the donor is willing to forego the income tax deduction part of the deal, can he assign an IRA to charity? An IRA is not *per se* non-assignable. One type of assignment is prohibited by the Code: if Participant pledges his IRA as security for a loan, it ceases to be an IRA and is treated as having been distributed to Participant. § 408(e)(4). The fact that one particular type of assignment is dealt with, and "punished," in § 408 implies that *other* assignments do *not* result in loss of IRA status. However, the IRS has made clear in various regulations that, in its view, the assignment of an IRA, although effective to transfer the account, causes it to lose its special tax characteristics. See discussions at ¶ 4.5.01, ¶ 5.5.07.

"The Charitable IRA Rollover Bill" has been a perennial proposal in Congress, though it has yet to become law. This proposal would allow individuals to transfer their IRAs to charity during life. While the donor would not be allowed an income tax deduction for the gift, he would also not have to recognize any income upon making the transfer. For comment on this proposal, see "Why Not Allow Lifetime Charitable Assignments of Qualified Plans and IRAs?" by Frank M. Burke, *Tax Notes* 7/7/97, page 121.

Until that legislation is passed, however, the only choice for someone who wishes to give his retirement plan to charity while he is still alive is to take a distribution from the plan and then give the same amount to charity. *Theoretically*, the charitable deduction should offset the income, so there would be no net income tax on the plan distribution; in real life, however:

A.   The percentage-of-income limits on the charitable deduction, the alternative minimum tax, state tax laws (which may not allow charitable deductions), and the limits on itemized deductions conspire to make it difficult in many cases to eliminate the income tax on large retirement plan distributions turned over to charity;

B.   Someone under age 59½ generally must pay the 10% penalty (see Chapter 9) if he takes a distribution even if the purpose of the distribution is to fund his charitable gift; and

C.   Someone who uses a retirement plan distribution to fund a CRT (¶ 7.5.04) to provide a lifetime income for himself and/or his spouse does not get a deduction equal to the entire amount placed in the trust, since only part of it is a charitable gift.

7.6.02 *Unrelated business taxable income (UBTI)*

Although charities are generally exempt from income tax, they are taxed on their "unrelated business taxable income" (UBTI). § 511. If retirement plan distributions were considered UBTI, there would be no income tax advantage to leaving such benefits to charity. The consequences would be even more drastic in the case of a Charitable Remainder Trust. A CRT is generally exempt from income tax if it meets all the requirements of § 664. However, a CRT is *not* income tax-exempt in any year that it has *any* UBTI. § 664(c).

PLR 9253038 involved a CRT that was to be named as beneficiary of retirement benefits. The IRS ruled that the trust in question qualified as a Charitable Remainder Trust and thus was tax-exempt so long as it did not have any UBTI. Some practitioners take this ruling as implying that retirement plan distributions are *not* UBTI, although the ruling did not specifically say that.

7.6.03 *Gift of ESOP "qualified replacement property" to a CRT*

The Code allows a business owner, if various requirements are met, to sell stock of his company to an "employee stock ownership plan" (ESOP), then reinvest the proceeds in marketable securities ("qualified replacement property"), without paying income tax on the sale. § 1042. The untaxed gain carries over to the qualified replacement property and the capital gain tax thus deferred will be paid when the taxpayer "disposes of" the qualified replacement property.

A disposition of the qualified replacement property "by gift" does not trigger this "recapture" provision, but since the Code doesn't define "gift," there is some question whether transferring qualified replacement property to a Charitable Remainder Trust (which is not totally a "gift" if the donor retains an income interest) is considered a gift for this purpose. PLR 9732023 answered this question favorably to the taxpayer involved in that ruling, concluding that "the contribution of the qualified replacement property to the charitable remainder unitrust will not cause a recapture of the gain deferred by the Taxpayers under section 1042(a)...."

Unfortunately, even aside from the fact that a private letter ruling cannot be relied on as precedent, the language of the ruling is ambiguous and limited. It says: "In the present case, the transfer of the [qualified replacement property] to the charitable remainder unitrust constitutes a disposition of such property with the meaning of section 1042(e) of the Code. However under the facts of the present case, no gain is realized by the Taxpayers on the transfer...," with no indication of *why* no gain is realized. Presumably the rationale is that the transfer is a gift, and therefore excepted from the recognition of gain.

7.6.04 *Net unrealized appreciation of employer securities*

The Code gives special favorable treatment to distributions of employer securities from a qualified plan. Any growth in value of such securities which has occurred between the time the plan originally placed the securities in the employee's account and the time of the distribution is called "net unrealized appreciation" (NUA). Under certain circumstances, NUA is not taxed at the time of the distribution; rather, taxation is postponed until the stock is later sold. See ¶ 2.4.

A retired employee who holds stock with not-yet-taxed NUA has the same options that other individuals owning appreciated stock have when they wish to diversify their investments and/or increase the income from their portfolios: either sell the stock, pay the capital gain tax and reinvest the net proceeds; or, contribute the stock to a Charitable Remainder Trust (¶ 7.5.04) reserving a life income, thus avoiding the capital gain tax and generating an income tax deduction besides. See PLR 1999-19039.

7.6.05 *Charitable pledges (and other debts)*

If the client names a creditor as beneficiary of his retirement benefits, so that the benefits will be used to satisfy the client's debt to that creditor, the IRS would treat this as generating taxable income *to the client's estate*. Although generally retirement benefits are taxed to the person who "receives" them (in this case the creditor) (see ¶ 2.1.01), the IRS would say that the estate "received" the IRD, because the estate's debt was canceled when the benefits passed to the creditor.

A charitable pledge that remains unfulfilled at death may, depending on applicable state law, constitute a debt enforceable against the estate. See, *e.g.*, *Robinson v. Nutt*, 185 Mass. 345, 70 N.E. 198 (1904) (unpaid written charitable subscription enforced as a debt against the estate due to charity's reliance), and *King v. Trustees of Boston University*, 420 Mass. 52, 647 N.E. 2d 1196 (1995). However, a charitable pledge is *not* considered a debt for federal income tax purposes. Rev. Rul. 64-240 (1964-2 C.B. 172). Therefore, making retirement benefits payable to a charity as beneficiary, in fulfilment of a charitable pledge, will not cause the estate to realize income when the charity collects the benefits, regardless of whether the pledge was enforceable as a debt against the client's estate.

7.7 Summary of Planning Principles

1.   For a client who wishes to make charitable gifts upon his death, there are tax advantages to using retirement benefits to fulfill those gifts.

2.   Despite the tax advantages of funding charitable bequests with retirement benefits, such gifts have some pitfalls and complications, particularly if the benefits flow through a trust, or if part of the benefits will pass to individual beneficiaries.

3.   Making benefits payable to a Charitable Remainder Trust may maximize the value of the benefits to the family if the alternative is an immediate fully taxable distribution of the benefits at the Participant's death.

4.   The tax laws involved in charitable giving are just as complicated and technical as the rules dealing with retirement benefits, and when the two areas overlap the results are often unclear.

8

Disclaimers; Life Insurance; Grandfather Rules

Disclaimers have proven useful in post mortem planning for benefits. Life insurance held in a retirement plan poses unique challenges. Obscure "grandfather rules" can be beneficial to the few who qualify to use them.

8.1 Qualified Disclaimers of Retirement Benefits

8.1.00 *Overview of disclaimers of benefits*

A disclaimer is the refusal to accept a gift or inheritance. Federal tax law recognizes that a person cannot be forced to accept a gift or inheritance. Therefore, a disclaimer (provided it meets the requirements of § 2518; ¶ 8.1.01) is not treated as, itself, a taxable transfer. § 2518(a). Since the person making the disclaimer never accepted the property in the first place, the theory goes, he never owned it and therefore he could not have given it away.

Example: Mary dies, leaving her $100,000 IRA to Maureen as primary beneficiary. Maureen is already wealthy and does not want the money. Maureen disclaims the IRA by means of a disclaimer that meets all the requirements of § 2518 ("Qualified Disclaimer") and applicable state law. Under applicable state law, disclaimed property passes as though the disclaimant had predeceased the transferor (i.e., as if Maureen had predeceased Mary). Accordingly, the IRA passes as a result of Maureen's disclaimer to the contingent beneficiary of the IRA, who is Maureen's poor cousin Pat. Even though Maureen has voluntarily parted with her right to receive a substantial sum of money, an action that normally would be considered a gift, Maureen has *not* made a gift under the gift tax law. In contrast, if Maureen had "accepted" the IRA (for example, by withdrawing all the money from it and putting it in her bank account; see ¶ 8.1.05), and then written a check to Pat for $100,000, she would have made a taxable gift.

Disclaimers can be very useful in *post mortem* planning for retirement benefits, as examples in ¶ 8.2 show. Unfortunately, many practitioners seem to have an oversimplified view of disclaimers; not every refusal to accept an inheritance is a *qualified* disclaimer, entitled to the blessings of § 2518. This ¶ 8.1 explains the critical *income tax* effects of disclaimers (¶ 8.1.02), and examines the requirements for a "qualified disclaimer," with emphasis on (i) how these requirements apply to disclaimers of retirement benefits and (ii) requirements that are often overlooked or misunderstood.

8.1.01 *Requirements of a Qualified Disclaimer under § 2518*

The following are the requirements for a Qualified Disclaimer under § 2518:

A.   The disclaimer must be irrevocable, unqualified (unconditional) and in writing. § 2518(b), § 2518(b)(1). Yes that's right: in order to be qualified, the disclaimer must be unqualified! Verbal, revocable and conditional disclaimers are not Qualified Disclaimers.

Example: Harriet wants to disclaim two IRAs she has inherited. She writes to the first IRA provider that she disclaims IRA # 1, "provided such disclaimer will not make me ineligible for Medicaid." This disclaimer is not "unconditional," so it is not a Qualified Disclaimer. She telephones a representative of the custodian of IRA # 2 and tells him she refuses to accept IRA # 2 and wants no part of it. This is not a Qualified Disclaimer because it is not in writing.

B.   The written disclaimer must be delivered to "the transferor of the interest, the transferor's legal representative, the holder of the legal title to the property to which the interest relates, or the person in possession of such property." Reg. § 25.2518-2(b)(2). See ¶ 8.1.12.

C.   The disclaimer must be delivered to the foregoing party(ies) within nine months after the transfer that created the interest that is being disclaimed (or, if later, nine months after the disclaimant attains age 21). § 2518(b)(2); ¶ 8.1.11. In the case of retirement plan death benefits, the date of the transfer is normally the date of death, but see ¶ 8.2.09.

D.   The disclaimant must not have "accepted the interest disclaimed or any of its benefits." § 2518(b)(3). See ¶ 8.1.05 through ¶ 8.1.10.

E.   The property must pass, as a result of the disclaimer, *to someone other than the disclaimant.* Exception: property can pass to the decedent's spouse as a result of the disclaimer, even if she is also the person making the disclaimer. § 2518(b)(4). See ¶ 8.2.05.

F.   The property must pass, as a result of the disclaimer, to whoever it passes to *without any direction on the part of the disclaimant.* Disclaimers in favor of the spouse are NOT excepted from this rule. § 2518(b)(4). See ¶ 8.2.06.

8.1.02 *Income tax treatment of Qualified Disclaimers*

§ 2518 recognizes Qualified Disclaimers "for purposes of this subtitle." § 2518 is part of Subtitle B of the Code, "Estate and Gift Taxes." Income taxes are governed by Subtitle A. Except for a minor provision dealing with disclaimers of powers by a trust beneficiary (§ 678(d)), there is no Code provision dealing with the effectiveness of disclaimers *for purposes of Subtitle A.*

The IRS Chief Counsel's office has filled the statutory gap, at least with respect to certain disclaimers of retirement benefits. GCM 39858 (9/9/81) ruled that a disclaimer of retirement benefits, if it met all requirements of § 2518 and applicable state law, is effective to shift the income tax on the benefits from the disclaimant (the person originally entitled to the benefits) to the person who receives the benefits as a result of the disclaimer. This GCM also held that such a disclaimer is not an "assignment or alienation" of plan benefits of the type forbidden by § 401(a)(13).

Thus, at least for Qualified Disclaimers that are valid under applicable state law, we can be sure that a disclaimer will not be treated as an assignment of income or of plan benefits (either of which could cause disqualification of the plan and/or immediate taxation of the income in question).

8.1.03 *State law requirements of disclaimers*

It is very important for the disclaimer to comply with the applicable state law. The question of which state's law the disclaimer of a qualified plan benefit or IRA must comply with is beyond the scope of this book; leading candidates include the state of Participant's domicile and the state where the retirement plan is administered. If in doubt comply with both.

If the disclaimer is not valid under applicable state law, it may not be effective to transfer the ownership of the disclaimed property away from the disclaimant.

Example: Tanya files a purported disclaimer of an IRA she has inherited from her father. Although it is an unconditional written refusal to accept the property, and it is filed with the right person and within the required time frame, the applicable state law says that a disclaimer of an IRA is not valid unless it is notarized and Tanya's disclaimer is not notarized. The effect under the applicable state law is that Tanya still owns the IRA. Her disclaimer is not a Qualified Disclaimer.

Theoretically it is possible for a disclaimer to be qualified under § 2518 even though not valid under state law; see § 2518(c)(3). However, under the IRS's interpretation of § 2518(c)(3), this could happen only if the state law dictates who will receive the disclaimed property in the event of an invalid disclaimer; see Reg. § 25.2518-1(c)(3), Examples 1 and 2. Thus, it would seem that this is rarely likely to actually occur. See also ¶ 8.2.08 regarding possible conflicts between disclaimers that are valid under state law and ERISA.

8.1.04 *Non-qualified disclaimers*

GCM 39858 did not purport to decide the income tax effects of a disclaimer that was either *not qualified* under § 2518 or *not valid under state law*.

The IRS has at least once treated a non-qualified disclaimer of a qualified retirement plan as effective to transfer the income tax burden of the retirement benefits to the person who took as a result of the disclaimer. See PLR 9450041. Nevertheless, a non-qualified disclaimer is clearly outside the safe harbor of GCM 39858.

This point is critical: there are cases when it does not really matter, for *gift tax purposes*, whether a disclaimer is qualified or not, but when the disclaimed property is income-taxable, as retirement plan distributions generally are (¶ 2.1.01), it is normally vital to have the disclaimer recognized for *income tax* purposes. See example at ¶ 8.2.05. If the disclaimer does not meet the requirements of § 2518, it may not be effective to shift the taxable income.

While the income tax effect of non-qualified disclaimers and disclaimers that are not valid under state law is uncertain, we have a safe harbor regarding the income tax treatment of a disclaimer that is valid under state law and qualified under § 2518. The rest of this ¶ 8.1 discusses how to meet the requirements of § 2518 in connection with disclaimers of retirement benefits. ¶ 8.2 discusses the planning uses (and pitfalls) of Qualified Disclaimers of retirement benefits.

8.1.05 *What constitutes "acceptance": overview*

One requirement of a Qualified Disclaimer is that the disclaimant must not "have accepted the interest disclaimed or any of its benefits." § 2518(b)(3). "Acceptance is manifested by an affirmative act which is consistent with ownership...." Examples of such an affirmative act include accepting "dividends, interest or rent from the property," "directing others to act with respect to the property" and "acceptance of any consideration in return for making the disclaimer." Reg. § 25.2518-2(d)(1). For exception for certain fiduciary actions, see ¶ 8.1.06.

Here are the easy clear examples of what does constitute acceptance. Assume Alpha dies and leaves 100 shares of Omega stock to each of his three children, Beta, Gamma and Delta. Under the terms of Alpha's will, If a child predeceases Alpha, or disclaims the bequest of stock, that child's share passes to that child's issue if any, otherwise to the surviving children (or their issue).

A.   Beta receives a check for $10, representing the quarterly $.10-per-share dividend on his 100 shares of Omega stock. He endorses the dividend check, and deposits it in his bank account. Beta is deemed to have accepted *the stock* because he accepted *the income from it*, so he cannot later disclaim the stock. See Reg. § 25.2518-2(d)(4), Examples (6), (11). The proper way to disclaim an income payment in the form of a check is return the check uncashed along with a written disclaimer. Reg. § 25.2518-2(c)(5), Ex. (6).

B.   Gamma intends to disclaim all of his inheritance from Alpha, so it will pass to Gamma's children, but he thinks Omega stock is a terrible investment for them to own, so he calls his broker and instructs the broker to sell the 100 shares of Omega that were left to Gamma. Gamma has *exercised control* over the stock, and so cannot later make a Qualified Disclaimer of the stock (or of the proceeds of the sale of the stock). See Reg. § 25.2518-2(d)(4), Example (4), and ¶ 8.2.04.

C.   Delta makes a deal with Beta that Delta will disclaim Delta's 100 shares of Omega stock if Beta disclaims some other property. By accepting *consideration* for his disclaimer, Delta is deemed to have exercised control over the property he is purporting to disclaim, and so he is deemed to have accepted the Omega stock. His disclaimer will not be qualified. Reg. § 25.2518-2(d)(1)(last sentence); Reg. § 25.2518-2(d)(4), Example (2).

On the other hand, certain actions do not constitute "acceptance." Acceptance must involve some action on the part of the beneficiary. Mere passive title-holding is not acceptance. For example, under many states' laws, if a decedent's real estate is bequeathed to a beneficiary, the title to that real estate automatically vests in the beneficiary on the death of the decedent. This automatic vesting does not constitute acceptance by the beneficiary, and does not prevent the beneficiary from making a Qualified Disclaimer of that real estate. Reg. § 25.2518-2(d)(1). See ¶ 8.1.07 and ¶ 8.1.08 for how this concept applies to retirement benefits.

8.1.06 *Limited exception for certain fiduciary actions*

This ¶ 8.1.06 discusses whether a person who is both a beneficiary and a fiduciary of the property can disclaim an interest *as beneficiary* despite having taken certain actions regarding the property in his capacity *as fiduciary*. For discussion of disclaimers by a fiduciary *in his capacity as fiduciary* see ¶ 8.2.07.

Actions taken by a person who is both a beneficiary and a fiduciary "in the exercise of fiduciary powers to preserve or maintain the disclaimed property" do not constitute acceptance *as beneficiary*. Reg. § 25.2518-2(d)(2).

Example: Mother dies. Her will leaves her house to her three children A, B and C, and names C as executor. To fulfill his duties as executor under applicable state law, C arranges for insurance, security and maintenance for the house. These actions taken as executor would not preclude his disclaiming his interest as beneficiary.

This exception can easily lead practitioners astray. This is a very limited exception for which the IRS provides no examples in the regulations. The only fiduciary powers blessed are "to preserve or maintain the disclaimed property." Conspicuous by their absence from the list are such fiduciary powers as selling assets and allocating assets among beneficiaries' shares.

Also remember that any exercise of discretionary powers *to direct the enjoyment of the property*, even if exercised in a fiduciary capacity, would preclude a Qualified Disclaimer of the property by the individual in his personal capacity, unless the exercise of discretion is limited by an ascertainable standard. Reg. § 25.2518-2(e)(1)(next-to-last sentence). See ¶ 8.2.06.

�ֆֆ֍ֆ

Now we turn to how these rules apply to retirement benefits. No rulings or cases discuss what constitutes "acceptance" of a retirement plan death benefit, so we must analogize from cases, regulations and rulings involving other forms of property.

8.1.07   *Titling of the account does not determine acceptance*

The fact that a retirement plan account is retitled in the name of the beneficiary after the death of Participant does not in and of itself mean the beneficiary has accepted the account. See Reg. § 25.2518-2(d)(4), Example (6); PLR 8817061 (a surviving spouse's filing an election to take a statutory share of the decedent's estate did not constitute acceptance of the statutory share; the spouse could disclaim part of the statutory share); PLR 9214022.

Example: Rachel dies, leaving her IRA (which is held at Brokerage Firm X) to her husband Isaac. Isaac promptly calls Brokerage Firm X and informs them of Rachel's death. Brokerage Firm X retitles the account "Rachel, deceased, IRA, for the benefit of Isaac, beneficiary." Brokerage Firm X sends Isaac paperwork explaining the account agreement, its fees, and his rights regarding rollover, investments and so forth. If this is all that happens, Isaac has not accepted the IRA. But: If Isaac gives Brokerage Firm X any instructions regarding the account, such as buying or selling investments, he has accepted the account (or at least those investments; see ¶ 8.1.09). If he names a successor beneficiary for his interest, see ¶ 8.1.10. If he takes a withdrawal from the account, see ¶ 8.1.09. If he elects to treat the inherited IRA as his own IRA (see ¶ 3.2.05) he has accepted it.

8.1.08 *Automatic deposit of benefits not acceptance*

It is common for a participant to arrange his IRA or other retirement plan so that periodic distributions are automatically deposited directly in his bank account. If the bank account is a joint account co-owned with the retirement plan beneficiary, the mere continuation of the automatic deposits after Participant's death would not, *in itself*, constitute acceptance of the retirement plan, or even of the amounts deposited, by the beneficiary, since there has been no action by the beneficiary.

Example: George receives monthly distributions of $2,500 from his IRA. These are automatically transferred, by the IRA provider, by electronic means, to the bank account George owns jointly with Martha, who is also named as beneficiary of the IRA. George dies on June 27. Two more monthly payments of $2,500 are transferred from the IRA to the bank account after George's death (on July 1 and August 1). When the IRA provider is notified of George's death, it ceases making the automatic transfers. Martha is not deemed to have accepted George's IRA just because of the continuation of the monthly automatic deposits, even though they were transferred into an account in her name, because she is not the one who directed that they be so transferred. These deposits were initiated by George, not Martha.

Although the continuation of automatic distributions does not in and of itself create "acceptance" by the beneficiary, however, the waters quickly get muddied if the surviving account owner/beneficiary exercises control over the joint bank account funds after the Participant's death. For example, suppose Martha in the above example writes some checks on the (formerly) joint bank account, or withdraws some cash from it, after George's death, and later decides she wants to disclaim the IRA distributions that were placed in the account after George's death. (If she wants to keep those payments but disclaim the *rest* of the IRA, see ¶ 8.1.09.)

If she wants to say she never accepted the post-death automatic distributions from George's IRA, she presumably has to prove that the money she spent from that account after George's death did *not* come out of the post-mortem IRA distributions. If, after George's death and prior to the disclaimer, the balance in the account ever dipped below the then-cumulative total of the post-death transfers from the IRA, then Martha will not be able to argue that she did not accept the IRA distributions. So, for example, if in July, after the first $2,500 post-death automatic deposit came in from the IRA, the balance in the account dipped below $2,500, that would mean Martha must have spent some of the money from the IRA distribution. If she spent it, she accepted it.

On the other hand, if the account balance always stayed equal to or higher than the cumulative total of post-death IRA distributions, Martha should succeed in her claim that she never touched those distributions and so never accepted them. See PLR 2000-03023.

8.1.09 *Taking a distribution as acceptance of the entire plan*

If the beneficiary accepts a distribution from the plan, does that necessarily constitute an "acceptance" of the *entire* plan, precluding a Qualified Disclaimer of the rest of the plan? This problem becomes acute when a Participant who has passed his Required Beginning Date dies near the end of the year, not having taken his Minimum Required Distribution (MRD) for the year. The beneficiary may feel rushed to take the MRD to avoid a penalty, but then, with more leisure to consider the matter, wish to disclaim the rest of the benefits. What the beneficiary would like to do in this situation is claim he has made only a partial acceptance of the inherited retirement plan.

The Code permits partial disclaimers. A person may disclaim "any interest" in property. § 2518(a). Reg. § 25.2518-3 is entirely devoted to disclaimers of "less than an entire interest." Several types of partial disclaimers are recognized, including a disclaimer relating to "severable property."

Severable property is "property which can be divided into separate parts each of which, after severance, maintains a complete and independent existence. For example, a legatee of shares of corporate stock may accept some shares of the stock and make a qualified disclaimer of the remaining shares." Reg. § 25.2518-3(a)(1)(ii).

When a beneficiary inherits an estate, or a joint securities account, the beneficiary has inherited in effect a collection of severable property. The beneficiary can take some assets from the inherited collection and refuse others. See Reg. § 25.2518-3(d), Ex. 17. The IRS has in rulings allowed beneficiaries to accept some assets from an estate, trust or joint investment account and later disclaim other assets. The favorable rulings (PLRs 8113061, 9036028 and 8619002) support the conclusion that a beneficiary may take a distribution from a typical self-directed IRA (which is, like an estate or a joint investment account, essentially a collection of severable property) without being deemed to have accepted the entire account and therefore without being precluded from disclaiming all or part of the rest of the account. (The only exception would be if the distributions taken could somehow be construed as representing the "income" of the entire account; see ¶ 8.1.05.)

If the beneficiary thinks of this issue in advance, he can either execute a partial disclaimer before taking the distribution, or at least send in to the IRA provider, along with the request for a distribution, a written statement that the beneficiary is not accepting the entire account, just the amount of this distribution.

Taking a distribution *would* preclude a later disclaimer if the retirement benefit is not a collection of "severable" property. For example, suppose the retirement plan in question is a Defined Benefit Plan, and the form of death benefit is a life annuity of $100 per month. As soon as the beneficiary accepts the first $100 check, he has accepted the entire benefit, because there is no way to "sever" the annuity.

8.1.10 *Naming a successor beneficiary as acceptance*

A beneficiary's designating a successor beneficiary for his interest in the account is probably not "acceptance." "The exercise of a power of appointment to any extent by the donee of the power is an acceptance of its benefits" (Reg. § 25.2518-2(d)(1)) but this apparently does not include an executory exercise; see Reg. § 25.2518-2(d)(4), Example (7), in which B has a testamentary power of appointment under A's trust, and executes a will which would exercise the power, but then makes a Qualified Disclaimer of the power before he dies.

8.1.11 *Deadline for Qualified Disclaimer*

At one level the deadline for disclaimers of retirement benefits is simply stated ("nine months after Participant's death"), but when stated with all its exceptions and wrinkles the rule is more complicated: § 2518(b)(2) states that the disclaimer must be delivered "not later than the date which is 9 months after the later of--(A) the day on which the transfer creating the interest in such person is made, or (B) the day on which such person attains age 21." Now the wrinkles:

First, the deadline is measured from *the date of the transfer* that created the interest being disclaimed. Normally, in the case of retirement plan death benefits, the date of transfer is the date of Participant's death, but there are cases in which the transfer arguably occurred prior to Participant's death; see ¶ 8.2.09. *The rest of this ¶ 8.1.11 assumes the time period starts running at Participant's death.*

Second, if a beneficiary is under the age of 21 years at the time of Participant's death, the deadline for that beneficiary to deliver his Qualified Disclaimer is nine months after the beneficiary reaches age 21. For the relation of this exception to the determination of Participant's "designated beneficiary" (for purposes of the minimum distribution rules discussed in Chapter 1) see ¶ 8.2.01.

Third, the fact that the deadline for finalizing the identity of the designated beneficiary for MRD purposes is September 30 of the year after the Participant's death does NOT mean that the deadline for making a qualified disclaimer is extended to that date; the MRD rules have no effect whatever on the deadline for a qualified disclaimer.

Fourth, if the deadline for delivering the disclaimer falls on a Saturday, Sunday or legal holiday (see Reg. § 301.7503-1(b) for definition), the deadline is extended to the next day which is not a

Saturday, Sunday or legal holiday. Reg. § 25.2518-2(c)(2).

Fifth, in rules borrowed from the deadline for filing tax returns, the IRS provides that "a timely mailing of a disclaimer" to the correct person (¶ 8.1.12) "is treated as a timely delivery." Reg. § 25.2518-2(c)(2). See Reg. § 301.7502-1(c)(1), (2), and (d), for requirements of "timely mailing."

8.1.12 *To whom is the disclaimer delivered?*

§ 2518(b)(2) requires that the disclaimer be "received by the transferor of the interest, his legal representative, or the holder of the legal title to the property to which the interest relates." Reg. § 25.2518-2(b)(2) adds one more candidate, "the person in possession of such property," but adds no further elucidation and no examples.

In the case of retirement benefits, the disclaimer cannot be delivered to "the transferor" (Participant) because he is dead, so that leaves "his legal representative" (i.e., the executor or administrator of Participant's estate), "the holder of the legal title to the property" and "the person in possession." The legal title to retirement benefits is generally held by the trustee (of a qualified plan or individual retirement trust) or custodian (of an individual retirement account or 403(b) mutual fund account), who also has "possession" of the retirement plan's assets.

The "or" in the Code and Regulation makes it appear that § 2518(b)(2) would be satisfied if the disclaimer is delivered *either* to the executor or administrator of Participant's estate *or* to the trustee or custodian of the retirement plan, in other words, that you have a choice of where to send the disclaimer. However, it is possible that, without specifically so stating, the government intends that the correct person to send the disclaimer to depends on the type of property; in other words, you can't just send it to any of the above, you have to send it to the right recipient. See Reg. § 25.2518-2(a)(3) and Reg. § 25.2518-2(c)(2), both of which speak of delivery to "*the person*" described in Reg. § 25.2518-2(b)(2), as though in the case of any particular asset there is only one possible recipient of the disclaimer and as though the menu of recipients in Reg. § 25.2518-2(b)(2) is only to accommodate different types of property, not to imply that for any type of property you can choose any of the foregoing.

Regardless of which destination would satisfy § 2518(b)(2), it is normally *also* necessary to comply with applicable state law requirements, which may have different or more specific requirements about where the disclaimer must be delivered (¶ 8.1.03). Also, in the case of a qualified retirement plan, check whether the plan has its own requirements about disclaimers and comply with those (see ¶ 8.2.08).

For what it's worth, in PLR 9016026 a qualified disclaimer of qualified plan benefits was filed with the employer and the plan trustee; in PLR 9226058, a qualified disclaimer of an IRA was filed with the Probate Court. Other letter rulings discussing qualified disclaimers don't say where the disclaimers were filed.

8.2 Planning with Disclaimers

Disclaimers have proven to be of great value in "cleaning up" beneficiary designations where the deceased Participant named the "wrong" beneficiary. Disclaimers have been used to redirect benefits to the surviving spouse (so she can roll them over), and to create funding for a credit shelter trust that would otherwise have no assets. Under the minimum distribution regulations, disclaimers are important in establishing the life expectancy payout period; see ¶ 1.8.03. *Post mortem* planning flexibility can be increased if the possibility of disclaimers is planned for in the drafting stage, although excessive reliance on possible future disclaimers is discouraged (¶ 8.2.04).

8.2.01 *Changing the "designated beneficiary"*

As explained in Chapter 1, § 401(a)(9)(B) requires that retirement benefits be distributed within a certain period of time after Participant's death. If the benefits are payable to a "designated beneficiary," that period of time is the life expectancy of the designated beneficiary. If the benefits are left to an individual ("Primary Beneficiary") who disclaims the benefits, and as a result of the disclaimer the benefits pass to a different individual ("Contingent Beneficiary"), which one of them is Participant's "designated beneficiary"?

The minimum distribution regulations specify that qualified disclaimers *are* given effect in determining who is the designated beneficiary. Reg. § 1.401(a)(9)-4, A-4(a). The designated beneficiary "will be determined based on the beneficiaries designated on the date of death who remain beneficiaries as of September 30 of the calendar year following the calendar year of the employee's death." That date is called in this book the "Designation Date." See ¶ 1.8. "Accordingly, if a person disclaims entitlement to the employee's benefit, pursuant to a disclaimer that satisfies section 2518 by that September 30 thereby allowing other beneficiaries to receive the benefit in lieu of that person, the disclaiming person is not taken into account in determining the employee's designated beneficiary." Reg. § 1.401(a)(9)-4, A-4(a).

Thus, it is clear that an older beneficiary (such as a surviving spouse or child) can disclaim the benefits and allow them to pass to a younger contingent beneficiary (such as a child or grandchild) and the younger beneficiary will then be "the" designated beneficiary whose life expectancy becomes the Applicable Distribution Period, provided the disclaimer is a "qualified disclaimer" under § 2518, and occurs prior to the Designation Date.

Note the following:

A.   This regulation does NOT extend the deadline for making a qualified disclaimer. See ¶ 8.1.11.

B.   If the beneficiary is under age 21 at the time of Participant's death, the deadline for such beneficiary's Qualified Disclaimer is nine months after his 21st birthday. ¶ 8.1.11. This could well be later than the Designation Date. A disclaimer (even if qualified) that does not occur until after the Designation Date is *not* effective to change the "designated beneficiary" for purposes of computing required distributions after Participant's death (see ¶ 1.8.01).

8.2.02 *Funding credit shelter trust*

In PLR 9442032, Participant named Spouse as primary beneficiary and his trust as contingent beneficiary. The trust provided that all IRA benefits had to be allocated to the marital trust, over which Spouse had a general power of appointment. No assets passed to the credit shelter trust. "To enable [the] estate to fully utilize the available unified credit," Spouse, as beneficiary of the IRA, disclaimed her interest in the IRA, and then, as beneficiary of the marital trust, disclaimed her general powers over the marital trust. As a result of these disclaimers, the IRA was now payable to a trust of which she was merely the life income beneficiary, with no general power of appointment. Then, as executor, she made a fractional QTIP election for the IRA and the trust. The non-elected portion of the IRA and marital trust became in effect the credit shelter trust.

8.2.03 *Salvaging spousal rollover*

If Participant dies having named the "wrong" beneficiary (typically, in published rulings, a trust), it may be possible to get the benefits to Spouse (so she can roll them over) by having the trust (or other "wrong" beneficiary) disclaim the benefits. This strategy works if, as a result of the disclaimer, the benefits pass outright to Spouse either as contingent beneficiary, or (more typically) as the "default" beneficiary under the plan (i.e., the person who, according to the governing provisions of the plan or IRA agreement, takes the benefits if Participant fails to name a beneficiary).

If Participant's "estate" is the default beneficiary under the plan, this strategy still works *if* (as a result of the disclaimer) the benefits will pass outright to Spouse as residuary beneficiary under Participant's will or by intestacy. See ¶ 3.2.09. Unfortunately, this strategy does not work if Spouse will not get the benefits as a result of the disclaimer (for example, if the benefits will pass to the estate as a result of the disclaimer, and Participant's will or the state intestacy law would cause the estate to pass to Participant's children rather than to Spouse).

In PLR 9045050, Participant named a trust as his beneficiary. Spouse was a trustee of the trust. Upon Participant's death, Spouse, as trustee, made a Qualified Disclaimer of the benefits. As a result of the disclaimer, the benefits passed to Spouse outright rather than to the trust, and she rolled them over. PLR 199913048 was similar except that Spouse was not named as trustee of Participant's trust, but the named trustee declined to serve and the probate court appointed Spouse as "special trustee." Acting as special trustee, she disclaimed the benefits (with court approval) as did all other beneficiaries of Participant's trust, and the IRA passed to Spouse as the default beneficiary under the plan. Note that the IRS in this ruling did not regard the other named trustees' refusal to serve, or the court's appointment of Spouse as special trustee, or the court's approval of the disclaimer by Spouse as trustee (which one guesses was required by local law to make the disclaimer effective) as constituting *post mortem* actions that made someone other than Participant the transferor of the benefits to Spouse.

In PLR 9450041, benefits were redirected from a marital trust to Spouse via a chain of qualified and non-qualified disclaimers; the rollover was allowed.

8.2.04 *Building disclaimers into the estate plan: pitfalls*

It is wise, at the estate planning stage, to anticipate the possibility of disclaimers. For example, Participant may be trying to choose between naming Spouse as beneficiary, to achieve deferral of income taxes via a spousal rollover, on the one hand, and naming a credit shelter trust as beneficiary, on the other hand, to take full advantage of his unified credit. Each choice has its merits (see full discussion at ¶ 10.5) and a clear "winner" may not be apparent during the planning phase.

Participant may decide to make the benefits payable to Spouse as primary beneficiary, because his main goal is to provide for Spouse's financial security (for example), but provide that, if Spouse disclaims the benefits, the benefits will pass to the credit shelter trust. If funding the credit shelter trust appears to be the more attractive alternative at the time of Participant's death, Spouse can activate the credit shelter plan by disclaiming the benefits, which will then pass to the credit shelter trust as contingent beneficiary. PLR 9320015 contains an example of this type of planning.

While it is wise to consider the possibility of disclaimers, the apparent flexibility of disclaimers can tempt planners to rely excessively on future disclaimers as a way of carrying out the estate plan. One justification for this approach is that it avoids the need to spend time analyzing the choices at the planning stage. Thus, professional fees are lower—at the planning stage. The estate plan relies on the fiduciaries and beneficiaries to make the decisions later, when a more informed choice can be made.

Before making important estate planning goals dependent on prospective disclaimers by beneficiaries or fiduciaries, the planner needs to weigh carefully the risks and drawbacks of relying on disclaimers. Contrary to the impression some practitioners have, disclaimers are not a simple solution. This ¶ 8.2.04 describes several issues that exist with disclaimers of any type of property. ¶ 8.2.05 and ¶ 8.2.06 explain two essential elements of a Qualified Disclaimer that are often misunderstood or overlooked. ¶ 8.2.08 and ¶ 8.2.09 discuss particular problems that arise with disclaimers of retirement benefits.

1.   One requirement of a Qualified Disclaimer is that the disclaimant must not have "accepted" the disclaimed property. See ¶ 8.1.05 through ¶ 8.1.10 for what constitutes acceptance. Exercising investment control over the account would constitute acceptance; thus, if a beneficiary is considering making a disclaimer, the beneficiary must not make any investment changes in the account prior to the disclaimer.

2.   Disclaimers generally have an inexorable deadline of nine months after the date of death. ¶ 8.1.11. Thus, an estate plan which depends on disclaimers is extremely dependent on rapid action *post mortem*, especially if an IRS ruling is required.

3.   No matter how cooperative and disclaimer-friendly the proposed disclaimant may have been during the planning stage, the emotional turmoil caused by Participant's death, or other factors, could cause him or her to have a change of heart and not sign a disclaimer when the time comes.

4.   If estate taxes will be due on the disclaimed property, who will pay them? The decedent's will may contain a tax payment clause that may not operate correctly if there is a disclaimer.

8.2.05 *Property must pass to "someone other than" disclaimant*

§ 2518(b)(4) requires that the property must pass, as a result of the disclaimer, either to the *surviving spouse* or to *someone other than the disclaimant*.

Example: Donna is named as primary beneficiary of her brother's IRA. Within nine months of his death she disclaims the IRA. As a result of her disclaimer, the IRA passes to the contingent beneficiary of the IRA. The contingent beneficiary is a charitable remainder unitrust (¶ 7.5.04) of which Donna is the only non-charitable beneficiary. Since the IRA is not passing to "someone other than the disclaimant," and since Donna is not the spouse of the IRA owner, this disclaimer is not a Qualified Disclaimer (unless she also disclaims all interests in the charitable remainder unitrust). For *gift tax purposes* the fact that her disclaimer is not qualified makes no difference. Even though her non-qualified disclaimer is treated as a gift for gift tax purposes there are no adverse consequences, because the donee is a qualified charitable remainder trust (under § 664) of which the only beneficiaries are herself and a charity. Gifts to yourself or charity are not subject to gift tax. However, the fact that her disclaimer is not qualified means that the *income tax treatment* of the IRA is not within the safe harbor of GCM 39858. She may be liable for income taxes on the full value of the IRA (if the disclaimer is treated as an assignment of the right to receive income in respect of a decedent under § 691; see ¶ 2.2.05).

This requirement is frequently overlooked, as planners cheerfully expect (*e.g.*) children to disclaim benefits that will then pass to a trust of which children are beneficiaries. Passing the benefits by disclaimer from the outright beneficiary to a trust only works if the outright beneficiary is (a) Spouse or (b) not a beneficiary of the trust.

8.2.06 *Property must pass "without direction" by disclaimant*

§ 2518(b)(4) also requires that the property pass, as a result of the disclaimer, to whoever it passes to *without any direction on the part of the disclaimant*. Disclaimers in favor of the spouse are NOT excepted from this rule.

Example: Emil disclaims an IRA left to him by his late wife, Randa. As a result of his disclaimer, the IRA passes to the contingent beneficiary of the IRA, which is a trust created by Randa. Although Emil is not a beneficiary of this trust, he is the trustee, and as such has the power to distribute principal, in his discretion as trustee (without any ascertainable standard), among the trust beneficiaries (Randa's children). Since the IRA is not passing "without direction on the part of the disclaimant," this disclaimer is not a Qualified Disclaimer (unless Emil disclaims his powers as trustee, or disclaims his right to be the trustee).

If the surviving spouse who is named as outright beneficiary of Participant's retirement benefits is to disclaim, she cannot thereafter retain any discretionary distribution powers over the disclaimed benefits (unless limited by an ascertainable standard). For example, if Spouse is disclaiming benefits which will then pass to a credit shelter trust for issue, she cannot be a trustee of that trust if the trustee has, say, discretionary power to "spray" the trust among Participant's issue; nor can she have a power of appointment enabling her to, *e.g.*, decide which issue of Participant will receive the trust after her death. Thus, taking advantage of the flexibility of disclaimers may eliminate the use of other, even more flexible *post mortem* planning tools, such as a spousal power of appointment.

8.2.07 *Disclaimers by fiduciaries of estates and trusts*

There is scant authority on the subject of disclaimers by fiduciaries (in their capacity as fiduciaries). There can be state law obstacles, such as a requirement of court approval or a requirement of specific language in the document authorizing disclaimers.

The requirement that property must pass "without any direction" on the part of the disclaimant (¶ 8.2.06) would presumably preclude a disclaimer from one discretionary trust to a second discretionary trust with the same trustees. The requirement that property must pass "to someone other than" the disclaimant (¶ 8.2.05) presumably bars a disclaimer by a trust in favor of another trust that has the same beneficiaries, or in favor of individuals (other than the spouse) who are also beneficiaries of the disclaiming trust.

The preceding statements deal with disclaimers by the trustee of a trust that is named as beneficiary of retirement benefits. When retirement benefits are payable to *Participant's own estate*, the IRS has ruled that Participant's executor may not disclaim the benefits because Participant had "accepted" his own retirement benefits. PLR 9437042. In this ruling, Participant had named his estate as beneficiary of his retirement plan; if the estate had been allowed to disclaim, the benefits would have passed to Spouse as default beneficiary under the plan.

8.2.08 *Disclaimers and the plan administrator*

One concern is whether a plan administrator of a qualified retirement plan ("QRP") might cite ERISA requirements in refusing to recognize a disclaimer. A plan administrator might take the position that the plan requires the benefits to be paid to the beneficiary named by Participant, and the plan has no authority to pay the benefits to someone else if the named beneficiary is in fact living; that ERISA requires the plan to be administered in accordance with its terms; that ERISA requires the plan to be administered for the exclusive benefit of the participant and his beneficiaries, and the taker-by-disclaimer is not a "beneficiary"; and that ERISA preempts state laws including disclaimer statutes.

In the author's view, this is not a correct interpretation of ERISA. QRP documents generally provide that the interpretation of the plan and administration of the trust are governed by state law to the extent not contrary to (or preempted by) ERISA. If the applicable state law permits disclaimers, the plan is required to give effect to them, in the author's view, unless the plan contains a specific provision to the contrary. All trustees, not just ERISA trustees, are required to administer their trusts in accordance with the terms of the trust instrument; most non-ERISA trust instruments say nothing one way or the other about disclaimers, but no one argues that trustees generally are entitled (let alone required) to ignore legally valid disclaimers. An ERISA trust is not different from any other trust except to the extent federal law requires it to be. In GCM 39858 (9/9/81), the IRS recognized that disclaimers do not violate ERISA. The IRS has blessed disclaimers of QRP benefits in numerous letter rulings; see, *e.g.*, 9016026, 9247026 and 2001-05058.

In a similar vein, the IRS has recognized that a plan must conform to a state's "slayer" statute, and not pay benefits to the person who murdered the participant, even if that person is named as the beneficiary under the plan. See, *e.g.*, PLR 8908063.

On the other hand, the Supreme Court has upheld a QRP's refusal to follow a state statute that would have voided a beneficiary designation in favor of an ex-spouse. *Egelhoff v. Egelhoff*, 121 S. Ct. 1322, 532 U.S. 141 (2000). The Court cited ERISA's preemption and the need for uniform national rules for plan administration. Furthermore, in GCM 39858, while the IRS strongly endorsed the validity of disclaimers of QRP benefits, the approval was limited to disclaimers that satisfy the requirements of § 2518 and of state law (though the IRS has allowed the transfer of QRP benefits by *non*-qualified disclaimer at least once; see PLR 9450041). When confronted with a disclaimer, the administrator should consider obtaining an opinion of counsel that the disclaimer meets the requirements of applicable state law and § 2518.

Note that an employer who wanted to help (rather than frustrate) employees and their families could easily eliminate any possible ERISA-state law conflict by providing in the plan document that disclaimers would be given effect, and establishing reasonable procedures for verifying and implementing disclaimers.

These issues are of no concern to IRA administrators, since IRAs are not subject to ERISA and its pre-emption rule.

8.2.09 *REA and deadline for Qualified Disclaimers*

A Qualified Disclaimer must be made within a certain time period "after the...date of the transfer creating the interest" being disclaimed. ¶ 8.1.11. The period is measured "with reference to the transfer creating the interest in the disclaimant." A transfer occurs when there is a "completed gift" (in the case of an inter vivos transfer), or (in the case of a transfer at death, or a transfer that becomes irrevocable at death) as of the date of death. Reg. § 25.2518-2(c)(3)(i).

So far, we have looked at retirement benefits under the assumption that the date of Participant's death is the starting point for measuring the time period during which a Qualified Disclaimer must be made. However, in any situation in which a beneficiary acquires rights in Participant's benefits earlier than the date of death we need to consider whether the time starts earlier.

Federal law gives married persons certain rights in each other's retirement benefits. See ¶ 3.4. Thus, under a pension plan, Spouse acquires vested rights in Participant's benefits at the same moment Participant does (or upon their marriage, if the marriage occurred when Participant was already in the plan). If Spouse acquired rights in Participant's benefits more than nine months before the date of death, is it too late for her to disclaim these benefits when Participant dies?

§ 2503(f) provides that *certain* spousal waivers of retirement benefits are exempt from gift tax. Specifically, § 2503(f) says that, "If any individual waives, *before the death of a participant*, any survivor benefit, or right to such benefit, *under § 401(a)(11) or 417* [REA benefits, in other words], such waiver shall not be treated as a transfer of property by gift for purposes of this chapter" (emphasis added). Thus, the Code has a specific exemption from gift tax for *certain* spousal waivers, namely, waivers (1) of REA-guaranteed survivor benefits (2) that occur before the death of the participant. Does this mean that:

1.   Waivers of *other* spousal plan benefits *are* taxable gifts? Many plans, for administrative reasons, give spouses more benefits than REA strictly requires. Although the statutory exemption is limited to REA-guaranteed benefits, presumably the IRS would

not attempt, in the case of a spousal waiver, to assess gift tax on the "enhanced" value of any plan spousal benefits over the strict minimum guaranteed by REA. However, there is no authority on this question one way or the other.

2.   Spousal waivers that occur *after* the participant's death *are* taxable gifts? No. The IRS announced in GCM 39858 (9/9/81) that § 2503(f) does not imply Congressional intent to impose gift tax on spousal waivers that occur *after* Participant's death: "no inference should be drawn from § 2503(f) that a disclaimer of plan benefits *after* the participant's death should receive unfavorable tax treatment simply because Congress provided for favorable gift tax treatment if plan benefits are waived *before* the participant's death."

GCM 39858 involved a spousal disclaimer of REA-guaranteed benefits. The IRS stated that: "There is no evidence that Congress intended to preclude a spouse from disclaiming or renouncing benefits under a qualified plan payable after the participant's death." In view of the IRS's strong policy statement in this GCM, it appears the IRS has answered, for now, any questions that might exist about the disclaimer of REA-guaranteed benefits: such benefits can be the object of a Qualified Disclaimer, according to GCM 39858.

8.2.10 Practical issues in disclaimers of retirement benefits

Here are some tips for dealing with and planning for qualified disclaimers of benefits:

A.   How to do partial disclaimers. If making a partial disclaimer, review Reg. § 25.2518-3, which discusses and gives examples of disclaimers of part of an inheritance by: disclaiming one or more separate interests in property while retaining others (Reg. § 25.2518-3(a)(1)(i); § 25.2518-3(d), Ex. (21)); disclaiming some "severable" property and accepting other severable property (see discussion at ¶ 8.1.09 and Reg. § 25.2518-3(a)(1)(ii); § 25.2518-3(d), Ex. (1), (3)); disclaimer of an undivided portion (Reg. § 25.2518-3(b); § 25.2518-3(d), Ex. (20)); and disclaimer of a pecuniary amount (or of everything except a pecuniary amount) (Reg. § 25.2518-3(c); § 25.2518-

3(d), Ex. (16)-(19)). Follow the "successful" examples as closely as possible, and comply with state law requirements.

B.   Keep the disclaimer short and sweet. It's tempting to recite, in the disclaimer, who will receive the property as a result of the disclaimer, but it's not a good idea. Whenever you mention who the property is passing to, it looks like the disclaimant is either trying to direct who will receive the property or trying to make the disclaimer conditional on the property passing to those recipients, either of which actions would make the disclaimer not qualified under § 2518. For an example of another type of extraneous language causing problems in a disclaimer, see TAM 8240012 (disclaimer of a pecuniary amount; disclaimant added the words "in cash or in kind"; IRS ruled this language did not sufficiently identify the assets disclaimed). See Form 5.2 in Appendix B for sample disclaimer language.

C.   Know where the property will end up before you disclaim it. Investigate THOROUGHLY who will receive the property as a result of the disclaimer. A child (*e.g.*) may assume that if he disclaims an inheritance from father this will cause the inheritance to pass to mother, only to find out later that the disclaimer caused the property to pass partly to mother and partly to some distant relatives of father. In the case of a retirement plan, normally a disclaimer by the primary beneficiary will cause the property to pass to the contingent beneficiary and a disclaimer by all named beneficiaries will cause the benefits to pass to the default beneficiary under the plan document.

D.   Consider having the disclaimer occur at the trust level. If it is anticipated that a beneficiary might want to make a "formula" disclaimer (*e.g.*, a surviving spouse as primary beneficiary disclaiming an amount sufficient to fully fund Participant's credit shelter trust), consider the practicalities of drafting such a formula, getting the plan administrator to accept it and then carrying out its terms all within a brief nine-month window after Participant's death. If that looks like it might be difficult to accomplish, or if there is any other reason to anticipate the plan administrator may pose obstacles to the disclaimer

(¶ 8.2.08), consider naming a trust as primary beneficiary, with the spouse as outright beneficiary under the trust. She can then disclaim interests in the *trust* as necessary to achieve the desired result. She will only need to deal with the (friendly, expert, understanding) trustee of Participant's trust and you sidestep the problems of dealing with the (cold, bureaucratic, non-knowledgeable) plan administrator.

E.   Naming different contingent beneficiaries for death, disclaimer. Is it permissible to name one contingent beneficiary to take in case of disclaimer by the primary beneficiary, and a different contingent beneficiary to take in case of death of the primary beneficiary? The most common use of this dual designation of contingent beneficiary should not pose any problem to anyone, and that is where for example: (1) the primary beneficiary of an IRA is Spouse and (2) the contingent beneficiary of the IRA in case of Spouse's disclaimer is a trust of which Spouse is a life beneficiary ("Trust") and (3) the contingent beneficiary of the IRA in case of Spouse's death is the same person (or group of people) who is the remainder beneficiary of Trust at Spouse's death. The purpose of the dual contingent-beneficiary-designation on the IRA in this case is simply to allow Spouse to disclaim as outright beneficiary of the IRA, while keeping her interest as beneficiary of Trust; if she were *also* to disclaim her interest as beneficiary of Trust, the IRA would then pass to exactly the same people as would be the contingent beneficiaries of the IRA if Spouse had predeceased Participant.

In other words, even though it appears that Participant is naming "different" contingent beneficiaries on his IRA depending on whether Spouse predeceases him or disclaims the benefits, he really isn't. He's just allowing Spouse to decide what form she wants to take the benefits in (as outright beneficiary or as life beneficiary of a trust), which is perfectly alright under § 2518. It would be stupid to provide that Trust is also contingent beneficiary of the IRA *in case of wife's death*, because Trust won't even exist if Spouse predeceases Participant. In case of an IRA provider who refuses to accept the dual beneficiary designation in this situation, just name Trust as contingent beneficiary in both cases, then on Participant's death if Spouse predeceased the trustee of Trust will simply direct the IRA custodian to send the assets directly to the remainder beneficiaries of the trust (see ¶ 6.1.06).

8.2.11 *Disclaimers: summary of planning principles*

1.   Upon the death of a client, all plan and IRA beneficiary designations should be reviewed as soon as possible. Either: (a) no benefits should be distributed to any beneficiary until this review is completed or (b) if a beneficiary wants to take a distribution (or must do so to comply with the minimum distribution rules) the request for the distribution should be accompanied by a statement that the beneficiary is not thereby accepting the entire account (just the amount distributed). No beneficiary should exercise investment (or other) control over inherited plan benefits until this review is completed. If any beneficiary designation appears undesirable, consider the use of Qualified Disclaimers to redirect benefits to the "right" beneficiary.

2.   When preparing beneficiary designations as part of the estate planning process, be sure to name a contingent as well as a primary beneficiary. Consider whether a different contingent beneficiary should be named in case of a disclaimer by, as opposed to the death of, the primary beneficiary.

3.   When choosing among competing considerations in naming a primary beneficiary, the client should make the choice based on the relative priorities the client assigns to the choices (such as "financial security of spouse" versus "saving estate taxes for children"). To allow maximum flexibility after the client's death, name the second choice as contingent beneficiary.

4.   When a disclaimer is anticipated at the estate planning stage, take steps beforehand to facilitate that process, including: spousal waiver of REA rights, if needed; clear instructions to the beneficiaries regarding the choices that will be available to them and what considerations should be applied in making the choice; granting disclaimer authority to fiduciaries, along with guidelines for exercise of the power to disclaim; and review the plan documents, § 2518 requirements, and state law to make sure these pose no obstacles to the proposed disclaimers.

8.3 Plan-Owned Life Insurance: Income Taxes

This Section explains the income tax rules applicable to the plan Participant and his beneficiaries when life insurance is held in a qualified retirement plan ("QRP"). These consequences are contrasted with (a) the tax treatment of non-life insurance plan benefits and (b) the tax treatment of life insurance that is not held in a QRP.

This ¶ 8.3 also discusses the difficult choices regarding the policy that arise at the Participant's retirement. ¶ 8.4 discusses the estate tax consequences and other planning considerations involved when dealing with plan-owned life insurance.

This book discusses plan-owned life insurance *from the perspective of the Participant*. Rules that are of concern only at the plan level (such as the limits on how much life insurance may be purchased in a QRP, and ERISA fiduciary investment rules) are beyond the scope of this book. For other sources, see the Bibliography. Similarly, the analysis of insurance products is beyond the scope of this book.

8.3.01 *Income tax consequences during employment*

Generally, an employee pays no income tax on his employer's contributions to a retirement plan, or on plan earnings, until these are actually distributed to him. However, if the employer contributions (or plan earnings) are used to purchase *life insurance* on the employee's life, then the employee *does* become currently taxable on part of the retirement plan contributions or earnings. Reg. § 1.402(a)-1(a)(3).

§ 72(m)(3)(B) and Reg. § 1.72-16(b) govern the tax treatment of life insurance contracts purchased by QRPs when (a) the premium is paid with deductible employer contributions or with plan earnings and (b) the policy proceeds are payable to Participant or Participant's beneficiary. The amount includible in Participant's gross income (regardless of whether or not the amount is "vested") is determined, each year the policy is held in the plan, in two steps: First determine the "amount of life insurance protection." Second determine the amount "applied to purchase" such life insurance.

The amount of life insurance protection that the plan is deemed to have purchased for the employee in any year is the amount of the *death benefit* payable under the policy ("at any time during the year"), minus the *cash surrender value* of the policy (determined as of the end of the year). Reg. § 1.72-16(b)(3). This amount is often called the "net amount at risk" or "pure insurance." (If the amount of the policy death benefit changes during the year, the author has not discovered any source explaining whether the death benefit is considered the highest amount in force at any time during the year or rather is pro-rated.)

Once the amount of life insurance protection is thus determined, the IRS next tells us how much of the employer contribution and plan earnings are treated as the amount applied to purchase this life insurance protection. The IRS has issued the following pronouncements on this subject. While these pronouncements focus primarily on "split-dollar" insurance arrangements (which have no application to retirement plans), they also contain value-of-insurance-coverage rules applicable to insurance held in a qualified plan:

1.   **Rev. Rul. 55-747**, 1955-2 C.B. 228, provided a table, called "P.S. 58," that was to be used to calculate the amount includible in Participant's gross income. This ruling was later modified by Rev. Ruls. 66-110, 1966-1 C.B. 12, and 67-154, 1967-1 C.B. 11, which expanded Table P.S. 58 and also provided that the insurer's lowest published rate for one-year term insurance available on an initial issue basis for "all standard risks" could be used if that rate was lower than the "P.S. 58 cost." Generally, the insurer's published term rates are considerably lower than the P.S. 58 Table rates. Although the "P.S. 58-or-insurer's-actual-rates-if-lower" regime lasted for several decades, there was a continuing problem: while the P.S. 58 table rates were unrealistically high, some parties were tempted to use alleged "insurer's actual rates" that were unrealistically low, in the sense that the insurer rarely if ever sold 1-year term insurance at such rates. Apparently, some insurers created policies designed for the sole purpose of artificially lowering the insured-participant's reportable income.

2.   **Notice 2001-10**, 2001-5 I.R.B. 459, took official notice that the P.S. 58 table rates were too high; revoked Rev. Rul. 55-747; published a new table, "Table 2001," with considerably lower rates; and announced the Service's intention to issue further rules on this subject, and to prevent abuse of the "insurer's actual rates" alternative.

3.　　　　**Notice 2002-8**, 2002-4 I.R.B. 398, revoked Notice 2001-10 (except for Table 2001, which was re-issued), and announced that the IRS would issue proposed regulations providing "comprehensive guidance" on the subject of split-dollar life insurance, as well as "further guidance" on the tax treatment of insurance held in qualified plans. In the meantime, Notice 2002-8 (Part III, 2) provides "interim guidance" on the tax treatment of life insurance held by a qualified plan, summarized in the next paragraph. The split dollar proposed regulations were issued in July 2002 (Prop. Reg. § 1.61-22) but did not address insurance held in qualified plans, so apparently Notice 2002-8 remains in effect until some "further guidance" is issued on this topic.

Under Notice 2002-8, for 2002 and later years (unless and until changed by the promised future "guidance"), the amount reportable as the value of the employee's current insurance protection under a plan-owned policy must *either* be determined under Table 2001 *or* (if certain conditions are met) be based on the insurer's actual term rates, if lower. Here are the details:

Table 2001: "For arrangements entered into before the effective date of future guidance, taxpayers may use" the premium rates contained in Table 2001 (which was re-issued in Notice 2002-8) to determine the value of current life insurance protection provided in a qualified plan. There is no authority to use the old P.S. 58 rates set forth in Rev. Rul. 55-747 for this purpose for taxable years ending after 2001. (There would be no advantage to using the higher P.S. 58 rates for this purpose anyway, since that would only result in higher taxable income to the employee.)

Insurer's published rates: Taxpayers may continue to determine the value of current life insurance protection under a qualified plan by using the insurer's lower published premium rates "that are available to all standard risks for initial issue one-year term insurance." However, the IRS reserves the right to take away this option altogether, in its future regulations, for "arrangements entered into" after the effective date of such future regulations. For arrangements entered into before the effective date of future regulations, the insurer's actual term rates can continue to be used, but will be subject to a new and presumably tighter regime, namely:

For any arrangement entered into after January 28, 2002, the IRS (for years after 2003) "will not consider an insurer's published premium rates to be available to all standard risks who apply for term insurance unless (i) the insurer generally makes the availability of such rates known to persons who apply for term insurance coverage...and (ii) the insurer regularly sells term insurance at such rates to individuals who apply for term insurance...through the insurer's normal distribution channels." Thus, new "arrangements" must meet this stricter standard, beginning in 2004, if the parties want to use the insurer's lower term rates. If this standard is not met, the employee will have to report income based on the Table 2001 rates. Policies already in place prior to January 29, 2002, will apparently not have to meet this strict standard of proof; however, it is not clear what standard of proof will apply to such pre-January 29, 2002, policies, since there was no such detailed definition of "insurer's one-year term rates" prior to Notice 2002-8.

In the rest of this Chapter, "Current Insurance Cost" is used as shorthand for "the amount Participant is required to include in gross income because of the plan-held life insurance." In any particular case, this amount may be the rate from Table 2001, or the insurance company's actual term rates if lower, whichever is applicable. Here are additional details regarding computation of the Current Insurance Cost:

1.   Group term life insurance: The actual premium of a group term life policy, rather than the Table 2001 cost, is considered the Current Insurance Cost; see Rev. Rul. 54-52, 1954-1 C.B. 150. Note that group term policies (like Table 2001) provide varying premiums based on the age of the employee.

2.   Individual term policy: It is not clear whether the Notice 2002-8 rules apply to individual *term* life insurance policies, or only to policies that provide something (such as cash value or annuity benefits) in addition to the pure insurance protection. Possibly, the actual premium of a term life policy, rather than the Table 2001 cost, is considered the Current Insurance Cost, as was true for a group policy under Rev. Rul. 54-52. However, an individual term policy (unlike a group policy) would typically have a level premium for a fixed period of years, so it is not clear that Rev. Rul. 54-52 applies to such policies.

3.   When is the "arrangement entered into?" Presumably the "arrangement is entered into" when the retirement plan purchases the life insurance policy. It is not clear whether modifying an existing plan-owned policy, or swapping it for a replacement policy, would be considered entering into a new arrangement.

8.3.02 *Cost of current insurance protection: assorted facts and rules*

Here is a collection of miscellaneous rules regarding, and fascinating facts about, the effects of inclusion of the Current Insurance Cost in the employee's income:

A.   Deemed income increases with age: The amount of currently taxable income generated by a plan-owned policy typically rises as the employee gets older because term rates go up with age. On the other hand, if the cash surrender value of the policy increases over the years, this increase will reduce the pure insurance protection (total death benefit under policy minus cash surrender value), which in turn would reduce the Current Insurance Cost.

B.   True cost to the employee: Inclusion of the Current Insurance Cost in the Participant's gross income means that the Participant must find the cash elsewhere to pay the resulting income tax. For example, a person in the 45% tax bracket (considering federal, FICA, state and local income taxes) must earn $818 of taxable salary to pay the income tax on $1,000 of Current Insurance Cost. For this individual, the tax on $1,000 of Current Insurance Cost is $450. He must earn $818 of taxable salary in order to have, after income taxes, the $450 of cash he needs to pay the tax on the Current Insurance Cost.

C.   Deemed income continues even if premiums stop: The Participant's obligation to pay income tax on the Current Insurance Cost continues even if the plan stops paying premiums on the policy (which can happen if the policy premiums are paid through policy dividends).

D.   Accumulated CIC becomes basis in the policy: The amount included in Participant's gross income over the years on account of the Current Insurance Cost is considered his "investment in the contract" and in effect becomes his "basis" in the policy. See ¶ 2.1.04. Participant is entitled to recover this basis tax-free, but only if the policy itself is distributed to him. If the policy lapses, or is surrendered for its cash surrender value at the plan level, Participant's "basis" disappears and cannot be offset against other plan distributions. Thus, the payment of income taxes over the years on the Current Insurance Cost generates a "basis" that may or may not be recouped later. Reg. § 1.72-16(b)(4). On the other hand, since the "Current Insurance Cost" is supposed to represent the annual cost of pure insurance protection, it is surprising the IRS allows it to be used as "basis" for any purpose; it is really an expense. Some speculate that the IRS will disallow the use of accumulated Current Insurance Cost as "basis" when it issues the "further guidance" promised in Notice 2002-8 (¶ 8.3.01).

E.   Owner-employee does not get any basis: An "owner-employee" (see "Keogh plan," Glossary) does not get to treat even the Current Insurance Cost as an investment in the contract. Reg. § 1.72-16(b)(4).

F.   Deemed income not subject to 10% penalty: The Current Insurance Cost that the employee must include in his gross income each year is not a "distribution" to the employee for purposes of the 10% penalty on premature distributions (see Chapter 9). IRS Notice 89-25, 1989-1 C.B. 662, A-11.

G.   Deemed income does not count towards required distributions: The Current Insurance Cost does not count towards any minimum distribution the Participant is required to take under § 401(a)(9). Reg. § 1.401(a)(9)-5, A-9(b)(6).

8.3.03 *Income tax consequences to beneficiaries*

When the Participant dies, and the insurance proceeds are paid out to his beneficiaries, § 72(m)(3)(C) dictates that the distribution is treated as a retirement plan distribution (taxable under § 402/§ 72; see

Chapter 2), rather than as a distribution of life insurance proceeds (tax-exempt under § 101(a)) to the extent of the policy's cash surrender value immediately prior to the employee's death. Thus, to the extent of the cash surrender value, life insurance proceeds are treated the same as all other retirement plan distributions, which are normally subject to income tax when paid out to the beneficiaries after Participant's death. Only the pure insurance protection portion of the distribution is tax-exempt under § 101(a).

Despite the fact that Participant might have been taxable on *more* than the cash surrender value if the policy had been distributed to him during life (¶ 8.3.05), the regulations state that only the cash surrender value is treated as gross income to the beneficiaries. Also, the beneficiaries are entitled to deduct the amount of Participant's "basis" in the policy (¶ 8.3.01) from the amount otherwise includible in their gross income. See Reg. § 1.72-16(c)(3), Ex. 1.

This treatment of plan-owned life insurance compares unfavorably with the treatment of insurance policies purchased outside of retirement plans, death benefits under which are received by the beneficiaries 100% income tax-free. § 101(a).

8.3.04 Issues at retirement: the "rollout"

If the Participant does not die while still employed, then, upon retirement, he will typically face some thorny issues regarding the life insurance policy.

The IRS generally requires that life insurance policies be either converted to cash or distributed to Participant at "retirement." This is one of the constellation of plan qualification requirements known as the "incidental benefit rule," the gist of which is that a retirement plan is supposed to provide retirement benefits, and may provide other or additional benefits only to the extent they are "incidental." See Rev. Rul. 54-51, 1954-1 C.B. 147, as modified by Rev. Ruls. 57-213, 1957-1 C.B. 157, and 60-84, 1960-1 C.B. 159.

If the life insurance policy is <u>distributed</u>, it cannot be rolled over to an IRA because an IRA cannot own life insurance (¶ 8.4.05). <u>Converting the policy to cash</u> would mean that the plan either sells the policy for cash, or terminates the policy by surrendering it to the insurance company (in exchange for which the insurance company would pay the plan an amount of cash equal to the policy's cash surrender value).

So, at retirement, Participant must either take the policy out of the plan as a distribution (thus probably losing further income tax deferral; see ¶ 8.3.05), or buy the policy from the plan (which requires coming up with the cash to do so; see ¶ 8.3.06), or terminate the policy by surrendering it to the insurance company (which means loss of the policy's insurance protection).

Buying or taking distribution of the policy from the plan is popularly referred to as the "rollout" of the policy (not to be confused with a "rollover"). See ¶ 8.4.04, E, for discussion of a planning idea that hinges on the policy's having a low valuation at the time of the "rollout."

The unpleasant choices at retirement can be postponed *if* the plan is a profit sharing plan *and* the policy was paid for only with funds held in the plan for more than two years, because such funds are not subject to the "incidental benefit rule." See Rev. Rul. 60-83, 1960-1 C.B. 157. In this situation, Participant can leave the policy in the plan along with his other benefits and withdraw it later (subject to the minimum distribution rules; Chapter 1). The policy will continue to generate annual taxable income to him (¶ 8.3.02, C).

In contrast, if the employee buys his life insurance *outside* of the retirement plan to begin with, the issues at retirement simply do not arise. *All* retirement benefits can be cleanly rolled over to an IRA and taken out when Participant feels like it (subject to the minimum distribution rules). Participant does not face the unpleasant choice between surrendering the policy, buying it from the plan or taking it out as a taxable distribution.

8.3.05 *Rollout option #1: Plan distributes policy to Participant*

If the policy is distributed to Participant, Participant must include in gross income the "fair market value" of the policy. Reg. § 1.402(a)-1(a)(1)(iii). This ¶ 8.3.05 discusses how to determine the policy's fair market value. Regardless of how the fair market value is determined, the amount includible in Participant's gross income can be reduced by his "basis" or investment in the contract; see ¶ 8.3.02, D.

The "fair market value" of a life insurance policy is *generally* its cash surrender value. Reg. § 1.402(a)-1(a)(2). However, if "the total policy reserves [established by the insurer to cover the death benefit, advance premium payments, etc.] ...represent a much more accurate approximation of the fair market value of the policy," Participant is required to include the amount of the policy reserves, rather than the cash surrender value, in gross income. The reserves represent a much "more accurate approximation of the fair market value of the policy" if the policy's reserves "substantially exceed" the policy's cash surrender value. Notice 89-25, Q&A 10, 1989-1 C.B. 662.

This is hardly a bright line test. How much larger than the cash surrender value must the reserves be before the reserves are deemed to "substantially exceed" the cash surrender value? In the Notice's example, the reserves were 3.8 times greater than, and were held to "substantially exceed," the cash surrender value. It appears that, if the policy is to be distributed *or sold* to Participant, the following steps are required:

1.   Determine the policy's cash surrender value.

2.   Obtain from the insurer a statement of the value of all policy reserves as of the proposed date of distribution of the policy.

3.   If (2) "substantially exceeds" (1), use (2) as the policy's value.

4.   If (2) does not "substantially exceed" (1), use (1) as the policy's value.

5.   If (2) exceeds (1), but it is unclear whether (2) "*substantially*" exceeds (1), obtain a ruling regarding which figure to use.

A discrepancy between the cash surrender value and the "policy value" may create problems at the *plan* level, possibly affecting the plan's qualification, according to Notice 89-25. Those issues are beyond the scope of this book.

On the bright side, these IRS pronouncements do not seem to require that the Participant's actual health be taken into account (except to the extent it is reflected in the policy reserves). There is no suggestion that, for purposes of determining the *income tax* value of a policy distributed to the insured-Participant, a higher value must necessarily be assigned if the Participant is no longer insurable at the same rates that applied when the policy was purchased.

One untested planning idea is for Participant to take a distribution of the policy, sell the policy to the beneficiaries (avoiding the transfer-for-value rule; see ¶ 8.4.02), and then roll the sale proceeds over to his IRA. Although generally a Participant must roll over the same property he received from the distributing plan, IRS Publication 590 seems to recognize an exception for property that the Participant sells after receiving it from the distributing plan, permitting the sales proceeds to be rolled over instead. See ¶ 2.5.08.

8.3.06 *Rollout Option #2: Plan sells policy to Participant*

If the policy is distributed to Participant (¶ 8.3.05), then all further opportunity to defer income taxes on the amount represented by the policy value is lost (unless the "untested planning idea" mentioned at the end of ¶ 8.3.05 is tried and works). For this reason, Participant may look at the possibility of purchasing the policy from the plan. Although this requires Participant to come up with some cash from other sources, it does allow him to continue deferring income tax on the amount represented by the policy value. Participant will own the policy (which he can transfer to an irrevocable trust, if he wants to remove the proceeds from his gross estate); and the plan will own cash, which can then be distributed to Participant and rolled over to an IRA for maximum continued deferral.

Buying the policy from the plan may create an ERISA problem. ERISA § 406(a) (29 U.S.C.§ 1106(a)) prohibits the sale of plan assets to a "party in interest." The definition of "parties in interest" includes categories one would expect, such as plan fiduciaries, the employer, and officers, directors and 10% owners of the employer. It also includes, surprisingly, any *employee* of the employer. ERISA § 3(14) (29 U.S.C. § 1002(14)). Thus, as an initial proposition, the sale of a life insurance policy from the plan to the insured employee is a "prohibited transaction."

IRC § 4975 has its own set of prohibited transaction rules, prohibiting sales between a plan and a "disqualified person"; however, a mere employee of the employer is not a disqualified person under § 4975. However, if (as would usually be the case in this type of transaction) Participant has more relationships with the employer than merely being an employee (for example, if Participant *is* "the employer," or directly or indirectly owns more than 50% of the employer, or is an officer of the employer, etc., etc.), then the sale of an insurance contract would be a prohibited transaction under IRC § 4975 as well as under ERISA § 406.

The Department of Labor has issued a "Prohibited Transaction

Class Exemption" which exempts such sales if certain requirements are met. PTE 1992-6, 2/12/92, 57 Fed. Reg. 5190; amended 9/3/02, 67 Fed. Reg. 56,313. This exemption exempts the transaction from both IRC § 4975 and ERISA § 406. Thus, if the desired approach is to have Participant buy the policy from the plan, there are two ways that this might be accomplished:

1.   Comply with PTE 1992-6; or,

2.   If Participant does not have any connection with the employer or the plan except as an employee, it might be worth exploring the possibility that the sale is not a "prohibited transaction" once Participant retires and ceases to be an employee. Consult an ERISA specialist before embarking on this course.

To comply with PTE 1992-6 when the *insured participant* is buying the policy from the plan, the following two requirements must be met. (If the purchaser is someone *other than* the participant-insured, there are additional requirements; see ¶ 8.4.02.)

1.   The contract would, but for the sale, be surrendered by the plan. PTE 92-6, II(c). This requirement is not a problem, if Participant is retiring, for the type of QRP that is *required* to sell or surrender the policy at that point (¶ 8.3.04). Also, according to *RIA Pension & Profit Sharing 2d* ¶ER408-4.15, the Department of Labor considers this condition satisfied if the Participant's plan account is "self-directed" as to investments, and the Participant directs the sale to occur, provided the Participant is not subject to "undue influence" in that decision. The author has been unable to locate this DOL position in the text of PTE 92-6 as it is reproduced in *RIA Pension & Profit Sharing 2d* at ¶93,211.

2.   The price must be "at least equal to the amount necessary to put the plan in the same cash position as it would have been [sic] had it retained the contract, surrendered it, and made any distribution owing to the participant on [sic] his vested interest under the plan." PTE 92-6, (II(e). *This requirement does not permit any price reduction for the Participant's basis* (¶ 8.3.02, D).

8.4 Plan-Owned Life Insurance: Other Aspects

This Section explains the estate tax aspects of holding life insurance in a retirement plan, the planning principles regarding such insurance, and the rules regarding IRAs and life insurance.

8.4.01 *Estate tax avoidance: the life insurance subtrust*

For the estate tax-conscious client, an important consideration in buying life insurance is to keep the insurance out of the insured's estate (and the estate of his spouse, if any), to increase the value of the benefits for subsequent beneficiaries (typically the client's children). If the policy is purchased *outside* the retirement plan, it is easy to accomplish this goal. The client creates an irrevocable trust for the benefit of his intended beneficiaries; and the trustee buys the policy. The policy proceeds are never part of either spouse's estate. If the policy is bought through a retirement plan, in contrast, it is doubtful whether the proceeds can be kept out of the estate of the Participant.

Generally, the estate tax treatment of retirement plan benefits is governed by § 2039. However, § 2042 governs the estate tax treatment of life insurance, even if the insurance is held inside a retirement plan. § 2039(a). Life insurance is subject to estate tax if it is payable to the insured's estate, or if the insured owns any "incident of ownership." § 2042. To keep plan-held life insurance out of the Participant's estate, therefore, it is necessary to deprive Participant of such "incidents of ownership" as the powers to name the beneficiary of the policy or surrender or borrow against the policy, and a 5% or more reversionary interest in the policy. § 2042(2); Reg. § 20.2042-1(c)(2).

Some practitioners believe this goal can be accomplished by establishing a "subtrust," defined as "an irrevocable life insurance trust slotted within the trust otherwise used to fund the pension or profit sharing plan" (from "The Qualified Plan as an Estate Planning Tool," by Andrew J. Fair, Esq., published by Guardian Life Insurance Company of America, New York, NY, 1995) (Pub. No. 2449).

The merits of the subtrust have been debated in numerous publications. See Zaritsky, H., and Leimberg, S.R., *Tax Planning with Life Insurance* (see Bibliography for full cite), sections 6.08[2][f] and 6.08[4][b], and articles cited in the Bibliography. Some writers conclude that the subtrust works to keep policy proceeds out of the estate, without disqualifying the underlying retirement plan. Other writers argue that either the existence of the subtrust disqualifies the plan, or, if the plan *is* qualified, it is impossible for Participant not to have estate-taxable incidents of ownership in the policy. To date, there is no published ruling or case either upholding or denying the estate tax exclusion for life insurance held in a retirement plan subtrust. Thus, use of this device must be considered risky; if the subtrust does not work, up to 50% of the policy proceeds could be lost to estate taxes.

The bottom line: if estate taxes are important to the client, buy the life insurance outside of the retirement plan. If the insurance must be bought inside the plan for some reason, consider using the subtrust technique, which may work to keep the proceeds out of the estate.

Even if the subtrust device does keep the death benefit out of the gross estate if Participant dies prior to retirement, new problems arise once Participant reaches retirement. If he then either buys the policy out of the plan (¶ 8.3.06), or receives it as a distribution (¶ 8.3.05), Participant is right back in the position of owning the policy. The next subsection discusses strategies people use to try to get the policy out of the plan, *and* out of the employee's estate, without triggering § 2035(a)'s three-year waiting period for estate tax exclusion.

8.4.02 *Avoiding estate tax inclusion at "rollout"*

As discussed at ¶ 8.3.04-¶ 8.3.06, the normal course is for the retirement plan to sell or distribute the policy to Participant at retirement. Participant may wish at that point to transfer the policy to his intended beneficiaries (or to an irrevocable trust for their benefit) to get the proceeds out of his estate for estate tax purposes. Since giving away the policy would not remove the proceeds from Participant's estate until three years after the gift (§ 2035(a)), practitioners look for an alternative way to get the policy into the hands of the beneficiaries (or trust) without the three-year waiting period. The obstacles to success in this endeavor are discussed in this ¶ 8.4.02; for further discussion of ways to deal with this "vastly over-exaggerated problem," see Ratner, C.L., and Leimberg, S.R., "Planning Under the New Split-Dollar Life Insurance Prop. Regs., Part 2" *Estate Planning*, Dec. 2002 (Vol. 29, No. 12, p. 603), at 606.

Since the plan cannot distribute benefits to anyone other than Participant during Participant's lifetime (because of the "exclusive benefit rule," § 401(a)(2)), the only ways the policy can be moved from the plan to the intended beneficiaries without triggering the three-year rule are for the plan (1) to sell the policy to the intended beneficiaries, or (2) distribute (or sell) the policy to Participant who then sells it to the beneficiaries. Such sales raise several issues (in addition to the question of where the beneficiaries will get the money to buy the policy):

A.   Transfer for value. The first problem is the "transfer for value" rule of § 101(a)(2). Life insurance proceeds (net of consideration paid for the policy) are taxable income to a recipient who acquired the policy in a transfer for value unless an exception applies. The purchase of the policy from Participant, or from the plan, by the beneficiaries (e.g., Participant's children, or an irrevocable trust for the benefit of Participant's spouse and/or children) would be a "transfer for value," causing the eventual death benefit to be taxable income instead of tax-exempt income. However, the transfer for value rule does not apply if the policy is bought by the insured, a partner of the insured or a partnership in which the insured is a partner. § 101(a)(2)(B). So, the plan could sell the policy to a partnership in which Participant and his intended beneficiaries are the partners, to avoid the transfer for value problem.

B.   Incidents of ownership in partnership-owned insurance. The next question is whether life insurance that is owned by a partnership in which Participant is a partner is includible in Participant's gross estate. As a partner, does Participant have "incidents of ownership" in a policy owned by the partnership? If the beneficiary of the policy is not the *partnership itself*, then the policy proceeds are included in the insured partner's estate under § 2042. Rev. Rul. 83-147, 1983-2 C.B. 158. However, if the proceeds are payable to or for the benefit of the *partnership*, the insured does not necessarily have any incidents of ownership; see, *e.g.*, PLR 200214028. This letter ruling involved a business partnership in which an unrelated individual was a one-third partner; whether the rules applicable to such an arms' length business partnership would also apply to a family partnership formed solely for the purchase of life insurance has not been tested. Nevertheless, this is a promising route to explore when buying an insurance policy from a retirement plan. Steve Leimberg, Esq., one of the nation's

leading experts on estate planning with life insurance, suggests
that the parties consider including in the partnership agreement
a provision barring any partner from any decisions with respect
to insurance the partnership owns on his/her life. A discussion
of partnership-owned life insurance is beyond the scope of this
book. See Bibliography for other resources.

C.   Sale to a "defective grantor trust." Another alternative is for
Participant to sell the policy, for its fair market value, to a
"defective grantor trust," *i.e.,* a trust all of which is deemed to
be "owned" (for income tax purposes) by Participant under the
"grantor trust rules" of § 671-§ 677. The theory is that a
transaction between Participant and his grantor trust is not
treated as a sale (and therefore there is no transfer for value)
because Participant and the trust are regarded as "one taxpayer"
for income tax purposes. Rev. Rul. 85-13, 1985-C.B. 184. The
trust could be structured so it would not be included in
Participant's estate. Exploration of this idea is also beyond the
scope of this book. See Bibliography.

D.   What is the proper price? The regulations discussed at ¶ 8.3.05
govern the determination of the policy's "value" for purposes
of a sale or distribution of the policy to the participant himself.
These regulations do not purport to apply to a sale of the policy
to the policy beneficiaries (whether the sale is made by the
Participant or by the plan). If the Participant is in poor health,
and would not, at the time of the sale to the beneficiaries, be
insurable at the same rates that applied when the policy was
issued, the IRS may raise questions regarding the sale if cash
surrender value or policy reserves are used to establish the
price. For example, a bargain sale to the trust could result in a
taxable gift.

E.   Prohibited transaction aspects. The third problem is the
prohibited transaction rules of ERISA. The Department of
Labor's class exemption, PTE 1992-6 (¶ 8.3.06), exempts the
sale of a life insurance policy by the plan from various
prohibited transaction rules if certain requirements are met. The
requirements that must be met if the purchaser of the policy is
the participant-insured himself are described at ¶ 8.3.06. If the

sale is to someone *other than* the Participant, and would be a prohibited transaction if not exempted, the following additional requirements must be met, in addition to those discussed at ¶ 8.3.06:

1.   The buyer may be a "relative" of the insured participant, or (under an amendment to the PTE, adopted 9/3/02 retroactive to 1992), a "trust established by or for the benefit of" the insured participant or a relative. PTE 92-6, I(a), I(b).

2.   The buyer must be the beneficiary of the policy. PTE 92-6, II(b).

3.   The Participant is "first informed of the proposed sale and is given the opportunity to purchase such contract from the plan, and delivers a written document to the plan stating that he or she elects not to purchase the policy and consents to the sale by the plan of such policy to such" relative or trust. PTE 92-6, II(d).

"Relative" for purposes of the exemption means either a relative as defined in § 3(15) of ERISA (29 U.S.C. § 1002(15)) and IRC § 4975(e)(6) (spouse, ancestor, lineal descendant or spouse of a lineal descendant), *or* a sibling or a spouse of a sibling. PTE 92-6, II(b).

Note that the PTE's definition of permitted buyers does not mention partnerships. If the strategy is to sell the policy from the plan directly to a partnership, the plan's ERISA counsel will have to determine whether the transaction is a prohibited transaction and, if it is, seek a DOL exemption for it. These issues can be avoided by having the plan sell or distribute the policy to Participant, and having Participant make the sale to the partnership.

8.4.03 *Second-to-die insurance*

Buying a second-to-die ("joint and survivor life") policy inside a retirement plan raises additional problems. Trying to minimize estate taxes on a second-to-die insurance policy (insuring the lives of Participant and Spouse) owned by a QRP involves considerable complexity.

If the policy is purchased *outside* the plan, the only legal paperwork required to avoid estate and gift tax is the drafting of one irrevocable trust to buy the policy, plus "Crummey" notices. If the policy is bought *inside* a retirement plan, on the other hand, one widely distributed booklet recommends a strategy that involves one trust, either three or four separate life insurance policies, and possibly a family partnership to deal with all the issues involved trying to keep the policy proceeds out of both spouses' estates.

Another, minor, complication is that there is no IRS table indicating how to calculate the amount to be included in Participant's gross income for QRP-owned second-to-die insurance. Table 2001 (¶ 8.3.01) covers only single life policies. Notice 2002-8 provides that "Taxpayers should make appropriate adjustments" to the Table 2001 rates "if the life insurance protection covers more than one life." Insurance experts do not find this computation difficult, despite the absence of any official guidance.

The Department of Labor has indicated that PTE 92-6 applies to second-to-die insurance policies on the life of the employee and his/her spouse as well as to single life policies on the life of the employee.

8.4.04 *Reasons to buy or not to buy life insurance inside the plan*

Here are reasons why people incur the complications of buying life insurance inside a retirement plan:

A.   Client uninsurable: The client is rated or uninsurable, and wants to buy insurance, and there is a policy available through the plan which the client can purchase without evidence of insurability.

B.   Favorable group policy available through plan. The plan may have a negotiated group insurance rate that is lower than Participant could obtain by buying insurance outside the plan.

C.   Increase defined benefit plan contribution: It is possible in some cases that the purchase of insurance, as an "incidental benefit," could increase permitted contributions to a defined benefit plan (or help absorb some funds in an overfunded defined benefit plan). See discussion in the McFadden/Leimberg article cited in the Bibliography.

D.   Only available money is in the plan: The client needs life insurance but has no money to pay for it outside the retirement plan. In this case, however, it is still advisable to look at the possibility of taking some money out of the plan to buy the insurance. Unless there is some reason the client cannot conveniently get money out of the plan (such as unacceptable level of tax on plan distributions; creditor or marital problems; plan doesn't permit it), the purchase of insurance outside the plan may be more tax-effective.

E.   Reduce plan value prior to distribution: Insurance is sometimes purchased inside a retirement plan as a way of (temporarily, it is hoped) depressing the value of the retirement plan, in order to reduce income taxes. For at least the first few years of the policy's existence, the cash surrender value of a whole life insurance policy is, in many cases, though not always, less than the amount of the premiums paid to purchase the policy, due to the commissions and other up-front costs involved. Thus, the value of this "investment" is typically less than the value of other investments that could have been made with the same amount of money. The vital second step of this approach is that, when the policy reaches its lowest point of value relative to what has been invested, the policy is distributed (¶ 8.3.05) or sold (¶ 8.3.06) to Participant. The distribution (or sale) transaction is less costly than it would have been had the plan invested in something other than life insurance, due to the depressed value of the policy. The vital third step of this approach is that, sometime after the "rollout," the policy increases rapidly in value so that at the end of the day the Participant still has a profitable investment. Obviously there is no guarantee that the life insurance policy (or any other investment) will increase in value at some future date. While this idea basically "works," it is not a reason to buy insurance the Participant otherwise doesn't want to buy. It might be a reason to buy an insurance policy *that the Participant wants to buy anyway* inside the plan rather than outside the plan, especially if Participant is near the point at which he must start to take required distributions (Chapter 1). A danger with this technique is that, to sell policies, some insurers may become overly aggressive in touting "temporarily depressed value" policies (with clever "trademarked" names), and Participants will buy these policies in their plans solely to take advantage of the artificial and temporary low value. A legitimate "incidental" tax benefit of owning insurance in the plan is being turned into the sole reason to buy insurance and a reason to invest 100% of your plan in it, and the participant is blinded to the desirability of purchasing only investments that always maintain solid value. Eventually, the IRS will have to crack down as it did on the "insurer's actual one-year term rates" (¶ 8.3.01, 1). In the meantime, parties to these transactions are risking ERISA violations and plan disqualification issues; see discussion in the recommended article, "Fully Insured (412(i)) Pension Plans: the Good, the Bad and the Ugly," by John J. McFadden and Stephan R. Leimberg, *Estate Planning* 2003 (full cite in Bibliography).

F.   Buy policy with "tax-deductible dollars": Sometimes a Participant is urged to buy insurance inside his retirement plan because this mode of purchase enables him to "buy insurance with tax-deductible dollars." This is not a valid reason to buy life insurance. *Any* investment bought inside a retirement plan is bought with "tax-deductible dollars." There is nothing special about buying insurance as opposed to stocks, bonds or money market funds with the tax-deductible dollars inside the retirement plan. In fact, buying life insurance makes the "dollars" in the plan *less* "tax-deductible" than they otherwise would be, because insurance necessitates Participant's paying income tax on the Current Insurance Cost (¶ 8.3.01).

8.4.05 *IRAs and life insurance*

A requirement of a valid IRA is that "No part of the [IRA's] funds will be invested in life insurance contracts." § 408(a)(3).

The guaranteed death benefit under an annuity contract generally does not violate § 408(a)(3). Specifically, "An individual retirement account may invest in annuity contracts which provide, *in the case of death prior to the time distributions commence*, for a payment equal to the sum of the premiums paid or, if greater, the cash value of the contract." Reg. § 1.408-2(b)(3) (emphasis added).

When a Participant wants to buy life insurance, and the only money he has available to use for this purchase is inside an IRA, he has the following choices:

1. Roll money to a QRP: One approach is to "roll" money from the IRA into a QRP, where it can be used to buy insurance (since QRP's aren't subject to the prohibition of § 408(a)(3)). The liberalized rules that apply after 2001 regarding what type of plan a distribution may be rolled into (¶ 2.5) should make it easier for Participants to roll IRA money into a QRP for purposes of purchasing life insurance. This easy solution is not so easy for an IRA owner who doesn't happen to participate in a QRP that accepts rollovers and permits insurance purchases.

2. Create a QRP to roll money into. If the IRA owner has no QRP available, but does have a business, some planners recommend having the business start a QRP so that the IRA owner can roll his IRA money into it (and buy insurance). In view of the many drawbacks of plan-owned insurance, and the costs and burdens of starting a QRP the Participant would not otherwise want, it is hard to believe that it would not be more cost-effective to simply take the money out of the IRA, pay tax on it, and use what's left to buy the life insurance. If the promoter of the plan insists that the QRP route is preferable, it may be because the actual goal is to use the depressed-value-rollout discussed at ¶ 8.4.04, E. That goal in turn raises questions about whether the newly-created retirement plan really is "qualified" (it may not be if it was adopted with the deliberate intention of terminating it in a few years when the insurance policy value is depressed; see McFadden/Leimberg article, Bibliography).

3. Entity-owned insurance: Another approach is for the IRA not to own the insurance directly, but rather to own an interest in an entity (such as a partnership) which in turn owns the insurance policy. Clearly, *at some point*, an entity shields the policy from being considered an asset of the IRA. For example, if the IRA owns a share of stock of General Motors, and General Motors owns an insurance policy on the life of the IRA owner, there is no reason to fear that the IRA has done something forbidden. On the other hand there is no guidance regarding what degree of control by the IRA or what other factors might be considered sufficient to cause an entity-held life insurance policy to be

deemed held by the IRA, causing disqualification of the IRA. Under Department of Labor regulation § 2510.3-101, if an IRA owns an equity interest in a non-publicly traded investment entity such as a family partnership, the assets held by entity are generally deemed assets of the retirement plan (i.e., the intervening entity is ignored) for purposes of determining who is a fiduciary of the plan's assets. The IRS has never suggested applying this prohibited transaction concept for purposes of § 408(a)(3), but they might do so someday. Unless the IRS perceives severe abuse, such a rule would presumably be prospective only.

4.   Take a taxable distribution: Finally, Participant could simply take the money out of the IRA, pay income tax on the distribution, and buy the insurance with what's left. If Participant is under 59½, the distributions should be arranged as a "series of substantially equal periodic payments" to avoid the 10% premature distributions penalty; see Chapter 9. This solution is simpler and less risky than some of the schemes being proposed to enable the purchase of life insurance inside a new QRP and avoids all the difficulties of the "rollout" (¶ 8.3.04-¶ 8.3.06).

8.4.06 *Borrowing on a plan-owned policy*

If a QRP borrows against a life insurance policy, the plan may become subject to income tax on "unrelated business taxable income" (UBTI). See § 408(e)(1), § 511, PLR 7918095.

8.4.07 *Planning principles with plan-owned life insurance*

1.   Use insurance to fund credit shelter trust. The "pure insurance portion" of a life insurance policy held by a QRP is income tax-free to the death beneficiary; see ¶ 8.3.03. So, if it is possible under the plan to designate a different death beneficiary for the life insurance policy proceeds, on the one hand, and any other plan death benefits, on the other, determine how much of the life insurance proceeds would be subject to income tax if the client died today, *i.e.*, the cash surrender value of the policy (less Participant's basis if applicable; see ¶ 8.3.02, D). If the cash surrender value is relatively small, and the client has

insufficient other assets to fully fund a credit shelter trust, consider naming the credit shelter trust as beneficiary of the plan-held policy. Since most of the proceeds would be income tax-free, the usual drawbacks of funding a credit shelter trust with plan benefits (see ¶ 10.5) would be minimized. The rest of the plan benefits, being fully income-taxable (¶ 2.1.01), could be left to the surviving spouse, who could roll them over to an IRA and continue to defer income taxes. See Form 3.1, Appendix B.

2. Can taxable and tax-free proceeds be left to different beneficiaries? Is it possible to further fine-tune the beneficiary designation for the life insurance policy, to the extent of directing that the income-taxable portion (pre-death cash surrender value, minus Participant's basis) will be paid to Spouse, and the "pure death benefit" portion and return of basis would pass to the credit shelter trust? It is not clear that such a beneficiary designation would be effective, as far as the IRS is concerned, to allocate the income-taxable portion to one beneficiary and the income-tax-free portion to the other. Although there is no IRS pronouncement on the subject, the IRS might require the taxable and tax-free parts of the policy proceeds to be allocated among the recipients in proportion to what each receives from the contract.

3. Spousal rollover (and Roth conversion?) of insurance proceeds. Consider making life insurance proceeds payable to Spouse, who can then roll over them over tax-free to her own retirement plan (¶ 3.2). § 402(c)(2), (c)(9). Note that, as a result of EGTRRA 2001, Spouse is now allowed to roll over the income tax-exempt portion of the proceeds to an IRA as well as the income-taxable portion. Spouse may consider this a favorable way to increase her own retirement savings, and having a substantial basis (¶ 2.1.04) in her IRA may enable Spouse to convert the IRA to a Roth IRA (see Chapter 5) at a relatively low income tax cost.

4. Buy insurance outside plan to save estate taxes. In general, it is better to buy life insurance outside the retirement plan if estate taxes are a consideration. While the "subtrust" device may offer a chance of keeping plan-owned insurance out of Participant's estate, it is at best an unproven technique. See ¶ 8.4.01. Definite estate tax exclusion can be easily obtained for insurance owned outside the plan. With estate tax rates of up to 50%, this factor will weigh heavily,

especially for older and wealthier participants.

5.   <u>Buy favorable group insurance in plan</u>. Especially if the client is not insurable at standard rates, investigate the availability of group insurance through his retirement plan (and elsewhere).

6.   <u>Consider subtrust for plan-held insurance</u>. If life insurance is owned by the client's retirement plan, investigate the "subtrust" (¶ 8.4.01) as a way of keeping the policy proceeds out of the gross estate.

7.   <u>Plan ahead for the rollout</u>. Be sure the client is aware of, and develops a realistic plan for, the issues that will arise regarding "rollout" of the policy at retirement. ¶ 8.3.04-¶ 8.3.06. Consider ways to get/keep the policy out of the client's gross estate following rollout, without triggering the "three year rule" of § 2035, while avoiding a "transfer for value" or "prohibited transaction."

8.5 Grandfather Rules

Chapter 1 describes the "minimum distribution rules" of § 401(a)(9) as they are in 2003. Today's rules have evolved through a number of mutations over the years. At several stages of this evolution, "grandfather" exceptions were created, so that today some individuals have benefits that are wholly or partly exempt from the rules. The 1999 edition of this book (pages 376-386) contains a history of this evolution. This ¶ 8.5 discusses three grandfather rules that are exceptions to the minimum distribution rules of § 401(a)(9), namely: the "TEFRA 242(b) election" (¶ 8.5.02), and two grandfather rules created by the Tax Reform Act of 1986 (¶ 8.5.03)—but leaves out the history lesson.

¶ 8.5.04 discusses another obscure grandfather rule, the continued availability of the estate tax exclusion for retirement benefits of certain individuals.

Other grandfather rules are discussed in Chapter 2: the former ability of non-spouse beneficiaries to roll over inherited benefits (¶ 2.5.05); and "10- year averaging" and "20% capital gain" income tax treatment for certain lump sum distributions (¶ 2.3.07-¶ 2.3.12).

8.5.01 *Why estate planners need to know the grandfather rules*

The grandfather rules are important for several reasons:

1.   Although the grandfather rules affect few clients, significant tax savings can be achieved for some of those who are eligible for grandfather treatment. The planner needs to be aware of these opportunities.

2.   A client may be postponing taking MRDs because he qualifies (or believes he qualifies) for a "grandfather" exception from the minimum distribution rules (Chapter 1). The planner needs to be able to verify that the client does or does not qualify for the exception he is claiming.   .

3.   If a client qualifies for a beneficial grandfather rule, the planner should be aware of what actions would cause loss of entitlement to the benefits of the grandfather rule so that these actions can be avoided (or can be taken only if the benefits of the action outweigh the benefits of continued qualification for the grandfather rule).

4.   The planner sometimes encounters a client who has not or may not have taken MRDs he was required to take in past years. The planner may conclude that the client will have to take catch-up distributions and/or be liable for a penalty (¶ 1.10.02). Before jumping to the conclusion that a penalty is owed, consider the possibility that for some or all of the years in question the client may have qualified for a grandfather rule, and so may not have been required to take distributions.

8.5.02 *TEFRA 242(b) elections: validity and effect*

TEFRA (1982) significantly expanded the minimum distribution rules. For plan years beginning after 1983, § 401(a)(9) would apply to *all* qualified retirement plans (previously it had applied only to Keogh plans). Under the pre-TEFRA lifetime distribution rules, no distributions were required prior to retirement; TEFRA (and the Tax Reform Act of 1984, which "cleaned up" the TEFRA changes via many retroactive amendments) added a requirement that 5% owners would have to start distributions at age 70½ even if still employed. TEFRA also added requirements for distributions after the employee's death (there had been none previously).

TEFRA contained a grandfather rule, § 242(b)(2), which provided that a plan will not be disqualified "by reason of distributions under a designation (before January 1, 1984) by any employee of a method of distribution...(A) which does not meet the requirements of [§ 401(a)(9)], but (B) which would not have disqualified such [plan] under [401(a)(9)] as in effect before the amendment" made by TEFRA. Under TRA '84 the TEFRA grandfather rule was continued. Accordingly, the TRA '84 changes would not apply to "distributions under a designation (before January 1, 1984) by any employee in accordance with a designation described in section 242(b)(2) of [TEFRA] (as in effect before the amendments made by this Act)." TRA '84, § 521(d)(2)-5. The minimum distribution regulations continue to recognize the validity of TEFRA 242(b) elections. Reg. § 1.401(a)(9)-8, A-13 through A-16.

As a result of the many changes brought by TEFRA, there was a flurry of activity among sophisticated plan participants trying to make a "designation" by December 31, 1983 that would enable them to continue to use the older, more liberal rules. The benefits of a participant who made a proper and timely "designation" would not be subject to the new minimum distribution rules.

Theoretically, participants with "242(b) designations" can postpone the start of required distributions past age 70½, until retirement, even if they own more than 5% of the employer (¶ 1.3.02), and their death benefits are not subject to the "5- year rule" (¶ 1.5.04) or the "at-least-as-rapidly" rule (§ 401(a)(9)(B)(i)). In other words, theoretically, a Participant who has a TEFRA 242(b) election in place can enjoy more income tax deferral for his plan benefits than the usual minimum distribution rules would allow, especially if he is a 5% owner (¶ 1.3.05). Unfortunately, TEFRA 242(b) designations have not proved as useful as originally expected for several reasons:

(a)   The requirements for a valid "designation" (as set forth in IRS Notice 83-23, 1983-2 C.B. 418, 11/15/83) are quite restrictive: "The designation must, in and of itself, provide sufficient information to fix the timing, and the formula for the definite determination, of plan payments. The designation must be complete and not allow further choice." P. 419. This does not mean the designation may not be amendable or revocable. Rather, the designation must be self-executing, requiring no further actions or designations by Participant to determine the size and date of distributions. Many purported TEFRA 242(b) designations do not meet this test.

(b)   Also, Participant generally cannot carry over a 242(b) designation from one plan to another. Rolling over QRP benefits protected by a 242(b) designation into an IRA causes loss of the 242(b) protection. However, grandfather protection is not lost if benefits are moved to another QRP without any election on the part of Participant (*e.g.*, as a result of a plan merger), if the transferee plan accounts for such benefits separately. Reg. § 1.401(a)(9)-8, A-14, A-15.

(c)   TEFRA 242(b) designations generally attempted to defer distributions for as long as possible. This turned out to be counterproductive, because an unrealistically long proposed deferral made it more likely that an individual grandfathered from the minimum distribution rules by a 242(b) election would want to make withdrawals sooner than his "designation" indicates. However, "any change in the designation will be considered to be a revocation of the designation." Notice 83-23, p. 420 (next to last sentence).

(d)   If the 242(b) designation is revoked, drastic results ensue. In effect the grandfathered status is revoked retroactively, and Participant is required to take "make-up distributions"—withdraw from the plan all the prior years' distributions he had skipped. Reg. § 1.401(a)(9)-8, A-16.

Thus, a participant relying on a TEFRA 242(b) designation lives in a perilous state. The longer he defers his distributions, the larger becomes the "make-up" distribution which will be required if he ever changes his mind and modifies the designation.

8.5.03 *Other MRD "grandfathers," including pre-1987 403(b) plans*

Under the Tax Reform Act of 1986 , the minimum distribution rules were extended for the first time to 403(b) plans; and the exception permitting non-key or non-5% owner employees to postpone distributions until actual retirement was eliminated (only to be reinstated 10 years later; see ¶ 1.3.02). Two new grandfather rules were created to accommodate these changes; however for reasons explained in the next two paragraphs, these are of little significance, and accordingly they are not explained in depth here. The two grandfather rules created by TRA '86 are:

First, a non-5% owner who was *born on or before June 30, 1917*, would still be entitled to defer commencement of distributions until actual retirement, even though TRA '86 eliminated that right for non-5% owners born after June 30, 1917. Presumably nobody needs this grandfather rule anymore because in 1996 Congress reversed the rule *again* so that, now, as before 1986, *all* non-5% owners, whether born before, on or after June 30, 1917, can postpone distributions until actual retirement; see ¶ 1.3.02. If full explanation of this rule is needed, see pp. 381-382 of the 1999 edition of this book (or pp. 228-229 of the 1996 edition).

Second, TRA '86 made the minimum distribution rules applicable, for the first time, to all 403(b) plans, but made this rule prospective only by exempting any pre-1987 403(b) plan balance from the new regime, provided such balance is accounted for separately. The pre-'87 account balance, while not subject to the full panoply of today's minimum distribution rules, is still subject to the more primitive predecessor of today's rules, the "incidental death benefit" rule.

The significance of this grandfather rule has diminished over the years. The pre-1987 grandfather amount is a frozen, fixed-dollar amount; investment earnings and gains do not increase the grandfathered balance (though distributions in excess of required distributions *decrease* it). With the passage of time, additional contributions to the plan and investment growth make the pre-1987 balance an ever-smaller percentage of the overall plan balance. It is unlikely to be a significant planning factor. If full explanation of this rule is needed, see pages 382-386 of the 1999 edition of this book, or the even fuller explanation at pages 230-238 of the 1996 edition.

8.5.04 *The federal estate tax exclusion lives!*

Once upon a time IRC § 2039 provided an unlimited federal estate tax exclusion for most kinds of retirement benefits. The exclusion was reduced to $100,000 by TEFRA '82 and repealed by TRA '84. However a grandfather clause was included in TRA '84 for both laws; then § 1852(e)(3) of TRA '86 made major substantive retroactive amendments to these grandfather clauses. The retroactive

TRA '86 changes made it much easier to qualify for the exclusion than it was under the original grandfather provision in TRA '84.

However, no regulations were issued after the TRA '86 amendments. The casual researcher may find only the strict TRA '84 grandfather rules (as embodied in IRS Temp. Reg. § 20.2039-1T, 1/29/86) under which only participants who were "in pay status" and had "irrevocably elected a form of benefits" by 1982 or 1984 still qualified for the exclusion. But TRA '86 simply *repealed* those two requirements and substituted others. Thus Temp. Reg. § 20.2039-1T is nugatory.

The best explanation of this tangle appears in PLR 9221030. The current requirements for a decedent's estate to be eligible for a total (or $100,000) estate tax exclusion, as stated by the IRS in this ruling, are:

1.   A decedent who separated from service before 1983, and dies after 1984, without having changed the "form of benefit" before his death, will be entitled to 100% exclusion of the benefit. A change of beneficiary is fine; it is a change of the *form of payment* of the benefit that triggers loss of the exclusion.

2.   If the decedent separated from service after 1982 but prior to 1985, and did not change the form of benefit between the time of separation from service and the time of death, the estate is still entitled to the exclusion but it is limited to $100,000.

Both of these exclusions under the retroactive amended grandfather clause are available *regardless* of whether the election of form of benefits was irrevocable, and *regardless* of whether the benefits were "in pay status" on December 31, 1984 or any other particular date.

9

Distributions Before Age 59½

What distributions the 10% penalty under § 72(t) applies to and how to avoid it

9.1 10% Penalty on Pre-Age 59½ Distributions

An individual who is under age 59½ and wants to withdraw money from his retirement plan faces a special obstacle: the 10% penalty imposed by § 72(t) on retirement distributions received prior to age 59½. This ¶ 9.1 describes various details of the penalty. ¶ 9.2 and ¶ 9.3 discuss a highly useful and flexible exception to the penalty, the "series of substantially equal periodic payments" (SOSEPP). ¶ 9.4 explains the requirements of the other 11 exceptions to the penalty.

For application of the penalty in connection with Roth IRAs, see ¶ 5.6; in connection with spousal rollover, see ¶ 3.2.02.

9.1.01 § 72(t): penalty for "early" or "premature" distributions

§ 72(t) generally imposes a 10% additional tax on retirement plan distributions made before the Participant attains age 59½. This additional tax is usually referred to as the "10% penalty" on "early distributions" or "premature distributions."

The § 72(t) penalty was added to the Code by the Tax Reform Act of 1986 and has been amended several times. The IRS has not issued regulations under § 72(t), presumably because it has given up trying to keep up with Congress's changes. The Service's position is revealed in IRS publications, IRS Notices, cases and private letter rulings. However, many aspects of the penalty (and its ever-growing list of exceptions) are not clear.

The 10% "additional tax" is not intended to be a punishment for wrongdoing, but merely a disincentive for early distributions (to encourage saving not only *for* but *until* retirement). The idea is to remove some of the benefits of tax-free accumulation if the accumulated funds are not used for their intended purpose.

9.1.02 *What types of plans the penalty applies to*

§ 72(t)(1) says that the penalty applies to any distribution from a "qualified retirement plan (as defined in § 4974(c))." § 4974(c)'s definition of "qualified retirement plan" includes 401(a) plans (true "qualified" retirement plans) as well as 403(b) arrangements and IRAs (both of which are not normally included in the term "qualified retirement plan"). (It also includes other types of plans not dealt with in this book.) *Although § 72(t) includes all of these plans in the term "qualified retirement plan," in this Chapter the term "qualified retirement plan" ("QRP") refers only to plans qualified under § 401(a), as distinguished from 403(b) arrangements and IRAs.*

Note that the plan in question does not have be "qualified" at the time of the distribution for the penalty to apply, as long as it was once a qualified plan. *Powell v. Comm'r*, 129 F.3d 321 (4th Cir. 1997).

9.1.03 *Distributions of employer stock*

An employee who receives employer stock in a lump sum distribution from a qualified plan is entitled to certain favorable tax treatment regarding the "net unrealized appreciation" in the stock. See ¶ 2.4. If the employee is under age 59½ at the time of the distribution, the 10% penalty will apply to the portion of the distribution that is includible in the employee's gross income. It will not apply to the income resulting from later sale of the stock. See ¶ 2.4.01.

9.1.04 *10% applies to amount included in gross income*

The penalty is not necessarily 10% of the total distribution. Rather, the 10% is calculated only with respect to "the portion of [the distribution] which is includible in gross income." § 72(t)(1); Notice 87-16, 1987-1 C.B. 446. To the extent the distribution is income tax-free because (for example) it represents the return of Participant's own after-tax contributions (¶ 2.1.04), or because it is rolled over to another plan or IRA in a qualifying rollover (¶ 2.5), it is also penalty-free. See, *e.g.*, PLR 9253049 (because a pre-age 59½ IRA distribution was excluded from the taxpayer's gross income by virtue of the U.S.-U.K. tax treaty, it was also not subject to the 10% penalty); PLR 9010007 (tax-free rollover not subject to penalty).

Other than the fact that the penalty applies only to the portion of a distribution that is includible in gross income, the 10% penalty has nothing to do with the income tax treatment of the distribution. Nevertheless, the § 72(t) exceptions are a source of confusion to clients and practitioners who wrongly conclude that distributions that are *penalty-free* under § 72(t) are also *income tax-free*.

9.1.05 *IRA contributions withdrawn before tax return due date*

If an IRA contribution for which no deduction has been taken is withdrawn from the account (together with the net earnings on that contribution) before the due date (including extensions) of the Participant's tax return for the year in which the contribution was made, the withdrawal of the *contribution* is not a taxable distribution (§ 408(d)(4)) and accordingly is also not subject to the penalty. However, any *income earned on the contribution* that is included in the corrective distribution will be subject to the penalty (unless it qualifies for one of the exceptions; ¶ 9.2, ¶ 9.4). IRS Notice 87-16, 1987-1 C.B. 446; *Hall v. Comm'r*, T.C. Memo 1998-336. IRS Publication 590, "Individual Retirement Arrangements (IRAs)" (2000), at page 21.

9.1.06 *Enforcement of the penalty by IRS and courts*

The IRS eagerly seeks to collect the penalty wherever it applies. People who take money from their retirement plans apparently unaware that the penalty exists are of course caught by the penalty. A more sympathetic case (though not to the IRS) is presented by people who did not know they had received a distribution, or who had reason to believe the distribution in question was tax-free, and then find out the hard way that not only have they received a taxable distribution but it is subject to a penalty.

This can happen, for example, to a person who takes a loan from a retirement plan but fails to meet the requirements of § 72(p), so that the loan is treated as a taxable distribution rather than a loan; Notice 87-13, 1987-1 C.B. 432, Q-20; *Plotkin v. Comm'r*, T.C. Memo 2001-71. It evidently happened to many members of the Maryland State Teachers' Retirement System, when their pension plan was reorganized and they received distributions that they were told (by their employer) could be rolled over tax-free to IRAs. Wrong. Each misled teacher under age 59½ had to pay the penalty. See, *e.g.*, *Thompson v. Comm'r*, 71 TCM 3160 (1996).

It happens to people whose attempts to roll over retirement plan distributions are held for one reason or another not to constitute "qualified rollovers"; see, *e.g.*, *Rodoni v. Comm'r*, 105 T.C. 29 (1995) (husband's distribution rolled over into IRA in the name of wife). It happened to Ben Moon who correctly rolled over his entire distribution check, but did not realize that 20% tax had been withheld from the distribution. Since he had therefore rolled over only 80% of the distribution, he was liable for income taxes and the 10% penalty on the part that had been paid directly to the IRS. The court had no sympathy for him, saying that the 20% withholding tax had been widely publicized (citing a Rutgers Law Journal article). *Moon v. U.S.*, U.S. Ct. Fed. Claims 95-702T, 7/9/97; 97-2 USTC 50,668.

Adding to the fun, the penalty may itself generate *another* penalty, if its existence means the taxpayer underpaid his estimated taxes. Notice 87-13, Q-20.

The Tax Court impartially enforces the penalty, occasionally expressing sympathy for the taxpayers, but declining to modify the clear words of the statute. See, *e.g.*, *Deal v. Comm'r*, T.C. Memo 1999-352, in which the IRS erroneously told Ms. Deal by phone that the penalty did not apply to her distribution, so she did not roll it over; the IRS later assessed the penalty and the Tax Court upheld it.

Only on rare occasions has the penalty not been applied when the taxpayer did not fit into any of the exceptions. Certain involuntary distributions have escaped the penalty; see ¶ 9.4.10. In one case, *Duralia v. Comm'r*, T.C. Memo 1994-269, the IRS apparently forgot to assess the penalty.

Though the IRS is relentless in collecting the penalty, it has been very flexible in granting advance rulings to taxpayers seeking to withdraw from their accounts under the "series of equal payments" exception; see ¶ 9.2.05. If the taxpayer seeks an advance ruling for his distribution, the IRS knows it will not collect any income taxes on the distribution unless it agrees that there will be no 10% penalty (because the taxpayer won't take the distribution without the ruling). The moral of the story: seek an advance ruling if a proposed pre-age-59½ distribution does not squarely fit within an exception.

9.1.07 *Bankruptcy, community property, life insurance*

For a discussion of whether the penalty is dischargeable in bankruptcy, see *In re Mounier*, KTC 1998-464 (S.D. Cal. 1998).

The taxable income from an IRA distribution, and the 10% penalty if applicable, are imposed on the IRA owner solely (not on the IRA owner and his or her spouse), even if the IRA is community property. *Bunney v. Comm'r*, 114 T.C. 259, 262 (2000); *Morris v. Comm'r*, T.C. Memo 2002-17.

When a qualified retirement plan purchases life insurance on the life of a plan participant, § 72(m)(3) generally requires that the cost of the insurance protection be included currently in the participant's gross income. ¶ 8.3.01. However, this deemed income is not treated as a distribution for purposes of § 72(t) and the 10% penalty does not apply. IRS Notice 87-16, 1987-1 C.B. 446, A-11.

9.1.08 *Overview of the exceptions to the penalty*

There are 12 exceptions to the penalty, so many individuals are able to withdraw funds from their plans prior to age 59½ without penalty. The exceptions are not the same for all types of retirement plans. For example, some exceptions available for qualified plans and 403(b) arrangements are *not* available for IRA distributions. Other exceptions apply *only* to IRAs. Some exceptions apply differently depending on the type of plan involved.

Most of the exceptions have limited usefulness for planning purposes because they are triggered only in particular hardship situations (death, disability) or depend on a particular use of the funds distributed (college tuition, health insurance premiums, "first time" home purchase). However, there is no "hardship exception" *per se* to this penalty; *Gallagher v. Comm'r*, T.C. Memo 2001-34; *Deal v. Comm'r*, T.C. Memo 1999-352. See, e.g., *Baas v. Comm'r*, T.C. Memo 2002-130, and *Czepiel v. Comm'r*, T.C. Memo 1999-289, aff'd. by order (1st Cir., Dec. 5, 2000), in which participants who had been incarcerated due to failure to pay child support, and withdrew funds from their retirement plans in order to get out of jail, had to pay the 10% penalty on their withdrawals; and *Robertson v. Comm'r*, T.C. Memo 2000-100 (need to withdraw funds for "subsistence" is not an exception to the penalty).

One exception stands out as a useful planning tool: the "series of substantially equal periodic payments."

9.2 Exception: "Series of Equal Payments"

9.2.01 *Series of substantially equal periodic payments (SOSEPP)*

The penalty does not apply to a distribution that is "part of a series of substantially equal periodic payments (not less frequently than annually) made for the life (or life expectancy) of the employee or the joint lives (or joint life expectancies) of such employee and his designated beneficiary." § 72(t)(2)(A)(iv). While at first this appears to be a rather narrow window, in fact it is a wide open door, because:

1.   Liberalized rollover rules introduced in 1992 (§ 402(c)) make it possible in many cases to create an IRA of the desired size to support the series (see ¶ 9.2.12) by taking that amount of money out of a profit sharing plan, even while still employed, and rolling the money over tax free to the IRA (see ¶ 2.5).

2.   The payments do not in fact have to continue for the Participant's entire life or life expectancy period, but only until the individual reaches age 59½, or until five years have elapsed, whichever occurs later. ¶ 9.3.02.

3.   The IRS allows several methods for determining the size of the "equal payments." See ¶ 9.2.05.

This is the most significant exception for planning purposes. All the other exceptions are tied to a specific use of the money (home purchase, college tuition), or to some type of hardship situation (death, disability), or are otherwise narrowly limited. In contrast, everyone who has an IRA (or who can get one via a rollover from some other type of plan) can use the SOSEPP exception. See the "Quentin" case study in Chapter 11 for an example of use of this exception.

Participants in qualified plans can also use this exception to take a series of payments *from* the qualified plan, but only if they have separated from service. § 72(t)(3)(B). If Participant is still employed, he cannot take a SOSEPP from a QRP; but if the QRP permits in-service distributions Participant can roll a distribution over to an IRA and take the SOSEPP from the IRA. "Separation from service" is not required for a SOSEPP from an IRA.

There is one significant limitation on the SOSEPP exception: if the series of payments is "modified" before the five years are up (or before the Participant reaches age 59½, if he started the SOSEPP more than five years before reaching age 59½), *all* payments in the series lose the shelter of the exception, and the penalty applies, retroactively and with interest, to all pre-age 59½ distributions. See ¶ 9.3.

9.2.02 *How this exception works*

The SOSEPP exception starts from the premise that there is a fund of money (the retirement plan account) that will be gradually exhausted by a series of regular distributions over the applicable period of time. The "applicable period of time" is (i) the life expectancy of the Participant or (ii) the joint life expectancy of the Participant and his designated beneficiary. Thus, the SOSEPP must be designed so that, *if* it continued for that period of time (which it won't; see ¶ 9.3.02), it would exactly exhaust the fund.

Note that § 72(t)(2)(A)(iv) itself does not say that the SOSEPP must be designed to *exhaust* the account over the applicable time period; it says only that the equal payments must be "made for" the applicable period of time. This wording clearly would preclude a series of equal payments that would exhaust the fund *before* the end of the applicable time period, but would not necessarily preclude a series of equal payments that would be too small to exhaust the fund. For example, if payments of $50,000 per year would exhaust the account over the taxpayer's life expectancy, why could he not take equal annual payments of any amount *up to* $50,000 per year? § 72(t)(2)(A)(iv)'s wording appears to permit him to take, say, $25,000 per year, so long as the payments were equal every year and continued for the required period of time.

However, the IRS's interpretation of this exception is that the SOSEPP must be designed to exhaust the fund over the applicable time period. See Notice 87-16, 1987-1 C.B. 446, A-12, and PLR 9805023. The Participant cannot take annual distributions that are too small to exhaust the account, even if they are equal, regular, payments designed to continue over the applicable time period. Fortunately, if the individual's benefits are in an IRA, it is very easy to get around this limitation; see ¶ 9.2.12.

9.2.03 *Notice 89-25 (A-12) and its successor, Rev. Rul. 2002-62*

IRS Notice 89-25 (A-12), 1989-1 C.B. 662, laid out three methods a taxpayer could use to compute the payments in his SOSEPP. The three methods are usually called the "required minimum distributions" (RMD) method (i.e., any method that "would be acceptable" for computing required distributions under § 401(a)(9)), the "amortization" method (similar to a level payment mortgage amortized over the applicable life expectancy) and the "annuitization" method (annuitizing the retirement account over the applicable life expectancy).

Revenue Ruling 2002-62, 2002-42 I.R.B. 710, which supercedes Notice 89-25 (A-12), continues the same three methods but with changes. Rev. Rul. 2002-62 changes or clarifies the rules regarding which life expectancy tables, interest rate and account balance may be used in designing a SOSEPP. As a result, much prior thinking about how to set up a SOSEPP is obsolete. Under the new regime, greater specificity in the rules comes at the price of some loss of flexibility.

Rev. Rul. 2002-62 applies to any SOSEPP commencing on or after January 1, 2003, and "may be used for distributions commencing in 2002." Shortly after issuing the Ruling, the IRS posted a document called "FAQs regarding Revenue Ruling 2002-62" at its web site, which is "for general information only and should not be cited as any type of legal authority." You can find these "IRS FAQs" on the web at www.rothira.com or at www.irs.gov/retirement/article.

9.2.04 *Steps required to initiate a SOSEPP*

To take advantage of the SOSEPP exception, the taxpayer must make several choices about the design of the series:

A. Choose one of the three permitted methods (RMD, amortization or annuitization). ¶ 9.2.05.

B. Choose a life expectancy table (single, joint with beneficiary, or "Uniform Lifetime Table"). ¶ 9.2.06-¶ 9.2.08.

C. If using the amortization or annuitization method, choose an interest rate. ¶ 9.2.09.

D. Choose an initial account balance valuation date. ¶ 9.2.10.

E.   Decide whether payments will be monthly, quarterly or annually. See ¶ 9.2.11.

The big decisions are *choice of method* and *choice of life expectancy table*. These choices are interrelated, not sequential. For example, the Participant could decide that certainty of payment size is his highest priority (in which case he would choose the amortization method and the Single Life or Uniform Lifetime Table), or conversely that the ability to vary payments was his major goal (in which case he would lean towards the RMD method and the Joint and Survivor Life Table). The other choices (interest rate and initial valuation date) are then interwoven with the big choices to arrive at the exact payment amount.

Although the IRS methods for calculating the payments appear easy, and software programs (see Appendix C) make them appear even easier, consider hiring an actuary to design the series if the amounts involved are substantial. Actuarial calculations can easily be bungled by non-actuaries; see, *e.g.*, PLR 9705033 (penalty imposed because the required payments were improperly calculated by the client's "independent third-party financial advisor"). Also, a good actuary can design a series that will most precisely achieve the client's goals (such as small or large payments and the ability to add another series later). See the "Quentin" case study, Chapter 11.

Even the IRS states that the amortization and annuitization methods "generally require professional assistance." IRS Publication 590, "Individual Retirement Arrangements (IRAs)" (2000), page 20.

9.2.05 *The three methods: RMD, amortization, annuitization*

The taxpayer has a choice of three IRS-approved methods for the design of his SOSEPP (the end of this ¶ 9.2.05 discusses getting IRS approval for other designs):

RMD method: Under the RMD method, the "series" payments are calculated in the same manner as required distributions under § 401(a)(9): the account balance (revalued annually) is divided by a life expectancy factor each year to produce the required payment. See Chapter 1. "Under this method, the account balance, the number from the chosen life expectancy table and the resulting annual payments are redetermined for each year." Rev. Rul. 2002-62, Sec. 2.01(a). Because this method requires annual revaluation of the account, payments fluctuate with investment performance. If the account grows in value, the payments will increase. If the investments decline in value, the payments shrink also. Annual revaluation can be seen as an advantage because it means the account will never be "wiped out," as can occur with the other two methods. The drawback of the RMD method is the unpredictability of the payments. Smaller payments might occur inconveniently just when the taxpayer needs more income. Higher payments could be required in a year when he is in a high bracket. Once the taxpayer has chosen the RMD method, he can never change to either of the other methods. The only controls the taxpayer can maintain over the size of the payments are through his choice of beneficiary—*if* he elected to use the Joint and Survivor Life Table (see ¶ 9.2.07), and, possibly, through his annual choice of valuation date; see ¶ 9.2.10.

Amortization ("Fixed amortization") method: Under this method, the taxpayer chooses a reasonable interest rate (see ¶ 9.2.09), and a life expectancy table (¶ 9.2.06-¶ 9.2.08.), then takes regular payments as if the account were a self-amortizing level payment mortgage (except that he is receiving, rather than making, the payments). Once the amount of the first payment is determined, the payments never vary, regardless of the investment performance of the account. However, the taxpayer does have the option, in any year after the first year, of switching to the RMD method. See ¶ 9.3.04.

Annuitization ("Fixed annuitization") method: Under this method, the taxpayer chooses a reasonable interest rate (¶ 9.2.09), and single or joint life expectancy, then divides the account balance by an annuity factor, as if the account were being annuitized over the applicable life expectancy. "The annuity factor is derived using the mortality table in Appendix B [of Rev. Rul. 2002-62] and using the chosen interest rate." Once the amount of the first payment is determined, the payments never vary, regardless of the investment performance of the account. However, the taxpayer does have the option, in any year after the first year, to switch to the RMD method. See ¶ 9.3.04.

Note that there is little difference between the amortization and annuitization methods:

A.   It is easier to calculate the payments under the amortization method. The annuitization method requires an actuary or math whiz, or just use one of the excellent software programs that do this such as NumberCruncher® or Brentmark® (Appendix C).

B.   Under Notice 89-25 (A-12), the IRS had formerly allowed greater flexibility in mortality assumptions for taxpayers using the annuitization method. See ¶ 9.2.06, # 1. That flexibility has been removed, eliminating this difference.

C.   It is not clear whether the hypothetical 10-years-younger beneficiary concept applies to the annuitization method. See ¶ 9.2.06, # 6.

However, beyond these minimal differences, both these methods (despite providing slightly different payment amounts) are pretty much the same, providing permanently fixed payments year after year, with the possibility of wiping out the account through the fixed payments and the saving possibility of switching to the RMD method to avoid that (see ¶ 9.3.04).

There *is* a significant difference between these two methods, with their *fixed* payments, and the RMD method, which has *variable* payments. If the taxpayer wants variable payments he selects the RMD method. If the taxpayer wants fixed payments, he selects the annuitization or amortization method (depending which gives him the size of payment he prefers), knowing he can always switch later to the RMD method.

The "three methods" are not the only possible ways to design a SOSEPP; however, if varying from these pre-approved models it is necessary to obtain advance approval from the IRS via a private letter ruling. See IRS FAQs (¶ 9.2.03), last question.

Prior to Rev. Rul. 2002-62 the IRS had granted approval of several variations in SOSEPP design. For example, in PLR 9816028 (1/21/98), the Participant's SOSEPP was based on the annuity method, but called for the payments to increase by 3% annually as a "cost of living adjustment." PLRs 9747045, 9723035 and 9536031 also involved regular payments that were to be "equal" except for an annual 3% cost of living adjustment. In PLR 9531039, the taxpayer was allowed to redetermine the life expectancy factor, interest rate factor and account balance each year. In PLR 9021058, the taxpayer was allowed to redetermine the interest rate factor and account balance each year.

9.2.06 *Participant must choose one of three life expectancy tables*

Rev. Rul. 2002-62 provides that the taxpayer using the RMD or amortization method must select one of three life expectancy tables for calculating his SOSEPP: the Single Life Table, the Joint and Survivor Life Table or the Uniform Lifetime Table.

The Single and Joint and Survivor Life Tables are contained in Reg. § 1.410(a)(9)-9 (A-1, A-3). The Uniform Lifetime Table (showing the joint and survivor life expectancy of the taxpayer and a hypothetical beneficiary who is 10 years younger than the taxpayer) is contained in Appendix A of Rev. Rul. 2002-62. It is an expanded version of the Uniform Lifetime Table contained in Reg. § 1.410(a)(9)-9 (A-2), but with the ages extended down to age 10. The Single Life and Uniform Lifetime Tables are also in Appendix A of this book.

Note the following:

1.   No more "reasonable mortality table." Notice 89-25 permitted use of any "reasonable mortality table" under the annuitization method. Rev. Rul. 2002-62 takes away that option, and supplies its own table of mortality factors that must be used in determining payments under the annuitization method. Rev. Rul. 2002-62, Sec. 2.02(a).

2.   Actual beneficiary doesn't matter with Single, Uniform tables. If the taxpayer elects to use the Single Life or Uniform Lifetime Table, it will make no difference (either at the commencement of the series or at any time thereafter) who is designated as beneficiary of the retirement account. Whether the beneficiary is old or young, individual or non-individual, makes no difference. Changing the beneficiary later in the series makes no difference. Thus, the Single Life or Uniform Lifetime Table should be selected if the taxpayer wants the greatest possible predictability as to how his distributions will be calculated, and wants to be able to change his beneficiary without having that change impact the size of his SOSEPP payments.

3.   Joint Survivor Table uses actual beneficiary. If the taxpayer elects the Joint and Survivor Life Table, then the factor used to determine the first payment in the series is based on the joint life expectancy of the taxpayer and his ACTUAL beneficiary. Rev. Rul. 2002-62, Sec. 2.02(b). If the taxpayer is using the RMD method, then the beneficiary (for purposes of determining the factor under the Joint and Survivor Life Table) is redetermined every year. Under the annuitization or amortization method, subsequent changes of beneficiary will have no effect on the payments so long as the Participant continues using that method—but if he switches in mid-stream to the RMD method (¶ 9.3.04), and is required to or chooses to continue using the Joint and Survivor Life Table, then his subsequent payments would be determined using the joint life expectancy of himself and his actual beneficiary.

4.   How to determine "actual beneficiary." Under the Joint and Survivor Life Table, the "actual beneficiary" is determined as of January 1 of the distribution year in question, using the same rules as apply for determining the designated beneficiary for minimum distribution purposes. E.g., naming a non-qualifying trust would be treated as having "no designated beneficiary," or if multiple beneficiaries are named the oldest one's life expectancy is used. See ¶ 1.7 for details on how to determine the designated beneficiary. When the Participant has elected the Joint and Survivor Life Table, but has no designated beneficiary on January 1 of the year in question, the Single Life Table is used. Rev. Rul. 2002-62, Sec. 2.02(b).

5.   Choice of table is (sometimes?) permanent. Once the taxpayer has selected his life expectancy table, that selection can never be changed if the taxpayer is using the RMD method and the SOSEPP commenced after 2002. Rev. Rul. 2002-62, Sec. 2.02(a) (last two sentences). For SOSEPPs that commenced prior to 2003, see ¶ 9.3.05. Of course, if the taxpayer is using the annuitization or amortization method the life expectancy table cannot be changed so long as he continues using that method, because the payments are fixed. If the taxpayer begins a SOSEPP using the amortization or annuitization method, and then in a later year switches to the RMD method, see ¶ 9.3.05.

6.   Availability of uniform table concept with annuitization method. It is not clear whether, under the annuitization method, the taxpayer can use his joint life expectancy with a hypothetical 10-years-younger beneficiary (as is allowed with the other methods) or only with his actual beneficiary. The Ruling says that the annuity period is "the life of the taxpayer (or the joint lives of the individual and beneficiary)." Under the amortization and RMD methods, distributions are determined using the "chosen life expectancy table" (Rev. Rul. 2002-62, Sec. 2.01(a), (b)), and Sec. 2.02(a) says that any of the three life expectancy tables may be used "to determine distribution periods." However, the life expectancy tables and the "distribution period" concept do not apply to the annuitization method. Further IRS clarification is needed.

9.2.07 *Joint/Survivor table provides possibility of future changes*

The first choice to be made is between a predictable life expectancy factor (as provided by the Single Life Table or Uniform Lifetime Table) or a variable life expectancy factor (as potentially provided by the Joint and Survivor Life Table).

The Participant who wants maximum control over the size of his payments, and who can tolerate risk and complexity, would gravitate towards the Joint and Survivor Life Table, because with this table (combined with the RMD method) the taxpayer can affect the size of his payments by changing his designated beneficiary:

Example: Ben wants to take a SOSEPP with relatively large payments and maximum flexibility for future change. To get the largest SOSEPP payments, he chooses the annuitization method, chooses the Joint and Survivor Life Table, and names his grandmother as his beneficiary. The joint life expectancy of Ben and his grandmother is virtually the same as Ben's single life expectancy, which is the shortest possible payout period under any method. Since naming his grandmother has obviously undesirable consequences in terms of RMD results after his death, he may buy life insurance to cover the accelerated income tax risk of his premature death, or maybe Ben just names grandmother as his beneficiary on December 31 each year and changes the beneficiary to his children on January 2 of the next year, and hopes he doesn't die on January 1. In later years, if Ben wants to decrease his SOSEPP payments, he may be able to do so by switching to the RMD method and naming his children directly as his beneficiaries on January 1. This will give him a larger life expectancy factor from the Joint and Survivor Life Table. A larger life expectancy factor will lead to smaller SOSEPP payments—unless the account balance has increased to the point that the increase wipes out the effect of using a larger divisor.

Example: Billy has less risk tolerance than Ben. The first thing he notices about the Joint and Survivor Life Table is that it depends on determining who is his actual beneficiary under the minimum distribution regulations (and, if using the RMD method, making that determination again every year). This could make his payments fluctuate unexpectedly in an undesirable manner. For example, if he names his same-age spouse as beneficiary, and expects to withdraw the account based on their joint life expectancy, but then his wife predeceases him, his children would become his beneficiaries. His payments would drop sharply because the children are so much younger. He is also concerned about the possibility that he might not correctly determine who is the "designated beneficiary" under the minimum distribution regulations, and an incorrect determination in any year could be deemed a "modification" of the SOSEPP, resulting in a substantial penalty. Billy like many other taxpayers would not welcome this type of uncertainty and risk in their planning, and so would steer away from the JSL table/RMD method combination.

9.2.08 *Predictable factors: Single Life, Uniform Lifetime Tables*

Once a taxpayer has decided to forego the risks and rewards of using the Joint and Survivor Life Table, his only choice is between the Single Life Table and the Uniform Lifetime Table. The only difference between these tables is the size of the annual payment relative to the size of the account. If you prefer larger payments, choose the Single Life Table. If you prefer smaller payments, choose the Uniform Lifetime Table. Under both tables, there is no possibility of changing to a different table later (for possible exception see ¶ 9.3.05, D), and there is no possibility of affecting the size of the payments by changing the designated beneficiary (compare ¶ 9.2.07).

With both of these tables, you find the appropriate factor for the first year's payment based on the Participant's age on his birthday in that year. Rev. Rul. 2002-62, Sec. 2.02(a). If using the RMD method, you then go back to the originally-chosen table every year to get that year's factor, based on the Participant's new age. If using the amortization or annuitization method, you don't go back to the table every year because the payments are fixed in amount.

9.2.09 *What interest rate assumption is used*

There is no interest rate assumption under the RMD method. The RMD method involves annual revaluation of the account balance, so investment performance is taken into account only in retrospect.

For the amortization and annuitization methods, it is necessary to choose an interest rate (representing the hypothetical projected investment return on the account during the period of the SOSEPP). The Participant may use "any interest rate that is not more than 120 percent of the federal mid-term rate (determined in accordance with section 1274(d) for either of the two months immediately preceding the month in which the distribution begins)." Rev. Rul. 2002-62, Sec. 2.02(c). These rates may be found at the IRS web site www.irs.gov/tax_regs/fedrates.html, as well as at www.tigertables.com and www.leimbergservices.com.

Note the following:

1.   New maximum interest rate. Prior to the issuance of Rev. Rul. 2002-62, the IRS did not prescribe either a safe harbor or a maximum interest rate. Notice 89-25 (A-12) required only that the taxpayer use a rate "that does not exceed a reasonable interest rate on the date payments commence." In letter rulings the IRS had approved rates as high as 120% of the applicable federal long-term rate (PLR 9747045). *The flexibility to use "any reasonable rate" does not exist for SOSEPPs commencing after 2002; 120% of federal mid-term is now the ceiling.*

2.   7520 rate is not a safe harbor. The § 7520 rate (used for valuing life estates and remainders for estate and gift tax purposes) is the federal mid-term rate *rounded to the nearest 2/10ths of a percent.* § 7520(a). Since the § 7520 rate could be rounded *up*, the § 7520 rate for a month could be higher than the absolute ceiling set in Rev. Rul. 2002-62.

9.2.10 *What account balance is used*

Whichever method the taxpayer is using, he must apply a certain factor to an account balance. The account balance "must be determined in a reasonable manner based on the facts and circumstances." Rev. Rul. 2002-62, Sec. 2.02(d).

Under all three methods, the Participant must select a valuation date for the first year's payment. The IRS provides an example the gist of which is that any date from the last prior year end to the day before the distribution would be fine. There is no specific prohibition against using a date earlier than the last prior year-end, but it would seem that the prior year-end (or any subsequent valuation date, up to the date of the first distribution) would be a safe harbor.

This reasonable approach gives taxpayers time to do their planning based on a particular valuation date (such as the last prior year-end) without having to rush to get the payments started before the next monthly valuation arrives, while also giving them the flexibility to make a last minute change in the valuation date (prior to the first SOSEPP payment) if violent market fluctuations make the last prior year-end value no longer realistic.

Under the *amortization and annuitization* methods, the account balance is determined only once, at the beginning of the series. Since the payments do not fluctuate, there is no need to look at the account balance again after the first year.

Under the *RMD method* the account balance is redetermined annually. Must taxpayer use the same valuation date for this purpose every year? No, according to Rev. Rul. 2002-62: From the IRS example of a SOSEPP commencing on July 15 of year 1 using the RMD method from an IRA that had daily valuations: "For subsequent years, under the required minimum distribution method, it would be reasonable to use the value *either* on the December 31 of the prior year *or* on a date within a reasonable period before that year's distribution." Sec. 2.02(d) (emphasis added).

However, the subsequently-issued IRS FAQs (see ¶ 9.2.03) contain an entirely different statement: "The account balance may be determined in any reasonable manner *that is used consistently.*" (Emphasis added.) The FAQs provide an example ("Mr. B") suggesting that whatever valuation date is used in the first year (e.g., prior year-end balance) must be used in subsequent years. It is outrageous that the IRS issues an authoritative pronouncement (a Revenue Ruling), then almost immediately issues "informal" guidance that directly contradicts its own authoritative guidance.

9.2.11 *Monthly, quarterly or annual payments?*

The "periodic payments" must be paid at regular intervals at least annually. Rev. Rul. 2002-62, Sec. 1.02(b). Though Rev. Rul. 2002-62 and its follow-up "FAQs" use only annual payments in their examples, monthly payments are at least as popular (see, e.g., PLRs 2002-14029, 2002-14034, 2002-03072). Quarterly payments would be another suitable choice.

9.2.12 *Applying the SOSEPP exception to multiple IRAs*

Must all IRAs be treated as one IRA for purposes of computing the payments? Or can one IRA be isolated from other IRAs owned by the same participant and used as a basis for these distributions?

§ 408(d)(1), which governs IRAs, provides that IRA distributions are includible in gross income "in the manner provided under § 72." § 408(d)(2) then provides that: "For purposes of applying section 72 to any amount described in paragraph (1)...(A) all individual retirement plans shall be treated as 1 contract, [and] (B) all distributions during any taxable year shall be treated as 1 distribution...." However, this provision states that it applies for the purpose of determining how much of any distribution is *included in gross income* (the subject of § 408(d)). There is no provision requiring that IRAs be aggregated for purposes of the *penalty* under § 72(t).

Similarly, the IRS, in Notice 89-25, A-7, states that "For purposes of determining the taxation of IRA distributions, all IRAs maintained for an individual must be aggregated and treated as one IRA," but the IRS has never applied this *income tax* rule for purposes of the § 72(t) *penalty* and the SOSEPP exception.

For purposes of structuring a SOSEPP, the taxpayer has several choices: the series can be based on all of his IRAs, aggregated; or on some of the IRAs aggregated, with others excluded; or on one IRA to the exclusion of others. As the IRS said in PLR 9747039, "If a taxpayer owns more than one IRA, any combination of his or her IRAs may be taken into account in determining the distributions by aggregating the account balances of those IRAs. *The specific IRAs taken into account are part of the method of determining the substantially equal periodic payments....*" (Emphasis added.)

All IRAs aggregated: In each of PLRs 9830042, 9824047, and 9545018, all of the taxpayer's IRAs were aggregated for purposes of computing the series payments. However, the rulings do not state that this aggregation was a requirement of the favorable rulings. The taxpayers may simply have wanted to aggregate all their IRAs.

Some IRAs aggregated, others excluded: In PLR 9816028 the taxpayer had numerous IRAs, seven of which were aggregated to form the basis of his proposed SOSEPP and the rest of which were not to be counted. In PLR 9801050 the taxpayer had several IRAs, three of which were aggregated to form the basis of his proposed SOSEPP and the rest of which were not to be counted. The IRS ruled favorably in both cases, requiring only that the series payments had to be made from the aggregated IRAs and not from the other accounts.

Take series from one IRA, not aggregated with others: In PLR 9818055 the taxpayer was taking a SOSEPP from one of her two IRAs. In PLR 9812038 the taxpayer was taking a SOSEPP from one of his three IRAs and wanted to start a second SOSEPP from a new, fourth, IRA, to be created by transfer of funds from one of the other IRAs (not the IRA that was already supporting the first SOSEPP). The IRS permitted this, and the ruling specifically stated more than once that the taxpayer's IRAs were not aggregated. In PLR 9747045 the taxpayer's IRS-approved SOSEPP was taken from one of her two rollover IRAs and not the other; the two were not aggregated.

These rulings indicate that the taxpayer must choose, at the beginning of his SOSEPP, either to aggregate or not to aggregate individual retirement accounts for purposes of designing and paying out the series. The SOSEPP can be based on one of several IRAs, on all of the taxpayer's IRAs on an aggregated basis, or on some IRAs aggregated with others excluded.

Whichever accounts are included in the initial design of the SOSEPP must be the sole source of payments in the series. Once the SOSEPP begins, funds must not be transferred *out of* the IRAs that are being used to support the series (except to make payments that are part of the series), or *into* any IRA that is part of the support for the series.

The ability to choose which IRAs will be aggregated in determining the size of the periodic payments gives the client tremendous flexibility. See the "Quentin" case study, Chapter 11. This flexibility is not unlimited, however. Although it is acceptable to have two IRAs, and use only one of them to support the SOSEPP, the IRS forbids using only *part* of an IRA to support a series. PLR 9705033. Since the taxpayer can easily get to the same result by dividing one IRA into two, this prohibition is little more than a trap for the unwary.

The author has found no rulings or other sources dealing with the aggregation of 403(b) arrangements or qualified retirement plans for purposes of applying the SOSEPP exception.

9.2.13 *Starting a second series to run concurrently with the first*

A taxpayer receiving a SOSEPP from one or more IRAs may initiate a *second* series of equal payments from a different IRA. See, e.g., PLR 9812038, discussed at ¶ 9.2.12, in which the taxpayer was receiving a SOSEPP from "IRA # 1." After that SOSEPP had been under way for a while, he was allowed to begin a second SOSEPP from a different IRA, "IRA # 4," that had been created just for the purpose. PLR 9747039 is another favorable ruling about starting a second SOSEPP from a different IRA.

However, the taxpayer may not start a second SOSEPP from the same IRA (or plan) that is already supporting the first SOSEPP; such a second series would constitute an impermissible "modification" of the first series (see ¶ 9.3.01).

9.2.14 *Procedural requirements*

There is no specific format for electing one of the three methods. There is no requirement that any of the elections or choices be in writing, or that notice of any choices be delivered to anyone in particular.

For each year that a pre-age 59½ distribution is received, the taxpayer must complete Form 4329 (attached to the Participant's Form 1040), and check off that the SOSEPP exception applies, but for now there is no requirement to attach any demonstration of compliance with the requirements of that exception. Needless to say, it is advisable to document the choices and the computations, to demonstrate that any pre-age 59½ distribution qualifies for the SOSEPP exception, because the burden of proof is on the taxpayer.

In one audit, here is what the IRS asked the taxpayer to produce to prove that his payments qualified for the SOSEPP exception: "we need...worksheets that you prepared (or an explanation) concerning your determination of the period over which the periodic payments would be made and the statements reflecting the periodic payments that were made from the date first made to the present. ...We need to see the documents between 1993 and the present to ensure that the distributions still qualify for the exception." *Evans v. Comm'r*, T.C. Memo 1999-33.

9.2.15 *How planning and investment professionals use § 72(t)*

The flexibility of the SOSEPP exception to § 72(t) offers planning opportunities. The series of payments can help a client under age 59½ achieve financial, investment and estate planning goals.

For example, actuary and retirement expert Bruce Temkin suggests the following program for an under-age 59½ client who needs money to start a business: First, the client refinances his residence. He uses the loan proceeds to cover the immediate financial need. Then he takes from his IRA a SOSEPP (with the size of the payments matched to the mortgage payments) to repay the mortgage. There will be no penalty, and the tax-deductible mortgage interest will reduce the income tax on the IRA distributions.

A mutual fund firm's brochure for financial advisors suggests using familiarity with § 72(t) as a marketing technique. An advisor can "use 72(t) to generate sales" by helping clients who have taken early retirement set up a segregated IRA (to support a SOSEPP to pay for living expenses) and meanwhile preserve tax deferral for the rest of the retirement funds in another IRA (presumably invested by the advisor).

Individuals have used pre-age 59½ distribution programs to finance early retirement, or just to achieve a better estate balance when IRA assets constituted a disproportionate share of the estate. One individual believed that making capital gain-generating investments *outside* his IRA would be more favorable tax-wise than continuing to make tax-deferred ordinary income-generating investments *inside* the IRA, so he took a series of equal payments to finance these capital gain investments. A § 72(t) series of equal payments may also be used to fund life insurance premium payments.

Another Temkin idea: Suppose your clients are a young couple. Right now, their estates consist mainly of large IRAs, but they expect to inherit substantial sums in the future from their parents. In view of their eventual expected estate tax problem, they would like to begin making annual gifts to their own children. § 72(t) allows them to take out enough from their IRAs each year to fund their annual gifting program, without penalty.

9.3 Making Changes after SOSEPP Has Begun

9.3.01 *Severe penalty for modification of series*

If the Participant "modifies" his series of payments before he has completed the required series duration (¶ 9.3.02) he is severely punished. His qualification for the SOSEPP exception is retroactively revoked, and he owes the penalty for all series payments he took prior to age 59½, with interest.

If a taxpayer makes a forbidden modification of his series of equal payments, his "tax for the 1st taxable year in which such modification occurs shall be increased by an amount, determined under regulations, equal to the tax which (but for paragraph (2)(A)(iv)) would have been imposed [under § 72(t)], plus interest for the deferral period." § 72(t)(4)(A).

§ 72(t)(4)(B) defines the "deferral period" over which interest must be calculated, but its definition doesn't make much sense. It is: "the period beginning with the taxable year in which (without regard to paragraph (2)(A)(iv)) [which contains the SOSEPP exception] the distribution *would have been includible in gross income* and ending with the taxable year in which the modification" occurs. This shows that even Congress is confused between "penalty-free" (what the § 72(t) exceptions are all about) and "income tax-free" (which § 72(t) has no bearing on), since *any* distribution from the retirement plan "would have been includible" in the Participant's gross income, regardless of whether it qualified under paragraph (2)(A)(iv).

For how to determine when the no-modifications period ends, see ¶ 9.3.02. For the effect of divorce, see ¶ 9.3.08. For death and disability exceptions to the no-modifications rule, see ¶ 9.3.03. For the ability to switch to the RMD method in mid-stream without such change being treated as a modification, see ¶ 9.3.04. For other events that have been found to be or not to be a modification, see ¶ 9.3.06 and ¶ 9.3.07.

9.3.02 *When the no-modifications period begins and ends*

The beginning date of the no-modifications period is the date of the first payment in the series. The ending date is the fifth anniversary of the date of the first payment in the series, or, *if later*, the date on which the Participant attains age 59½. § 72(t)(4)(A). Once this ending date is passed, payments may be freely taken from the plan without penalty (or the series may be suspended—*i.e.*, the Participant can STOP taking payments).

Note that the ending date of the five years is not simply the date of the fifth year's payment. The five years ends on the *fifth anniversary of the first payment.* In the case of *Arnold v. Comm'r*, 111 T.C. No. 250, the taxpayer, at age 55, took the first of a series of equal annual payments of $44,000 in December 1989. He took the second, third, fourth, and fifth payments in the series in January 1990, 1991, 1992, and 1993, respectively. In September 1993 he turned 59½, and, thinking he had now completed his greater-of-five-years-or-until-age-59½ requirement (because he had taken all five of the annual required payments and was over age 59½), he took another distribution of $6,776 in November 1993 from the same IRA.

The Tax Court, citing legislative history regarding how to calculate the five-year period, held that this $6,776 distribution was an impermissible modification of the SOSEPP because it occurred during the five years beginning on the date of the first distribution. Therefore, the taxpayer's qualification for the SOSEPP exception was retroactively revoked, and he owed the 10% penalty, plus interest, on all five of his $44,000 distributions!

9.3.03 *Exceptions for death or disability*

If the series is modified "by reason of death or disability" there is no penalty. § 72(t)(4)(A). IRS Publication 590, "Individual Retirement Arrangements (IRAs)" (2000) echoes this, saying that a modification does not result in penalty if the "change from an approved distribution method is because of the death or disability of the IRA owner" (p. 20). Presumably death automatically ends the requirement of continuing the series, since death benefits are exempt from the penalty (¶ 9.4.01). Regarding "disability," first, such disability presumably must be the type of total disability that justifies penalty-free distributions (see ¶ 9.4.02). It is not clear whether the occurrence of such a disability *automatically* ends the requirement of continuing the series, or whether the Participant must somehow demonstrate that the series had to be modified *because* of the disability—for example, by showing that the Participant had to increase his distributions because of his disability.

9.3.04 *Changing to RMD method is not a modification*

Apparently many taxpayers took advantage of the SOSEPP exception during the 1990's, using the annuitization or amortization methods. The stock market declines of 2000-2002 placed many such individuals in a difficult position: if they kept taking their payments at the rate originally established, the retirement account would be reduced to nothing, not only prior to death but even prior to age 59½.

Rev. Rul. 2002-62 allows a Participant using the annuitization or amortization method to change to the RMD method. Because the RMD method requires annual revaluation of the account balance, a downturn in the account value will translate into a reduction in the subsequent year's payment. Thus, the series payments will shrink along with the account value and the account will never run dry.

There are other reasons besides a stock market downturn why a Participant might want to switch to the RMD method. If the investments perform substantially better than the growth assumption used in designing the SOSEPP, switching to the RMD method allows the Participant to increase his payments. As noted above (¶ 9.2.07), a Participant who elected to use the Joint and Survivor Life Table can, if using the RMD method, manipulate the size of his payments by changing his designated beneficiary.

9.3.05 *How to switch to RMD method: requirements and example*

Here are the requirements for a Participant who is using the annuitization or amortization method to switch to the RMD method from Rev. Rul. 2002-62, Sec. 2.03(b):

A.   He must have used the annuitization or amortization method for the first year's distributions under the SOSEPP. He can then switch to the RMD method in the second or any subsequent year.

B.   The switch, once made, is irrevocable. The switch is effective for the year in which it is made and all subsequent years. Any further changes will be considered "modifications."

C.   When he switches, it appears probable that he must continue to use the same life expectancy table (¶ 9.2.06) that his series was originally based on, IF his SOSEPP commenced in 2003 or later. However, this point is not quite clear in the Revenue Ruling. The last two sentences of Sec. 2.02(a) say: "*In the case of the required minimum distribution method*, the same life expectancy table that is used for the first distribution year must be used in each following year. Thus, if the taxpayer uses the single life expectancy table *for the required minimum distribution method* in the first distribution year, the same table must be used in subsequent distribution years." The italicized words create the impression that this rule does not apply to someone who is making a switch to the RMD method from the annuitization or amortization method; in other words, this wording suggests that when someone switches to the RMD method he can *also* choose a new life expectancy method. But Sec. 3 creates the opposite impression, stating that a person who is taking a series *that commenced prior to 2003* can change "at any time to the required minimum distribution method, *including use of a different life expectancy table*." This wording suggests that a person whose series commences after 2002 may not switch to a different life expectancy even if he switches to the RMD method. Further IRS clarification is needed.

D.   A person whose annuitization or amortization method SOSEPP commenced *prior to 2003* can switch to the RMD method at any time, "including use of a different life expectancy table." Rev. Rul. 2002-62, Sec. 3.

Example: Susanna began an annual-payment SOSEPP in 1999 at age 54, using the amortization method. Based on the reasonable interest rate assumption supplied by the actuary who designed the series, her annual payments from the IRA (which was then worth $2 million) were $110,000. By 12/31/01, the account value had declined to $1.4 million. By 9/30/02 the account value had declined to $800,000. Susanna (who had not yet taken her 2002 distribution as of 9/30/02) switched to the RMD method in 2002, the year she turns 57. Because her SOSEPP commenced prior to 2003, she can choose a life expectancy table as part of her switch to the RMD method. The beneficiary of her IRA on 1/1/02 is her husband who also turned 57 in 2002.

If she uses the 9/30/02 valuation date to calculate her 2002 distribution, her life expectancy factor choices look like this:

$800,000 ÷ Factor from Single Life Table for age 57 (27.9) = $28,674.

$800,000 ÷ Factor from Uniform Lifetime Table for age 57 (39.7) = $20,151.

$800,000 ÷ Factor from Joint and Survivor Life Table for ages 57 and 57 (33.7) = $23,739.

If she uses the 12/31/01 valuation date to calculate her 2002 distribution, her life expectancy factor choices look like this:

$1,400,000 ÷ Factor from Single Life Table for age 57 (27.9) = $50,179.

$1,400,000 ÷ Factor from Uniform Lifetime Table for age 57 (39.7) = $35,264.

$1,400,000 ÷ Factor from Joint and Survivor Life Table for ages 57 and 57 (33.7) = $41,543.

Because of the wide fluctuation in value she has quite a range of choices (from $20,151 to $50,179) for the first year. She chooses the Uniform Lifetime Table and 12/31/01 valuation date, and accordingly takes a distribution of $35,264 in 2002. She will have to stick with the Uniform Lifetime Table for the rest of the no-modifications period, which expires when she reaches age 59½ in about two years.

9.3.06 What other changes do NOT constitute a modification?

The following changes in a SOSEPP have either been ruled not to be prohibited modifications, or have occurred without negative comment in cases or rulings involving other issues:

A. When the paying agent, as part of a change in its computer systems, changed the date of monthly payments in a series to the first day of the month (instead of the last day of the preceding month), the change was ruled to be "ministerial," and not a "modification," even though the change meant that the recipient's income would include one fewer payment for the year the switch was made. PLR 9514026.

B.   The taxpayer in PLR 9221052 was receiving monthly payments from a money purchase pension plan. When that plan terminated in the middle of his SOSEPP, he sought to roll over the termination distribution to an IRA and continue paying himself the monthly payments from the IRA. The IRS ruled that this change would not constitute a modification.

C.   In the case of annual payments, it apparently does not matter exactly when during the year the payment is taken; in other words it does not have to be on the anniversary of the first payment to avoid having a "modification." See Rev. Rul. 2002-62, Sec. 2.02(d). See PLR 9747039, in which the IRS ruled that the taxpayer would qualify for the exception "if [he] received at least five annual payments of $510,000 from IRA Y (at least one during each of the years 1997, 1998, 1999, 2000 and 2001) and does not otherwise modify his IRA distribution scheme." See also *Arnold v. Comm'r*, discussed at ¶ 9.3.02, where the taxpayer took his first annual payment in December of 1989 and his subsequent annual payments in January each year, and the opinion contains no negative comment on this procedure.

D.   As noted, the amortization and annuitization methods provide for fixed payments. If investment performance is poor, these payments might exhaust the account. Running out of money due to taking the payments called for by a properly designed annuitization or amortization SOSEPP will not be considered a "modification" of the series. Rev. Rul. 2002-62.

9.3.07 *What changes DO constitute a modification?*

Examples of prohibited modifications of a SOSEPP include:

1.   Terminating the series (*i.e.*, ceasing to take the payments). See PLR 9818055.

2.   Taking an extra payment (*i.e.*, a payment that is over and above

the payments required as part of the series) from the plan or IRA that is supporting the series (see *Arnold v. Comm'r*, discussed at ¶ 9.3.02).

3. Probably, changing from annual payments to quarterly or monthly payments (or vice versa), even if the total payments for the year add up to the right amount. There is no authority or precedent for the proposition that the size of individual payments in the series does not matter so long as the annual total is the same each year.

4. "[A]ny nontaxable transfer of a portion of the account balance to another retirement plan" will be a modification of the series. Rev. Rul. 2002-62, Sec. 2.02(e)(ii). See ¶ 9.3.08 for effect of this rule on a divorce-related division of the retirement account.

5. Changing how the payments in the series are determined:

Example: In PLR 9821056, taxpayer retired at 47 and started a series of equal annual payments from his IRA. These payments were based on his then-life expectancy, existing account balance and projected rate of return. Five years later he wanted to recalculate the rest of the required payments, based on his new life expectancy and account balance and a new projected rate of return that reflected the actual investment experience of the account (which had been much more favorable than originally projected). He sought a ruling from the IRS that this would not be a "modification," on the theory that the change amounted to merely an adjustment to reflect actual experience, and the series was in fact continuing exactly as before. Unfortunately for him, the IRS ruled that "such a proposed change in payments...would be a modification."

Ironically, this taxpayer probably could have designed his series initially to build in the flexibility the IRS did not allow him to add later. For example, in PLR 9531039 the IRS approved an annuitization-method SOSEPP that called for the annual redetermination of the so-called "equal payments" based on the individual's redetermined life expectancy, account balance and interest rate. Alternatively, this taxpayer could have kept some of his IRA money in another account, separate from the account supporting the SOSEPP, and used the second IRA to start a second SOSEPP later (¶ 9.2.13). Especially with younger clients, it is desirable to build flexibility into the program.

9.3.08 *Effect of divorce on the SOSEPP*

If the Participant gets divorced in the middle of his SOSEPP, the odds are that his spouse will be awarded a share of the IRA (or other retirement plan that is supporting the SOSEPP). What happens to his SOSEPP in that case?

Usually the spouse's share is given to her by means of a tax-free transfer to the spouse's account, under a QDRO (§ 414(p)) or the IRA equivalent (§ 408(d)(6)). Rev. Rul. 2002-62 gave the IRS the perfect opportunity to say that, in the event of such a tax-free transfer of a portion of a SOSEPP-supporting IRA or other plan to the Participant's spouse, the Participant could reduce his SOSEPP payments by the same proportion as the amount of the account transferred to the spouse. Or that a Participant could switch to the RMD method in that event, so his payments would automatically adjust downwards.

Unfortunately the IRS did not say either of those things. Instead they said just the opposite: "any nontaxable transfer of a portion of the account balance to another retirement plan" WILL be a modification of the series. Rev. Rul. 2002-62, Sec. 2.02(e)(ii). Thus, every taxpayer in this situation <u>must</u> seek a letter ruling (with attendant filing fees and legal fees; extra costs people do not need when they are getting divorced), not only to change the amount of their SOSEPP payments, but even to avoid having the divorce-transfer itself be considered a modification.

Prior to Rev. Rul. 2002-62, the IRS had dealt sensibly with this situation in letter rulings. In PLR 9739044, a taxpayer got divorced after commencing his SOSEPP. The IRAs supporting the series were community property. The divorce court divided the IRAs and gave half of each to the taxpayer's ex-wife. Both spouses then apparently continued the SOSEPP, with each of them taking (from his or her respective share of the formerly unified IRAs) one half of the required annual distribution. The IRS ruled that, because the division of the IRA between the spouses was non-taxable under § 408(d)(6), and in view of the "continuous compliance with the requirements of § 72(t)(2)(A)(iv)," there was no modification.

The three taxpayers in PLRs 2002-02074, 2002-02075 and 2002-02076 were receiving SOSEPPs from their IRAs. They were losing respectively 50%, 40% and 45% of their IRAs to their spouses in divorce proceedings. The IRS allowed them to reduce their SOSEPP payments by 50%, 40% and 45% respectively, without such reductions being considered a modification. A similar proportionate reduction of SOSEPP payments was allowed in PLR 2002-14034.

9.4 The Other Eleven Exceptions to the Penalty

We now turn to the other exceptions to § 72(t)'s penalty. Although these lack the broadly applicable planning possibilities of the SOSEPP, each can be useful in particular situations.

9.4.01 *Death benefits*

A distribution "made to a beneficiary (or to the estate of the employee) on or after the death of the employee" is exempt from the penalty. § 72(t)(2)(A)(ii). This exception applies to distributions from all types of plans. Thus death benefits may be distributed penalty-free from a qualified plan, 403(b) arrangement or IRA, regardless of whether the *beneficiary* receiving the benefits is over 59½ and regardless of whether the *participant* had attained age 59½ at the time of his death.

Despite the unique clarity of this exception, it generates confusion for the following reason: If a surviving spouse rolls over benefits inherited from the deceased spouse to the surviving spouse's *own* IRA, the rolled-over funds lose the characteristic of "death benefits," and become simply part of the surviving spouse's own retirement account. Thus, distributions from the rollover IRA will once again be subject to the § 72(t) penalty rules if the surviving spouse is under age 59½—even if the deceased spouse was over age 59½ when he died. See ¶ 3.2.02 for further discussion.

9.4.02 *Distributions "attributable" to total disability*

A distribution that is "attributable to the employee's being disabled" is not subject to the penalty. § 72(t)(2)(A)(iii).

"Disabled" is defined in § 72(m)(7): it means "unable to engage in any substantial gainful activity by reason of any medically determinable physical or mental impairment which can be expected to result in death or to be of long-continued and indefinite duration. An individual shall not be considered to be disabled unless he furnishes proof of the existence thereof [sic] in such form and manner as the

Secretary may require." Note that the definition requires *total* disability. In PLR 2002-14029, a disabled taxpayer sought approval for a SOSEPP (¶ 9.2); presumably he was not disabled enough to qualify for the disability exception.

Reg. § 1.72-17A(f)(1), (2), (interpreting § 72(m) as it applies to lump sum distributions to self-employed persons) provides the following further elaboration on this definition: "In determining whether an individual's impairment makes him unable to engage in any substantial gainful activity, primary consideration shall be given to the nature and severity of his impairment. Consideration shall also be given to other factors such as the individual's education, training, and work experience. The substantial gainful activity to which section 72(m)(7) refers is the activity, or a comparable activity, in which the individual customarily engaged prior to the arising of the disability or prior to retirement if the individual was retired at the time the disability arose." Although the IRS's own regulation says that the "gainful activity" referred to is the individual's customary activity or a comparable one, IRS Publication 590, "Individual Retirement Arrangements (IRAs)" (2000) (at page 20) erroneously says you must be able to "furnish proof that you cannot do *any* substantial gainful activity because of your physical or mental condition" (emphasis added).

Another IRS requirement in Publication 590, "Individual Retirement Arrangements (IRAs)" (2000) is that "A *physician* must determine that your condition can be expected to result in death or to be of long continued and indefinite duration" (emphasis added). This requirement is not waived for those whose religious beliefs prohibit them from hiring physicians; the Tax Court points out that the regulation does not impair the free exercise of religion, it just makes such exercise more expensive in some cases. *Fohrmeister v. Comm'r*, 73 T.C. Memo 2483, 2486 (1997).

Reg. § 1.72-17A(f) also lists certain impairments, such as "Damage to the brain or brain abnormality which has resulted in severe loss of judgment, intellect, orientation, or memory," which are said to "ordinarily," but not "in and of themselves," result in the necessary impairment.

An individual suffering from depression was not "disabled" where he continued his normal occupation (securities trading). *Dwyer v. Comm'r*, 106 T.C. 337 (1996). Earning a salary and starting an engineering business are both activities that are "inconsistent with the exigencies of the statutory definition of disability." *Kovacevic v.*

Comm'r, 64 TCM 1076 (1992) (another depression case).

What does it mean that the distribution must be "attributable" to the disability? Contrast this wording with § 402(d)/(e)(4)(A) (the definition of "lump sum distribution"), which gives lump sum distribution status to an otherwise-qualifying distribution made "after the employee has become disabled," without any requirement that the distribution be "attributable to" the disability.

If the distribution is from an employer plan, and is specifically triggered by a provision in the plan calling for distribution of benefits in case of total disability, then the distribution is clearly "attributable" to the employee's being disabled. If the plan does not specifically provide for disability benefits, but does provide for distribution of benefits upon termination of employment, and the cause of the termination of employment was the employee's disability, once again it would appear the distribution is "attributable" to the employee's being disabled.

But what if the termination of employment occurred long before the disability struck? Or what if the distribution is from an IRA, distributions from which can be taken at any time without regard to either disability or termination of employment? In Publication 590, "Individual Retirement Arrangements (IRAs)" (2000), the IRS reiterates (at page 18) that the distribution from an IRA must be "because" of the disability to qualify for this exception. Some commentators assume that any distribution to a totally disabled person is automatically exempt from the penalty. However, it is possible that the IRS will require the Participant to demonstrate that the distribution was *necessitated* by the disability (*e.g.*, to substitute for employment income lost due to the disability).

9.4.03 *Distributions to pay deductible medical expenses*

Distributions after 1996 from any type of plan are penalty-free "to the extent such distributions do not exceed the amount allowable as a deduction under § 213 to the employee for amounts paid during the taxable year for medical care (determined without regard to whether the employee itemizes deductions for such taxable year)." § 72(t)(2)(B). "During the taxable year" presumably means "during the taxable year in which the distribution is received."

This exception may increase the medical problems of the Participant by giving him a severe headache. Medical expenses are deductible under § 213 only to the extent such expenses exceed 7.5% of adjusted gross income. § 213(a). But the plan distribution *itself* is includible in gross income and thus decreases the "amount allowable as a deduction."

Example: Cathy's adjusted gross income for the year, before taking any distribution from her IRA, is $100,000. Cathy is 53. She has medical expenses of $10,000. Her medical expenses are deductible to the extent they exceed 7.5% of $100,000 or $7,500, so (again before considering any IRA distribution) she can deduct $2,500 of her medical expenses. She withdraws $2,500 from the IRA to help pay those medical expenses. However, the IRA distribution increases her adjusted gross income to $102,500, thus *decreasing* her permitted medical expense deduction to $2,312.50 ($10,000 of medical expenses minus [$102,500 X 7.5%=$7,687.50]=$2,312.50). So she owes the 10% penalty on $187.50 of the distribution (total penalty $18.75).

To avoid the penalty, while still taking advantage of the ability to withdraw from the plan to pay deductible medical expenses, the individual would have to perform a circular calculation, so that the distribution does not exceed [total medical expenses] minus 7.5% of [distribution plus other adjusted gross income]. Of course this assumes that the individual can determine his adjusted gross income and medical expenses to the penny on or before December 31 of the year in question, since a distribution must be matched with medical expenses incurred in the year of the distribution, not some preceding year.

9.4.04 *QRPs, 403(b) plans: separation from service after age 55*

A distribution from an employer plan made to an employee "after separation from service after attainment of age 55" is exempt from the penalty. § 72(t)(2)(A)(v). This exception is available for qualified plans and 403(b) plans, but not for IRA distributions. § 72(t)(3)(A).

An employee who separates from the company's service *before* age 55 is not entitled to use this exception; an employee who quits, retires or is fired before he reaches age 55 cannot simply wait until age 55 and then take a penalty-free distribution. The exception is available for distributions "made to you after you separated from service with your employer if the separation occurred during or after the calendar year in which you reached age 55." IRS Publication 575, "Pension and Annuity Income" (1997) (at page 32). Note that although IRS Publication 575 and Notice 87-13, 1987-1 C.B. 432, A-20, both state that the exception applies to separations from service occurring on or after *January 1* of the year the employee reaches age 55, § 72(t) itself limits the exception to distributions made after separations occurring after the actual 55th birthday.

Also, the distribution must occur after the separation from service, not before. *Humberson v. Comm'r*, 70 TCM 886 (1995).

9.4.05 *QRPs, 403(b) plans: QDRO distributions*

Distributions from a qualified retirement plan or 403(b) arrangement (but not from an IRA) made to an "alternate payee" under a qualified domestic relations order ("QDRO") (see § 414(p)(1)) are exempt from the early distributions penalty. § 72(t)(2)(C). This book does not cover QDROs.

9.4.06 *ESOPs only: certain stock dividends*

This Chapter generally does not cover special rules applicable to "employee stock ownership plans" ("ESOPs"). Under § 404(k), a company can take a tax deduction for dividends paid on stock that is held by an ESOP, and the ESOP can pass these dividends out to the plan participants, if various requirements are met. Such dividend payments are not subject to the 10% penalty. § 72(t)(2)(A)(vi).

9.4.07 *IRAs only: health insurance premiums for the unemployed*

In years after 1996, an unemployed individual can take penalty-free distributions from his IRA (but not from a qualified plan or 403(b) arrangement) to pay health insurance premiums. § 72(t)(2)(D). Here are the specific requirements for this exception:

The person must have separated from his employment, and, as a result of that separation, must have "received unemployment compensation for 12 consecutive weeks under any Federal or State unemployment compensation law." The distributions must be made during the year "during which such unemployment compensation is paid or the succeeding taxable year." Presumably this phrase does not imply that the 12 consecutive weeks' worth of unemployment compensation must all be received in the same taxable year, but presumably it does mean that the unemployed person does not become eligible until the year the 12 consecutive weeks are completed.

Does this clause mean that the unemployed person can take penalty-free distributions only in one year—*either* the year he completes the 12 weeks of unemployment benefits *or* the following year? Or does it mean that penalty-free distributions may be taken in both years? The IRS has offered no enlightenment.

The maximum distribution under this exception in any taxable year is the amount paid for "insurance described in § 213(d)(1)(D) [medical and long term care insurance] with respect to the individual and the individual's spouse and dependents." Also, the distribution must be made either while the individual is still unemployed or, if he becomes employed again, less than 60 days after he has been re-employed.

The IRS, in regulations, can permit a self-employed individual to use this exception "if, under Federal or State law, the individual would have received unemployment compensation but for the fact the individual was self-employed." No such regulations have been issued.

9.4.08 *IRAs only: distributions to pay expenses of higher education*

The 10% penalty will not apply to IRA distributions that do not exceed the taxpayer's "qualified higher education expenses" for the taxable year of the distribution. This exception is not available for distributions from qualified plans or 403(b) arrangements. § 72(t)(2)(E).

The distribution in question must be made after 1997 and be to pay for education provided in "academic periods" beginning after 1997; see IRS Notice 97-53, 1997-40 IRB 6, for full details. The distribution must be to pay for education furnished to the taxpayer or his spouse, or to any child or grandchild of either of them. (It's pretty fast work for a taxpayer under age 59½ to have college-age grandchildren.)

This exception borrows definitions from the Code section allowing various tax breaks to "qualified state tuition programs" (§ 529(e)(3)) for the type of expenses covered ("tuition, fees, books, supplies, and equipment required for the enrollment or attendance of a designated beneficiary at an eligible educational institution") and eligible institutions. "Eligible Institutions" include "virtually all accredited public, non-profit, and proprietary post-secondary institutions," according to Notice 97-60, 1997-46 IRB 1, Sec. 4, A-2.

Notice 97-60 provides many other details regarding this exception, including the fact that room and board are among the covered expenses if the student is enrolled at least half-time.

To the extent the education expenses in question are paid for by a scholarship, federal education grant, tax-free distribution from an Education IRA (§ 530), tax-free employer-provided educational assistance, or other payment that is excludible from gross income (other than gifts, inheritances, loans or savings), they cannot also be used to support a penalty-free IRA distribution. § 72(t)(7)(B), § 25A(g)(2); Notice 97-60, Sec. 4, A-1.

9.4.09 IRAs only: distribution to help purchase someone's first home

"Qualified first-time homebuyer distributions" from an IRA are not subject to the penalty. § 72(t)(2)(F). An individual can withdraw from his IRA (but not from a qualified plan or 403(b) arrangement) up to $10,000, without paying the 10% penalty, if the distribution is used "before the close of the 120th day after the day on which such payment or distribution is received to pay qualified acquisition costs with respect to a principal residence of a first-time homebuyer who is such individual, the spouse of such individual, or any child, grandchild, or ancestor of such individual or the individual's spouse." § 72(t)(8)(A). For such a small exception, this one is quite complicated. Note the following:

The $10,000 is a lifetime limit. It applies to the person making the withdrawal (the IRA owner), not the person buying the home.

Example: Mom and Dad, both age 54, want to help Junior, age 27, buy his first home. All three of them have IRAs. Mom and Junior each withdraw $10,000 penalty-free from their respective IRAs, and Dad withdraws $5,000 from his IRA penalty-free, to help pay for Junior's new home. (Note each will have to pay *income taxes* on these withdrawals; only the 10% penalty is waived.) The following year, Sis, age 25, wants to buy *her* first home. But Mom can't dip into her IRA penalty-free to help Sis out because Mom has already used up her $10,000 lifetime limit for such withdrawals. Dad still has $5,000 left that he can withdraw penalty-free to help Sis buy her home; otherwise, Sis is on her own.

"Principal residence" has the same meaning as in § 121 (exclusion of gain on sale of principal residence). § 72(t)(8)(D)(ii). § 121 itself does not contain a definition of "principal residence." Reg. § 1.121-1(b) says the determination depends on all the "facts and circumstances"; refer to that regulation if there is doubt as to whether a particular residence is the homebuyer's principal residence.

"Qualified acquisition costs" are the costs of "acquiring, constructing, or reconstructing a residence", including "usual or reasonable settlement, financing, or other closing costs." § 72(t)(8)(C).

A "first-time homebuyer" is not someone who has literally never owned a home before. It is a person who has had no "present ownership interest in a principal residence during the 2-year period ending on the date of acquisition of the" residence being financed by the distribution. If the homebuyer is married, both spouses must meet this test. § 72(t)(8)(D).

The "date of acquisition" is the date "a binding contract to acquire" the home is entered into, or "on which construction or reconstruction of such a principal residence is commenced"—but, if there is a "delay or cancellation of the purchase or construction" [what about *re*construction?] and, solely for that reason, the distribution fails to meet the 120-day test, the distribution can be rolled back into the IRA; AND the rollover back into the IRA will be a qualified tax-free rollover, even if it occurs more than 60 days after the distribution, so long as it occurs within 120 days of the distribution, AND the rollover back into the IRA will not count for purposes of the one-rollover-per-year limit of § 408(d)(3)(B). § 72(t)(8)(E). What could be simpler!

Finally, to the extent the distribution in question qualifies for one of the *other* exceptions (*e.g.*, a distribution to pay higher education or deductible medical expenses, or health insurance premiums for an unemployed person, or on account of death or total disability, or part of a SOSEPP), it will not count as a "first-time homebuyer" distribution even if it is used to pay expenses that would qualify it for the first-time homebuyer exception. § 72(t)(2)(F).

9.4.10 *IRS levy on the account*

Generally, even an involuntary distribution is subject to the penalty. IRS Notice 87-13, 1987-1 C.B. 432. However, over the protests of the IRS, the Tax Court has excused certain taxpayers from the penalty when their benefits were seized by the government. See, *e.g., Murillo v. Comm'r*, 75 T.C. Memo 1564 (1998); this case contains references to earlier cases on point. For distributions after 1999, there is some statutory relief from this situation: If the retirement plan is taken by an IRS levy under § 6331, the forced "distribution" will not be subject to the 10% penalty. § 72(t)(2)(A)(vii).

9.4.11 *Return of certain excess contributions*

Certain excess contributions to "cash-or-deferred-arrangement" plans (such as 401(k) plans) may be distributed penalty-free if various requirements are met. See § 401(k)(8)(D) and § 402(g)(2)(C).

9.5 Summary of Planning Principles

1.   Be aware that distributions (even inadvertent distributions) to a Participant under age 59½ generally trigger a 10% penalty.

2.   If a client wants to take money from a retirement plan prior to age 59½, refer to this Chapter to determine whether he qualifies for an exception. Note carefully the requirements of any possibly applicable exception (*e.g.*, make sure it is available for the type of plan involved). Do not expect the exceptions to operate in a logical, fair and consistent manner.

3.   If a client has an IRA (or can create one by rollover from another type of plan), consider the highly flexible "SOSEPP" exception as a possible funding source for gifting programs, life insurance premium payments and other expenditures. Consider hiring an actuary to help design a substantial or creative SOSEPP. In general, create the smallest possible separate IRA to support the desired size of payment, and preserve as much flexibility as possible for future changes in the client's needs. See the Quentin case study, Chapter 11.

4.   The penalty does not apply to post-death distributions, but a surviving spouse who rolls over death benefits to her own retirement plan loses the exemption for death benefits.

10

The "How To" Chapter

How to do "life and death planning" for clients' retirement benefits in various situations, and ideas for dealing with some perennial problems in this field

The preceding nine chapters explain what the law is. This Chapter reassembles some of the information from the point of view of what a practitioner might do with clients: guidance on distributions during life (¶ 10.1); ideas for fixing a trust that does not comply with the minimum distribution rules (¶ 10.2); disability planning for retirement benefits (¶ 10.3); checklist of issues in advising beneficiaries (¶ 10.4); and drawbacks of funding a credit shelter or QTIP trust with retirement benefits (and suggested ways around the problem) (¶ 10.5).

10.1 How to Take Lifetime Distributions

This ¶ 10.1 answers the question "Should I withdraw money from my retirement plan—even if I don't have to?" (listing both tax and non-tax reasons to take non-required distributions), and provides practical tips for taking required distributions.

10.1.01 *Taking out extra: to reduce taxes*

If money could stay in the retirement plan for a long enough period of time, the economic benefits of long-term tax-free investing would probably outweigh ANY tax advantage that might accrue by taking the money out right now. However, it may not be possible to leave the money in the plan long enough to reap these rewards for many reasons, such as: the minimum distribution rules (Chapter 1), which require distribution of the plan assets at a certain point; or the plan doesn't offer a long-term payout option (¶ 1.5.09); or the beneficiaries will have to withdraw the money right after Participant's death to pay estate taxes, or to spend. Weigh the advantages of whatever income tax deferral is *realistically* available against the following possible tax advantages of Participant's taking out of the plan, right now, more than is required:

Participant is in an unusually low tax bracket this year. In this case, also consider Roth IRA conversion instead of a straight distribution, if Participant qualifies. See ¶ 5.4. In fact, the option of converting to a Roth should always be kept in mind for any Participant who qualifies; see Chapter 5 for list of reasons to convert to a Roth and eligibility requirements.

Participant could take a distribution that would qualify for an especially low tax rate, such as a distribution of employer securities with "net unrealized appreciation" (¶ 2.4), or special averaging treatment (¶ 2.3).

Participant wants to make gifts to reduce his future estate taxes and the only source of funds is the retirement plan. The estate tax savings may outweigh the income tax advantages of leaving money in the plan. This strategy would appeal to someone who does not expect the estate tax to be repealed prior to his death.

If Participant's life expectancy is severely shortened (e.g., terminal illness), and it is expected that the estate will be subject to estate taxes, see ¶ 2.2.08, ¶ 2.4.08 and ¶ 5.5.06 for planning strategies.

If there are no non-retirement plan assets to fund a "credit shelter trust" in case of Participant's death, consider withdrawing funds now so such a trust could be funded with after-tax dollars (see ¶ 10.5.03, Solution H, for more on this).

Match withdrawals to large charitable gifts to obtain a charitable income tax deduction. In this situation, also keep an eye on the "Charitable IRA Rollover Bill" (see ¶ 7.6.01).

If there is life insurance in the retirement plan, consider removing it so the policy can be transferred to an estate tax-free insurance trust; see ¶ 8.4.01. Also consider removing a life insurance policy (or any other plan asset) from a plan at any time that you believe its current value is relatively low. See ¶ 8.4.04, E, and "Dr. Della" case study (Chapter 11).

If Participant has underpaid his estimated taxes and is coming up on the end of the year, consider taking a withdrawal from the retirement plan and having the plan administrator send 100% of the distribution to the IRS as withheld income taxes. See ¶ 2.1.08.

Whenever contemplating a tax-saving strategy that involves Participant's taking more out of a retirement plan than is required, keep financial planning in mind. If client's primary need is to have money to live on during retirement, leaving the money in the plan may be the best way to accomplish that goal, even if in the long run it may cost the surviving beneficiaries more taxes.

Consider also the other drawbacks of taking money out of a retirement plan, that may or may not apply in any particular case, such as: loss of creditor protection: (money inside a retirement plan may qualify for protection from claims of creditors; taking the money out of the plan may increase vulnerability); loss of future income tax deferral on the funds withdrawn; and loss of any special "grandfather" status that may be applicable (see ¶ 8.5).

10.1.02 *Taking out extra: non-tax reasons*

If Participant needs cash for living expenses or other goals, and must choose between (1) selling appreciated assets that he holds outside the plan and (2) taking the money out of a retirement plan, which should he do? Selling assets outside the plan causes lower immediate taxes if the profit is taxed as long-term capital gain (because the tax is only 20% of the gain portion of the sale price) than taking a plan distribution (normally fully taxable as ordinary income; see ¶ 2.1.03 for exceptions). However, the appreciated assets, if held until Participant's death rather than being sold, will get a "stepped-up basis" at Participant's death (if he dies before 2010; or, in many cases, even if he dies after 2009), while the retirement benefits will not (¶ 2.2.01)—so taking the money from a retirement plan may result in lower income taxes over the long term.

Non-tax reasons to consider taking money out of a retirement plan include balancing assets between retirement and non-retirement plan investments: because retirement plan assets are especially vulnerable to government policy whims (such as changing tax rates or distribution rules), a person who has almost all his assets inside retirement plans might want to take some assets out when it is reasonably favorable to do so, in order to build up the possibly less vulnerable non-retirement plan side of his balance sheet.

A Participant could withdraw funds from a profit sharing plan to avoiding the necessity of obtaining spousal consent to Participant's choice of a death beneficiary (see ¶ 3.4.03); or, prior to marriage, from any QRP to avoid giving his future spouse REA rights (¶ 3.4).

If Participant is under age 59½, structure the distributions as a "series of substantially equal periodic payments" (¶ 9.2) or other form of distribution that is exempt from the 10% premature distributions tax (¶ 9.4).

Consider also the other drawbacks of taking money out of a retirement plan listed at ¶ 10.1.01 (last sentence).

10.1.03 *How to take minimum required distributions*

Take minimum required distributions (MRDs) as late in the year as possible, to maximize income tax deferral. With late-in-the-year MRDs, consider having the plan administrator or IRA provider send the entire amount to the IRS as withheld income taxes (see ¶ 2.1.08).

If using the late-in-the-year distribution strategy (especially if combining it with the withholding strategy), Participant must be careful not to die before taking the distribution. Death before taking the distribution would make the withholding strategy impossible, and also would set the beneficiaries up for a penalty because they might not have enough time before year-end to complete the MRD.

When commencing MRDs from an employer plan, if the employee has both an "employee contribution account" and an "employer contribution account" in the plan, use the former to satisfy the MRD requirement for both accounts, to maximize the tax-free portion of MRDs (see ¶ 1.9.03). This strategy does not work with IRAs (see ¶ 5.4.10-¶ 5.4.12).

If an IRA holds a hard-to-value asset such as a limited partnership, and Participant is concerned that the IRS might decide the asset is worth more than Participant thinks it is, Participant can be sure he will avoid the 50% penalty (¶ 1.10.02) by taking a proportionate share of that asset as part of his MRD. For example, if the MRD for the year is 1/26th of the prior year end value, Participant can be sure he is taking "enough" of that hard-to-value asset by distributing a 1/26th interest in the asset to himself shortly after the prior-year-end valuation date (and of course also taking out 1/26th of the other assets in the account). This will not avoid underpayment of income taxes if the IRS later decides the asset is undervalued on the IRA's books; it just avoids the § 4974 penalty (because, regardless of what the value of the asset turns out to be, Participant took the required proportion of it). To avoid costly annual appraisals and get the problem behind him, Participant could withdraw the hard-to-value asset entirely.

In general, consider taking distributions in kind to avoid commissions for selling securities.

As to which assets to take out of the plan to satisfy the MRD requirement, choose those you consider most likely to have capital gain-type appreciation in the future, e.g., choose a stock you think is temporarily depressed in price instead of a bond that generates taxable interest but is considered unlikely to increase in price. By removing the stock investment you consider "temporarily" undervalued, you pay tax on the current value (which you think is low), and enjoy capital gain treatment for the expected price rebound. Keep good records of the date of distribution value, as that will be your basis in the distributed securities going forward.

If Participant has multiple IRAs, consider taking all of each year's MRD from only one of them, using Notice 88-38 (¶ 1.9.01). This is administratively easier than taking MRDs from a multitude of accounts, and can be a painless way to close out smaller accounts.

The first year's MRD from a QRP can be combined with a special deal such as NUA (¶ 2.4) or special averaging treatment (¶ 2.3.06). If Participant is eligible for either of these, the deal should be reviewed as soon as possible, because once he has taken a MRD (or any other distribution) in one taxable year these special deals will no longer be available in subsequent years (unless there is a new triggering event), all as explained in ¶ 2.3.

10.2 How to Fix a Non-complying Trust

This ¶ 10.2 provides ideas for what to do with a trust that "flunks" the minimum distribution trust rules (¶ 6.2, ¶ 6.3) after Participant's death.

10.2.01 *Fixing trust while Participant is living*

If a proposed trust has both charitable and non-charitable beneficiaries, and the existence of charitable remainder beneficiaries may cause the trust to flunk the trust rules, see ¶ 7.3.02 and ¶ 7.3.03 for ways to fix the problem.

10.2.02 *After death, before Designation Date*

First, consider whether having the trust comply with the trust rules is an important goal (see ¶ 7.3.03, A). If it *is* an important goal, consider whether it is possible to fix the problem before the "Designation Date" (September 30 of the year after the year of Participant's death; ¶ 1.8) by actions such as the following:

Distribution: If the problem is that the trust has one or more non-individual beneficiaries, consider whether these beneficiaries' interests could be eliminated prior to the Designation Date by distribution (¶ 1.8.05). This solution works to eliminate older beneficiaries and non-individual beneficiaries (such as the estate or charity) who are entitled to amounts that can be ascertained and distributed by the Designation Date.

Disclaimer: Consider whether a charitable or other non-individual (or older) beneficiary would be willing to disclaim its interest; or whether a trustee could disclaim an interest or power. See Chapter 8.

Trust reformation: With proceedings in the Court having jurisdiction of the trust, it may be possible to have the trust reformed, divided into separate trusts or otherwise re-engineered so that the trust that receives the benefits, as of the Designation Date, complies with the trust rules, even if the trust did not comply with such rules on the date of death. While post-death actions to modify a trust are normally *not* effective to accomplish such goals as, e.g. qualifying for the marital deduction, the regulations specifically allow recognition of post-death changes for purposes of the minimum distribution rules. ¶ 1.8.01. Unfortunately, the regulations do not state whether a trust reformation completed prior to the Designation Date is effective to change the trust terms for minimum distribution purposes. Some (all?) reformations could be considered "adding a new beneficiary," a post-death change that is specifically *not* allowed under the final regulations. Reg. § 1.401(a)(9)-4, A-4(a).

10.2.03 *Other ideas*

1.   **Spousal rollover**. The IRS, in its rulings, has been liberal in permitting the spouse to roll over benefits even when Spouse was not named directly as beneficiary, so long as Spouse had the absolute right (as beneficiary of an estate or trust) to receive the benefits. ¶ 3.2.09.

2.   **Wait and see**. If Participant died before his RBD (¶ 1.3), and you believe that the trust should qualify for the life expectancy payout method, but the result is not clear under the regulations, use a "wait and

see" approach. Begin distributions based on the assumption that the trust qualifies, and that the installments-over-life-expectancy method is available. This means making annual installment distributions, beginning by the end of the year after the year of Participant's death, based on the life expectancy of the oldest trust beneficiary. Once four years have elapsed, review the situation again. By then there may be case law, or new IRS guidance providing a new or clearer answer. If the question has been answered unfavorably to your trust, or if it still is ambiguous and you do not want to seek an IRS ruling, you can still comply with the 5-year rule and distribute all benefits by December 31 of the year that contains the fifth anniversary of Participant's death.

3.   **Fight the IRS.** Occasionally the courts have thrown out an IRS regulation as being beyond the scope of statutory authority.

10.3 How to Plan for Disability

10.3.01 *Can benefits be assigned to revocable living trust?*

Can a retirement plan permit Participant to direct the payment of lifetime benefits (disability and retirement) to his revocable living trust? Two Code sections at first appear to pose obstacles to such assignments. § 401(a)(13) prohibits any "assignment" of QRP benefits; however, a voluntary, revocable assignment is not an "assignment" for this purpose, so *this* Code section is not a problem. Reg. § 1.401(a)-13(e). Unfortunately, § 72(p)(1)(B) treats all "assignments" of qualified plan benefits as loans from the plan, apparently taxable as distributions, and neither § 72(p) nor regulations thereunder suggests an exception for a voluntary revocable assignment.

In the author's view, an "assignment" to a revocable trust should not be treated as an assignment for purposes of either § 72(p) or § 401(a)(13) because Participant and his revocable trust are treated as "one person" for income tax purposes under the grantor trust rules (§ 671-§ 677). See Rev. Rul. 85-13, 1985-1 C.B. 184. However, there has been no IRS pronouncement specifically blessing this application of the Rev. Rul. 85-13 principle.

10.3.02 *Power of attorney*

The client's power of attorney should at a minimum enable the power holder to receive benefit checks and endorse them. It can go further and give the holder the power to make elections as to the form and timing of benefits (subject to the rights of client's spouse) but this would necessarily involve the power holder in making choices between the client and the beneficiary of death benefits under the plan. Giving the power to designate a beneficiary of plan death benefits gives even greater responsibility to the power holder. See Form 5.1, Appendix B.

Consider the possibility that the power-holder may have to carry out rollovers when the client is disabled. Carrying out a rollover may involve opening a new IRA (to receive the rolled over distribution), which means naming beneficiaries for the newly-opened account; or may involve substantially increasing the benefits going to the beneficiaries of the recipient account and decreasing the benefits going to the beneficiaries of the distributing account. Problems can be avoided by anticipating the rollover and instructing the power-holder regarding the choice of beneficiary. Consider the following scenarios:

Scenario 1: Participant has significant benefits in a QRP. The plan offers only the lump sum distribution form of death benefit. Participant expects that, when he retires, he will roll the benefits over to an IRA that will offer the life expectancy payout option to Participant's beneficiaries. What will happen if Participant becomes mentally disabled before he retires, when the money is still in the QRP? The distribution and rollover must be carried out, if at all, by Participant's guardian or conservator, or by the holder of Participant's durable power of attorney (DPOA). *Participant's power of attorney should give the power-holder the power to demand, receive and roll over distributions from the QRP and instruct the power-holder who to name as beneficiaries of the rollover IRA.*

Scenario 2: Participant's beneficiary designation form leaves her benefits to her husband as primary beneficiary. Both spouses' expectation is that husband will roll the benefits over to his own IRA and name the children as his beneficiaries. What will happen if husband is mentally disabled when Participant dies? The distribution and rollover must be carried out, if at all, by husband's guardian or conservator, or by the holder of husband's DPOA. *Husband's power of attorney should give the power-holder the power to demand, receive and roll over distributions from plans inherited from Wife, and instruct the power-holder who to name as beneficiaries of the rollover IRA.*

It is advisable to get the client's IRA provider or plan administrator to approve the form of any power of attorney dealing with the benefits. For example, file the power with the client's beneficiary designation and ask the custodian to say in writing that they will honor the form unless they receive notice that it is no longer valid. The point is to get them on board to recognize this particular document, rather than find out after the fact that they won't accept it.

The pre-approval process may be a realistic option only in cases of large individually managed IRAs. In the case of smaller accounts and/or mutual fund IRAs, see if the IRA provider has its own form of power of attorney or will accept a power of attorney if it is filed "pre-need." Unfortunately, some practitioners report that some IRA providers' standard form power of attorney may be too limited to be useful (e.g., not permitting withdrawals from the account).

10.4 How To Represent Beneficiaries

The following discussion assumes you are asked to help one or more non-spouse beneficiaries (for example, a deceased Participant's children) with an inherited IRA that offers the life expectancy payout method of distribution (¶ 1.2.01). If the surviving spouse is a beneficiary, see Chapter 3 instead.

When advising a beneficiary who has inherited an IRA or other retirement plan, you need to cover five issues: the minimum distribution rules (planning opportunities and compliance); establishing separate accounts (if there are two or more beneficiaries); whether a plan-to-plan transfer is needed; the IRD deduction; and naming a successor beneficiary.

10.4.01 *MRDs: planning, compliance*

Minimum required distributions from an inherited retirement plan present both planning opportunities (helping the beneficiaries take advantage of the life expectancy payout method) and compliance challenges (making sure the beneficiaries take out the annual required distribution).

If the plan does not offer the life expectancy payout, and the plan is an IRA, see ¶ 10.4.03. If it's a QRP, ask the plan to purchase a non-assignable fixed or variable annuity contract and distribute *that* to the beneficiaries. See Gorin, S., "Giving to the Grandchildren: Annuities are a great way to pass along QRP benefits to non-spouses," *Trusts & Estates* (Sept. 2002, p. 43), and PLR 2002-44023.

Planning: Explain the valuable income tax deferral opportunity offered by the "life expectancy payout method." See "Lena and Tina" example (¶ 1.2.01). Consider using software (Appendix C) to provide projections and illustrations of the financial rewards of this method.

Compliance: If the Participant died on or after his or her RBD, the first step is to determine whether the Participant withdrew the entire MRD for the year of death; if not, the beneficiary(ies) (not the estate of the Participant—unless the estate is the beneficiary) must take that distribution before the end of the year in which death occurred. The year-of-death MRD is computed using whatever method the Participant used during life. See ¶ 1.5.03.

Once the beneficiaries sign up for the life expectancy payout method, be sure there is someone responsible to calculate the minimum distribution annually and make sure it gets paid. This could be a good occasion for an annual meeting with these clients.

Supervise the transition of the account from the decedent's ownership to the beneficiary's ownership with eagle eyes. The IRA provider's staff may not be aware of the critical issues involved in this step. If the IRA provider issues a check to the beneficiary (who cashes it), or transfers funds from the inherited account to the beneficiary's own IRA, you are faced with a completed distribution (or a distribution followed by an illegal rollover).

Make sure that the IRA provider keeps the IRA titled as an "inherited" IRA. There is no particular required wording for this; the only requirement is that the account documentation must make clear that (even though the beneficiary now owns the account) this is not the "beneficiary's" IRA. The beneficiary cannot contribute to this account for example. Acceptable methods of titling include "John Doe, deceased, for the benefit of Richard Roe, beneficiary," and "Richard Roe, as beneficiary of John Doe, deceased." The name of the deceased Participant should appear somewhere, with indication that beneficiary owns this account merely as beneficiary of the original Participant.

The Social Security number on the account should be the

beneficiary's, despite private letter rulings saying that the decedent's number should be used. See IRS Instructions for Form 1099-R (2001), p. R-5 ("Beneficiaries" section). The opening of the account does not, in itself, require the IRA provider to report anything to the IRS, but the IRA provider needs the beneficiaries' TINs because it will have to file Form 1099-R annually to report whatever distributions are made from the new account to a beneficiary.

If the account was inherited from a Participant who died prior to issuance of the new proposed and/or final minimum distribution regulations in 2001/2002, see also ¶ 10.4.06.

10.4.02 *Establishing separate accounts*

If there are multiple beneficiaries, and their interests are fractional (e.g. "Equally to my four children"), they may want to treat the inherited benefit as "separate accounts" for MRD purposes, so that each beneficiary can use his or her own life expectancy to compute MRDs. For this purpose, the separate accounts must be "established" no later than December 31 of the year after the year of the Participant's death. This can easily be done with inherited IRAs by having the IRA provider divide the inherited IRA into several separate inherited IRAs, one for each beneficiary. See ¶ 1.7.06. As long as each beneficiary's separated inherited account is the right value (e.g., all accounts should initially be of equal value if the IRA was left equally to several children), they can even pick and choose which investments would go into which beneficiary's separated account. If a trust was named as beneficiary, see ¶ 6.3.13 regarding separate accounts.

Also consider physical division of the IRA post mortem for reasons *other than* § 401(a)(9), such as to permit each beneficiary to "self-direct" the investment of his portion of the IRA.

10.4.03 *Plan-to-plan transfers*

The beneficiary of an inherited IRA may want to transfer it to a different IRA provider. This can be done by means of a direct transfer by one IRA custodian (or trustee) to another IRA custodian (or trustee), from one inherited IRA (the IRA that was actually inherited) to another "inherited IRA" (that isn't really inherited, it is a newly opened account in the name of the deceased participant). Even if there is no change of custodian or trustee, changing the account from one big account payable to multiple beneficiaries into multiple smaller accounts, each payable to one beneficiary, is considered a plan-to-plan transfer.

The IRS has no problem with these transfers PROVIDED: the transferee account is still titled as an inherited IRA, not the beneficiary's "own" IRA (see ¶ 10.4.01); and the assets go DIRECTLY from one IRA custodian (or trustee) to the other IRA custodian (or trustee). The WRONG way to do this is for the first IRA provider to give a check to the beneficiary, which he or she then deposits in the other IRA. This would be a "rollover," not a "plan-to-plan transfer," and (though the transactions look pretty much alike to most people) a non-spouse beneficiary CANNOT roll over an inherited IRA (¶ 2.5.05), so that procedure would be fatal.

Rev. Rul. 78-406, 1978-2 C.B. 157, provides the legal authority allowing plan-to-plan transfers to take place even where a "rollover" would not be permitted. See, e.g., PLRs 2000-28040, 2000-28041.

10.4.04 *Don't forget the IRD deduction*

If Participant's estate was subject to federal estate tax, a beneficiary who has to pay income tax on distributions from Participant's retirement plan is entitled to an income tax deduction for the estate taxes paid on the inherited benefit. Calculation of this deduction is complex and uncertain (see ¶ 2.2.07-¶ 2.2.11), but the main problem with the deduction is (apparently) beneficiaries don't know about it and so don't take it. This is a big waste of money.

In an estate that was subject to a substantial estate tax, the effect of the "IRD deduction" is to lower the beneficiary's tax bracket on plan distributions. The beneficiary should take that into consideration when he needs some spending cash. If the beneficiary's choice is to take money from an inherited IRA or from his own IRA, the distribution from the inherited IRA will be subject to lower income taxes because of the IRD deduction. Also, a distribution from an inherited IRA is never subject to the 10% "premature distributions" penalty even if the beneficiary is under age 59½. ¶ 9.4.01.

10.4.05 *Naming a successor beneficiary*

Once the beneficiary has settled into a nice long-term life expectancy payout for the inherited IRA, he needs to consider what will happen to that account if he dies before the end of the life expectancy payout period. The IRS (and, now, most major IRA providers) recognize that a beneficiary can designate his own "successor beneficiary," to take over the account in case the original beneficiary dies before he has withdrawn all of the benefits. ¶ 1.9.02.

Designating a successor beneficiary should be part of a complete and coordinated estate plan for the beneficiary, and should be done as soon as possible after the beneficiary inherits the IRA.

10.4.06 *Beneficiaries of pre-2001 decedents*

The final minimum distribution regulations provide substantially increased income tax deferral opportunities for many individuals who were taking required distributions from retirement plans they inherited from deceased participants—even for beneficiaries of decedents who died prior to the issuance of the final regulations (2002), if the account is still in existence.

The final regulations apply for purposes of determining required minimum distributions for calendar years beginning on or after January 1, 2003, even if the employee died prior to January 1, 2003. Thus, all individuals receiving required distributions from inherited retirement plans, *regardless of how long ago the original Participant died*, must switch to the new rules no later than 2003. For illustration of how this works, see PLR 2002-48030 and the example at ¶ 1.1.06.

10.5 How to Fund a Credit Shelter Trust

This ¶ 10.5 discusses the problem of "how to fund a credit shelter trust" (see Glossary) when all or most of the client's assets are in the form of retirement plans. While in some cases the problem can be solved while still achieving all of the client's estate planning goals (see ¶ 10.5.03, Solutions B and C), in other cases the client will have to choose between mutually exclusive competing objectives (see ¶ 10.5.03, Solutions A, D, H and J).

A typical client statement of goals might be "I want to provide maximum financial security for my surviving spouse, and minimize estate taxes, and achieve maximum income tax deferral of my retirement benefits." The following list of "drawbacks" illustrates that, when retirement benefits are the only asset available to fund the "credit shelter trust," this client can easily achieve any two of these goals, but usually cannot achieve all three.

Finally, some ideas that are advanced as solutions to this problem may not work as well as hoped (or at all) (see ¶ 10.5.03, Solutions E, F, G, I and K).

¶ 10.5.05 discusses the virtually identical drawbacks (and solutions) involved in funding a QTIP trust with retirement benefits.

10.5.01 *What the problem is and who has it*

There are significant income tax disadvantages to using income-taxable retirement benefits to fund a credit shelter trust of which the surviving spouse ("Spouse") is a beneficiary. These income tax disadvantages (1) may reduce or eliminate the estate tax savings that is supposed to be obtained by using a credit shelter trust and/or (2) may reduce the amount of money Spouse has available to live on as compared with leaving the benefits outright to Spouse.

The problem arises when you have a married couple old enough and rich enough to care about estate taxes, but (as to one or both spouses) the credit shelter trust cannot be fully funded on the first death without using retirement benefits.

The following lists of drawbacks assumes that the retirement plan in question consists of pre-tax money. "Solution G" in ¶ 10.5.03 discusses whether converting a traditional IRA to a Roth IRA would eliminate the drawbacks (it wouldn't).

10.5.02 *Drawbacks of funding trust with benefits*

Here are the drawbacks of funding a credit shelter trust with retirement plan death benefits when Spouse is a beneficiary of the trust:

1.   *Distributions start sooner after Participant's death (loss of income tax deferral, part 1).* Benefits paid to a credit shelter trust will have to be distributed, generally speaking, beginning within one year after Participant's death (but see ¶ 10.5.03, Solution D). If Spouse were named as beneficiary individually, and rolled the benefits over to an IRA, she wouldn't have to take any distributions until she reached age 70½. If Spouse received the benefits personally and did *not* roll them over, she wouldn't have to take distributions until the year Participant would have reached age 70½. Thus, making benefits payable to

a credit shelter trust often results in less income tax deferral because distributions have to commence sooner than would otherwise be the case. This drawback is not a factor if both spouses are at, near or past age 70½.

2. *Faster distributions during Spouse's life (loss of income tax deferral, part 2)*. Benefits paid to a credit shelter trust will have to be distributed over the single life expectancy of the oldest beneficiary of the trust. This is the *best case* scenario for benefits paid to a trust, and assumes the IRS's "trust rules" (¶ 6.2) are complied with. This will produce a much more rapid distribution of the benefits than would be required if the benefits were payable to Spouse personally, Spouse rolled them over to an IRA, and withdrew MRDs using the Uniform Lifetime Table (¶ 1.4.01). Since the Uniform Lifetime Table is equivalent to the joint life expectancy of Spouse and a hypothetical beneficiary 10 years younger than Spouse, the Uniform Lifetime Table provides smaller required distributions than the single life expectancy of Spouse.

3. *Faster distributions after Spouse's death (loss of income tax deferral, part 3)*. If Spouse received the benefits personally and rolled them over to an IRA, she could name younger generation individuals as designated beneficiaries of the rollover IRA. After her death, the remaining benefits in the IRA could be paid out over the life expectancy of the younger-generation beneficiaries. In contrast, benefits paid to a credit shelter trust will have to be distributed over the single life expectancy of the oldest beneficiary of the trust (Spouse) even after that oldest beneficiary has died.

4. *Higher income taxes on benefits paid to trust*. To the extent benefits are paid to the credit shelter trust and kept in the trust (i.e., not immediately distributed out to individual beneficiaries; see ¶ 6.1.03), they will be taxed at the *trust's* income tax rate. Thus, for many families, making the benefits payable to a trust will cause them to be taxed at a higher rate than if the benefits were paid to individual beneficiaries.

5.   *"Wasting" part of the exemption paying income taxes.* If the credit shelter trust is funded with a retirement plan (other than a Roth IRA; see ¶ 10.5.03, Solution G), the trust will have to pay income taxes on the retirement plan distributions as they are received. ¶ 2.1.01. Part of Participant's estate tax exemption will be "wasted" paying income taxes. In contrast, if the credit shelter trust is funded with non-income-taxable assets, the trust receives the full exemption amount, undiminished by income taxes. This factor may not be significant if the retirement benefits are the only asset available. However, this is a serious consideration to very wealthy individuals whose total assets exceed the anticipated estate tax exemption levels; see ¶ 10.5.03, Solution H.

6.   *Life expectancy payout may not be available except via spousal rollover.* The preceding drawbacks are inherent in the tax law. This drawback is not inherent in the law, but is a problem under some retirement plans: many (perhaps most) qualified retirement plans do not permit any form of death benefit other than a lump sum distribution. ¶ 1.5.09. With this type of plan, usually the only way to achieve the advantages of a life expectancy payout is to have the lump sum distribution paid outright to Spouse who rolls it over. (See ¶ 10.4.01, second paragraph, for another idea.)

7.   *Spousal consent may be required to name a beneficiary other than Spouse.* Under virtually all qualified plans, Participant cannot designate a credit shelter trust (or any other beneficiary who is not Spouse) without Spouse's consent (see ¶ 3.4) as to either part or all of the plan benefit. (IRAs and some 403(b) plans are not subject to this requirement.)

10.5.03 *Solutions: the good, the bad and the useless*

Here are the choices available to respond to the problem.

A.   **Leave the benefits outright to spouse; underfund the credit shelter trust.** This eliminates Drawbacks 1-7. The drawback of this solution is possibly increased estate taxes on the second death due to "wasting" the first spouse's estate tax exemption.

This solution is appropriate if: Client cares more about Spouse's financial security than about saving estate taxes for future beneficiaries. Or, client believes that both spouses will probably live long enough so that increasing exemptions, decreasing assets and/or estate tax repeal will eliminate estate tax concerns, and therefore prefers reasonably definite income tax advantages over remote estate tax savings. Or, after running the numbers, client and planner conclude that the net tax savings of a credit shelter trust (projected estate tax savings minus projected income tax loss) would be not worth the trouble. If using this solution, the option of funding a credit shelter trust can be kept alive by naming the credit shelter trust as contingent beneficiary to the extent Spouse disclaims the benefit. Also, the couple could divide their non-retirement assets equally between them, so that, regardless of which spouse dies first, *some* assets will go into the estate tax-saving credit shelter trust of the first spouse to die.

The disclaimer non-solution. Many planners suggest that *the* solution to the problem is to name Spouse as primary beneficiary, and credit shelter trust as contingent beneficiary in case of Spouse's disclaimer; then expect that on Participant's death Spouse will disclaim a sufficient amount to fill up the credit shelter trust. This "disclaimer" estate plan does not eliminate the problem of funding a credit shelter trust with retirement benefits. If the situation hasn't changed when Participant dies, activating the credit shelter trust by having Spouse disclaim the retirement benefits will have EXACTLY the same drawbacks as naming the credit shelter trust as beneficiary in the first place (but now with the added complications of carrying out a qualified disclaimer). The disclaimer plan is no more than a useful backstop, to be activated if (when Participant dies) something has changed: for example, if Spouse's financial situation has improved (she won the lottery?), or the tax laws, at the time of Participant's death, have changed so that having the retirement benefits pass to the credit shelter trust would no longer have a negative effect on the spouse's financial security.

B.   **Leave the benefits directly to the younger generation.** This does not eliminate Drawback 1; distribution of benefits will still have to begin within one year after Participant's death. This solution does eliminate Drawbacks 2 and 3 by going directly to the (long) life expectancy of the younger generation. This solution can eliminate Drawback 4 if the benefits go outright to the younger generation or go to a conduit trust (¶ 6.3.08) for them (so benefits are taxed at their individual rates rather than trust rates). It does not eliminate Drawback 5, 6 or 7. This solution is appropriate if: Providing for Spouse's financial security is not a goal, or if Spouse's financial security is well provided for without this retirement benefit.

C.   **Community property solution.** This is an excellent solution that works perfectly (eliminates Drawbacks 1-6) IF the couple have enough non-retirement assets to fund a credit shelter trust for one spouse, but not both, AND the retirement plan in question is an IRA. The goal in such a situation is to have the non-retirement assets wind up in the estate of the first spouse to die (where they can be used, with none of the listed drawbacks, to fund decedent's credit shelter trust) and to have the retirement plan end up in the hands of Spouse (who can roll it over and get the advantages of longer term income tax deferral etc.). This goal can be achieved in non-community property states only if the couple can correctly guess which spouse is going to die first (see "Solution I"). In some community property states, such guessing is unnecessary. Participant and Spouse can sign a contract agreeing that all their assets (including the IRA) are "aggregate" community property, and assigning all their assets to a joint trust. The IRA is made payable to the joint trust. Then, on the first death, regardless of which spouse dies first, the survivor gets to choose which assets he (or she) will take from the joint pot as his (or her) share of the community property, and can simply walk away with those assets, leaving the rest of the assets to constitute the deceased spouse's share of the community property (and to pass into the deceased spouse's credit shelter trust). So the survivor says "I'll take the IRA as my share" and keeps it (or, if it belonged originally to the deceased spouse, rolls it over to a new IRA in the survivor's name), and lets the non-IRA assets pass to the deceased spouse's credit shelter trust. This solution does not work even in community property states if the retirement plan is subject to ERISA, because the Supreme Court has held that

ERISA's spousal protection rules (¶ 3.4), when applicable, preempt community property law. Non-community property state residents may be able to achieve the same advantages by transferring their property to an Alaska Community Property Trust. See "Alaska Enacts an Optional Community Property System Which Can Be Elected by Both Residents and Nonresidents," by David G. Shaftel and Stephen E. Greer, 25 ACTEC Notes 206 (1999).

D.   **Conduit Trust: trust is required to pass out to Spouse all retirement plan distributions as they are received by the credit shelter trust.** The conduit trust (¶ 6.3.08) eliminates Drawback 4: the high trust income tax rates applicable to IRD distributions paid to the credit shelter trust as principal are avoided by having the credit shelter trust pass out to Spouse all distributions the trust receives from the retirement plan, as the trust receives them. The result is that the retirement plan distributions will be taxed to Spouse at her (low) rate, rather than to the trust at its (high) rate. The trust terms would require that the Trustee distribute to Spouse all retirement plan distributions received by the trust, as and when they are received by the trust (regardless of whether these distributions are defined as income or as principal for trust accounting purposes; ¶ 6.1.07). This is called a "conduit trust," and under the minimum distribution regulations, this trust could: postpone the commencement of required distributions until the decedent would have reached age 70½ (just as Spouse could have done had she been named directly as beneficiary) (which can provide substantial income tax deferral *if* Participant died well before reaching age 70½, thus eliminating Drawback 1); recalculate Spouse's life expectancy for purposes of MRDs to the trust (meaning that if the trustee takes only MRDs there is guaranteed to be something—not necessarily very much—left in the trust when Spouse later dies); and (if Participant and Spouse *both* die before the end of the year Participant would have reached age 70½) (not a very common scenario) the subsequent distributions to the younger generation remainder beneficiaries would be based on their life expectancy, not Spouse's (eliminating Drawback 3 in that unusual scenario). The first problem with this approach is that the bulk of the retirement plan will be paid out over Spouse's life expectancy. If all plan distributions are distributed out to Spouse as the trust receives them, there will be little left in that credit shelter trust when Spouse dies, assuming she lives for all or most of her IRS-defined life expectancy. Few estate tax dollars will have been saved, because the retirement plan has been added to Spouse's estate just as if you had named her directly as beneficiary—but without the advantages of the spousal rollover. If you want to save estate taxes, you must provide that the credit shelter trust does NOT distribute the original value of Participant's retirement plan to Spouse. Keeping this money IN the credit shelter trust (and out of Spouse's estate) is the whole point of having a credit shelter trust. Thus this approach makes sense in only a very small number of situations where, for example, Spouse has a short life expectancy, but Participant does not want to cut her out entirely because she may need the money; and it is understood that the credit shelter trust device will save estate taxes only if Spouse dies prematurely. The second problem with this approach is that it solves only one of the drawbacks of using a credit shelter trust to receive Participant's retirement plan distributions—the high trust income tax rates (# 4). It partly solves Drawback 1, and in rare cases Drawback 3, but does not eliminate Drawbacks 2, 5, 6 or 7. The third problem with this approach is that it builds the whole trust on the assumption that the trustee will be able to and will want to take distributions from the retirement plan based on today's minimum distribution rules. If the minimum distribution rules change, to require a faster payout than is required under today's rule, the credit shelter trust could end up with nothing in it in short order after Participant's death.

E.   **Spray trust for the benefit of Spouse and issue.** Another approach is to give the trustee discretion to distribute funds from the credit shelter trust to Spouse or issue to minimize overall income taxes paid. With this approach, the trustee could eliminate Drawback 4 (high trust income tax rates) by passing retirement plan distributions out to Spouse and/or the issue, depending on who was in the lowest income tax bracket. This approach does not eliminate Drawbacks 1, 2, 3, 5, 6 or 7. Furthermore, to the extent income taxes are reduced by distributing the income to Spouse, her estate taxes are correspondingly increased (because she ends up owning assets that were supposed to stay in the credit shelter trust); this defeats the purpose of the credit shelter trust (as discussed under "Solution D"). On the other hand, to the extent income taxes are reduced by passing the retirement plan distributions out to *issue*, the money is no longer available for Spouse's needs; and if she didn't need the money in this trust, why didn't you just make it payable to the issue in the first place and get the benefit of their long life expectancy? Again, this seems likely to be a realistic solution in very few cases, though there seems to be no harm in giving the trustee discretion to distribute to issue in a non-conduit credit shelter trust established for the primary benefit of Spouse.

F.   **Have Participant buy life insurance to replace the credit shelter trust.** Buying a $1 million life insurance policy through an irrevocable trust, funded with annual "Crummey power" gifts, is not really a "solution" to the problem, because at the end of the day there is still nothing in the client's credit shelter trust. If Participant could figure out a way to fund his credit shelter trust, he could do both things—fund the credit shelter trust and *also* make lifetime gifts to an irrevocable insurance trust. However, a life insurance policy and irrevocable trust can be a good "consolation prize" for a person who has the problem we are discussing. It could, for example, be a good way to provide for the increased estate taxes generated by Solution A.

G.   **Converting to a Roth IRA, and using that to fund the credit shelter trust.** This eliminates Drawback 5 (wasting exemption paying income taxes): by paying the income taxes before death, Participant assures that the credit shelter trust can be funded with "after-tax dollars," namely the Roth IRA. Unfortunately, the Roth IRA does not solve the "loss of deferral" problems: The Roth IRA, if made payable to the credit shelter trust of which Spouse is the life beneficiary, would have to be distributed over Spouse's single life expectancy. If the Roth were left to Spouse outright, she could roll it over to her own Roth IRA and then there would be no required distributions until Spouse's death. Thus, Drawbacks 1, 2 and 3 are not eliminated. The way to maximize the value of a Roth IRA conversion is (i) do not withdraw from it during Participant's life; then either (ii) make it payable at death directly to children or grandchildren, so it is paid out over the (long) life expectancy of a young beneficiary or (iii) make it payable outright to Spouse, and she rolls it over and allows it to accumulate during *her* life, then *she* makes it payable at *her* death directly to children or grandchildren, so it is paid out (after her death) over the (long) life expectancy of a young beneficiary. A credit shelter trust that benefits Spouse for life can never use the younger beneficiaries' life expectancy; a Roth IRA payable to such a trust must be entirely distributed over the life expectancy of Spouse. So Participant would be paying the price of a Roth conversion (immediate loss of the money used to pay income tax on the conversion) without getting the benefit (long term tax-free payout over younger beneficiary's life expectancy). Drawback 7 does not apply to a Roth IRA.

H. **Cash out enough of the IRA now to fund a credit shelter trust with after-tax dollars.** Participant could withdraw enough money from the retirement plan now, during life, to leave him with $1 million after paying the income tax on the withdrawal. If he is over 59½, he could make this withdrawal without paying a penalty. Then he could leave the $1 million non-retirement plan fund to the credit shelter trust and the remaining balance of the retirement plan to Spouse, who could roll it over to her own IRA. The major attraction of this option is that none of Participant's federal estate tax exemption would be "wasted" paying income taxes, because the credit shelter trust would be funded entirely with after-tax dollars, so Drawback 5 is eliminated. This approach does not solve Drawbacks 1, 2 and 3 (loss of income tax deferral)—rather it totally sacrifices income tax deferral in favor of greater estate tax savings. This option may be attractive: if Participant is approaching his RBD (so he will have to begin taking large distributions soon anyway—by accelerating the distributions a few years, he would gain the peace of mind of having the credit shelter trust fully funded with non-retirement plan dollars); or if Participant is about to die (so he can be sure the benefits of the move—funding the credit shelter trust with after-tax dollars—would be realized soon); or if Participant has a strong propensity to invest in capital gain and growth-type investments which would be eligible for a stepped-up basis if held outside the retirement plan; or the family is way overweighted in retirement plan assets (for example Spouse also has a multi-million dollar retirement plan). This plan would be less attractive if Participant's major concern is creditors' claims (assets may be more easily protected inside the retirement plan); or if he is likely to be in a lower income tax bracket in later years (maybe he lives in a high income tax state now and is planning to move to a low tax state); or if this is the only asset in the family and there is major concern about whether Participant will have enough to live on during retirement; or if Participant has a tendency to spend any dollars that are not inside a retirement plan.

I.   **Put all non-retirement assets in the name of the spouse who will die first.** Some planners believe they can predict which spouse will die first. Such a planner simply causes all the non-retirement assets to be put in that spouse's name, so they can be used to fund the credit shelter trust when that spouse dies; the retirement plan can then be left to (or kept by) the surviving spouse. Needless to say this plan can produce disastrous results if the wrong spouse dies first, especially if *all* the assets are in the other spouse's name. If the spouses die in the correct order, this plan eliminates Drawbacks 1-7; but the community property solution (C) is a far better way to accomplish the result if it is available, and it doesn't require a crystal ball.

J.   **Leave the benefits to a traditional credit shelter trust.** If the best form of distribution of the benefits is a lump sum distribution, not rolled over (this could be the case if for example the entire plan balance consists of low-basis employer stock; see ¶ 2.4), it may not make much difference whether the distribution is paid to Spouse or a credit shelter trust. Similarly, if the alternative is leaving the benefits to a QTIP trust (not to the spouse outright), there's little difference in terms of drawbacks between leaving the benefits to a QTIP trust or a credit shelter trust (as explained at ¶ 10.5.05). Also, if Spouse is not much older than the remainder beneficiaries, then Participant can name a credit shelter trust as beneficiary of the retirement plan, and have Spouse be a beneficiary of that trust, without suffering Drawback 3; however, Drawbacks 1, 2, 4, 5, 6 and 7 still exist.

K.   **Make the credit shelter trust a 678 grantor trust.** This idea does not work. The approach that has been suggested by some practitioners is this: use § 678(a)(1) (see ¶ 6.3.09) to cause Spouse to be treated as the "owner" of the trust property for income tax purposes by making her the sole trustee with power to distribute principal to herself for her health, education, maintenance and support ("HEMS" power). Since § 678(a)(1) says that a person who has power to pay funds to herself is treated as the "owner" of such funds for income tax purposes, and since § 678(a)(1) does not contain any apparent exceptions for a power limited by an ascertainable standard, Spouse would have to be treated as the owner of the trust principal by virtue of her power to pay such principal to herself (even though it is limited by an ascertainable standard). Yet this power is not broad enough to cause the trust principal to be included in Spouse's estate on her subsequent death because it meets the definition of a non-general (therefore non-taxable) power of appointment under § 2041. The problem with this idea is that, even though § 678 does not contain an *explicit* exception for powers limited by an ascertainable standard, the courts have found an implied one. When the IRS has sought to cause a surviving spouse to be taxable on trust income because of some right of lifetime withdrawal she holds, the courts have interpreted § 678 as applying only to a truly unrestricted right to withdraw from the trust. See *Blattmachr* [Bibliography], § 3:4.5, n. 159. In other words, the courts have interpreted § 678 just the opposite of the way it is interpreted by practitioners encouraging this approach. Accordingly, if Spouse's power to withdraw principal from the trust is limited by a HEMS standard, she is *not* taxable on the trust's income from retirement plan distributions treated as principal merely by virtue of holding that power.

10.5.04 *Credit shelter trust of non-participant Spouse*

So far we have been looking at the problem of a married couple where one or both spouses have, as their only asset available to fund a credit shelter trust, a retirement plan. As the problem has been framed up to this point, both spouses have (or can have, if assets are rearranged slightly) sufficient assets to fund their respective credit shelter trusts, if retirement benefits are used for that purpose.

Now we turn to the problem of a couple in which one spouse has *no* assets, and the other spouse's assets are entirely in the form of retirement benefits. This case poses an additional problem: how to fund a credit shelter trust if the non-participant Spouse dies first, since she has no assets in her name.

In a *non-community property state*, there are only two ways to solve this problem. One is for Participant, while he and Spouse are both still living, to cash out (and pay tax on) enough of his retirement plan to give Spouse $1 million of after-tax money to fund her credit shelter trust. The other is for the spouses to get divorced or legally separated, and have Spouse take part of Participant's retirement plan by means of a QDRO (§ 414(p)) (or the IRA equivalent of a QDRO under § 408(d)(6)). Few clients are willing to pay enormous current income taxes (or get divorced) just to receive a speculative estate tax benefit down the road—especially since it would all be wasted effort if the non-participant Spouse does *not* die first!

In a *community property* state there is slightly more flexibility, if the retirement plan is an IRA. If the IRA can be treated as community property, the parties could sign an agreement recognizing this asset as aggregate-basis community property, then the non-participant Spouse in her will could leave part of her share of Participant's IRA to her credit shelter trust (up to whatever amount is necessary to fully fund it) and the balance to Participant. Then, *if* the non-participant Spouse dies first, Participant could cash out as much of the non-participant Spouse's share of his IRA as necessary to fund non-participant Spouse's credit shelter trust, pay income tax on it, and transfer whatever's left to the credit shelter trust of the deceased non-participant Spouse.

Note that, even in a community property state that recognizes a non-participant Spouse's ownership of part of the IRA, there is *no way* that Participant can transfer any of the non-participant Spouse's share of *Participant's* IRA to *non-participant Spouse's* credit shelter trust without paying income tax on it. But at least if the IRA is community property Participant can, if, as and when non-participant Spouse predeceases him, transfer some of his IRA to her credit shelter trust without having the transfer be treated as a gift by him. In a non-community property state there is *no* way, even if Participant is *willing* to pay income taxes, to get funds from Participant's IRA to non-participant Spouse's credit shelter trust without gift tax consequences once non-participant Spouse has died.

10.5.05 *Funding QTIP trust with retirement benefits*

In a "second marriage" situation where a client wants to leave assets for the life benefit of Spouse, but ultimately have the funds pass to his children by a prior marriage; or any situation in which a client wants to leave assets in a life trust for Spouse's benefit rather than outright to Spouse for tax or non-tax reasons; the usual solution is a "QTIP" trust. ¶ 3.3.04. Leaving retirement benefits to a QTIP trust has exactly the same drawbacks as leaving benefits to a credit shelter trust for Spouse's life benefit (see ¶ 10.5.02, Drawbacks 1-7), except for # 5 (wasting credit shelter amount) which doesn't apply to the QTIP trust. See ¶ 3.3.10 and the Koslow case study (Chapter 11).

Here are the solutions available to respond to the problem; some are similar to the "credit shelter trust" problem solutions listed at ¶ 10.5.03. The following discussion assumes Participant wants the trust to qualify for the federal estate tax marital deduction as a QTIP trust, but the problems don't change even if the estate tax is repealed.

A.   **Leave the benefits outright to Spouse.** This eliminates all the listed drawbacks. The disadvantage of this solution is whatever disadvantage the client perceived would exist if benefits were left outright to Spouse. For example, if Spouse has total control of the benefits, Spouse may not choose to leave the benefits to client's children of a prior marriage (in which case consider Solution B or D instead). Or, client may perceive that Spouse cannot be expected to handle a large outright bequest properly (in which case consider Solution C). Solution A is appropriate if: Client cares more about Spouse's financial security than about protecting the future beneficiaries; or if, after running the numbers, client concludes that the income tax drawbacks of the QTIP trust are so substantial that they outweigh whatever benefit client wanted to obtain from the QTIP trust.

B.   **Leave some benefits outright to spouse and some outright to the children.** With a QTIP trust, Spouse has a life interest and children have a remainder interest. The combined value of their respective interests equals 100% of the value of the retirement plan. Participant could leave some of the benefits outright to Spouse and some outright to the children (or to a trust for their exclusive benefit). If Spouse takes full advantage of the spousal rollover and the children take full advantage of the life expectancy payout option, both Spouse and children should end up with substantially more dollars in their pockets than they would if they received theoretically the same relative amounts as life and remainder beneficiaries of a QTIP trust. Only the IRS loses. See Koslow case study, Chapter 11.

C.   **Conduit Trust: trust is required to pass out to Spouse all retirement plan distributions as they are received by the QTIP trust.** The advantages and problems of this solution are discussed at ¶ 10.5.03 (Solution D). This solution is not appropriate for someone whose goal in establishing a QTIP trust was to preserve principal for the children, because (unless Spouse dies prematurely) Spouse ends up with the lion's share of the retirement plan—but without the income tax deferral advantages of the spousal rollover. This solution may be suitable if Participant wants a QTIP trust only because Participant believes that Spouse cannot suitably handle a substantial outright bequest, but Participant does not have the same concerns about Spouse's ability to handle a stream of distributions from a conduit trust.

D.   **Leave benefits outright to Spouse, leave other assets to (and maybe buy life insurance for) children.** This eliminates all the listed drawbacks and can be a good solution for a Participant whose reason for wanting a QTIP is to protect children by a prior marriage.

E.   **Converting to a Roth IRA, and using that to fund the QTIP trust.** The advantages and drawbacks of this solution are discussed at ¶ 10.5.03 (Solution G).

F.   **Name Spouse as beneficiary, on the condition that she will name Participant's children as beneficiaries of her rollover IRA.** This frequently-advanced idea is a non-starter. First, the children are not at all protected by Spouse's assurance that she will name them as beneficiary of her rollover IRA. Unless they force Spouse into some kind of court proceedings, how will they know if she complied? But even if she complied, she has agreed to basically nothing, since she can withdraw all funds from that rollover IRA without anyone's consent or knowledge. Once the funds have been withdrawn from the IRA she can spend them, or she can leave them to anyone she chooses, and the children will get nothing. If Participant leaves benefits to Spouse on the condition (enforced by a separate agreement, since no plan administrator, would be able to accommodate such a condition) that she *not* spend them, and that she will leave either the benefits themselves or the proceeds thereof to Participant's children, then he has created a terminable interest that will not qualify for the marital deduction (¶ 3.3.02).

G.   **Cash out the retirement plan and leave after-tax proceeds to a QTIP trust (or roll the benefits over to an IRA and leave that to a QTIP trust).** This would eliminate Drawback 7 in the case of some profit sharing plans (which require spousal consent in order to name a non-spouse beneficiary, but do not require spousal consent for Participant to withdraw funds from the retirement plan during life) (see ¶ 3.4.03). If Participant either is over 59½ or rolls the distribution over to an IRA, he could make this withdrawal without paying a penalty (see Chapter 9). This does not eliminate any other drawback.

H.   **Leave the benefits to a traditional QTIP trust.** If the best form of distribution of the benefits is a lump sum distribution, not rolled over (for example the entire plan balance consists of low-basis employer stock; ¶ 2.4), it may make no difference whether the distribution is paid to Spouse or a QTIP trust.

11

Case Studies

Case studies illustrating some typical situations in estate planning for retirement benefits

Dr. Della: Estate taxes on large retirement plan balance

Dr. Della is 68. She has a $5 million IRA, a home worth $800,000 and few other assets. Currently, her three children are named as beneficiaries of the IRA. She wants to leave all her assets to the three children, and name you, her estate planning attorney, as executor of her estate. She also wants to save taxes. She is concerned about the large minimum distributions she will face in a few years when she reaches age 70½.

Before considering ways to *reduce* taxes, you first face the question of how estate taxes will be paid. Della's "estate" for estate tax purposes is $5.8 million, but her "probate estate" (the assets her executor would control) is only $800,000 (the value of the house), because the IRA would pass directly to her children as the named beneficiaries. The executor of the estate will be liable for about $2 million of estate taxes, but most of Della's assets will be in the hands of the children, not the estate. The executor might have to sue the children to collect their share of the estate taxes. Whoever Della nominates as her executor might well refuse to accept the appointment if he/she/it figures out prior to accepting the position that the estate's liabilities (estate taxes on a $5.8 million taxable estate) exceed the value of the estate's only asset (the $800,000 house).

To avoid putting the executor in this difficult position, make sure the person who is primarily responsible for paying the estate taxes has control of the money. For example, make the IRA payable to a trust, and make sure the trustee is the same as the executor of the estate. That way, the executor can be sure the friendly trustee (himself) does not run away with the IRA money before taxes are paid. See ¶ 6.2.13 for problems of paying estate taxes out of a trust named as beneficiary.

Or, make the three children co-executors as well as beneficiaries, so they are primarily as well as secondarily liable for the estate taxes.

Another approach is for Della to buy life insurance to assure the availability of funds to pay estate taxes. Again, she will need to be sure that the life insurance proceeds end up in the hands of the person who will need them to pay the estate tax.

Next Della invites everyone she knows to send her ideas for how to reduce the estate tax value of her IRA (and/or how to reduce the income tax impact of required minimum distributions). Here are the ideas she has received so far:

Roll the IRA back into a corporate retirement plan, then buy life insurance inside the plan, then distribute the policy out of the plan after a few years when the policy value is lower than the sum of premiums paid. The idea here is that, for the first several years of its existence, a life insurance policy is worth less than you paid for it; it takes many years for the cash value to catch up to what it would have been had you invested in (say) bonds rather than life insurance. See ¶ 8.4,04, E, for discussion of the merits and drawbacks of this idea. An IRA cannot hold life insurance, so the possibility of using this scheme depends on having a qualified retirement plan (QRP) you can roll the IRA into. In Della's case, she would have to go to work for a company that had a plan that would permit her to roll her IRA into it and also would permit the purchase of life insurance in the plan.

Invest in a venture capital, research or real estate development partnership or other form of investment that temporarily reduces the value of the plan. This is a variation on the buy-life-insurance plan, but is more useful to the client who has no QRP available which can buy life insurance, or who does not want to buy life insurance. The idea is to invest the IRA in something that the client believes will be a profitable investment *over the long term,* but that *temporarily* declines in value right after the investment is made. The decline in value is due to a lack of transferability or lack of marketability of the investment during a lockup phase while the venture is still in the start-up stage. There are two essential ingredients to success with this approach. The first is that, while the investment is still in its reduced-value stage, the client must either (a) die or (b) withdraw the investment from the plan. The second is that the investment must later (after the client's death, or after the client has withdrawn the asset from the retirement plan) grow in value sufficiently to make up for its initial decline.

  Transfer IRA assets to family limited partnership. The idea here is to form a family partnership (FLP) among the IRA (which contributes all its investments to the FLP), the IRA owner (as general partner, perhaps) and (say) the client's children. The goal is to get the same "valuation discounts" for the investments inside the IRA as clients get for their outside-the-IRA investments by contributing same to FLPs. The main obstacle is whether having the IRA enter into a partnership with the IRA owner and other related parties constitutes a "prohibited transaction" under § 4975. This is a subject for analysis by an ERISA lawyer, not an estate planning specialist. Department of Labor Advisory Opinion # 2000-10a illustrates the analysis to be followed when determining whether a transaction of this type is a prohibited transaction. In that opinion the DOL stated that there were three separate prohibited transaction rules that could potentially be violated by investment of IRA assets in a FLP. The DOL found that the particular transaction in question was not a violation of *one* of those rules, but reserved judgment as to whether the later operation of the partnership might violate the other two rules. To read the opinion, go to the DOL web site www.dol.gov./dol/pwba/public/programs/ori, and select opinion 2000-10a. For an excellent discussion of all the issues, see Bray, C.P., and Kearns, D.B., "The Family Limited Partnership As An Asset Of The IRA," *Trusts & Estates* 8/98 (page 93).

  Valuation discount for built-in income taxes. Certain appraisers will give an opinion that the value of an IRA should be discounted to reflect the income taxes that must be paid on any distributions. The IRS does not agree with this valuation idea; see TAM 2002-47001. I agree with the IRS on this one; see Choate, N., "Estate Tax Valuation of Retirement Benefits," *Trusts & Estates,* May 2002, p. 16.

Felicia Fallon: Planning for post-death lump sum distribution

  Felicia Fallon is 66. She has $8 million in total assets: $3 million in the qualified retirement plan (QRP) of her employer, and another $5 million of liquid investments and residential real estate.

  She has two children, ages 48 and 45, and several grandchildren. The children are well provided for financially. While the children are to be the principal beneficiaries of her estate, Felicia has some interest in charitable giving. She has already used up her estate tax and GST tax exemptions through lifetime gifts.

Under her employer's QRP, the only option for distribution of death benefits to a non-spouse beneficiary is a lump sum in cash. ¶ 1.5.09. The plan does not permit distribution of annuity contracts in lieu of cash. Felicia does not plan to retire until she is age 75, but the plan prohibits her from taking any distributions prior to separation from service. Thus, if she dies prior to her projected retirement nine years from now, whoever receives her plan benefits will receive them in a lump sum. There is no possibility of a life expectancy payout to her designated beneficiaries.

In preparing Felicia's estate plan, we compare two possible scenarios. The first is making the benefits payable to the children. They withdraw all funds from the QRP within one year after Felicia's death, pay the income taxes, and invest what's left. The calculations show that after 44 years (which is the average joint and survivor life expectancy for two people age 48 and 45, according to the IRS Joint and Survivor Life Table; see ¶ 1.2.04) the ultimate net value to family of this scenario is $11,083,390.

The other alternative is to have the benefits distributed to a charitable remainder unitrust (CRT) that would pay a 6% unitrust payout to the children for their joint lifetime and for the life of the survivor. The advantage of this scenario is that the CRT pays no income tax on the distribution it receives (¶ 7.5.04). The children would then receive, for life, the income from the entire $3 million fund. They would have to pay income taxes on these distributions. On the death of the surviving child all funds remaining in the CRT would go to Felicia's favorite charity.

In addition to eliminating income taxes on the lump sum distribution, this approach produces an estate tax charitable deduction to Felicia's estate for the value of the remainder interest. After 44 years, the accumulated value of the estate tax savings from this deduction, and the accumulated value of distributions from the CRT, total $12,195,566. This is more than $1 million *more* than the children would have had they received the plan outright on Felicia's death!

These numbers suggest that leaving the benefits to a CRT does not "penalize" the children substantially or at all, making it an especially appealing approach to funding Felicia's charitable gifts. The calculations in this example are based on the following assumptions: Felicia Fallon dies in December 1999. Felicia's other assets total $5 million, so her total estate is $8 million. All estate taxes are paid out of the non-retirement assets. The state death tax on her estate is exactly equal to the maximum credit for state death taxes allowed against her federal estate taxes. The two Fallon children are in the 39.6% tax bracket for all income. All the family's and CRT's investments earn 6% income, fully taxable.

While these projections are interesting (since they seem to show that the family makes a profit from a charitable gift), there are many limitations to such projections. For example, the calculations assume a 6% rate of income, year in and year out, on all investments. Actual investment return might be less or more than 6% in any particular year. Investments can also decline in value. Furthermore, the calculations assume that the entire 6% consists of interest and dividends taxable as ordinary income; in real life, it is probable that some of the investments *outside* the retirement plans would be invested for capital gain and that part of the return would therefore be capital gain. Capital gain is not taxed currently, but only when the asset is sold; and when it is sold, the tax rate on capital gain is lower than on other kinds of income.

The projections assume a 39.6% tax rate for all individuals. It is possible that some individuals would be in a lower bracket. A higher bracket could apply if state income taxes are figured in; and federal rates will probably change over the period of the projections.

The CRT scenario assumes that at least one child lives for 44 years. If both of them die before the 44 years are up, the entire trust at that point moves to the charity. Thus, in case of premature death, the value to the family of the "CRT scenario" would probably be *lower* than the value of the "outright to children" scenario. The children can overcome this risk by buying decreasing term insurance on their lives; or, Felicia could decide that this risk is not of concern to her.

The CRT scenario assumes a 6% payout rate to the children and that the trust earns exactly 6% each year. The scenarios assume that there is a separate fund, outside the retirement plan, of $3,838,700. This would be the amount needed at Felicia's death to pay the estate taxes if all the benefits are paid to the family. If the benefits are paid to a CRT, the estate taxes would be reduced, so some of this fund would be available for the family, rather than going to pay estate taxes, and that has been figured into the value of the CRT scenario.

Ken Koslow: QTIP trust (second marriage)

Ken Koslow is a 62-year-old executive, with two children by his first marriage, ages 36 and 33. His second wife, Karen, is also an executive; she is 54.

Ken wants to leave his life insurance to his children, his house to his wife, and all of his retirement benefits to a QTIP trust. The trust would pay income to Karen for life and on her death the balance would pass to his children.

Ken's assets consist of:

House - joint with spouse	$ 450,000
Qualified retirement plan	1,200,000
IRA	600,000
Non-plan investments	500,000
Life Insurance	500,000
Total	$3,250,000

The problem with this proposal is that paying his retirement benefits to a QTIP trust has many tax disadvantages; see ¶ 3.3.10, ¶ 10.5.05.

A non-tax disadvantage of leaving retirement benefits to a QTIP trust is that Ken's children would have a long wait for a little money. Karen is only 18 years older than Ken's oldest child. Thus it is likely that Ken's children themselves will be "old" before they see anything from the marital trust. Karen's life expectancy is currently about 30 years under the IRS tables. Since the IRS tables are "unisex," they do not reflect Karen's above-average life expectancy as a female. Thus the children can expect, based on average life expectancy, to wait *at least* 30 years before they get any benefits from their father's retirement plan. In the meantime Karen and the children are left competing with each other regarding the investment policies of the trust.

Using software, we project that the eventual value of the benefits to the family under the QTIP scenario (leaving all benefits to a QTIP trust) is $5,526,000 after 30 years. (Assumptions are discussed in more detail below.) Of this amount, assuming Karen dies in 30 years, $1,087,000 would pass to the children (being the then-remaining principal of the marital trust) and $4,439,000 would be held by Karen's estate (representing the accumulated distributions to her from the marital trust). There would be no dollars left inside the retirement plans.

This proposed scenario was compared with the "outright scenario," under which there would be no QTIP trust. The $1.2 million of QRP benefits would be made payable to Karen personally, and the $600,000 IRA would be payable directly to Ken's children. Ken would make sure his life insurance and investments outside the plan were sufficient to pay the estate taxes on the benefits passing to the children.

This scenario has many advantages over the QTIP scenario. Each beneficiary would have total control of his or her own share of the benefits, without having to compete for the attention of the trustee of the QTIP trust. The children could use their long life expectancies to measure MRDs of their benefits.

Karen could roll over her share of the benefits to an IRA in her own name and defer the commencement of distributions until she reached age 70½. She would name her nieces as her designated beneficiaries on the rollover IRA. No benefits would be subject to the high income tax bracket of a trust.

Another advantage of this approach has to do with the practicalities of plan distribution options. QRPs very often do not permit an installment payout to any beneficiary other than a surviving spouse. ¶ 1.5.09. Thus, if QRP benefits are made payable to a marital trust, the plan may not permit the trust to draw those benefits out over the life expectancy of the oldest trust beneficiary. If the benefits are payable to Karen personally, by contrast, she can roll them to an IRA which has whatever payout distribution options she wants. ¶ 3.2.

Furthermore, QRPs are subject to "REA" (¶ 3.4), meaning that the benefits cannot be distributed to someone other than the spouse without her consent. By making the QRP benefits payable to Karen personally, Ken avoids the need for obtaining her consent, which would be required to make the benefits payable to a QTIP trust or some other beneficiary. Since REA does not apply to IRAs, Ken can make the IRA payable to his children without Karen's consent (subject to any requirements of state law or prenuptial agreements they may have signed). Last but definitely not least: both Karen and the children would end up with *substantially more dollars* in their pockets, as the following pages demonstrate.

The following projections assume that all investments earn 7% pre-tax, whether inside or outside a retirement plan, and that all plan distributions, net of income tax, are accumulated rather than spent. The results compare values of the accumulated funds at the end of 30 years.

Scenario 1: All benefits ($1.8 million) left to a QTIP trust.

Th QTIP trust distributes all of its trust accounting income annually to Karen Koslow as required by the marital deduction rules. Each plan distributes to the trust, each year, the greater of the income for that year or the MRD required for that year based on the life expectancy of Karen Koslow. The trust then distributes the income portion of the distribution to Karen personally; principal distributions (i.e. the minimum distribution amount, to the extent it exceeds the income distribution; see ¶ 3.3.06) are retained in the trust fund as principal. It is assumed that the trust and Karen are both in the 39.6% bracket at all times (even though Karen's bracket might drop after her eventual retirement). After 30 years here are the results:

Amount held in a retirement plan in Karen's name: $0.

Amount held in Karen's name personally (accumulated income distributions from the QTIP trust): $4,439,000.

Amount held in the QTIP trust (passing to children): $1,087,200 (gross of $1,800,000 paid to marital trust, minus 39.6% tax)

Total value to family: $5,526,000

Assuming Karen were to die at this point, the QTIP trust would pass to the children (actually, it would be subject to estate tax on Karen's death; however, for purposes of illustration, these scenarios assume that all estate taxes on both spouses' estates are paid by some other source of funds).

Scenario 2: QRP benefits paid to Karen, IRA to children.

Here are the assumptions used in Scenario 2:
One of Ken's children will probably be in the 31% bracket; the other would probably be in the 36% bracket. To compromise these differences, an overall tax rate of 33.5% on the children's benefits is used. The trust and Karen are always in the 39.6% bracket (even though Karen's bracket might drop after her eventual retirement).
The IRAs would be distributed gradually to the children over the 46.4-year life expectancy of the oldest child. This would call for

very small minimum distributions especially in the early years, but each child's income from this source would gradually increase. By the time the children reach their 60's, *each* would be receiving distributions of $40,000 per year (and growing) from the IRA fund. It would be a major source of retirement funding for them.

Karen would take the plans payable to her as a lump sum and roll them over to her own IRA. She would then defer all distributions until her age 70½, when she would start withdrawing benefits using the Uniform Lifetime Table (¶ 1.4.01).

Under this scenario here is what each beneficiary would have in 30 years: The children's accumulated personal funds (outside the IRA) would be, for both children together, $1,419,000, consisting of the accumulated after-tax MRDs from the inherited IRA. In addition, they would have $1.509 million *still inside* the IRA, to be distributed to them over the next 17 years. Contrast this with their having $1,087,000 outside of an IRA and *nothing* inside a retirement plan under Scenario 1. Increase in value to children: $1,841,000.

	Scenario 1: Benefits to Marital Trust	Scenario 2: QRP to Karen; IRA to Children	Increase:
Karen holds:			
In IRA	-0-	4,164,000	
Outside IRA	4,439,000	2,771,000	
Total	4,439,000	6,935,000	2,496,000
Children Hold:			
In IRA	-0-	1,509,000	
Outside IRA	1,087,000	1,419,000	
Total:	1,087,000	2,928,000	1,841,000
Total Value to Family:	5,526,000	9,863,000	4,337,000

Karen would have, in 30 years, accumulated $2.771 million *outside* of her rollover IRA from the accumulated MRDs, and would still have $4.164 million *inside* her rollover IRA. Thus her combined value would be $6.935 million, vs. $4.439 million under Scenario 1. Increase to Karen: $2,496,000.

Note: under Scenario 2 a substantial portion of Karen's and the children's money would still be inside an IRA and would not yet have been taxed, whereas under Scenario 1 all of the money would be after-tax. But, under Scenario 2, even if Karen totally liquidated her IRA 30 years from now (as opposed to continuing to distribute it gradually to herself over 15 more years), her after-tax value would be $5.286 million, which is still $847,000 *more* than under Scenario 1.

Summary: If all benefits are left to a QTIP trust, all beneficiaries are *substantially worse off* than if some benefits are left to Karen outright and some to the children outright.

Quentin: Early retirement with "SOSEPP"

Quentin, age 56, is cutting back his workload. He is changing his position at his firm from full time managing director to part time consultant. He will still see a few clients, work on the marketing committee and drive a company car, but he will turn over the reins (and the nights and weekends work) to his successors.

To finance this plan, Quentin figures he needs an annual income of $150,000 over and above the paycheck he will receive from the firm. Since his profit sharing plan at the firm has $5 million in it, he figures he can afford his proposed agenda—*if* he can get money out of the retirement plan at a reasonable cost. He knows he has to pay income tax on the plan withdrawals but would like to avoid the 10% penalty.

First, Quentin looks at what would happen if he took money directly out of his company plan and put it in his bank account. *If* he were completely retiring now, he could withdraw from the company plan without penalty, because there is an exception to the 10% penalty for distributions from a qualified plan upon separation from service at age 55 or later (¶ 9.4.04). But this exception is not available to Quentin because he is not terminating his employment; he is just cutting back, not leaving.

The next thing he investigates is the possibility of taking a "series of substantially equal periodic payments" (SOSEPP) from the company plan. But this avenue, too, is blocked, because this exception is not available for distributions from a qualified plan unless there has been a "separation from service," and Quentin is not separating from service.

Quentin's solution is to (1) take a partial distribution of his benefits from the company plan, (2) roll the distribution over to an IRA, then (3) use the rollover IRA to support a SOSEPP to him that will satisfy the requirements of § 72(t). ¶ 9.2. He hires an actuary to determine what size fund would be needed to produce equal annual payments of $150,000 over his life expectancy, and generally to help him design the SOSEPP. The actuary suggests the following strategy to get Quentin his $150,000 per year:

First, create the *smallest possible* separate rollover IRA needed, within IRS guidelines, to support a $150,000 per year payout to Quentin. Unless there is a serious risk of totally depleting the entire account prior to the end of the age 59½-five year no-modifications period (¶ 9.3.01), it is desirable to use the smallest possible IRA because the less money that is tied up in this IRA (where it must remain untouched for five whole years, except for distributions required for the series), the more money is left in his company plan. The money that is still left in Quentin's *company* plan can be withdrawn freely after he reaches age 59½ in three years, without penalty, and without contaminating the series of equal payments Quentin is receiving from the IRA. Also, if it turns out that Quentin, before reaching age 59½, needs more money than the series is providing, he can always take *another* distribution from the company plan and use it to establish *another* rollover IRA, and use that second IRA to establish a new SOSEPP. ¶ 9.2.13.

In contrast to this, if all or most of his retirement plan money is tied up in the IRA that is supporting the SOSEPP, he will have little or no flexibility to increase his distributions if it turns out that he needs more money in the next five years than he now expects.

Now that we know the goal is to get level payments of $150,000 per year, for five years, using the smallest possible rollover IRA, several decisions become easy. First, it is necessary to decide which of the three IRS-approved methods (¶ 9.2.05) will be used to calculate the SOSEPP. The IRS's "minimum distribution" method is out; it does not produce the level, predictable payments Quentin is looking for. So the choice narrows down to the annuitization or amortization method.

Second, as between a joint or a single life expectancy, Quentin should use the single life expectancy; the shorter the payout period, the smaller the fund needed to produce $150,000/year over that payout period. Third, the actuary will use the highest interest rate permitted (see ¶ 9.2.09), for the same reason. Finally, the actuary will use whichever of the two remaining methods (amortization or annuitization) produces a higher payment for a given fund.

Note that Quentin's program for taking penalty-free early distributions is possible only because his company's profit sharing plan allows in-service withdrawals for employees who have attained age 55. Not all plans allow such withdrawals. If Quentin's plan did not permit any in-service withdrawals there would be no way he could access his retirement plan without quitting his job. This is a reminder that the flexibility of an IRA that is "custom-made" to support a SOSEPP is available only to participants who *have* IRAs to begin with, or who can get money from other types of retirement plans into an IRA.

Appendix A: Tables

1. <u>The Uniform Lifetime Table</u>

Table for Determining Applicable Distribution Period (Divisor)			
Age	Distribution period	Age	Distribution period
70	27.4	93	9.6
71	26.5	94	9.1
72	25.6	95	8.6
73	24.7	96	8.1
74	23.8	97	7.6
75	22.9	98	7.1
76	22.0	99	6.7
77	21.2	100	6.3
78	20.3	101	5.9
79	19.5	102	5.5
80	18.7	103	5.2
81	17.9	104	4.9
82	17.1	105	4.5
83	16.3	106	4.2
84	15.5	107	3.9
85	14.8	108	3.7
86	14.1	109	3.4
87	13.4	110	3.1
88	12.7	111	2.9
89	12.0	112	2.6
90	11.4	113	2.4
91	10.8	114	2.1
92	10.2	115 and up	1.9

This table must be used by all taxpayers to compute lifetime required distributions for 2003 and later years, unless the sole beneficiary is the participant's more-than-10-years-younger spouse. See ¶ 1.4. This table may not be used: by beneficiaries of a deceased participant (except in year of participant's death); or for years prior to 2002 (optional for 2002).

For each "Distribution Year," determine: (A) the account balance as of the preceding calendar year end; (B) the participant's age on his or her birthday in the Distribution Year; and (C) the "applicable distribution period" (divisor) for that age from the above table. "A" divided by "C" equals the minimum required distribution for the Distribution Year.

2.   <u>Uniform Lifetime Table, Younger Ages</u>: For pre-age 59½ SOSEPPs using "RMD Method." See ¶ 9.2.08. Do NOT use this table for computing MRDs to beneficiaries.

Taxpayer's Age:	ADP:	Taxpayer's Age:	ADP:
21	75.3	43	53.4
22	74.3	44	52.4
23	73.3	45	51.5
24	72.3	46	50.5
25	71.3	47	49.5
26	70.3	48	48.5
27	69.3	49	47.5
28	68.3	50	46.5
29	67.3	51	45.5
30	66.3	52	44.6
31	65.3	53	43.6
32	64.3	54	42.6
33	63.3	55	41.6
34	62.3	56	40.7
35	61.4	57	39.7
36	60.4	58	38.7
37	59.4	59	37.8
38	58.4	60	36.8
39	57.4	61	35.8
40	56.4	62	34.9
41	55.4	63	33.9
42	54.4	64	33.0

3.   <u>Single Life Expectancy Table</u>. For computing required distributions after Participant's death (see ¶ 1.2.04, ¶ 1.5). Use this table to compute MRDs to beneficiaries.

Ages 0 to 57

Age	Life Expectancy	Age	Life Expectancy
0	82.4	29	54.3
1	81.6	30	53.3
2	80.6	31	52.4
3	79.7	32	51.4
4	78.7	33	50.4
5	77.7	34	49.4
6	76.7	35	48.5
7	75.8	36	47.5
8	74.8	37	46.5
9	73.8	38	45.6
10	72.8	39	44.6
11	71.8	40	43.6
12	70.8	41	42.7
13	69.9	42	41.7
14	68.9	43	40.7
15	67.9	44	39.8
16	66.9	45	38.8
17	66.0	46	37.9
18	65.0	47	37.0
19	64.0	48	36.0
20	63.0	49	35.1
21	62.1	50	34.2
22	61.1	51	33.3
23	60.1	52	32.3
24	59.1	53	31.4
25	58.2	54	30.5
26	57.2	55	29.6
27	56.2	56	28.7
28	55.3	57	27.9

Single Life Table, cont.

Ages 58 to 111+

Age	Life Expectancy	Age	Life Expectancy
58	27.0	87	6.7
59	26.1	88	6.3
60	25.2	89	5.9
61	24.4	90	5.5
62	23.5	91	5.2
63	22.7	92	4.9
64	21.8	93	4.6
65	21.0	94	4.3
66	20.2	95	4.1
67	19.4	96	3.8
68	18.6	97	3.6
69	17.8	98	3.4
70	17.0	99	3.1
71	16.3	100	2.9
72	15.5	101	2.7
73	14.8	102	2.5
74	14.1	103	2.3
75	13.4	104	2.1
76	12.7	105	1.9
77	12.1	106	1.7
78	11.4	107	1.5
79	10.8	108	1.4
80	10.2	109	1.2
81	9.7	110	1.1
82	9.1	111+	1.0
83	8.6		
84	8.1		
85	7.6		
86	7.1		

4. <u>Tax on Various Lump Sum Distributions</u>. Chart prepared by Ed Slott, CPA; see Appendix C for Ed's *IRA Advisor* newsletter.

If Your Lump Sum Distribution is:	10 Year Averaging Tax Is:
$100,000	14,471
150,000	24,570
200,000	36,922
250,000	50,770
275,000	58,270
300,000	66,330
318,833	72,733
350,000	83,602
375,000	93,102
400,000	102,602
450,000	122,682
500,000	143,682
550,000	164,682
600,000	187,368
650,000	211,368
700,000	235,368
750,000	259,368
800,000	283,368
850,000	307,368
900,000	332,210
1,000,000	382,210

For meaning of this Chart, see ¶ 2.3.08.

Appendix B
Forms

Table of Contents

INTRODUCTION; DRAFTING CHECKLIST

Introduction; Drafting Checklist

This Appendix contains sample forms which can be used by practitioners as a starting point for drafting their own forms for various clients and situations. In drafting forms to dispose of retirement benefits, keep in mind the following points:

1.   Impress on the client that the "Designation of Beneficiary Form" is just as important a legal document as a will or trust. Often, more of the client's assets are controlled by this form than by his will. An improperly drafted (or missing) beneficiary designation form could cost the client's estate and family thousands of dollars in taxes, lost deferral opportunities and increased settlement costs.

2.   Read the applicable sections of the "Account Agreement" establishing the client's IRA or Roth IRA, to make sure the beneficiary designation and payout method the client desires are permitted. In the case of a qualified retirement plan (QRP) benefit, read the "Summary Plan Description" or the description of available benefit payout options in the employer-provided beneficiary designation form, then check conclusions with the Plan Administrator. In case of doubt read the actual plan documents.

3.   There are certain issues in the disposition of death benefits that need to be considered and covered. While some IRA providers now cover these matters in their printed IRA documents, others do not. If these matters are *not* covered in the IRA agreement or QRP documents, they can be covered in the beneficiary designation form:

A.   Who chooses the form of death benefits, the client-participant or the beneficiary? In the forms in this Appendix, the beneficiary chooses the form of death benefit (see Section 3.01 in the Master Beneficiary Designation forms, 2.1 and 2.2).

B.   On the death of the Participant, the primary beneficiary is entitled to the benefits. If the beneficiary does not withdraw them immediately, what happens to benefits that are still in the IRA (or QRP) when the *primary beneficiary* dies? Will they pass to a new beneficiary designated by the primary beneficiary? Do they now belong to the primary beneficiary's estate, so they pass under his or her will? See

¶ 1.9.02. The Master Beneficiary Designation Forms in prior editions of this book specified that the beneficiary could name his or her own beneficiary. That part of the form has been dropped in this edition because experience showed that the provision doesn't help if the Plan doesn't allow beneficiaries to name their own beneficiaries, and is unnecessary if the Plan does allow beneficiaries to name their own beneficiaries.

      C.   In the case of an IRA (or Roth IRA), can the beneficiary transfer the benefits to another IRA (or Roth IRA) still in the name of the deceased Participant? See Section 3.08 of the IRA/Roth IRA Master Beneficiary Designation Form (Form 2.1) and ¶ 2.5.01.

4.   Problems frequently arise with IRA providers when practitioners submit beneficiary designation forms that place unsuitable duties on the IRA provider. Most IRAs are custodial accounts, under which the IRA provider's duties are limited to custodial and tax reporting services, and the provider's fees are nominal. Administrators of most company retirement plans also are not set up to monitor and administer employees' retirement benefit accounts individually. There are IRA providers who offer "individual retirement trusts" (IRTs), which are identical in all tax attributes to IRAs, but are structured as trusts rather than custodial accounts. The IRT provider is the trustee of the IRT, and as such often provides a higher level of services than the typical IRA account contemplates. The IRT provider's fees would also typically be higher if it is providing trust services rather than just custodial services. Unless the client's particular IRA or IRT provider is set up to provide individual services customized for that client (with appropriate charges), the provider cannot be expected to do much more than send out benefit checks in specified proportions to beneficiaries whose names, addresses and Social Security numbers are listed in the beneficiary designation form. Here are some "do's and don't's" for avoiding problems with the plan or IRA administrator:

      A.   Don't require the administrator to make legal judgments. A form that says "I leave the benefits to X unless he disclaims the benefits by means of a qualified disclaimer within the meaning of section 2518," appears to require the plan administrator to determine whether the disclaimer is qualified under § 2518 before it can decide who to pay the benefits to. Compare Form 3.1.

B.   <u>Don't require the administrator to carry out functions of an executor or trustee</u>. For example, if you say "I designate my son as beneficiary, to receive only the minimum required distribution each year," you are requiring the plan administrator to control the beneficiary's withdrawals. Most IRAs have no mechanism for restricting the beneficiary's withdrawals. If you want to restrict the beneficiary's withdrawals or make them conditional in any way ("beneficiary can withdraw funds as needed for education"; "beneficiary can withdraw funds so long as she has not remarried") you must either (i) leave the benefits to a trust (so the trustee can enforce the conditions); or (ii) find an IRA provider that offers accounts which allow restricted withdrawal provisions (and probably charges accordingly).

C.   <u>Don't require the administrator to determine amounts dependent on external facts</u>. If it is necessary to include, in your beneficiary designation form, a formula that is dependent on external facts (for example, "I leave my grandchild an amount equal to my remaining GST exemption," or "I leave to the marital trust the minimum amount necessary to eliminate federal estate taxes"), do this in a way that does not make the IRA provider responsible to apply the formula. Provide that a beneficiary or fiduciary will certify the facts to the IRA provider, who can rely absolutely on such certification. See, e.g., Section II(B) of Form 3.3(A).

D.   <u>Do avoid redundant or contradictory lists of definitions and payout options</u>. The lists of definitions in Forms 2.1 and 2.2 are intended to be used with IRAs and retirement plans which have (as many do) no or incomprehensible defined terms. If the plan document already has suitable and clear definitions of "primary beneficiary," "death benefit," "the account" and other terms, using a different set of definitions may just create confusion.

5.   Consider whether you wish to alter the applicable presumptions in case of simultaneous death. See ¶ 3.1.02.

6.   If the disposition is intended to qualify for the marital deduction, include language to that effect. See Section 3.07 in the Master Beneficiary Designation forms (2.1 and 2.2); and several others, including Form 7.4; and ¶ 3.3.05, ¶ 3.3.14.

7.   Consider the extent to which you need to define any terms such as "issue *per stirpes*," or "income"; and/or specify which state's law shall be used to interpret terms you use in the form. It is highly likely that the QRP or IRA agreement specifies that the law of the sponsor's state of incorporation will be used. Since that may well not be the state in which your client lives (or dies), there is a potential for problems if the client's chosen disposition depends on a definition which varies from state to state. Although you cannot change the governing law of the "plan," a statement that the language *of the beneficiary designation* will be interpreted according to the laws of a particular state should be accepted in the sense that it will lead to the correct determination of the client's intent. See Section 3.04, Forms 2.1, 2.2.

8.   Follow the required formalities of execution. Most IRAs are simply custodial accounts. As such, they may be considered "probate" assets of Participant's estate in some states. Some states do not recognize a disposition of certain forms of retirement benefits unless executed with the formalities of a will.

9.   The choice of a contingent beneficiary should not be overlooked. For example:

A.   If benefits are being made payable to a trust, to take advantage of Participant's unified credit while providing life benefits for the surviving spouse, consider naming the trust as primary beneficiary only if the spouse survives. Consider naming the children (assuming that is Participant's choice as contingent beneficiary) directly as contingent beneficiaries if the spouse does not survive, to avoid the complications of running benefits through a trust (see Form 3.5(A)).

B.   Consider whether different contingent beneficiaries should be named depending on whether the primary beneficiary actually dies before Participant, or merely disclaims the benefits (see Form 3.6).

10.   Whenever a trust is named as beneficiary, see the Trust Drafting Checklist at ¶ 6.1.05, and be sure to file the required documentation (see Forms 6.1 and 6.2). Some beneficiary designation forms in this Appendix in which benefits are left to a trust describe the trust as "the [TRUST NAME] Trust [optional:, a copy of which is attached hereto]."

The phrase "a copy of which is attached hereto" is optional, and would be used solely to identify the trust that is named as beneficiary. Attaching a copy of the trust to the beneficiary designation form does NOT satisfy the "documentation requirement." You could choose to identify the trust by other means (*e.g.*, "under agreement dated 1/1/98") instead of attaching a copy of the trust to the beneficiary designation form. No matter how you choose to identify the trust which is named as beneficiary, you ALSO must comply with the documentation requirement; see ¶ 6.2.09-¶ 6.2.10 and Forms 6.1 and 6.2.

11. It is strongly advised to include complete contact information for the beneficiaries, or they and the IRA provider may never find each other; and also to require the administrator to provide information to the participant's executor. See Section 3.02, Forms 2.1 and 2.2.

12. Finally, don't focus on taxes and minimum distributions to the exclusion of basic drafting issues. If the spouse is named as beneficiary, is that only if he/she is married to Participant at time of death?...or does divorce revoke the designation of spouse? If any beneficiary predeceases Participant, does his/her share pass instead to the surviving beneficiaries, or to his/her own issue, or to someone else?

1. SIMPLE BENEFICIARY DESIGNATION FORM

Who might use this form: This form may be suitable for a client who wants to leave benefits outright to his spouse if living, otherwise to his children equally (and issue of deceased children). This form is included primarily for use with (1) retirement plans that are of relatively small value and (2) retirement plans that already contain, in the plan documents, the estate plan-friendly additional provisions included in the longer Master Beneficiary Designation forms (2.1 and 2.2). If the benefit is of substantial value, either absolutely or relative to the rest of the client's estate, and the plan documents do not have provisions dealing with the important estate planning issues covered in the longer forms, it would be advisable to use the longer forms.

1.1   Simple Beneficiary Designation: Spouse, Then Children (or Issue)

DESIGNATION OF BENEFICIARY

TO: [Name of IRA or Roth IRA Provider or Plan Administrator]
FROM: [Name of Participant]
RE: [IRA or Roth IRA No._____] or [or Name of Plan]

1.   I hereby designate as my beneficiary, my spouse, [SPOUSE NAME], whose date of birth is [SPOUSE BIRTHDATE], to receive all benefits payable under the above [account] [plan] in the event of my death.

2.   If my spouse does not survive me, I designate as my beneficiaries, in equal shares, such of my children as shall survive me; provided, that if any of my children does not survive me, but leaves issue surviving me, such issue shall take the share such deceased child would have taken if living, by right of representation. My children are:

Name   Address   Date of Birth   Social Security Number   Phone

[alt. 1: pay minor's benefits to a custodian]
3.   Any benefits becoming distributable to a person under the age of twenty-one (21) years shall be distributed to such person's surviving parent, if any, otherwise to my oldest then living child, as custodian for such person under the Uniform Transfers to Minors Act. Such custodian shall be entitled to act for the minor in all respects with regard to the benefits.

[alt. 2: pay minor's benefits to Participant's trust; make sure the trust instrument has suitable provision to receive this payment and hold it for the particular minor beneficiary who is entitled to it]
3.   Any benefits becoming distributable to a person under the age of twenty-one (21) years shall be distributed to the Trustee then serving as such under the [NAME OF TRUST] created by [Agreement/Declaration/Instrument/my Will] dated [date of trust

instrument] [optional:, a copy of which is attached hereto], to be held and administered for the benefit of such person as provided therein.

4.   Regardless of who is named as beneficiary above, you shall provide to the executor, administrator or other duly appointed representative of my estate such information regarding me, my account or my beneficiary(ies) as such representative may reasonably request in connection with the performance of his, her or its duties as such representative.

Signed this _____ day of _____, 20 ___.

_____
Signature of Participant

2.   MASTER BENEFICIARY DESIGNATION FORMS: MORE COMPLEX PROVISIONS

How to use these forms: These Master Beneficiary Designation forms are meant to be used with all beneficiary designation forms provided in Sections 3 and 4 of this Appendix. Form 2.1 is meant to be used with IRAs (traditional and Roth). Form 2.2 is for QRPs. Make sure the IRA agreement does not contradict anything contained in these forms before using them. Some IRA providers now cover these matters in their printed IRA documents, making it unnecessary to repeat the provisions in the beneficiary designation form.

Other notes: Drafters will not use all of these provisions in every beneficiary designation form. Section 3.03 can be omitted if no minors can possibly become beneficiaries. Section 3.05 could be dispensed with if it is not likely there will be multiple beneficiaries. Section 3.07 can be omitted if Participant is not naming his spouse as beneficiary or contingent beneficiary. For discussion of the reason behind Section 3.07, see ¶ 3.3.14. These provisions, like all forms, are intended as examples only, and should be modified as necessary for individual clients. Also, note that a particular IRA provider or QRP administrator may not be willing to accept some of these provisions.

2.1   Master Beneficiary Designation: Traditional or Roth IRA

DESIGNATION OF BENEFICIARY

TO: _____

      Name of Custodian or Trustee of the Account

FROM: _____

      Name of Participant

RE: Account No. _____

I.   Definitions

The following words, when used in this form and capitalized, shall have the meaning indicated in this Section.

"Account" means the "Individual Retirement Account," "Individual Retirement Trust," "Roth Individual Retirement Account" or "Roth Individual Retirement Trust" referred to above, which is established and maintained under § 408 or § 408A of the Code.

"Administrator" means the IRA custodian or trustee named above, and its successors in that office.

"Agreement" means the account agreement between the Administrator and the undersigned establishing the Account.

"Beneficiary" means any person or entity entitled to ownership of all or part of the Account as a result of my death (or as a result of the death of another Beneficiary), whether such person or entity is a Primary, Contingent or Successor Beneficiary.

"Contingent Beneficiary" means the person(s) I have designated in this form to receive the Death Benefit if my Primary Beneficiary does not survive me (or disclaims the benefits).

"Death Benefit" means all amounts payable under the Account on account of my death.

The "Personal Representative" of any person means the duly appointed guardian or conservator of such person, or executor or administrator of such person's estate, who is serving as such at the applicable time.

"Primary Beneficiary" means the person or persons I have designated in this form to receive the Death Benefit in the event of my death.

"Successor Beneficiary" means a person entitled to receive the balance of another Beneficiary's benefits if such other Beneficiary dies before distribution of all of his or her share of the Death Benefit.

II.   Designation of Beneficiary

[Here insert the chosen designation of beneficiary provision, from Section 3 or 4 of this Appendix B, or elsewhere.]

III.   Other Provisions [dispense with any of these that are not appropriate in view of the choice of beneficiary or that are not necessary because already covered in the IRA provider's documents governing the Account]

3.01   Form of Benefit Payments after my Death. Except as may be otherwise specifically provided herein, or in the Agreement, or by applicable law, each Beneficiary shall be entitled to elect the form and timing of distribution of benefits payable to him or her.

3.02   Information to be provided to Personal Representative. The Administrator shall provide to my Personal Representative any information such representative shall request in connection with the performance of such representative's duties (including the preparation of any tax return) regarding the benefits, the terms of the account, and the beneficiaries, including information as to matters prior to such representative's appointment, to the same extent and on the same terms that such information would have been provided to me had I requested it. Any beneficiary, by accepting benefits hereunder, shall be deemed to have consented to the release of information to my Personal Representative as provided in the preceding sentence.

3.03   Payments to Minors. If any Beneficiary becomes entitled to ownership of any part of the Account at a time when he or she is under the age of twenty-one (21) years, such ownership shall instead be vested in the name of such Beneficiary's surviving parent, if any, otherwise in the name of my oldest then living child if any, otherwise in the name of some other person selected by my Personal Representative, as custodian for such Beneficiary under the Uniform

Transfers to Minors Act of the state of my domicile at death, and such custodian shall have the power to act for such Beneficiary in all respects with regard to the Account.

3.04   Governing Law. The law of the State of _____ shall apply solely for the purpose of interpreting my intent as expressed in this Designation of Beneficiary form. This provision is not intended to amend or supercede any governing law provision in the Agreement with respect to the interpretation and administration of the Agreement.

3.05   Multiple Beneficiaries. If there are multiple Beneficiaries entitled to ownership of the Account simultaneously, I direct that each such Beneficiary's proportionate share of the Account shall be treated as a separate account, payable solely to such Beneficiary, within the meaning of Treasury Regulation § 1.401(a)(9)-8, A-3, and that the Account shall be deemed divided (as of the date of my death) into separate accounts, in proportion to the relative amounts payable to the respective Beneficiaries, with one such separate account payable to each of my Beneficiaries for purposes of determining the amount required to be distributed to each Beneficiary under § 401(a)(9) of the Internal Revenue Code. So long as the separate accounts remain commingled, all investment gains and losses incurred in the Account shall be allocated among the separate accounts in proportion to the relative values of the separate accounts. A distribution from the Account to any Beneficiary (or a transfer from the Account to a separate individual retirement account, still in my name, and payable to such Beneficiary) shall be charged to that Beneficiary's separate account (reducing its value for purposes of subsequent allocations of investment gains or losses). The Beneficiaries shall be entitled, by joint written instructions to the Administrator, to have the Account partitioned into multiple Accounts, corresponding to each Beneficiary's separate account, as of or at any time after my death, to the maximum extent such division is permitted by law to occur without causing a deemed distribution of the Account. Following such partition the newly created separated Accounts shall be maintained as if each were an Account in my name payable solely to the applicable Beneficiary, and no Beneficiary shall have any further interest in or claim to any Account other than the separate Account representing his or her interest.

3.06   Allowing Beneficiary to Appoint Investment Manager. The Beneficiary may designate an Investment Manager for the Account (or, if the Account has been partitioned pursuant to the preceding provisions hereof, such Beneficiary's separated Account). Upon receipt of written authorization from the Beneficiary, and until receiving notice that such authorization is revoked, the Administrator shall comply with investment instructions of the Investment Manager in accordance with the Beneficiary's authorization.

3.07   Preservation of marital deduction. If my spouse survives me, this paragraph shall apply to any portion (or all) of the Account as to which my spouse is the Beneficiary or as to which my spouse becomes the Beneficiary by virtue of the death of (or a disclaimer by) a prior Beneficiary. My spouse, as such Beneficiary, shall have the right, exercisable solely by my spouse, annually or more frequently (in my spouse's discretion), to require distribution to my spouse of all income of the Account, and also shall have the power, exercisable by my spouse alone and in all events, at any time or times and from time to time, to appoint all of the principal of the Account (including undistributed income) to my spouse. Rights given to my spouse under this paragraph shall be in addition to and not in limitation of any rights given to my spouse by law, by the Agreement or by other provisions hereof. My spouse shall have sole responsibility for determining the "income" and "principal" of the Account. The Administrator's responsibility under this section is limited solely to distributing to my Spouse any amounts my Spouse has instructed the Administrator to distribute to my Spouse.

3.08   Transferring Account. The Beneficiary shall have the right to have the Account (or, if the Account has been partitioned pursuant to the preceding provisions hereof, such Beneficiary's separated Account) transferred to a different individual retirement account or trust, of the same type ("traditional" or "Roth") as the Account, still in my name, with the same or a different custodian or trustee, if at the applicable time such transfer is permitted by law to occur without causing a deemed distribution of the Account.

Signed this _____ day of _____, 20 ___.

_____
Signature of Participant

> Receipt of the above beneficiary designation form is hereby acknowledged this ___ day of _____, 20 ___.
>
>
>   _____
>   Name of Custodian or Trustee
>   By:_____
>   Title

2.2   Master   Beneficiary   Designation   Form: Qualified Retirement Plan

WARNING: If Participant is married, spousal consent is required if anyone other than spouse is named as beneficiary. See ¶ 3.4.

> ### DESIGNATION OF BENEFICIARY
> TO: _____
>   Name of Trustee or Plan Administrator
> FROM: _____
>   Name of Participant
> RE: _____
>   Name of Retirement Plan
>
>
> I.   Definitions
>
>   The following words, when used in this form and capitalized, shall have the meaning indicated in this Section.
>   "Administrator" means the Plan Administrator or Trustee named above, and its successors in such office.
>   "Beneficiary" means any person entitled to receive benefits under the Plan as a result of my death (or as a result of the death of another Beneficiary).
>   "Contingent Beneficiary" means the person(s) I have designated in this form to receive the Death Benefit if my Primary Beneficiary does not survive me (or disclaims the benefits).
>   "Death Benefit" means all benefits payable under the Plan on

account of my death.

The "Personal Representative" of any person means the duly appointed guardian or conservator of such person, or executor or administrator of such person's estate, who is serving as such at the applicable time.

"Plan" means the qualified retirement plan or other retirement arrangement described at the beginning of this form.

"Primary Beneficiary" means the person designated in this form to receive benefits under the Plan on account of my death.

"Successor Beneficiary" means a person entitled to receive the balance of another Beneficiary's benefits if such other Beneficiary dies before distribution of all of his or her share of the Death Benefit.

II.   Designation of Beneficiary

[Here insert the chosen designation of beneficiary provision, from Section 3 or 4 of this Appendix B, or elsewhere.]

III.   Other Provisions [dispense with any of these that are not appropriate in view of the choice of beneficiary or that are not necessary because already covered in the plan documents governing the benefits]

3.01   Form of Benefit Payments After My Death. Except as may be otherwise specifically provided herein, in the Plan, or by applicable law, each Beneficiary shall be entitled to elect the form and timing of distribution of any benefits payable to such Beneficiary.

3.02   Information to be provided to Personal Representative. The Administrator shall provide to my Personal Representative any information such representative shall request in connection with the performance of such representative's duties (including the preparation of any tax return) regarding the benefits, the Plan, and the beneficiaries, including information as to matters prior to such representative's appointment, and including copies of Plan documents and returns, to the same extent and on the same terms that such information would have been provided to me had I requested it. Any beneficiary, by accepting benefits hereunder, shall be deemed to have consented to the release of information to my Personal Representative as provided in the preceding sentence.

3.03   Payments to Minors. If any Beneficiary becomes entitled to benefits under the Plan at a time when he or she is under the age of twenty-one (21) years, such benefits shall be instead payable to such Beneficiary's surviving parent, if any, otherwise to my oldest then living child, if any, otherwise to some other person selected by my Personal Representative, as custodian for such Beneficiary under the Uniform Transfers to Minors Act, and such custodian shall have the power to act for such Beneficiary in all respects with regard to the benefits to which such Beneficiary is entitled.

3.04   Governing Law. The law of the State of _____ shall apply solely for the purpose of interpreting my intent as expressed in this Designation of Beneficiary form. This provision is not intended to amend or supercede any governing law provision in the Plan with respect to the interpretation and administration of the Plan.

3.05   Multiple Beneficiaries. If there are multiple Beneficiaries entitled to ownership of the Death Benefit simultaneously, I direct that each such Beneficiary's proportionate share of the Death Benefit shall be treated as a separate account, payable solely to such Beneficiary, within the meaning of Treasury Regulation § 1.401(a)(9)-8, A-3, and that the Death Benefit shall be deemed divided (as of the date of my death) into separate accounts, in proportion to the relative amounts payable to the respective Beneficiaries, with one such separate account payable to each of my Beneficiaries for purposes of determining the amount required to be distributed to each Beneficiary under § 401(a)(9) of the Internal Revenue Code. So long as the separate accounts remain commingled, all investment gains and losses shall be allocated among the separate accounts pro rata, that is, in proportion to the relative values of the separate accounts. A distribution to any Beneficiary shall be charged to that Beneficiary's separate account (reducing its value for purposes of subsequent allocations of investment gains or losses). The Beneficiaries shall be entitled, by joint written instructions to the Administrator, to have the Death Benefit partitioned into multiple Accounts, corresponding to each Beneficiary's separate account, as of or at any time after my death, to the maximum extent such division is otherwise permitted by the Plan and by law (without causing a deemed distribution of the Death Benefit). Following such partition the newly created separated Accounts shall be maintained as if each were a Death Benefit in my name payable solely to the applicable Beneficiary, and no Beneficiary shall have any further interest in or claim to any Death Benefit other than the separate account representing his or her interest.

3.06   Allowing Beneficiary to Appoint Investment Manager. The Beneficiary may designate an Investment Manager for the Death Benefit (or, if the Death Benefit has been divided pursuant to the preceding provisions hereof, such Beneficiary's share of the Death Benefit). Upon receipt of written authorization from the Beneficiary, and until receiving notice that such authorization is revoked, the Administrator shall comply with investment instructions of the Investment Manager in accordance with the Beneficiary's authorization.

3.07   Preservation of marital deduction. If my spouse survives me, this paragraph shall apply to any portion (or all) of the Death Benefit as to which my spouse is the Beneficiary or as to which my spouse becomes the Beneficiary by virtue of the death of (or a disclaimer by) a prior Beneficiary. My spouse, as such Beneficiary, shall have the right, exercisable solely by my spouse, annually or more frequently (in my spouse's discretion), to require distribution to my spouse of all income of the Death Benefit, and also shall have the power, exercisable by my spouse alone and in all events, at any time or times and from time to time, to appoint all of the principal of the Death Benefit (including undistributed income) to my spouse. Rights given to my spouse under this paragraph shall be in addition to and not in limitation of any rights given to my spouse by law, by the Plan or by other provisions hereof. My spouse shall have sole responsibility for determining the "income" and "principal" of the Death Benefit. The Administrator's responsibility under this section is limited solely to distributing to my spouse any amounts my spouse has instructed the Administrator to distribute to my spouse.

3.08   Honoring Disclaimers. Notwithstanding the foregoing, if a Beneficiary disclaims all or any portion of any interest in the Death

Benefit to which such Beneficiary would otherwise be entitled under the foregoing provisions hereof, by means of a written disclaimer that appears to be a qualified disclaimer within the meaning of § 2518 of the Internal Revenue Code, then that Beneficiary shall be deemed (as to the interest so disclaimed) to have predeceased me, the interest so disclaimed shall pass as if such Beneficiary had predeceased me and the Beneficiary who takes the interest so disclaimed shall be "my beneficiary" under the Plan for purposes of the requirement that benefits be paid to "my beneficiary." This provision shall not be construed to prevent an interest disclaimed by my spouse from passing to my spouse by other means.

Signed this _____ day of _____, 20 ___.

_____
Signature of Participant

Receipt of the above beneficiary designation form is hereby acknowledged this ___ day of _____, 20 ___.

_____
Name of Plan Administrator or Trustee
By:_____
Title

3.   SEVEN WAYS TO LEAVE BENEFITS TO THE MARITAL AND/OR CREDIT SHELTER SHARE

3.0   Explanation of the marital/credit shelter forms, including the "Minimum Marital Share Override" and "State Death Tax Override" clauses

Each of the following forms is a beneficiary designation designed to leave benefits to a marital or credit shelter share, or to split benefits between a marital and credit shelter share. These can be inserted into "Part II" of the appropriate "Master Beneficiary Designation Form" (Form 2.1 for a traditional or Roth IRA, Form 2.2 for a QRP) in the preceding section of this Appendix. Related provisions to be included in the client's trust instrument, when applicable, follow the beneficiary designation form.

Optional "Minimum Marital Share Override" clauses

In view of the changing exemption amounts under the federal estate tax, and the scheduled repeal (and reinstatement?) of that tax, formula clauses based on federal estate tax concepts may not work as intended (or at all). Under several of the marital/credit shelter formulas in this Appendix, if no "override" clause were added, nothing at all would go into the marital share if the estate tax were not in effect at the Participant's death. Because that result could be contrary to the client's intent, each of those forms includes an optional "**Minimum Marital Share Override**" provision, which provides that a certain minimum amount or percentage must be allocated to the marital share regardless of what the estate tax-based formula says.

This point must be discussed with the client before the estate plan is drafted: How much would you choose to leave to your spouse (or marital trust) if it is not necessary to leave *anything* to your spouse (or marital trust) to eliminate estate taxes on your estate? If the client is leaving assets to the spouse (or marital trust) only because that disposition is necessary to gain maximum federal estate tax deferral, the estate plan does not need a Minimum Marital Share Override. If, on the other hand, client wants the spouse (or the marital trust) to receive a certain minimum dollar or percentage amount regardless of what the federal estate tax happens to provide when client dies, it is necessary to include a Minimum Marital Share Override clause to carry out the client's intent. Each of the following forms includes such an optional clause if appropriate. The "Other Notes" at the beginning of each form explain whether that particular form includes an optional Minimum Marital Share Override clause and why or why not.

Needless to say, the client's estate plan must be reviewed regularly in light of all changes in the estate tax and other applicable laws that may affect it. Including a Minimum Marital Share Override in the trust instrument does not resolve all the possible issues concerning federal estate tax repeal or increased exemptions. The purpose of the Minimum Marital Share Override in these forms is simply to assure that a marital/credit shelter formula clause does not inadvertently, due to estate tax repeal or increased estate tax exemptions, leave to the spouse (or marital trust) less than the client intends the spouse (or marital trust) to receive.

Optional "State Death Tax Override" clauses

For many decades prior to EGTRRA 2001, the federal estate tax allowed a credit for state death taxes. The maximum credit was determined by a table. Most states adopted an estate tax equal to this credit amount. EGTRRA reduces and gradually eliminates the credit over several years; see discussion at ¶ 2.2.07, 3. This federal law change has the indirect effect of reducing state revenues. Many states are responding by enacting additional death taxes. As state death taxes decouple from the federal estate tax, a marital clause based solely on the federal estate tax may not minimize state death taxes. When this dichotomy applies, the client may have to choose between minimizing all death taxes on the first death and minimizing federal estate taxes on the second death. Some clients (especially if they are very wealthy, don't expect that the federal estate tax will really disappear before the surviving spouse dies, and face a relatively modest state death tax) will want to continue to use a federal-tax-only formula, assuring the lowest possible overall federal estate taxes on both estates even if that means incurring some "unnecessary" state death taxes on the first death.

Other clients (especially if they think the federal estate tax is likely to disappear by the time the surviving spouse dies and/or if the state death tax that would apply on the first death could be substantial) may prefer to pay as little tax as possible on the first death and take their chances regarding what happens at the second death. For this second group, the marital/credit shelter formula clauses in this Appendix offer an alternative formula clause, the **"State Death Tax Override"** clause, that makes the marital share whatever is necessary to minimize both federal AND state death taxes on the first death. Whether this clause is suitable for a particular client depends on that client's objectives as well as the particular form of state death tax adopted by that client's state.

3.1   Life Insurance to Credit Shelter Trust, Rest to Spouse

Who would consider using this form: Any client who holds life insurance inside his QRP, and wants the insurance proceeds payable to a trust (*e.g.,* to "fill up" a credit shelter trust), but wants the surviving spouse to be able to roll over the non-insurance portion of the benefits.

Warning: A client whose plan-held insurance is held in a "subtrust" (¶ 8.4.01) cannot designate the beneficiary for the policy.

Other notes: Under this form the amount each beneficiary receives is not dependent on an estate tax-driven formula. The credit shelter trust gets the insurance proceeds and the spouse gets the rest of the benefits, regardless of whether the federal estate tax exists or what the federal estate tax exemption amount is. Therefore, it is not necessary to include a Minimum Marital Share Override.

3.1   Beneficiary Designation Form

II.   <u>Designation of Beneficiary</u>

    A.   <u>Primary Beneficiary</u>

If my spouse, [SPOUSE NAME], survives me, the Death Benefit shall be distributed to the following Primary Beneficiaries:

1.   Any amount payable under any contract of life insurance on my life shall be paid to [TRUSTEE NAME], as Trustee of the [TRUST NAME] Trust, under Agreement of Trust dated [TRUST DATE] [optional:, a copy of which is attached hereto].

2.   The balance of the Death Benefit shall be paid to my spouse.

    B.   <u>Contingent Beneficiary</u>

If my spouse does not survive me (or to the extent my spouse disclaims any benefits otherwise distributable to my spouse under section A above), I direct that 100% of the Death Benefit (or the amount disclaimed as the case may be) shall be paid to [TRUSTEE NAME], as Trustee of the "Family Trust" of the said [TRUST NAME] Trust.

3.2   Benefits Payable to "Pourover" Trust, Under Which Assets Are Divided Between a Marital Share (Paid to Spouse Outright) and a Credit Shelter Trust by a Fractional Formula. Benefits Allocated to Marital Share

Who would consider using this form: Client who expects to need to use some or all of his retirement benefits to "fill up" a credit shelter trust, and wants any benefits not needed for that purpose paid to the spouse outright so she can roll them over. See ¶ 10.5.

Drawbacks of this form: Under this form and the related trust provision, the trustee is required to fund the marital share with retirement benefits to the maximum extent possible, and then is required to distribute the marital share outright to the spouse on her request. This approach is based on IRS private letter rulings, permitting the surviving spouse to roll over benefits which pass to her through a trust, if she has the unfettered right to withdraw the benefits. ¶ 3.2.09. Since this IRS policy has so far appeared only in private letter rulings, there is no guarantee the IRS will continue to recognize such rollovers, although it appears likely (and correct under the Code) that such rollovers will be allowed.

Other notes: This form names only the trust as beneficiary, regardless of whether the spouse survives. If the entire trust is to be distributed to Participant's issue outright on the death of the surviving spouse, consider naming the trust as primary beneficiary only if the spouse survives, and naming the issue directly as beneficiaries if the spouse does not survive. See form 3.5 for an example of this approach. Because this Form 3.2 has different dispositive provisions for the marital share (paid outright to spouse) and the credit shelter share (held in trust), an optional Minimum Marital Share Override provision is included in the trust form.

3.2(A) Beneficiary Designation Form

II.   Designation of Beneficiary

A.   Primary Beneficiary

I hereby designate as my Primary Beneficiary, to receive 100% of the Death Benefit in case of my death, [TRUSTEE NAME]

(hereinafter "my Trustee"), as Trustee of the [TRUST NAME] Trust, under Agreement of Trust dated [TRUST DATE] [optional:, a copy of which is attached hereto].

B.   Distribution of Benefits to Spouse

My Trustee is directed under the said Agreement of Trust to allocate the Death Benefit, pursuant to a formula, between my spouse and the "Family Trust" established under said Agreement of Trust. My Trustee is further directed or permitted under said Agreement of Trust to cause the part of the Death Benefit so allocated to my spouse to be (i) distributed outright to my spouse or (ii) transferred directly to an "individual retirement account" (or other eligible retirement plan) in my spouse's name. Accordingly, if the Administrator is so instructed by my Trustee, the Administrator shall, with respect to the amount indicated by my Trustee, (i) distribute such amount outright to my spouse or (ii) transfer such amount directly to an "individual retirement account" (or other eligible retirement plan) in my spouse's name.

3.2(B) Related Trust Provisions

__.   Payments After My Death

Upon my death, the Trustee shall hold and administer all property of the Trust, including any amounts received or receivable then or later as a result of my death or otherwise, as follows:

.01   If my spouse does not survive me, the Trustee shall designate all of such property as the "Family Trust," to be held and administered as provided in Article __.

.02   If my spouse survives me, the Trustee shall divide the said property into two separate shares, to be designated respectively the Marital Share and the Family Trust. The two separate shares shall be funded pursuant to the following formula. If application of the formula results in assets being allocated to only one of the shares instead of both, the Trustee shall fund only such one.

[Version 1: minimize federal estate tax only:]

.03   The Trustee shall allocate to the Marital Share a portion of the Remaining Trust Property determined by multiplying the Remaining Trust Property by a fraction. The numerator of the fraction shall be the smallest amount necessary, if allowed as a marital deduction, to eliminate (or minimize, if it is not possible to eliminate) the federal estate tax otherwise payable by reason of my death, reduced by the value of all other items included in my estate which qualify for the federal estate tax marital deduction and which pass or have passed to my spouse otherwise than under this provision. The denominator of the fraction is the value of the Remaining Trust Property. For purposes of this formula:

(i)   It shall be assumed with respect to property not passing under this trust that my Executor will elect to treat as "qualified terminable interest property" all property eligible for such treatment.

(ii)   The "values" of assets shall be their values as finally determined for purposes of the federal estate tax on my estate.

(iii)   The "Remaining Trust Property" means all property of this trust that is included in my federal gross estate, reduced by the amount of any debts, expenses of administration, specific and pecuniary bequests and death taxes payable out of such property.

(iv)   The federal estate tax credit for state death taxes shall be taken into account only to the extent its use does not increase the state death taxes otherwise payable on my estate.

[Version 2: **State Death Tax Override**: minimize both federal and state death taxes at the first death:]

.03   The Trustee shall allocate to the Marital Share a portion of the Remaining Trust Property determined by multiplying the Remaining Trust Property by a fraction. The numerator of the fraction shall be the smallest amount necessary, if allowed as a marital deduction, to eliminate (or minimize, if it is not possible to eliminate) the federal estate tax otherwise payable by reason of my death, or, if greater, the smallest amount necessary, if allowed as a marital deduction, to eliminate (or minimize, if it is not possible to eliminate) any state estate or inheritance tax otherwise payable by reason of my death, reduced (in either case) by the value of all other items included in my estate which qualify for the applicable marital deduction and which pass or have passed to my spouse otherwise than under this provision. The denominator of the fraction is the value of the Remaining Trust Property. For purposes of this formula:

     (i)   It shall be assumed with respect to property not passing under this trust that my Executor will elect to treat as "qualified terminable interest property" all property eligible for such treatment.

     (ii)   The "values" of assets shall be their values as finally determined for purposes of the applicable tax.

     (iii)   The "Remaining Trust Property" means all property of this trust that is included in my estate for purposes of such tax, reduced by the amount of any debts, expenses of administration, specific and pecuniary bequests and death taxes payable out of such property.

     (iv)   The federal estate tax credit for state death taxes shall be taken into account only to the extent its use does not increase the state death taxes otherwise payable on my estate.

[optional: **Minimum Marital Share Override**: this can go with either version of subparagraph .03: "Notwithstanding the foregoing, the numerator of the fraction shall not be less than [here insert the minimum dollar amount the client wants the marital share to receive]" or "Notwithstanding the foregoing, the fraction applied to determine the portion of the Remaining Trust Property allocated to the Marital Share shall not be smaller than [here insert the minimum fractional or percentage amount the client wants the marital share to receive]."

     .04   All property not allocated to the Marital Share pursuant to the preceding formula shall be designated as the Family Trust, and administered as provided in Article __.

     .05   In selecting which assets shall be used to fund which share, the Trustee shall, to the maximum extent possible, allocate tax-favored retirement plans to the Marital Share and assets other than tax-favored retirement plans to the Family Trust. A "tax-favored retirement plan" means an individual retirement account (within the meaning of § 408 of the Internal Revenue Code (the "Code")), Roth individual retirement account (within the meaning of § 408A of the Code), qualified retirement plan (within the meaning of § 401(a) of the Code), "tax-sheltered annuity" (described in § 403(b) of the Code) and similar plans, accounts and arrangements.

.06   The Marital Share shall be distributed to my spouse, outright and free of trusts. To the extent that all or part of any tax-favored retirement plan is allocated to the Marital Share pursuant to the foregoing provisions, the Trustee may (and shall, if requested to do so by my spouse) cause such plan (or part thereof) to be paid directly from such plan to my spouse as beneficiary, or shall (if so requested by my spouse) cause such plan (or part thereof) to be transferred directly from such plan into another retirement plan account in my spouse's name, without the intervening step of transferring it to this Trust.

3.3   All Benefits Payable to a "Pourover" Trust, Under Which Assets are Divided Between a QTIP Marital Trust and a Credit Shelter Trust by a Fractional Formula; Drafter May Choose to Specify Allocation of Benefits to Marital Trust, Credit Shelter Trust or Neither

Who should consider this form: A client who does not want any benefits paid to the spouse outright and whose trust will be allocated between a marital trust and a credit shelter trust by a fractional formula. The related trust provisions contain two alternatives for funding these shares. One version requires benefits to be allocated to the marital share to the extent possible; the other requires benefits to be allocated to the credit shelter share to the extent possible. A third option is to omit both versions of paragraph .06 and allow the trustee to choose which assets to use to fund which share (but see ¶ 7.4.08).

Drawbacks of this form: No spousal rollover is possible under this form.

Other notes: If the trust named as beneficiary under this form has different dispositive provisions for the marital share and the credit shelter share (e.g., spouse is sole beneficiary for life of the marital share while the credit shelter trust is a "spray" trust for spouse and issue) determine whether including the optional Minimum Marital Share Override provision is necessary to carry out the client's intent.

3.3(A) Beneficiary Designation Form

II. Designation of Beneficiary

A. Primary Beneficiary

I hereby designate as my Primary Beneficiary, to receive 100% of the Death Benefit, [TRUSTEE NAME] (hereinafter "my Trustee"), as trustee of the [TRUST NAME] Trust, under Agreement of Trust dated [TRUST DATE] [optional: , a copy of which is attached hereto].

B. Division of Benefit

Under the terms of said Agreement of Trust, my Trustee is directed, if my spouse survives me, to divide the assets of said Trust into two separate trusts, to be designated the "Marital Trust" and the "Family Trust." If so instructed by my Trustee, the Administrator shall divide the Death Benefit into two separate accounts (within the meaning of Treasury Regulation § 1.401(a)(9)-8, A-3), both still in my name, one payable solely to the Marital Trust as Beneficiary and the other payable solely to the Family Trust as Beneficiary; or, in accordance with such instructions, shall designate the entire Death Benefit as payable to one of said trusts. The Administrator shall have no responsibility to determine the correctness of my Trustee's instructions regarding such allocation, and shall have no liability whatsoever to any person for complying with my Trustee's said instructions. The beneficiaries of the Marital Trust and Family Trust shall look solely to my Trustee for enforcement of their rights under the said Trusts.

C. Benefits Payable to Marital Trust

With regard to any portion of the Death Benefit so allocated to the Marital Trust, there must be distributed to the Marital Trust in each year, beginning with the year of my death, from the Marital Trust's portion of the Death Benefit, at least the net income of the Marital Trust's portion of the Death Benefit for such year accrued after my death. My Trustee, and not the Administrator, shall have sole responsibility for determination of the amount of such income, and directing the distribution of such amount to the Marital Trust.

3.3(B) Related Trust Provisions

___.   Payments Upon My Death

Upon my death, the Trustee shall hold and administer all property of the Trust, including any amounts received or receivable then or later as a result of my death or otherwise, as follows:

[here, copy sections .01 through .04 from form 3.2(B), including the optional **Minimum Marital Share Override** if appropriate, but change "Marital Share" to "Marital Trust", and add:]

.05   The Marital Trust shall be held and administered as provided in Article ___.

[Use one or the other of the following optional funding provisions, or neither, **but not both**]

[optional funding provision: alternative 1]

.06   Any death benefit under any "qualified retirement plan," individual retirement account, Roth IRA or similar tax-favored retirement arrangement that is payable to this Trust shall be allocated to the Marital Trust to the maximum extent possible within the limits of the preceding formula.

[optional funding provision: alternative 2]

.06   Any death benefit under any "qualified retirement plan," individual retirement account, Roth IRA or similar tax-favored retirement arrangement that is payable to this Trust shall be allocated to the Family Trust to the maximum extent possible within the limits of the preceding formula.

[here insert Form 7.4, or otherwise take steps to qualify for the marital deduction; see ¶ 3.3.05]

3.4   Benefits Payable to Marital Trust That Is Part of a "Pourover" Trust with a Pecuniary Marital Formula

Who should consider using this form: A client who wants to use a pecuniary marital formula for his marital/credit shelter share division because it is easier to administer; who wants his retirement benefits paid to a marital trust, and not outright to his spouse; and whose retirement benefits will probably not be needed to fund the credit shelter share. By making the benefits payable directly to the Marital Trust, the client avoids having the pecuniary formula applied to the benefits (see ¶ 2.2.05), avoids the complexity of transferring the retirement benefits from a "funding" trust into a Marital or Family Trust, and avoids having to use a fractional formula for any assets.

The preferred simplicity of administration which comes from using a pecuniary formula does not have to be sacrificed just because part of the trust will consist of retirement benefits. Under this form, the retirement benefits do not go through the pecuniary funding formula—the benefits bypass the formula and go straight into the Marital Trust.

Drawbacks: If the retirement benefits turn out to be a greater amount than is required, as a marital deduction gift, to eliminate estate taxes, then this form would overfund the marital share. That problem can be solved easily post mortem by a fractional QTIP election, or, less easily, by a disclaimer by the marital trust. Also, no spousal rollover is possible under this form.

Other notes: If the trust named as beneficiary under this form has different dispositive provisions for the marital share and the credit shelter share (e.g., spouse is sole life beneficiary of the marital share while credit shelter trust is a "spray" trust for spouse and issue) determine whether including the Minimum Marital Share Override is necessary to carry out the client's intent. Under this Form 3.4, the spouse is guaranteed to get at least the amount of the retirement benefits, because those are allocated to the marital trust *regardless* of what happens under the formula, so the question is whether the client wants the marital trust to be sure to receive the *greater* of (1) all the retirement benefits or (2) a specified dollar amount.

3.4(A) Beneficiary Designation Form

II.   Designation of Beneficiary

A.   Primary Beneficiary

I hereby designate as my Primary Beneficiary, to receive 100% of the Death Benefit, [TRUSTEE NAME], as trustee of the [MARITAL TRUST NAME] Marital Trust, established under Agreement of Trust dated [TRUST DATE] [optional:, a copy of which is attached hereto].

B.   Form of Distribution of Benefits

After my death, there shall be distributed to the Beneficiary, in each year, so long as my spouse is living, whichever of the following amounts is the greatest:

(a)   the net income of the Death Benefit for such year;

(b)   the Minimum Distribution Amount for such year; or

(c)   such amount as the Beneficiary shall direct by written instructions to the Administrator.

The Beneficiary, not the Administrator, shall have sole responsibility for determining the amounts under subparagraphs (a), (b) and (c).

3.4(B) Related Trust Provisions

___.   Payments After My Death

Upon my death, the Trustee shall hold and administer all property of the Trust, including any amounts received or receivable then or later as a result of my death or otherwise, as follows:

.01   If my spouse does not survive me, the Trustee shall designate all such property as the "Family Trust" to be held and administered as provided in Article ___.

.02   If my spouse survives me, the Trustee shall divide the said property into two separate trust funds, to be designated the Marital Trust and the Family Trust, pursuant to the following formula. If application of the formula results in assets being allocated to only one of the trusts instead of both, the Trustee shall fund only such one.

(a)   The Trustee shall allocate to the Marital Trust all benefits payable under any "qualified retirement plan," "individual retirement account" (other than Roth IRAs), or similar retirement plan, annuity or arrangement, as well as any assets that are payable by the terms of my will, beneficiary designation form or otherwise directly to the Marital Trust.

(b)   The Trustee shall allocate to the Marital Trust such additional amount, if any, as is necessary to bring the total value of the Marital Trust up to the Optimum Marital Amount. To the extent there is a choice of assets, this gift to the Marital Trust shall be funded to the extent possible only with assets or the proceeds of assets that qualify for the applicable estate tax marital deduction. The Marital Trust shall be held and administered as provided in Article ____.

[alt. 1: no Minimum Marital Share Override; minimize federal estate tax only]

(c)   The "Optimum Marital Amount" means the smallest amount which, if it passed to my spouse in a manner qualifying for the federal estate tax marital deduction, would eliminate the federal estate tax on my estate (or minimize such tax, if it is not possible to eliminate it), reduced by the value of any property passing to my spouse otherwise than under this trust to the extent such property qualifies for the federal estate tax marital deduction (or would so qualify if my Personal Representative so elected). In computing the Optimum Marital Amount, the federal estate tax credit for state death taxes shall be taken into account only to the extent its use in the foregoing formula does not increase the state death taxes otherwise payable on my estate. If the amount passing to my spouse would have no effect on the computation of the federal estate tax on my estate (for example, because such tax has been repealed) the Optimum Marital Amount shall be zero.

[alt. 2: includes Minimum Marital Share Override and State Death Tax Override]

(c)   The "Optimum Marital Amount" means the greatest of the following three amounts: (1) the smallest amount which, if it passed to my spouse under this trust in a manner qualifying for the federal estate tax marital deduction, would eliminate the federal estate tax on my estate (or minimize such tax, if it is not possible to eliminate it); or (2) the smallest amount which, if it passed to my spouse under this trust in a manner qualifying for the marital deduction, would eliminate any state estate or inheritance tax applicable to my estate (or minimize such tax, if it is not possible to eliminate it); or (3) $[here insert the minimum combined dollar amount the client wants to have pass to the spouse and the marital trust], reduced by the value of any property passing to my spouse otherwise than under this trust. In computing the Optimum Marital Amount, the federal estate tax credit for state death taxes shall be taken into account only to the extent its use in the foregoing formula does not increase the state death taxes otherwise payable on my estate.

(d)　　All property not allocated to the Marital Trust pursuant to the preceding formula (or, if no property is allocable to the Marital Trust pursuant to preceding formula, then all property of the Trust) shall be designated as the Family Trust, to be held and administered as provided in Article ____.

[here insert Form 7.4, or otherwise take steps to qualify for marital deduction; see ¶ 3.3.05.]

3.5　Benefits Payable to "One Big QTIP Trust" if Spouse Survives; Trustee Can Divide the Trust; Issue are Contingent Beneficiaries

Who would use this form: The client who wants all income of his benefits paid to his spouse for life, but wants principal remaining at the spouse's death to pass to beneficiaries selected by client. This form leaves all the benefits to "one big QTIP trust," with the trustee having discretion either to make a fractional QTIP election, or to divide the trust into two separate trusts at the client's death, with the QTIP election being made for only one of them, whichever seems best at the time. Participant's issue are named directly as contingent beneficiaries if spouse does not survive Participant.

Drawbacks: See ¶ 10.5.05, and *Koslow* case study, Chapter 11.

Other notes: The trust Form 3.5(B) allows the trustee to divide the trust into two or more separate trusts. Generation skipping transfer tax implications of division of a trust into two or more trusts are beyond the scope of this book. Since under this form the dispositive provisions are not affected either by federal estate tax repeal, or by the amount of the federal estate tax exemption, or by state death taxes (because the terms of the marital and credit shelter shares are identical) it is not necessary to include a Minimum Marital Share Override or State Death Tax Override.

3.5(A) Beneficiary Designation Form

II.   Designation of Beneficiary

    A.   Primary Beneficiary

I hereby designate as my primary Beneficiary, to receive 100% of the Death Benefit, if my spouse survives me, [TRUSTEE NAME], as Trustee of the [TRUST NAME] Trust under Agreement of Trust dated [TRUST DATE] [optional:, a copy of which is attached hereto].

    B.   Form of Distribution of Benefits

After my death, there shall be distributed to the Beneficiary, in each year, so long as my spouse is living, whichever of the following amounts is the greatest:

    (a)   the net income of the Death Benefit for such year;

    (b)   the Minimum Distribution Amount for such year; or

    (c)   such amount as the Beneficiary shall direct by written instructions to the Administrator.

The Beneficiary shall have sole responsibility for complying with these instructions as to the Form of Distribution of Benefits. The Administrator shall have no responsibility or liability to calculate the amounts specified above or to see that they are distributed. Any person who claims that the distributions called for above have not been properly made shall look solely to the Beneficiary for satisfaction of such claim.

    C.   Contingent Beneficiary

I hereby designate as my Contingent Beneficiary, to receive 100% of the Death Benefit if my spouse does not survive me, my issue surviving me, by right of representation.

3.5(B) Related Trust Provisions

__.   Payments After My Death

Upon my death, the Trustee shall hold and administer all property of the Trust, including any amounts received or receivable then or later as a result of my death or otherwise, as follows:

.01   If my spouse does not survive me, the Trustee shall designate all of such property as the "Family Trust," to be held and administered as provided in Article __.

.02   If my spouse survives me, the Trustee shall pay to my spouse the net income from the date of my death, at least quarter annually, for life.

.03   If this Trust is the beneficiary of death benefits under any "individual retirement account," "Roth IRA," "qualified retirement plan," or similar tax-favored retirement arrangement or annuity (the "Plan") the Trustee must withdraw from the Plan, in each calendar year, and deposit in this trust fund, at least whichever of the following amounts is the greater: (a) the Plan's net income for such year; or (b) the "minimum distribution amount" required to be withdrawn from such Plan under § 401(a)(9) of the Internal Revenue Code or other Code provisions or applicable law. This paragraph .03 shall not be deemed to limit the Trustee's power and right to withdraw from the Plan in any year more than the greater of the said two amounts.

.04   Upon the death of my spouse, the principal, as it may then exist, shall be held, administered and distributed as provided for property of the Family Trust under Article __.

.__   Division of the Trust

The Trustee in its discretion may divide the trust into two or more separate shares, each such separate share to be administered as a separate trust on all the same terms provided herein for the undivided trust fund. I anticipate that the Trustee will exercise its discretion under this Article for reasons of administrative convenience, or in order to recognize different characteristics the separate shares or trusts will have for purposes of certain taxes.

3.6   Benefits Payable to Spouse, "Disclaimable" to Credit Shelter Trust; Different Contingent Beneficiary Depending on Whether Spouse Predeceases or Disclaims

Who would consider using this form: A client who does not have sufficient non-retirement plan assets to fully fund a credit shelter trust, but nevertheless wants to leave the benefits to his spouse and allow the spouse to make the ultimate decision whether to (a) keep the benefits and roll them over to an IRA or (b) disclaim some or all of the benefits and allow them to flow to the credit shelter trust.

Drawbacks: See ¶ 8.2.04.

Other notes: Since under this form the surviving spouse is sole beneficiary of the benefits, and benefits pass to the credit shelter trust only to the extent the spouse chooses voluntarily to disclaim them, it is not necessary to include a Minimum Marital Share Override to assure spouse receives a certain amount. How much spouse receives is entirely within spouse's own control.

3.6   Beneficiary Designation Form

II.   Designation of Beneficiary

   A.   Primary Beneficiary

   I hereby designate as my Primary Beneficiary, to receive 100% of the Death Benefit, my spouse, [SPOUSE NAME], if my spouse survives me.

   B.   Contingent Beneficiary in Case of Disclaimer

   If my spouse survives me, but disclaims the Death Benefit (or part of it), I hereby designate as my Contingent Beneficiary, to receive the part (or all) of the Death Benefit so disclaimed, [TRUSTEE NAME], as Trustee of the [TRUST NAME] Trust, under agreement dated [TRUST DATE] [optional:, a copy of which is attached hereto].

   C.   Contingent Beneficiary in Case of Death

   If my spouse does not survive me, I hereby designate as my Contingent Beneficiary, to receive 100% of the Death Benefit, my issue surviving me, by right of representation.

3.7   Benefits Payable to Credit Shelter Trust, "Disclaimable" to Spouse

Who would consider using this form: A client who does not have sufficient non-retirement assets to fund a credit shelter trust, and expects to use his retirement benefits for that purpose, but wants to leave the door open for a spousal rollover because he thinks that (a) there might possibly be sufficient other assets to fund the credit shelter trust by the time he dies so the retirement benefits won't be needed after all or (b) even if there are not sufficient other assets to fund the credit shelter trust when he dies the rollover might appear at that time likely to produce a better overall tax and financial picture for his beneficiaries (see ¶ 10.5). This client does not want to make the benefits payable to the spouse and "disclaimable" to the credit shelter trust because he does not want to make the estate plan dependant on spouse's disclaimer.

Drawbacks of using this form: Do not use this form without first investigating applicable state law on disclaimers by fiduciaries.

Other notes: By using this form, the client has already decided that he is willing to have spouse receive no benefits (since under this form benefits pass to the surviving spouse only to the extent the credit shelter trust chooses voluntarily to disclaim them). Accordingly, it is not necessary to include a Minimum Marital Share Override to assure spouse receives a certain amount. How much spouse receives is within the control of the trustee of the credit shelter trust.

3.7(A) Beneficiary Designation Form

II.   <u>Designation of Beneficiary</u>

A.   <u>Primary Beneficiary</u>

I hereby designate as my Primary Beneficiary, to receive 100% of the Death Benefit [TRUSTEE NAME] (hereinafter "my Trustee"), as Trustee of the [TRUST NAME] Trust, under Agreement of Trust dated [TRUST DATE] [optional:, a copy of which is attached hereto].

B.   <u>Alternative Primary Beneficiary</u>

If and to the extent that my Trustee disclaims any of the Death Benefit, I name as my Primary Beneficiary, for the portion (or all) of the Death Benefit so disclaimed, my spouse, [SPOUSE NAME], if my spouse survives me.

3.7(B) Related Trust Provisions

.__ Disclaimers by Trustee

.01 The Trustee shall have the power and authority, without the approval of any court, and without the consent of any beneficiary, to disclaim (refuse to accept) all or part of any property or interest in property that is payable to the trust by gift, devise, inheritance, bequest or otherwise, if the Trustee, in its discretion, determines that such disclaimer is in the best interest of beneficiaries of this Trust or will otherwise help achieve the objectives of this Trust.

.02 In exercising its discretion under this Article, the Trustee shall be entitled to presume that any benefit conferred on an individual is likewise a benefit to the descendants of that individual, and shall bear in mind my objective of minimizing taxes for my family as a whole.

---

4. OTHER BENEFICIARY DESIGNATION FORMS

4.1 Spouse is Primary Beneficiary; Children are Contingent

This is a designation of spouse if living otherwise children (or their issue), suitable for use with Forms 2.1 and 2.2.

II. Designation of Beneficiary

A. Primary Beneficiary

I hereby designate as my Primary Beneficiary, to receive 100% of the Death Benefit, my spouse, [SPOUSE NAME], if my spouse survives me.

B. Contingent Beneficiary

If my spouse does not survive me, I hereby designate as my Contingent Beneficiary, to receive 100% of the Death Benefit, my children surviving me, in equal shares; provided, that if any child of mine does not survive me, but leaves issue surviving me, such issue shall take the share such deceased child would have taken if living, by right of representation.

4.2   Designating Children (Or Their Issue) as Beneficiaries

This is a designation of living children (and issue of deceased children) as the primary beneficiaries, suitable for use with the Master Beneficiary Designation forms (Forms 2.1 and 2.2).

II.   Designation of Beneficiary

I hereby designate as my Primary Beneficiary, to receive 100% of the Death Benefit, my children surviving me, in equal shares; provided, that if any child of mine does not survive me, but leaves issue surviving me, such issue shall take the share such deceased child would have taken if living, by right of representation.

5.   MISCELLANEOUS FORMS

5.1   Power of Attorney Dealing with Retirement Benefits

This clause could be added to the client's power of attorney or set up as a separate power of attorney just dealing with benefits:

5.1   Power of Attorney Dealing with Retirement Benefits

[This clause could be added to the client's power of attorney or set up as a separate power of attorney just dealing with benefits. The precise form and formalities of execution need to be appropriate for the applicable jurisdiction and the participant's circumstances. For any significant retirement plan benefit, determine in advance whether the plan will honor this form; some IRAs, for example, require customers to use a particular form prepared by the IRA provider.]

My Agent shall have the power to establish one or more "individual retirement accounts" or other retirement plans or arrangements in my name.

In connection with any pension, profit sharing or stock bonus plan, individual retirement arrangement, Roth IRA, § 403(b) annuity or account, § 457 plan, or any other retirement plan, arrangement or annuity in which I am a participant or of which I am a beneficiary (whether established by my Agent or otherwise) (each of which is hereinafter referred to as "such Plan"), my Agent shall have the following powers, in addition to all other applicable powers granted by this instrument:

1.   To make contributions (including "rollover" contributions) or cause contributions to be made to such Plan with my funds or otherwise on my behalf.

2.   To receive and endorse checks or other distributions to me from such Plan, or to arrange for the direct deposit of the same in any account in my name or in the name of [NAME OF CLIENT'S LIVING TRUST].

3.   To elect a form of payment of benefits from such Plan, to withdraw benefits from such Plan, to make contributions to such Plan and to make, exercise, waive or consent to any and all elections and/or options that I may have regarding the contributions to, investments or administration, of, or distribution or form of benefits under, such Plan.

[alt. 1: Power-of-attorney holder can choose beneficiary]

4.   To designate one or more beneficiaries or contingent beneficiaries for any benefits payable under such Plan on account of my death, and to change any such prior designation of beneficiary made by me or by my Agent; provided, however, that my Agent shall have no power to designate my Agent directly or indirectly as a beneficiary or contingent beneficiary to receive a greater share or proportion of any such benefits than my Agent would have otherwise received unless such change is consented to by all other beneficiaries who would have received the benefits but for the proposed change. This limitation shall not apply to any designation of my Agent as beneficiary in a fiduciary capacity, with no beneficial interest.

[alt. 2: Power-of-attorney holder is to name a particular beneficiary]

4.   To designate my spouse, [SPOUSE NAME], if living, otherwise my issue surviving me by right of representation, as beneficiary of any benefits payable under such Plan on account of my death.

5.2   Disclaimer of All Interests in an IRA

DISCLAIMER OF INDIVIDUAL RETIREMENT ACCOUNT

TO: [Name of IRA or Roth IRA Provider] and [Name(s) of deceased
          Participant's executor(s) or administrator(s)]

FROM: [Name of Beneficiary who is disclaiming]

RE: [Identify the IRA or Roth IRA being disclaimed; e.g., include
          account number and repeat name of the IRA provider firm]

IN THE NAME OF THE LATE: [Name of deceased Participant]

          I hereby unconditionally disclaim and refuse to accept any
interest in the above-described individual retirement account left to me
as beneficiary by the late [Name of deceased Participant]. I hereby
certify that I have not accepted the interest hereby disclaimed or any
benefits of such interest.

Signed this _____ day of _____, 20 ___.

_____
                    [Name of Beneficiary who is disclaiming]

[Include any formalities of execution, such as witnesses, notarization,
etc. required by applicable state law or by the IRA provider.]

---

6.   FORMS TO COMPLY WITH THE DOCUMENTATION REQUIREMENT OF IRS "TRUST RULES" WHEN TRUST IS NAMED AS BENEFICIARY OF RETIREMENT BENEFITS

6.1   Cover Letter: Post-Death Distributions: If Copy of Trust Is Given to the Plan

          See ¶ 6.2.09. By October 31 of the year after the year of the
Participant's death (or October 31, 2003, if later), the trustee of the trust
that is named as beneficiary must send a copy of the trust (or the
alternative "certification"; see Form 6.2) to the plan administrator.
Although there is no requirement that any particular form accompany
the copy of the trust, the following form can be used as a cover letter to
accompany a copy of the trust sent to the plan administrator after the
Participant's death:

To the Plan Administrator:

Enclosed herewith is a copy of the actual trust document for the trust, of which the undersigned is the trustee, that is named as a beneficiary of [NAME OF DECEASED PARTICIPANT] under the [NAME OF RETIREMENT PLAN].

Signed:_____

Trustee

6.2 Certification Form: Post-Death Distributions: If Copy of Trust Is NOT Given to the Plan

If the trustee does not send a copy of the trust itself to the plan administrator (see Form 6.1), the trustee of the trust that is named as beneficiary must send the plan administrator the following certification:

To the Plan Administrator:

The late [NAME OF DECEASED PARTICIPANT] named the [NAME OF TRUST] ("the Trust"), established under instrument of trust dated [DATE OF TRUST], of which the undersigned is the trustee, as beneficiary of his/her death benefits under the [NAME OF RETIREMENT PLAN] ("the Plan"). In accordance with Treasury Regulation § 1.401(a)(9)-4, A-6(b):

(i) I hereby certify that the following is a complete list of all beneficiaries of the Trust with respect to the trust's interest in the Plan (including contingent and remainderman beneficiaries, with a description of the conditions on their entitlement), as of September 30 of the calendar year following the calendar year in which [NAME OF DECEASED PARTICIPANT] died.

[The following is this author's interpretation of what the IRS is looking for when it requires "a complete list of all beneficiaries of the Trust"; this is not an official form. The following assumes a trust for the life benefit of Participant's spouse, with remainder to Participant's issue who are living at the death of the spouse; it assumes there are such issue living at Participant's death, and that no person has the power to vary the identity or relative shares of the beneficiaries.]

"Current beneficiary(ies): The participant's spouse, [NAME OF SPOUSE], who is entitled to all income of the trust for life, plus principal distributions if needed for medical expenses or support. If at any time during the spouse's life there is no child of the participant (and no issue of a deceased child of the participant) living, the trust terminates and is distributed to the spouse outright and free of trusts.

"Remainder beneficiary(ies) (entitled to benefits upon the death of the participant's spouse, if they survive the spouse): The participant's children in equal shares, with issue of any deceased child to take the share such deceased child would have taken had he/she survived the participant's spouse; these beneficiaries take the trust property outright and free of trust on the death of the spouse. The names, addresses, Social Security numbers and dates of birth of the participant's currently living children are: [INSERT].

(ii) I certify that to the best of my knowledge: the above list is correct and complete; and that, within the meaning of Treas. Reg. § 1.401(a)(9)-4, A-5(b), paragraphs (1), (2) and (3), the trust is valid under applicable state law, all beneficiaries of the trust are identifiable and the trust was irrevocable by its terms as of the participant's date of death.

(iii) I agree to provide to you a copy of the Trust instrument upon demand.

Signed:_____
Trustee

7.   TRUST PROVISIONS DEALING WITH BENEFITS

7.1   Administration During Donor's Life; Irrevocability

The purpose of including this language is to assure that the trust is a "grantor trust" as to the Participant and to make it clear to any plan administrator that the "Second rule" (irrevocability; ¶ 6.2.07) is complied with. This form is not suitable for a testamentary trust.

___. Administration During my Life

.01   The Trustee shall distribute to me such amounts of the principal or income of the trust (including all thereof) as I may request from time to time, or (if I am legally incapacitated) as my guardian, conservator or other legal representative may request on my behalf.

.02   I reserve the right to amend or revoke this trust by one or more written and acknowledged instruments delivered to the Trustee during my lifetime. This trust shall become irrevocable at my death.

7.2   Insulating Retirement Assets From Estate Claims

Notwithstanding any other provision hereof, except as provided in this paragraph, the Trustee may not, on or after September 30 of the calendar year following the calendar year in which my death occurs, or on or after such earlier date as shall be established by IRS regulations or other guidance as the final date for determining whether this trust meets the requirements for treatment of the trust's beneficiaries as if they had been named directly as beneficiary of any retirement plan payable to this trust (the "Designation Date"), distribute to or for the benefit of my estate, any charity or any other non-individual beneficiary any Retirement Benefit payable to this trust under any qualified retirement plan, individual retirement account or other retirement arrangement subject to the "minimum distribution rules" of § 401(a)(9) of the Internal Revenue Code, or other comparable provisions of law. It is my intent that all such Retirement Benefits held by or payable to this trust on or after the Designation Date be distributed to or held for only individual beneficiaries, within the meaning of § 401(a)(9) and applicable regulations. Accordingly I direct that such benefits may not be used or applied on or after the Designation Date for payment of my debts, taxes, expenses of administration or other claims against my estate; nor for payment of estate, inheritance or similar transfer taxes due on account of my death. This paragraph shall not apply to any bequest or expense which is specifically directed to be funded with Retirement Benefits by other provisions of this instrument.

7.3　Excluding Older Adopted "Issue"

Notwithstanding any other provision hereof or of state law, the a person's "issue" shall not include an individual who is such person's "issue" by adoption if such individual (i) was so adopted after my death and (ii) is older than the oldest other beneficiary of this trust who was a living member of said class at my death.

7.4　Marital Deduction Savings Language

If any marital trust created by this instrument becomes the beneficiary of death benefits under any "individual retirement account," "Roth IRA," "qualified retirement plan," or similar tax-deferred retirement arrangement or annuity (the "Plan") the Trustee must withdraw from the Marital Trust's share of the Plan, each year, at least whichever of the following amounts is the greater:

A.　　the net income of the Marital Trust's share of such Plan for such year; or

B.　　the "minimum distribution amount" required to be withdrawn from such share under § 401(a)(9) of the Internal Revenue Code or other applicable law.

This paragraph shall not be deemed to limit the Trustee's power and right to withdraw from the Marital Trust's share of the Plan in any year more than the greater of the said amounts.

7.5　Defining "Retirement Benefit"

The following definition is very broad and would encompass variable annuities and so-called "non-qualified" deferred compensation arrangements. It is not the only possible definition. If retirement benefits are a significant asset in your client's estate, review this definition to make sure that it includes all types of benefits your client has, and that it works properly with any other special provisions you intend to include to deal with the client's retirement benefits.

In this instrument, the term "Retirement Benefit" means any benefit or amount that is owned by or payable to this trust under: an individual retirement account ("IRA") as defined in § 408; a Roth IRA as defined in § 408A; a "deemed" IRA or Roth IRA under § 408(q); an annuity or mutual fund custodial account under § 403(b); a pension, profit sharing, stock bonus or other retirement plan that is qualified under § 401(a); any other retirement plan or arrangement that is subject to the "minimum distribution rules" of § 401(a)(9), or equivalent rules under any other Code section; any annuity; or any plan or arrangement of deferred compensation for services. The plan, trust, account or arrangement under which any Retirement Benefit is held for or payable to this trust is referred to as a "Retirement Plan."

7.6   Accounting for Retirement Benefits

.01   General Principles. This Article shall govern the Trustee's accounting for Retirement Benefits. In general, a Retirement Benefit shall be deemed an asset of the Trust, increases or decreases in its value shall be allocated to income or principal of the Trust as provided herein, and distributions from the Retirement Benefit shall be accounted for as provided herein.

.02   Certain Individual Account Plans. With respect to a "self-directed" IRA or Roth IRA, or any other individual account Retirement Plan for which the Trustee receives such reporting of the investment activity in the Retirement Plan that the Trustee can readily determine the "income" and "principal" of the Trust's interest in the Retirement Plan in accordance with normal trust accounting principles, the Trustee shall account for the Trust's interest in the Plan as if the applicable Plan assets were owned by the Trust directly.

.03   Fixed Benefit Plans. With respect to any Retirement Benefit that consists of the right to receive one or more payments of a fixed amount on one or more certain dates, the Trustee shall treat the inventory value of the Retirement Benefit as principal, and all subsequent increase in value shall be treated as income, accruing over the time between the date of the inventory value and the date of payment, at the rate of interest used to discount such payment to present value for purposes of determining its inventory value.

.04   All Other Plans. With respect to any other Retirement Benefit, the Trustee shall treat the inventory value of the Retirement Benefit as principal, and allocate any subsequent increases in value (or charge decreases in value) to income or principal in accordance with any reasonable method selected by the Trustee and consistently applied to the Trust's interest in such Plan, including:

1.   A method specified in any "Uniform Principal and Income Act" or other state law governing trust accounting for retirement benefits or deferred compensation.

2.   In the case of a plan similar to the type of plan specified in paragraph .02 (or .03) above, the method specified in said paragraph .02 (or .03) adapted as necessary.

3.   Any method used in the Internal Revenue Code or Treasury regulations to distinguish between "ordinary income" and "return of principal" (or corpus) with respect to similar assets.

.05   Treatment of Distributions from Plan. When a distribution is received from a Retirement Benefit, and, at the time of such distribution, under the foregoing rules, the Retirement Benefit is composed of both income and principal, such distributions shall be deemed withdrawn first from the income portion of the Retirement Benefit, until such income portion is exhausted, except to the extent the Trustee chooses to charge such distribution to the principal portion of the Retirement Benefit.

.06   Definition of Inventory Value. In the interpretation of this Article, the "inventory value" of a Retirement Benefit shall mean:

        A.   In the case of a Retirement Benefit that becomes payable to (or is owned by) this trust as of the date of the donor's death, its "fair market value" determined in accordance with the rules applicable for valuing such interests for purposes of the federal estate tax (as in effect at the donor's death, or, if such tax does not then exist, as in effect on the date hereof). As is true under such rules, such value shall be determined without regard to any applicable restrictions that limit the ability to transfer such Retirement Benefit and without regard to the income taxability of future distributions from the Retirement Benefit; or,

        B.   In the case of a Retirement Benefit that becomes payable to this trust as of a date after the date of the donor's death (for example, by transfer from another fiduciary), its "fair market value" shall be its value as of the donor's death determined as provided in the preceding subparagraph, adjusted as necessary for distributions, expenditures and receipts that occurred between the date of the donor's death and the date of transfer to this trust; or, if the trustee cannot determine its value in that manner, its "fair market value" shall be its value as of the date it becomes an asset of this trust, determined as provided in the preceding subparagraph, provided, in the case of a Retirement Benefit transferred to this Trust from another fiduciary (such as the donor's Personal Representative) accrued income so transferred shall be treated as income and shall not be included in "inventory value."

7.7   Establishing a "Conduit Trust" for One Beneficiary

From and after my death, this trust shall be held for the benefit of [Name of individual trust beneficiary] (hereinafter referred to as the "Beneficiary"). Each year, beginning with the year of my death, my Trustees shall withdraw from any Retirement Benefit the Minimum Required Distribution for such Retirement Benefit for such year, plus such additional amount or amounts as the Trustee deems advisable in its sole discretion. All amounts so withdrawn (net of expenses) shall be distributed to the Beneficiary, if the Beneficiary is then living. If the Beneficiary is then deceased, my Trustees shall instead distribute to [Name(s) of remainder beneficiary(ies)] the amount which would have been distributed to the Beneficiary had the Beneficiary been living.

The following definitions shall apply in administering this trust: The Minimum Required Distribution for any year shall be, for each Retirement Benefit: (1) the value of the Retirement Benefit determined as of the preceding year-end, divided by (2) the Applicable Distribution Period; or such greater amount (if any) as the Trustee shall be required to withdraw under the laws then applicable to this Trust to avoid penalty. If my death occurred before my "required beginning date" with respect to such benefit, the Applicable Distribution Period means the life expectancy of the Beneficiary. If my death occurred on or after my "required beginning date" with respect to such benefit, the Applicable Distribution Period means the life expectancy of the Beneficiary, or (if longer) my remaining life expectancy. Notwithstanding the foregoing, if my death occurred on or after my "required beginning date" with respect to such Benefit, the Minimum Required Distribution for the year of my death shall mean (a) the amount that was required to be distributed to me with respect to such Benefit during such year, minus (b) amounts actually distributed to me with respect to such Benefit during such year. Life expectancy, and the meaning of "required beginning date" and other terms in this paragraph, shall be determined in accordance with § 401(a)(9) of the Internal Revenue Code of 1986, as amended and Treasury regulations thereunder.

Appendix C

Resources

This Appendix lists software, newsletters and other resources available to help professionals in planning for their clients' retirement plan benefits. For books, see the Bibliography. Prices, ordering information and features change constantly, so check with the vendor before placing an order.

Software

Most providers offer a downloadable demo at their web sites.

Brentmark Pension & Roth IRA Analyzer® (v. 8.00). $395. Includes 6 months' free maintenance; $129 annual update fee. Powerful feature-filled software to help planners analyze proposed plan distribution strategies from QRPs, IRAs and Roth IRAs (comparing up to 4 scenarios simultaneously), including income tax, estate tax and spousal rollover aspects. Also analyzes whether it is worthwhile to convert a traditional IRA to a Roth IRA and computes pre-59½ SOSEPP distributions. It's easy to use right out of the box—maybe deceptively so; the ideal user is an experienced planner with some training to understand the impact that changing assumptions has on outcome. I use Brentmark's mini program, Pension Distributions Calculator (v. 6.30, $149), for quick minimum distribution projections. Brentmark Software, Inc., 3505 Lake Lynda Drive # 212, Orlando FL 32817-8327; 1-800-879-6665 or 407-306-6160; www.brentmark.com. The Brentmark web site has lots of free information and useful links; the top web site for professionals on retirement distributions planning.

MRD-Determinator® 3.0. This product of the outstanding brain of Guerdon Ely, the financial planner and math whiz, is designed to do all MRD calculations as well as projections comparing possible distribution scenarios. MRD-Determinator provides more help than other programs in understanding the rules applicable in a particular case. It is geared toward compliance and investment advice. This Excel-based program is focused on the timing of plan distributions more than overall estate planning. $395, includes one-year support; $235 annual fee after that. Net Worth Strategies, 960 SW Disk Drive Ste B, Bend,

OR 97702, 541-383-3899, www.NetWorthStrategies.com.

Steve Leimberg's NumberCruncher®. $395 plus shipping (annual updates $99). This is not primarily a retirement distributions analysis product, but it does pre-59½ SOSEPP distribution calculations. The program is fast and extremely easy to use. The printout shows the assumptions used in making the calculations, which is extremely helpful. NumberCruncher also does "almost 100" other estate planning calculations. Indispensable tool for estate planners. Leimberg & LeClair Inc., PO Box 1332, Bryn Mawr, PA 19010, (610) 924-0515. Order at www.leimberg.com.

Newsletters

Ed Slott's IRA Advisor. Ed Slott, CPA, is one of America's most knowledgeable retirement benefits experts, plus he writes beautifully and is a great speaker. Each issue has in-depth discussion of practical retirement tax info by top practitioners. $89.95 for twelve 8-page issues per year (plus back issues). Sent by regular mail (800-663-1340), or download (and find lots of other useful info) at www.irahelp.com.

Choate's Notes, by Natalie B. Choate. Published irregularly, free for now, sent by regular mail to customers of Ataxplan Publications and to professionals who request it by handing in business card at a Natalie Choate seminar (or sign up at www.ataxplan.com). Each issue contains a short article on some aspect of planning for retirement benefits, plus other info of interest to estate planning professionals.

Steve Leimberg's Employee Benefits and Retirement Planning Newsletter. E-mail-only. Analysis of breaking news as it happens, such as private letter rulings, cases, and legislation. Written by Bob Keebler, CPA, Noel Ice, Esq., Barry Picker, CPA, me and others, edited by the incomparable Steve Leimberg. Includes "LawThreads," which summarizes recent exchanges on estate planning topics from various professional listservs; and 24-hr access to extensive database. $19.85 per month (includes all four of Steve's newsletters). Indispensable. Visit one-time free or subscribe at www.leimbergservices.com.

Seminars

I have not evaluated these seminars, but am providing this list in response to many requests.

Who Should Be Beneficiary of Your IRA? A turnkey seminar for professionals to provide to clients and prospects. Schumacher Publishing, 800-728-2668, www.estateplanning.com (where this PowerPoint seminar is hidden under the tab "print products"). $695.

For other turnkey PowerPoint seminars for professionals, see www.power-presentations.net. Power Presentations, 8535 E. Hartford Dr. # 104, Scottsdale AZ 85255, (480) 325-8464.

Steve Leimberg, Esq., who is an outstanding seminar instructor himself, in addition to being a nationally recognized expert on estate planning, retirement benefits, and life insurance, and a major supplier of helpful tools for our industry, also has ready-to-go seminars for estate planners at www.Leimberg.com.

Other Resources

Laminated card, 9" X 11.5", with color charts summarizing the minimum distribution rules: Lifetime distributions on one side, post-death on the other. $19.85 for one (includes shipping). For info, call 801-273-3310 or e-mail jackmcm@unidial.com

Barry Picker's Guide to Retirement Distribution Planning, by Barry C. Picker, CPA/PFS, CFP. 40-pages. Clear, complete, accurate explanation of minimum distribution choices clients face. Includes checklist, worksheets and tables. Perfect to give to a client with substantial retirement assets; also good introductory text for pros. $24.95, plus $1.75 S&H (total $26.70); plus NY state & city tax if applicable. 800-809-0015 or www.BPickerCPA.com.

The new best book for non-professionals is *The Retirement Savings Time Bomb and How to Defuse It...A 5-Step Action Plan for Protecting Your IRAs, 401(k)s and Other Retirement Plans from Near Annihilation by the Taxman"* by Ed Slott, CPA (Viking, 2003; $24.95).

Bibliography

Estate Planning is a magazine published by Warren Gorham & Lamont, 31 St. James Ave., Boston, MA 02116.

"TMP" refers to the "Tax Management Portfolio" series published by the Bureau of National Affairs, Inc., 1231 25th St., N.W., Washington, D.C. 20037. A publication date is not provided for books in this series because they are kept up to date by annual supplements.

"CCH" is Commerce Clearing House, Inc., 4025 W. Peterson Ave., Chicago, IL 60646-6085. www.cch.com or 800-449-8114.

ACTEC Journal is published by the American College of Trust and Estate Counsel, 3415 S. Sepulveda Boulevard Suite 330, Los Angeles, CA 90034, 310-398-1888; www.actec.org.

Prior editions of this book (*Life and Death Planning for Retirement Benefits* by Natalie B. Choate, 3d ed. 1999 or 4th edition 2002), may be purchased for $39.95 plus shipping by calling 617-951-8995.

General note on sources: All statements in this book are based on the author's research using primary sources supplemented by secondary sources, with the exception of matters relating to the income tax treatment of trusts. Because the purpose of this book is only to highlight issues particularly involved when retirement plan benefits are paid to a trust, not to explain all the extremely complex rules of trust income taxation, I have relied on two secondary sources regarding this subject, namely, Blattmachr, J.G., and Michaelson, A.M., *Income Taxation of Estates and Trusts*, 14th Ed. (2000), (Practicing Law Institute Press, 810 Seventh Ave., New York, NY 10019) (cited as "*Blattmachr*") and Zaritsky, H. and Lane, N., *Federal Income Taxation of Estates and Trusts*, (third Edition, 2000; Warren, Gorham & Lamont) (cited as "*Zaritsky*"). I strongly recommend these books to those seeking information regarding the income taxation of trusts.

Introduction: Books and Other Resources on Retirement Plans and Estate Planning Generally

The best book for lawyers on tax-oriented estate planning is *Estate Planning Law and Taxation* (Fourth Edition, with 2001 Supplement) by Professor David Westfall and George P. Mair, Esq., published by Warren, Gorham & Lamont.

The best one-volume reference work for ERISA questions is *The Pension Answer Book,* by Stephen J. Krass, Esq. Mainly deals with "employer" issues such as the design, funding and qualification of retirement plans, but several chapters have material on distributions. Also covers prohibited transactions. A Panel Publication of Aspen Publishers, Inc., 7201 McKinney Circle, Frederick, MD 21704, 800-638-8437; www.panelpublishers.com. Current price is $199 per year, discount available if purchased at a trade show.

For 403(b) plans in general and TIAA-CREF plans in particular, see *Understanding TIAA-CREF* (Oxford Univ. Press 2000; $27.50) by Irving S. Schloss, Esq., and Deborah V. Abildsoe.

Estate and Gift Tax Issues for Employee Benefit Plans (TMP 378) and *An Estate Planner's Guide to Qualified Retirement Plan Benefits* (American Bar Assoc., Section of Real Property, Probate and Trust Law, 1992), both by Louis A. Mezzullo, Esq. are excellent overviews of the subject. The former also covers subjects not covered in this book, including non-qualified deferred compensation plans, QDROs, and gift and estate tax issues.

For treatment of annuities, non-qualified plans, and many other distribution topics not covered in this book, I recommend CCH's *Retirement Benefits Tax Guide*, 2d ed., by Thomas F. Rutherford, J.D.

Chapter 1:   Minimum Distribution Rules

Practical Application of the Retirement Distribution Rules, by Seymour Goldberg, CPA, MBA, JD (IRG Publications, 2001) is the latest work from the MRD expert who started it all. $59 (includes shipping) plus NY state tax if applicable. 800-808-0422.

Chapter 2:   Income Tax Matters

For more about IRD, see Alan S. Acker, *Income in Respect of a Decedent*, TMP 862.

For more discussion of lump sum distributions, see Frederick J. Benjamin, Jr., Esq., *Qualified Plans: Taxation of Distributions*, TMP 370-2d; *Taxation of Distributions from Qualified Plans*, by Diane Bennett *et al.*, Warren, Gorham & Lamont, ch. 5.1; and 2001 CCH *Standard Federal Tax Reporter,* ¶ 18,217A.082.

For more on what to do for clients who have company stock in their retirement plans, get the audiotape "Sophisticated Tax Planning

Opportunities with Employer Securities Held Within Qualified Plans" (with written materials), by Robert Keebler CPA, $29.95 plus $4 shipping, plus WI tax if applicable; send check to Virchow Krause & Co., LLP, PO Box 11997, Green Bay, WI 54307-1997; call 920-490-5607 for further information.

Chapter 3:   Marital Matters

For more on spousal waivers under REA, see Lynn Wintriss, Esq. "Practice Tips: Waiver of Rights Under the Retirement Equity Act and Premarital Agreements," 19 *ACTEC Journal*, no. 2, Fall 1993.

"The 'Probate Law' of ERISA," by Mary Moers Wenig, Esq., in *Estate Planning Studies*, April 1996 issue (page 5), newsletter published for members of the bar by State Street Bank and Trust Company, 225 Franklin St., Boston MA 02101 (thoughtful and well written review of the background of REA and how it has been interpreted by the courts).

For more on community property issues regarding retirement benefits, see "Practicalities of Post-Mortem Distribution Planning for Community Property Retirement Benefits and IRAs—Trusts as Beneficiaries, Separate Shares and Aggregate Theory Agreements," by Edward V. Brennan, Esq., *California Trusts and Estates Quarterly*, Vol. 5, No. 4 (Winter 1999).

Chapter 4:   Retirement Benefits and the Non-Citizen Spouse

For requirements of the marital deduction when the surviving spouse is not a U.S. citizen, see CCH *Federal Estate and Gift Tax Reporter*, ¶ 7045 *et seq.*

Chapter 5:   Roth IRAs

Mervin M. Wilf, Esq., authored several articles regarding Roth IRAs in *Estate Planner's Alert* (newsletter published by Research Institute of America): "The Roth IRA: A New Estate Planning Opportunity,", October 1997, page 11; "Roth IRAs: Second Chance for Distribution Planning after Age 70½ (Nov. 1997, p. 9); "Roth IRA AGI Threshold: Per Spouse or Per Couple?" (Dec. 1997, p. 6); and "Roth IRA Rollover Amounts should be Limited" (Jan. 1998, p. 5). See also his "Innovative Estate Planning Strategies Using Roth IRAs," *Estate Planning* March/April 1998 (Vol. 25, No. 3) page 99.

M.M. Wilf, Esq., "Regs Ignore 'Repeal' of Incidental Death Benefit Rule for Roth IRAs," *Pension & Benefits Week* 10/5/98, p. 5.

Michael J. Jones, CPA, "Roth IRA Gifts May Terminate Income Tax Benefits," *Tax Notes*, 6/1/98, p. 1156,

For a discussion of the hidden pitfalls built into the assumptions used in financial and tax planning software, see *The Terrible Truth About Investing* by Bruce J. Temkin (Fairfield Press, 1998; 1-888-820-5958; $24.95 plus shipping), p. 223.

For treatment of Roth IRAs in layman's language, complete with economic analysis and financial projections see the *Roth IRA Book: An Investor's Guide*, by Gobind Daryanani, Ph. D. (Digiqual Inc., Bernardsville, NJ, 1998; $34.95). Call toll-free 877-Roth911, or visit www.rothirabook.com.

Another book with financial analysis of Roth IRAs is R.S. Keebler, CPA, MST, *A CPA's Guide to Making the Most of the New IRAs* (AICPA). Also visit www.RothIRA.com or read *Roth to Riches* by John D. Bledsoe (Legacy Press, $19.95).

Chapter 6:   Trusts as Beneficiaries of Retirement Benefits

For fiduciary income tax, see Blattmachr and Zaritsky books recommended at the beginning of the Bibliography, and *Preparing Fiduciary Income Tax Returns*, by Jeremiah W. Doyle IV, Esq., *et al.* MCLE, 10 Winter Place, Boston, MA 02108, 1997.

The problem of trust accounting for retirement benefits is the subject of "IRA Distributions to a Trust After the Death of the IRA Owner—Income or Principal?" by Jeremiah W. Doyle, Esq., *Trusts & Estates*, Vol. 139, No. 9, p. 38 (Sept. 2000).

Chapter 7:   Charitable Giving with Retirement Benefits

Books:
The Harvard Manual on Tax Aspects of Charitable Giving, by the late David M. Donaldson, Esq., Carolyn M. Osteen, Esq., et al.(8th edition, 1999) is a magnificent summary of charitable giving techniques, with citations, written from the point of view of counsel for the charitable donee. The Harvard University Office of Planned Giving, Cambridge, MA 02138, 800-446-1277 (donation of $105, check only).

Conrad Teitell, Esq., is one of the country's top experts in the tax law of charitable giving, and fortunately for the rest of us he is also a prolific author and superb public speaker. For a complete catalogue of his books, newsletters and amazing seminars, call 800-243-9122.

Articles and seminar outlines:

Blattmachr, J.G., "Income in Respect of a Decedent," 12 *Probate Notes* 47 (1986). This excellent article discusses numerous strategies for reducing taxes on retirement benefits and other IRD, including charitable dispositions.

Burke, F.M., "Why Not Allow Lifetime Charitable Assignments of Qualified Plans and IRAs?" *Tax Notes* 7/7/97.

Hicks, Z.M., "Charitable Remainder Trust may be more Advantageous than a Qualified Plan," *Estate Planning* (5-6/90, p. 158). This is about using a CRUT *instead of* a qualified plan as an accumulation/payout vehicle for retirement.

Hoyt, C.R., "How to Structure Charitable Bequests from a Donor's Retirement Plan Account"; seminar outline, 2000.

Mezzullo, L.A., "Using an IRA for Charitable Giving," March/April 1995 *Probate & Property*, the Journal of the ABA Section of Real Property, Probate and Trust Law, p. 41.

Mulcahy, T.W., "Is a Bequest of a Retirement Account to a Private Foundation Subject to Excise Tax?," *Journal of Taxation*, August 1996.

Newlin, Charles F., "Coping With the Complexity of Separate Shares Under the Final Regs.," *Estate Planning*, July 2000 (Vol. 27, No. 6, p. 243).

Shumaker, R.L., and Riley, M.G., "Strategies for Transferring Retirement Plan Death Benefits to Charity," 19 ACTEC Journal, no. 3, p. 162 (1993), and follow-up comments published in 20 ACTEC Journal, p. 22 (1994). Compares the economic effects of various ways of funding a $1 million charitable gift from a $4 million estate, including the use of retirement benefits.

Shumaker, R.L. (with Riley, M.G.), "Charitable Deduction Planning with Retirement Benefits and IRAs: What Can Be Done and How Do We Do It?," American Bar Association Section of Real Property, Probate and Trust Law meeting outline, August 1995.

Chapter 8:   Disclaimers; Life Insurance; Grandfather Rules

DISCLAIMERS: See, generally, on disclaimers, the CCH *Federal Estate and Gift Tax Reporter;* or the RIA *Federal Tax Coordinator 2d;* or Mary Moers Wenig, Esq., *Disclaimers* (TMP 848).

LIFE INSURANCE: See generally, Zaritsky, H., and Leimberg, S.R., *Tax Planning with Life Insurance*, Warren, Gorham & Lamont.

For an excellent discussion of life insurance in the retirement plan, see Beverly R. Budin, Esq., *Life Insurance*, TMP 826.

For excellent discussion of the merits of the latest (as of 2003) ideas for retirement plans and life insurance, see "Fully Insured (412(i)) Pension Plans: the Good, the Bad and the Ugly," by John J. McFadden and Stephan R. Leimberg, *Estate Planning*, Winter 2003

Regarding "subtrusts," see: "The Qualified Plan as an Estate Planning Tool," by Andrew J. Fair, Esq., booklet distributed by Guardian Life Insurance Co. Of America, 201 Park Ave. South, New York, NY 10003; "Estate Tax on Life Insurance Held in Qualified Plans," by Mervin M. Wilf, Esq., in *Retirement Plan Trio* seminar 6/22/95, materials published by ALI-ABA, 4025 Chestnut St., Philadelphia, PA 19104-3099 (Publ. No. Q239); "IRS opens the way toward favorable estate and income tax treatment of plan distributions," by Kenneth C. Eliasberg, Esq., *Estate Planning* (7/83, p. 208); "Subtrusts and Reversionary Interests: A Review of Current Options," by I. Meyer Pincus, L.L.B., *Journal of the American Society of CLU & ChFC* (9/92, p. 64); "Excluding Qualified Plan Insured Incidental Death Benefits from the Participant's Gross Estate; Minority and Non-Stockholders," by Jonathan Davis, Esq., *The Estates, Gifts and Trusts Journal* (9-10/83, p.4); "Excluding Defined Benefit Plan Insured Death Benefits from the Gross Estate -- Sole and Majority Shareholders," by Jonathan Davis, Esq., *Tax Management Compensation Planning Journal* (5/84, p. 123).

Chapter 9:   Pre-Age 59½ Distributions

Toolson, Richard B., "Structuring Substantially Equal Payments to Avoid the Premature Withdrawal Penalty," *Journal of Taxation*, Nov 1990, page 276.

Glossary

This book assumes the reader is familiar with estate planning concepts and retirement plan terminology. This Glossary provides brief definitions of certain terms in these specialized fields to accommodate readers who do not have expertise in both fields. Terms that are an integral part of tax planning for retirement benefits (such as "rollover" and "IRD") are defined in the text dealing with that topic.

The Glossary is in two sections: the "Estate Planning Glossary" and the list of "Types of Retirement Plans."

Estate Planning Glossary

Credit shelter trust (sometimes also called "**Bypass Trust**"). The Code allows each person a tax credit that may be applied to gift or estate taxes otherwise due on transfers by that person. To the extent the credit is not used for lifetime transfers, it is available to shelter the person's estate from estate taxes. Because it may be applied to either gift or estate taxes, it is referred to as a "unified" credit.

The maximum credit allowed for deaths or gifts in 2003 is equal to the estate tax on a taxable estate of $1 million. Therefore, the effect of the credit is that each person can transfer up to $1 million free of gift or estate taxes to his children, or any other beneficiary who is not the person's spouse or a charity. (*Unlimited* amounts may be transferred tax-free to the spouse or charity.) The credit/exemption equivalent is scheduled to increase gradually over the years so that, for deaths in 2009 and later, the exemption is $3.5 million, leading to repeal of the estate tax altogether for deaths in 2010 (and reinstatement of the tax under the law as in effect in 2001, for deaths in 2011 and later).

Basic tax-oriented estate planning for a husband and wife involves making sure that each spouse takes full advantage of the federal estate tax exemption, most commonly by having the first spouse to die leave the exemption amount either to the children or grandchildren directly, or to a trust for their ultimate benefit. The surviving spouse may be a beneficiary of this trust, but does not have sufficient control over it to make it includible in his or her estate. Thus, this trust escapes estate tax at both deaths: it is not taxed in the first spouse's estate because it was sheltered by the decedent's unified credit; it is not taxed in the surviving spouse's estate because he or she does not own it. Because such a trust is "sheltered" by the first spouse's unified credit, this type of trust is called a "credit shelter trust." It is also called a "bypass trust" because it "bypasses" the surviving spouse's taxable estate and goes (eventually) to a younger generation tax-free.

Fractional bequest. A bequest or gift expressed as a fraction or percentage of a fund. A typical fractional bequest: "I bequeath my estate in equal shares to my children surviving me." A fractional bequest may be in the form of a formula, for example: "The Trustee shall pay to the Marital Trust a portion of the trust property determined by multiplying the value of the trust (as of my date of death) by a fraction, the numerator of which is the smallest amount necessary (if left to my spouse) to eliminate the estate tax on my estate, and the denominator of which is the total value of the trust."

Generation Skipping Transfer (GST) Tax. The estate tax applies to all assets transferred by a decedent at death. The decedent's estate pays estate taxes, and then distributes whatever is left to the beneficiaries of the estate—typically the decedent's children. In the normal course of events, the children themselves die some decades later and the same assets are taxed *again* before being passed along to the children's own children. To avoid having assets be subject to estate taxes in every generation, a grandparent might leave assets directly to grandchildren (to "skip" the estate taxes at the child's generation level), or to a trust which would benefit the children's generation for their lifetimes but not be included in the children's estates. Such "generation skipping trusts" are an important and valid way to reduce the estate tax burden on a family. The generation skipping transfer (GST) tax (Chapter 13 of the Internal Revenue Code) allows each person to transfer up to an exemption amount in the form of "generation skipping transfers," but imposes a tax, at a rate equal to the highest estate tax rate, on generation skipping transfers that exceed that limit. The amount of the exemption is $1,060,000 as of 2001. The exemption may increase through COLAs in 2002 and 2003; it is scheduled to increase in the years 2004-2009, leading to repeal of the GST tax in 2010 (and reinstatement in 2011 under EGTRRA's sunset provision).

Grantor Trust. Generally speaking, a trust is a separate taxpayer. It files its own tax returns and pays income tax on its income at special trust rates. (The only exception is that income distributed to the beneficiaries of the trust will normally be taxed at the beneficiary's rate rather than the trust's rate.)

However, in certain cases, the Code ignores the trust as a taxable entity and treats the income and deductions as belonging directly to the "grantor" (the person who contributed the money to the trust). The most common example is a "revocable living trust," under which the grantor can take the assets back any time he wants to. The Code ignores the trust during the grantor's life and treats its income and deductions as belonging directly to the grantor. There are many less obvious examples, and quite a number of complicated rules under § 671-§ 677, under which part or all of a trust's income may be taxable directly to the grantor (or, under § 678, to the beneficiary). See ¶ 6.3.09. If a person is treated as the owner of all of a trust's assets under these rules, transactions between the trust and the deemed owner are ignored for tax purposes because in effect they are regarded as "one taxpayer." Rev. Rul. 85-13, 1985-1 C.B. 184.

Pecuniary bequest. A bequest or gift of a specific sum of money, for example: "I bequeath $10,000 to my son." A pecuniary gift may be in the form of a formula which produces a specific dollar amount, such as: "The Trustee shall pay to the Marital Trust an amount of money or other property equal in value to the smallest amount necessary, if taken as a marital deduction, to eliminate the federal estate tax on my estate." This is in contrast to a fractional bequest (*q.v.*).

Power of appointment. A power given by one person (the original transferor) to another person (the power holder) to decide who will receive property. Example: A trust provides that Wife will receive the income of the trust during her life, and at her death the principal will be distributed among Husband's issue "as Wife shall appoint by her will." Wife has a power of appointment over the principal.

Types of Retirement Plans

This section explains the different types of retirement plans discussed in this book.

What's most confusing about the various types of plans is that there is not one set of mutually exclusive categories; there are different overlapping classifications for different purposes. For example, "qualified retirement plans" are divided into two types (defined benefit and defined contribution) for purposes of the limits (under § 415) on what may be contributed or accrued for a Participant, but into three types (pension, profit sharing and stock bonus plans) for purposes of plan aggregation under § 402 (definition of lump sum distribution). Profit sharing and stock bonus plans must be Defined Contribution Plans, but a pension plan may be either a Defined Contribution Plan or a Defined Benefit Plan. An ESOP can be either a profit sharing plan or a stock bonus plan; a Keogh plan can be any type of Qualified Retirement Plan other than a stock bonus plan or ESOP.

In general, the types of retirement plans this book deals with share the following universal characteristics:

1.   Each is a formal arrangement for accumulating capital for the primary purpose of financing the owner's retirement.

2.   The arrangement is funded with contributions from the owner's earnings (or from the owner's spouse's earnings), or with contributions made directly by the owner's employer.

3.   Investment earnings accumulated "inside" the arrangement are not subject to income tax so long as they remain "inside" (unlike capital accumulated outside a retirement plan, the earnings on which are taxed as they are realized).

4.   In order to receive this special tax benefit, the arrangement must comply with an array of tax rules and other requirements.

5.   One set of tax rules that all these plans must comply with (with some slight variations) is the minimum distribution rules of § 401(a)(9) (Chapter 1).

Beyond those universal characteristics, however, retirement plans come in a variety of flavors. The commonly-encountered types of retirement plans covered by this book vary widely in terms of the rules to which each type is subject, such as limits on contributions, tax treatment of distributions, when distributions are permitted, spousal rights, the likely availability of different planning devices, grandfather rules, creditors' rights, and so on.

An in-depth discussion of the rules applicable to the different types of retirement plans is beyond the scope of this Glossary. The purpose of this Glossary is to explain the differences among the various types of plans only to the extent such differences are likely to have an impact on planning choices.

403(b) arrangements or plans. These retirement plans are available only to tax-exempt employers. These plans are similar to Qualified Retirement Plans (QRP) in that the employee is not taxed currently on the plan contributions or earnings, but is taxed only as distributions are made to him. One difference is that the plan assets will be solely in the name of the employee, like an IRA. Another difference is that 403(b) money can be invested in only two types of investments: annuity contracts purchased by the employer and issued in the name of the employee; and "regulated investment companies" (mutual funds) held by a bank (or other approved institution) as custodian for the employee.

The main differences between 403(b) plans (also sometimes called in this book "403(b) arrangements") and other plans from a tax planning perspective are that a 403(b) plan distribution is never eligible for treatment as a "lump sum distribution" under § 402 (¶ 2.3) and the minimum distribution rules apply slightly differently; see ¶ 8.5.03.

Defined Benefit Plan. Under a Defined Benefit Plan, also called a "defined benefit pension plan," the employer promises to pay the employee a specific pension, starting at retirement, and continuing for the employee's life. Social Security is an example of a "Defined Benefit Plan." Typically, the amount of the pension is based on a formula, such as "a monthly pension for life, beginning at age 65, equal to 1/12th of 1% of final average compensation times years of service, reduced by 10% for each year of service less than 10 if the employee has less than 10 years of service, and up to an annual maximum of 40% of career average compensation." The formula may be extremely elaborate, partly (inevitably) because it must include the "415 limits" (the limits under § 415 on what may be accrued for an individual employee) but also because, for example:

A.   The formula may award different percentages of compensation for different years (e.g., "1% of compensation for years 1965-1970, .75% of compensation for years 1971-1985 "); such a formula usually reflects changes in the benefit formula over the years.

B.   The formula may award a lower percentage for compensation below the FICA wage base than for compensation in excess of the FICA wage base.

C.   The formula will contain adjustments for early or late retirement. For example, if the annual pension promised is "25% of average compensation, beginning at age 65," but the plan permits early retirement at age 55, there will be a reduction in the percentage amount for each year prior to age 65 that the employee retires. The two pension amounts will nevertheless be "actuarially equivalent" because a lower rate paid for more years is equivalent in value to a higher rate paid for fewer years.

Once the formula is established and the plan adopted, the employer then hires an actuary, who tells the employer, each year, how much must be contributed to the plan to amortize the employer's future obligations to retiring employees under the plan. The actuary is essentially required to predict the future: how many employees will stick around long enough to actually collect the promised pension? Along the way, how many wage increases will these employees have, that will boost the employer's obligations under the pension plan? How long will the retired employees live (and have to be paid by the plan) after retirement? How much will the plan's investments earn?

The law specifies some of the assumptions, such as a maximum and minimum interest rate that the actuary is permitted to use. Also, even if the employer designs the plan so that it starts off with a huge unfunded liability for past service, the employer is not permitted to pay off the entire unfunded liability at once. However, the law requires the employer to fund the plan to a specified extent each year. As a result, the actuary must produce not one but two contribution amounts for the employer's consideration each year—the legally required minimum contribution and the legally permitted maximum contribution.

The employee is guaranteed to receive the stated pension; a federal agency (the Pension Benefit Guaranty Corporation) insures employee pensions under Defined Benefit Plans. Any investment risk falls on the employer (and investment profits benefit the employer). Thus if the plan's investments do well one year, the employee's projected pension does not increase (but the employer may get by with a smaller contribution). Likewise, if the plan's investments decline in value, the employer may have to contribute more money to shore up the plan, but the employee is protected.

Defined Benefit Plans generally are of greater value to older employees (older than approximately age 50) than to young employees, just because of the time value of money. Even if their eventual projected pensions are the same amount, say $36,000 per year starting at age 65, the value is greater to the employee who will be receiving that sooner. $36,000 a year starting in 10 years (how the pension looks to the 55 year-old employee) is a more significant asset than $36,000 a year starting in 30 years (how the pension looks to a 35 year-old employee). The older employee's pension looks more valuable to the employer too, who has to contribute more for the older employee than for the younger.

Defined benefits plans were once the normal form of retirement plan for American businesses. Their overall popularity has declined (especially among small businesses) due to increasingly complex tax rules applicable to these plans and due to the lower cost and more easily understandable appeal of Defined Contribution Plans. However, Defined Benefit Plans remain attractive to the one-person business as a way of maximizing tax-deductible retirement contributions. If the business owner/sole employee is over age 50, approximately, a Defined Benefit Plan will give him a larger annual tax-deductible contribution than the limit under a defined contribution plan.

From an *estate planning perspective*, the Defined Benefit Plan has the following distinctive features:

First, the employee does not have an "account" in a Defined Benefit Plan the way he does in a Defined Contribution Plan. The employee's benefit statement for the Defined Benefit Plan will typically say the employee's "accrued benefit" under the plan is (e.g.) "$1,450 a month," of which (say) "80% is vested." What this means is that the employer has already obligated itself to provide for this employee (if the employee *keeps on working* until retirement age) a pension of $1,450 per month for life starting at the employee's "normal retirement age" under the plan (usually, 65); and if the employee *quits right now*, he's vested in 80% of that, meaning that at normal retirement age he would receive 80% of $1,450 per month.

The benefit statement may or may not contain more details such as: how much of a pension the employee would receive if he retired early (if the plan offers "early retirement"); and (of great significance in estate planning), whether the employee will be permitted upon retirement to withdraw the lump sum equivalent of the accrued pension, or what death benefit, if any, would be available for the employee's beneficiaries, which brings us to the second significant factor in planning for defined benefit pension benefits: Planners should be prepared for the fact that some Defined Benefit Plans do not offer the option of taking a lump sum equivalent in cash (or that the client may have already chosen an annuity option and foreclosed his ability to take a lump sum equivalent). Thus there will not be the ability to "roll over" benefits from this plan to an IRA.

Also, some Defined Benefit Plans provide no benefits at all after the death of the employee (or after the deaths of the employee and surviving spouse). Defined Benefit Plans are targeted purely at financing *retirement*, and (by law) may offer death benefits only "incidentally." Some Defined Benefit Plans are structured so that, if an employee dies prematurely, the money that was set aside to fund that employee's pension goes back into the general fund to finance the benefits of other employees, rather than passing to the deceased employee's heirs. There is nothing illegal or immoral about this; a plan structured this way is able to offer better retirement benefits to all employees.

Other Defined Benefit Plans *do* permit the employee, upon retirement, to take his benefits out of the plan in the form of a lump sum in cash, the value of which is "actuarially equivalent" to the value of the employee's vested pension under the plan. However, planning is not necessarily any easier in this situation. The employee in this type of plan will have to choose between a life annuity and a one-time cash distribution. If the employee is married, the complexity of the decision is compounded by the spouse's rights to a survivor annuity (see ¶ 3.4).

This decision involves certain hazards. For example, remember that what is guaranteed to the employee is the monthly pension stated in the plan, *not* the equivalent lump sum value. The equivalent lump sum value is determined by discounting the projected stream of future pension payments back to its present cash value based on a certain discount rate (the interest rate that plan investments are assumed to earn in the future). If interest rates are rising as the employee approaches his retirement, the lump sum value of the pension will decline commensurately. This process can be extremely upsetting to an individual who is facing retirement and closely counting his available funds, and then finds out on the day he retires that the lump sum he is getting from the pension plan is smaller than it would have been if he had retired six months earlier, due to an increase in interest rates in the meantime. Thus employees should not regard the lump sum equivalent of their defined benefit pension plans as an asset in hand until it actually is in hand.

Furthermore, the employee's life expectancy and that of his spouse should influence the decision. If the employee's health is poor, a life annuity may be a bad choice. On the other hand, if health is better than average, the annuity options may be attractive, especially if the plan subsidizes certain annuity options (such as the joint and survivor annuity with the spouse). If the benefits in the plan are substantial, an actuary should be consulted to help the employee evaluate the choices under the plan; this is not a job for the estate planner.

Key points for the estate planner: expect a benefit statement that discusses a pension payable at retirement, rather than a current value; determine whether the plan offers any death benefit beyond the required spousal annuity; and, as the client approaches retirement, consider hiring an actuary to assist in the evaluation of benefit alternatives.

Defined Contribution Plan. A Defined Contribution Plan is, along with the "Defined Benefit Plan," one of the two broad categories of Qualified Retirement Plan. Defined Contribution Plans are also called "individual account plans." § 414(i). Under a Defined Contribution Plan, the employer may commit to making a certain level of contribution to the plan (such as "10% of annual compensation," an example of a money purchase pension plan formula), or (under a profit sharing plan) may make such contributions periodically on a discretionary basis or based on profit levels. Profit sharing plans, money purchase pension plans, 401(k) plans, target benefit plans and ESOPs are examples of Defined Contribution Plans.

Once the employer has contributed to the Defined Contribution Plan, the contributions are allocated among "accounts" for the individual employees who are members of the plan. What the employee will eventually receive from the plan is determined by (a) how much is allocated to his account under the contribution formula and (b) what is the subsequent investment performance of that account. The employer does not guarantee any level of retirement benefits. If the plan's investments do well, the profits will increase the employee's account value. If the plan's investments do poorly, the employee will receive less at retirement.

If the plan is "self-directed," each participant makes the investment decisions for his or her own account in the plan, from a menu of alternatives permitted by the plan. The menu may be very broad or may be limited to a small number of mutual funds. If the plan is not self-directed, the investments are determined at the plan level by the trustee of the plan.

Key points for estate planners: Participant's retirement benefits will normally be in the form of a lump sum distribution of the account balance, which Participant can then roll over to an IRA, although certain defined contribution plans offer annuities or instalment payouts.

ESOP (Employee Stock Ownership Plan). An ESOP is a Qualified Retirement Plan primarily designed to invest in stock of the sponsoring employer. Over the years, trying to head off the workers' revolution predicted by Karl Marx, Congress has tried to encourage employee ownership of the means of production, and one of its enticements is the ESOP. ESOPs have various liberalized rules compared with other retirement plans, most of which are of interest only to the employer-sponsor and not to estate planners.

Key points for estate planners: Distributions of company stock to an employee from an ESOP or any other retirement plan are eligible for certain favorable tax treatments if various requirements are met. See ¶ 2.4. Thus, if a client's retirement plan holds employer stock, all options should be considered before that stock is disposed of. However, an ESOP is not required to distribute the stock to the employee. An ESOP is allowed to permit only cash distributions. Thus the fact that an employee has a retirement account with employer stock in it does not mean the employee is going to be eligible for the special treatment.

Individual Account Plan. A plan in which individual accounts are maintained on the plan's books for plan participants, with the result that each participant obtains the profits (or bears the losses) of his own account. IRAs, Roth IRAs, SEP-IRAs and Defined Contribution Plans are individual account plans, but a Defined Benefit Plan is not.

Individual Retirement Account (IRA). An IRA is not a Qualified Retirement Plan under § 401(a). Rather, it is a private "individual" retirement plan created under § 408. An IRA can be structured as a trust (§ 408(h)) or as a custodial account (§ 408(a)); the tax treatment is exactly the same.

Keogh Plan. A "Keogh plan" (or "H.R. 10 Plan") is a qualified retirement plan that covers one or more self-employed individuals.

Thus, a "Keogh plan" is Qualified Retirement Plan (QRP) established by an unincorporated employer (partnership or sole proprietor) for the benefit of the partners and employees of the partnership, or for the benefit of the sole proprietor and his employees. Any type of QRP other than an ESOP or stock bonus plan may be a "Keogh plan."

While this term (which never appears in the Code) is still used by self-employed persons to describe their retirement plans, almost all of the once-significant distinctions between plans adopted by corporations and plans adopted by the self-employed were eliminated by the Tax Reform Acts of 1984 and 1986, and the Unemployment Compensation Amendments of 1992. To read about what the differences used to be, see Reg. § 1.401(e).

There are still some differences of interest to planners, however. This summary gives an overview; for the nuances and exceptions, see the cited Code sections. Note that some of the differences are applicable to all "Self-employed persons" while others apply only to the "Owner-employee."

Definitions: A "Self-employed person" is an individual who has self-employment income. § 401(c)(1). In contrast, a "common law employee" (or, as the Code calls it, "an individual who is an employee without regard to § 401(c)(1)") is an employee of someone else (not himself). An "Owner-employee" is the sole proprietor of an unincorporated business, or a partner "who owns more than 10 percent of either the capital interest or the profits interest" in the partnership. § 401(c)(3). So, all Owner-employees are Self-employed persons, but not all Self-employed persons are Owner-employees.

This author has not found a clear rule as to *when* the 10% test (for determining Owner-employee status) is applied; do we test only at the end of the plan year? Or must we determine whether the individual owned more than 10% of the capital *at any time during* the year? And is the test applied yearly? Or is the individual considered *forever* an Owner-employee if he was *ever* an Owner-employee?

Lump sum distributions: A lump sum distribution (LSD) may qualify for special tax treatment. See ¶ 2.3, ¶ 2.4. A LSD is a distribution of Participant's entire account balance within one calendar year following the most recent "triggering event." "Triggering events" are: for EVERYBODY, turning age 59½ or dying; for Self-employed persons ONLY, becoming disabled; and for common law employees ONLY, separation from service. § 402(d)(4)(A).

Premature distributions: A distribution from an employer plan made to an employee "after separation from service after attainment of age 55" is exempt from the 10% "premature distributions" penalty (see Chapter 9). Although § 72(t) does not specifically exclude the Self-employed from using this exception, it is not clear what would constitute "separation from service" for a sole proprietor.

Premature distributions, continued: In years after 1996, a person who has "received unemployment compensation for 12 consecutive weeks under any Federal or State unemployment compensation law" can take penalty-free distributions from his IRA to pay health insurance premiums. § 72(t)(2)(D). The IRS, in regulations, can permit Self-employed persons to use this exception. No such regulations have yet been issued.

Life insurance: Generally, if a Qualified Retirement Plan maintains a life insurance policy on the life of Participant, Participant must include the cost of the current insurance protection in his income each year; see ¶ 8.3.01. Unlike other Participants, however, an Owner-employee does not get to treat the accumulated cost (that he has paid tax on) as an "investment in the contract" (basis) for income tax purposes. Reg. § 1.72-16(b)(4); ¶ 8.3.02.

Pension Plan. A Pension Plan is a type of Qualified Retirement Plan under which the employer is *obligated* to make annual contributions, or, as the Code puts it, it is a plan "subject to the funding standards of section 412." The required annual contribution may be determined by an actuarial formula based on the promised benefits (Defined Benefit Plan), or may be simply a percentage of employees' compensation each year (Money Purchase Pension Plan), or may be derived from an actuarial formula involving benefits that are projected but not guaranteed (Target Benefit Plan). A pension plan is contrasted with a Profit Sharing Plan or Stock Bonus Plan, under which the employer's contributions are discretionary or linked to profits.

Key points for estate planners:

1. A pension plan may not permit "in-service distributions" (distributions of benefits prior to Participant's death, disability or separation from service), unless Participant has met the requirements for "retirement" (typically a minimum age and number of years of service). Even though a pension plan MAY

permit in-service distributions if the employee has met the requirements for retirement, however, many do not permit any distributions until actual retirement.

2. Pension plans must offer the qualified joint and survivor annuity as the normal form of retirement benefit for most married employees, and the qualified pre-retirement survivor annuity as the normal form of pre-retirement death benefit for most married employees, and these forms cannot be altered without spousal consent; see ¶ 3.4.

3. All pension plans are considered "one plan" for purposes of determining whether there has been a distribution, within one calendar year of the recipient, of the employee's entire balance in "the" plan under § 402(d) (lump sum distributions; ¶ 2.3.04), even if they are not the same type of pension plan (e.g. a Defined Benefit Plan and a money purchase plan).

Profit Sharing Plan. A Profit Sharing Plan is a type of Defined Contribution Plan under which the employer's contributions are either entirely discretionary or are fixed to a certain percentage of profits. Most 401(k) plans and some ESOPs are profit sharing plans. The key differences between profit sharing plans, on the one hand, and pension plans, on the other, are as follows:

1. A profit sharing plan MAY (subject to certain limits) permit "in-service distributions," that is to say, distributions to Participant prior to his separation from service and prior to his meeting the plan's requirements for "retirement." The significance of this for estate planning is that profit sharing funds may be available for certain planning purposes (such as rolling over some of the funds to an IRA, to support a "series of substantially equal periodic payments" under § 72(t); ¶ 9.2), even while the employee is still employed. However, it should be noted that most profit sharing plans do *not* in fact permit in-service distributions. This may be due to a historical accident: at one time, plans were very strict about when distributions were permitted because of concern about "constructive receipt"—the doctrine under which an individual is taxed on income he has a right to receive whether or not he actually takes

the income. Although amendments to § 402 have eliminated the need for concern about constructive receipt (see ¶ 2.1.01), by providing that retirement benefits generally are taxed only when actually distributed, most plans still provide that there are no distributions prior to retirement. Another possible reason employers keep this requirement is that they want to encourage (or force) employees to leave the money in the plan and not dissipate it prior to retirement.

2.   While the "incidental benefit rule" (¶ 8.3.04) imposes limits on how much life insurance a QRP may buy, this limit does not apply to funds that have been in a profit sharing plan for more than two years. Thus, if Participant wants to buy life insurance, the profit sharing plan may be a possible source of funds. A profit sharing plan, of course, may choose not to permit the purchase of life insurance even when the law allows it.

3.   While pension plans are *always* subject to REA's QJSA and QPSA requirements, profit sharing plans can qualify for a limited exemption. See ¶ 3.4.03.

Qualified Retirement Plan. A "Qualified Retirement Plan" (QRP) means a retirement plan that meets the requirements of § 401(a) (i.e., is "qualified" under § 401(a)). Since § 401(a) has more than 30 separate requirements, some of which cross reference other lengthy Code sections, it is no mean feat to be qualified under § 401(a). Most of the requirements (such as the requirement that the plan not discriminate in favor of highly compensated employees; requirements specifying which employees must be covered and how quickly their benefits must vest; limits on contributions prior to the employer's bankruptcy) are of little concern to the estate planner who is helping an employee plan for the distribution of his or her benefits. However, it is helpful to be aware of certain § 401(a) concepts that create the landscape in which all Qualified Retirement Plans must function. For example:

A.   A QRP is established and maintained by the "sponsor" of the plan. Normally, the sponsor of the plan is the employer of the employees who are covered by the plan, but it could also be a labor union or an association of employers. The employer could be a sole proprietor or partnership, in which case the plan is not only a QRP it is a "Keogh plan."

B.   The assets of the QRP generally must be kept in a separate trust for the "exclusive benefit" of the employees and their beneficiaries.

C.   If all the rules are complied with (including the § 415 limits on how much may be *contributed* to the plan each year, and the separate limits in § 404 on how much of each year's contribution may be deducted for income tax purposes), the employer gets a tax deduction for its contributions to the plan. However, the employee does not have to include the plan benefits in his or her gross income until he or she receives a distribution from the plan (¶ 2.1.01).

D.   The plan must prohibit the assignment or alienation of benefits by the employee. § 401(a)(13)(A).

E.   The plan must contain provisions required by REA. ¶ 3.4.

F.   The plan must not discriminate in favor of highly compensated employees, but contributions or benefits that bear a uniform relation to compensation are not considered discriminatory, even though higher-paid employees thereby receive greater contributions or benefits. Actually, the plan is required to discriminate *against* highly compensated employees, since contributions are generally based on compensation but compensation in excess of $200,000 per year (as of 2003) doesn't "count." Also, some discrimination against lower-paid employees is permitted, in that an employer may choose to "take credit" for the Social Security taxes it pays for employees.

There are several types of Qualified Retirement Plans (QRPs).; see Defined Benefit Plan, Defined Contribution Plan, ESOP, Pension Plan and Profit Sharing Plan.

Index

ORDER FORM
Save your book! Photocopy this form....

FORMS ON DISK

Now, all the forms in *Life and Death Planning for Retirement Benefits* plus several more that didn't fit into the book, are available ready to plug into your word processor and use in your practice. All beneficiary designation and election forms and related trust provisions, plus a "plan termination assignment" and all four IRS model spousal consent forms are included, in 8.5" x 11" page size. Provided for your convenience to save typing, meant to be used in conjunction with the book, so no instructions are included. Format: WordPerfect 8.0 and Word 2000, 3.5" disk.

Price: $49.95 (includes shipping and handling). Please add $2.50 Mass. sales tax for Mass. delivery.

      Yes, please send me "Forms on Disk." $ 49.95
      For Mass. delivery, add $2.50 Mass. sales tax $_____

      TOTAL $_____

Photocopy this order form, fill out the copy, and mail it to:
               Ataxplan Publications
               P.O. Box 1093-F
               Boston, MA 02103-1093

Name: _____

Company name:_____

Address:_____

City: _____ State: _____ Zip:_____-_____

Telephone: (___) _____

Payment:
□ Check
    Credit card: □ Visa □ Mastercard
Card number: _____

Name on card: _____Exp. date_____/__

Signature (required for credit card orders):

_____

NOTES

Order Form
Save your book! Photocopy this form....

Life and Death Planning for Retirement Benefits

✳   Fax order: (419) 281-6883   @   Web orders: **www.ataxplan.com**

☎   Telephone orders: Call Toll Free: 1(800) 247-6553. Have your
AMEX, Discover, VISA or MasterCard ready.

✉   Mail orders: Send check payable to "Book Masters" to:
               BookMasters, Inc.
               30 Amberwood Parkway
               Ashland, OH 44805

**Please send me____copies of Life and Death Planning for
Retirement Benefits (5th edition, 2003) at $89.95, plus $7.00 shipping,
each.** I understand that I may return any books for a full refund for any
reason, within 90 days.

Name: _____
Company name:_____
Address:_____
City: _____ State: _____ Zip: _____ - _____
Telephone: (___) _____

Sales tax:
Please add 5% sales tax for books shipped to a Massachusetts address.
Please add required sales tax for books shipped to an Ohio address.

Shipping: $7 charge is for UPS ground. For overnight service, inquire.

Payment:
□ Check payable to "BookMasters"
Credit card: □ Visa, □ MasterCard, □ AMEX, □ Discover
Card number: _____
Name on card: _____Exp. date____/__

Signature (required for credit card orders):

_____
Call *toll free* and order now